# CASTLES AND THE ANGLO-NORMAN WORLD

*Norman Connections partners and conference speakers, 16 May 2012.*

# CASTLES

AND THE

# ANGLO-NORMAN WORLD

*Proceedings of a Conference held at Norwich Castle in 2012*

*Edited by*

John A. Davies, Angela Riley, Jean-Marie Levesque
and Charlotte Lapiche

The Norman Connections Project has been supported by

Norfolk Museums Service · NORMAN CONNECTIONS · france (manche channel) england interreg · European Regional Development Fund The European Union, investing in your future · Fonds européen de développement régional L'union Européenne investit dans votre avenir · Supported using public funding by ARTS COUNCIL ENGLAND · heritage lottery fund LOTTERY FUNDED

Oxbow Books
*Oxford & Philadelphia*

Published in the United Kingdom in 2016 by
OXBOW BOOKS
10 Hythe Bridge Street, Oxford OX1 2EW

and in the United States by
OXBOW BOOKS
1950 Lawrence Road, Havertown, PA 19083



Hardcover Edition: ISBN 978-1-78570-022-4
Digital Edition: ISBN 978-1-78570-023-1

A CIP record for this book is available from the British Library

Library of Congress Cataloging-in-Publication Data

Names: Davies, John A. (John Arthur), 1955- | Riley, Angela. | Levesque, Jean-Marie. | Lapiche, Charlotte. | Norman Connections Project.
Title: Castles and the Anglo-Norman world : proceedings of a conference held at Norwich Castle in 2012 / edited by John A. Davies, Angela Riley, Jean-Marie Levesque and Charlotte Lapiche.
Description: Oxford : Oxbow Books, 2015. | "The Norman Connections Project." | Includes bibliographical references and index.
Identifiers: LCCN 2015027267 (print) | LCCN 2015028294 (ebook) | ISBN 9781785700224 (hardback) | ISBN 9781785700231 (digital) | ISBN 9781785700231 (epub) | ISBN 9781785700248 ( mobi) | ISBN 9781785700255 (pdf)
Subjects: LCSH: Castles--England, Southern--Congresses. | Castles--France--Normandy--Congresses. | Excavations (Archaeology)--England, Southern--Congresses. | Excavations (Archaeology)--France--Normandy--Congresses. | Normans--England, Southern--Congresses. | Normans--France--Normandy--Congresses. | Architecture, Anglo-Norman--Congresses. | England, Southern--Antiquities--Congresses. | Normandy (France)--Antiquities--Congresses.
Classification: LCC DA660 .C32 2015 (print) | LCC DA660 (ebook) | DDC 942.202--dc23
LC record available at http://lccn.loc.gov/2015027267



Printed in the United Kingdom by Short Run Press, Exeter

For a complete list of Oxbow titles, please contact:

UNITED KINGDOM
Oxbow Books
Telephone (01865) 241249, Fax (01865) 794449
Email: oxbow@oxbowbooks.com
www.oxbowbooks.com

UNITED STATES OF AMERICA
Oxbow Books
Telephone (800) 791-9354, Fax (610) 853-9146
Email: queries@casemateacademic.com
www.casemateacademic.com/oxbow

Oxbow Books is part of the Casemate Group

Front cover: Dover Castle, Kent. © Robert Liddiard
Back cover: Eastward view in St John's Chapel. © John Crook

# CONTENTS

## Part II
### The Castles in Context



## Part III
### Recent Archaeological Research



## Part IV
### Presenting the Sites



## Part V
### Sculpture and Objects

# CONTRIBUTORS

STEVEN ASHLEY FSA
Finds Archaeologist, Norfolk Historic Environment Service
steven.ashley@norfolk.gov.uk

BRIAN AYERS FSA
Honorary Senior Lecturer, School of History,
University of East Anglia
Honorary Secretary, Society of Antiquaries of London
b.ayers@uea.ac.uk

PROFESSOR DAVID BATES FRHistS, FSA, FHA
Professorial Fellow, School of History
University of East Anglia
david.bates@uea.ac.uk

PETER BERRIDGE
Formerly Head of Colchester and Ipswich Museum Service
peterjberridge@yahoo.co.uk

PIERRE BOUET
Directeur Honoraire, Office Universitaire d'Etudes Normandes,
Université de Caen Basse Normandie
pfbouet@free.fr

RICHARD BROWN
Senior Project Manager, Oxford Archaeology South
richard.brown@oxfordarch.co.uk

NICOLA COULTHARD
Chef du Service Archéologie, Conseil Général du Calvados
Chargé de Cours, Université de Caen Basse-Normandie et Université de Reims Champagne-Ardenne
nicola.coulthard@calvados.fr

DR JOHN CROOK FSA
Independent Architectural Historian and Photographer
Consultant Archaeologist to Winchester Cathedral
and the College of St George, Windsor
john@john-crook.com

DR JOHN A. DAVIES FSA
Chief Curator and Keeper of Archaeology, Norfolk Museums Service
john.davies@norfolk.gov.uk

FRANÇOIS FICHET DE CLAIRFONTAINE
Inspecteur des Patrimoines, Ministère de la Culture
et de la Communication
Formerly Conservateur Régional de l'Archéologie
de Basse-Normandie, Direction Régionale des Affaires Culturelles
francois.fichet-de-clairfontaine@culture.gouv.fr

DR JON GREGORY
Lecturer in Landscape History, School of History,
University of East Anglia
j.gregory@uea.ac.uk

BÉNÉDICTE GUILLOT
Ingénieur Chargé de Recherches, Institut National de Recherches Archéologiques Préventives
benedicte.guillot@inrap.fr

DR ROLAND B. HARRIS FSA
Independent Buildings Archaeologist
Norwich Cathedral Archaeologist
roland@roland-harris.com

PROFESSOR SANDY HESLOP FSA
Professor of Visual Arts, School of World Art Studies,
University of East Anglia
t.heslop@uea.ac.uk

DR EDWARD IMPEY FSA
Director-General and Master, Royal Armouries
Formerly Director of Heritage Protection and Planning,
English Heritage
edward.impey@armouries.org.uk

CHARLOTTE LAPICHE
Directrice Adjointe du SPIC, Château Guillaume
le Conquérant, Falaise
Chef du Service du Patrimoine, Falaise
charlotte.lapiche@falaise.fr

PASCAL LEROUX
Attaché de Conservation, Musée de Normandie / Château de Caen
pleroux@caen.fr

JEAN-MARIE LEVESQUE
Conservateur en Chef, Musée de Normandie / Château de Caen
jmlevesque@caen.fr

DR ROBERT LIDDIARD FSA
Senior Lecturer, School of History, University of East Anglia
rob.liddiard@uea.ac.uk

DR PAMELA MARSHALL FSA
Retired Lecturer and Specialist in the Archaeology of Standing Buildings
Formerly Chair of UK Castle Studies Group and Member of the Comité Permanent of the European Château Gaillard Colloque
p.marshall752@btinternet.com

JOHN MCNEILL FSA
Lecturer, History of Art, Department of Continuing Education, Oxford University
Honorary Secretary, The British Archaeological Association
jsmcneill@btinternet.com

JOSEPH MASTROLORENZO
Archéologue en Architecture
mastrolorenzo@wanadoo.fr

DR MARC MORRIS
Freelance Historian and Broadcaster
marcgmorris@gmail.com

BENOÎT PANOZZO
Médiateur Culturel, Château Guillaume le Conquérant, Falaise
benoit.panozzo@falaise.fr

DR ELIZABETH POPESCU FSA
Post-Excavation and Publications Manager, Oxford Archaeology East
elizabeth.popescu@oxfordarch.co.uk

ANGELA RILEY
Project Officer, Norfolk Museums Service
angela.riley@norfolk.gov.uk

# ACKNOWLEDGEMENTS

We are grateful to the many individuals who have supported both the Norman Connections project and Castles Conference (16–17 May 2012), and who share our enthusiasm for Anglo-Norman heritage.

Norman Connections was led by Ed Woollard and coordinated by Marie Pandolfo at Medway Council. Their assistance was vital in ensuring a smooth and successful conference. We are equally appreciative for the support of other members of the project team: Mathias Dilys, Pascal Leroux, Antoine Verney, Régine Turgis, Sarah Belsom, Kevin Boorman, Philip Wise and Tom Hodgson. We are particularly grateful to Mathias for his help with translations.

Our colleagues Tim Pestell and Emma Taylor have provided assistance throughout the project, conference and subsequent Norwich Keep symposium; Tim also chairing a session on Romanesque architecture and artefacts.

The conference was made possible thanks to European funding and guidance from Samuel Lesart, Interreg Facilitator. Close partnership work established key and valuable links on both sides of the Channel and enabled a presence of leading specialists in the worlds of castles and Anglo-Norman history, archaeology and architecture. This publication is the result of continued collaborative work.

We would like to sincerely thank all of the contributors to the conference, including Richard Eales and Jean Mesqui, and to this volume. Brian Ayers, Rob Liddiard and Sandy Heslop provided regular advice during the planning stage of the conference, site tours and professional knowledge throughout. Philip Dixon also generously offered support at all stages. Special thanks go to Professor David Bates, who delivered the keynote lecture and who, here, provides our foreword.

Finally, we would like to extend our thanks to the people who attended the Norwich conference and subsequent symposium and who continue to visit our historic sites.

*John A. Davies, Angela Riley, Jean-Marie Levesque and Charlotte Lapiche*

May 2014

# PREFACE

## *George Nobbs*

I am both honoured and delighted to have been invited to write the preface for this volume on the theme of Anglo-Norman castles and their surroundings. It contains an impressive collection of articles by English and French specialists who are both passionate about the subject and internationally recognised.

Originally built as a royal palace some 900 years ago, Norwich Castle was a fitting location for the conference held in 2012. Events following the Conquest of 1066 had a great impact on the city of Norwich, in terms of its landscape, wealth and administration. During the Norman period, this culturally rich and inspiring city was one of the largest in England, later becoming the second city after London. Much of its medieval heritage remains intact, with other foundations of the period being the Cathedral and marketplace. It is a mark of its reputation as an important regional centre and the capital of a great province that it has been twinned with Normandy's own capital of Rouen.

English and French castles have long been of great interest to scholars, students and the general public. Those represented by the *Norman Connections* project are some of the key heritage and tourism attractions of their regions. Great stone fortresses, they provided a stronghold, witnessed historic battles and sieges and were part of much wider castle precincts. Today they remain symbols of Norman power and prestige. In both countries they were once, but are no longer, the symbol of a foreign military presence, where first Normans in England and later English armies in France used them to control local populations. Today, in a way that our ancestors surely could never have envisioned, they are much-loved landmarks, and old friends to local populations that have taken them to their hearts over the centuries.

This book features new research on other important subjects such as the White Tower in London and the Exchequer Hall in Caen, as well as the famous Bayeux Tapestry. This outstanding surviving work of art is and will remain synonymous with the Battle of Hastings and documents, to some accuracy, this pivotal moment in English and French history. Together, this collection of articles helps us understand these historically significant sites and tells us what they originally looked like and how they related to their environments and their impact on 'town-planning'. We also gain an insight into what can be learned from archaeological excavations, the study of buildings and the discovery of artefacts, as well as how this knowledge can be best presented to the public.

*Norman Connections* is a wonderful example of cross-border collaboration and demonstrates the importance of maintaining historical and cultural links between our countries. It is perhaps symbolic that Norwich's Norman Castle itself contains many works on Normandy which artists from the famous Norwich School of Artists produced in the years immediately following the Anglo-French peace in 1814 when people, long kept apart by war, rushed to flock across the Channel to revisit each other's architectural gems. Our castles were then, as now, principal attractions. Continued cross-Channel partnership working has huge potential to raise interest from funders and visitors for further developments of these sites. I hope that this publication helps to achieve that.

*Councillor George Nobbs*
*Leader of Norfolk County Council*

# INTRODUCTION

## Introducing Norman Connections

*John A. Davies, Angela Riley, Jean-Marie Levesque and Charlotte Lapiche*

In 2008 a group of professionals from the worlds of museums, historic castles and regional tourism, based in the south and east of England and Normandy, came together with the aim of enhancing the understanding, study, presentation and promotion of our common Norman heritage, through our historic monuments. The partnership represent the towns of Caen, Falaise and Bayeux, Calvados Tourisme and the Conseil Général du Calvados in France as well as Colchester Borough Council, Hastings Borough Council, Medway Council and Norfolk County Council in England. Together we represent the Norman castles at Caen, Falaise, Colchester, Hastings, Rochester and Norwich, and the Bayeux Tapestry Museum. In 2010, under the banner of *Norman Connections*, the partnership obtained funding from the *Interreg IVA France (Channel) – England* cross-border co-operation programme in order to achieve an initial phase of development at our historic sites. Medway Council has been the lead partner throughout the life of the project.

The *Norman Connections* project was structured from the outset to jointly develop knowledge of the historic monuments associated with the partnership and their context in the Anglo-Norman world, while developing ways to achieve a better identity for our shared heritage across the whole cross-Channel region. We initially sought to increase knowledge about our sites for the purposes of the staff working at them, and where possible for the purposes of ongoing academic research, while in all cases our eventual aim has been to provide an improved awareness and interpretation of the sites for our visitors.

The partnership castles not only share a common heritage in their Norman origins, but also in their evolution through time on both sides of the Channel. Ancient medieval fortresses, abandoned and destined as romantic ruins or army barracks, and in some cases prisons, our castles are today protected monuments. They present museum displays and exhibitions and are the subject of archaeological research, restorations and grand developments. Therefore, by studying their history and engaging in joint development projects, we can find points of comparison and enrich the knowledge of one site with answers to questions posed by another.

It is in this context that the Norman Connections Castles Conference was developed. Planning started in 2011, with the conference being held on 17 and 18 May 2012, at Norwich Castle Museum & Art Gallery. Papers were delivered by experts from the partner sites and leading scholars from both France and England, in French and English. Simultaneous translation was provided. The conference opened with discussion of the partner castle sites of Norwich, Colchester, Rochester, Hastings, Caen and Falaise, including both summaries of current knowledge and new research. Subsequent sessions covered the subjects of the evolution of Anglo-Norman castles, the architecture and archaeology of Norman monuments, recent excavations, Romanesque architecture and artefacts, the Bayeux Tapestry and the presentation of historic sites to the public. Additional contributions have been provided by David Bates, Brian Ayers and Pamela Marshall for this publication.

Phase I of *Norman Connections* ended in 2014, with improvements for visitors having been achieved across our sites. Our joint legacy includes the creation of a bilingual website *www.normanconnections.com*, digital 3D reconstructions of our castles and the enabling of a regular exchange of museum objects for exhibition between the partners. Our joint work will continue. The project has stimulated new questions about all of our sites. *Norman Connections* has established the way forward for future research, an even better presentation of our sites, a fuller understanding of the wider Anglo-Norman landscape and greater appreciation of our shared heritage throughout our cross-Channel region, at the heart of Europe.

En 2008, un ensemble de professionnels des musées, châteaux historiques et institutions touristiques régionales, tous situés au sud et à l'est de l'Angleterre et en Normandie, se sont réunis dans le but mettre en valeur la connaissance, l'étude, et les actions de médiation et de promotion consacrées aux monuments historiques du patrimoine normand. Ce partenariat rassemble les villes de Caen, Falaise et Bayeux, Calvados Tourisme (le Comité Départemental du Tourisme du Calvados) et le Conseil Général du Calvados, en France, ainsi que le Colchester Borough Council, le Hastings Borough Council, le Medway Council et le Norfolk County Council en Angleterre. Il concerne les châteaux normands de Caen, Falaise, Colchester, Hastings, Rochester et Norwich, et le Musée de la Tapisserie de Bayeux. En 2010, sous l'étendard du projet *Norman Connections*, ce partenariat a obtenu le soutien du programme de coopération transfrontalière *Interreg IVA France (Manche) – Angleterre*, dans le but d'accomplir une première phase de développement au bénéfice. Le Medway Council s'est constitué chef de file des partenaires pour toute la durée du projet.

Dès son origine, la structure du projet *Norman Connections* a été conçue dans le but de développer les connaissances autour des monuments historiques associés dans le partenariat, et de leur contexte dans les mondes anglo-normands, tout en créant des outils permettant une meilleure identification de ce patrimoine commun à la région transmanche. L'intention initiale était d'améliorer la formation des personnels, d'apporter si possible de nouvelles ressources à la recherche et dans tous les cas de renforcer l'intérêt du public et de faire progresser la médiation auprès de nos visiteurs.

En effet, la situation des châteaux concernés par le partenariat ne présente pas seulement un patrimoine commun dans son origine normande mais aussi dans son évolution à travers le temps des deux côtés de la Manche: vieilles forteresses médiévales, abandonnées au destin des ruines romantiques ou devenus des casernes, et parfois même des prisons, nos châteaux sont aujourd'hui des monuments protégés, ils accueillent des musées et des expositions et font l'objet de recherches archéologiques, de restaurations et de mises en valeur spectaculaires. C'est donc aussi en étudiant leur histoire sur toute la durée et en échangeant sur des projets communs d'aménagements et de développements qu'on peut trouver des points de comparaison enrichissant la connaissance d'un site des réponses aux questions posées sur un autre.

C'est dans ce contexte que la conférence sur les châteaux du projet Norman Connections a été conçue. Les préparatifs ont commencé en 2011, et la conférence s'est tenue les 17 et 18 mai 2012 au Norwich Castle Museum & Art Gallery. Les communications ont été données par les responsables des sites du partenariat et des chercheurs anglais et français de premier plan, et présentées en anglais et en français en traduction simultanée. La conférence s'est ouverte sur une discussion autour des châteaux du réseau de partenaires: Norwich, Colchester, Rochester, Hastings, Caen et Falaise, et plus particulièrement sur l'état des connaissances à leur sujet, ainsi que l'actualité de la recherche en cours. Les sessions suivantes ont traité de l'évolution des châteaux anglo-normands en général, de l'architecture et de l'archéologie des monuments normands, des fouilles récentes, de l'art et des collections d'époque romane, de la Tapisserie de Bayeux ainsi que des méthodes de médiation auprès du grand public. David Bates, Brian Ayers et Pamela Marshall ont bien voulu en outre apporter des contributions supplémentaires à la présente publication.

Une première étape du travail en commun des partenaires de *Norman Connections* s'est terminé en 2014, par la mise en place d'importantes améliorations pour l'accueil des visiteurs. Parmi ces réalisations figurent la création d'un site internet bilingue *www.normanconnections.com*, la modélisation de maquettes numériques en 3D des châteaux et des échanges pour des expositions et les espaces d'interprétation. Notre travail commun continuera. Le projet a stimulé l'émergence de nouvelles questions autour des sites partenaires. *Norman Connections* a véritablement ouvert la voie vers de nouvelles recherches et une meilleure médiation pour les sites. Il a enfin permis de mieux appréhender l'étendue du paysage anglo-normand et de son patrimoine commun dans cette région transmanche, au cœur de l'Europe.

# FOREWORD

## Living in the twelfth-century cross-Channel empire

*David Bates*

The metamorphosis of the 'Norman Connections Castles Conference' into a volume bearing the title *Castles and the Anglo-Norman World* is an interesting commentary on the way in which their subject has evolved over the last half century. The replacement of 'Norman' with 'Anglo-Norman' and the deletion of 'Connections' mirror a process that has been ongoing among historians since the 1970s, albeit with the insertion of a few distorting prisms in place on the way that I will leave to one side. The year 1976, with the publication of John Le Patourel's *The Norman Empire* and R. H. C. Davis's *The Normans and their Myth*, marks a convenient starting-point in this historical debate, with a consequence of the process I am referring being that we can legitimately question what we mean by the phrase 'Norman castle'.[1] Or indeed query whether we should describe Norwich Castle as a Norman castle. While this might seem like semantic nit-picking, it is, I would argue, absolutely fundamental to focusing our minds on the central political, social, and cultural issues that provide essential context for this book's subject and to grasping just how important this volume is to our understanding of the cross-Channel world brought into existence by Duke William of Normandy's conquest of the kingdom of the English in 1066, and which lasted until the conquest of the duchy of Normandy by the French king Philip Augustus in 1204.

John Le Patourel's *The Norman Empire* argued that the study of Normandy and England must be undertaken as a unity, with unity and assimilation being the titles of major chapters in his book. Although innovative in its thesis, and for my present purpose absolutely fundamental because it introduced into the discourse the dynamic signified by the word colonisation and therefore the processes of evolving change associated with it, it arguably also continued an Anglophone tradition encapsulated in the work of his contemporaries David Douglas and R. Allen Brown, which, in Douglas's words, emphasised 'the unity of the Norman achievement'.[2] This tradition was one that went back to the work of Charles Homer Haskins and indeed beyond his time into the 19th century; it was Haskins in 1916, in the published version of a series of lectures given in the United States, who supplied the stunning statement that Normandy was 'the mother of a greater Normandy in England, Sicily, and in America'.[3] Ralph Davis's *The Normans and their Myth* was a short illustrated scholarly polemic that set out to wreak havoc with this notion of a single unified pan-European Norman world. But, for all that its arguments might seem revolutionary and that it did provoke the discussions of identity that are still ongoing, it too belonged in a tradition that stressed enduring and developing differences between Normandy and England, a theme that was central to a book that is almost contemporary with Haskins', namely, Sir Maurice Powicke's *The Loss of Normandy*. This approach also has elements in common with a distinguished Francophone historiography that can at times turn Normandy and the Normans into the victims of their achievement.[4] These debates about cultural and personal identity have also found their way into the discourse of scholars working on castles, and also into the publications of archaeologists in general, with the work of Naomi Sykes being one notable example.[5]

In one of his four Presidential Lectures to the Royal Historical Society in the 1970s, Sir Richard Southern made the statement that 'the mistake is often made of looking for evidence of a historical revival only in the histories it produces'. This was followed by a call to take into account every type of evidence.[6] Given that Southern's subject was historical writing, it is hardly surprising that he did not proceed to explore the implications of his advice. That the inter-disciplinarity required to do so is arguably beyond the powers of any individual is yet another reason why this volume is important. As an observation it does, however, inexorably take us back to the 1960s and Brian Davison's denial that a single unified culture of Norman castle-building existed, and to his argument that the *motte*, as a regular feature thereof, was a phenomenon that emerged in England after 1066, and not in Normandy before it.[7] François Fichet de Clairfontaine's essay in this volume both shows just how much work has been done since the 1960s in Lower Normandy alone and invites a renewed cultural and typological analysis. And, on fast-forward, they both take us into the first decades of the 21st century and to multiculturalism, with its acknowledgement that culture can rarely be defined simply in relation to a monochrome national and ethnic identity. And, from there, as the social scientists would nowadays argue, to the study of life-histories as the route to the understanding of values and identity.[8] And further from there to both the logical corollary of this statement, which is that buildings have lives that can be studied in the same way as those of human beings, and to the recent call for more 'interplay between castle studies and other areas of scholarship.[9]

In what might at first seem like a historian's timid retreat, I am now going to turn to one of the great historical writers of the 12th century, Orderic Vitalis. One of Ralph Davis's provocative statements with reference to Orderic was 'it is a frightening thought that one eloquent historian might impose an idiosyncratic view on all his successors, compelling them to consider that disparate conditions and disjointed events were really part of an "inherent unity"',[10] to which my response would be that, if anybody imposed anything on anybody, it was 19th- and 20th-century attitudes to nationality and ethnic identity that did the imposing. Born in England of mixed parentage in 1075, sent to the abbey of Saint-Evroult in southern Normandy as a 10-year-old child to become an oblate, Orderic in fact had views on his personal identity and on the collective identity of the Normans that were complex and which would merit renewed exploration. Although he lived almost all of his adult life in Normandy and at the start of Book V of his great work, the *Historia Ecclesiastica*, he declared that his objective was to write a history of the Normans for the Normans, he called himself *Ordricus angligena*, emphasising to the end of his life his English descent from his mother, and subsequently being entered in Saint-Evroult's calendar under his English name. He manifestly empathised profoundly throughout his life with the humiliation of the people among whom he had spent his childhood.[11] His self-identity and inner life might therefore be thought to have differed radically from the public responsibilities he believed he had to undertake as a historian. When it comes to values and identity, he provides an instant warning based on the life of one individual, albeit a truly remarkable one, against thinking that either can be presented in a simplified way when viewed through the medium of the many thousands of lives touched by the cross-Channel empire.[12] To describe him as 'Norman' or 'English' is for obvious reasons misleadingly facile. To resort to the word Anglo-Norman has its merits, but can also be thought feeble to the point of being meaningless because it slides over many hidden depths.

The central importance of this volume is that it both continues the distinguished tradition of analysing individual sites, as well as, at the same time, providing material to examine the wider picture of connections, networks, and cultural transfer that are at the cultural heart of the *Norman Connections* project. Thus, the essay by Edward Impey and John McNeill encapsulates architectural themes that have parallels with those of Orderic's life, in that we are dealing with a form of migration from England to Normandy that has implications for imperial identity. The Salle de l'Echiquier at Caen is seen by them both as a prototype for the export of an English style of domestic architecture, the hall, to Normandy and, when taken alongside the great hall constructed at Westminster at the same time, as an expression of what I would term an imperial architecture; that these two highly innovative buildings were built in close proximity to the churches where William the Conqueror had been crowned king of the English and was buried surely cannot be accidental. The phenomenon is certainly not Norman, but, it is not English either; when account is taken of its ambition and scale, it is a specialised product of a new imperial world brought into existence in 1066.[13] The essay by Pamela Marshall shows just how complex this world was.

Processes of change over time involving cultural aspirations and influences from far beyond the frontiers of Normandy and England are part of the arguments set out in the essay by Jon Gregory and Robert Liddiard; the choices made by individual aristocrats and their architects can be shown to draw on western European influences that affected both Normandy and England, as of course they had been doing in the centuries before 1066. To return for a moment to written documents and to a process of dissemination that drew on an English base, the history of the writ and the writ-charter is one that demonstrates an expansion of a specific form throughout parts of northern France, as well as into the kingdom of Scots and elsewhere in the British Isles.[14] If we then go back to Le Patourel and Davis for a moment, we can see that what we are dealing with in all this does not have the cultural uniformity of a Norman empire and a culturally Norman inspiration as Le Patourel defined them, but that, at the same time, it does possess a unifying multiculturalism for which the activities of the Normans were the central cathartic force which therefore goes against Davis' critique.

To develop my theme further through a case-study that has manifestly not been selected at random, it can be seen that the processes that these changes epitomise are very evident in the 11th- and 12th-century histories of Norwich and East Anglia. Norwich Castle keep, for example, differs greatly from the two earlier large stone keeps built in England, namely, the White Tower of London and Colchester, and has affinities with similar buildings on the river Loire. The east-facing loggia of Bigod's Tower has elements in common with the early 9th-century Visigothic royal hall near Orvieto and the precursor of the great arch beneath the tower has been suggested as being the mid-11th-century imperial palace at Goslar.[15] If the predominant influence on the design of Norwich Cathedral is unquestionably the church of William the Conqueror's monastic foundation of Saint-Etienne of Caen, the size of the building and its decoration draw on multiple inspirations that lie far beyond the frontiers of the duchy of Normandy, as well as on many drawn from contemporary England.[16] Like several of the other great churches of post-1066 England, it is much larger than anything built in contemporary Normandy and, indeed than almost anywhere else in western Europe. Its decoration shows influences from Durham and the sections of Canterbury Cathedral rebuilt by St Anselm.

It is also relevant to my theme that the tortuous process that led to the location of the bishopric in Norwich was an entirely English one, the result of the defeat of the attempt by the bishops of East Angles to locate their see in the abbey of Bury St Edmunds; the main participants might have come from Normandy and northern France, but the foundations of their arguments drew on English precedent and conditions.[17] Exchanges across the North Sea that continued and developed pre-existing connections are also of great importance to the architectural history of post-Conquest East Anglia. Thus, while the western block still partly visible at Ely cannot necessarily be thought of as a straightforward early borrowing from the churches of the Empire, it is beyond doubt that they were the sources on which it and other major churches were drawing, and that some aspects of the design had links with old St Peter's in Rome.[18] At a less elevated level, the origin of the famous round towers of the parish churches of Norfolk and Suffolk may draw partly on the new cathedral at Norwich and the abbey church of Bury St Edmunds, but what is certain is that such towers proliferated around the peripheries of the North Sea, and nowhere else, in the 12th century.[19] But for all that we can see East Anglia as an importer of multiple cultural influences; it also became an exporter, most notably through the huge increase in the renown of the cult of St Edmund. It is intriguing to note that Herman the archdeacon's late 11th-century account of the miracles of St Edmund is a prime source for the history of Barfleur, a Norman coastal town with no discernible pre-1066 history, whose fortune seems to have been made by the vastly expanded number of Channel crossings that followed on from the conquest of 1066.[20]

In terms of individual and collective life-stories, the impact on the citizens of Norwich of these vast building campaigns and the associated increase in the city's territorial area is superficially an obvious one, although not an entirely straightforward one. Little Domesday Book waxed eloquent on the effects of the construction of the castle that preceded the present one by commenting of the indigenous population that 'those fleeing and the others remaining have been entirely ruined'.[21] Yet the work must in due course have brought jobs and relative prosperity to many.[22] Elizabeth Popescu's essay in this volume deepens enormously knowledge of the specifics of this process. At the same time, the extensive use of Caen stone in the construction of both cathedral and keep must have benefitted economically and financially those who worked in the quarries at Caen and the mariners responsible for transporting the stone. An imprecise, but extremely evocative, comment on the situation is supplied by Brian Ayers' assessment that 'colossal' quantities of stone must have been moved by sea to Norwich.[23] Although interpretation of the 12th-century history of the quarries at Caen presents problems, it would be good to think that some rudimentary quantification might be possible on the basis of the Norwich evidence that could convert architectural history into economic and social history.[24] What this analysis does show is that it was not just the aristocratic cross-Channel elite that had an interest in the continuation of the cross-Channel empire. It added dimensions to many lives and it created new vested interests. Even if the life-stories of those who laboured in the quarries at Caen and of the builders who did the work at Norwich can never be written, the history of the buildings and of the landscape can make a significant contribution to opening up our understanding of what they might have been like.

As with all empires, the ultimate determinant of rise and fall was the commitment of the imperial elite in the face of opposition from within and outside. The life-stories of the aristocratic elite with cross-Channel landholdings are therefore of central importance. Although much-studied, their history is one that merits further work that concentrates on long-term processes and the infrastructures of power. For me, it is particularly striking not just how the massively wealthy topmost elite perpetuated itself over generations and was constantly renewed, but how it reacted to crisis; the cross-Channel emphasis of so much activity during the civil war between King Stephen and the Empress Matilda is a phenomenon whose importance is not always appreciated.[25] With their networks and cultural links that stretched far beyond the frontiers of Normandy and England, these immensely powerful men and women were significant agents of the multiculturalism I want to emphasise. A fine symbolic expression of imperial values in operation in the later 12th century is provided by the similarities in the appearance of the two keeps at Conisbrough and Mortemer, both built Hamelin Plantagenet, by marriage between 1164 and 1202 the inheritor of the Warenne family's interests in England, Normandy and Flanders.[26]

The conquest of 1066 created new identities for the many who acquired lands in England. That, for example, so many of the first generation of settlers in Cambridgeshire at a relatively humble social level have been shown to have adopted English toponyms before the making of Domesday Book is just one illustration of how newcomers came to identify themselves with the localities in which they had acquired lands.[27] However, when life-stories are created, it can be shown that this apparent integration into new places did not mean that they necessarily ceased to be participants in the cross-Channel empire. A new identity that was actually a cross-Channel one is supplied by William of Malmesbury's reference to the *Vituli* family, who had possessions in Southampton and Caen, as a special breed of men associated with ships and the sea (*genus hominum nauticorum*); so significant indeed were they as a group that they could persuade Earl Robert of Gloucester, the Empress Matilda's great supporter, not to attack Southampton.[28] In all these instances, to try again to pin down an identity as either Norman or English is to engage in simplification; analysis in terms of a diaspora should indeed make us expect that an identity that might be thought of as either English or Norman could revert to a previous form in a subsequent phase of a life-cycle or in the next generation.[29] A single, apparently isolated, reference can indeed draw attention to dimensions of individual and collective life-histories that might otherwise have been thought non-existent. Thus, the case-study that alerted me to the potential of this line of analysis, the gathering of the widow and descendants of Richard de Reviers at the abbey he had effectively founded at Montebourg in western Normandy more than 30 years after his death in the year 1107.[30] And, returning to the subject of architecture, John Crook's article on the capitals in St John's chapel in the White Tower of London pinpoints again the presence of multicultural stylistic identities, with the cushion capitals undoubtedly deriving inspiration from north-eastern France, rather than Normandy. As also, although his main focus is on the chronology of the construction of the White Tower of London, do sections of Roland Harris's article. And so finally, now leaving behind both buildings and written documents, does Steven Ashley's essay that covers a remarkable range of elite objects, including, for example, horse harness pendants and buckles.

With the take-over of England's economic resources after 1066 by the invading newcomers being quite extraordinarily comprehensive, it is entirely justifiable to refer to the cross-Channel polity as 'the empire of the Normans', on the grounds that the core of the invading force and the new cross-Channel elite came from Normandy and identified themselves as Normans. But, as we do this, we need also to keep in mind not only the well-known point that a good proportion of these newcomers did not come from Normandy at all, but rather from other regions of northern France, but the arguably even more important one that the empire was born plural. William the Conqueror was crowned 'king of the English' and in the history of English church architecture we have the 'Saxo-Norman overlap'.[31] What we can for convenience call English themes were culturally present from the start, even if, in relation to the history of power in a highly abstract form that completely failed to protect the aristocracy of the pre-Conquest kingdom.[32] And the response to the subsequent pressures on Wales, Scotland, and Ireland produced a mixture of enforced change, cultural transfer, and the robust assertion of pre-existing identities. The overall process of course must take into account what Robert Bartlett has conveniently termed 'European change', the wider currents that to greater or lesser degrees affected everyone, including Normandy and the Normans.[33] All, in other words, constitute an argument for studying multiple life-stories – including those of buildings – to deepen understanding of the multicultural history of the cross-Channel empire.

My final point is to re-emphasise that empire and multiculturalism brought change to Normandy. It undoubtedly brought wealth from England into the duchy, on a scale that Mathieu Arnoux has set out an argument in favour of a Norman industrial revolution.[34] But it is evident too that empire came with a price attached. Alongside the triumphalism associated with military victories and an awareness of a pan-European expansion in which individuals from Normandy had played leading roles, there is also the shock expressed in the story first told by Orderic and elaborated in the 1160s by Wace about the surrender of Caen to Henry I in 1105, without a blow being struck on behalf of his older brother, the legitimate Duke of the Normans, Robert Curthose. Orderic reported that the English manor granted in recognition by Henry was known as 'the Traitors' Manor' and that it was soon relinquished. Wace added that the place of surrender was one where nothing had since grown, a permanent reminder to all who passed by it of divine disapproval.[35] The creation of empire had brought civil war to Normandy in a way that was resented. Yet it also brought absorption of themes from the periphery into a new imperial identity, most notably in the rapid assimilation of Geoffrey of Monmouth's stories of the British King Arthur into the mainstream of cross-Channel imperial identity. The prime agents in this process in the 1140s and 1150s seem to have been Robert of Torigni, prior of Le Bec and later, from 1154 until 1186, abbot of Le Mont Saint-Michel, and Wace, through the earlier of his two *magna opera*, the *Roman de Brut*.[36] Let us remember the surprise of the historian Henry of Huntingdon, who was based in England and who identified it as his homeland, when he visited Robert of Torigni at Le Bec in 1139 and made his first acquaintance there with Geoffrey's work, despite the fact that it had been written in England.[37] The history of Norman Gothic architecture, recently magisterially surveyed by Lindy Grant, provides an illustration of cultural change flowing into the duchy from within the French kingdom. A complex topic, it mixes conservatism, a conscious archaism that might be thought to try to continue a great Norman past, and the adoption of revolutionary new influences from the mid-12th-century architectural power-house that was the Ile-de-France.[38] Once more therefore we have a mixture of multiculturalism and a strong Norman identity.

In Wace's life, like Orderic's, we have a story that consists of both the triumphalism of empire and of profound ambivalence about its impact. They articulate a rich tapestry that can only be understood through examining their lives as a whole and, as such, they illuminate the well-known huge potential of such histories and lives. Exactly the same potential, however, is present in the history of buildings and demonstrates why international collaborations of the kind exemplified by this volume are the indispensable foundation for the understanding of phenomena that transcend national boundaries. They take us into a world of multiculturalism that is notably different from the dominant discourse of the period up until the 1970s and which is, of course, very much still with us. These essays both deepen knowledge and suggest many lines of further enquiry for the future.

## Vivre dans l'empire transmanche du douzième siècle

La transformation d'un colloque intitulé en anglais 'Norman Connections Castles Conference', dont la traduction en français approximative est la 'Conférence sur les Châteaux liés aux Normands' en un volume intitulé *Châteaux et le Monde Anglo-Normand* est un commentaire intéressant sur la manière dont le sujet du volume a évolué au cours des dernières cinq décennies. Le remplacement de 'normand' par 'anglo-normand' et le fait d'avoir supprimé 'connections' révèlent un processus chez les historiens qui a vécu depuis les années 1970, même si c'est avec l'insertion de quelques prismes déformants en chemin, dont je ne parlerai pas. L'année 1976, avec la publication du livre de John Le Patourel *The Norman Empire* et de celui de R. H. C. Davis intitulé *The Normans and their Myth*, marque un tournant intéressant dans ce débat historique, la conséquence du processus auquel je fais référence étant que nous pouvons légitimement nous interroger sur le sens de 'château normand'.[1] Ou effectivement on peut se demander si on doit décrire le château de Norwich comme un château normand. Certes, cela peut être interprété comme 'couper les cheveux en quatre', sémantiquement parlant. À mon avis cependant, il est tout à fait fondamental de nous concentrer sur les questions politiques, sociales et culturelles centrales qui forment le contexte principal du thème de cet ouvrage et de percevoir l'importance de ce volume dans la compréhension du monde transmanche qui a vu le jour après la conquête du royaume anglais en 1066 par Guillaume de Normandie, et qui a perduré jusqu'à la conquête du duché de Normandie par le roi de France, Philippe Auguste, en 1204.

*The Norman Empire* de John Le Patourel soutenait que l'étude de la Normandie et de l'Angleterre doit être entreprise comme une unité, l'unité et l'assimilation étant les titres de deux des principaux chapitres de son livre. Bien qu'innovant dans sa thèse, et pour mon objet ici, absolument fondamental parce qu'il a introduit dans le discours la dynamique portée par le terme de colonisation, et de ce fait les processus de changement évolutif qui en sont des corollaires, il a sans doute aussi repris une tradition anglophone que l'on retrouve dans l'œuvre de ses contemporains, David Douglas et R. Allen Brown, qui selon les mots de Douglas, mettait l'accent sur 'the unity of the Normandy achievement'[2] (l'unité de la réussite normande). Cette tradition remontait à l'œuvre de Charles Homer Haskins et en fait au-delà de cette époque, jusqu'au XIXe siècle; ce fut Haskins en 1916, dans la version publiée d'une série de cours dispensés aux États-Unis, qui affirma de façon surprenante que la Normandie était 'la mère d'une plus grande Normandie en Angleterre, Sicile et en Amérique'.[3] L'ouvrage de Ralph Davis, *The Normans and their Myth* déclencha une petite polémique entre académiciens, et sema le chaos, de par cette notion d'un monde normand paneuropéen unique et unifié. Mais, cet ouvrage, aux arguments d'apparence révolutionnaire et qui a entraîné des discussions sur l'identité se poursuivant encore aujourd'hui, était lui aussi ancré dans une tradition qui soulignait des différences de toutes sortes entre la Normandie et l'Angleterre, thème central de l'ouvrage de Sir Maurice Powicke *The Loss of Normandy*, presque contemporain de celui de Haskins. Cette approche a également des éléments en commun avec une éminente historiographie francophone qui peut parfois transformer la Normandie et les Normands en victimes de leur réussite.[4] Ces débats sur l'identité culturelle et personnelle ont aussi trouvé leur place dans le discours des intellectuels qui travaillent sur les châteaux, et également dans les publications des archéologues en général, l'œuvre de Naomi Sykes en étant un exemple notable.[5]

Dans un de ses quatre Cours Présidentiels à la *Royal Historical Society* dans les années 1970, Sir Richard Southern a déclaré que 'on fait souvent l'erreur de chercher les preuves d'un renouveau historique dans les histoires qu'il produit', suite à quoi il invite à prendre tous les témoignages en compte.[6] Étant donné que le sujet de Southern était l'écriture de l'histoire, il n'est guère surprenant qu'il n'ait pas commencé à explorer ce qu'impliquaient ses conseils. C'est parce que l'interdisciplinarité nécessaire va bien au-delà des pouvoirs de toute personne que ce volume est important. Mais, en qualité d'observation, il nous ramène inexorablement dans les années 1960 au refus de Brian Davison d'admettre qu'il existait une culture unique et unifié de construction de châteaux normands, et à son argumentation que la motte, qui en est une caractéristique traditionnelle, était un phénomène qui est apparu en Angleterre après 1066, et non pas avant en Normandie.[7] L'essai de François Fichet de Clairfontaine dans ce volume montre précisément le travail fait depuis les années 1960 en Basse Normandie seule et appelle également à une nouvelle analyse culturelle et typologique. Et, de la sorte, tous deux nous emmènent déjà dans les premières décennies du XXIe siècle et le multiculturalisme, avec sa reconnaissance que la culture peut rarement se définir simplement par rapport à une identité ethnique et nationale monochrome. Et, à partir de là, comme le diraient aujourd'hui les scientifiques sociaux, vers l'étude des histoires de la vie comme chemin vers la compréhension des valeurs et de l'identité.[8] Et à partir de là, vers le corollaire logique de cette affirmation, à savoir que les bâtiments ont une vie qui peut être étudiée de la même manière que celle des humains, et vers la récente invitation à davantage 'd'interaction entre les études des châteaux et d'autres domaines d'études.[9]

Dans ce qui pourrait au premier abord passer pour un retranchement timide d'historien, je vais maintenant me tourner vers l'un des plus grands écrivains historiques du XIIe siècle, Orderic Vital. Une des affirmations provocantes de Ralph Davis, faisant référence à Orderic était 'c'est terrifiant de penser qu'un historien éloquent puisse imposer une vision idiosyncratique à tous ses successeurs, les obligeant à envisager que des conditions disparates et des événements sans rapport entre eux fassent en fait partie d'une 'unité inhérente''.[10] Ce à quoi ma réponse serait que, si quiconque imposait quoi que ce soit à quiconque, ce sont en fait les attitudes des XIXe et XXe siècles vis-à-vis de l'identité nationale et ethnique qui imposaient cela. Orderic était né en Angleterre, de parents mixtes, en 1075, envoyé à l'abbaye de Saint-Evroult dans le sud de la Normandie, à l'âge de 10 ans, pour qu'il entre dans comme oblat, il avait en fait une analyse complexe de son identité personnelle et de l'identité collective des Normands qui mériterait d'être explorée à nouveau. Bien qu'il ait vécu presque toute sa vie d'adulte en Normandie et qu'au début du Livre V de son grand ouvrage, *L'Histoire Ecclésiastique*, il déclare que son objectif était d'écrire une histoire des Normands pour les Normands, il se nommait *Ordricus angligena*, soulignant, jusqu'à la fin de sa vie, le fait qu'il descendait des Anglais par sa mère. Il fut ensuite entré dans le calendrier de Saint-Evroult sous son nom anglais. Manifestement il était en profonde empathie, et ce pendant toute sa vie, avec l'humiliation du peuple au milieu duquel il avait passé son enfance.[11] Sa propre identité et sa vie intérieure étaient sans doute très différentes des responsabilités publiques qu'il croyait devoir entreprendre en tant qu'historien. Quand on parle de valeurs et d'identité, il donne un avertissement qui s'appuie sur la vie d'une personne, même s'il s'agit d'un être vraiment remarquable, et il prévient qu'il ne faut pas penser que l'une ou l'autre puisse être présentée de manière simplifiée en l'analysant par le biais de milliers de vies affectées par l'empire transmanche.[12] Il est trop facile et trompeur de le décrire comme 'normand' ou 'anglais', et ce pour des raisons évidentes. Choisir le terme 'anglo-normand' a ses avantages, mais peut aussi sembler faible, voire insignifiant, parce qu'il passe par-dessus de nombreuses profondeurs cachées.

L'importance centrale de ce volume est qu'il poursuit la tradition remarquable d'analyse des sites individuels tout en fournissant au même temps du matériel pour examiner le spectre plus large des liens, réseaux, et transferts culturels qui sont au cœur culturel du projet 'Norman Connections'. Ainsi, l'article rédigé par Edward Impey et John McNeill incorpore les thèmes architecturaux qui correspondent à ceux de la vie d'Orderic, dans la mesure où nous parlons d'une certaine forme de migration de l'Angleterre vers la Normandie qui a des implications pour l'identité impériale. La Salle de l'Echiquier à Caen est perçue par eux comme à la fois un prototype pour exporter un style anglais d'architecture nationale, le hall, vers la Normandie et, quand on le compare au grand hall construit à Westminster à la même époque, comme une expression de ce que j'appellerais l'architecture impériale; ce ne peut être le fruit du hasard que ces deux bâtiments très innovants aient été construits tout près des églises où Guillaume le Conquérant a été couronné roi d'Angleterre et a été enterré. Le phénomène n'est pas du tout normand mais il n'est pas non plus anglais; lorsqu'on tient compte de son ambition et de son échelle, c'est un produit spécialisé d'un monde impérial nouveau qui est né en 1066.[13] L'essai de Pamela Marshall montre la complexité de ce monde.

Les processus de changement, qui au fil des ans ont impliqué des aspirations culturelles et des influences provenant de bien au-delà des frontières de la Normandie et de l'Angleterre, entrent dans la discussion exposée dans l'essai de Jon Gregory et Robert Liddiard ; les choix faits par les aristocrates individuels et leurs architectes sont influencés par l'Europe occidentale qui a influencé à la fois la Normandie et l'Angleterre, comme a aussi bien-sûr été le cas dans les siècles précédant 1066. Pour revenir un instant sur les documents écrits et au processus de dissémination qui s'appuyaient sur l'Angleterre, l'histoire de l'acte et la charte de l'acte démontre bien une expansion d'une forme spécifique dans les régions du nord de la France, ainsi que dans le royaume d'Écosse et ailleurs dans les îles britanniques.[14] Si on revient pendant un instant à Le Patourel et Davis, on voit que tout cela n'a pas l'uniformité culturelle d'un empire normand et l' inspiration culturelle normande telles que les définissait Le Patourel, mais qu'en même temps, il existe un multiculturalisme unifiant résultant des activités des Normands, force cathartique centrale, ce qui va donc à l'encontre de la critique de Davis.

Pour développer plus avant mon thème par une étude de cas qui n'a manifestement pas été choisie au hasard, on voit que les processus que ces changements mettent en avant sont très évidents dans l'histoire des XIe et XIIe siècles de Norwich et de l'East Anglia. Le donjon du château de Norwich, par exemple, est très différent des deux grands donjons de pierre construits en Angleterre, à savoir la Tour Blanche de Londres et Colchester, et ressemble à des constructions similaires sur la Loire. La galerie qui donne sur l'est de la Tour de Bigod partage des éléments avec le hall royal wisigoth du début du IXe siècle près d'Orvieto et le précurseur de la grande arche sous la tour est, dit-on, le palais impérial du milieu du XIe siècle de Goslar.[15] Si l'influence prédominante sur les décors de la cathédrale de Norwich est sans aucune discussion possible, l'église de la fondation monastique de Guillaume le Conquérant de Saint-Etienne de Caen, la taille du bâtiment et sa décoration s'inspirent de multiples autres édifices bien au-delà des frontières du duché de Normandie, ainsi que de l'Angleterre contemporaine.[16] Comme plusieurs autres grandes églises de l'Angleterre d'après 1066, elle est bien plus grande que tout ce qui a été construit dans la Normandie contemporaine et en fait presque partout en Europe occidentale. Sa décoration révèle des influences de Durham et les parties de la cathédrale de Cantorbéry reconstruites par St Anselm.

Ce qui est aussi important pour mon thème est que le processus tortueux qui a mené au site de l'évêché à Norwich était totalement anglais, résultant de la défaite de la tentative, par les évêques d'East Anglia, d'asseoir leur siège dans l'abbaye de Bury St Edmunds ; les principaux participants venaient peut-être de Normandie et du nord de la France, mais les bases de leurs arguments s'appuyaient sur un précédent et des conditions anglais.[17] Les échanges dans la Mer du Nord qui se poursuivaient et développaient des liens pré-existants ont également une grand importance pour l'histoire architecturale de l'East Anglia après la Conquête. Ainsi, alors que le bloc occidental encore en partie visible à Ely ne peut pas nécessairement être vu comme un véritable emprunt précoce des églises de l'Empire, il ne fait aucun doute que c'étaient là les sources d'inspiration d'autres églises importantes, et que certains aspects des décors étaient liés à la vieille basilique St Pierre de Rome.[18] A un niveau moins élevé, l'origine des fameuses tours rondes de certaines églises paroissiales du Norfolk et du Suffolk est peut-être à trouver dans la nouvelle cathédrale de Norwich et l'église abbatiale de Bury St Edmunds, mais ce qui est certain est que ce type de tour a proliféré autour de la Mer du Nord, et nulle part ailleurs, au XIIe siècle.[19] Mais d'après ce que l'on voit, l'East Anglia en sa qualité d'importateur de multiples influences culturelles, est également devenue exportateur, plus particulièrement par l'énorme augmentation de la renommée du culte de St Edmund. Il est surprenant de noter que le rapport de l'archidiacre Herman, à la fin du XIe siècle, sur les miracles de St Edmund, est une source essentielle de l'histoire de Barfleur, ville côtière normande qui n'a apparemment aucune histoire avant 1066, et dont la fortune semble avoir été créée par le nombre croissant de traversées de la Manche suite à la conquête de 1066.[20]

En termes d'histoires de vies individuelles et collectives, l'impact de ces vastes campagnes de constructions sur les habitants de Norwich, ainsi que l'accroissement de la surface de la ville qui en découle, est important en surface du moins, même si ce n'est pas assez simple qu'on peut croire. Le volume qu'on appelle Little Domesday Book nous fournit d'un commentaire éloquent des effets de la construction du château qui est l'ancêtre du château actuel, en disant de la population indigène que 'ceux qui partaient et les autres qui restaient ont été totalement ruinés'.[21] Pourtant le travail a dû à une certaine époque créer des emplois et une prospérité relative pour beaucoup.[22] L'essai d'Elizabeth Popescu dans ce volume approfondit considérablement la connaissance des détails de ce processus. Parallèlement, l'usage important de la pierre de Caen dans la construction de la cathédrale et du donjon a dû profiter économiquement et financièrement à ceux qui travaillaient dans les carrières de Caen et aux marins chargés du transport de ces pierres. Un commentaire imprécis, mais extrêmement évocateur de la situation vient de l'évaluation de Brian Ayers: des quantités 'colossales' de pierres ont sans doute été transportées par la mer jusqu'à Norwich.[23] Bien que l'interprétation de l'histoire du XIIe siècle sur les carrières de pierres de Caen présente des problèmes, il serait bon de penser qu'on peut procéder à une certaine quantification sur la base de la preuve de Norwich qui pourrait transformer l'histoire architecturale en une histoire économique et sociale.[24] Ce que cette analyse montre est que ce n'était pas uniquement une élite aristocratique transmanche qui avait intérêt à ce que l'empire transmanche perdure. Ce dernier apportait davantage d'horizons à de nombreuses personnes et créait de nouveaux intérêts directs. Même si l'histoire de ceux qui travaillaient dans les carrières de Caen et construisaient Norwich ne peut s'écrire, l'histoire des bâtiments et du paysage peut contribuer de manière importante à comprendre ce que cela représentait.

Comme pour tous les empires, l'élément déterminant ultime de la montée et de la chute fut l'engagement de l'élite impériale face à l'opposition venant de l'intérieur tout comme de l'extérieur. L'histoire de l'élite aristocratique qui détenait des terrains transmanche est donc extrêmement importante. Bien que son histoire ait été souvent étudiée, elle demande davantage de recherches concentrées sur les processus à long terme et les infrastructures du pouvoir. Pour moi, ce qui est particulièrement frappant, ce n'est pas seulement comment une élite supérieure excessivement riche a survécu pendant des générations et s'est renouvelée constamment, mais comment elle a réagi face à la crise; les actes politiques transmanche ont été beaucoup en évidence pendant la guerre civile entre le roi Etienne et l'Impératrice Mathilde, un phénomène dont l'importance n'est pas toujours appréciée.[25] Avec leurs réseaux et liens culturels qui s'étendaient bien au-delà des frontières de la

Normandie et de l'Angleterre, ces hommes et ces femmes, immensément puissants, étaient des agents importants du multiculturalisme que je veux souligner. Une belle expression symbolique des valeurs impériales qui fonctionnaient à la fin du XIIe siècle vient des similitudes dans l'aspect des deux donjons de Conisbrough et Mortemer, tous deux construits par Hamelin Plantagenet, par mariage entre 1164 et 1202, héritier des intérêts de la famille Warenne en Angleterre, Normandie et Flandre.[26]

La conquête de 1066 créa de nouvelles identités pour tous ceux qui acquéraient des terres en Angleterre. Par exemple, le fait que tant de personnes de la première génération de colons du Cambridgeshire, à un niveau social relativement peu élevé, aient adopté des toponymes anglais avant la création du Domesday Book, n'est qu'une illustration de la façon dont les nouveaux arrivants se sont identifiés aux lieux où ils avaient acquis des terres.[27] Cependant, lorsqu'on crée l'histoire des vies, on voit que cette intégration apparente dans de nouveaux endroits ne signifiait pas pour autant qu'ils n'étaient plus actifs dans l'empire transmanche. Une nouvelle identité qui était en fait une identité transmanche, est donnée par la référence de Guillaume de Malmesbury à la famille *Vituli*, qui avait des biens à Southampton et Caen, comme une race spécifique d'hommes associée aux bateaux et à la mer (*genus hominum nauticorum*); il s'agissait d'un groupe si important qu'ils réussirent à convaincre le comte Robert de Gloucester, grand partisan de l'Impératrice Mathilde, de ne pas attaquer Southampton.[28] Dans tous ces cas, essayer de trouver une identité soit normande, soit anglaise relève de la simplification; une analyse en termes de diaspora doit en fait nous convaincre que ce qui était vu comme soit anglais, soit normand, pouvait revenir à une forme précédente dans une phase suivante d'un cycle de vie ou dans la génération suivante.[29] Une référence unique, apparemment isolée, peut en fait attirer l'attention sur les dimensions des vies individuelles et collectives qui, autrement, auraient pu être considérées comme n'existant pas. Ainsi, une étude de cas m'a fait comprendre le potentiel de ce point de vue: la réunion de la veuve de Richard de Reviers et de ses descendants, plus de 30 ans après sa mort en l'an 1107, à l'abbaye qu'il avait en fait fondée à Montebourg dans l'ouest de la Normandie.[30] Et, pour en revenir au sujet de l'architecture, l'article de John Crook sur les chapiteaux dans la chapelle de St Jean dans la Tour Blanche de Londres souligne à nouveau la présence d'identités stylistiques multiculturelles, les chapiteaux cubiques tirant incontestablement leur inspiration du nord-est de la France, plutôt que de la Normandie. Il en va de même, bien que l'axe essentiel soit sur la chronologie de la construction de la tour Blanche de Londres, pour des paragraphes de l'article de Roland Harris. Et ainsi, pour finir, laissant de côté les constructions et les écrits, l'article de Steven Ashley qui couvre un ensemble remarquable d'objets de cette élite, comme par exemple, les sécurités et boucles des harnais des chevaux.

Les nouveaux arrivants s'emparant de presque toutes les ressources économiques de l'Angleterre après 1066, il est totalement justifié de parler du régime transmanche comme de 'l'empire des Normands', puisque le cœur de la force d'invasion et de la nouvelle élite transmanche venait de Normandie et s'identifiaient aux Normands. Mais, ce faisant, il faut aussi garder à l'esprit la chose suivante: outre le fait qu'une bonne proportion de ces nouveaux arrivants ne venait pas de Normandie du tout, mais plutôt d'autres régions du nord de la France, l'empire, qui plus est, était né pluriel. Guillaume le Conquérant a été couronné 'Roi des Anglais' et dans l'histoire architecturale des églises, il y a cette période qui est appelé 'saxo-normande'.[31] Ce que, pour des raisons pratiques, nous pouvons appeler les thèmes anglais, se retrouvait culturellement depuis le début, même si, par rapport à l'histoire du pouvoir dans une forme tout à fait abstraite qui a totalement échoué dans sa protection de l'aristocratie du royaume pré-conquête.[32] Et la réponse aux pressions qui en découlèrent sur le Pays de Galles, l'Écosse et l'Irlande produisit un mélange de changements en vigueur, de transferts culturels et l'affirmation forte d'identités préexistantes. Le processus général doit bien entendu prendre en compte ce que Robert Bartlett a appelé de manière pratique le 'changement européen', les courants plus larges qui, à des degrés plus ou moins importants, ont affecté tout le monde, y compris la Normandie et les Normands.[33] En d'autres termes, tout ceci constitue un argument pour étudier de nombreuses histoires – y compris celles des bâtiments – pour avoir une meilleure connaissance de l'histoire multiculturelle de l'empire transmanche.

Pour finir, je voudrais souligner à nouveau que l'empire et le multiculturalisme ont transformé la Normandie. Ils ont sans doute apporté de la richesse au duché depuis l'Angleterre, à tel point que Mathieu Arnoux a développé une argumentation en faveur d'une révolution industrielle normande.[34] Mais il est également fort évident que l'empire ne fut pas gratuit. Certes il y eut le triomphalisme associé aux victoires militaires et une prise de conscience d'une expansion paneuropéenne dans laquelle des personnes de Normandie avaient joué un rôle important, mais il y a aussi le choc exprimé dans l'histoire racontée à l'origine par Orderic et développée dans les années 1160 par Wace sur la reddition de Caen à Henri I en 1105, sans un seul coup porté pour le compte de son frère aîné, le duc de Normandie légitime, Robert Curthose. Orderic a raconté que le manoir anglais attribué en reconnaissance par Henri fut appelé 'le Manoir des Traitres' et qu'il fut vite rendu. Wace ajouta que le lieu de la reddition était un endroit sur lequel rien ne poussa par la suite, souvenir permanent pour tous ceux qui y passaient de la désapprobation divine.[35] La création de l'empire avait apporté la guerre civile à la Normandie, à contre cœur. Mais il avait aussi apporté l'absorption de thèmes provenant de la périphérie vers une nouvelle identité impériale, plus particulièrement dans l'assimilation rapide des histoires de Geoffroi de Monmouth du roi britannique Arthur dans l'identité impériale transmanche. Les agents principaux de ce processus dans les années 1140 et 1150 semblent avoir été Robert de Torigni, prieure du Bec et par la suite, de 1154 à 1186, abbé du Mont Saint-Michel, et Wace, à travers le premier de ses deux *magna opera*, le *Roman de Brut*.[36] N'oublions pas la surprise de l'historien Henri de Huntingdon, basé en Angleterre et qui en parlait comme de son pays natal, lorsqu'il rendit visite à Robert de Torigni au Bec en 1139 et tomba pour la première fois sur l'œuvre de Geoffroi, en dépit du fait qu'elle avait été écrite en Angleterre.[37] L'histoire de l'architecture gothique normande, récemment étudiée magistralement par Lindy Grant, est une illustration du changement culturel qui pénétrait dans le duché en provenance du royaume de France. Un sujet complexe, mélangeant conservatisme, archaïsme conscient qui pourrait être perçu comme une tentative de poursuivre un passé normand brillant, et adoption de nouvelles influences révolutionnaires provenant de ce berceau architectural qu'était l'Ile de France à partir du milieu du XIIe siècle.[38] Une fois encore donc, nous avons un mélange de multiculturalisme et de forte identité normande.

Dans la vie de Wace, comme dans celle d'Orderic, nous avons une histoire qui consiste en triomphalisme de l'empire et profonde ambivalence en ce qui concerne son impact. Ces éléments forment une riche tapisserie qui ne peut être comprise qu'en examinant leurs vies dans leur ensemble et illustrent ainsi l'immense potentiel connu de ces histoires et de ces vies. On retrouve exactement ce même potentiel dans l'histoire des bâtiments et cela démontre pourquoi les collaborations internationales, comme soulignées dans ce volume, sont la base indispensable à la compréhension de phénomènes qui transcendent les frontières nationales. Ils nous entraînent dans un monde multiculturel qui est très différent du discours prédominant de la période antérieure aux années 1970 et qui est, bien entendu, toujours présent aujourd'hui. Ces essais approfondissent la connaissance et suggèrent de nombreuses pistes de recherches pour l'avenir.

## Notes

1 Le Patourel 1976; Davis 1976, passim, with the basic thesis set out at pp. 12–5. As a critique of Davis's book, Loud 1982 (reprinted in Loud 1999, chapter I) remains fundamental.

2 Douglas 1969, p. 14.

3 Haskins 1916, p. 3.

4 Powicke 1961, pp. 297–307; Musset 1982, pp. 292–4. Note in particular, 'l'équilibre ancien entre Angleterre et Normandie se reverse complètement, au bénéfice de l'Angleterre' (p. 294). The argument is also clearly set out in Jouet 1983, pp. 17–9 (nb, 'c'est la dilution progressive au sein d'un empire dont elle n'est plus l'inspiratrice unique', at p. 19), with the arguments repeated in Jouet 2007, pp. 3–8. The argument was also one of the pillars of Davis 1976, with statements such as 'Once England had become the principal residence of most Normans' (p. 123).

5 Sykes 2005; 2007. For a survey, Creighton 2009.

6 Southern 1973, p. 249 (Bartlett, ed. 2004, p. 72).

7 Davison 1969.

8 This is one of the central themes of Bates 2013.

9 Higham 2010, p. 11.

10 Davis 1976, p. 15.

11 Chibnall 1969–80, pp. 3 and 6–9 (*inspirante Deo Normannorum gesta et euentus Normannis promere scripto sum conatus*); Chibnall 1984, p. 3, note 2. On Orderic's childhood, Chibnall 1984, pp. 3–11. For the calendar, Bibliothèque Nationale de France, ms. lat. 10062, fo. 19v; cit, Hingst 2009, p. xix.

12 On Orderic and identity, see further, Bates 2013, pp. 31–2.

13 Fernie 2000, chapter 2; Bates 2013, pp. 23–7.

14 Hagger 2009, pp. 181–206; cf, Bates 1985, pp. 266–84. See also Broun 2005, pp. 164–83; Crouch 2009, pp. 75–90.

15 For all this, Heslop 1994, pp. 11–2 and 32. See further his essay in this volume.

16 Fernie 1993, pp. 107–55.

17 Most recently, Licence 2012, and especially at pp. 155–7.

18 Plant 2013. For the general thesis of England's greater openness, Grant 1994, pp. 121–6; Fernie 2000, pp. 120–4.

19 Heywood 2013.

20 Musset 1983, p. 51.

21 Farley 1783, p. 2, fos. 116v–18r.

22 See Campbell 2004, pp. 39–45.

23 Ayers 1990, p. 223. That the statement is inclusive of Barnack and Caen does not detract from its force.

24 Dujardin 1998, pp. 1 and 190–5.

25 Bates 2013, pp. 113–5 and 151–2.

26 Sands, Braun and Loyd 1936; Brindle 2012, pp. 64–5.

27 Lewis 1993, and see especially pp. 20–1 and 23–5; Bates 2013, p. 40–2.

28 King and Potter 1998, pp. 128–9.

29 Bates 2013, pp. 29 and 181–3.

30 Bearman 1994, no. 8; Bates 2013, pp. 15–17.

31 Fernie 2000, pp. 209–19.

32 Bates 2013, pp. 90–2.

33 Bartlett 1994, passim, with the central arguments at pp. 1–3. Among stimulating reflections on this theme is Pryce 2007.

34 Arnoux 2007, pp. 231–4.

35 Chibnall 1969–80, pp. 6 and 78–9; Burgess 2004, pp. 336–7, lines 11285–11308; Urbanski 2008. For the site at which the surrender took place, Jean-Marie 2000, pp. 23, 52–3 and 214.

36 This is of course a subject on which there is a huge literature. For comments in relation to this article's theme and references to the central literature, Bates 2012, pp. 182–4; Bates 2013, pp. 53–6.

37 Greenway 1996, pp. 558–9.

38 Grant 2005, pp. 67–95.

## Bibliography


### *Primary Sources*

Bearman, R., ed. (1994) *Charters of the Redvers Family and the Earldom of Devon 1090–1217*, Devon and Cornwall Record Society, New Series, Vol. 37 (Exeter).

Burgess, G. S., trans. (2004) *The History of the Norman People: Wace's Roman de Rou* (Woodbridge, Boydell).

Chibnall, M., ed. and trans. (1969–80) *The Ecclesiastical History of Orderic Vitalis*, 6 vols, Oxford Medieval Texts (Oxford).

Farley, A., ed. (1783) *Domesday Book, seu Liber Censualis Willelmi primi regis Angliae*, 2 vols (London).

Henry of Huntingdon *Historia Anglorum (The History of the English People)*, D. E. Greenway, ed. and trans. (1996) Oxford Medieval Texts (Oxford).

William of Malmesbury, *Historia Novella: The Contemporary History*, E. King, ed. and K. R. Potter, trans. (1998) Oxford Medieval Texts (Oxford ).

### *Secondary Sources*

Arnoux, M. (2007) 'L'événement et la conjuncture. Hypothèses sur les conditions économiques de la conquête de 1204', in A-M. Flambard Héricher and V. Gazeau, ed., pp. 227–38.

Ayers, B. S. (1990) 'Building a fine city: the provision of flint, mortar and freestone in medieval Norwich', in D. Parsons, ed., pp. 217–28.

Bartlett, R. J. (1994) *The Making of Europe: Conquest, Colonisation and Cultural Change, 950–1350* (London, Penguin).

Bartlett, R. J., ed. (2004) *History and Historians: Selected Papers of R. W. Southern* (Oxford, Penguin).

Bates, D. (1985) 'The earliest Norman writs', *English Historical Review* 100, pp. 266–84.

Bates, D. and Curry, A., ed. (1994) *England and Normandy in the Middle Ages* (London and Rio Grande, Hambledon Press).

Bates, D. (2012) 'Robert of Torigni and the *Historia Anglorum*', in D. Roffe, ed., pp. 175–84.

Bates, D. and Liddiard, R., ed. (2013) *East Anglia and its North Sea World in the Middle Ages* (Woodbridge, Boydell).

Bates, D. (2013) *The Normans and Empire* (Oxford, Oxford University Press).

Bautier, R. H. *et al.*, ed. (1982) *La France de Philippe Auguste. Le Temps des Mutations. Actes du Colloque International organisé par le CNRS* (Paris, CNRS).

Brindle, S. (2012) 'The Keep at Conisbrough Castle, Yorkshire', *Château Gaillard* 25, pp. 61–74.

Broun, D. (2005) 'The Adoption of Brieves in Scotland', in M. T. Flanagan and J. A. Green, ed., pp. 164–83.

Campbell, J. (2004) 'Norwich before 1300', in C. Rawcliffe and R. Wilson, ed., pp. 29–48.

Chibnall, M. (1984) *The World of Orderic Vitalis* (Oxford, Clarendon).

Creighton, O. H. (2009) 'Castle studies and the European medieval landscape: traditions, trends and future research directions', *Landscape History* 30, pp. 5–20.

Crook, D. and Vincent, N., ed. (2009) *Records, Administration and Aristocratic Society in the Anglo-Norman Realm* (Woodbridge, Boydell).

Crouch, D. (2009) 'Between three realms: The Acts of Waleran II, Count of Meulan and Worcester', in D. Crook and N. Vincent, ed., pp. 75–90.

Davis, R. H. C. (1976) *The Normans and their Myth* (London, Thames & Hudson).

Davison, B. K. (1969) 'Early earthwork castles: a new model', *Château Gaillard* 3, pp. 37–47.

Douglas, D. C. (1969) *The Norman Achievement* (London, Eyre & Spottiswoode).

Dujardin, L. (1998) *Carrières de Pierre en Normandie. Contribution à l'étude historique et archéologique des carrières de pierre à bâtir à Caen (Calvados) et en Normandie aux époques mediévale et moderne*, 3 vols (doctoral thesis, University of Caen).

Fernie, E. (1993) *An Architectural History of Norwich Cathedral* (Oxford, Clarendon).

Fernie, E. (2000) *The Architecture of Norman England* (Oxford, Oxford University Press).

Flambard Héricher A-M. and Gazeau, V., ed. (2007) *1204: la Normandie entre Plantagenêts et Capétiens* (Caen, CRAHM).

Flanagan, M. T. and Green, J. A., ed. (2005), *Charters and Charter Scholarship in Britain and Ireland* ((Basingstoke, Palgrave Macmillan).

Grant, L. (1994) 'Architectural relationships between England and Normandy, 1100–1204', in D. Bates and A. Curry, ed., pp. 117–29.

Grant, L. (2005) *Architecture and Society in Normandy 1120–1270* (New Haven and London, Yale University Press).

Hagger, M. (2009) 'The earliest Norman writs revisited', *Historical Research* 82, pp. 181–206.

Haskins, C. H. (1916) *The Normans in European History* (London, Boston and New York).

Heslop, T. A. (1994) *Norwich Castle Keep: Romanesque Architecture and Social Context* (Norwich, Centre of East Anglian Studies).

Heywood, S. (2013) 'Stone building in Romanesque East Anglia', in D. Bates and R. Liddiard, ed., pp. 256–69.

Higham, R. (2010) 'Castle studies in transition: a forty year reflection', *Archaeological Journal* 167, pp. 1–13.

Hingst, A. J. (2009) *The Written Word: Past and Place in the Work of Orderic Vitalis* (Notre Dame, University Press).

Jean-Marie, L. (2000) *Caen aux XIe et XIIe siècles. Espace urbain, pouvoirs et société* (Caen, Editions La Mandragore).

Jouet, R. (1983) *Et la Normandie devint française* (Paris, Editions Mazarine).

Jouet, R. (2007) 'Avant-propos: Faut-il commémorer 1204?', in A-M. Flambard Héricher and V. Gazeau, ed., pp. 3–8.

Le Patourel, J. (1976) *The Norman Empire* (Oxford, Clarendon).

Lewis, C. P. (1993) 'The Domesday Jurors', *Haskins Society Journal* 5, pp. 17–45.

Licence, T. (2012) 'Herbert Losinga's trip to Rome and the Bishopric of Bury St Edmunds', *Anglo-Norman Studies* 34, pp. 151–68.

Loud, G. (1982) 'The *Gens Normannorum* – Myth or Reality', *Anglo-Norman Studies* 4, pp. 104–16 and 204–9.

Loud, G. (1999) *Conquerors and Churchmen in Norman Italy.* Variorum Collected Studies Series (Aldershot).

Musset, L. (1982) 'Quelques problèmes posés par l'annexion de la Normandie au domain royal français', in R. H. Bautier *et al.*, ed., pp. 291–309.

Musset, L. (1983) 'Barfleur, plaque tournante de l'Etat anglo-normand', *Annuaire des cinq départements de la Normandie* 141, pp. 51–7.

Parsons, D., ed. (1990) *Stone: Quarrying and Building in England AD 43–1525* (Chichester, Phillimore).

Plant, R. (2013) 'Romanesque East Anglia and the Empire', in D. Bates and R. Liddiard, ed., pp. 270–86.

Powicke, F. M. (1961) (2nd ed.) *The Loss of Normandy 1189–1204: Studies in the History of the Angevin Empire* (Manchester, University Press).

Pryce, H. (2007) 'Welsh rulers and European change, *c.* 1100–1282', in H. Pryce and J. Watts, ed., pp. 37–51.

Pryce, H. and Watts, J., ed. (2007) *Power and Identity in the Middle Ages: Essays in Memory of Rees Davies* (Oxford, Oxford University Press).

Rawcliffe, C. and Wilson, R., ed. (2004) *Medieval Norwich* (London and New York, Hambledon).

Roffe, D., ed. (2012) *The English and their Legacy 900–1200: Essays in Honour of Ann Williams* (Woodbridge, Boydell).

Sands, H., Braun, H. and Loyd, L. C. (1936) 'Conisbrough and Mortemer', *Yorkshire Archaeological Journal* 32, pp. 147–59.

Southern, R. W. (1973) 'Aspects of the European tradition of historical writing: 4. The sense of the past', *Transactions of the Royal Historical Society*, 5th series 23, pp. 246–63. Reprinted in R. Bartlett (2004).

Sykes, N. (2005) 'Zooarchaeology of the Norman Conquest', *Anglo-Norman Studies* 27, pp. 185–97.

Sykes, N. (2007) *The Norman Conquest: A Zooarchaeological Perspective*, British Archaeological Report International Series 1656 (Oxford).

Urbanski, C. (2008) 'Apology, protest and suppression: interpreting the surrender of Caen (1105)', *Haskins Society Journal* 19, pp. 137–53.

Vincent, N. ed. (2009) *Records, Administration and Aristocratic Society in the Anglo-Norman Realm: Papers commemorating the 800th Anniversary of King John's Loss of Normandy* (Woodbridge, Boydell).

# Part I

# The Norman Connections Castles

# 1

# Norwich Castle

*Elizabeth Popescu*

## Résumé

*Cet article approfondira l'interprétation archéologique du château de Norwich et de ses remparts, un joyau de son époque. Son donjon normand impressionnant a été décrit comme étant, sur le plan architectural, une des constructions les plus ambitieuses de son temps en Europe occidentale. Il a été parmi les 40 premiers châteaux urbains à être construits avant 1100, et sa surface s'étend sur une grande partie du territoire de Norwich qui est devenue l'une des villes majeures d'Angleterre en 1066. Pendant presque un siècle, Norwich a été l'unique château royal dans le Norfolk et le Suffolk et a exercé les fonctions de centre administratif dans une région extrêmement riche. Une importante clôture de terres relevant directement de la couronne – les "droits" ou "libertés" (Fee ou Liberty) du château – était délimitée dans la proximité immédiate du château et la juridiction royale a été maintenue dans cette enceinte jusqu'en 1345. Deux grands murs d'enceinte furent érigés au sud et au nord-est de cet enclos, devenue plus tard la rue de Castle Meadow. Une barbacane fut ajoutée au XIIIe siècle. Au milieu du XIIIe siècle, le château de Norwich se trouvait au cœur d'une ville fortifiée plus vaste que Londres, son développement étant influencé par le cours caractéristique de la rivière Wensum.*

*Dans le cadre de la construction d'un centre commercial souterrain, des travaux d'excavation importants ont été menés sur le site du château entre 1987 et 1991 par l'unité d'archéologie du Norfolk: à l'époque, il s'agissait du plus grand projet de ce type en Europe du Nord. Cet essai prend en compte les résultats des fouilles en relation avec l'impact du château sur la topographie de la ville actuelle, et retrace le développement du donjon et de ses remparts dans leurs phases de bois et de pierre, avec une attention particulière portée sur les périodes de construction les plus importantes entre environ 1067–70 et 1122. On inclut un bref résumé de la manière dont le château et son enclos (Fee) ont continué d'influencer le développement du cœur historique de Norwich jusqu'à notre époque.*

## Introduction

Norwich Castle was one of the finest Norman fortifications in England. Its great Norman keep or donjon has been described as 'architecturally the most ambitious secular building [of its time] in western Europe' (Heslop 1994, p. 66). It was one of more than 40 urban castles established before 1100, and overlies a substantial part of what had become one of the dominant towns in England by 1066. By the mid-14th century, it lay at the heart of a walled city larger than London, the distinctive shape of which was influenced by the course of the River Wensum (Figure 1.1). Norwich was to remain the only royal castle in Norfolk and Suffolk for nearly a century, serving as the administrative centre of an extremely wealthy area. A substantial precinct of Crown land (*Feodum Castelli*: Fee or Liberty of the castle) was defined immediately around it and royal jurisdiction was maintained over the enclosure until 1345. Within the Fee, two large baileys were laid out to the south and north-east, the latter being known as the Castle Meadow (Figure 1.2). A barbican complex was added in the 13th century. At its largest extent, the entire castle precinct encompassed about 9.3 hectares (23 acres).

Recognition of the site's national importance led to its scheduling in 1915 (SAM Norfolk 5), the protected area being extended in 1983 to enclose much of the Fee. Despite eventual landscaping for a Cattle Market most of the south bailey remained open space. Redevelopment for a retail centre – named Castle Mall – led to a major excavation by the Norfolk Archaeological Unit between 1987 and 1991 (covering 2.3 hectares, 5.7 acres; Site 777N): at the time of excavation, this was the largest project of its kind in northern Europe. Further excavations took place at Golden Ball Street in 1998. The results from both sites are published in two monographs (Parts I and II; Shepherd Popescu 2009a and b), supplemented by occasional papers on zooarchaeology (Part III: Albarella *et al.* 2009) and additional documentary evidence relating to the 71 medieval properties that lay within the Castle Fee (Part IV; Tillyard *et al.* 2009). The project also has a digital aspect, which provides full details of the various cemeteries

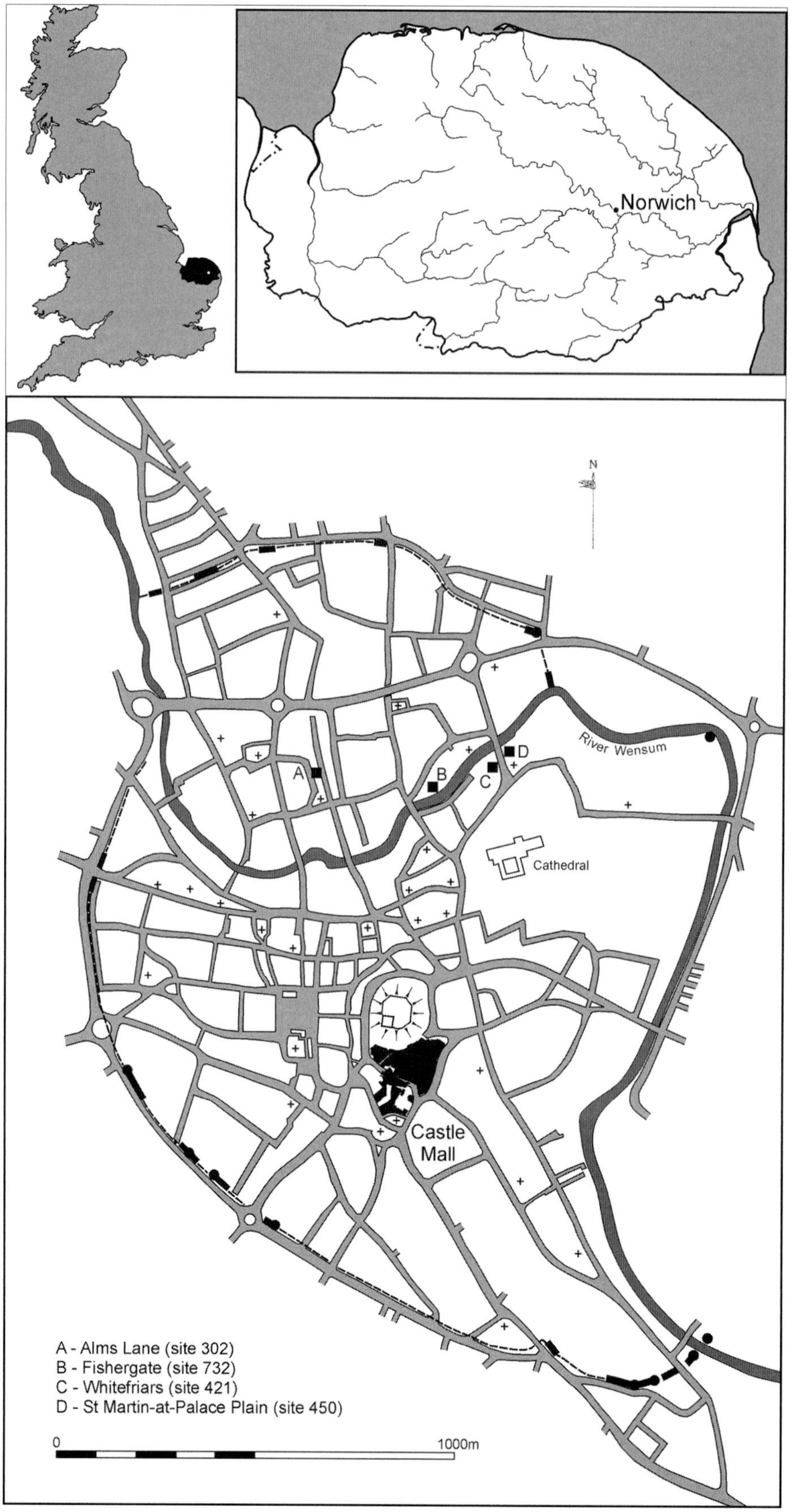


*Figure 1.1. Location of Norwich and of the Castle Mall and Golden Ball Street sites (Norfolk Museums Service).*

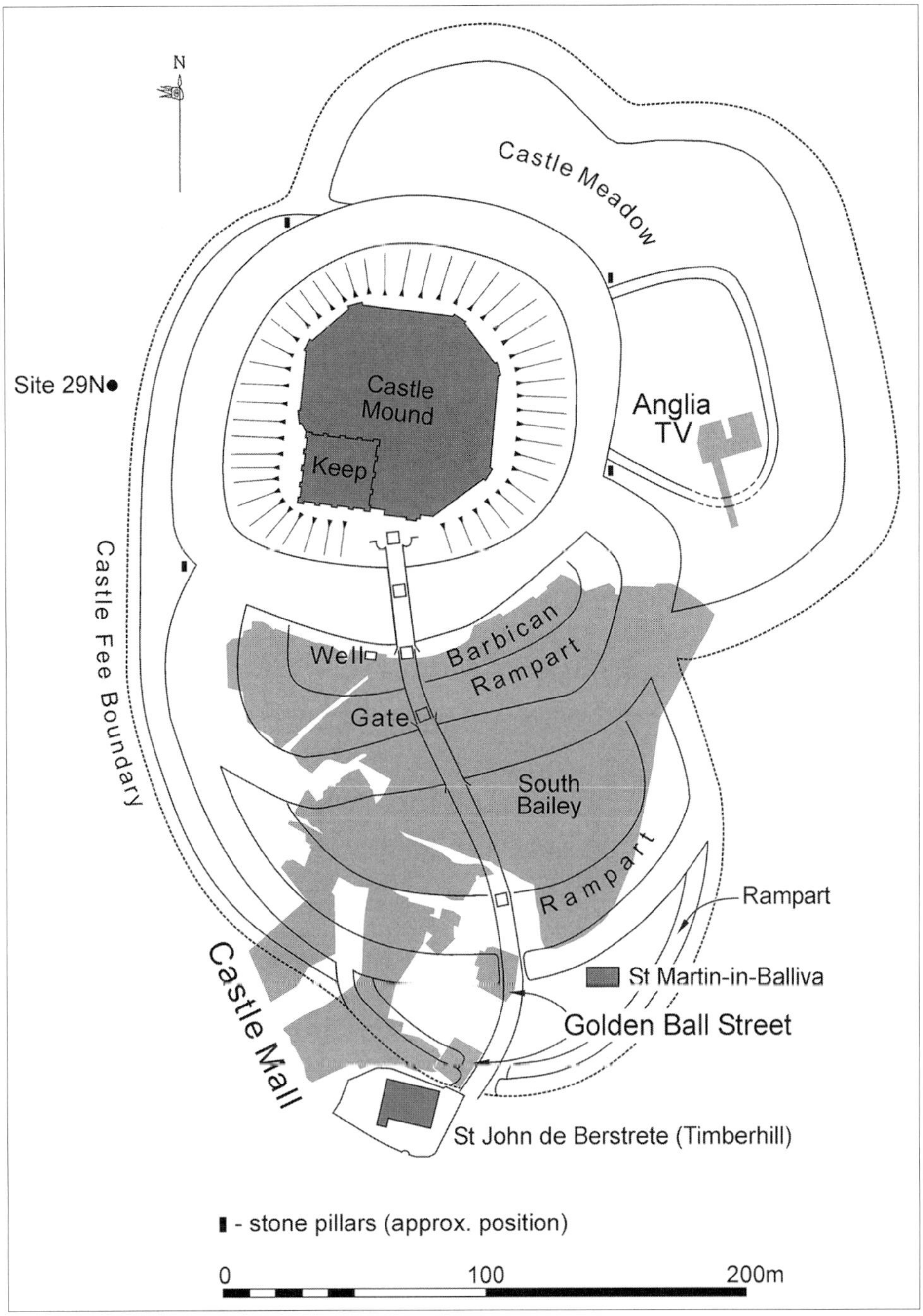


*Figure 1.2. Plan of excavated areas at Castle Mall and Golden Ball Street, showing modern street names and the footprint of the excavations against the castle defences (Norfolk Museums Service).*

at the site (Part V; Shepherd Popescu 2009c). An additional report on supplementary excavations at the castle mound in 1999–2001 is in preparation (Wallis, forthcoming).

### Natural topography

Contrary to popular opinion Norfolk, and more particularly Norwich, are not flat. The city is dominated by two areas of high ground: Mousehold Heath to the north-east and the Ber Street ridge to the south. The site selected for the castle had a naturally dominant position, lying at the northern end of the Ber Street ridge: one obvious suggestion for the origin of the street name refers to the limit of the Saxon burh (Armitage 1912, p. 174), although another suggestion is that it derives from the Old English (WSax) *beorg* or Angle *berg* meaning 'hill' or 'mound' (Hudson 1896, p. 17; Sandred and Lindström 1989, p. 88). To the west of the castle site a stream – the Great Cockey – ran northwards to the Wensum in its own valley. This watercourse later separated the castle precinct from the Norman market place to the west, at the same time defining much of the eastern edge of the Jewish Quarter.

## The pre-Conquest landscape

### *Middle Saxon Needham?*

Norwich Castle has long been believed to overlie part of the pre-Conquest settlement of *Needham*, one of five hamlets or villages founded in the 8th to 9th century that had, by the 11th century, coalesced to form the town of Norwich. The place-name implies a poor homestead or meadow (Sandred and Lindström 1989, pp. 140–1). Although the initial findings of the excavation did not appear to indicate direct activity in the area during the Middle Saxon period, burials in a cemetery beneath the barbican rampart were later radiocarbon dated to the 8th to 9th centuries. *Needham* may have consisted of little more than a collection of farmsteads (Green and Young 1981, p. 10) and the presence of an early cemetery and finds in the vicinity of the castle supports the suggestion that pre-urban settlements began in Norwich during the 8th century (Ayers 1994, p. 22). Indeed, small concentrations of Middle Saxon finds occur within the local 'settlement' area.

### *The two* Burhs

Norwich's emergence as a town may be rooted in the probable period of Danish occupation (*c.* 870 to *c.* 917) and in the Anglo-Scandinavian period that followed re-conquest by the West Saxon kings. The presence of a defended area of possible Danish origin on the north bank of the River Wensum (*Northwic*) was originally postulated on the basis of surviving street pattern (Carter 1978, fig. 7). This D-shaped enclosure may have been of similar character to those recorded elsewhere (such as Bedford and Lincoln), possibly re-used – as at Ipswich – to form a 10th-century burh (Ayers 1997, p. 59).

New information suggests that at Norwich two 'burhs' may have opposed each other across the River Wensum (Figure 1.3), similar double burhs being known at many urban centres such as Ipswich, Thetford and Cambridge. The limit of Norwich's southern burh may be reflected in the curving line of Mountergate (formerly Inferior Conesford), running northwards across the cathedral precinct to meet the river just to the east of Whitefriars bridge (cf. Atkin and Carter 1985; Atkin 1993). An extension of this line to the west of King Street runs along the former course of Stepping Lane and Rising Sun Lane (cf. 1883 OS map), to the junction with Golden Ball Street. West of this point, the castle defences obliterated any topographical indicators of this putative boundary. The western limit of settlement was probably defined by the contours of the Great Cockey stream valley, its position mirroring the known defence on the river's north bank. Recent work south of Stepping Lane confirms the presence of a substantial ditch in the anticipated position of the Late Saxon defence (Site 26577N; Penn 1999; Lloyd *et al.* 2002). Any continuation to the east and west has not yet been located, although a ditch and bank observed immediately to the west of the castle have been interpreted as demarcating the Castle Fee boundary and/or that of the burh (see below).

On the basis of the evidence summarised above, the burh ditch would be expected to have run directly across the Castle Mall site: although the recorded evidence provides no apparent evidence for its presence, a line across the western and southern part of the site was clearly significant and was repeated by the castle earthworks.

### *The Late Saxon town*

Recent evidence has revised the plan of Late Saxon Norwich, with evident regularity to the east of King Street (Emery 2007), probably the result of the combined effects of local topography and proximity to the town's economic centre (Figures 1.3 and 1.4). Whether this more regular settlement was established during the Late Saxon period or whether it was a post-Conquest development remains uncertain. Of course, such regularity does not necessarily imply planning as unplanned settlements (i.e. those not deliberately laid out as an entity) 'could also appear regular owing to the constraints imposed by natural or relict features acting as morphological frames' (Biddle 1975, p. 31). At the castle site, to the west of King Street, no planning is evident, with growth now being seen as a much more organic process rooted in the Middle Saxon period.

There is no specific indication of a high status area – possibly part of the demesne of the Earl of East Anglia, Ralph de Gael/de Guader – beneath the castle. Undoubtedly the 27 Late Saxon buildings found at Castle Mall correlate with some of the 98 houses or properties that Domesday Book notes were swept away by castle construction: 'on that land of which Harold had the jurisdiction, there are 15 burgesses and 17 empty dwellings which are in the occupation of the castle. Also in the Borough there are 190 dwellings empty in this [area] which was in the King's and the Earl's jurisdiction and 81 in the occupation of the castle' (Brown 1984, p. 116b (1.61)). Norwich is one of eleven towns recorded by Domesday as suffering damage, destruction or abandonment of buildings as a result of castle construction: at several other urban centres, settlement destruction has been recorded archaeologically without documentary reference. The remains of several building types were found at the Norwich site, including sunken-featured buildings of urban form. These add to the corpus of similar structures found beneath castle defences elsewhere (e.g. Oxford and Northampton, Hassall 1976, p. 251, fig. 9; Poore 2004, figs 20, 28 and 29; Wilson and Hurst 1962–3, p. 322). Nearly three hundred pre-Conquest pits were associated with the Norwich buildings, material within their fills indicating a wide range of activities, including pottery manufacture. Most of the previous evidence for pottery manufacture comes from kiln sites in a 'suburban' area to the west of the Late Saxon town (Atkin *et al.* 1983). The findings at Castle Mall (which include a possible drying kiln, wasters and pottery dumps) may represent an earlier industry, with the previously known kilns perhaps indicating later (i.e. 10th- to early 12th-century) production. Some of the vessels may represent a transitional stage (*c.* 1000 to *c.* 1067–70) of specialised forms, which evolved prior to the development of fully developed early medieval wares.

The relatively sparse occupation in the Castle Mall area contrasts with the more regular settlement pattern now

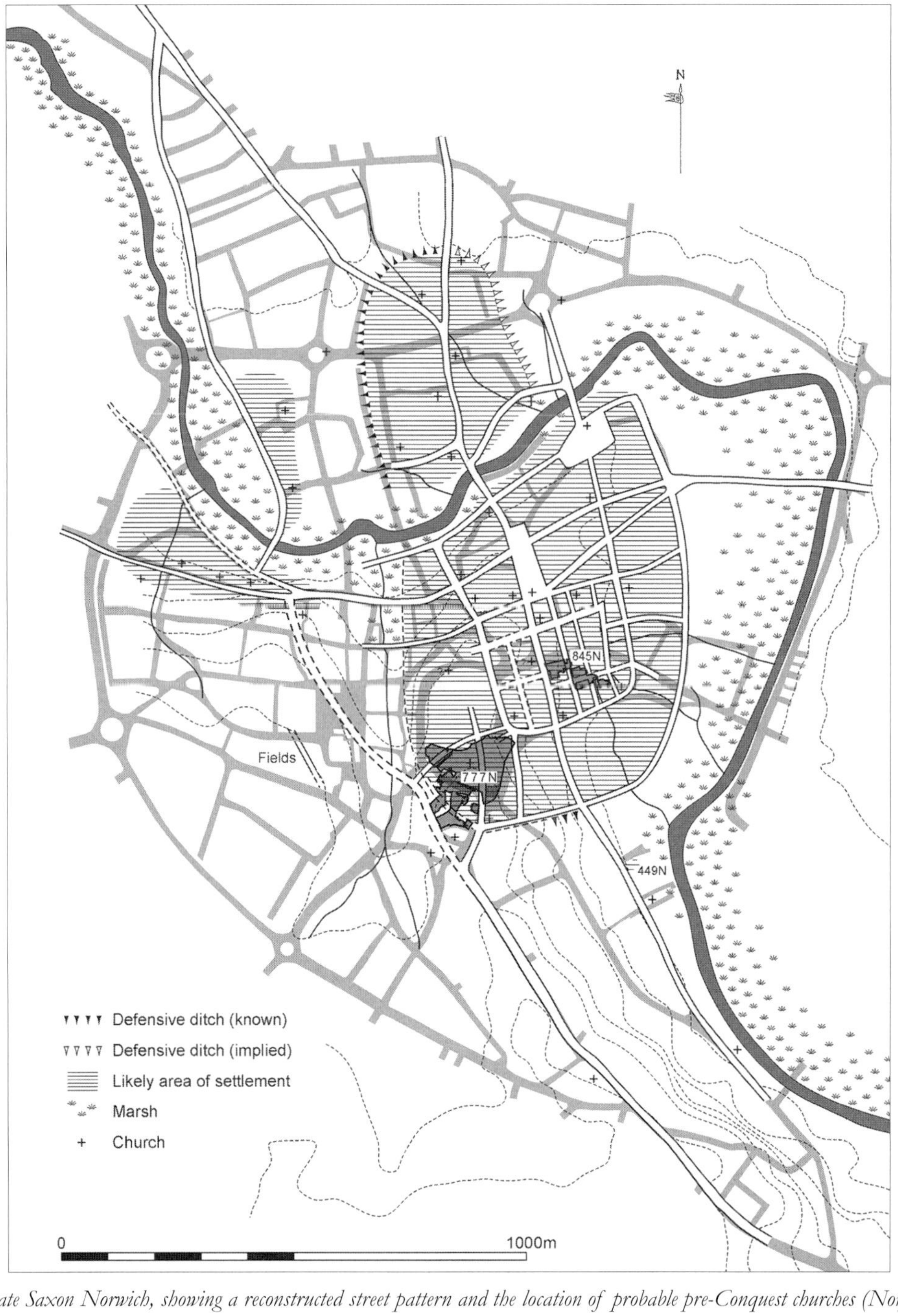


*Figure 1.3. Map of Late Saxon Norwich, showing a reconstructed street pattern and the location of probable pre-Conquest churches (Norfolk Museums Service).*

*Figure 1.4. Reconstruction of the Late Saxon (11th century) settlement in the vicinity of the later castle, viewed from the south-west, with the Great Cockey stream in the foreground (Norfolk Museums Service).*

evident to the east of King Street. The discovery of silver refining and other evidence associated with minting just to the east of Norwich Castle at the Mann Egerton site (Site 845N; Emery 2007) may argue for the beginnings of truly urban activity during the 10th to 11th century, with its origins in the late 9th century. Pottery from the Castle Mall site does not discount activity at the site during much of the 10th century and occupation may have been well-established by *c.* 980, when the now dominant settlement of *Norwic* was documented in the *Liber Eliensis.*

### *Churches and cemeteries*

Norwich had at least 46 churches and chapels (81% of its subsequent total of parish churches) by the time of the Domesday Survey in 1086 (Morris 1989, p. 169). Archaeological evidence suggests that as many as six churches and cemeteries may have been engulfed by the castle, one of which – St Martin in Balliva – was eventually enclosed within the south bailey to remain in use after the conquest, when it became the castle's parish church (Blomefield 1806, vol. II, p. 121). A timber church of unknown dedication was excavated at the Anglia Television site in 1979, within the area that became the Castle Meadow (Site 416N; Ayers 1985).

Just outside the southern entrance to the castle defences lay the church of St John at the Castle Gate/de Berstrete, which still survives (as St John the Baptist, Timberhill; Figure 1.2). It was first mentioned in the mid-12th century, although the extant building may have superseded an earlier church. Its excavated burials have been radiocarbon dated to at or just before the conquest. Non-metric traits (variations from the 'normal' skeletal anatomy) suggest a link between this group and that from another cemetery which was swept away by the south bailey (at Farmer's Avenue). This *may* indicate displacement of the latter church and cemetery by the castle and population movement to St John's parish. The most unusual aspect of this latter cemetery is the presence of a high level of leprosy, possibly affecting 35 out of the total excavated group and indicating a much higher incidence than would normally be expected from an urban parish cemetery. The position of this church and cemetery raises key issues relating to urban topography. Before the Conquest, the church may have lain outside one of the entrances to the southern burh, mirroring later examples at Oxford, Wallingford and Wareham (Morris 1989, p. 214). After establishment of the castle, it would have lain immediately adjacent to the castle gate on the main approach route along Ber Street. Such a position outside the town but adjacent to one of the main thoroughfares was the classic location for *leprosaria* (cf. Chichester; Magilton *et al.* 2008, fig. 4.1). No direct association with a *leprosarium* is, however, suggested for the St John's group.

## Norwich Castle

### *The local context*

By the end of 1067 William I had completed the defences of Sussex and was free to move further north (Chibnall 1993, p. 13). The date of Norwich Castle's foundation is undocumented, although it may have occurred during the construction of 'castles widely throughout this nation' in 1067 (ASC (D), *sub anno* 1066; Swanton 2000, p. 200) or the following year: William's military expedition to East Anglia in the autumn of 1068 saw the construction of castles at Lincoln, Cambridge and Huntingdon (Orderic Vitalis (OV) ii.185; Chibnall 1969, p. 219). Its defences were certainly well established when it was subjected to a prolonged siege in 1075 (detailed below). Norwich was William's only East Anglian castle: its isolation is clear on Figure 1.5, which indicates its setting against castles documented to have been founded immediately after the Conquest. Norwich Castle lies towards the eastern end of the southern line of Norfolk castles – the end of routes from Cambridge, London and Suffolk (Figure 1.6). It was both a strategic focus and a political objective as a major source of wealth and centre of administration.

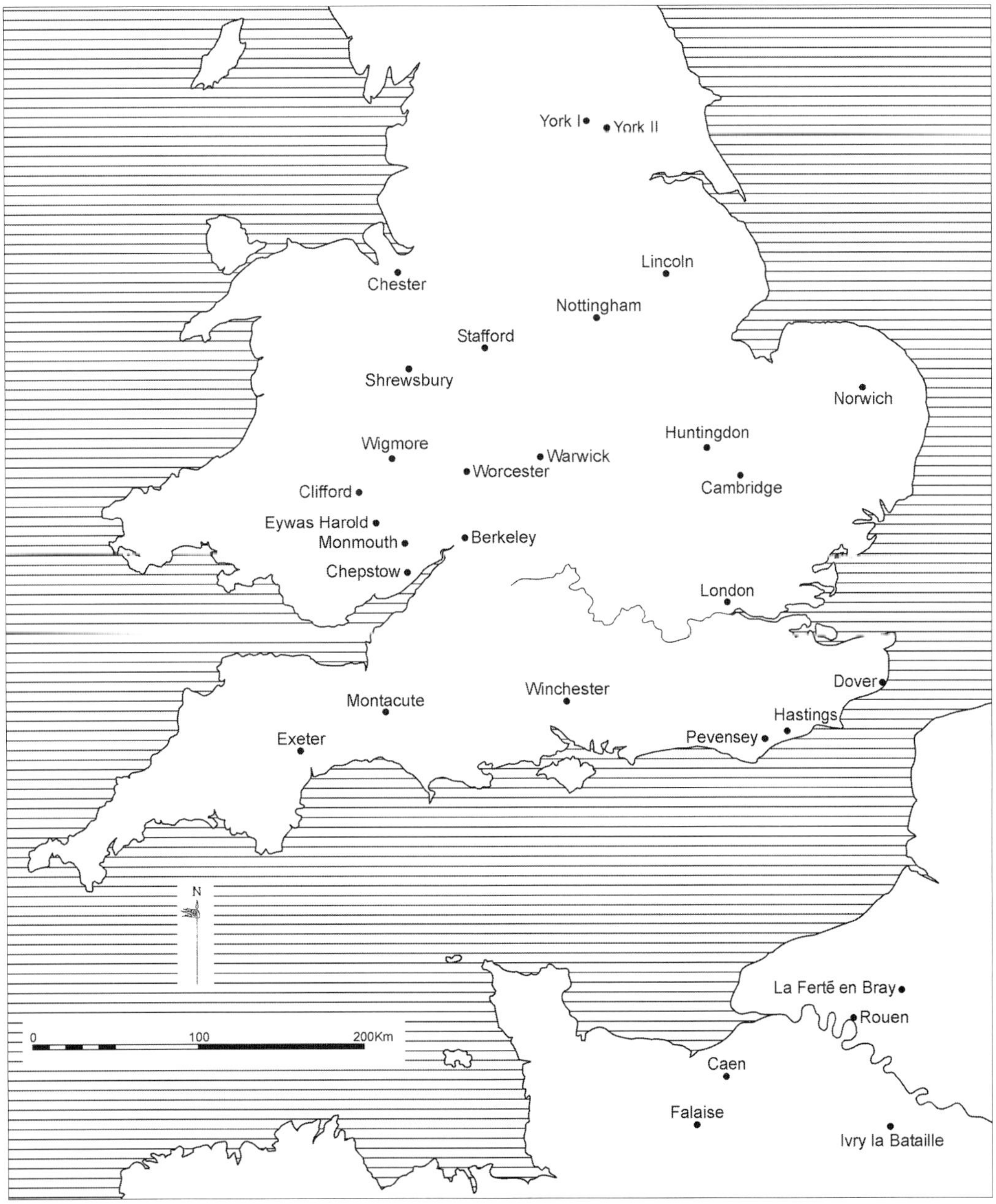


*Figure 1.5. Documented Anglo-Norman castles of the period 1066–1070 (after Higham and Barker 1992, fig. 2.19) and Normandy castles mentioned in the text, showing the location of Norwich (foundation date undocumented) (Norfolk Museums Service).*

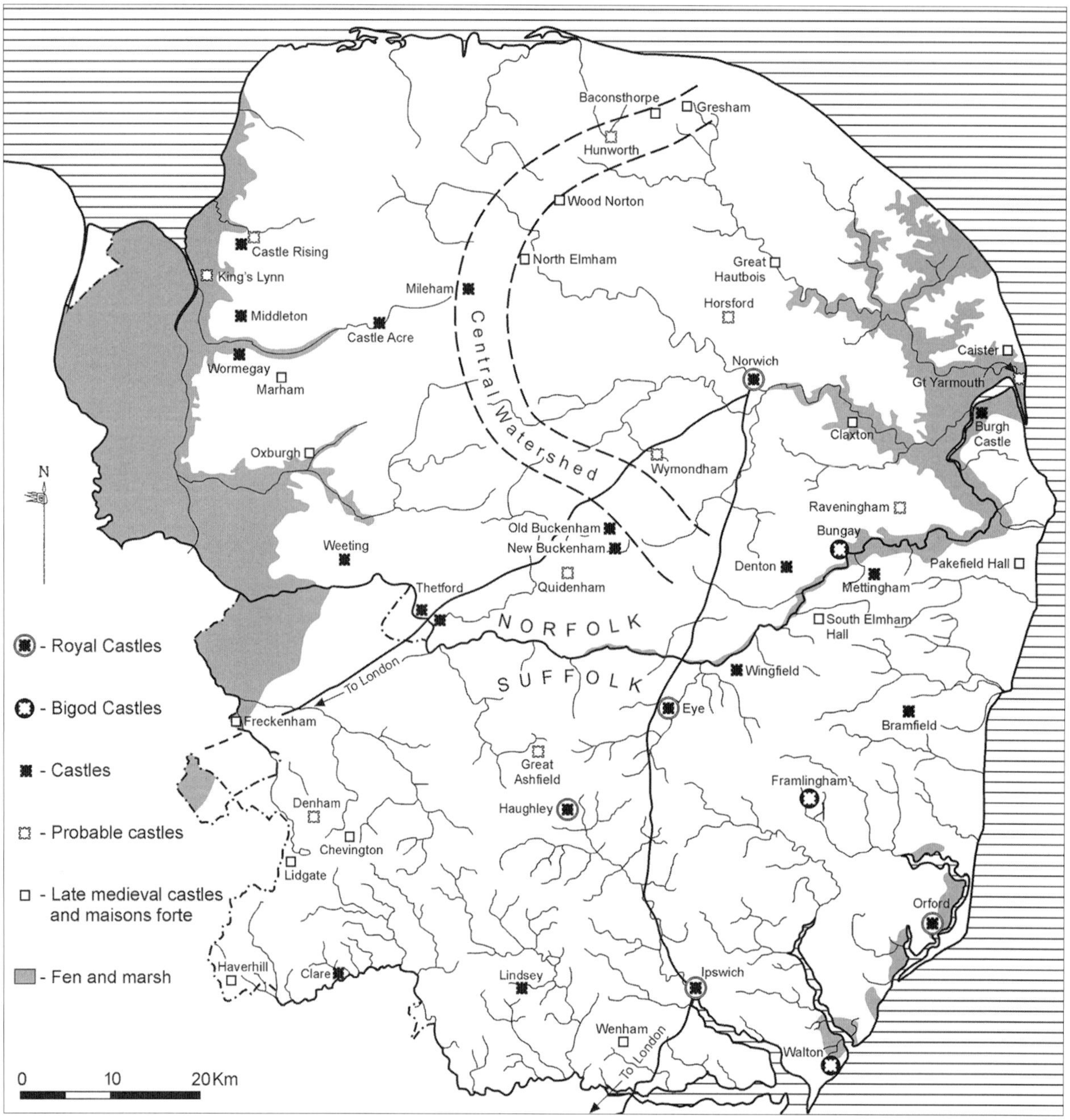


*Figure 1.6. Norfolk and Suffolk castles (Norfolk Museums Service).*

### *Antiquarians and early research*

Antiquarian study of Norwich Castle's defences began with Neville in 1575. Earlier plans of the defences, summarised in Figure 1.7, can now be reconsidered against the excavated evidence. The historic plan sequence begins with the three concentric ditches and outer barbican postulated by Wilkins in 1796 (pl. xxiii, p. 146). Harrod produced the first definitive plan of the castle's two baileys (Harrod 1857, map p. 133), while Beecheno explored the extent and complex history of the Castle Fee (MS 1908). Understanding of the castle's defences immediately before the Castle Mall project was primarily based on Campbell's map, drawing on antiquarian observations and extremely limited excavation (Campbell 1975, p. 8, fn. 89 and maps 2–3). Such modern maps of the defences (cf. Carter *et al.* 1974, fig. 7; Carter 1978, fig. 7; Green 1990, fig. 2) were necessarily summary in form. Several of the postulated ditches subsequently proved to be in the wrong place (see below). Others were the wrong size or incorrectly identified: the ditch interpreted as the south bailey defence at Site 150N (Carter *et al.* 1974; Atkin 2002) has now been reinterpreted as the barbican ditch, while the undated ditch recorded as the north-east bailey ditch at the Anglia Television site (Site 416N; Ayers 1985) is now known to have lain enclosed by a massive outer ditch.

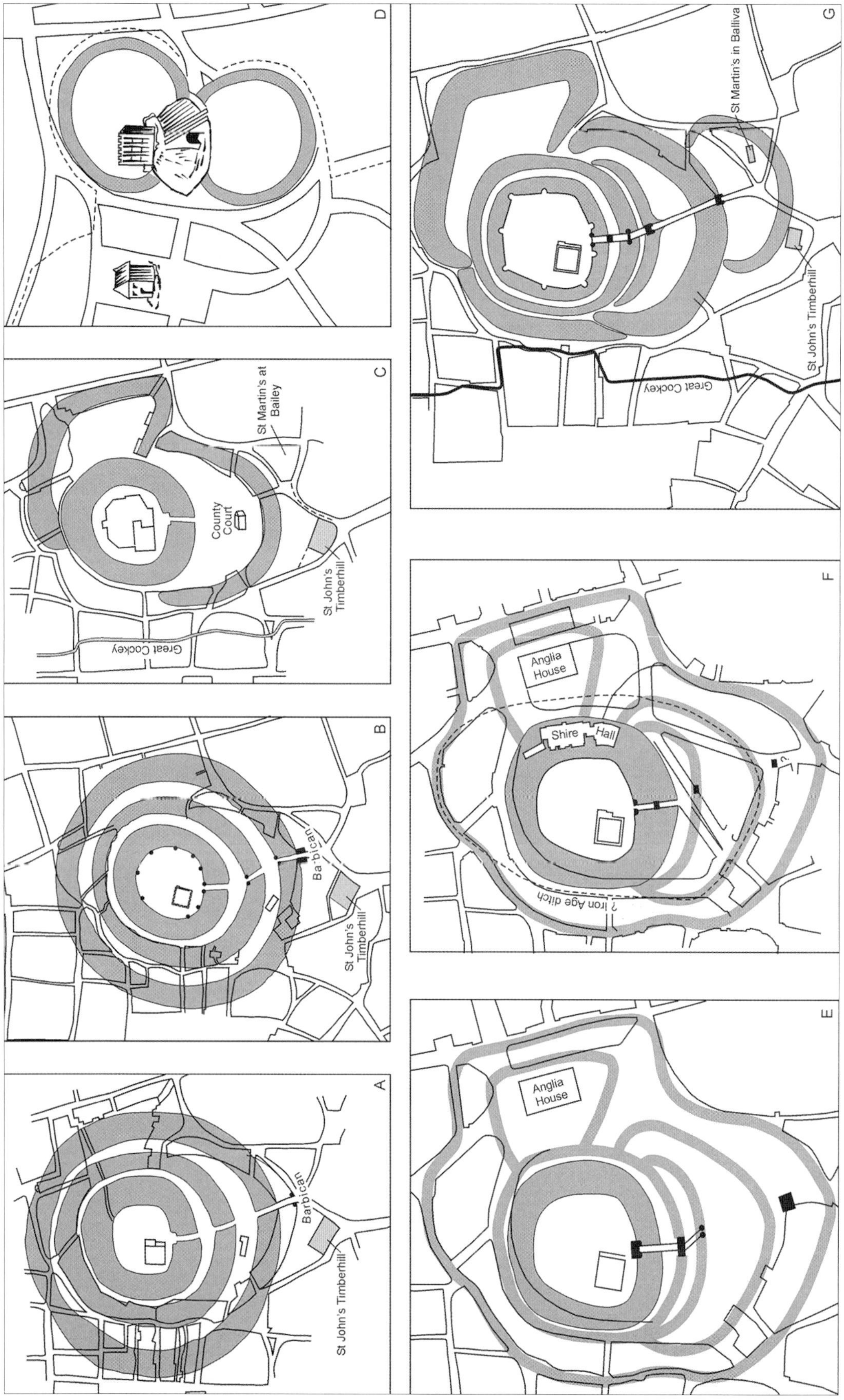


*Figure 1.7. Previous interpretations of the defences of Norwich Castle: A = Wilkins 1796 (after plate xxiii, 146); B = Woodward 1847; C = Harrod 1857 (after map p. 133); D = Hudson 1896 (after map iii); E = Green 1966; F = Carter et al. 1974 (after fig. 7); G = Campbell 1975 (after maps 2 and 3).*

The castle precinct provides the basis for the modern street pattern and can be traced in earlier maps (e.g. Cleer 1696 and Hochstetter 1789), although Beecheno's warning against relying too extensively on the position of houses and streets to indicate the position of castle ditches holds true (Beecheno MS 1908, pp. 11–2). It is now evident that while some roads do mirror the outer line of the ditches relatively well, others do not relate to their original form at all.

## *The impact of castle construction*

Norwich was chosen as the site of a major royal castle due to a combination of financial, political and geographical factors. By the time of the Conquest, it was the fourth largest town in England and, undoubtedly, there was a symbolic aspect to the construction of its castle. It is one of ninety-three Norman castles documented in England before 1100, almost half of which were urban (Drage 1987, p. 117; Eales 2003, pp. 47–53). Of these, 'no less than twenty were built within or against the defences of a town' (Pounds 1990, p. 57). In eight of the latter examples, the castle was placed inside an Anglo-Saxon burh and Norwich may conform to this model. It was once suggested, however, that the defences of Norwich's southern burh continued southwards along the line of Ber Street, only the western stretch of the castle's defences reusing the putative earlier boundary (Armitage 1912, p. 174 and fig. 23; Baggs 1963, p. 3). It now appears that any such pre-Conquest ditch probably swung eastwards, the castle being built in the south-western corner of existing settlement (Figure 1.8). The castle site is naturally dominant, lying at the northern end of a ridge of high ground (the Ber Street escarpment).

The French Borough and new market were laid out to the west of the castle, probably before 1075, on agricultural land that was at least partially owned by Earl Ralph (Brown 1984, 1.66, 118a). Land ownership in the Norwich Castle area before 1066 remains obscure and acquisition of the castle site may have had more to do with geography and topography than with previous land tenure. While seizure of land for the construction of castles is known, particularly in urban contexts, and purchase is evident largely at rural castles (Liddiard 2000, p. 25), granting is perhaps most likely to have been the case at Norwich.

While construction of the castle was eventually to boost Norwich's fortunes, the initial detrimental effects on the general populous are clear. Archaeological evidence confirms the Domesday reference that earlier settlement was obliterated during site clearance (above). The impact of the construction of both castle and cathedral stretched over a wide area of the southern part of the town and a concomitant marginalisation and decline has been noted at the Mann Egerton site (Emery 2007).

## *The timber phase (c. 1067 to c. 1094)*

Thanks to recent research at sites such as Hen Domen (Higham and Barker 2000) and Stafford (Darlington 2001), along with the seminal overview by Higham and Barker (1992), the potential strength and sophistication of early castles has now been recognised. Nothing was previously known of the defences of the timber phase of Norwich Castle: the new research indicates an initially simple form, which quickly became complex (Figure 1.9). This is one of very few major urban castles in England where the timber phase has yet been investigated in any detail. While no archaeological evidence for the postulated timber tower of the late 11th century has yet been recovered (Ayers, this volume; Wallis, forthcoming), its remains may lie preserved beneath the second *motte*, constructed in association with the great masonry donjon (*c.* 1094 to *c.* 1121–22). The presence of an early *motte* had long been suggested: its dimensions and form have now been confirmed).

Amongst those named in the Domesday Survey who may have been associated with the construction of the timber castle were Herbert the ditcher and Rabel, possibly the engineer or architect of the first castle. The architect of the stone donjon remains unknown. Rabel was probably the same Radbel *artifex* who held several properties in the county (Harvey 1975, p. 148; Blomefield 1806, II, p. 18, n. 2), and possibly Rabel *Carpentarius* (Rye 1921, p. 23).

Several interpretations of the layout of Norwich Castle's earliest defences (i.e. pre-1075) are possible. The first earthworks appear to have consisted of a simple possible palisaded bank and ditch enclosure 'necessarily constructed at great speed in a situation of extreme danger' (English 1995, p. 48). Davison proposed that England's very earliest castles (*c.* 1066–8) may have been ring-works with a bank and ditch, to which a *motte* and bailey was perhaps added later (Davison 1969; cf. Winchester, Biddle 1990, pp. 470–88). Once the outer precinct was defended, the *motte* could be constructed in safety, perhaps a very short time after the excavation of the ditch. The acreage enclosed by Norwich's first castle remains uncertain, although an enclosure of *c.* 6.2 hectares (*c.* 15.4 acres) can be postulated.

Its defences were first tested in 1075. During that year Earl Ralph married Emma, the daughter of William Fitzosbern and sister of Roger of Breteuil. With another of William's barons (Earl Waltheof), Ralph and Roger conspired at the wedding feast to rebel against the king on his return from abroad. Lanfranc, the archbishop-regent, was warned of the rebellion and assured the king in a letter that he could deal with the rebels, ultimately setting siege to Norwich Castle for three months. Ralph eventually escaped to secure his lands in Brittany, leaving his bride in charge of a large force of his Breton followers. After the siege, Lanfranc was obliged to allow the Bretons to depart honourably when famine threatened. He wrote to William again:

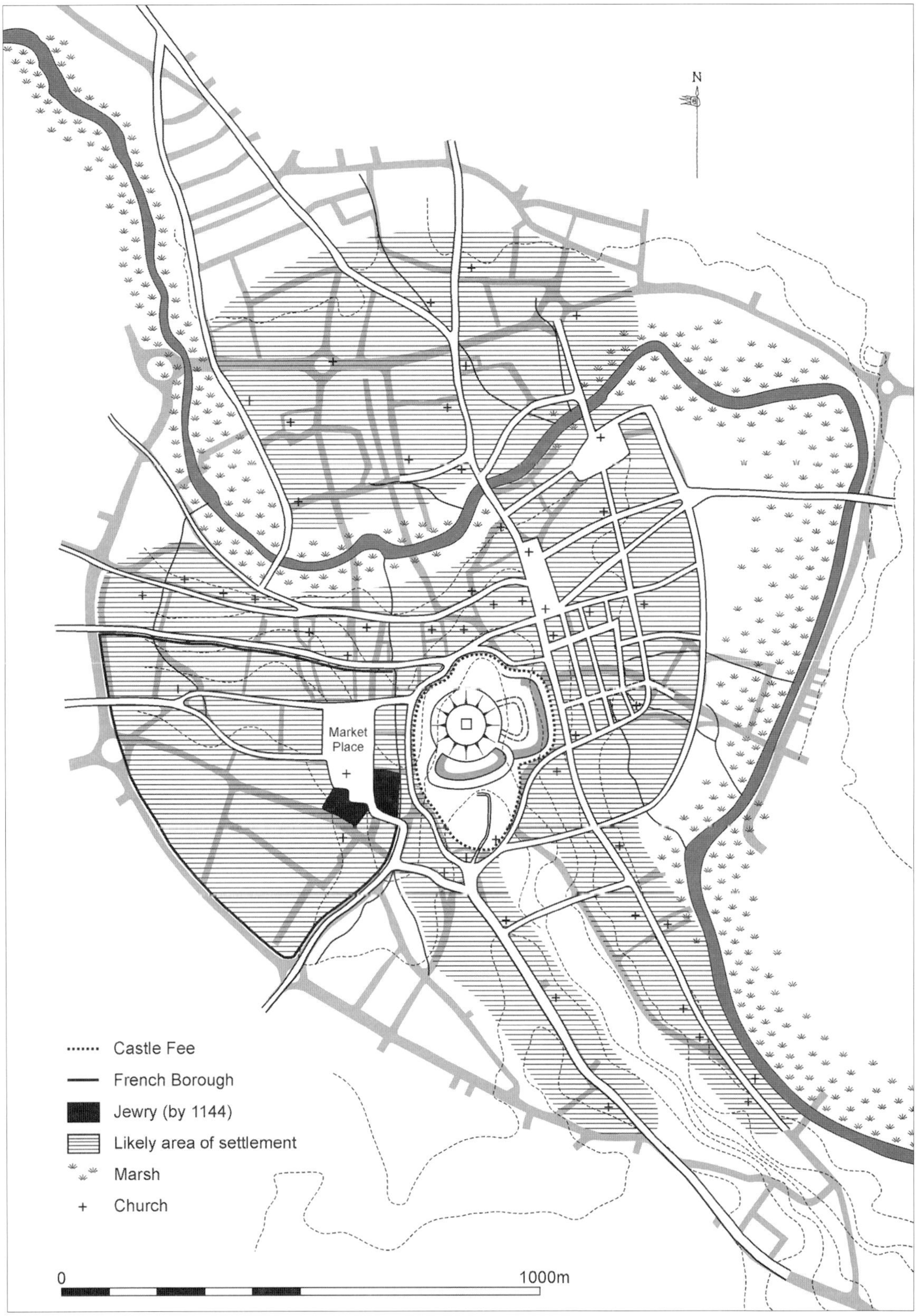


*Fig. 1.8. Map of Early Norman Norwich showing reconstructed street pattern, Norman churches and the impact of the creation of the first castle and French Borough (Norfolk Museums Service).*

*Figure 1.9. Reconstruction of the early Norman castle, viewed from the south-west. The postulated timber keep is depicted on its small motte with an associated flying bridge (Norfolk Museums Service).*

> Norwich Castle is surrendered and the Britons [Bretons] who were in it … life being granted to them with limbs have sworn that within forty days they will go out from your Kingdom and moreover will not enter it without your license ... In the same castle have remained… 300 men in armour with armour with them, with Crossbowmen and many artificers of machines (MS Cotton, Nero A., VII, fo. 26bb, British Museum).

The use of 'every kind of engine of war' may have included bombardment machines (such as the mangonel and balista), siege towers and battering rams (Morillo 1994, pp. 138–9). Despite the extended duration of the siege there is no evidence in either the documentary or archaeological record for a siege castle at Norwich.

Orderic Vitalis states that during the siege, the army received daily reinforcements along with ample supplies of food and other necessities, which would have relied heavily on good roads and water-borne transport (OV ii, 317; Morillo 1994, p. 128). The Norwich siege was exceptional in terms of its length; few others at this date lasted so long. Most ranged between four and six weeks although the siege of Arundel in 1102 was comparable to the Norwich case (Morillo 1994, p. 144; OV vi.22). The extended duration of both sieges may be due to the fact that no other tasks were required of the army at the time, meaning that the siege did not have to be accelerated by the use of force (Morillo 1994, p. 143). The burial of a small hoard of William I pennies, discovered at Nos. 13–15 London Street in 1972 (Site 215N) has previously been attributed to this event, although this no longer seems likely (Clough 1973).

Early alterations to the defensive scheme may link to the events of 1075. New evidence suggests subdivision of Norwich's south bailey as a secondary phase of the timber castle, coeval with the insertion of two previously unknown sets of double-ditches defending probable bridge landings (Figures 1.10A and 1.11). The resultant plan indicates the significance of the southern approach to Norwich Castle from an early date and demonstrates the complexity and strength of the defences. This period may have seen the addition of the north-east bailey/Castle Meadow and concomitant loss of the church recorded at Anglia Television. The lack of evidence for any major castle entrances facing the French Borough, the English Borough and the cathedral (from *c.* 1094) remains puzzling and the issue of the displacement of Norwich Castle in relation to the old town remains an issue for future study.

Evidence for formalised 'settlement' within the Castle Fee has proved elusive, although materials recovered from ditch fills and the contents of 84 pits demonstrate the nature of activities (e.g. grain storage and processing, disposal of possible stable waste and bone-/ horn-working) and local environment within the *enceinte* of the initial castle. Faunal

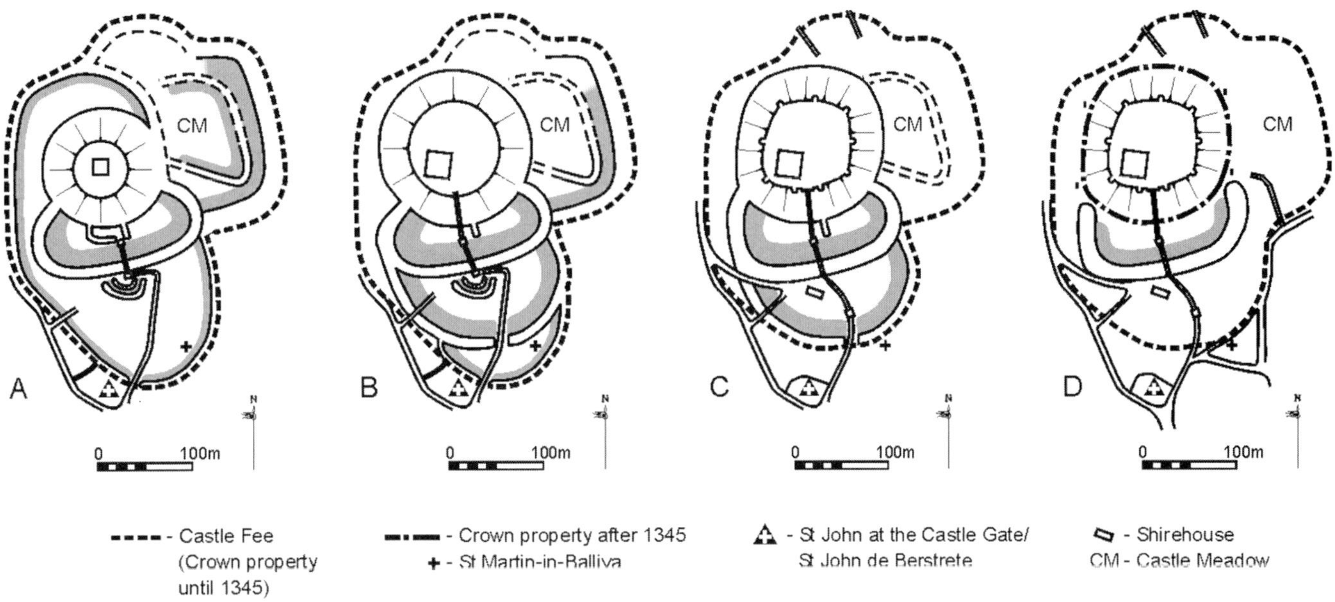


*Figure 1.10. Summary of the major defensive alterations: A =* c. *1075; B =* c. *1094–1122; C =* c. *1250–1300; D =* c. *1345 (Norfolk Museums Service).*

*Figure 1.11. Excavation of one of the crescentic ditches defending the bridge landing in the timber castle phase (Norfolk Museums Service).*

remains from the timber castle phase include cats (which had been skinned) and dogs which had apparently been eaten, perhaps in relation to the siege.

'A distance of only a couple of hundred metres put a castle beyond the range of bowshot and siege weaponry' (Creighton 2002, p. 35) and the reconstructed timber phase at Norwich (Figure 1.9) places the first *motte c.* 250m from the southern limit of the defences: the ease of accessibility on this side may explain the distance of the southern defence from the *motte* in relation to its other sides, which were physically constrained by the local topography. A similar distance was maintained in the stone phase.

While the baileys of English castles were generally curvilinear, they were occasionally constructed with square sides (King 1991, p. 43). The distinctive square shape of the eastern side of Norwich's Castle Meadow was dictated by the presence of a pre-existing road – Superior Conesford (King Street) – forming one of the main arterial routes into the city. The bailey infilled an 'insula' of the Late Saxon town (Figure 1.8), although its spatial relationship to the core of the old town remains curious. New evidence from Castle Mall adds significantly to the understanding of this bailey, perhaps confirming previous suggestions that it was a secondary addition. The awkwardness of earlier interpretations of its form, first presented as sub-triangular by Harrod (1857, map p. 133) and followed by Campbell (1975, maps 2 and 3), Ayers (1985, fig. 2) and Atkin (2002, fig. 1), is notable. It was once suggested that 'the anachronistic position of this bailey was already recognised by the time that the keep was built and that there was therefore no need to bring it into a co-ordinated defensive network' (Ayers 1985, p. 6). The impressive sequence of ditch recuts recorded at Castle Mall does, however, indicate co-ordination in planning and considerable investment in labour, implying the presence of concentric ditchwork here as well as in the south bailey. Both this and the scale of the outer ditchwork (at a maximum of 20–27m wide and 8.5–9.5m deep) refute the previous suggestion that the bailey was militarily weak (e.g. Pounds 1990, p. 126).

A possible embanked north gate within the Castle Meadow (leading onto London Street and thence to the cathedral) may help to explain the kink in the edge of the Castle Fee boundary at this point. No firm conclusion can be drawn until such time as archaeological evidence becomes available, although the bulge replicated in the modern street pattern – which survives as an area of raised ground – may result from the influence of natural contours in the Late Saxon or Norman periods (cf. Woodward 1847), or from earthworks yet to be discovered.

### *The stone phase (*c. *1094 to* c. *1121–22)*

The building or re-building of English castles in stone began within a generation of the Norman Conquest (Allen Brown 1966–9, p. 87). The layout of the new defences at Norwich is shown in Figures 1.10B and 1.12, and a reconstruction as they may have appeared in *c.* 1121/22 is given in Figure 1.13.

Norwich is one of six urban castles of late 11th and early 12th centuries with a stone donjon and Class I *motte*, the latter classified as those over 10m high (Drage 1987, p. 121 and fig. 54). 'The largest *mottes*, like those of Conisborough and Norwich, could ... carry a complete inner ward together with its keep' (King and Alcock 1969, p. 95): this upper bailey at Norwich enclosed *c.* 2.3 acres, making it England's largest *motte* in terms of surface area. Clearly, the new constructional phase would have taken considerable time to complete and consideration of the labour and time necessary to adapt existing earthworks for the new defences has been estimated: the grand total for both *mottes*, for example, amounts to 22,421 days (cf. Pounds 1990, fig. 1.6; 24,000 days), which may need to be tripled to reach anything like a realistic estimate (bringing the total for the *motte* alone to 67,263 days; 336 days for a team of 200 men). Documentary evidence attests to the continued strengthening and repair of the defences throughout the 12th century.

Work on the donjon began at around the time that England's first palace-keeps at the White Tower (London) and Colchester were nearing completion (Drury 2002, p. 218). As a royal palace, Norwich's new donjon was far more elaborate than its predecessors and, together with the cathedral church, provided the foundation for a distinctive regional architectural style (Heslop 1994). The Norman French sobriquet *Blanchefleur* possibly used for the new Norwich donjon was noted by antiquarians, but has thus far been overlooked by recent scholars. Although the French names of castles are often associated with their topographical setting (Creighton 2002, p. 69), Norwich is perhaps an example of the naming in relation to young girls (Sandy Heslop, pers. comm.) and the name probably reflects the whiteness of the new Caen stone donjon. The main approach was always from the south and 'it is tempting to interpret in a symbolic sense the fact that the keep looked towards London' (Heslop 1994, p. 8).

Construction of the new donjon required enlargement of the *motte*, both in terms of vertical height and lateral widening, and recent excavation confirms the complexity of this extension (Figure 1.14). The somewhat curious position of the building on the south-western corner of the *motte* – dominating the skyline of the new French Borough rather than the old town – can now be at least partially explained as a matter of practicality: it overlies the more stable area of the pre-existing mound.

Despite the pessimism of antiquarians, archaeological excavation has demonstrated that the *c.* 40m long Norman bridge remains substantially intact beneath refacing: it was first documented when repaired in the late 12th century. High quality footings were founded over 4m below the modern base of the *motte* ditch (Figure 1.15), the bridge's original height being masked by centuries of refuse deposition. In its original form, the underside of the arch would have stood over 11m above the base of the contemporary *motte* ditch.

A substantial well (nearly 30m deep; Figure 1.16) lay within the courtyard at the foot of the *motte* bridge, providing a supplementary source of water to another well within the donjon. The sinking of a deep well was a costly task and it is curious that no mention of the well(s) is made in the documentary record for Norwich Castle.

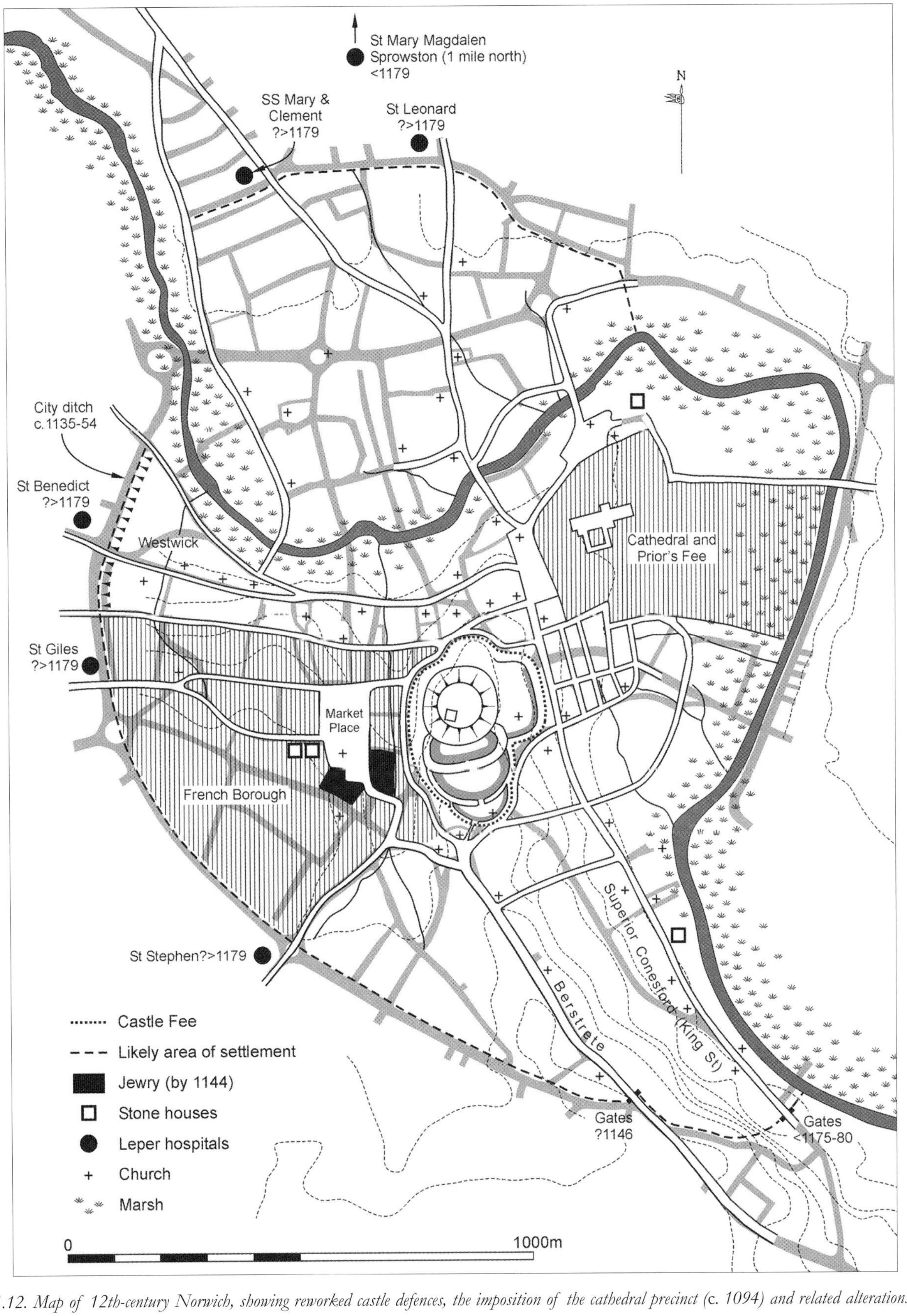


*Figure 1.12. Map of 12th-century Norwich, showing reworked castle defences, the imposition of the cathedral precinct (c. 1094) and related alterations to street pattern (Norfolk Museums Service).*

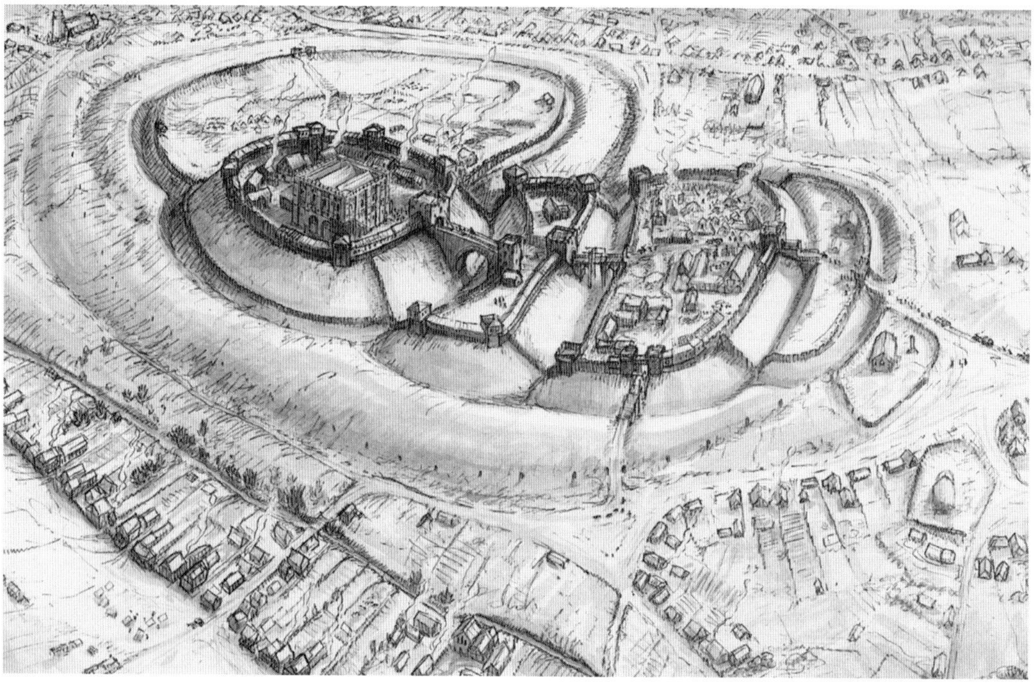

*Figure 1.13. Reconstruction of the Norman (12th-century) castle, viewed from the south-west. The new masonry donjon lies on its enlarged motte, with revised ditchwork and additional masonry structures added to the defences of the south bailey (Norfolk Museums Service).*

Twelve large fragments of a probable 12th-century gatehouse were found, which once stood at the entrance to the courtyard housing the well at the foot of the bridge (Figure 1.17). These indicate a structure of comparable dimensions to the gate at Castle Acre (Coad and Streeten 1982, p. 164 and figs 9 and 14).

Accompanying the new masonry elements, the ditchwork was reshaped and enlarged (Figure 1.10B). A new south bailey ditch (14m wide by 5.5m deep) was inserted (Figure 1.18), the earlier ditch further south (demarcating the initial possible Fee boundary) perhaps being re-cut to form a hornwork around the south gate. Elements of the south bailey rampart survived up to 2m high. The north-east bailey's outermost ditch was also recut, its infilling providing evidence for livestock grazing, brewing activity and a possible lime kiln. The castle's major ditches began to be infilled during the 12th century, resonating with findings at other castle sites (Creighton 2002, p. 138).

Although the presence of the south bailey was recognised by antiquarians, the fact of 'the site being mostly covered with buildings &*c*. [*sic*] it cannot be traced so as to mark out its form with the same precision as the inner [*motte*] and middle [inner bailey/barbican] vallums' (Wilkins 1796, p. 149). Previous plans of the ditch placed it considerably north of its actual position (Figure 1.7), an inevitable error resulting from placing too much reliance on the position of topographical indicators to demonstrate the position of earthworks. A major discovery is that both the Castle Fee and south bailey ditches were crossed by causeways which 'were presumably less satisfactory from a military point of view than a timber bridge' (King 1991, p. 56).

### *Artefactual evidence*

Rich material culture is unexpectedly sparse at most early castle sites and such is the case at Norwich. Here, all categories combine to indicate a typical urban – rather than castle – assemblage. The site is a reversal of the norm where, in the absence of historical data, status is often inferred from material culture and the morphology of archaeological features; had the royal and military status of the site not been known prior to the excavations, it would certainly not be inferred from the finds – although the scale of the ditches would have flagged up its defensive character. The point is made clear from an examination of the distribution of finds by site period (Figure 1.19). The main phases of active castle life (Periods 2 and 3) have the lowest level of small finds – the figure for the timber phase (Period 2) is elevated by a group of more than 200 bone strips indicating the manufacture of combs. As in the previous period, few finds of any status were associated with the stone phase of the castle – the relatively meagre quantity of 12th-century finds that were recovered relate largely to diversions (including a nine men's morris gaming board and a bone die) and indicate a relatively lowly diet including cheap fish – which together suggest the rather mundane everyday life of the garrison.

*Figure 1.14. Excavations through the front of the motte in 1999–2001, prior to insertion of a new lift shaft (Norfolk Museums Service).*

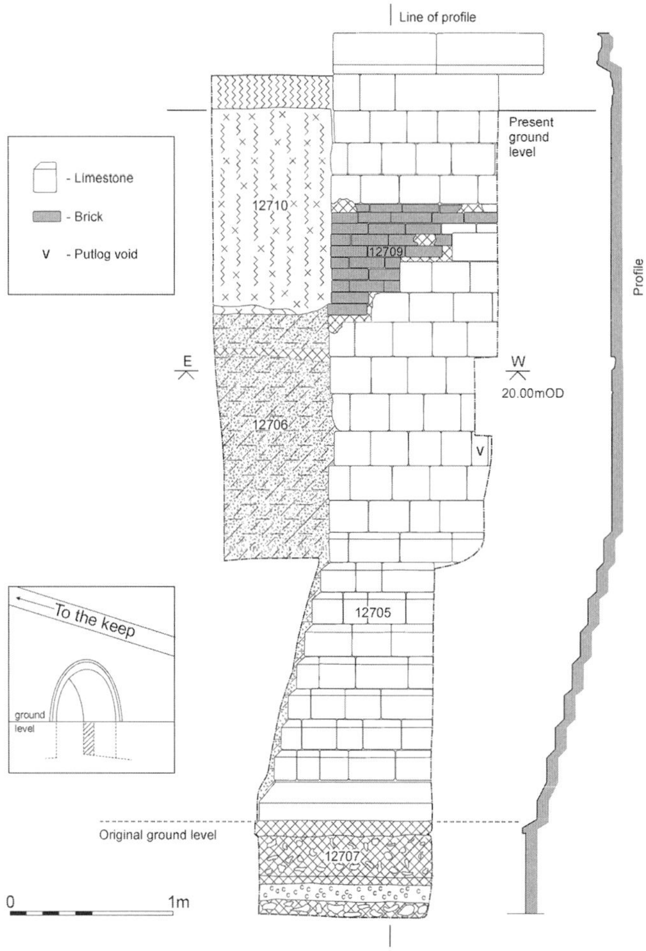


*Figure 1.15. Period 3.1: North-facing elevation of the motte bridge, showing chamfered limestone plinths at its base and their level in relation to modern ground surface (Norfolk Museums Service).*

## The character and history of the Castle Fee

No other British Castle Fee appears to have been subjected to such detailed scrutiny as has now been possible at Norwich (Shepherd Popescu 2004; 2009a and b; Tillyard *et al.* 2009). At *c.* 9.3 hectares (*c.* 23 acres), the Norwich Fee was one of the largest urban castle enclosures in Britain (see Creighton 2002, fig. 7.2 for comparisons of scale). In a Norfolk context, Norwich Castle's precinct was twice that of Castle Rising and three times that of Castle Acre (Figure 1.20). Little was previously understood of the early development of this area and its inter-relationship with the other elements of the castle. Although the Fee apparently existed during the 12th century, it remains uncertain exactly when and over what area it was first laid out (cf. the Liberties of the Tower of London; Keevill 2004, p. 12). From a probable origin as a late 11th-century ditch, the boundary may have developed to be demarcated by armorial plaques in the 13th century and eventually by stone posts, which perhaps remained active markers throughout the period *c.* 1345 to 1805.

Earlier investigation of the Fee was limited to largely unpublished documentary evidence: the new research has permitted linkage between the topographical, archaeological, documentary and historical evidence for specific tenements, in particular the 14 Castle Fee and eight city properties encompassed by the excavations (see below). Direct correlations between documented individuals/events and archaeological evidence have been attempted.

It appears that the original 'Men of the Fee' supplemented the regular garrison in time of attack and had special rites and privileges. A colourful account of the defence of the castle during the 1170s is given in the *Liber Cartarum et Placitorum*:

> When the [Pikars] *Picards* ... came into England and took the city of Norwich, and besieged the castle of the said city, then entered the men of the Fee ... into the castle,

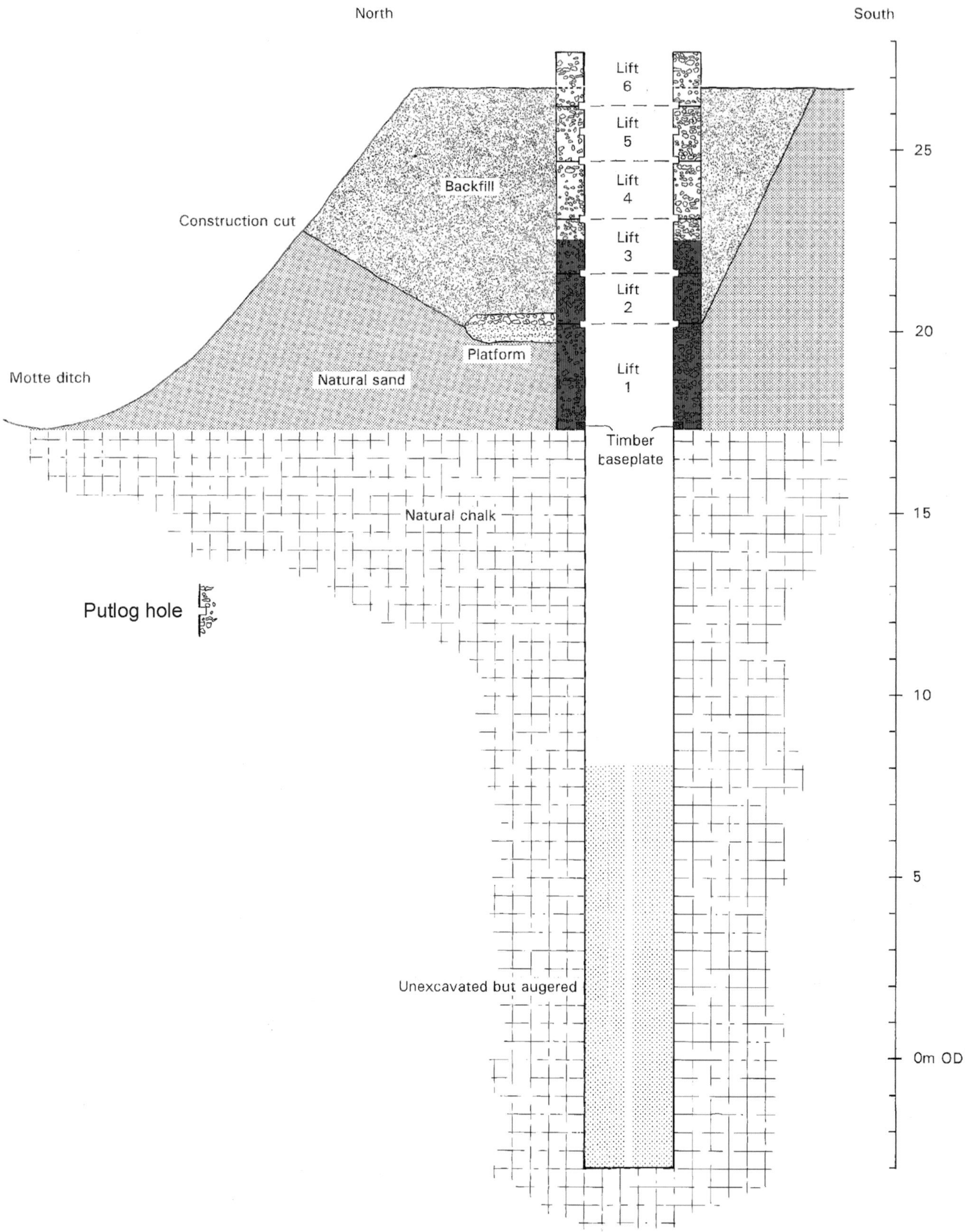


*Figure 1.16. Period 3.1: Elevation of interior of the Norman well, showing puttlog holes and timber curb at base (Norfolk Museums Service).*

*Figure 1.17. The site during excavation, showing part of the Norman gatehouse which collapsed after undermining by a post-medieval quarry (Norfolk Museums Service).*

> and saved the castle honourably to the use of the king which it then was. For some of them were good men of arms, some good arbalisters, some good archers, and the others forcible in defence, wherefore all those which were then and since infeoffed have enjoyed their franchises, and ought so to do most honourably in all points (Kirkpatrick, MS 42; quoted by Woodward 1847, p. 31).

The reference to the 'Men of the Fee' entering the castle is interesting as it implies a distinction between the outer part of the Castle Fee, within which these men may have been housed, and the defensive features set within it. A similar settlement is known at Chester, where the Fee encompassed a hamlet (Pounds 1990, fig. 8.7).

The Castle Fee remained an administrative entity for many centuries: extant Castle Fee rent lists span the period from 1397 to 1626, with the first documented exchange in

*Figure 1.18. The south bailey ditch during excavations at Golden Ball Street (Norfolk Museums Service).*

1255 (Tillyard *et al.* 2009). Tensions between city and Fee inhabitants are evident, the rite of sanctuary being one of the stated reasons behind the transfer of the baileys to the city in 1345 (Hudson and Tingey 1906, pp. 23–4): the transfer engendered a process of sale and conversion to leases which continued until the 18th century.

### Later alterations (to c. 1345)

Norwich Castle was adapted to suit the military needs of the 13th century. By the middle of the century, with the construction or enlargement of the city ditch, the castle lay at the heart of the city (Figure 1.21 and 1.22), although such may have been the case from the latter part of the 12th century. Considerable castle works included excavation of the barbican ditch, the insertion of drum towers and a new gate on the castle bridge, construction of a new hall adjacent to the donjon, provision of a curtain wall and towers around the top of the *motte*, repairs to the gaol and construction of the Shirehouse.

Construction of the Norwich barbican has been associated with the capture of the castle by Louis, Dauphin of France in 1216 (Reeve 1992, p. 23): a date in the range *c.* 1224 to *c.* 1250 now seems probable, both in terms of the specific evidence at the site and the broader context of barbican construction. Documented barbicans of the period include those at Bristol (1220), Lincoln (1224–5),

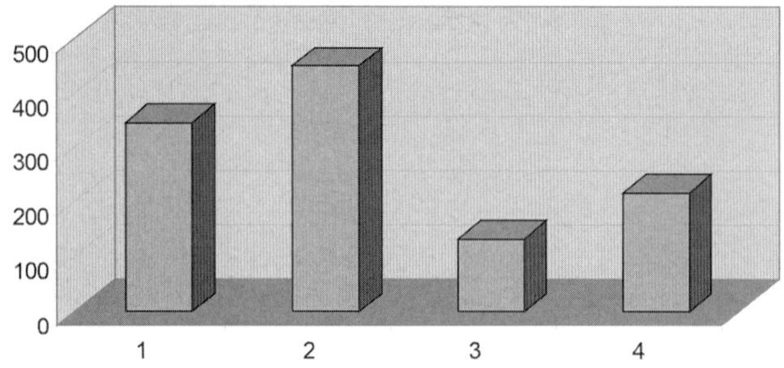


*Figure 1.19. Bar chart showing finds by period: Period 1 = Late Saxon; Period 2 = Timber Castle; Period 3 = Stone Castle; Period 4 = late 12th century–c. 1345 (Norfolk Museums Service).*

Shrewsbury (1233–4), Dover (1243), Scarborough (1243), Windsor (1249–50) and Marlborough (1250–51) (Allen Brown, Colvin and Taylor 1963, I, p. 118). While the presence of the Norwich ditch had long been known, its staggering scale has now been revealed and the first calculations of associated earth-moving and labour rates attempted. The new ditch would have been about 27m wide by more than 10m deep (Figures 1.10C and 1.23), making it larger than the city ditch. Where they recognised its existence, earlier plans of the castle defences hypothesised a narrow barbican (Figure 1.7). New evidence indicates that it was wider internally than previously supposed, enclosing the Norman well (which remained functional) and two gates.

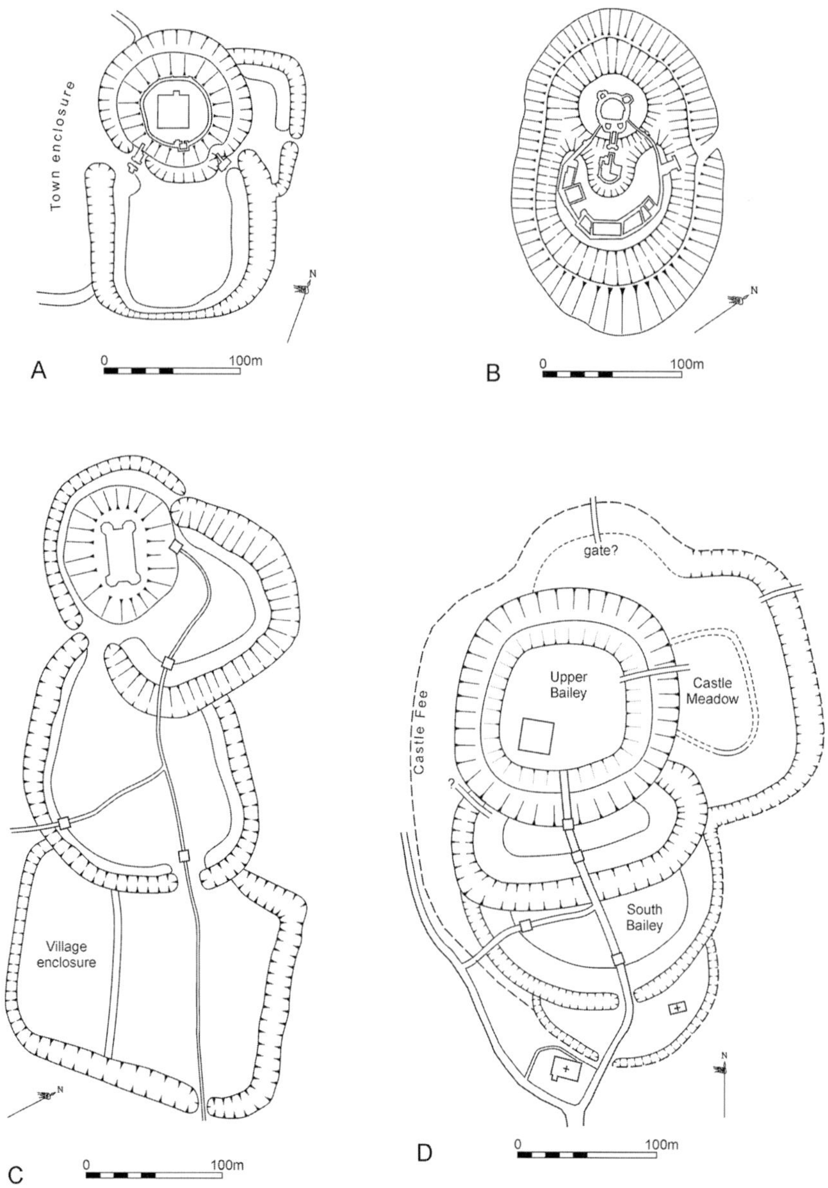


*Figure 1.20. Comparison between Norwich Castle and other castles: A = Castle Acre (after Coad and Streeten 1982, fig. 3); B = Sandal (after Mayes and Butler 1983, fig. 8); C = Stafford (after Darlington 2001, fig. 7); D = Norwich (c. 1120s) (Norfolk Museums Service).*

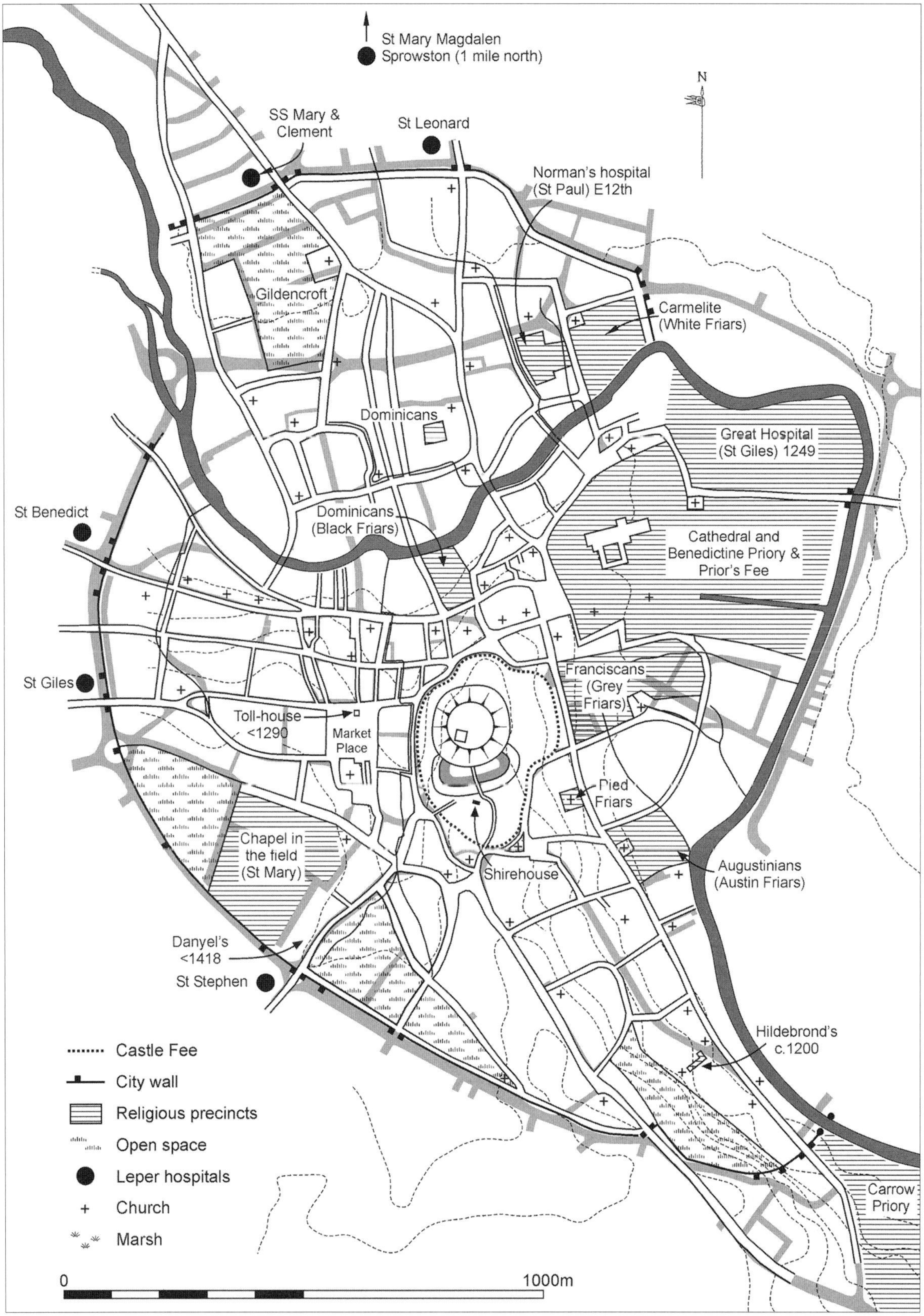


*Figure 1.21. Map of pre-1345 Norwich (Norfolk Museums Service).*

*Figure 1.22. Reconstruction of Norwich Castle during the 13th century, with the new barbican defences and the curtain wall with towers around the top of the motte (Norfolk Museums Service).*

*Figure 1.23. The 13th-century barbican ditch during excavation (Norfolk Museums Service).*

No physical evidence for the massive rampart survived, much of the area having been levelled in the landscaping campaigns of the 18th and 19th centuries. Most of its fills were post-medieval, indicating regular clearance in earlier times despite ample documentary evidence for illicit refuse deposition.

Changes in the conduct of warfare during the later 13th and early 14th century meant that although the buildings within Norwich's upper bailey were maintained as a fortress, administrative centre and prison, the importance of the outer baileys diminished, especially so with completion of the city walls (1297–1344). Many urban castles were used as courts and gaols in the later medieval period. Such limitations of use allowed other features of castles to decay: 'The paucity of royal finance, which affected ... royal castles, contributes to this decline. Archaeology has yet to record this process with the eloquence or detail of contemporary surveys' (Drage 1987, p. 127). The work at Castle Mall has duly found evidence for such processes. Physical evidence has been recovered for documented encroachment into the baileys (which began before 1221) and the cemetery of St John (first documented in 1297). As is detailed below, commercial development of properties closest to the roads, particularly for craft activities, is readily apparent.

By *c.* 1300, Norwich had fallen to the middle rank of castles, few castles of the period being consistently maintained (Drage 1987, p. 123), and it was no longer used as a royal residence by the latter half of the 14th century.

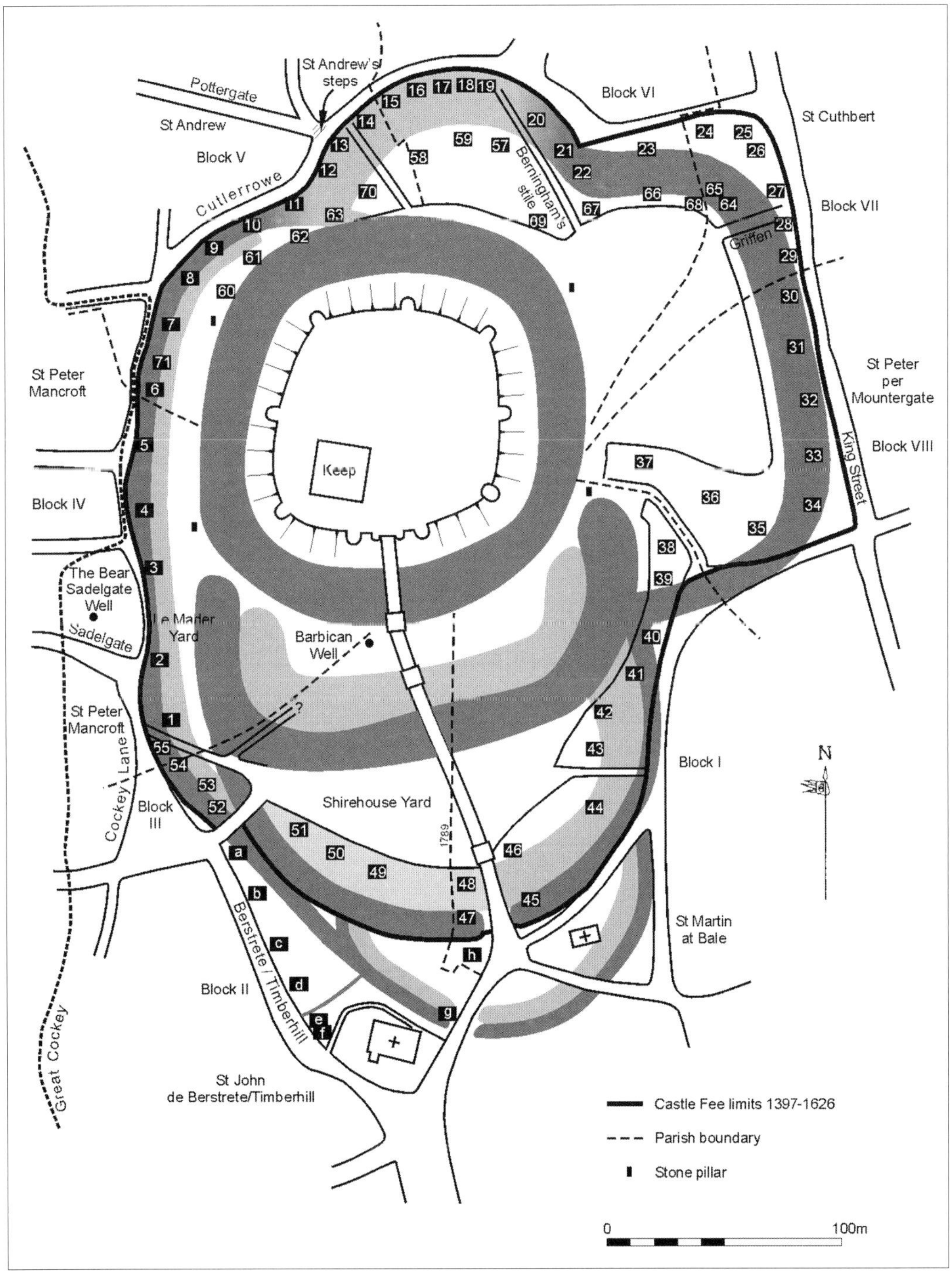


*Figure 1.24. Documented properties around Norwich Castle 1397–1626: Properties have been numbered according to the first Castle Fee rent list (Plots 1–55), with additional numbers given in the order in which the grants made appear in the Norwich Domesday Book (NRO Case 17) (Norfolk Museums Service).*

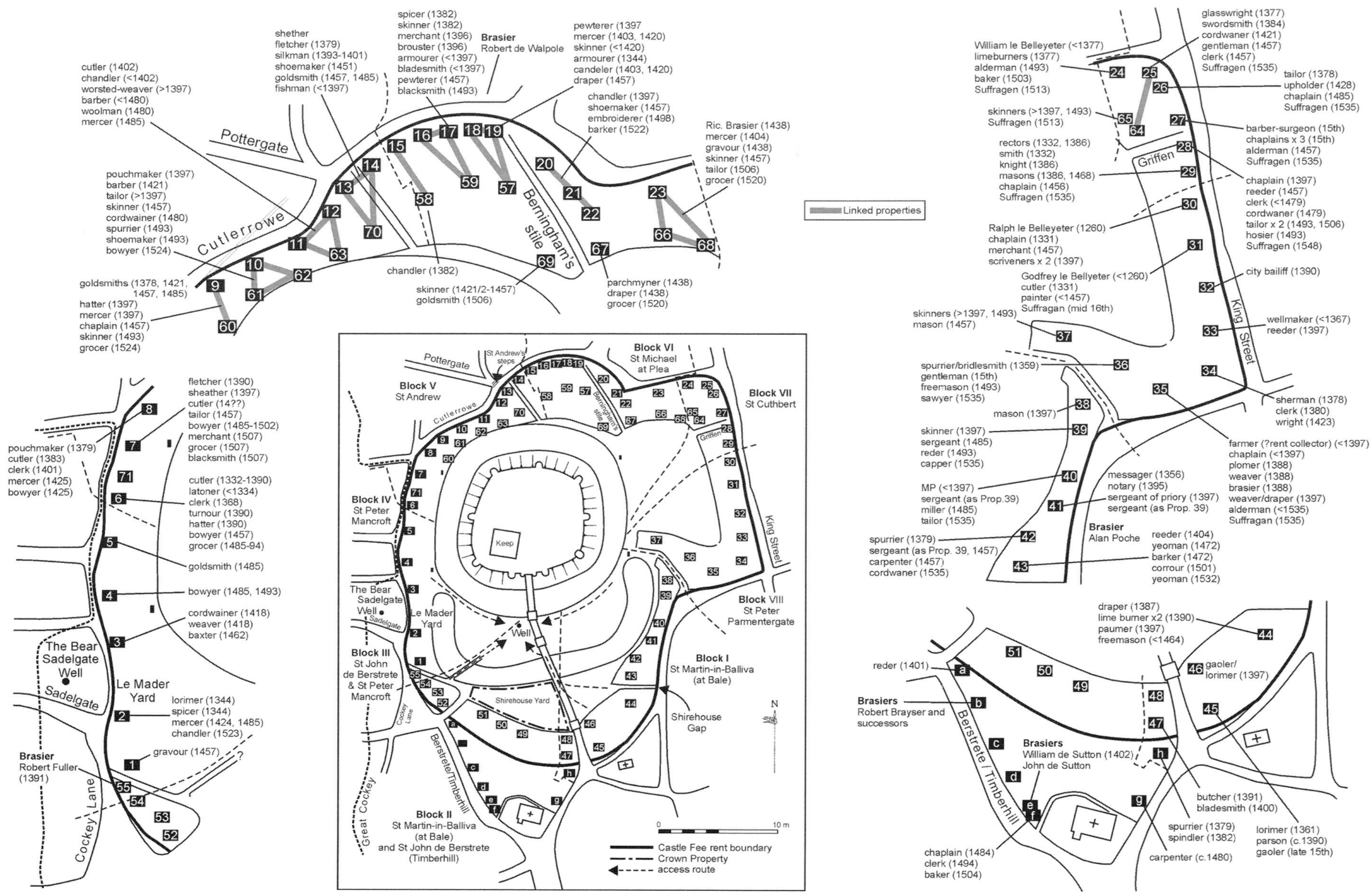


*Figure 1.25. Documented trades around the Castle Fee from the late 14th century to* c. *1530. Note that some references are to the same individual at different properties (Norfolk Museums Service).*

### *Castle Fee artisans*

The Castle Fee rent lists form a directory of ownership/occupancy of relevant properties (Figure 1.24) and have been linked to Kelly's trade groups (1983) to consider local economic activity: this analysis emphasises the high potential of linking documentary, cartographic and archaeological evidence at urban sites. A wide range of artisans worked around the fringes of the castle (Figure 1.25) and waste from virtually all of these trades found its way into the Norman well at the foot of the castle bridge, perhaps suggesting that the disposal was licensed. Numerous trades and professions were active within the Fee, including silkmen, armourers, blacksmiths and swordsmiths, bow and arrow makers, leather colourers, spur makers and saddlers. For example, in 1465 at Castle Fee Property 6, John Roper, a bowmaker left to William Nobbs, his next door neighbour at Property 7, all the tools and stock in his shop, including 60 bow-staves (NCC Will 6 Cobbald).

The prolific dumping of waste from these trades into the well (around 181 tonnes) may be a reflection of the city authority's attempts to keep the barbican and *motte* ditches clear: archaeological evidence indicates that – despite the documentary references to its continued occurrence – very little waste of the period was present in the barbican ditch which remained substantially open at this time. By the mid-16th century, the sheriff was still spying on those dumping muck into the *motte* and barbican ditches.

Highlighting just one aspect of the massive assemblage from the well, the most conclusive evidence from the animal bone refuse of a particular craft is provided by the remarkable group of goose wing bones. Goose wing tips were valued for their primary feathers and a minimum of 270 left and 122 right wing tips were recovered from the well, along with many other wing bones and matted lumps of feathers. The bias towards the left wing may indicate that these are the residue from a quill-dresser workshop, these being the preferred wing for right-handed quill users (as the feather curves away from the eye). An alternative is that the bias may link to the fletching of arrows, during which feathers from a single wing would have been used. The behaviour of incorrectly fletched arrows, which do not fly true, is known amongst archers as 'flirting'. Evidence for arrow manufacture in the locality comes both from documentary evidence for the presence of fletchers and bowyers and from the discovery of part-made armour-piercing arrows within the well fills.

This was the period of the longbow, when arrows were in high demand and when arms and raw materials had to be supplied to the Crown for its military campaigns. In 1417, six feathers from every goose within twenty southern English counties was to be supplied to the Tower, while the following year sheriffs were commanded to supply 1,190,000 goose feathers by Michaelmas (Cal. Pat. Rolls, 1416–22, 178; cited in Hardy 1994, p. 168).

### *Castle decline*

After the release of the castle baileys to the city in 1345 (Figure 1.10D), they were heavily exploited for quarrying, craft activities and refuse disposal, although the donjon and other buildings on the mound remained in use. Small sums were spent on the maintenance of Norwich Castle's remnants in the latter part of the 14th and into the 15th century but they were an increasing target for robbing. By the 16th century all the towers were in decay and by the end of the 17th century serious cracking of the donjon walls was apparent. Most of the curtain wall had disappeared by the end of the 17th century and excavation of a vast quarry led to the collapse of one of the castle gatehouses (Figure 1.17). The 18th century saw repairs to the bridge and donjon, although decline of the ditches continued.

The castle keep remained in use as a prison until 1888 and the county courts functioned there until the late 20th century. Pressure for space within the city's great market eventually led to the transfer of the livestock market to the baileys in 1616, where it remained until the 1960s.

## Conclusions

In conclusion, the recent research at Norwich Castle has permitted a detailed investigation of the great fortification of Norwich Castle over its long history. For urban studies more generally, the opportunity to investigate the social, economic and historical context of an urban royal castle, set within the framework of the Castle Fee, is currently unparalleled in England. Beecheno – the local antiquarian who was born within the Fee – once despaired that there was 'little scope for novelty in description, or fresh discovery' at Norwich Castle after the ravages of the centuries (Beecheno 1888, p. 1). Thankfully, this has not proved to be the case.

## Acknowledgements

The illustrations are by David Dobson (plans) and Nick Arber (reconstructions).

## Bibliography

Albarella, U., Beech, M., Locker, A., Moreno-García, M., Mulville, J. and Curl, J., with Shepherd Popescu, E. (2009) *Norwich Castle: Excavations and Historical Survey 1987–98. Part III: A Zooarchaeological Study,* East Anglian Archaeology Occasional Paper 22.

Allen Brown, R., Colvin, H. M. and Taylor, A. J., ed. (1963) *The History of the King's Works*, Vols I and II (London, HMSO).

Allen Brown, R. (1966–9) 'The Norman Conquest and the Genesis of English Castles', *Château Gaillard* 3, pp. 1–14.

Armitage, E. S. (1912) *The Early Norman Castles of the British Isles* (London).

Atkin, M. (1993) *Norwich, History and Guide* (Stroud, A. Sutton).

Atkin, M. (2002) 'Excavations within the Castle Fee, South Conesford', in M. Atkin and D. H. Evans, *Excavations in Norwich 1971–78: Part III*, East Anglian Archaeology 100, pp. 68–75.

Atkin, M. W., Ayers, B. S. and Jennings, S. (1983) *Waterfront Excavations and Thetford Ware Production,* East Anglian Archaeology 17.

Atkin, M. and Carter, A. (1985) 'General Introduction', in M. Atkin, A. Carter and D. H. Evans, *Excavations in Norwich 1971–1978 Part II*, East Anglian Archaeology 26, pp. 1–6.

Ayers, B. S. (1985) *Excavations within the North-East Bailey of Norwich Castle, 1979,* East Anglian Archaeology 28.

Ayers, B. S. (1994) *English Heritage Book of Norwich* (London, Batsford).

Ayers, B. S. (1997) 'Anglo-Saxon, Medieval and Post-Medieval (Urban)', in J. Glazebrook, ed., *Research and Archaeology: A Framework for the Eastern Counties,* East Anglian Archaeology Occasional Paper 3, pp. 59–66.

Ayers, B. S. (2016) '…traces of the original disposition of the whole'. Excavated evidence for the construction of Norwich Castle keep, this volume.

Baggs, A. P. (1963) *A Suggested Location for Norwic,* Norfolk Research Committee Bulletin 15.

Beecheno, F. R. (1888) *Notes on Norwich Castle* (Norwich, privately printed).

Beecheno, F. R. (1908) *Notes on the Ditches of Norwich Castle* (unpublished manuscript).

Biddle, M. (1976) 'The Evolution of Towns: Planned Towns before 1066', in M. W. Barley, ed., *The Plans and Topography of Medieval Towns in England and Wales,* Council for British Archaeology Research Report 14, pp. 19–32.

Biddle, M. *et al.*, ed. (1990) 'Object and economy in Medieval Winchester', *Winchester Studies* 7.ii (Oxford, University Press).

Blomefield, F. (1806) *The History of the City and County of Norwich* (Norwich, privately printed).

Brown, P., ed. (1984) *Domesday Book: 33 Norfolk (Part 1)*, in J. Morris, ed. (Chichester, Phillimore).

Campbell, J. (1975) 'Norwich', in M. D. Lobel, ed., *Historic Towns* (London).

Carter, A. (1978) 'The Anglo-Saxon origins of Norwich: the problems and approaches', in *Anglo-Saxon England* 7 (Cambridge, University Press).

Carter, A., Roberts, J. P. and Sutermeister, H. (1974) 'Excavations in Norwich, 1973: Norwich Survey Third Interim Report – The Background to the Excavations – Conesford and the Street Pattern', *Norfolk Archaeology* 39, pp. 63–71.

Chibnall, M., ed. (1969) *The Ecclesiastical History of Orderic Vitalis*, Vol. II, books III and IV (Oxford, Clarendon Press).

Chibnall, M. (1993) *Anglo-Norman England 1066–1166* (Oxford, Blackwell).

Clough, T. H. Mc K. (1973) 'A small hoard of William I type I pennies from Norwich', *British Numismatic Journal* 43, pp. 142–3.

Coad, J. G. and Streeten, A. D. F. (1982) 'Excavations at Castle Acre Castle, Norfolk, 1972–77: country house and castle of the Norman Earls of Surrey', *Archaeological Journal* 139, pp. 138–301.

Creighton, O. H. and Heigham, R. (2005) *Medieval Town Walls: an Archaeological and Social History of Urban Defence* (Tempus).

Darlington, J., ed. (2001) *Stafford Castle: Survey, Excavation and Research 1978–1998: Volume 1 – The Surveys* (Stafford Borough Council).

Davison, B. K. (1969) 'Early earthwork castles: a new model', *Château Gaillard* 3, pp. 37–47.

Drage, C. (1987) 'Urban castles', in J. Schofield and R. Leech, *Urban Archaeology in Britain*, Council for British Archaeology Research Report 61, pp. 117–32.

Drury, P. (2002) 'Norwich Castle Keep', in G. Meirion-Jones, E. Impey. and M. Jones, ed., *The Seigneurial Residence in Western Europe AD c800–1600*, British Archaeological Report International Series 1088.

Eales, R. (2003) 'Royal Power and Castles in Norman England', in R. Liddiard, ed., *Anglo-Norman Castles* (Boydell Press).

Emery, P. (2007) *Norwich Greyfriars, Excavations at the Former Mann Egerton Site, Prince of Wales Road, Norwich, 1992–1995,* East Anglian Archaeology 120.

English, B. (1995) 'Towns, mottes and Ring-works of the Conquest', in A. Ayton and J. L. Price, ed., *The Medieval Military Revolution: State, Society and Military Change in Medieval and Early Modern Europe* (London).

Green, B. (1970) *Norwich Castle, A Fortress for Nine Centuries* (Norwich, Jarrolds).

Green, B. (1990) *Norwich Castle: a Guide to the Castle as it was in about AD 1200*, Norfolk Museums Service Information Leaflet.

Green, B. and Young, R. M. R. (1981) *Norwich: the Growth of a City* (Norfolk Museums Service).

Hardy, R. (1994) 'The longbow', in A. Curry and M. Hughes, *Arms, Armies and Fortifications* (Woodbridge, Boydell).

Harrod, H. (1857) *Gleanings among the Castles and Convents of Norfolk* (Norwich).

Harvey, J. H. (1975) *Medieval Craftsmen* (London).

Hassall, T. G. (1976) 'Excavations at Oxford Castle 1965–73', *Oxoniensia* XLI, pp. 232–305.

Heslop, T. A. (1994) *Norwich Castle Keep: Romanesque Architecture and Social Context* (Norwich, Centre of East Anglian Studies).

Higham, R. and Barker, P. (1992) *Timber Castles* (London, Batsford).

Higham, R. and Barker, P. (2000) *Hen Domen, Montgomery: a Timber Castle on the English-Welsh border: a final report* (Exeter, University Press).

Hudson, W. H. (1896) *How the City of Norwich Grew into Shape.*

Hudson, W. H. and Tingey J. C., ed. (1906), *The Records of the City of Norwich* I (Norwich).

Keevill, G. (2004) *The Tower of London Moat: Archaeological Excavations 1995–1999*, Historic Royal Palaces Monograph 1 (Oxford Archaeology).

Kelly, S. (1983) 'The economic topography and structure of Norwich c. 1300', in S. Kelly, E. Rutledge and M. Tillyard, *Men of Property: an Analysis of the Norwich Enrolled Deeds 1285–1311* (Centre of East Anglian Studies).

King, D. J. C. (1991) *The Castle in England and Wales: an Interpretative History* (London and New York, Routledge).

King, D. J. C. and Alcock, L. (1969) 'Ringworks of England and Wales', *Château Gaillard* 3, pp. 90–111.

Liddiard, R. (2000) *Landscapes of Lordship: Norman Castles and the Countryside in Medieval Norfolk, 1066–1200*, British Archaeological Report 309.

Lloyd, R., Holmes, M. and Soden, I. (2002) *Excavations at King Street, Norwich (831 and 26577N): Assessment and Updated Project Design*, Northamptonshire Archaeology (unpublished).

Magilton, J., Lee, F. and Boylston, A., ed. (2008) *Lepers outside the gate: Excavations at the cemetery of the Hospital of St James and St Mary Magdalene, Chichester, 1986–87 and 1993*, Council for British Archaeology Research Report 158.

Mayes, P. and Butler, L. A. S. (1983) *Sandal Castle Excavations 1964–73* (Wakefield Historical Publications).

Morillo, S. (1994) *Warfare under the Anglo-Norman Kings 1066–1135* (Woodbridge, Boydell ).

Morris, R. (1989) *Churches in the Landscape* (London, Dent).

Penn, K. (1999) *Results of an Archaeological Evaluation at the former Brewery Site, King Street, Norwich*, NAU Client Report 342 (unpublished).

Poore, D. (2004) 'Latest Images from Oxford Castle', available at: www.oxfordarch.co.uk/pages/oxfordcastle_march04.htm.

Poore, D. (2004) 'Latest Images from Oxford Castle', available at: www.oxfordarch.co.uk/pages/oxfordcastle_march04.htm.

Poore, D. (2004) 'Latest Images from Oxford Castle', available at: www.oxfordarch.co.uk/pages/oxfordcastle_march04.htm.

Pounds, N. J. G. (1990) *The Medieval Castle in England and Wales* (Cambridge, University Press).

Reeve, J. (1992) 'Lost town and ditches', in B. S. Ayers, J. Bown and J. Reeve, *Digging Ditches* (Norwich, Norfolk Museums Service).

Rye, W. (1921) *Norwich Castle* (Holt).

Sandred, K. I. and Lindström, B. (1989) *The Place-Names of Norfolk*, Part 1 (London, The English Place-Name Society).

Shepherd Popescu, E. (2004) 'Norwich Castle Fee', *Medieval Archaeology* XLVIII, pp. 209–19.

Shepherd Popescu, E. (2009a) *Norwich Castle: Excavations and Historical Survey, 1987–98: Part I: Anglo-Saxon to c.1345*, East Anglian Archaeology 132.

Shepherd Popescu, E. (2009b) *Norwich Castle: Excavations and Historical Survey, 1987–98: Part II: c.1345 to Modern*, East Anglian Archaeology 132.

Shepherd Popescu, E. (2009c) *Norwich, Castle Mall* [data-set]. York: Archaeology Data Service [distributor] (doi:10.5284/1000173).

Tillyard, M. with Shepherd Popescu, E. and Ives, N. (2009) *Norwich Castle: Excavations and Historical Survey, 1987–98: Part IV: Property and People in the Documentary Record*, East Anglian Archaeology Occasional Paper 23.

Swanton, M. (2000) *The Anglo-Saxon Chronicles* (London, Phoenix Press).

Wallis, H. (forthcoming) *Excavations on Norwich Castle Mound 1999–2001*, East Anglian Archaeology.

Wilkins, W. (1796) 'Essay towards a History of Venta Icenorum and of Norwich Castle', *Archaeologia* XII, pp. 132–180.

Wilson, D. M. and Hurst, D. G. (1962–3) 'Medieval Britain in 1961', *Medieval Archaeology* VI–VII, pp. 306–49.

Woodward, S., ed. (1847) *The History and Antiquity of Norwich Castle* (London and Norwich).

# 2

# '...TRACES OF THE ORIGINAL DISPOSITION OF THE WHOLE'. EXCAVATED EVIDENCE FOR THE CONSTRUCTION OF NORWICH CASTLE KEEP

*Brian Ayers*

**Résumé**

*Cet article présente les résultats des fouilles entreprises en 1986 au sein du donjon du château de Norwich et vise à développer à la fois les travaux précédemment publiés sur la conception esthétique du donjon et l'étude analytique de la structure. Il résume les précédentes interventions sur le bâtiment, notamment l'enlèvement de grandes quantités de matériel accumulé dans les années 1880, avant de traiter de trois petites fouilles ciblées, deux dans le compartiment nord du rez-de-chaussée du donjon et une troisième dans le compartiment sud.*

*Les travaux ont permis d'avoir une meilleure compréhension des quatre murs extérieurs du donjon. Plus précisément, la fouille effectuée contre le mur nord a été particulièrement révélatrice, la structure du mur et la stratigraphie du sol indiquant un effondrement précoce et important du mur qui nécessita une reconstruction presque complète. Ensuite, la zone continua d'être instable, le sommet de la butte s'affaissant probablement vers l'est, et par la suite le mur nécessita une importante rénovation.*

*La fouille a également fait apparaître des changements dans la conception du donjon lors de sa construction. Les murs intérieurs du compartiment sud ont témoigné d'un changement de plan, une sous-division de ce compartiment étant postérieure à la construction initiale du puits. Une autre découverte importante fut celle d'une base de mur intermédiaire, probablement une petite arcade, dans le compartiment sud. Toutefois, l'observation la plus importante concerne peut-être celle du changement de technique de fondation à l'extrémité ouest du mur de refend qui divisait le donjon en compartiments nord et sud. Ce changement se produit exactement au point où, selon un plan de la fin du XVIIIe siècle, des murs en diagonale avaient été conservés au niveau du premier étage. Certains soulignent que ce changement de fondation du mur de refend, sans changement évident dans la structure bâtie de la partie inférieure conservée du mur lui-même, implique que l'on savait pendant la construction que le mur situé au-dessus de la zone en question n'était pas destiné à être un mur porteur. Par conséquent, la base de mur observée appuie l'idée d'une arcade disposée en diagonale au niveau du premier étage. Des murs en diagonale, à ce niveau, constitueraient un exemple unique dans les donjons romans connus d'Europe du Nord.*

*L'article conclut par des observations sur d'autres interventions récentes au château de Norwich et les implications pour la recherche méthodologie future au sein du donjon.*

## Background

In the early 1980s, a small committee of Norfolk County Council officers, with advisors from the Ancient Monuments branch of the then Department of the Environment (subsequently English Heritage), was set up to consider ways of improving understanding and presentation of Norwich Castle keep (NHER 30; TG23155 08500). As a necessary preliminary, Plowman Craven and Associates carried out a photogrammetric survey of the interior of the keep and, following this, Paul Drury was commissioned to undertake an analytical survey of the building during 1983–4, with the aim of elucidating so far as possible the original plan of the keep, how it was modified in construction, and how it was used. The balance of the capital sum provided by Norfolk County Council for this enabled the present writer to excavate within the keep in 1986 to resolve some uncertainties. Separately, Sandy Heslop of the University of East Anglia undertook a study of the design of the building.

Paul Drury's analysis of the evolution of the design and planning of the keep was published in 2002 while Sandy Heslop's assessment of the design aesthetic appeared in 1994. Drury's interpretation of the building, particularly its western end, was contested in part by Philip Dixon and Pamela Marshall who published their own interpretation at the same time as him and in the same volume. While reference was made by Drury to the 1986 excavations in his paper, he did not publish any detailed account of the work. To date therefore, the only publication is a summary account published by the writer the year after the work (Ayers 1987, pp. 21–3).

This present paper, in presenting the excavated results and discussing their implications, thus completes a process set in train some 30 years ago. Its title uses a quotation from Edward King, writing at the beginning of the 19th century. He was firmly (and erroneously) of the opinion that the Norwich Castle keep was 'Saxon' but he did note that 'although the timbers are at present removed, and only small sheds are built against the walls, yet traces of the original disposition of the whole may plainly be discovered, by any person accustomed to examine these kind of buildings ...' (King 1807, p. 41). This account details such traces and explores 'the original disposition'.

## Previous excavation within Norwich Castle keep

It is quite likely that numerous interventions have taken place within the ground-floor area of the keep from the late medieval period onwards. Repairs to the north wall of the building in the 18th century probably required a deep cut through accumulated deposits. The sinking of a well *c.* 1785 resulted in the archaeological observation (almost certainly erroneous) of a pre-mound road crossing the site (Hudson 1892, p. 30; Ayers 1985, p. 3) and the cutting of an entrance at ground-floor level in 1827 may have entailed the removal of archaeological material. The most major work, however, was clearly that undertaken under the supervision of Edward Boardman in 1888/9, when 2m or more of material appears to have been removed to establish the present ground-floor level.

Prior to the removal of soil by Boardman, a series of exploratory shafts were sunk by J. Brockbank, the City Architect. His notes, dated 16 May 1888, survive in the Castle Museum. Following the removal of late 18th-century prison buildings, he excavated in an attempt to locate the medieval well as marked by Wilkins on his plan of the keep (Drury 2002, fig. 14) but failed in this objective. He did, however, find the remains of the spine wall although he recorded this as being 'without footings'. Proceeding, he stated that, as far as excavated, 'no evidence has been procured to verify Wilkins' plan as to the oblique walls at the west end of the keep'.

Excavations were also undertaken in the south-eastern part of the keep, uncovering elements of the internal walls there. A third shaft found remains of a pier in the northern compartment. The material removal was also summarised:

> So far as the excavations have gone the soil thrown out is ordinary filling up material. A large quantity of bones, two boars tusks, fragments of pottery and moulded stone columns also a curious iron instrument have been exhumed but nothing further that calls for remark.

Finally Brockbank made three borings through the mound. He found that 'to a depth of about twenty-five feet [7.62m] below the present floor the mound is composed of soil of various kinds, including traces of old mortar'. Below that was 'a layer of clay three or four feet thick [0.91m to 1.22m] and below that was found an earthy sand very dark in colour'.

Two of the borings met an obstruction at 35 feet [10.67m] which could not be pierced. The third bore was eventually sunk to 42 feet [12.80m], finding natural sand at 10.67m and pure sand thereafter for a further 2.13m. Orders were given to fill in the shaft on 6 June 1888.

In contrast to Brockbank's account the major excavations undertaken by Boardman are very poorly documented. The Royal Archaeological Institute visited in August 1889 and some discussion of the desirability of excavations was held. It was subsequently noted that 'since the Castle was visited by the Institute a large portion of the interior has been excavated down to the original level [*sic*], but no further light has been at present thrown upon its history' (Anon 1889, p. 446). Photographs taken during clearance do survive, one of which shows two workmen standing on or next to the spine wall, armed with sledgehammer and pick! No report of the deposits removed was prepared. In 1890 the medieval well was excavated; again no report was prepared.

Subsequently three interventions in the 1970s are recorded (Figure 2.1). The first of these in 1972 was associated with drainage work when a pipe was laid north-to-south across the basement, through the doorway in the spine wall. A section of the disturbed deposits was drawn (Figure 2.2). The trench revealed a 'longitudinal' (east-to-west) foundation below both the hall and chamber, that is in the northern and southern compartments. The plinth of the spine wall adjacent to the doorway was seen (information in a letter from A. B. Whittingham to P. A. Faulkner, 12 October 1972). The section implies a probable early threshold. This excavation was notable for the discovery of a highly-decorated bobbin of walrus ivory (Beckwith 1973, pp. 277ff).

In 1974 two small excavations were undertaken in the north compartment (Figure 2.1, A.74 and B.74). The first of these, Trench A.74, was excavated at the foot of the east wall below an impost block subsequently examined by Drury (Drury 2002, p. 212, fig. 11). It uncovered a wall of flint which ran westward, presumably to continue as the similar wall uncovered in Trench B.74. This latter trench showed the wall to be associated with a pier base.

Finally, in 1975 emergency drainage work (associated with voids discovered at depth to either side of the 18th-century well) entailed the cutting of drainage trenches east of the well across the southern compartment. The salvage work of the 1970s was of particular value because it was generally well-recorded, demonstrated the depth of surviving deposits and provided information about the structure of the keep.

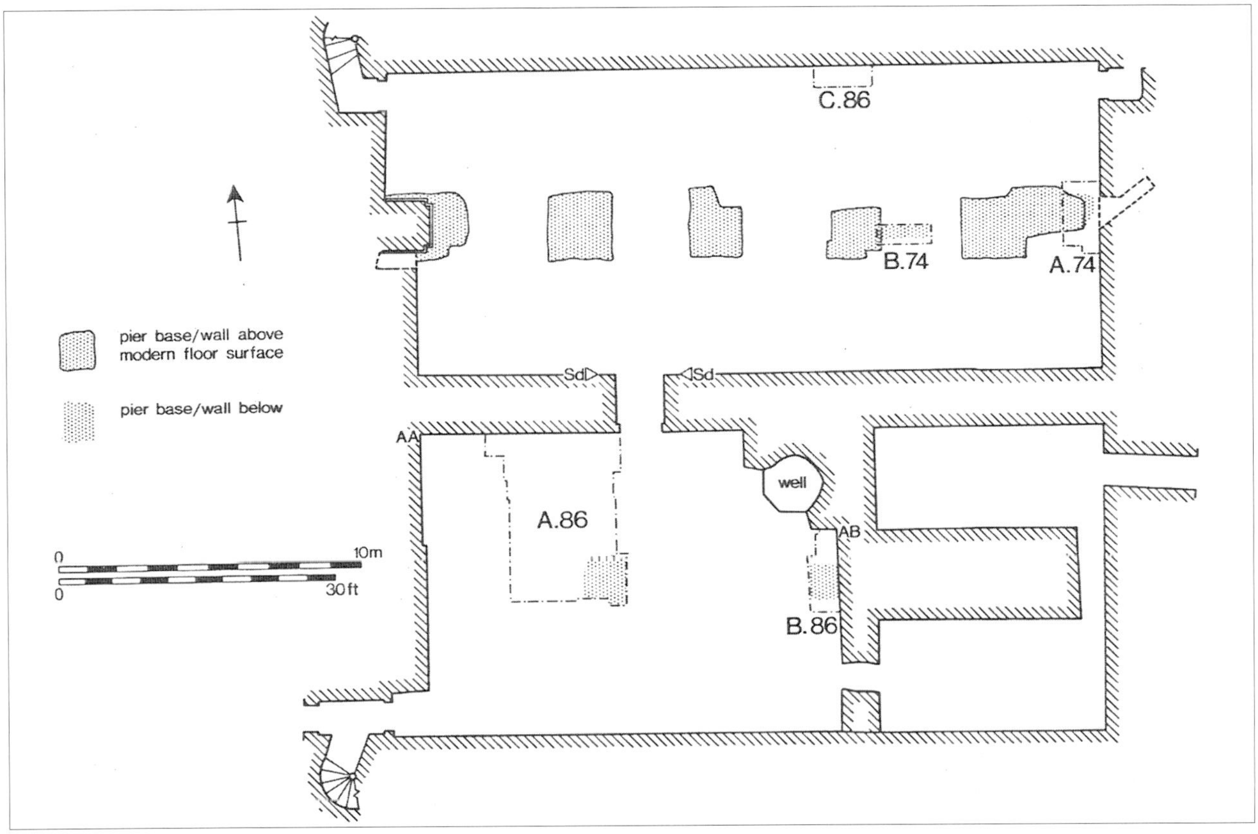


*Figure 2.1. Norwich Castle keep: location of 1974 and 1986 excavations.*

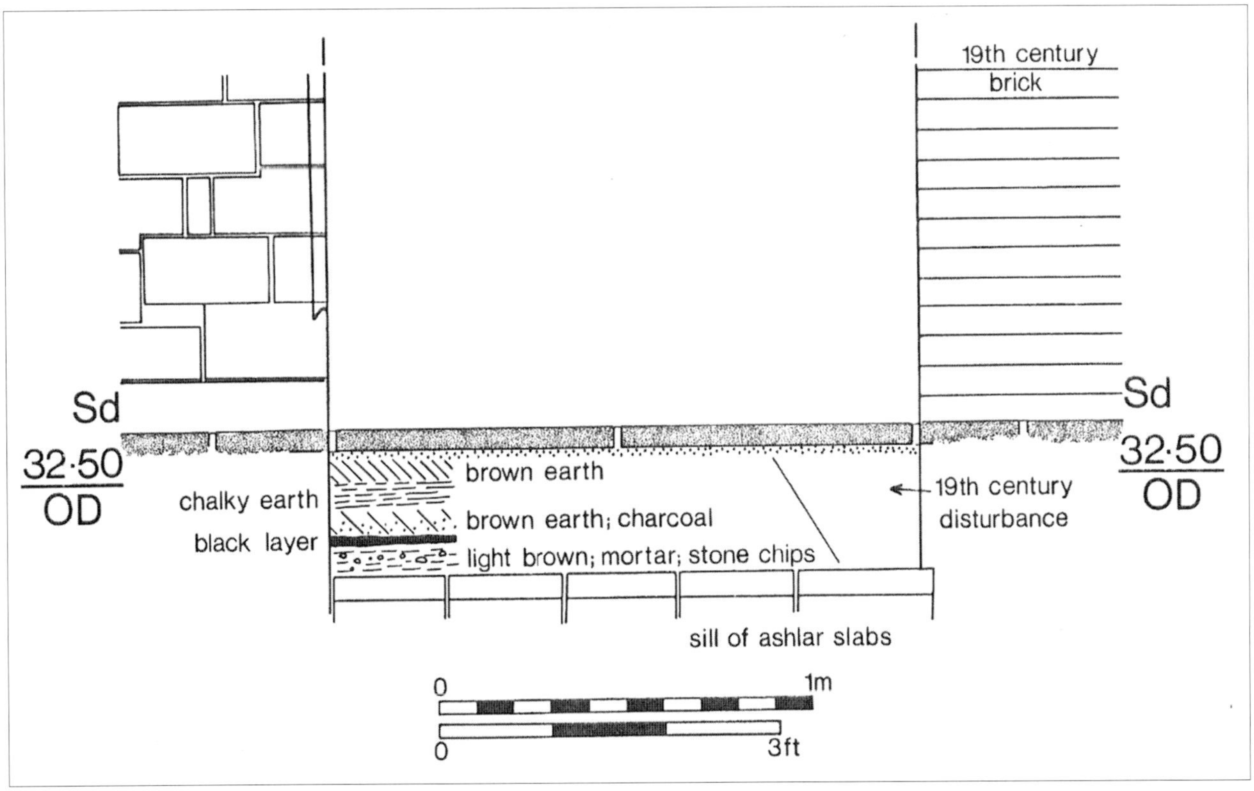


*Figure 2.2. Norwich Castle keep: 1972 section showing doorway in spine wall.*

## The 1986 excavation

Excavation took place in three areas within the ground-floor of the keep (Figure 2.1: A.86, B.86 and C.86), chosen to elucidate problems which had been identified by study of the upstanding fabric and records.

It would appear that accumulated material within the basement had reached a height in excess of 2m by the late 18th century (much of this accumulation no doubt consisting of demolition debris from internal walls and the roof), providing the surface upon which Sir John Soane constructed a free-standing gaol between 1789 and 1793 (Stroud 1984, pl. 46). Following demolition of Soane's building in 1888 removal of accumulated material established the ground-floor at approximately 32.5m OD (the surface varies).

Some 0.5m of occupation deposits survived the work of the 1880s and overlies the re-deposited top of the mound or *motte* upon which the keep stands. This mixed material is often difficult to separate from primary occupation surfaces. True natural deposits (of sand, gravel and chalk) lie in excess of 10m beneath the excavated areas and were clearly not reached during the work.

The excavation was undertaken using artificial light, generally 'natural' fluorescent tubes but also occasional spotlights. These may well have distorted soil colours (affecting Munsell notations in the excavation archive) but did not seem to impair stratigraphic analysis.

None of the excavations was large, Area A.86 being the greatest in size at 17m$^2$. Work was conducted using standard recording techniques on as open a plan as possible. Only two specific problems require noting here.

Firstly, excavation had to allow for modern features, that is access to the ground-floor spaces and continued use of the building above. This latter consideration meant that stanchions set into pits, to support Boardman's inserted floor, could not be undermined and excavation had to contract to avoid them. This was of greatest importance in the south-western corner of Area A.86 where the location of a stanchion prevented the full excavation of Pit *21*.

Secondly, wherever possible, deposits that could be identified as clearly pre-keep in date were not excavated. This was in order to preserve them for future, more large-scale work. It seems likely from observations made during the course of the excavation that such early deposits do survive, albeit mangled by later building work, and as such probably form the best single area of extant early Norman deposits on the mound. As the project was designed to examine the keep rather than these earlier levels, it seemed reasonable to record and then preserve them.

The following account of the excavated features is kept deliberately brief, concentrating upon the information pertinent to an understanding of the building. Finds recovered from the work are summarised in Appendix 1.

## Excavation features: Period I – pre-keep deposits (not illustrated – archive plan 5)

Evidence was recovered for pre-keep occupation in all three areas, the greatest extent of such deposits being in Area A.86. Here alternating layers of chalk and sand loam may have represented part of the mound although charcoal flecks were present in two contexts. These were superseded by deposits of silty sands and sand loam, all containing charcoal flecks and all cut by or predating the foundation trench for the spine wall of the keep.

Within B.86 only one level, a deposit of hard-packed chalk, was encountered while in C.86, against the north wall of the keep, silty sand loams were found to predate its construction, one deposit containing animal bone.

## Excavation features: Period II – the construction of the keep (Figures 2.3–2.6)

### *Area A.86*

Excavation adjacent to the east-to-west spine wall (*20*) uncovered a foundation trench (*51*) running from the east edge of the excavation westward for some 3.20m, cutting earlier deposits (Figure 2.3). It was packed with coursed flint rubble in sand (*52*), offset 0.35m to the south of the spine wall. The wall was constructed above (Figure 2.4). At the western end of trench *51* the wall continues westward above chalk *57* and thin deposits *56* and *55* rather than above a substantial foundation. Although the foundation technique changes, the structure of the wall does not, being coursed through in flint.

South of foundation trench *51* a large part of the area excavated was covered by a crumbly sand loam (*42*), probably the upcast from the trench itself. This deposit may have acted as a surface within the keep, some wear being evident in the centre; the area seems to have been repaired as traces of a possible crude cobbled surface (*43*) were uncovered (Figure 2.3).

A second east-to-west foundation trench (*53*) was then excavated and found to be packed with a footing of quarried flint (*54*) before being surmounted by a heavily-mortared foundation (*14*) (Figure 2.3). Unlike the footing below the spine wall, the foundation to *14* was not offset. It post-dated deposit (*42)* and had been cut by later intrusion and levelled flat (probably in the 19th century). However, a surviving fillet of mortar on the south face, together with the probable surface of deposit *42*, indicated that the base of the superstructure had been located at *c.* 32.35m OD. It is possible, therefore, that the excavated footing supported a wall of unknown height or function, located midway between the spine wall and the south wall of the keep.

Later intrusive robbing at the west end of foundation *14* suggests that such a wall was either removed or

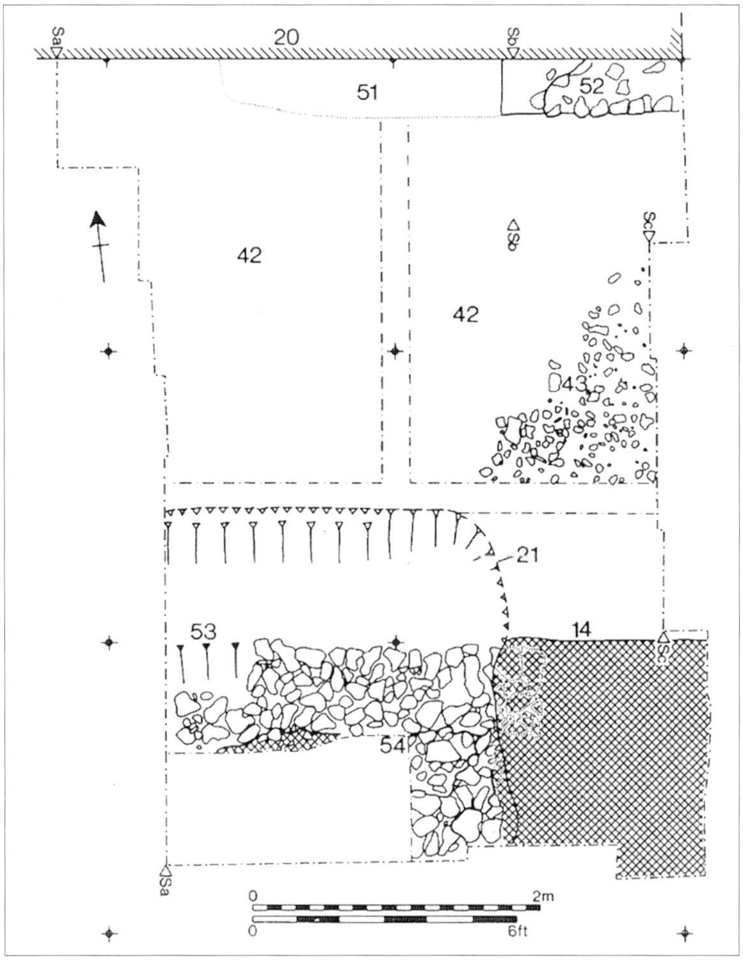


*Figure 2.3. Norwich Castle keep: Area A.86 phase II plan.*

supplemented by the provision of an arcade supported on large piers, one of which was placed within the area of the excavation (Figure 2.3) and also subsequently robbed. The robbing indicated the probable size of the pier, extending north and south of the earlier flint footing. The deposition of extensive layer *2*, consisting of mortar and flint as well as abundant small, fresh fragments of worked limestone, may have been associated with the construction of such piers and attendant vaulting.

## *Area B.86*

This trench (Figure 2.1), located in the western angle formed by walls numbered *108* (bounding the eastern edge of the excavation) and *109* (the south side of the well), revealed that, below present ground-floor level, these walls merely abut (the wall of the well – *109* – is the earlier) although they are keyed in higher up by means of dressed limestone quoins. The north-to-south aligned wall (*108*) was seen to be constructed above a foundation of three flint courses which were not offset. The lower courses of wall *109* could

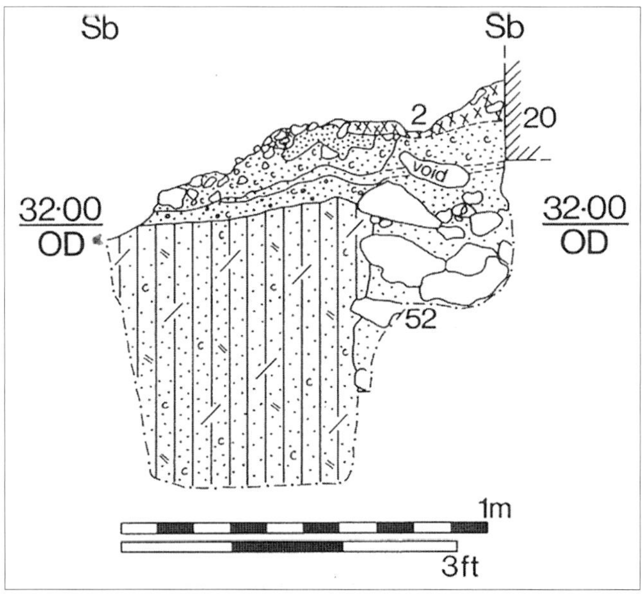


*Figure 2.4. Norwich Castle keep: Area A.86 showing offset foundation to the spine wall.*

not be seen because of a heavily-mortared flint feature of single course depth (*106*) (Figure 2.5) which ran westward from wall *108*, parallel to wall *109*. The bottom (visible) quoin of wall *109* ran behind this feature.

South of feature *106* a further, and larger, feature (*105*) was encountered. Constructed of flint and mortar it was of similar build to, and on the same alignment as, feature *14* in Area A.86. As such it must represent the eastern end of foundation *14*, abutting north-to-south wall *108*. A crack across *105*, 0.46m west of wall *108*, may represent settlement although this cannot have been due to differential settling above the foundation of *108* as this latter did not have an offset foundation. Feature *105* was abutted by loamy sand (*103*) to the south but deposits to the north had been removed by later intrusion.

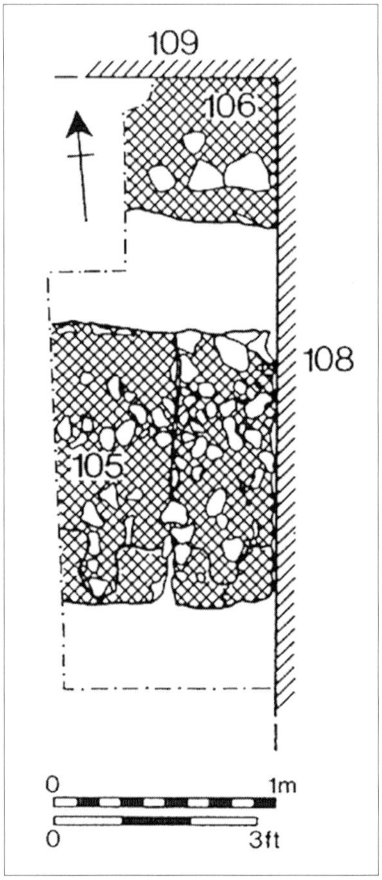


*Figure 2.5. Norwich Castle keep: Area B.86 phase II plan.*

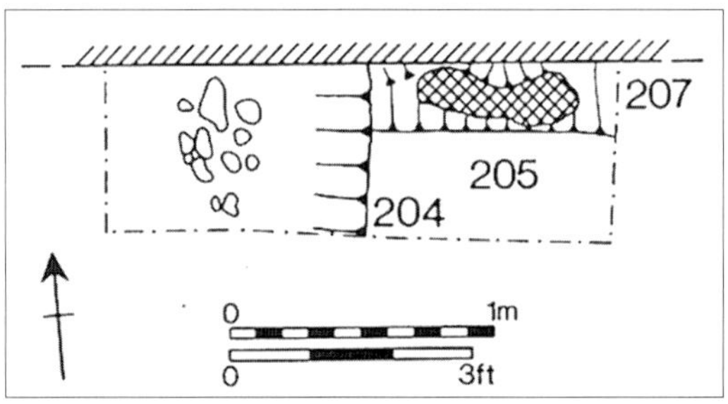


*Figure 2.6: Norwich Castle keep: Area C.86 phase II plan.*

### *Area C.86*

This trench (Figure 2.1), against the north wall of the keep, indicated that construction of the wall was a two-stage process. In the first stage, building commenced above a foundation trench (*207*), the wall being slightly uneven at the base but thereafter flat and rendered. However, it was subject to a substantial failure at an early date leading to a second stage where the wall was rebuilt west of a major crack with only the very bottom of the original wall surviving. This re-building involved the insertion of feature *204*, an incision to allow access to the work, thereby cutting earlier foundation *207* (Figure 2.6). The repair appears to have been built up against the crack although the western part is offset very slightly (between 15mm and 30mm) to the south, probably due to differential settlement (the offsetting was also observed for the surviving element of the first stage of construction).

## Excavation features: Periods III and IV – Late medieval and post-medieval alteration and use of the keep (Figure 2.7)

### *Area A.86*

Little evidence survived for usage of the ground-floor area during the medieval period. In the late 15th century, however, it is likely that wall/arcade *14* was demolished and at least partly robbed. A large pit (*21*) was excavated which cut the substantial structure of *14*, widening to both the north and south; full excavation was impossible due to a modern stanchion. This intrusion removed all of feature *14* that lay within its area save for the bottom course of flint foundation. The pit filled rapidly, primarily with destruction debris (*44*), but subsequently with a very uniform deposit (*13*) of dark brown sandy loam containing much animal bone and a good group of late medieval pottery (see below).

Elsewhere in this area, layer *2* was cut by a number of features, some of which appeared to be the remains of post-holes but the evidence was too scanty to allow interpretation. Two large pits (*10* and *8*) were excavated adjacent to the spine wall. These had the effect of removing all connecting stratigraphy between the wall and the remainder of the excavation save for a sliver of material between them which survived somewhat precariously. Pit *10* was cut immediately south of the offset foundation and, apart from possibly effecting some erosion to the upper courses, did not damage this footing. The lower part of the pit was square and contained much ash, clinker and charcoal

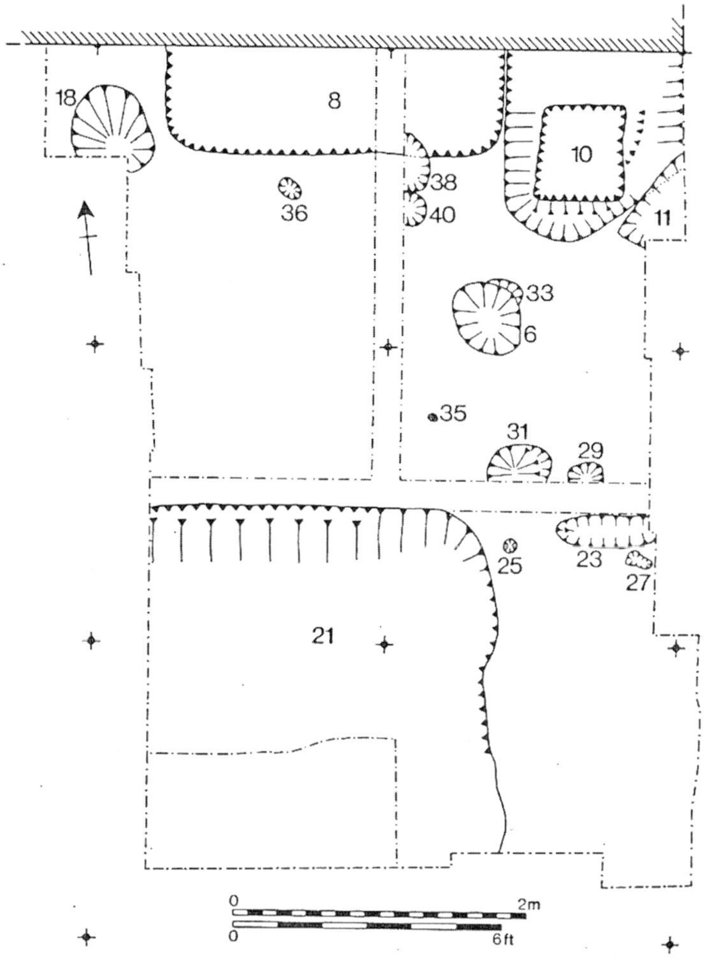


*Figure 2.7: Norwich Castle keep: Area A.86 phases III and IV plan.*

as well as two very large lumps of bonded brickwork which was almost certainly 19th-century in date. Pit *8* was more destructive, having been cut immediately adjacent to the spine wall. It removed the offset foundation in its entirety, only the very bottom of the foundation cut surviving below the base of the pit.

These pits, together with two smaller features *11* and *38*, were the latest to be uncovered by the excavation. Most of the area was then overlain by an homogeneous deposit (*1*) which, although it contained quantities of late medieval material, probably represented a levelling layer established at the end of the 19th century following the removal of soil and debris above the present ground-floor level during conversion of the building to a museum.

### *Area B.86*

A linear feature *107* was excavated between earlier features *105* and *106*. It contained quantities of dressed and decorated limestone, presumably destruction debris. Feature *105* itself was overlain by a deposit of fine loose and crumbly mortar before all levels were then overlain by *101*, a deposit similar to *1* in Area A.86.

### *Area C.86*

No medieval features survived in this area. The only deposit to be recovered was *201*, a levelling layer similar to *1* in Area A.86 and *101* in Area B.86 although there was very slight evidence to suggest the bottom of a cut to allow the stitched repair of the north wall of the keep.

## Concluding discussion

The recently-published works of Drury, Heslop, Dixon and Marshall together provide a comprehensive set of (occasionally contrasting) views for the likely construction history, design aesthetic and intended function of Norwich Castle keep. It is unlikely that, without major further detailed survey of the internal fabric, significant additional information will be recovered. However, the results of the 1986 excavation do provide insights into the problems of initial construction and changes in design during building. In addition, excavated evidence also contributes to discussion of the thorny question of the disposition of internal walls at the first-floor western end of the structure.

### *Initial construction – the main walls of the keep*

The 1986 work has enabled a better understanding of the four exterior walls of the keep (especially the north wall), together with the spine wall, all of which are bonded together. Specifically, excavation against the north wall, although the smallest intervention in 1986, was also one of the most revealing. The sequence has been described above but its implication is profound. The wall fabrics and soil stratigraphy seem to indicate an early and major failure of the north wall that required almost complete rebuilding. Subsequently the area continued to be unsound, the mound top probably subsiding eastward, and eventually the wall needed substantial stitching. It is also interesting to note that the north wall was the only one to be provided with an additional external buttress which would have both strengthened and masked the joint between the primary and rebuilt structures (Figure 2.8).

Failure of the north wall was probably accompanied by problems encountered during construction of the east wall. Here examination of the fabric above the principal door at first-floor level near the north-east angle of the building indicates subsidence which had to be levelled-up as building work proceeded. The reason for the difficulties is likely to have been the proximity of a ditch, the keep being built on an early mound which was subsequently extended. Such seems to be the evidence of excavations through the mound in 1999–2001 (Wallis, *in prep.*) while photographs taken in the 1960s (during extensive and otherwise unrecorded excavations for subterranean rooms as part of museum extensions) appear to show the steep tip-lines of an early mound (Shepherd Popescu 2009, pl. 6.4).

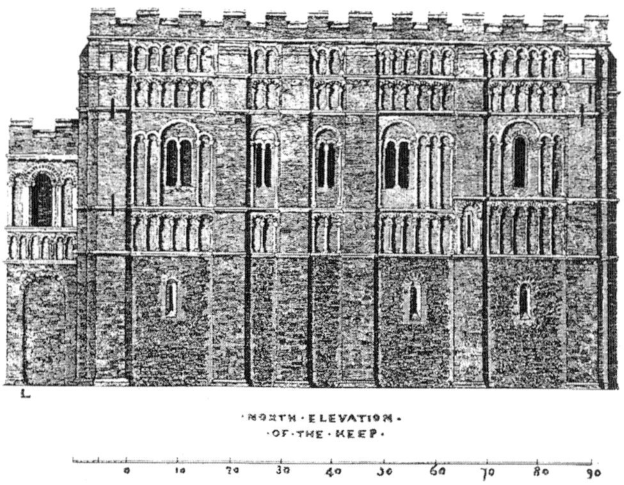


*Figure 2.8. Norwich Castle keep: north exterior elevation by William Wilkins 1795.*

The excavation did not throw any additional light on a likely date for the start of keep construction. This remains, on stylistic grounds, to be most probable in the reign of William Rufus (Heslop 1994, pp. 60ff). The primary build of the four main walls of the keep (together with its spine wall) is likely therefore to have occupied a pre-existing Conquest period mound which was subsequently extended to the east. This not only explains the apparently anomalous position of the keep with regard to the pre-existing Anglo-Scandinavian town (the centre of which on Tombland cannot be seen from the top of the building) but also suggests that evidence of earlier structures may survive beneath. Such is also the implication of deposits seen within the 1986 excavations.

### *Changes in design during construction of the keep*

The construction of internal walls *108* and *109* in the southern compartment was seen to be rather odd. These walls clearly abutted one another at a low level but were keyed-in higher up. The sequence of construction was east-to-west wall 109 followed by north-to-south wall *108* which was in turn abutted by the intermediary wall (here numbered *105* and subsequently the footing for the short arcade). Of additional interest in this area was the considerable number of dressed limestone fragments recovered from a later intrusion.

It has long been evident that wall *108*, together with the substantially thicker east-to-west aligned wall to its east (which lies beneath the area of the first-floor chapel), is a result of a change in plan during construction (wall *108* for instance is not bonded into the south external wall of the building but merely abuts it). The excavated evidence, however, demonstrated conclusively that wall *108* was an afterthought to the construction of the well-shaft but had been determined upon soon after work had started on raising the well-shaft towards first-floor level. Indeed, a probable sequence would now seem to be of a pre-existing well associated with creation of the mound and usage during a (lost) timber phase; a decision to extend the well-shaft upward as part of a new stone keep; and, finally, incorporation of the well-shaft into a re-design as the keep reached first-floor level.

An important discovery was the uncovering of an intermediary wall in the southern compartment. This seems to have been observed in 1972 and was clearly later than wall *108* and therefore also part of a re-design of the internal layout of the building. Very slight traces of material could be interpreted as forming part of a wall superstructure but, thereafter, its foundation seems to have been used as a linked footing for a short arcade. The evidence of pit *21* suggests that a large pillar or pier was constructed within (and slightly extending north and south from) its alignment before being robbed out in the late 15th century. The robber pit indicated the approximate dimensions of the pier. The short arcade thus provided would have had piers linked by a wall foundation in a manner similar to the foundation known in the northern compartment from the 1974 excavations.

Dating of the removal of the arcade to the late 15th century accords well with the known history of the castle. Certainly by the 18th century it is recorded that prisoners on the first floor could look down into the ground-floor exercise yard in the south-west corner of the building (Nick Arber, *pers. comm.*).

### *The western part of the keep*

The discovery of a change in foundation technique for the spine wall is of great interest. The change occurs at exactly that point where Wilkins' plan suggests diagonal walls survived at first-floor level. Evidence for such walls was specifically sought by Brockbank during his 1888 excavations. As noted above, he stated that, as far as excavated, 'no evidence has been procured to verify Wilkins' plan as to the oblique walls at the west end of the keep'. He added for clarity: 'I would repeat that no traces of the foundations of any oblique walls have been discovered.'

Taken together these statements imply that Brockbank excavated against the spine wall, that he was at the western end of the keep and that he was looking for foundations in the area below where walls are suggested on Wilkins' drawing. It is therefore probable that pit *8*, excavated in the A.86 trench was that inserted by Brockbank. Presumably his workmen did not recognise the offset foundation during excavation and the finished section would not have betrayed its existence to him. Pit *8* actually stopped marginally short of the change in foundation noted in the 1986 excavation but, even if it had not, it would be unreasonable to expect Brockbank to have recognised the likely significance of such a change.

That significance is, of course, a matter of interpretation. It is argued here that a change in foundation for the spine wall, without an obvious change in the built fabric of the wall itself, implies that it was known that the wall above the area in question was not intended to be load-bearing. At first-floor level it could, therefore, have branched in the singular manner suggested by Wilkins' plan. The lack of any ground-floor foundations for the resulting diagonal walls could be explained by the Y-shape thus created being one formed of branching arches from the spine wall, running to the interior face of the main western wall.

Diagonal walls in this location would be unique in the known Romanesque tower keeps of northern Europe. Dixon and Marshall doubt the accuracy of those drawings which show them (2002, p. 236) although they are careful not 'to dismiss the drawing out of hand'. Drury in contrast favours the existence of the walls (as arches; 2002, p. 216) and cites interpreted architectural evidence to support this. The evidence of the excavation would seem in turn to support the Drury position.

The 1986 excavations were planned with limited objectives in mind and were essentially subordinate to the architectural survey of the keep undertaken at the same time. However, the results complemented that survey, providing additional information which, as has been seen, helps interpretation of the construction and adaptation of the building. The deposits which yielded this information could only do so because of their remarkable degree of survival despite massive depletion at the end of the 19th century. However, the existence of such deposits also extends beyond their importance as a link to the standing monument. The construction of the keep can be viewed as a final stage in an evolving pattern of use on this part of the motte-top. While the building fulfilled many functions, some (if not many) affecting the below-ground archaeology, it also sealed earlier horizons. The 1986 excavation established that these horizons still exist, that they contain evidence of occupation and that, as such, they can probably be distinguished from the artificial mound make-up.

Work on Norwich Castle since 1986 has provided a massive new dataset for the entire complex, most of it now published (Shelley 1996; Shepherd Popescu 2009). However, other work on the keep remains unpublished including a small excavation adjacent to the interior of the west wall (Bradley and Gaimster 2001, p. 304; Wallis, *in prep.*) and a survey of the exterior faces of the building which, while inevitably mainly recording 19th-century re-facing, also recorded surviving elements of the original façade (NAU 2000, pp. 36–7).

The results of the 1986 excavations within the keep illustrate well that even localised and small-scale work, if it is planned carefully, can result in informative data which helps towards a greater understanding of the building. However, even such small interventions need to be added to the major loss of 2m of material during conversion of the building to a museum in 1889–94 and to other incidental losses of deposits due to cutting of easements. At the same time, the value of those deposits that survive is increasingly appreciated, not least because of the potential for exploration of pre-keep horizons. Accordingly, should any future excavation within the keep be mooted, there is a strong argument that, as well as using the best possible modern excavation and recording techniques (followed by prompt publication), any work should uncover as large an area as possible in order to understand as fully as possible the fragmentary nature of the levels.

## Appendix 1: the finds

### *Non-ceramic artefacts (by Val Fryer)*

A total of 29 small finds was recorded from Areas A.86 and B.86 (Area C.86 did not produce any small finds). All of the finds, with the exception of No. 1 below, are consistent with domestic and rubbish deposits. No small finds were recovered from Period 1 deposits, and the layers associated with the construction phases of the keep only produced an incomplete nail and an unidentifiable iron object. The occupation and alteration levels of Period III produced a copper alloy and iron barrel padlock, a copper alloy buckle plate and a small fragment of painted window glass. The majority of the small finds were recovered from the post-medieval features of Period IV. Notable amongst these are a gold finger ring (no. 10) and three bone pins. Only one object, No. 1, is illustrated here. A catalogue (ordered by period, small find number and context number) is kept with the excavation archive.

*Illustrated object (Figure 2.9)*

1. Gold finger ring with garnet set 'en cabochon' in an oval collet. There are rectangular mouldings where the hoop joins the bezel. The ring can be dated to the early 13th century (cf. Oman 1974, pl. 14A). Period IV S. F. 1. 1. (A.86).

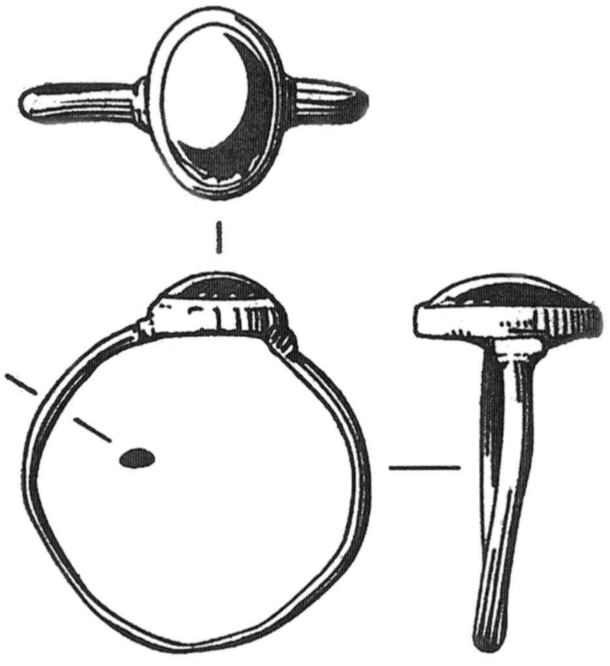

*Figure 2.9. Gold finger ring (drawing by the late Sue Margeson).*

### *The pottery (by Carolyn Dallas)*

A total of 2268 sherds were found in the 1986 excavations, of which trenches B.86 and C.86 produced only 19 and 68 sherds respectively. The pottery outlined below was recovered from Area A.86 and ranged from Saxo-Norman Thetford-type wares to sherds of 18th-century vessels but the assemblage consisted predominately of 14th- to 16th-century wares. Stratigraphically the vessels recovered from Pit *21* were most important and the significance of these is discussed separately below. The range of wares from A.86 can be summarised as follows:

1. Thetford-type. Five Saxo-Norman bodysherds in Periods I and Iii (0.2%).
2. Early medieval. Four possible bodysherds in Period II, and residually in Period IV (0.2%).
3. Medieval – late medieval unglazed wares (534; 25.2%). 13 jar rims, *c.* 11 vessels (Jennings 1981, fig. 15). The latest example is similar to LMT (see below). Some 22 jug rims were found (Jennings 1981, p. 48) of which three have twisted rod handles, and a further 19 bodysherds have applied strips or roulette decoration (Jennings 1981, fig. 17). One of the 28 sagging bases has a thumbed strip around the basal angle.
4. Medieval – late medieval glazed wares (813; 38.3%). These would seem all to be jugs, of which 1.7% are fully oxidised with yellowish lead glazes with copper spots. The rest are green-glazed, including some 20% which seem to be late medieval with oxidised, often purplish-red, surfaces and dark or mottled green copper glazes. At least two vessels in pit *21* have big narrow necks, and are probably baluster jugs, as are five bases in Periods III and IV. Some quarter of the green-glazed sherds are jugs from Grimston in north-west Norfolk (Jennings 1981, pp. 50–1). Decorated fragments include one arm of a face jug, sherds with iron-slip applied strips, and foliage decoration (Clarke and Carter 1977, pp. 206–10) and one sherd has ring-and-dot impressions with uniform green glaze; a number of sherds have cordons and grooves. The eight Grimston-type rims and the 14 sagging bases, usually thumbed intermittently, also are all jugs. Almost, if not all, of the Grimston-type jugs would seem to be late in the series (14th to 15th century), there are no other forms or material which are clearly late Grimston ware (16th century, (Clarke and Carter 1977, pp. 233–5), except one sherd with some internal glaze in Period IV. Also conspicuous among the glazed wares are some sherds (*c.* 6.4%) in Periods III and IV with a quantity of rounded quartz particles in a fine sandy, often slightly harsh, background. They are usually light grey and partly oxidised and seem to represent a number of vessels from the same source area. One curfew fragment with some chalk and oolitic particles has probably come from West Norfolk in the area of the Fen edge and King's Lynn:

some ten glazed jug sherds may be postulated as coming from a similar source. Other unclassified glazed sherds would also seem to be indigenous to Norfolk, including the east and south areas of the county, and all would seem to be from jugs (see also LMT (5) below).

5. Late medieval and transitional wares (Jennings 1981, pp. 61–2) (667 sherds; 31.40%). These are sandy with some mica, and usually oxidised. At least 16 rim and neck sherds would seem to be from jugs, and there are almost as many strap handles. In pit *21* there are rims from two pancheons, one skillet, six bowls (of types cf. Jennings 1981, figs 414 and 419), jars of which one is handled, one pipkin, one lid or bowl and a further nine bases (one with tripod leg), three handles and 27 bodysherds which belong to vessels with internal glaze such as these. The rest of the collection adds rims of three jars/pipkins, two bowls, nine bases and ten bodysherds with internal glaze.

The remaining LMT bases (over 30) and bodysherds are of undiagnostic forms, but some 16 sherds are rilled. Most are unglazed but some have orange or green glaze, usually in spots.

1. Continental imports (90 sherds, 4.2%).
   a) Early tin-glazed earthenware foot-ring base of a jug (from pit *21*). Spain, probably mature Valencian lusterware of 15th century date (Hurst *et al.* 1986, p. 42). Fine sandy fabric with brown and black inclusions (up to *c.* 12mm), buff with some pink in margins. Buff tin-glaze on all surfaces, cobalt blue line on exterior and narrower white lines standing out against decayed interior.
   b) Martincamp flask (one Type II from top of pit *21*). Buff core, light brownish-buff exterior, pink interior. 16th century (Hurst *et al.* 1986, p. 104).
   c) German stonewares (76 sherds, *c.* 66 to 67 vessels, 3.6%). There are two Langerwehe, 14 Raeren or Langerwehe/Raeren, and four Frechen sherds in Period IV. The remaining 56 sherds are from pit *21* comprising one Siegburg (possible jug), two Langerwehe, 25 Langerwehe?Raeren, and 27 Raeren and one ?Raeren. This last sherd is a plain, slightly sagging base some 8cm in diameter in dark grey/black unglazed stoneware with some finger-printed iron wash puddle inside. The other nine Langerwehe and Raeren type bases are frilled, and forms would seem to be mugs, two of which have crooked handles.
   d) Source uncertain. (Five sherds, one or two vessels from pit *21* and Period IV pit *8*). One jug rim, one bodysherd has handle stub and two others have internal dark green glaze hard, rather dense fabric with rounded quartz grains (often protruding) and some fine silver mica. Dark reddish-brown core, dark grey surfaces. It is possible that these vessels may be overfired local products as they resemble the local jugs in all but the density of their fabrics, which are often of near stoneware quality.
   e) Dutch red wares (Jennings 1981, pp. 134–6). At least seven sherds (from *c.* six vessels) in reddish-brown sandy fabrics may be Dutch glazed earthenware (in pit *21* and Period IV), including a collared rim bowl, a foot-ring fragment and a bodysherds of cauldron or pipkin.
2. Surrey white wares. One rim of a pipkin and one base (from Period IV pit *8*). Rim has one patch of green glaze and spots of light yellow glaze.
3. Glazed red earthenware (Jennings 1981, pp. 157–8). One small bodysherd with orange glaze (in Period IV pit *10*).
4. Post-medieval. Six sherds in Period IV, all 18th century. Includes one rim of a brown-glazed cup.

### *A note on Pit* 21 *(Period III)*

This feature accounts for nearly half of the pottery recovered from the excavations, being a group of some 958 sherds. It contained most of the continental imports including the tin-glazed earthenware from Spain, some Dutch red earthenware, and most of the German stoneware from the site (*c.* 48 vessels); the later Martincamp vessel lay on the surface.

The remaining sherds (93% of the group) would seem to be of East Anglian origin. A quarter of the sherds must be residual as they are of medieval date. These comprise medieval glazed jugs (Grimston type 9.3%, other 2.7%), unglazed wares (11.4% of which 1.6% are certainly jug fragments) or of uncertain, probably medieval, type (0.6%).

The remaining sherds are of late medieval and transitional types, including some 2.9% of harsh quartz-tempered fabrics (see group 4 above) and green-glazed sherds from both reduced and oxidised vessels. There are some 59 sherds (6.2%) which account for most of the sherds with the internal glaze mentioned above in Group 5 (jar, pipkin, skillet, bowl, pancheon), and there are 12 rims and eight handles which must belong to jugs (2.1%). Most of the bodysherds are from large vessels, and jugs and storage jars are more numerous than flatwares or smaller vessels such as pipkins. Any vessel estimate would be high, although sherds from the same vessels are present and occur in different layers within the feature.

The dating of pit *21* to *c.* 1500 stems from the combined facts that most of the local pottery dates to *c.* 1450–1500 (S. Jennings, *pers. comm.*) and that the German stoneware is mostly Raeren-type vessels. The type II Martincamp flask seems likely to post-date the Dissolution but, as it was not stratified within the feature, the earlier dating suggested by the other finds seems more probable.

### *General discussion of the pottery*

The nature of this ceramic assemblage is conditioned more by architectural and archaeological activity than by its domestic origins. It can be considered from three different aspects, only one of which, c), is truly significant:

a) Modern archaeological work has deliberately avoided disturbance to the mound itself beneath the keep so that the few sherds of Saxo-Norman pottery (in Periods I and II) are from test samples of layers rather than being truly representative of material originally present in daily use: no domestic assemblages were encountered.

b) Similarly, the 18th- to 19th-century levelling and alterations (Period IV) seems not to have disturbed the Saxo-Norman levels. They have turned up quantities of pottery dating from the 14th to late 15th centuries prior to the activity of Period III (see c) below). This pottery is almost all residual but must reflect the ceramics present during the later medieval Period. Most of the material is derived from Norfolk, and it is perhaps surprising that more regional and continental imports are not evident.

c) The large robbing pit *21*, Period III, also contains medieval and late medieval material, but is conspicuously different from the other contexts in having a much higher percentage of LMT, German stonewares and other continental imports. This relates to the immediacy of disposal forming a more cohesive group, but there is also residual pottery as the local medieval vessels cannot be contemporary with the Raeren stonewares and the pit must have cut into earlier layers, as did the features in Period IV.

This assemblage therefore only offers a slice of time, rather than a sequence or overall view of the domestic wares in use on the castle mound. It gives evidence of sources for 14th- to 15th-century pottery with the local products supplemented by fine wares from Spain, France, Holland and Germany. The main usefulness of this pottery, however, is as dating evidence for architectural activity of Periods II and III (*c.* 1500).

## Bibliography


Anon (1889) 'Proceedings at Meetings of the Royal Archaeological Institute', *Archaeological Journal* 46, pp. 438–56.

Ayers, B. S. (1985) *Excavations within the North-East Bailey of Norwich Castle*, East Anglian Archaeology 28.

Ayers, B. S. (1987) *Digging Deeper* (Norwich, Norfolk Museums Service).

Beckwith, J. (1973) 'A Romanesque Bobbin', in P. Bloch *et al.*, ed., *Intuition und Kunstwissenschaft. Festschrift für Harms Swarzenski zum 70.Geburtstag am 30. August 1973* (Berlin).

Bradley, J. and Gaimster, M. (2001) 'Medieval Britain and Ireland in 2000', *Medieval Archaeology* 45, pp. 233–379.

Clarke, H. and Carter, A. (1977) *Excavations in King's Lynn 1963–1970*, Society for Medieval Archaeology Monograph 12.

Dixon, P. and Marshall, P. (2002) 'Norwich castle and its analogues', in G. Meirion-Jones, E. Impey and M. Jones, ed., *The Seigneurial Residence in Western Europe AD c. 800–1600*, British Archaeological Report International Series 1088, pp. 235–43.

Drury, P. J. (2002) 'Norwich Castle Keep', in G. Meirion-Jones, E. Impey and M. Jones, ed., *The Seigneurial Residence in Western Europe AD c. 800–1600*, British Archaeological Report International Series 1088, pp. 211–34.

Heslop, T. A. (1994) *Norwich Castle Keep: Romanesque Architecture and Social Context* (Norwich, Centre of East Anglian Studies).

Hudson, W. H. (1892) 'Notes about Norwich before the close of the Thirteenth Century', *Norfolk Archaeology* 12, pp. 25–84.

Hurst, J. G. *et al.* (1986) 'Pottery produced and traded in north-west Europe 1350–1650', *Rotterdam Papers* VI.

Jennings, S. (1981) *Eighteen Centuries of Pottery from Norwich*, East Anglian Archaeology 13.

King, E. (1807) *Observations on Ancient Castles* (London).

Norfolk Archaeological Unit (2000) *Annual Review 1999–2000* (Norwich, Norfolk Archaeological Unit).

Oman, C. (1974) *British Rings 800–1914* (London, Batsford).

Shelley, A. (1996) 'Norwich Castle Bridge', *Medieval Archaeology* 40, pp. 217–26.

Shepherd Popescu, E. (2009) *Norwich Castle: Excavations and Historical Survey, 1987–98*, East Anglian Archaeology 132.

Stroud, D. (1984) *Sir John Soane, Architect* (London, Faber & Faber).

Wallis, H. (forthcoming) *Excavations on Norwich Castle Mound, 1999–2001*, East Anglian Archaeology.

# 3

# The shifting structure of Norwich Castle keep, 1096 to *c.* 1230

*T. A. Heslop*

**Résumé**

*Le donjon de Norwich était d'une conception ambitieuse dans son architecture et audacieuse dans sa structure, fondée sur une grande butte qui n'avait été construite que récemment. La capacité de cette plate-forme artificielle à soutenir le donjon était apparemment une source d'anxiété, ce qui s'est avéré justifié étant donné que le mur est a montré des signes d'affaissement. Le poids de ce mur fut réduit, les voûtes en diagonale des angles sud-est et nord-est ayant été supprimées, et de nouvelles fondations et arcades ont été construites pour soutenir l'étage principal au-dessus. Les fouilles récentes suggèrent que cela se produisit alors que le sous-sol du donjon était encore en construction (vers 1100). Dans le même temps, la taille de la chapelle fut augmentée et son plan modifié. Une cuisine fut créée, son foyer bloquant une tourelle d'escalier en spirale. Le puits fut prolongé jusqu'au premier étage. Ces reconfigurations coïncident avec le règne d'un nouveau roi, Henri Ier, dont l'administration peut avoir été responsable des décisions prises. Au XIIIe siècle, les piédroits d'arcade furent épaissis et des voûtes en maçonnerie furent ajoutées en remplacement du plancher de bois.*

Norwich Castle keep was probably built between 1096 and 1120. It stands on the largest artificial mound, or *motte*, of any English castle. The level 'platform' on its top is some 2.3 acres in extent, more than ten times the area needed to support the keep and its forebuilding, and effectively provides a spacious 'acropolis'. No other stone tower the size of Norwich was built on an artificial hill in the Norman period (i.e. before 1135). It is in several respects a megalomaniac project, and fits well with what we know of the ambitions of King William Rufus (1087–1100). A recent estimate of the time it would have taken to build the mound indicates a figure of about 50,000 man days and if the earthworks constituting the ditches and banks of the surrounding baileys in this phase are taken into account the overall figure rises to about 70,000 man days (Shepherd Popescu 2009, pp. 990–1). It is likely that this labour was unpaid and instead taken as part of the obligation known as *Trinoda neccesitas*, which included the construction and maintenance of fortifications (Allen Brown, Colvin and Taylor 1963, pp. 6–9 and 24–5). This would have placed a heavy burden on the local population by distracting them from more directly productive and profitable employment. The point is not just that the mound at Norwich would have been onerous to build, but that it is excessively so and further that it chimes well with the other extravagances of the project.

The interior arrangements and exterior embellishment of Norwich keep are more sophisticated than any earlier great tower we know about. This is immediately evident in the sheer quantity of freestone cut as ashlar walling, shafting, capitals and moulded voussoirs on the building which in my view were all intended from the outset (Heslop 1994). It was on a par with, or even surpassed, the most ambitious church buildings of the period, most pertinently Norwich Cathedral, and serves to indicate that secular authority was in no way less impressive than its sacred counterpart. On this reading, the rubble facing of the lower storey is differentiated hierarchically – denoting it as the basement, for storage – and it would anyway have been scarcely visible behind the palisade surrounding the top of the mound.

The designer of the building employed the English perch of 16ft 6in (5.03m) as a standard measure. Multiplications and divisions of it: 5ft 6in, 11ft, 16ft 6in, 22ft, 33ft, 55ft and 77ft occur in the plans of basement and first floor levels. Alongside this ran an almost obsessive application of the proportion 1 to root 2 (that is the relationship between the side of a square and its diagonal) in both the plan and the elevation. At the largest scale this explains the proportions of north and south façades (68ft × 96ft) apparently based on an awareness that the ratio of 12:17 and 17:24 are a very close approximation of root 2 and thus so are 68 (4 × 17) and 96 (4 × 24). But the same proportion also determines the relationships of lesser bay widths and levels on the exterior and interior. Thus the height of the first string course on the outside is 23ft 4in, which is 16ft 6in multiplied by √2 (1.4142), while on the interior at first floor level the string course is at 9ft 8in, which is 23ft 4in divided by 1 plus √2 (Heslop 1994, pp. 18–20 and 43–4).

The sheer ambition of the project was not without its dangers. Constructing a great stone tower on a newly raised mound, before the earth had time to consolidate, was clearly risky as the evidence of differential settlement was soon to show when the eastern wall began to lean outwards. This probably occurred very soon after work began on the keep, indeed within the first year or two and was to be one of the factors influencing various changes in the first few years of building. The effect of the insecure foundations can be seen in the north wall about 20ft (*c.* 6.1m) from the eastern corner where a large crack began to appear, causing a number of adjustments to be made. The intended window opening at this point was not built, an extra buttress was added to the exterior, and ashlar 'stitching' was inserted (Figure 3.1). Settlement also occurred in the south-east corner, though at a rather higher level and thus perhaps a building season or two later. Internally the junction of the south-eastern

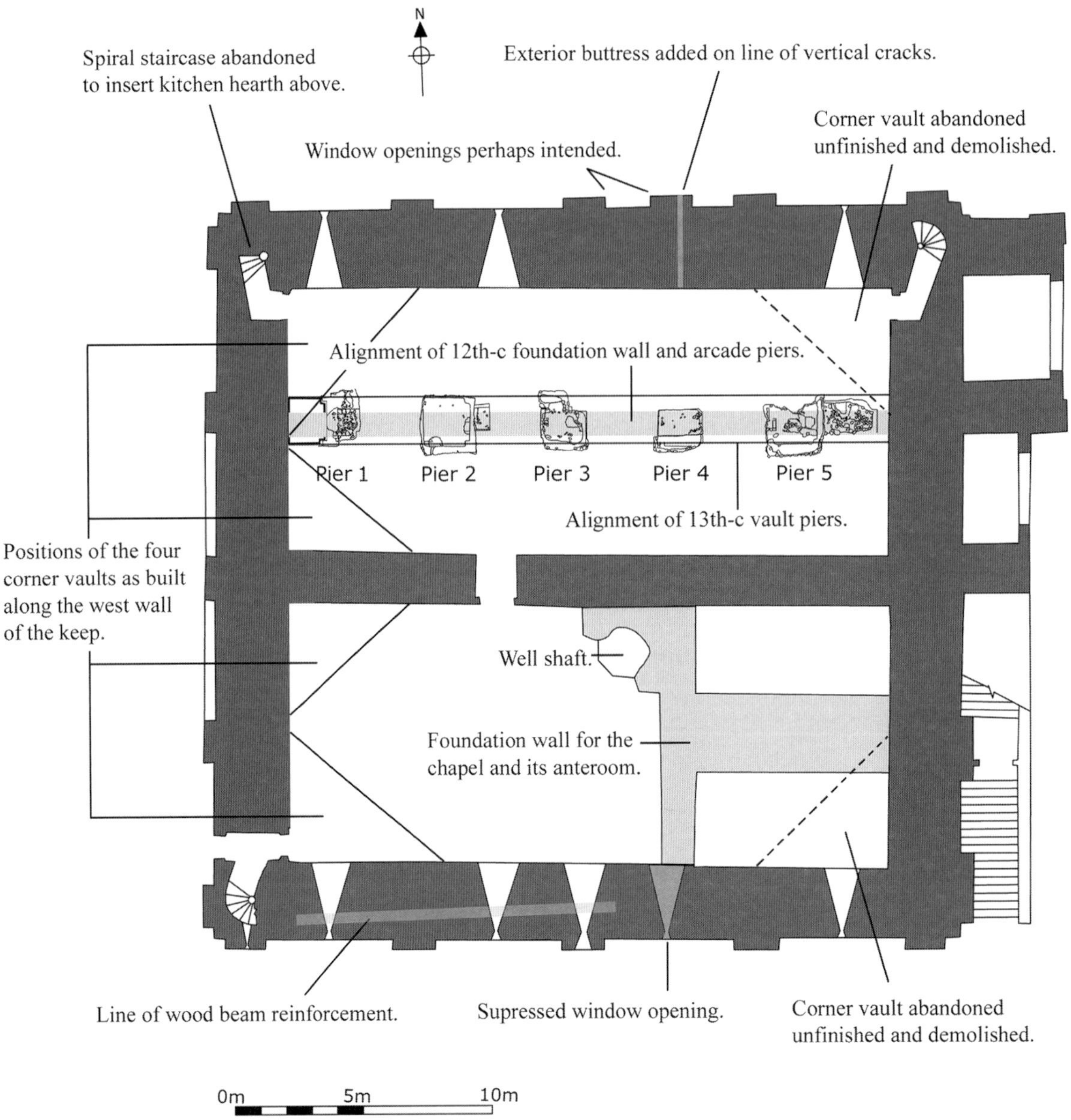


*Figure 3.1. Norwich Castle keep: plan of basement incorporating data from the 2013 cleaning and excavation in the northern compartment.*

vault and the south wall now leans markedly to the east, about 3° from the vertical. Just as in the north wall, the result here was an abandonment of the corner vault and the large window immediately west of it. But why was this north–south line a weak point in the building? The most likely answer is the earlier history of the site.

A castle had been created in Norwich soon after the Norman invasion of 1066 and briefly resisted a siege in 1075. If as seems likely this followed the motte and bailey pattern there will already have been a mound and this is probably still at the heart of the existing earthworks. The builders of the present keep would have been wise to use this earlier platform as the basis for their new foundations as it would have consolidated over the 20 years since it was constructed (Shepherd Popescu 2009, pp. 971–4). However, one explanation of what happened next is that the earlier mound was not quite big enough to support the size of the stone keep and that its east wall was too close to the edge of the slope down into the original surrounding ditch (Shepherd Popescu 2009, fig. 6.49). Uncertainty about the stability of the mound may well have encouraged the designer to make the keep symmetrical by positioning the spine wall across the middle of the plan to ensure an even distribution of weight. Another strategy was to embed tree trunks, horizontally, in the rubble core of the walls in order to give rigidity to the structure, though it is not certain that ploy was used from the beginning; it may only have been adopted when fissures began to appear in the fabric.

It is clear from the changes that took place when differential settlement manifested itself that lightening the load in this area was deemed necessary, and it was achieved in various ways. One was the suppression of the corner vaults against the east wall. Another, it is argued below, was the provision of additional foundations and supporting walls and arcades to distribute the weight of the building more generally within the footprint of the keep. Recent cleaning and minor excavation in the basement has, for the first time, clarified methods developed over time for supporting the main floor level, and these will be analysed once the details of the original scheme have been explained more fully.

The ashlar springing points of all the intended corner vaults in the building are part of the original fabric, about five feet above present basement floor level (Drury 2002, figs 7, 8 and 10); in other words, allowing for up to 6ft (1.8m) to be built each year, probably from late in the first or early in the second season of construction. Their forms make it certain that the east side of the keep was to have two such vaults, in the north-east and south-east corners, whereas the west side was to have four, two in the outer corners and two more, rather smaller ones, in the angles between the west wall and the central spine. Though physical evidence for this arrangement now survives only in the compartment north of the spine wall, the equivalent at the west end on the south side was extant in the late 18th century to judge from a plan showing that the vault abutting the spine had been provided with a wall across its entrance (Figure 3.2).

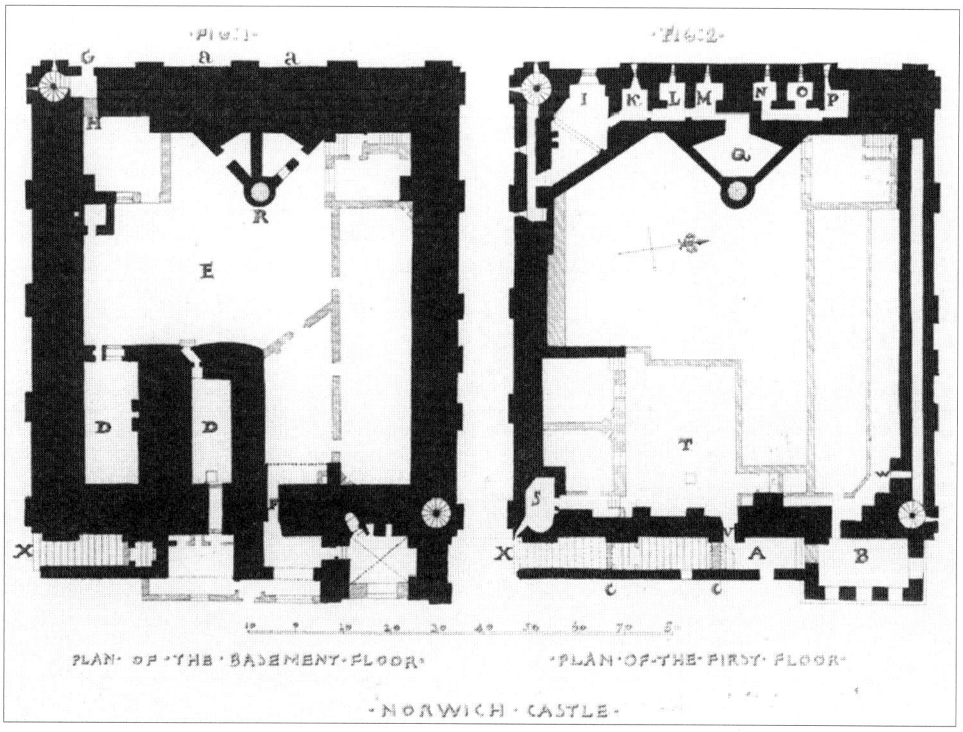


*Figure 3.2. Norwich Castle keep: plans of basement and first floor levels in 1797 (after W. Wilkins in Archaeologia XII).*

In the south-east corner, the diagonal vault construction was abandoned about 16ft (4.9m) above the ground, perhaps therefore at the end of season three. As noted above, its junction with the south wall is not vertical, suggesting subsidence to the east. It seems however that the stones cut for facing the arch fronting this vault had already been prepared and were on site; this would explain the impressive quantity of ashlar now to be found in the upper east wall of the basement, an area which would otherwise have been faced with flints as elsewhere at this level. Following this change of plan, a new support system was devised, involving broadly based foundation walls, to support the walls and arcade of the chapel and its anteroom above. The north-south foundation wall blocked a window opening originally envisaged in the south wall of the keep and its north end was extended to the west to encase the well shaft in order to take it up to the first floor. At the same level that the south-east corner vault was suppressed (about 16ft/4.9m), and thus in my view at the same date (cf. Drury 2002, p. 213), a change was also made in the north-west corner: even though there was no problem with subsidence, they abandoned building the spiral staircase. The curtailment of the north-west stair made possible the transformation of the first floor level into a kitchen, with the stairwell being capped and fitted out as a large cylindrical chimney above a generous hearth.

The overall effect, in this phase of work, was to double the floor area of the chapel, introduce an integral kitchen and give direct access to well water at the upper level, albeit at a curious location in the corner of the great chamber. I see these three changes as contemporary, and given a starting date of *c.* 1096–7 probably connected to a revision of the brief undertaken early in the reign of the new king, Henry I, arguably during the winter of 1100–1. It was probably at this time too that work was put in hand to provide arcading in the north and south compartments of the basement to support the great wooden floors spanning the building at first floor level. The span of the north and south compartments was almost 33ft (10m), so it would have been possible to carry the floor on substantial joists, provided enough timber of the requisite scantling was available. However, such timbers would have been very heavy, and the expedient of inserting an intermediary arcade would have allowed their size and weight to be reduced as well as providing additional load-bearing foundations for them.

*Figure 3.3. Norwich Castle keep:- view of the excavation on the east side of Pier 2, August 2013.*

In the south compartment of the basement, excavations undertaken by Brian Ayers in 1986 revealed that the east–west axial foundations butted up against the secondary wall built to carry the west wall of the redesigned chapel (Ayers, this volume, p. 36 and Figure 2.5), so it seemed that this foundation for the arcade was envisaged only after the revision of the south-east corner scheme. However, regardless of the details of their phasing, there is good evidence that they were conceived together. Revising the position of the cross wall to support the chapel had the disadvantage that the new position for the west wall of the chapel at first floor level impinged on the original space allocated to the great chamber, to the detriment of its proportions. So why was this position chosen? In general terms the answer is likely to be that the builders believed the ground beneath to be firm, quite possibly because it was within the perimeter of the top of the earlier mound, so the recent build up was quite shallow. More specifically its alignment matches that of Pier 4 in the newly conceived axial arcade supports in the northern compartment, the location of which stemmed from the equal spacing of Piers 2 to 5 inclusive. In other words, although the axial foundation in the south compartment butts up against the chapel foundation wall, it must be conceptually contemporary with the axial support system in the northern compartment which itself determined the position of the foundation for the west wall of the chapel (Figure 3.1). This proposition requires a more detailed examination, as too does determining the date when this occurred.

In the northern compartment a short section of the axial foundation wall was excavated in August 2013 on the east side of Pier 2 (Wallis 2014) (Figure 3.3). This foundation aligns exactly with the surviving lowest course of masonry extant for Piers 3 (Figures 3.4 and 3.5) and 4. Here ashlar blocks were carefully cut and laid to act as the shuttering of the rubble core for rectangular piers measuring 39" by 67" (99cm × 170cm). The dressing of the ashlar is very distinctive, with long, fine, horizontal cuts, apparently made by a sharp axe, worked across the surface parallel to the long sides of the rectangular face of the block. This same tooling is found elsewhere in the basement of the keep, but is not apparent at main floor level (Figures 3.5 and 3.6). This strongly implies that the axial supports were begun while the spine and north wall of the basement were still under construction, arguably within the first few seasons of work.

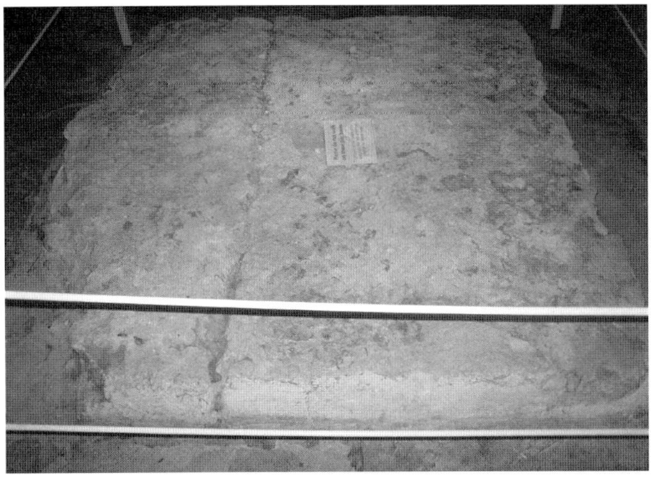

*Figure 3.4. Norwich Castle keep: Pier 3 from the west showing the fissure between the early 12th-century rectangular pier and its later raft extension.*

*Figure 3.5. Norwich Castle keep: Pier 3, detail of the horizontal tooling of the ashlar of the eastern face.*

At the west end of the northern compartment, on the same alignment as the rectangular piers, are remnants of an upward extension of the foundation into a flint rubble wall adjacent to Pier 1. The fabric of this wall is visually very similar to the foundation excavated next to Pier 2, and so it seems likely to be contemporary. If so, then for some reason the axial division of the compartment consisted of piers at the east end and a rubble wall at the west, with the change of system coinciding approximately with Pier 2. It will be argued in due course that the piers carried an arcade of four arches from Pier 2 to the east wall of the keep rather than rising sheer to support a large wooden beam, which is the alternative proposal currently shown in the reconstructions of this phase on display in the Museum (Figure 3.7).

The recent excavation suggested that the axial foundation was contemporary with a mortared floor some 15 inches (38.1cm) below the Victorian flagstones (Figure 3.8), though whether this early floor went under or ended up against the foundation was not quite clear; the latter seems more probable. So, provisionally, in 1101 or soon after, the axial foundation supporting the rectangular piers stood about 12 inches (30.5cm) proud of a mortar floor. This low foundation wall was itself capped off with mortar, presumably to help prevent it being eroded by people walking over it; this upward projection must have constituted an obstacle to traffic and a potential trip hazard, at least for a while.

This system for supporting the joists at main floor level was in use for several decades, but was replaced perhaps

*Figure 3.6. Norwich Castle keep: voussoirs in the basement north wall for the springing of the intended corner vault, detail of tooling.*

*Figure 3.7. Norwich Castle keep: model showing the basement and hall above.*

in the 1170s (Drury 2002, p. 211) though in my view in the 1220s by masonry vaults carried on more substantial cruciform piers measuring about 5ft 6in (1.67 m) across, the same as the length of the earlier piers. The western respond of this phase survives to a height of nearly eight feet and is made of large blocks of well-dressed ashlar with fine jointing between them. The shadow of these piers was clearly evident on the foundation rafts created to support Piers 2 (Figure 3.9), 4 and 5; their edges marked by a thin layer of Victorian cement. The implications of this evidence are that in the late 1880s, when the keep was cleared of the accumulated build-up of later deposits prior to its conversion into a museum, the lower courses of the 13th-century piers were discovered and their foundations consolidated. At some point soon thereafter this medieval stonework was removed, leaving the cement outline to indicate its form. Apart from Pier 1 (Figure 3.10), only Pier 3 retains any upstanding fabric of this period, and that is no more than a few inches of its flint rubble core.

The purpose of these cruciform piers was to take the weight of a masonry vault. As Paul Drury has persuasively argued, these ramped up to the spine wall and north wall of the keep (Drury 2002, p. 213), and the lower stages of the line they took can still be seen on the east wall, rising from the remains of a substantial Barnack limestone respond some 14ft (4.27m) above the top of the mound. Presumably the projecting elements of the cruciform piers carried arches, semi-circular on the east–west alignment and apparently quadrant arches to north and south as there are no traces of responds for semi-circular arches in the north wall. But why were they built – what was wrong with the earlier solution? One possibility is that the capture of the castle by the French in 1216 caused substantial damage to the fabric. If the evidence of very serious scorching on the underside of the forebuilding vault is from this period, it is quite possible that the wooden floor of the keep was damaged by fire and seen to be vulnerable. On this hypothesis, it would have been after the expulsion of the invaders and the restoration of English royal government that vaulting was inserted; some repair work is indeed accounted in the Pipe Roll for 1223. An alternative is that the massive expenditure of over £600 on the hall in the castle in the late 1280s relates in part to this vaulting (Allen Brown, Colvin and Taylor 1963, pp. 754–5) though the date seems too late for the style of the surviving stonework. A few finds from the mortar of the foundation rafts of this phase may help refine the dating. These included a tooth, some bone and sherds of pottery, including a piece of Grimston ware, all from Pier 2 (Wallis 2014).

The excavation of the east face of the foundation raft of Pier 2 (Figures 3.3 and 3.8) showed very clearly that it partly sat on top of the earlier foundation wall, but that where it projected to north and south it was taken down to the early mortar floor level. However there was no indication that these lower levels had been shuttered, either with wood or with laid flints as happens at the upper edges of the raft. It seems then that the lower levels of this mortar bed were simply poured into holes in the earth. This in turn suggests that there had been a levelling up of the floor to the top of the earlier foundation wall and that pits were created in this material to receive the fabric for the lowest 12in (30.5cm) or so of the new foundation rafts.

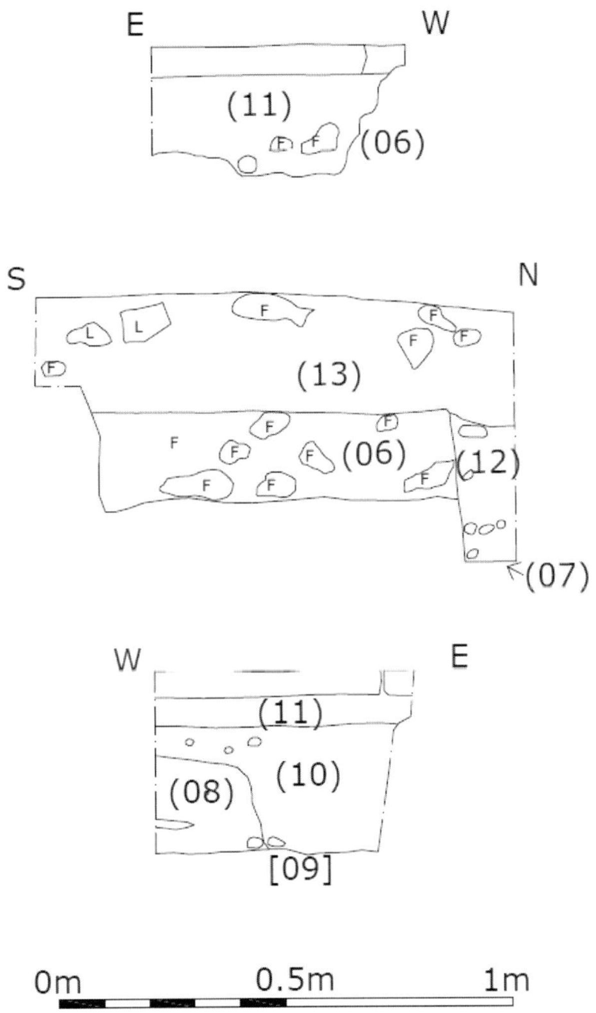


*Figure 3.8. Norwich Castle keep: section drawing of the excavation to the east of Pier 2, August 2013 (Heather Wallis). Features identified: (06) Section of linear foundation wall for rectangular piers,* c. *1100; (07) Apparently an early mortar floor,* c. *1100; (08) medieval deposit cut through by (12); (09) Cut line for the foundation of the Victorian stanchion; (10) Victorian infill around the stanchion foundation; (11) Victorian levelling deposit under flagstones; (12) medieval footing for flint and mortar raft above; (13) medieval flint and mortar raft for cruciform piers; Feature (06) is possibly capped with mortar – a brown-pink line visible at its summit and beneath (13).*

It is within the core of these rafts that the remains of at least the three easternmost of the old rectangular piers can be found, with the lowest course of ashlar facing surviving complete in Piers 3 and 4 from this phase (Figures 3.4 and 3.5). At 67 inches (1.70m) in length they are close to the 5ft 6in (1.67m) module used for the pilaster buttresses on the exterior of the north and south façades. These two piers are spaced 110 inches (2.79m) apart. At 111 inches (2.81m) to the east is the only extant piece of ashlar *in situ* in the raft for Pier 5. As the western face of this block is some 179 inches (4.55m) from the east wall of the keep, it implies that once again there was a pier about 67 inches (1.70m) long and a gap of around 112 inches (2.84m). In other words, the piers represent a regular sequence of equidistant supports. The anomaly is at the west end for, even allowing that the current west respond might encase an earlier pier, the gap would be a minimum of 152 inches (3.86m), way beyond the norm. Paul Drury suggested that the location of the first freestanding pier (Pier 2) was determined by the existing diagonal vaults which would obviate the need to continue the support system any further west (Drury 2002, p. 213). However the space between the vaults narrows gradually and not immediately west of this point, so some additional support for the main floor could usefully have been provided even here. Further, as noted above, the foundation wall continues to the west with some upstanding rubble walling on it as though at this end of the building the floor joists at first floor level were to be supported on a sub-spine flint wall rather than a pier and arch system. The best explanation currently available to account for the anomalies is that the location of Pier 2 had already been determined before the others further east were built or even thought of. Once the need

*Figure 3.9. Norwich Castle keep: Pier 2 showing the later raft foundation with the shadow of a cruciform pier outlined in cement.*

for them was identified they were spaced equally between Pier 2, already begun, and the inner face of the east wall. A thorough-going excavation through or underneath the 13th-century raft foundation of Pier 2 would be needed to confirm this hypothesis.

In the south compartment, the excavation undertaken in 1986 showed that, unfortunately, the equivalent pier there had been completely robbed out (Ayers, this volume, p. 35 and Figure 2.3). However, in other places to the south of the spine wall the evidence was revealing. As noted above, the cross wall foundation for the west wall of the (extended) chapel was located so as to leave room for a two bay arcade with the same size piers and intervening spaces as in the northern compartments. Taken together, all this evidence suggests that the position of the westernmost freestanding pier in both compartment preceded the axial foundations and the arcades they supported. But what might these piers have been designed for?

Different interpretations were offered in two papers published in 2002, by Paul Drury with Dominic Marner, and Philip Dixon and Pamela Marshall. The plans published by Drury (2002, figs 4 and 5) imply that their role was to extend up through the main floor level to act as a support for a mezzanine balcony. This is the scheme exemplified in the model still on show in the keep, and it makes general sense (Figure 3.7). However, it has to be pointed out that, if constructed as shown on the plans, the hypothetical square pier at first floor level would not sit on top of the surviving element in the basement but would oversail it by about 20 inches (50.8cm) to the east. With that caveat, it could still serve as a support for the mezzanine balcony, though that balcony would have to be set forward to overhang the pier's eastern edge by getting on for two feet. At this juncture, Castle Rising can be invoked as a parallel, for there a single cruciform pier in this position in the basement serves something like the same purpose (Figure 3.11). With this potential confirmation of the mid-12th-century arrangement at Norwich in view, the reconstruction proposed by Dixon and Marshall enters the frame.

*Figure 3.10. Norwich Castle keep: Pier 1.*

Castle Rising preserves its original arrangement at the west end of the northern compartment, with a slightly cruciform pier supporting transverse arches and two square, groin vaulted bays to create a platform for the rooms at main floor level. Drury saw this as a rationalisation of the oddities of the Norwich plan. Dixon and Marshall suggested that it more closely replicated what was actually built at Norwich because, in their view, the diagonal vaults at Norwich were 'supplemented' at an early date by vaulted square bays (Dixon and Marshall 2002, p. 236, fig. 1). In support of this, it might be pointed out that the peculiar positioning of the western respond at Norwich creates two square bays on plan, each with sides of about 166 inches (4.20m), well suited to receive masonry vaults like those at Rising. However, the difficulty at Norwich is if and when these square bays were actually vaulted. If built, the vaults have left no discernible trace on the fabric. More problematically, and as previously noted, the masonry of the western respond, with large block size, finely worked surfaces and very thin joints, looks 13th century, certainly not early 12th as Dixon and Marshall apparently wish it to be.

The function of this substantial vaulted structure in the basement would have been, in their view, to support a masonry wall and vaults at first floor level to create a 'waiting room' or antechamber for those seeking an audience in the great chamber. It would be a very large space for such a purpose, but more problematic archaeologically is that in (re)constructing it a certain amount of regularisation of the surviving data has taken place. To begin with, in order to align the proposed eastern wall of this first-floor room clear of the doors in the north and south walls of the keep, it is necessary to move it east of the eastern face the pier in the basement. Such 'oversailing' (of nearly two feet) might be sustainable, but it is disconcerting that Dixon's reconstruction drawing shows the wall rising sheer as though it were in perfect alignment with the column beneath (Dixon and Marshall 2002, fig. 3). There are other examples of idealisation in their proposal. The surviving springing point of the transverse arch in the south-west corner of the keep (Figure 3.12: space P8)

*Figure 3.11. Castle Rising keep: cruciform pier at the west end of the northern compartment of the basement.*

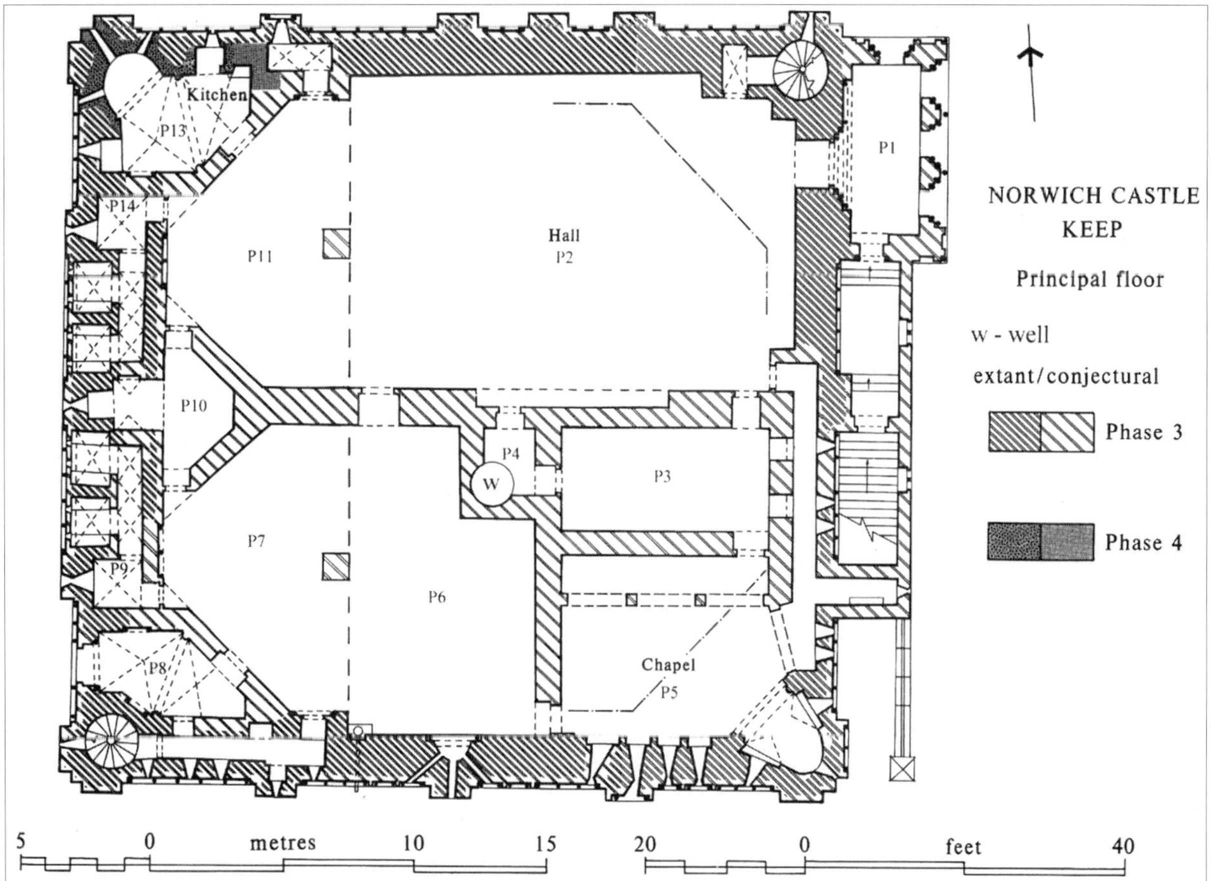


*Figure 3.12. Norwich Castle keep: reconstruction of the plan at first-floor level (after Drury 2002).*

shows the direction in which it was heading, at an angle of about 75° to the south wall: on the plan published by Dixon and Marshall (2002, fig. 4) this has been pushed close to 90°. A similar arrangement with an angle of about 75° can be inferred for the kitchen (Figure 3.12: space P13) where, in addition, an impost block and angled walling indicate the springing point of an arch or vault cell which simply does not feature in Dixon's and Marshall's reckoning. These actualities are, fortunately, mostly recorded and reconciled on the plan published by Drury, which odd though it may look I believe to be much more firmly founded in the archaeological evidence.

## Conclusions

As a result of the recent investigations, we are now in a position to add more detail as regards the thinking behind and chronology of the keep's development. Soon after work began, perhaps during the first season, the mound under the east wall was beginning to settle at its northern end and work ceased on the masonry vault in the north-east corner. In the south-east corner the effects of settlement were delayed for a further year or two. Once apparent, the corner vault was abandoned there too. New walls were built up from the ground to support the chapel at first floor level and axial foundation walls were created in the rest of the south compartment and across the full length of the north compartment upon which rectangular piers supporting arches and at least one stretch of flint rubble wall were built to carry the joists of the main wooden floor above. All of this served to spread the load of the building more evenly over the surface of the mound, and is likely to have been at least part of the motivation. The remarkable tooling of the extant ashlar of the rectangular piers is the same as that found elsewhere in the basement of the keep, but not higher up the building; it suggests that the new support structure was created before work had progressed to first floor level.

There are still two points worthy of attention. The first is that on the interior of the east wall of the keep today there are, as noted above, pieces of Barnack ashlar that can be understood as marking the positions on the wall of the respond for the later vaulting. However, slightly above these, and with different coursing alignments are three fragments of Caen limestone. Above these again, to either side are more pieces of cut stone, the inner faces of which are 39 inches (99cm) apart, the same as the width of the rectangular piers. All of these would have been obscured by the 13th-century vaulting and can have served no obvious purpose at this period in the building's development. One interpretation would thus be that these sorry fragments are the remnants of the easternmost arch of the arcade standing on the rectangular piers. The height of these cut stones suggests a springing point for the arches about 17ft (5.18m) above the early mortar floor. Assuming semi-circular arches with a diameter of 111 inches (2.81m), the apex of the arches would be about another 56 inches (1.42m) above that. That would leave a height of about 2 ft (61cm) for a continuous wall on top of the arches which would have carried the wall plate to support the ends of the floor joists. There is however one caveat. The position of the putative respond on the east wall does not align well with the rectangular piers. The reason may be that these were assumed by the mason constructing the respond to be in the middle of the northern compartment, whereas in fact they are displaced to the south. As a result, the mason placed his respond too far north. It does indeed seem that the alignment of Pier 5, in both its rectangular and cruciform phases, was skewed slightly to the north to accommodate this miscalculation. A detailed stone-by-stone survey of the interior walls of the keep is really needed in order to secure, or undermine, the position and status of these elements and indeed all the visible fabric of this important building.

The second point is more wide-reaching in its implications. There is still a debate about what a castle is and what a keep was, both functionally and ideologically, in so far as those two things can be distinguished. It is therefore worth being explicit about what is at stake in the case of Norwich and its early development. William Rufus was a showy monarch, with an eye for the latest fashions and other visible signs of power. He completed the White Tower in London, including its 'palace chapel', and constructed the wall around it, drawing on the labour services of surrounding counties (Harris 2008, pp. 30 and 43; Crook 2008, pp. 121–2). However, the greatest monument of his reign is Westminster Hall, which at 240 ft (*c.* 73m) long was the largest building of its type in northern Europe. William of Malmesbury noted that the king 'began and completed one very noble edifice, the palace in London, sparing no expense to manifest the greatness of his liberality' (William of Malmesbury 1998, IV.i). Those attending the inaugural banquet in the hall at Pentecost 1099 are supposed to have thought it 'a good size' (*satis magnam*) but others that it was too large. According to Henry of Huntingdon, Rufus responded by saying it was only half big enough (Henry of Huntingdon 1996, pp. 446–7). Henry also reworked the entry in the Anglo-Saxon Chronicle for 1097 claiming that Rufus 'had castles built on the borders of Wales' and 'harassed the shires in taxes (*tributis*) which never ceased for the building of the wall round the Tower of London, [and] for the building of the royal hall at Westminster' (Henry of Huntingdon 1996, pp. 444–5). It is abundantly clear that this king believed in architecture as a mode of regal display and the imposing mound and keep at Norwich thus fit his character as a patron and the date of his documented building activity very well.

The changes made to the design of Norwich keep in or very soon after Rufus's untimely death in 1100 are indicative of a shift in priorities. The outward show was retained but the reconfiguration of the interior suggested that domestic convenience and religious propriety were seen as important to the image of Henry I's monarchy. Unlike his brother Rufus, Henry was married and he and especially his wife were strong supporters of the Church, between them founding a number of monasteries, and supporting the foundation of many more. A bigger or smaller chapel, a kitchen or no kitchen, might seem like domestic details, but they are telling and it was the upgraded amenities that proved so attractive to the builders of Castle Rising (Goodall 2011, p. 113). At another level they are fundamental to perceptions of status. In the mid-1090s Norwich was being recreated as a cathedral city, with the second longest church in England. As William of Malmesbury wrote less than three decades later, the founding bishop, Herbert Losinga, transferred his see *ad insignem mercimoniis et popularum frequentia vicum*: 'to a town remarkable for its trade and large population' (William of Malmesbury 2007, pp. 240–1). Relatively isolated from the rest of England, its role as a regional capital was increasingly secure. In such circumstances the very visible presence of royal authority will have been deemed essential.

Norwich Castle keep can help us to understand not just what kind of shifts in priorities might be of concern in this case, but also what sort of place Norwich was perceived to be, its character and significance as a wealthy centre of trade both regionally and across the North Sea. It was because of its size and importance that it merited an architectural set-piece such as was the keep, and it is telling that no subsequent great tower ever rivalled the ostentation of Norwich.

## Acknowledgements

I am very grateful to Heather Wallis for her help with the interpretation of the archaeology in the basement and to the staff at the Castle Museum for facilitating the excavation.

## Bibliography

Allen Brown, R., Colvin, H. M. and Taylor, A. J., ed. (1963) *The History of the King's Works* (London, HMSO).

Crook, J. (2008) 'St John's Chapel', in E. Impey, ed., pp. 95–124.

Dixon, P. and Marshall, P. (2002) 'Norwich Castle and its analogues', in G. Meirion-Jones, E. Impey and M. Jones, ed., pp. 235–9.

Drury, P. J. (2002) 'Norwich Castle Keep', in G. Meirion-Jones, E. Impey and M. Jones, ed., pp. 211–34.

Goodall, J. (2011) *The English Castle 1066–1650* (New Haven and London, Yale University Press).

Harris, R. (2008) 'The structural history of the White Tower', in E. Impey, ed., pp. 29–94.

Henry of Huntingdon (1996) *Historia Anglorum (The History of the English People)*, D. E. Greenway, ed. (Oxford, Oxford Medieval Texts).

Heslop, T. A. (1994) *Norwich Castle Keep: Romanesque Architecture and Social Context* (Norwich, Centre of East Anglian Studies).

Impey, E., ed. (2008) *The White Tower* (New Haven and London, Yale University Press).

Meirion-Jones, G., Impey, E. and Jones, M., ed. (2002) *The Seigneurial Residence in Western Europe AD c. 800–1600*, British Archaeological Report International Series 1088.

Shepherd Popescu, E. (2009) *Norwich Castle: Excavations and Historical Survey, 1987–98*, East Anglian Archaeology 132.

Wallis, H. (2014) 'Cleaning and Excavation, Norwich Castle Keep Summer 2013', (unpublished report).

William of Malmesbury (2007) *Gesta Pontificum Anglorum*, M. Winterbottom, ed. (Oxford, Oxford Medieval Texts).

William of Malmesbury (1998) *Gesta Regum Anglorum*, R. A. B. Mynors, R. M. Thomson and M. Winterbottom, ed. (Oxford, Oxford Medieval Texts).

# 4

# Colchester Castle: 'Some tyme stronge and statelye, as the ruynes do shewe'

*Peter Berridge*

**Résumé**

*Cet article met l'accent sur la question la plus litigieuse concernant le château de Colchester, à savoir sa hauteur d'origine. Le point de vue couramment admis actuellement est que, avant les travaux de démolition entrepris par John Wheely à la fin du XVIIe siècle, il était composé à l'origine de trois étages. Toutefois, cet article met en avant une opinion alternative. Pour ce faire, un examen initial de l'évolution des idées est présenté. Ensuite, différentes formes de preuves sont abordées. Tout d'abord, la preuve documentaire, qui établit qu'aucune activité majeure de démolition n'eut lieu avant Wheely. Ensuite, diverses descriptions publiées avant la démolition sont présentées, lesquelles ne font aucune mention d'une ampleur exceptionnelle de l'édifice. Les activités de John Wheely sont traitées en détail, concluant que la période au cours de laquelle il a entrepris la démolition, peut-être quelques mois, fut très brève. Les différents éléments structurels présentés le plus souvent comme arguments en faveur de l'existence d'un étage supplémentaire sont ensuite examinés et il est démontré que des doutes importants existent sur tous ces points. En particulier, la galerie intérieure supposée au troisième étage s'avère être datée des XVIIIe et XIXe siècles et ne fait pas partie de la conception originale normande. Les problèmes d'utilisation d'éléments de comparaison avec d'autres donjons sont ensuite brièvement abordés et une analyse comparative des niveaux de plancher, entre la Tour Blanche et le château de Colchester, est présentée. Enfin, une série de représentations d'avant la démolition du château de Colchester est décrite et abordée, surtout le dessin d'un artiste flamand du XVIIe siècle, publié pour la première fois. Tous ces indices pris en considération, fournissent une argumentation convaincante pour la réinterprétation du château de Colchester en bâtiment à deux étages.*

Colchester Castle is a fascinating building with a long and involved history. Built on top of the foundations of a Roman temple, construction of the castle probably started in the late 1060s or early 1070s. In subsequent ages, different people placed their own interpretation on the structure. It has been developed, destroyed, re-built, added-to and adapted. An inevitable legacy is a relatively complex structural sequence which is now quite difficult for the expert, as well as for the general observer, to understand and unravel. Consequently, some significant areas of uncertainty and controversy over the structure remain, especially around the original height of the building. Sometime between 1684 and 1704, it is certain that part of the castle was demolished by John Wheely; but how much did he actually remove? Was it two floors higher, one floor higher, or in fact roughly the same height as today? The standard theory, from the 1970s to the present day, has been that it was originally three storeys high; one more than now. However, at different times, the other views have also been strongly championed and significant uncertainty still exists in relation to this key question. Consequently, this paper will focus on that issue and, in doing so, I will argue that it was only ever two-storeys high. This will be done by first rehearsing the changing views over the height, followed by a detailed discussion of the different forms of evidence.

At the outset, it is necessary to understand that Colchester Castle is not in any way a typical Norman keep. This is particularly illustrated by its size but more so by its highly unusual ground plan which involves essentially a north south rectangle with an apsidal projection at the south east corner which, in an upper floor, houses a chapel. This arrangement is shared by only one other keep in Britain; the White Tower. Until relatively recently they were the only two Norman keeps known to have this form, not just in Britain but in the whole of Europe, and so, not surprisingly, this also suggested a link between the two. The situation is now, however, very different as other examples have been found; most notably Ivry-la-Bataille in Normandy. Ivry not only shares the same unusual ground plan but has a construction date that is significantly earlier than the two English royal keeps. Consequently Colchester Castle and the White Tower can now be seen as part of a wider tradition (Fernie 2000, p. 66; Impey 2008, pp. 230–9).

Turning to the height issue, a starting point is a statement by the Reverend Philip Morant, published in 1748, which reads as follows:

> It suffered extremely from the ill-judged attempt of John Wheely, who purchased it of the late Robert Norfolk, Esq; with intent and upon condition to demolish it entirely, and make money of the materials. For this purpose, many of the Roman Bricks were taken away and sold, with most part of the free stone at the coins and in the inward arches of the building. A fine Well was destroyed, and the tops of the Towers and Walls forced down with screws, or blown up with gun-powder, and thrown upon the heads of the arched Vaults below, in such heavy weights, and with so great violence, as to break one of the finest of them, the remaining part of the Walls being so strongly cemented that the profit did not answer the charge of further demolition, he was forced to desist. (Morant 1748, p. 7)

Morant was of course writing about events that occurred before his birth and he only moved to Colchester in 1737. Consequently, his main source of information would have been word of mouth, though he did try to find documentary evidence. As well as the account of Wheely's activities, Morant also produced the first detailed description of Colchester Castle. In his own words, his intention was to produce, 'as exact and particular an account of the Castle as I can'. Many later authors of the 18th century would simply recycle Morant's description adding little or nothing new. Francis Grose is a good example of this (Grose 1783, Vol. 2, pp. 113–8). Something that is noteworthy about the account is that he does not mention the original height of the building which, while it has been noted before, still continues to surprise many when it is pointed out (Jenkins 1853b, p. 31; Nicholls 1889, p. 17). The phrase 'tops of the towers and walls were forced down with screws or blown up with gunpowder' does not need to imply the removal of a floor even though many later commentators have clearly inferred that it does.

The next stage in the developing ideas around the height of Colchester Castle was in 1774 when Joseph Strutt published a description of the building. Unlike several others Strutt, rather than rehashing Morant, conducted an independent examination of the building, as is clear from his description. Of particular significance is when describing the Great Stairs, in the south-west tower, he went on to write, 'the staircase leads you to the battlements, where you might formerly have passed round the whole work, a passage being made in the breadth of the wall at the top'. Perhaps most intriguingly of all, Strutt records a meeting with a person who remembered the castle before it was partially demolished. The relevant passage reads:

> I could not learn for certainty whether the top of the wall had been garretted or not, though an old man, who happened to be there when I was, informed me that he remembered something like embattlements at the top before it was so shamefully abused, great part of which were forced down with screws and gunpowder.

While it may seem implicit that Strutt believed that Colchester had one more floor, he does not state this anywhere in his account (Strutt 1774, pp. 26–9).

Not long after Strutt's account Edward King, in 1777, also produced a description of Colchester Castle. His description is important for a number of reasons but especially because it not only contains the second claim for the existence of the wall passage but also the first explicit statement that the demolition work had removed whole floors (King 1777, pp. 406–8). Following Strutt and King, from the latter part of the 18th through much of the 19th century there was a clearly a prevailing view that the castle was originally three storeys high. A contrary view was the two storey model put forward by the Reverends Henry Jenkins and George Buckler, linked to their view that the castle was largely a Roman building. This mid-19th-century controversy is one of the peculiarities of the history of the research of Colchester Castle and which, while misguided, generated a body of important structural observations from protagonists on both sides of the argument (Jenkins 1851, 1853a, 1853b, 1861, 1869; Buckler 1876, 1877, 1879, 1882; Cutts 1853).

The next major shift in interpretation was provided by J. H. Round, who in 1882 produced a landmark study of the building entitled *The History and Antiquities of Colchester Castle*. When considering the original appearance of the building he drew upon the work of Baron Cuvier, the famous 19th-century French comparative anatomist, who, in Round's own words, could 'construct a whole skeleton from a single bone'. Round believed that the same comparative method could be applied to Colchester Castle, using the White Tower as the model. Consequently, in his interpretation Colchester was originally four storeys high, with a double height Great Hall and Chapel, both starting on the second floor. By this time the evidence for the intramural gallery around the top of the first floor, as first noted by Strutt, had been disproved (this will be returned to later) and while Round envisaged such a gallery, he had this at the base of his fourth storey or third floor (Round 1882, p. 87).

At the same time as Round championed the four storey model George Clark, on examining the building, stated that 'there does not seem to have been a second floor'. This was in the context of a broader study of Norman castles and so is of particular note. Also around this time Nicholls came up with an interesting alternative idea, suggesting the possibility of a curtain wall, including windows, extending upwards to give the impression of a third storey but internally only extending up two storeys. This idea of windows looking over the roof space has now been shown to have been part of the original designs at both Castle Hedingham and, even more significantly, the White Tower. So Nicholls' proposal now seems prescient and is worthy of further consideration (Clark 1882; Nichols 1889, p. 17; Dixon and Marshall 1993; Harris 2008, pp. 76–85).

Round's four storeys view, however, prevailed for much of the 20th century before another major shift occurred. This change in attitude is well reflected in the different editions of a popular guidebook written by David Clarke, the first of which appeared in 1966, followed by two major revisions in 1980 and 1985. In the first edition he affirmed the idea of a four storey building but reintroduced the idea of the second-floor wall passage though, he did use the word 'probably' (Clarke 1966, p. 21). In the second revised edition he considered the building to have had 'at least three storeys' and in relation to the mural passage he had dropped the word 'probably', stating that it existed with certainty (Clarke 1980, pp. 17–8). In the third revised edition the building is firmly seen as having been originally three storeys with a double height Great Hall and a wall passage that extended around the entire circuit of the building (Clarke 1985, p. 17).

While Clarke made some significant contributions to the study of Colchester Castle, he was largely reflecting the interpretations of Philip Crummy and Paul Drury in relation to its height, both of whom favoured a three-storey model. Crummy, a significant figure both in the direct investigation and the interpretation of Colchester Castle, in 1980 attempted to bring together and summarise evidence for a structural interpretation. This involved producing plans of the different floor levels which in terms of the first and second storeys were based upon the work of the Royal Commission, with some additions. However, the plan of a presumed third storey was based on one published by the Reverend Cutts which spuriously shows a passageway around the entire circuit of the building (Crummy 1981, pp. 80–1).

In parallel with Crummy's research, Paul Drury was completing a major study of the castle. His work in two parts focused firstly on the Roman substructure and secondly on the post-Roman-to-modern history (Drury 1982; Drury 1984). These two works, along with Round's 1882 booklet, are the most important contributions to the study of Colchester Castle produced to date. In terms of the height debate Drury, in illustrating his idea of a three storey model, not only reproduced Crummy's plans but unfortunately also drew an east to west cross section of the building based on them. This cross-section gives the false impression of a walkway on the east wall even though there was no evidence for one, as will be discussed (Drury 1984, p. 318, fig. 9; p. 392, fig. 39; p. 394, fig. 40).

More recently, as part of a comparative study focused around the White Tower, Dixon has proposed an interesting alternative three storey model with no double-height rooms. This has the royal apartments on the third floor on the east side with the apartments of the constable below. The great attraction of this model is that it overcomes the problem of having the chapel and Great Hall on different floors and also resolves the very odd access arrangements to the third floor apartments in the eastern range (Dixon 2008, pp. 245–7).

These represent the changing views concerning the height of Colchester Castle. As can be seen, almost every possible variation has at one time been put forward. The prevailing view is now one of three-storeys, following the Crummy and Drury model. However, a consideration of new evidence has led me to the conclusion that it was only ever two-storeys high. The evidence falls into four broad areas: documentary sources (both unpublished and published), the demolition activity of John Wheely, physical traces within the building and pre-demolition depictions.

It is initially worth clarifying when the major demolition phase took place. When making presentations concerning the height issue, I have occasionally faced a response that no matter what evidence is produced relating to the late 17th century, an earlier unrecorded phase of demolition would make this irrelevant. This can, however, be countered by clear documentary evidence. In 1609 Colchester Castle was in a ruined state, as shown by the fact that it was listed in a document entitled *Certificate of His Majesty's Decayed Castells* (NA SP 14/49/82). However, in 1599, a detailed assessment of the castle was undertaken which included an estimate of what it would take to repair it, including the complete retiling of the main roof over the western half (ERO D/Dre Z3). Clearly, the roof must have been substantially extant at this point and it precludes any idea of an earlier phase of demolition in terms of removing whole floors. The main roof can be seen to have survived for several decades; until 1637 when an inquiry into the state of the building recorded: 'there hath lately fallen downe the roofe of a certain spacious roome King Coells Hall' (ERO D/DRc Z8).

It is only from the late 16th century that written descriptions of Colchester Castle appear in published form. These early accounts, including those by William Camden, William Smith, John Norden (from whom the title quote is derived), John Speed and John Aubrey, are very brief, normally consisting of a simple statement concerning the building's overall appearance along with some speculation over its construction date. These limited statements reflect the nature of the time and it is clear that the authors were not thinking about the need to record the building and set down a clear description for posterity. It was there for all to see, so why should they describe it in detail? The concept of the need for literary descriptions of such monuments did not develop until the 18th century. That there is no depth or detail to these descriptions, while not surprising in the context of the time, is still extremely frustrating given that they were written prior to the demolition work in the 1680s and 1690s (Camden 1586; Wheatley and Ashbee 1879, p. 24; Norden 1594; Speed 1611; Fowles 1980, pp. 460–1).

While the small number of pre-demolition descriptions are unfortunately all silent on the subject of the height, it is worth noting what they do not say. There is no mention of anything exceptional about Colchester Castle, though Smith, in 1588, did use the word 'marvellous'. If the building had originally been three or four storeys, to a person of the 16th and 17th centuries the building would have surely appeared to be truly immense; one of the biggest single structures they had ever seen. If it had been significantly higher it would surely have elicited greater comment. Despite the sparseness of early descriptions, the lack of reference to it being of exceptional size is significant. Descriptions made relatively soon after the demolition period are again notable for what they do not say. Daniel Defoe, who owned land in Colchester, makes no reference to the castle having been originally higher and even Joseph Strutt's pre-demolition witness only stated that he 'remembered something like embattlements at the top' but made no reference to additional height (Defoe 1724, pp. 45–6).

Turning to the activity of John Wheely, the often quoted passage by Morant is not fully clear in terms of the full extent of his demolition activity. In consequence, we have to consider other ways to help establish the extent. The first consideration is the timespan over which he conducted this work. The current view, as set out by Round, is that Wheely did not initially pursue his intention to demolish the castle but rather looked at other means of making money from the property and only began to seriously engage in demolition around 1695 (Round 1889, p. 150; RCHM 1922, p. 50; Pugh and Cooper 1994, p. 245). This is based on records of the Colchester Chamberlain for 1695 to 1699, relating to various payments to Wheely, including two for stone. That stone was being removed from the castle is shown by a bill, covering the period November 1697 to August 1698, which itemises payments to a haulier for carting five loads, weighing seven tons (ERO D/B5Aa 1/folio 35, 67, 71 and 77; ERO D/B5Ab 1/22; and ERO D/B5Aa 1/35 folio 83). Further documentary evidence that Wheely had stone available as a commercial commodity is revealed when, on 3rd December 1694, he secured a mortgage on the castle. Under the terms of the mortgage he received £330 from a Samuel Mott. The mortgage document contains the clause that Mott was entitled to ten tons of stone as part of the re-payment terms (ERO D/Y 2/2, 265).

Based on this evidence, it appears likely that the demolition period was spread over ten years, up to the time when Wheely sold the castle in 1704. This allows time for a considerable amount of destructive work to be undertaken. However, this scenario can now be shown to be wrong both in terms of the start date and the length of time over which it was carried out. The first point is that Round's interpretation was based on incomplete evidence, as the Chamberlain's Accounts are missing between 1684 and 1695. A similar gap exists within the Chamberlain's Bills and Vouchers. Consequently it is impossible to know whether Wheely was receiving payments for stone earlier than 1695. The second point concerns a print, entitled 'Meheaux's Prospect', which was published in 1697 (Figure 4.1). As part of a townscape

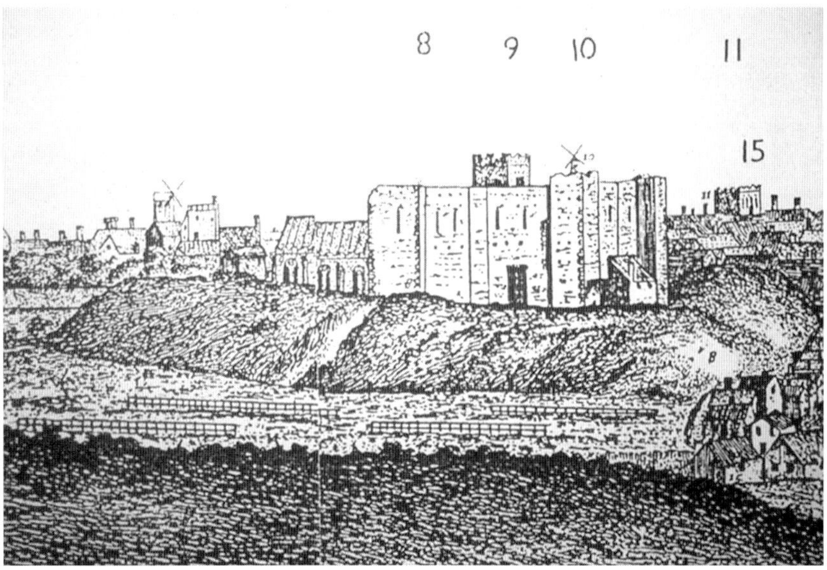


*Figure 4.1. Colchester Castle – Mehaux's Prospect, 1697 (detail).*

of Colchester the castle is clearly shown at the same height it is today, with all the corner towers demolished flush with the main walls. If we recognise the publication date of the print, even though the drawing upon which it was based would have been earlier, the point when demolition work (at least in terms of height) must have ceased must be pushed back by seven years, to 1697.

The second consideration is the use of the castle as a prison. Prior to Wheely purchasing the castle, its use as the county prison had ceased in 1667. However, it was still recognised that there was a need for a more local prison to serve the north-east of the county. In consequence, through an agreement between the County and Wheely, a prison was reopened in the castle in 1691. It occupied the whole eastern side, as it had done previously. Consequently, demolition work has to be pushed back to before this date, both for the practical problem of how a building could be demolished when part of it was being occupied and the fact that Wheely would no longer have had any right to carry out work on the eastern side when it was leased to the County.

The third line of evidence is that from April 1685, Wheely started to sub-let parts of the castle bailey to a variety of individuals. Most significantly, the first firmly dated agreement was with Edmund Hickringill, the Rector of All Saints Church in Colchester, for the area along the west side of the castle upon which he constructed a series of lean-to buildings, including a barn, a stable and two houses. This would have imposed a significant constraint on any demolition work on the western wall, which formed the back wall of these lean-to structures.

A fourth point is provided by the testimony put forward in a legal case of 1709. This included the statement: 'Wheely first bought the Castle to Demolish it & sell the materials & started soo to doo, but finding he could not compleat his designe afterwards purchased the inheritance'. If this can be accepted, then its implication is that Wheely's major demolition effort only lasted a very short time, between when he first leased the castle, on 10 March 1683, and the point he purchased it, on 20 April 1683 (ERO D/DRe L6).

One last factor to consider is the amount of time Wheely would have had available to conduct any demolition, as he was also involved in a wide range of other activities. This included work as a merchant, ironmonger and brasier, as he is described in various contemporary documents. He was also involved in an enterprise to improve the town's water supply, starting in 1684, in which he still retained an interest until at least 1694. He cultivated a field in the castle bailey. From early 1693 he took-on the role as gaoler, as well as the role as steward for Sir Isaac Rebow, which he was certainly undertaking in 1692, through to at least November 1702. Wheely and his family had at some point moved into the castle, where they lived in the old gaolers house, proving yet another strong dis-incentive for demolition work.

It should be stressed that this is not a completely revisionist review. Wheely did carry out some demolition work at the castle. Under the terms of his initial lease with Robert Norfolk, dated 10 March 1683, he had licence for just over a year, 'to fell downe, dig upp, & pull downe, take, cart, & carry away whatsoever stones, bricks, pavements, or rubbish, or other materials he can in ye aforesaid tyme'. That he did conduct some work is shown by the fact that he had stone to sell as evidenced by the Colchester Chamberlain's bills and accounts and that he could use stone as part of a mortgage agreement with Samuel Mott in 1694. That demolition work was going on at the castle is also shown by Richard Newcourt's irritation, on a visit in the late 17th century, when he could not view the execution spot of the royalist officers Lucas and Lisle because 'it lay buried under a great deal of Rubbish, thrown down from the Castle Wall' (Newcourt 1710, p. 168). On the basis that the building was only two-storeys high at that time, Wheely clearly took down the corner towers so that they were level with tops of the main walls, which themselves were lowered to the base of the battlements. He also clearly removed one of the two internal north–south walls; the demolition of which would have been greatly facilitated by the fact it was not bonded into the external wall at the north end and also by the fact that it probably consisted of a series of arches at both ground and first floor level rather than being a solid wall. All this would have provide him with a significant amount of stone and more than enough to account for the quantities contained in the various 1690s documents.

While evidence points to a more limited amount of demolition than has previously been assumed, structural evidence also needs to be considered. The first issue to consider is that of a possible mural passage running around the top of the first floor level. It can clearly be seen from drawings and photographs of the 19th and early 20th century but, unfortunately, today it is obscured by the roofing work of the 1930s and later. As already mentioned, Joseph Strutt, in 1774, was the first to describe this feature. It seemed to be evidence of a mural walkway familiar from a number of other castles, for example the White Tower (Strutt 1774, p. 27). The existence of such a walkway seemed to point to the existence of at least one further floor. While Strutt was not explicit on this point, a few years later, in 1777, Edward King, certainly was (King 1777, p. 408). However, in the 19th century, a number of people began to cast doubt on the passage, or rather its age. The first was Benjamin Strutt who, in 1803, considered that what was present on the west and north wall was 'of modern construction'. Others, such as Wright, soon came to the same conclusion (Strutt 1803, p. 162; Wright 1831, p. 314). The Reverend Henry Jenkins then developed the idea even further, interpreting the inner parapet as a kind of visitor safety barrier built in the 18th century (Jenkins 1853b, p. 30).

One of the most important contributions to this debate was provided by George Buckler who critically observed that the west wall walkway cut through the chimney flues of both of the original Norman fireplaces below. Consequently the walkway could only date to a period after the fireplaces were no longer in use (Buckler 1876, p. 39, fig. 14; Buckler 1877, pp. 61–4). Buckler's argument quickly gained acceptance as shown in the two 1882 reviews of Colchester Castle by Clark and Round. Round stated that it was a 'parapeted gangway, constructed in the last century' although he firmly believed that the castle should have such a gallery, though on a higher floor (Round 1882, pp. 85–6 and 102). Clark, viewing the evidence at around the same time, also came to the same conclusion that it was not original but rather 'built to make the walk safe' along the top of the wall (Clark 1882, p. 252). Soon afterwards Nicholls also considered the wall traces to be modern and strongly emphasised the evidence of the chimney flues (Nicholls 1889, pp. 16–17).

In consequence, it seems strange that there is a prevailing view that a wall passage did exist around the entire circuit of the castle at the top of the first floor level. This change of view came about during the late 1970s and early 1980s through the work of Crummy (and the plans that he produced) and Drury (who produced an east–west cross section of the building based on the plans). Neither Crummy nor Drury make any reference to the 19th-century discussion and were presumably unaware of its implications. In consequence of all of the repeated reproduction of the plans and section, the accepted view firmly shifted to the mural passage being an original Norman feature, even though there had in fact been no new discoveries (Clarke 1966, p. 21; Crummy 1981, pp. 80–1, fig. 67; Drury 1982, pp. 393–5; Drury 1984, p. 6; Crummy 1997, pp. 145–7; Fernie 2000, p. 65; Marshall 2009–10, p. 187).

In conclusion, it is clear that the path along the west wall is a later insertion, after the time that the fireplaces had gone out of use. This also seems to be the case in relation to the north wall, even though there is not the comparable evidence of the fireplace flues. Photographic evidence, particularly the work by T. C. Gall from the early 1930s, seems to show a constructional break and support the idea that the walling on top of the north wall is added. The logic, therefore, is that the wall walk along the west and north walls was constructed under the instruction of Charles Gray and that its function was to give a protected route to the room he had constructed on top of the north-east tower.

In relation to the east wall, the plan and section made by Crummy and Drury, reconstructs this as if a mural passage exists here. However, in no past description of the building has any structural evidence of a wall passage ever been noted there. In 1889, Nicholls, one of the few to discuss the matter (from direct observation) clearly stated that he saw no evidence of such a passage. Also significantly, in the case of the two east wall fireplaces, the flues are intact and not broken through in the same way as in the case of the west fireplaces. The absence of a wall walkway on the east can also be fully verified by examination of photographs taken prior to the re-roofing of the 1930s (Nicholls 1889, p. 17).

Having considered the west, east and north walls this leaves the south. The Reverend Cutts was the first to note traces of an inner wall indicating a wall passage here (Cutts 1853, Appendix vi). While Buckler has argued that the inner wall was built as part of the 18th-century re-roofing work, he is a lone voice and there has been universal acceptance of the passage along the south wall (Buckler 1876, p. 40). Today, from direct observation, it does seem clear that the inner wall, appears to be an original Norman construction. Such a walkway could, however, be accommodated in both a three-storey and a two-storey model. In the case of two storeys, the roofs would not sit directly on the outer edge but would rather be set back, as there would have been the practical requirement for a walkway between the outer wall and the roof edge. Whereas the three main roofs ran north-south, along the southern range there were probably two shorter east–west roofs. Consequently, the inner wall would have seated the southern edge of the westerly of these two roofs. The matter, however, still needs further detailed consideration and investigation, such as mortar analysis.

The next key structural element to consider is what has been claimed to be the remains of a window arch, where the west wall abuts the northwest tower. This was first noted in 1853 by Cutts, who considered that it proved 'beyond doubt, that Colchester Castle was, originally at least, one storey higher' (Cutts 1853, pp. 7–8). Soon afterwards, however, Buckler came to a very different conclusion, claiming that what was visible was rather 'the reveal of the embrasure, edged inside and out with tiles' and therefore indicating that the castle was only originally two storeys (Buckler 1876, pp. 39–40 and 63; Buckler 1882, p. 12). That the physical traces could elicit very divergent views is also well illustrated by Round, who claimed to see 'the jamb of a round-headed window, the tiles which form the spring of its arch', and Nicholls, who referred to 'the scarcely distinguishable remains of an arched opening' (Round 1882, p. 85; Nicholls 1889, p. 17).

Rex Hull made an important contribution to the window debate by stating that in the late 19th or early 20th century part of the window remains had collapsed. Unfortunately he gave no source for his statement, although he did make it clear that it was not based on personal observation (Hull 1982, p. 317). All subsequent commentators, largely on the basis of Hull's work, seem to have accepted the existence of this window, with some people mistakenly thinking that Hull had witnessed the collapse (Clarke 1966, p. 21; Crummy 1981, pp. 80–1; Fernie 2000, p. 65). The relevance is that if it can be accepted that a collapse had removed part of what was a window arch, then it would indicate either the existence of an additional floor or at least a curtain wall, such as seen at Castle Hedingham. Also, if part of it had really been lost, then it would mean that any independent observation based on the surviving structural remains today would be largely worthless.

So how can the existence of this window be tested? One way is to examine the large body of paintings, drawings, and photographs that pre-date this supposed collapse. The first relevant images are several early 19th-century oil paintings which show the area of the disputed window and which are accurate in all the features that can be observed today. The fact that there is no such evidence of a window arch is significant. Other depictions may also be examined, such as a very detailed pencil drawing by Sergeant, of 1845. These consistently show no difference from today. This also applies to the photographic record of the second half of the 19th century. It seems that there has not been any significant change to the appearance of this area from at least the mid-19th century. Consequently, Hull's reference to a significant collapse may be dismissed.

It is now therefore possible to return to the walling and make observations of the physical remains. There is clearly a stretch extending about two meters southwards from the north-west corner tower and which stands approximately 3m higher than the rest of the west wall. However, this may just indicate the original height of the battlements and represent the edge of an embrasure, as suggested by Buckler, rather than evidence of another floor. There are certainly a series of angled tiles at the top which some have taken as evidence of the beginning of a window arch but similar arrangements of tiles can be found elsewhere in the solid body of the walls. Also while there is a slight inward curvature in the centre of the masonry remnant which certainly visually strengthens the idea of a window, this is inconsistent with both the side of a window or an embrasure, as both would be vertical. This must be the result of weathering.

The last piece of structural evidence to consider is that of the supposed foundations of a chapel on the roof at the south-east corner. This idea started with Round, in 1882, who, because of his interpretation of the castle as a four storey building, expected to find the foundations of a chapel above the space he referred to as the Crypt. He also believed that a chapel would replicate the arrangement at the White Tower (Round 1882, pp. 88–9). He was unable to closely examine this area, which was obscured both by a roof, put there by Charles Gray, and building rubble that had accumulated under it. This was the situation until 1908 when there was a need to repair the roof. The rubble was then removed, which allowed the space underneath to be viewed properly. It revealed an east–west space with an apsidal end to the east and, within the thickness of the south-east tower buttress, a smaller east-west rectangular space with an apsidal end. There were six internal pilasters within the main apse. Understandably, following Round's interpretation, all of these features were taken to indicate the base of a chapel space with a small side-chapel. The Royal Commission soon accepted these structural remains as evidence of a third-storey chapel and also concluded that it must have extended up through two storeys (RCHM 1922, p. 54).

A further opportunity for detailed examination occurred in 1988 when it was decided to turn the space into a usable room. This investigation was conducted by the Colchester Archaeological Trust and, while the results have not as yet been fully published, a short popular account, along with a plan, was prepared. This was, however, largely based on St John's Chapel in the Tower, rather than new evidence. This has led to a false belief that physical traces were found. There is also a belief that column bases were discovered in the same relative positions as those at St John's Chapel. The plan and photograph of people standing in the locations of where columns might have stood contributed to this (Crummy 1989, 2). Philip Crummy is a proponent of a three storey building and chapel on the second floor. However, he noted 'in fact in all, there was little good evidence that the chapel had ever been built' (Crummy 1994, p. 6).

So, very little evidence was actually found. There was no evidence of columns or walls extending up above the second storey level on the north or west sides. What we do have is the external wall and a room within the thickness of the buttress on the south side. There is no other evidence of internal walls or other structural features associated with a chapel. So what does this mean? The walls in this space still need to be understood. This could simply be a single room representing an enlarged corner tower rather than a chapel.

In relation to structural evidence, one final area to consider is that of comparisons with other keeps. Comparative studies have to some degree bedevilled the study of Colchester Castle both in terms of the overall structure and with specific features. The idea that there is a standard model has featured in a number of interpretations of Colchester, with Round providing the most extreme example. A very important point to stress is that the late 11th and early 12th century was a period of great experimentation; so looking for exact parallels may be pointless. Previous comparative discussions have tended to roam far and wide. In chronological terms, they have been drawn from evidence of castles built a generation or more from the time of Colchester's construction. The one thing that is clear is that Colchester is not at all typical and an interesting suggestion is that it is more aligned to a royal palace than other tower keeps. Consequently, if we are looking for comparisons, then we should perhaps be looking at Carolingian castle-palaces rather than other English keeps (Colvin 1963, p. 32; Renn 1968, p. 35; Rowley 1983, p. 39; Heslop 1994, p. 56).

In discussing comparative evidence, an interesting area to consider is the amount of floor space available

| Comparative Floor areas | | | | |
|---|---|---|---|---|
| ***Colchester Castle*** | | ***White Tower*** | ***Colchester Difference*** | |
| Ground Floor | 1040m$^2$ | 720m$^2$ | + 320m$^2$ | + 45% |
| Four Storey Building with double height Great Hall and Chapel (after Round) | 3700m$^2$ | Three Storey 2160m$^2$ | + 1540m$^2$ | + 71% |
| Three Storey Building with no double height rooms (after Dixon) | 3120m$^2$ | | + 960m$^2$ | + 45% |
| Three Storey Building with double height Great Hall (after Crummy/Drury) | 2760m$^2$ | | + 600m$^2$ | + 28% |
| Two Storey Building (after the author) | 2080m$^2$ | | - 80m$^2$ | - 4% |

*Figure 4.2. Table of Colchester Castle and the White Tower floor areas.*

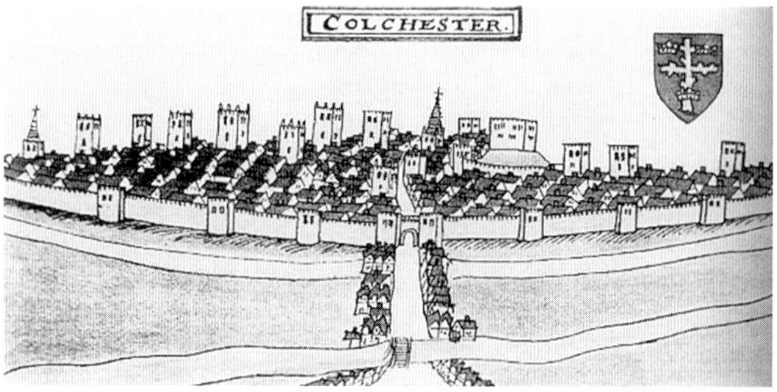


*Figure 4.3. Colchester Town: William Smith, 1588.*

when compared to the White Tower. Although Drury has previously made an attempt to assess this, I have made fresh calculations, which take account of the re-assessment of the original height of the White Tower. The comparisons, set out in the table, include revised height measurements for Colchester Castle.

When considering these results the first thing to note is just how much bigger Colchester is compared to the Tower. This is consistent across the differing interpretations of Round, Dixon and Crummy/Drury. Even with the smallest of the three interpretations Colchester is still approximately has an additional 600m$^2$ of floor space, making it around 28% bigger (Figure 4.2). It is of interest to ask what all of this extra space would have been used for? The problem of *excessive* space is, however, removed if we follow the model preferred by the author, as the size of the two buildings converge far more closely, with Colchester now the slightly smaller of the two.

The last source of information to consider concerning the original height of Colchester Castle comprises a number of pre-demolition depictions. While there are two town seals of the 14th and 15th centuries and a 15th-century marginal drawing on a manuscript that may show the castle, their interpretation is so difficult as to make them worthless (Studd 1994, p. 277; Crummy 1981, pp. 82–4; Marks and Williamson 2003, p. 266; Wheatley 2004, pp. 39–42; Caine 1898, pp. 320–1; Astley 1903, pp. 117–9). What is left are eight relevant images depicting the castle before the late 17th-century demolition. Starting with the earliest, there is a townscape by William Smith (Figure 4.3) that forms part of a work, dated to 1588, entitled *The Particular Description of England With views of some of the chief towns and armorial bearings of nobles and bishops* (Wheatley and Ashbee 1879, p. 24). It consists largely of coloured illustrations, particularly views of towns, although it also contains a charming prospect of Stonehenge. The depiction of Colchester shows the town from a vantage point to the east, looking across the river Colne and up East Hill. It is shown surrounded by walls, with a number of bastions, and the town's east gateway can be seen half way up East Hill. Within the town are a number of church towers and also the castle. It is shown as a two-storey building with no evident corner towers, two rows of windows and with crenellations surmounting the top of the walls. It also shows the bailey wall surviving intact along the east and part of the south sides and a surviving gate house on the south side. The depiction is clearly to a degree schematic and details of the town are also wrong. In particular, there is an excess of churches; while the number and location of the town wall bastions is incorrect.

As a consequence of its shortcomings, this image seems to have been dismissed as being of no or limited value, both in terms of the town and the castle (Crummy 2004, p. 8; Philips 2004, p. 52). This, however, may be too simplistic an assessment and in this respect it is worth considering another one of Smith's drawings; that of Stonehenge. That image is not by Smith, but seems to have derived from an earlier image (Piggott 1978, p. 10). Despite this, and the fact that it is inaccurate in a number of details, it is demonstrably Stonehenge and would have been immediately recognised as such by anyone familiar with the monument in the late 16th century, as it is to us today. So, should we not assume the same for the early image of Colchester? While it might be wrong in several specific details, could it not still be accurate enough to be recognised as Colchester to Smith's intended audience? Another significant point is that Smith's town drawings, and in particular the castles within them, are in each case individualised and distinctive. A depiction of Norwich Castle, for example, is very different to that of Colchester and it is also correct in terms of height. Rochester Castle is also very distinctive and is shown towering above its surrounding buildings, and proportionately looks correct. In a townscape of part of London, like Rochester, the White Tower is also similarly shown towering over the surrounding two-storey houses. Three rows of windows are also visible, and on the basis that the adjacent buildings would obscure the lower course of windows, then this can be seen as a relatively accurate depiction. Consequently, Smith's depiction of Colchester Castle, and the town, needs to be taken more seriously. It depicts an ancient walled town, on a hill with a river running below it, with a distinctive roof-scape dominated by church spires and towers and a castle. While inaccurate in some specific details, it clearly captures and successfully conveys the essence of the town. In consequence the same should apply to the castle image in that it displays the building as a relatively squat form; something that is further emphasised when it is compared to the tower-like appearance of both Rochester and the White Tower.

John Speed's great work *Theatre of the Empire of Great Britain* was published in 1611. It was common practice in cartographic circles at the time to re-use someone else's earlier map, often unacknowledged, as Speed certainly did. His map of Essex is a copy of an earlier one by Norden (Nicolson 1988, p. 12). Speed's great contribution, however, was his town plans, the majority of which seem to be his own work and, in some cases, the first known for a particular town (Skelton 1951; Nicolson 1988, p. 15). Included among these plans is one of Colchester, dated to 1610 (Figure 4.4), which is of particular importance for the study of the development of the town from the early 17th century onwards. Within the walled town is a depiction of the castle. As in the Smith drawing, this is a two-storey building, though this time with raised corner towers. There is no evidence of the apse and the main door, in the south side, is placed wrongly in the centre. It is, however, consistent with the evidence of the 1588 drawing in that it shows the survival of part of the bailey defences, particularly a gatehouse central to the south bailey wall and a short stretch of wall running just around the south-east corner.

To date, there has only been limited discussion of Speed's town plan in relation to the castle. In 1853 Cutts noted it and, while acknowledging the height indicated by the drawing, viewed it as being worthless (Cutts 1853, p. 31). Drury also briefly discussed it and considered that it did at least indicate a relatively squat building, even though it was unreliable in terms of detail (Drury 1982, p. 395). A number of other authors, though referring to it, do not comment in terms of the height of the building depicted (Clarke 1966, p. 17; Crummy 2004, pp. 12–3). As with the 1588 Smith drawing, however, it does seem to be worth considering it in more detail. For instance Speed's depiction can be compared with his other castle images. On this basis, unlike Smith, he does seem, in several instances, to have adopted a standard, stylised, castle form, which could argue against the value of his Colchester drawing. However, this is to a degree countered by some of his images which are individualistic, such as that of Rochester Castle. That is shown as a tower-like building and in relative terms seems to be an attempt to convey a fairly realistic depiction of the building. In isolation, Speed's image would carry little weight but together with Smith's earlier image and the subsequent ones to be discussed, it should not be dismissed so easily.

The next image to consider is on a Bay Seal dating to 1618. This is inscribed on one side 'English Colchester Saye 1618', while on the other there is a depiction of a castle which, it is logical to conclude, depicts Colchester Castle (Clarke 1985, p. 32; Philips 2004, p. 55). On this basis what we see is the south face of the building with the main doorway. This is reached by steps at the top of which is a standing figure and is in the correct relative position on the east side; not centrally as in the Speed image. There is no evidence of the apse; although this would not be so pronounced from a view from the south, such as this. In terms of the height, it again shows a two-storey building. A slight note of caution is that similar bay seals depicting castles in other towns are almost identical, including the presence of a central tower. This then raises the suspicion

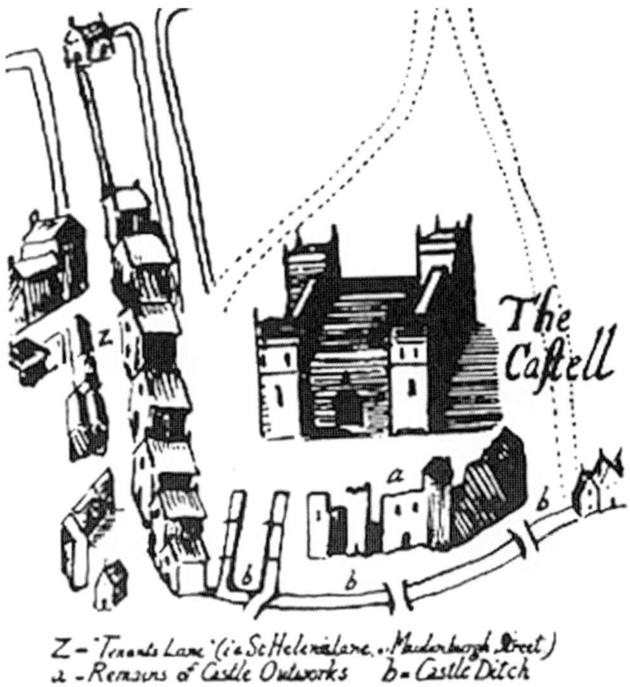


*Figure 4.4. Colchester Castle: John Speed, 1610 (detail from Town Plan).*

that what we are seeing is a standard and stylised castle depiction used by an engraver to produce bay seals for more than one town.

The next image chronologically, forms part of a plan entitled *The Plott of the Castle of Colchester in the Countie of ESSEX*, dated to 1622 (ERO D/DJ 1/3). Its purpose was to show the lands associated with the castle and to help establish the ownership rights at the time. The castle is depicted as a two-storey building but it has erroneous features including a central entrance, no corner towers, and most discordantly a constricted waist. Of the post-medieval images discussed so far, this is clearly the most schematic and generalised, and not an attempt to achieve anything like a lifelike representation. However, while the least convincing image, which on its own would clearly be seen as being of little value, taken in conjunction with all the other pre-Wheely views it may carry some weight, not least in that it once again shows a two-storey building.

In 1639 a work entitled *Histoire de L'entrée de le Reyne Mare de Roy tres-christian dans la Grande Bretagne* was published (De la Serre 1639). It is an account of the rather unhappy journey of Marie de Medici to England in 1637, when she was trying to seek refuge with her daughter and son-in-law, Queen Henrietta Marie and Charles I. Marie and her entourage, having landed at Harwich, progressed towards London and on the way stopped in Colchester. As well as a brief written description of the visit, there is also a drawing consisting of a view looking up East Hill and showing the Queen descending from her carriage (Benham 1901). The castle does appear in the image, but only just (Figure 4.5). It is shown peeping above the roofline of the houses on the north side of the street, with the crenellations topping the walls and raised corner towers just visible. Though the full height cannot be seen, what is clear is that it is not towering *above* the surrounding buildings.

*Figure 4.5. Colchester Town: Marie de Medici, 1637.*

While this image has been noted on several occasions before, only Philip Crummy has previously analysed it in detail. He concluded that it was most probably produced by an artist unfamiliar with Colchester and who drew it not from direct observation but rather as an extrapolation using Speed's 1610 map. This would limit its value in relation to the castle height debate. His argument centres around the similarity of the arrangement of the churches to Speed's plan, the fact that the Swan Inn (which is clearly depicted and is known to have been at the top of East Hill) is placed on the wrong side of the road and the artificially elevated viewpoint (Crummy 2004). His argument, however, does not hold-up for a number of reasons. Firstly, in relation to the Swan Inn, the artist clearly knew the rough location; information that could not possibly have been derived from Speed's map (Sier 1938). The artist had to have had some more direct knowledge of Colchester. Secondly, it was the norm for artists to artificially elevate the viewpoint and so it should not be used as evidence that the image might be hypothetical (Piggot 1978, p. 10). Once again, this image cannot be dismissed so lightly and remains worthy of further consideration.

In 1669 Cosimo the Third, Grand Duke of Tuscany, escaping from an unhappy marriage, was on a tour of England (Strathern 2003, p. 387). Along with Cosimo came a large entourage including a number of artists whose job was to create a pictorial record of the journey. Among the group was Count Lorenzo Magalotti, whose duty was also to provide a written account. However, it was not until 1821 that Magalotti's manuscript account was published, along with some prints derived from the artists' works. The relevance here is that in the second week of June 1669 Cosimo came to Essex, including Colchester. On the 11th Cosimo and his party travelled to Chelmsford, where they stayed for the night and in the morning of the 12th, most of the party went on to Colchester. Cosimo took a more leisurely day and only arrived in the town in the late afternoon. Undoubtedly the most important result of the visit was a drawing of a view of the town from the south-west (Figure 4.6). As with the Marie de Medici drawing, the castle is not shown towering above the surrounding buildings but just rises slightly above the general roofline. It is interesting to compare it with the second known panoramic view of the town, when the artist stood to the south. That was produced by Samuel and Nathaniel Buck and dates to 1741, a considerable time after the demolition. Though the image is based on a more easterly vantage point, it depicts the castle just poking up from behind St Nicholas church. It is very reminiscent of the earlier 1669 pre-demolition view. This seems difficult to equate with the idea of the castle having been originally one or more floors higher. Surely, if this was the case, then some significant difference should be discernible, between the pre-demolition and the post-demolition views, in terms of the relative height in relation to that of the surrounding buildings, especially the churches.

The next image forms part of a print published sometime in the 1660s entitled *An Orthographical Design of Several Views upon the Road*. Among the views is one of Colchester Castle which is clearly shown, once again, as a two-storey building surmounted by crenellations and with raised corner towers (Figure 4.7). Around it are some single-storey buildings but there is a clear view of one whole section of the castle wall. While the image is very small, literally postage stamp size, it does appear to be a high quality image. But is it reliable? In the bottom right hand corner of the print is written *'This Designe is to illustrate Cambdens Britannia that where he mentions such places the Curious may see them. Which is the Endeavour by God's assistance of Y. S. Daniel King'*. Also along the bottom is written *'souls by John Overton at the Whitehorse neere the fountain without Newgate'*. This text has led to confusion over the origin of the drawing and the artist. It is known that John Overton produced the print from drawings that had once belonged to Daniel King and that he came into possession of them on King's death in 1661. The title on the published engraving and the fact that the drawings comprising it clearly came from the effects of King have led some to assume that it was also drawn by him (Allen Brown and Colvin 1963, p. 616; Cob 1974, p. 300). However, more detailed assessments have attributed the overall drawing, upon which the print was based, to Wencelaus Hollar (Pennington 1982, p. 148; Griffiths 1998, p. 191). This matter of the original artist is not a minor pedantic point but is of critical importance in relation to the degree of reliance that can be placed on the drawing. Hollar was one of the major topographical draughtsmen of his day whereas King, by comparison, is a relatively minor figure who has been heavily criticised as an artist both in terms of his skill and accuracy. Ascribing the drawing to Hollar, therefore, means that far greater confidence can be placed on the details of the image. In terms of dating all we can say for certainty is that it must pre-date King's death in 1661 (Cob 1974, p. 299; Parry 1988, pp. 16–18; Mallalieu 1986, p. 179; Mackenzie 1998, p. 200; Griffiths 1998, p. 190).

While all of the images so far discussed have been individually questioned, and some are certainly suspect in relation to some particular details, as a group they are at least consistent in either showing a two-storey building or one just peeping up, not towering, above the surrounding houses. Together, they carry more weight and form an indicative body of evidence. Following these relatively well known images, we come to the last which, while unfortunately undated, must pre-date the demolition period.

*Figure 4.6. Colchester Town: Cosimo de Medici, 1669.*

*Figure 4.7. Colchester Castle: Wencelaus Hollar.*

That image was first described in 1889 by F. M. Nicholls, though at the time he did not fully realise its significance (Nicholls 1889, p. 9). It is a pencil and ink drawing entitled *il Castello, osio fortezza, di Colecester in Inghliterra*; one of two drawings donated on 11th January 1721 by George Holmes, in the collection of the Society of Antiquaries. It carries the signature of the artist '*Boul*'. In different handwriting, at the bottom of the sketch is written: *'Drawn by Mr Boul a Fleming who lived many years in Italy - & came to England & drew abundance of Views'*. It is in two parts, with the upper consisting of a view of the castle from the north-east (Figure 4.8). Other buildings are visible behind, including St Nicholas church. In the foreground are two male figures. Below the elevation is a rough outline plan, largely in pencil though with a few inked lines. It is, unfortunately, of no real value in interpreting the castle as it is clearly inaccurate in

*Figure 4.8. Colchester Castle: Boul (reproduced by kind permission of the Society of Antiquaries of London).*

some important details, especially in relation to the apsidal corner which is shown as a large circular tower. The upper drawing is, however, clearly of a very different standard, both compared to the plan and the other 16th- and 17th-century depictions. It is of high artistic merit as well as being demonstrably accurate in all important details that can be directly verified today.

Unfortunately it has not proved possible to find an exact match for the apparent signature or name of the artist from the standard reference works (Caplan 1982; Jackson 1991; Wilenski 1960; Turner 1998; Benezit 1999; De Maere and Wabbes 1994; Ris-Paquot nd). This is also true of a search involving a number of other criteria including: variants on the name such as Bol, Boel or Boule; a broad date range from the late 16th to the early 18th centuries; being Flemish; known to have visited Italy; and a recorded period in England. At present, the strongest candidate is an artist called Cornelius (or Cornelis) Boel who was born in 1589, possibly in Antwerp. (Croft-Murray and Hulton 1960, 201–2; Stainton and Wright 1987, 72)

The most important point to note in the drawing is that it shows Colchester Castle as a two storey building, with four corner towers raised above the height of the central walls, and with what looks like a roof structure on the north east tower. Most significantly, there are two pitched roofs, including chimneys, over parts of the main building. The larger of these roofs seems to extend over much of the length of the great hall. The second shorter roof is one of the two that would be expected over the southern apsidal block, though over which of the three spaces is difficult to be certain. While there is no date on the drawing and no definitive attribution to a specific artist, the drawing must still pre-date 1721, the year it was presented to the Society of Antiquaries. It must also depict the building before Meheaux's 1697 print, as by this time all evidence of roofs had gone and the corner towers had been reduced so that they were roughly flush with the main walls. Finally, the presence of some surviving roofs suggests that it pre-dates 1637, when the main roof was recorded to have collapsed. This drawing provides compelling evidence for the appearance and height of Colchester Castle prior to the demolition work of John Wheely.

Having discussed the various strands of evidence, what then can be concluded? The documentary evidence precludes an early unrecorded period of major demolition of the keep and demonstrates that the main roof survived through to the 1630s. In terms of what John Wheely actually did, both in terms of the length of time and the extent of any demolition work, was far more restricted than previously thought. It was apparent to Wheely that he could earn more from the castle as a standing building than a source of salvaged building material. Then, all of the main structural details that have been used as arguments for at least one further floor, while open to varying interpretations, can all be accommodated in a two-storey building. Lastly the pre-demolition depictions, while they can individually be questioned, together provide a powerful body of evidence supporting the view that the building was only ever two storeys high, though with raised corner towers. The Boul image is of particular importance as it seems to provide definitive evidence of the original height.

If Colchester Castle was only ever two storeys high, there remains one final question. Was this due to an initial design or was it the result of a modified plan? One of the well-known features of Colchester Castle is that after a period of initial construction there was a cessation of work and then commencement again, perhaps after more than a decade. This break in construction is known from two sources of evidence. There is a distinct change in the nature of the predominant building material used. Then, at the junction between building material types, there is evidence of in-filled crenellations around much of the circuit, seemingly indicating that it was a single-storey building for a period. At the point that construction recommenced to raise the building to its final height, an indication that there was some kind of modified plan is provided by a new observation concerning the garderobe in the east wall. If that had been planned as part of an initial design, then the garderobe chute, which opens out below the level of the constructional break, would have had to have been partially built during the first phase. However, from the external view, it seems very clear that in constructing the chute it was necessary to cut down into the wall and in the process break through one of the phase-one merlons. Therefore, this must have been an afterthought, as part of the second phase. If so, this could accommodate the view of those who have argued Colchester Castle should be at least three storeys high. It would imply that there was an *original intention* to build to such a height. In such a scenario, a possibility is that the garderobe was originally intended for one floor higher up but a change of plan reduced the original intended height, which necessitated modification. If there was such a change of plan, then this, in part, might be recognition of the folly of building such a grandiose structure, as a royal palace, in a location that, as events proved, was never going to be a main royal residence. Nevertheless, a two-storey Colchester Castle would still have been a magnificent building and an imposing symbol of Norman authority.

### *Abbreviations*

| | |
|---|---|
| ERO | Essex Record Office |
| NA | National Archives |
| RCHM | Royal Commission for Historic Monuments |

## Bibliography


Allen Brown, R. and Colvin, H. M. (1963) 'The Royal Castles 1066–1485', in H. M. Colvin, ed., *The History of the King's Work*, Vol. II, pp. 553–894 (London, HMSO).

Astley, H. J. D. (1903) 'Mediaeval Colchester – Town Castle and Abbey – from MSS in the British Museum', *Transactions of the Essex Archaeological Society*, n.s. XIII, pp. 117–37.

Bénézit, E. (1999) *Dictionaire Des Peintres, Sculpteurs, Dessinateurs et Graveurs*, 14 vols (Paris, Grund).

Benham, W. G. (1901) 'Marie De' Medici in Essex, 1638', *Essex Review* 10, pp. 200–8.

Buckler, G. (1876) *Colchester Castle A Roman Building, First Section.*

Buckler, G. (1877) *Colchester Castle A Roman Building, Second Section.*

Buckler, G. (1879) *Colchester Castle A Roman Building, Third Section.*

Buckler, G. (1882) *Colchester Castle A Roman Building, Fourth Section.*

Caine, C. (1898) 'Our cities: sketched 500 years ago', *Journal of the British Archaeological Association,* n.s. IX, pp. 319–21.

Camden, W. (1586) *Britannia.*

Caplan, H. H. 1982 *The Classified Directory of Artists' Signatures, Symbols and Monograms* (London, George Prior).

Clark, G. T. (1882) 'Some account of the keep of Colchester Castle', *Archaeological Journal* 39, pp. 239–56.

Clarke, D. (1966) *Colchester Castle: A history, description and guide* (place of publication, publisher?).

Clarke, D. (1980) (5th rev. ed.) *Colchester Castle: A history, description and guide* (place of publication, publisher?)

Clarke, D. (1985) (6th rev. ed.) *Colchester Castle: A history, description and guide* (place of publication, publisher?).

Cob, G. (1974) 'Daniel King: a lesser-known seventeenth-century etcher', *Antiquaries Journal* 54, pp. 299–301.

Colvin, H. M. (1963) 'The King's Works 1066–1154', in H. M. Colvin, ed., *The History of the King's Work*, Vol. I , pp. 19–50 (London, HMSO).

Croft-Murray, E. and Hulton, P. (1960) *The British Museum Catalogue of British Drawings, Vol. 1, 16th and 17th Centuries* (London, British Museum).

Crummy, P. J. (1981) *Aspects of Anglo-Saxon and Norman Colchester*, Colchester Archaeological Report 1 and Council for British Archaeology Research Report 39.

Crummy, P. J. (1989) 'The chapel on the roof', *Colchester Archaeologist* 2, pp. 12.

Crummy, P. J. (1994) 'The Castle that Eudo built', *Colchester Archaeologist* 7, pp. 1–7.

Crummy, P J. (1997) *City of Victory: the story of Colchester - Britain's First Roman Town* (Colchester, Colchester Archaeological Trust).

Crummy, P. J. (2004) 'The earliest known picture of Colchester?', *Colchester Archaeologist* 17, pp. 8–13.

Cutts, E. L. (1853) *Colchester Castle Not A Roman Temple.*

De La Serre, S. (1639) *Histoire de L'entrée de la Reyne Mare de Roy très-christian dans la Grande Bretagne.*

De Maere, J. and Wabbes, M. (1994) *Illustrated Dictionary of 17th Century Flemish Painters* (Brussles, La Renaissance de livre).

Defoe, D. (1724) *A Tour Thro' the whole Islands of Great Britain Divided in to Circuits or Journies.*

Dixon, P. (2008) 'The Influence of the White Tower on the Great Towers of the Twelfth Century', in E. Impey, ed., *The White Tower*, pp. 243–75, (New Haven and London, Yale University Press).

Dixon, P. and Marshall, P. (1993) 'The Great Tower at Hedingham Castle: a Reassessment', *Fortress* 18, pp. 16–23.

Drury, P. J. (1982) 'Aspects of the origins and development of Colchester castle' *Archaeological Journal* 139, pp. 302–419.

Drury, P. (1984) 'The Temple of Claudius at Colchester Reconsidered', *Britannia* 15, pp. 7–50.

Fernie, E. (2000) *The Architecture of Norman England* (Oxford, University Press).

Fowles, J., ed. (1980) *John Aubrey's Monumenta Britannica* (Milborne Port, Dorset Publishing Company).

Griffiths, A. (1998) *The Print in Stuart Britain 1603–1689* (London, British Museum Press).

Grose, F. (1783) (new ed.) *The Antiquities of England and Wales*, Vol. 2.

Harris, R. (2008) 'The structural history of the White Tower, 1066–1200', in E. Impey, ed., pp. 29–93.

Heslop, T. A. (1994) *Norwich Castle Keep: Romanesque Architecture and Social Context* (Norwich, Centre of East Anglian Studies).

Hull, M. R. (1982) 'Observations on the keep', in Drury, P. J. (1982) 'Aspects of the origins and development of Colchester castle', *Archaeological Journal* 139, pp. 317–23.

Impey, E. (2008) 'The Ancestry of the White Tower', in E. Impey, ed., pp. 227–41.

Jackson, R. (1991) *The Visual Index of Artists' Signatures and Monograms* (London, Foulsham).

Jenkins, H. (1851) 'Colchester Castle', *Journal of the British Archaeological Association* 6, p. 451.

Jenkins, H. (1853a) *Colchester Castle.*

Jenkins, H. (1853b) *Appendix to the Lecture on Colchester Castle together with a Reply to the Animadversions of the Rev. E. L. Cutts.*

Jenkins, H. (1861) *Colchester Castle shown to have once been The Templed Citadel which the Roman Colonists raised to their Emperor Claudius.*

Jenkins, H. (1869) (rev. ed.) *Colchester Castle shown to have once been The Templed Citadel which the Roman Colonists raised to their Emperor Claudius.*

King, E. (1777) 'Observations on Antient Castles', *Archaeologia* 4, pp. 364–413.

Mackenzie, I. (1998) (2nd rev. ed.) *British Prints* (Woodbridge, Antique Collector's Club).

Magalotti, L (1821) *Travels of Cosimo the third Grand Duke of Tuscany Through England During the Reign of Charles the Second (1669).*

Mallalieu, H. L. (1986) (2nd ed.) *The Dictionary of British Watercolour Artists up to 1920*, Vol. I (Woodbridge, Antique Collector's Club).

Marks, R. and Williamson, P., ed. (2003) *Gothic Art for England 1400–1547* (London, V&A Publications).

Marshall, P. (2009–10), 'The internal arrangements of the donjon at Colchester in Essex: a reconsideration', *Castle Studies Group Journal* 23, pp. 178–90.

Morant, P. (1748) *The History and Antiquities of the Most Ancient Town and Borough of Colchester in the County of Essex.*

Newcourt, R. (1710) *Repertorium Ecclesiasticum Parochiale Londinense.*

Nichols, F. M. (1889) 'Colchester Castle', *Transactions of the Essex Archaeological Society*, n.s. III, pp. 1–35.

Nicolson, N. (1988) 'Introduction', in *The Counties of Britain A Tudor Atlas by John Speed* (British Library), pp. 7–18.

Norden, J. (1594) *Speculi Britanniae Pars: an historical and chorographical description of the County of Essex*, Camden Society, O. S. 9, 1840.

Parry, G. (1988) *Hollar's England: a mid-seventeenth-century view.*

Pennington, R. (1982) *A Descriptive Catalogue of the Etched Work of Wenceslaus Hollar 1607–1677* Cambridge, University Press).

Phillips, A. (2004) *Colchester a History* (Stroud, Phillimore).

Piggott, S. (1978) *Antiquity Depicted: Aspects of Archaeological Illustration* (London, Thames & Hudson).

RCHM, (1922) *An Inventory of the Historical Monuments in Essex*, Vol. 3.

Renn, D. F. (1968) *Norman Castles in Britain* (London, John Baker).

Ris-Paquot [nd] *Dictionnaire Encyclopédique des Marques est Monogrammes.*

Round, J. H. (1882) *The History and Antiquities of Colchester Castle.*

Round, J. H. (1889) 'Some documents relating to Colchester Castle', *Transactions of the Essex Archaeological Society*, n.s. III, pp. 143–54.

Rowley, T. (1983) *The Norman Heritage 1066–1200* (London, Palladin).

Rudsdale, E. J. (1948) 'Some notes on the Siege of Colchester', *Essex Review* 57(228), pp. 161–72.

Sier, L. C. (1938) 'The 'Swan' Inn, Frere Street, Colchester', *The Essex Review* 47(88), pp. 194–8.

Skelton, R. A. (1951) 'Tudor town plans in John Speed's Theatre', *Archeaological Journal* 108, pp. 109–20.

Speed, J. (1610/1611) *Theatre of the Empire of Great Britain.*

Stainton, L. and Wright, C. (1987) *Drawing in England from Hilliard to Hogarth* (London, British Museum Press).

Strathern, P. (2003) *The Medici: Godfathers of the Renaissance* (London, Jonathan Cape).

Strutt, B. (1803) *The History and Description of Colchester.*

Strutt, J. (1774) *A Contemplative View of the Manners, Customs, Arms, Habits, etc. of the Inhabitants of England, from the arrival of the Saxons, till the Reign of Henry the Eighth.*

Studd, P. (1994) 'Arms, Insignia and Plate', in J. M. Cooper, ed., *A History of the County of Essex*, Vol. IX, Victorian County History, pp. 277–9.

Turner, J., ed. (1998) (rev. ed) *The Dictionary of Art*, 34 vols (New York, Oxford University Press).

Wheatley, A. (2004) *The Idea of the Castle in Medieval England* (Woodbridge, York Medieval Press).

Wheatley, H. B. and Ashbee, E. W., ed. (1879) *William Smith The Particular Description of England 1588 With Views of Some of the Chief Towns and Armorial Bearings of Nobles and Bishops.*

Wilenski, R. H. (1960) *Flemish Painters 1430–1830*, Vol. I (London, Faber & Faber).

Wright, T. (1831) *The History and Topography of the County of Essex Comprising Its Ancient and Modern History.*

# 5

# Rochester Castle

*Marc Morris*

**Résumé**

*Rochester, bâti juste après la conquête normande de 1066 par le demi-frère du conquérant lui-même, l'évêque Odo de Bayeux, a été dès l'origine un des plus importants châteaux d'Angleterre. Reconstruit en pierre durant la dernière décennie du XIe siècle, l'adjonction après 1127 de son immense tour élancée – de 125 pieds (38m) – le plus grand édifice de son genre en Europe occidentale, l'a radicalement transformée. La notoriété de Rochester tient aussi dans le drame de la période suivante. En 1215, au début de la guerre qui a conduit le célèbre roi Jean à sa répudiation de la Grande Charte, le château a été le lieu d'un des sièges les plus longs et les plus durs qu'ait connus l'Angleterre, une bataille qui s'est terminée de façon spectaculaire lorsque les armées de Jean ont ébranlé avec succès la grande tour, causant son effondrement partiel. A la fin du siècle et bien que la tour ait ensuite été réparée au début du XIIIe siècle, Rochester s'est détérioré d'une manière irrémédiable.*

With the completion of the Shard of Glass in London, England holds the record for the tallest building in Europe (at least for the time being). In the 12th century, it held a similar distinction with the great tower at Rochester Castle. Although surpassed in height by many cathedral spires, Rochester was the tallest castle tower in Christendom: from the base of its plinth to the top of its turrets it soars to 125 feet, or 38m (Figure 5.1 and 5.2). To walk its battlements today is a vertiginous experience, and anyone who has done so must sympathise somewhat with the celebrated diarist and sexual predator Samuel Pepys, who visited in 1665:

> 'I did there walk to visit the old Castle ruines', wrote Pepys in his diary for 2 October, 'and there going up I did upon the stairs overtake three pretty maids or women, and took them up with me, and did besarlas muchas vezes et tocar leur mains and necks, to my great pleasure: but Lord, to see what a dreadful thing it is to look down praecipices, for it did fright me mightily, and hinder me from much pleasure which I would have made to myself in the company of these three if it had not been for that.' (Goodall 2006, pp. 268–9).

As well as its superlative, emasculating height, Rochester is also famous as the setting for one of the greatest of all medieval sieges. In the autumn of 1215, the castle was attacked by the infamous King John for almost two months, a bitter struggle that resulted in the great tower being partially destroyed. The story was recently made into a low-budget action movie called *Ironclad*. The strapline 'Heavy metal goes medieval' tells you all you need to know about its historical and dramatic merits.

As with most towers of its type, the tower at Rochester was not contemporary with the foundation of the castle itself. Like most castle sites in England, Rochester was established during the reign of William the Conqueror: the first documentary reference to it comes in 1086, when it is mentioned in passing in the Domesday Book (Williams and Martin 2002, p. 6). Given its location, however, a foundation date closer to 1066 is highly likely. The town of Rochester sits on the Roman road from Dover to London – Watling Street – at the point where it crosses the River Medway. Watling Street is likely to have been the route taken by William the Conqueror as he advanced on London in the autumn of 1066 (Morris 2012a, pp. 193–5). At any rate Rochester would have been a strategically essential place for the Normans to protect from an early date. The first chronicle reference to the castle reveals that in 1088 it was in the hands of William's notorious half-brother, Odo of Bayeux. Odo had been placed in charge of Kent as early as the start of 1067, and in the same year, according to the Anglo-Saxon Chronicle, 'built castles far and wide throughout the land, oppressing the unhappy people' (Garmonsway 1972, pp. 200 and 223–4). Lastly, the shape of

*Figure 5.1. Rochester Castle keep (Medway Council).*

*Figure 5.2. Rochester Castle keep (Medway Council).*

Rochester's site conforms to the type constructed elsewhere by the Normans during the earliest phase of the Conquest, being a simple enclosure formed by hiving off a section of the town. As with other very early sites, there is no trace of a *motte* (English 1995, pp. 45–61).

Beyond the shape of its earthworks, little remains today of the 11th-century castle – as one would expect, given that the great majority of early Norman castles in England were constructed from wood. There is one section of wall on the west side of the bailey of an early date, which suggests that at some point soon after its foundation the whole circuit was rebuilt in stone. The obvious context for this rebuilding is the period immediately after William the Conqueror's death in 1087, at which point Odo of Bayeux rebelled against the newly crowned William Rufus, his nephew, with the result that Rochester was besieged and Odo was driven into exile. Around the same time, the city's bishop, Gundulf, struck a deal with Rufus that obliged him to carry out rebuilding work at the castle. The likeliest scenario is that the rebuilding followed the siege and entailed the replacement of an existing timber palisade with a wall of stone (Peats and Drury 2009, pp. 17–20).

Fortunately when it comes to the great tower we are on much firmer ground. A royal charter of 1127 shows that Rufus's successor, Henry I, struck a deal with the archbishop of Canterbury, William of Corbeil, granting him joint custody of the castle, and at the same time obliging him to build a tower there. The chronicler Gervase of Canterbury, writing later in the century, confirms that the archbishop built 'a noble tower of outstanding size'. Since the architecture is all of a piece, the assumption is that it was completed by the time of the archbishop's death in 1136, i.e. within a period of just nine years (Goodall 2006, pp. 265–7).

'A tower of outstanding size' is clearly a reference to Rochester's soaring height. At *base* it is comparatively small compared to other great towers – approximately 73ft × 74ft (22.25m × 22.56m), compared with, for instance, Norwich's 93ft × 110ft (28.34m × 33.53m), the Tower of London's 107ft × 118ft (32.61m × 35.97m), or Colchester's 110ft × 151ft (33.53m × 46.03m). This, coupled with its immense height, gives Rochester a slender appearance compared to its squatter contemporaries. In terms of design, it harks back to the donjon built 100 years or so earlier at Loches by Fulk Nerra, count of Anjou, though the influence is probably not direct. John Goodall has suggested the great tower at Corfe in Dorset as a possible intermediary between the two, along with perhaps a trio of castles built by Henry I's chief minister, Bishop Roger of Salisbury, at Sherborne, Devizes and Old Sarum. The common link between these towers is their incorporation in each case of a stone forebuilding, a unusual feature at this early date. Rochester's forebuilding is particularly large and sophisticated, communicating with the main body of the great tower at every level, and containing a chapel in the floor above the entrance – an arrangement which was to become typical, but which at the time was shared by only one other building, the contemporary tower at Portchester (Goodall 2006, pp. 273–4).

Rochester was pioneering in other ways. The holes around its wall head to support a wooden fighting platform appear to be original, which makes it the earliest castle in England to boast such a feature. Inside the tower, the space is divided into two by a cross-wall, as is the case with several other great towers. Rochester's cross-wall, however, is exceptional in breaking into columns at the level of its principal floor (other towers do this, but only at basement level). It seems that, initially at least, the designer envisaged that the two halves of the tower would combine at this level to produce a single grand chamber. But at some later stage, it was decided to block the openings between the columns with the insertion of a stone partition (a portion of it survives at the far end, an archway of a door). That this wall was not keyed in to the columns suggests it was an afterthought, but the fact that the archway matches the style of the rest of the build suggest that it was an afterthought that occurred soon after the initial construction was completed (Goodall 2006, pp. 272–3 and 284–5).

What really marks Rochester out as unique is its inclusion of an additional storey above the level of its principal chamber. No other great tower in England can boast such an addition (Figure 5.3). Some other towers – e.g. Richmond in Yorkshire – appear on the outside to have been large enough to have done so, but in fact their top floors were domestically redundant, and simply conceal countersunk roofs. The tower at Hedingham, closely modelled on Rochester, was originally like this: the top floor seen today is a creation of the 15th century, a late medieval example of loft conversion (Morris 2012b, pp. 69–70).

Since it would have been possible to create such a 'dummy' storey at Rochester, had height been the only concern, it begs the question: why did the designer bother to include a whole extra floor? John Goodall has proposed that it was included because of the castle's special status, being a joint concern of both the king and the archbishop of Canterbury. According to this interpretation, the lower two floors would constitute a suite for the archbishop, while the upper floor would be reserved for the use of the king. This is a clever solution, and works very well in purely symbolic terms. But there appear to be problems at a practical level – i.e. if we imagine both parties simultaneously in residence. As Goodall himself points out, there are no garderobes on the top floor, because of the gallery which runs continuously through the thickness of the wall immediately below. If both floors were occupied, in other words, the king would either have had to steal downstairs in the night to use the archbishop's facilities, or else to disregard convention and go out of the window. Neither scenario is wholly compatible with maintaining the majesty and mystique of monarchy (Goodall 2006, pp. 266–7, 289 and 291–3).

Was Rochester conceived as a military building? For several decades now, the trend in castle studies has been concerned to overturn old military orthodoxies, and stress the peaceable motives that underlay the design of such great towers (e.g. Coulson 2001). They were intended to project power symbolically, and to serve as palaces for their royal and aristocratic owners. Yet there is a danger, it seems to me, of pushing this argument too far. Contemporary chroniclers, when they wrote about such buildings, typically

*Figure 5.3. The cross-wall inside Rochester's great tower, which breaks into columns and arches at second-floor level.*

used phrases such as 'very strong' or 'virtually impregnable' (Morris 2012a, p. 66). The great tower at Rochester is certainly concerned with defence. At the lowest levels, its windows are small and narrow; only at the higher levels do they widen to let in more light. At the top of the tower, as we've already noted, there are holes to support hoarding, and this wall-head defence was presumably a permanent fixture. The forebuilding and the external stair leading up to it *were* designed to impress, but also to protect, including as they did a portcullis and a drawbridge. Because of the height of the building, the walls necessarily had to be very thick. These features may strike some as secondary or even incidental. But the fact remains that, when put to the test, Rochester proved extremely resilient.

In June 1215 the unpopular King John had been cornered by his political opponents and forced to concede that most famous of all English historical documents, Magna Carta. But for all its later fame, Magna Carta in its first incarnation was worthless. No sooner had the ink dried than John had dispatched messengers to the pope, who obliged him by declaring that the charter should be torn up. At that point the struggle between the king and his barons collapsed into outright civil war, with the rebels offering the crown to Louis, son of King Philip II of France. Since John was also looking for help from the Continent in the form of Flemish mercenaries, it was a war in which the southeast was a crucial theatre of conflict. Control of the castles of Kent became imperative for both sides (Warren 1997, pp. 236–46).

John had been trying to obtain control of Rochester since the start of the summer, but had been unable to persuade the archbishop of Canterbury to surrender it. In early October, the rebels, based in London, stole a march on the king and occupied the castle, presumably with the consent of the archbishop and his resident constable. It was a major coup, but the new rebel garrison had little time to savour it. Two days later John was outside the gates and the siege began.

To judge from the reports of contemporary chroniclers, the king gave Rochester as good a battering as he was able. We read of five great stone-throwing machines, which by this date must surely have been trebuchets, and a bombardment that did not cease day or night. But the king's barrage, although it must have had some effect on the morale of the defenders, apparently had little effect on the fabric of the castle. In the end John was forced to drive a mine under the southern corner of the great tower in the hope of causing a collapse. On 28 November, some 7 weeks into the siege, he sent a celebrated writ to his chief minister, Hubert de Burgh, urgently commanding the delivery to Rochester of forty bacon pigs 'the fattest and the least good for eating'. Their fat would fuel the fire in the mine under the castle, burning away the wooden pit props. And so it happened. The mine was collapsed, and with it almost a quarter of Rochester's great tower. Remarkably, this did not mark the end of the siege. The rebels inside the tower continued to fight on, using the cross-wall as a last line of defence. In the end it was the prospect of imminent starvation that persuade them to submit two days later. 'Living memory does not recall', wrote the contemporary Barnwell Annalist, 'a siege so fiercely pressed, and so staunchly resisted' (Morris 2012b, pp. 75–6 and 81–9).

The conclusion is quickly told. Despite his success at Rochester, John never mustered the courage for a decisive assault on the remaining rebels in London, and so the war ground on into 1216. The stalemate was not resolved until the following October, when the king contracted dysentery and died. Since John himself had been the principal cause of the war, his sudden removal opened the way for peace; it was far more difficult to justify rebellion against his blameless nine-year-old son, now crowned as Henry III. The new king's regents reissued Magna Carta, this time in good faith, and very soon peace was restored (Morris 2012b, pp. 90–3).

Restoring Rochester, however, took considerably longer. Repairs to the masonry were not completed until 1227, and another 5 years passed before it was re-floored and re-roofed. It was not in fact, a true restoration, more in the way of a repair job, for the quality of the new stonework is noticeably inferior to that of the original. The stone used for the fine details was not from Caen, as in the 1120s, but from Reigate (Goodall 2006, p. 268).

The design of the exterior was also different. Where there had once been a square corner, the king's masons replaced it with a round one. Round towers had become popular in England around the turn of the 12th and 13th centuries. Castle historians of old regarded this as a military development, arguing that round towers were more resistant to missiles and mining. Latterly we have been taught to regard this simply as a matter of changing architectural fashion. The rebuild at Rochester, however, suggests that, at least in this particular instance, the old school had it right. There seems to have been little concern here with aesthetics; the new round tower, to my eye at least, makes a considerable mess of what had been a handsome building. The concern was evidently to make the vulnerable southern corner of the great tower stronger – witness the new drum tower, with its two levels of arrowloops, inserted into the curtain wall at the same moment. Whether such a design actually meant the building was more resilient is besides the point; the point is that contemporaries believed that it did.

The patched-up Rochester enjoyed a protracted afterlife. After 1215 it was exclusively a royal castle – there was no longer any question of sharing ownership with Canterbury. The most sustained royal interest was shown by John's son, Henry III, who visited many times during his reign and who commissioned new royal apartments in the bailey – all now vanished, but described in some detail in the king's orders to his workmen. Towards the end of Henry's reign the castle was again besieged, in the course of the king's struggle against his celebrated brother-in-law, Simon de Montfort. Compared with the great siege of 1215, this one of 1264 was little more than a scuffle. Montfort spent a week trying to force out Rochester's royalist garrison before news of Henry's own advance sent him scurrying back to London. More damage was done by the defenders, who responded to Montfort's advance by destroying the king's new hall, presumably because it compromised the castle's defensibility.

The siege of 1264, however, did mark the beginning of Rochester's long decline. Very little was spent on repairs during the reign of Henry's son, the imperious Edward I, famed though he was a castle-builder in Wales. An inquiry of 1275 found that a good deal of Rochester's fabric had been pilfered by an earlier constable, John Potyn, who had carried off lead, stone, timber, an oriel window and some 3000 tiles. More was spent in the 14th century by Edward III and Richard II, but only on repairs to the great tower, and the mural towers in the bailey wall – the royal apartments within the bailey remained ruinous and derelict (Ashbee 2006, pp. 250–64).

Unsurprisingly, therefore, Rochester saw few royal visits in the centuries that followed. The reception of Henry VIII's fourth wife, Anne of Cleves, in 1540 was the last of any consequence. In the early 17th century James I gave the site to Sir Anthony Weldon and, as we've seen, Samuel Pepys described it as being in ruins in 1665. Two centuries later it was bought by the Corporation of the City of Rochester and its bailey laid out as a park. It is now managed – appropriately, given the terms on which its tower was originally built – as a joint concern by the city and English Heritage (Peats and Drury 2009, pp. 54–9, 69 and 73).

## Bibliography

Ashbee, J. (2006) 'The medieval buildings and topography of Rochester Castle', in T. Ayers and T. Tatton-Brown, ed., *Medieval Art, Architecture and Archaeology at Rochester*, British Archaeological Association Conference Transactions 28, pp. 250–64.

Coulson, C. (2001) 'Peaceable power in English castles', *Anglo-Norman Studies* 23, pp. 69–95.

English, B. (1995) 'Towns, mottes and ring-works of the Conquest', in A. Ayton and J. L. Price, ed., *The Medieval Military Revolution*, pp. 45–61 (London, Tauris).

Garmonsway, G. N., ed. (1972) *The Anglo-Saxon Chronicle* (London, Everyman).

Goodall, J. A. A. (2006) 'The Great Tower of Rochester Castle', in A. Ayton and J. L. Price, ed., *Medieval Art, Architecture and Archaeology at Rochester*, British Archaeological Association Conference Transactions 28, pp. 265–99.

Morris, M. (2012a) *The Norman Conquest* (London, Hutchinson).

Morris, M. (2012b) *Castle: A History of the Buildings that Shaped Medieval Britain* (London, Windmill).

Peats, R. and Drury, P. (2009) *Rochester Castle Conservation Plan, Part 1: Understanding and Significance*, (Chelmsford, The Paul Drury Partnership). Available at: http://www.visitmedway.org/xsdbimgs/Consul%20P1.pdf.

Warren, W. L. (1997) *King John* (New Haven and London, Yale University Press).

Williams, A. and Martin, G. H., ed. (2002) *Domesday Book: A Complete Translation* (London, Penguin).

# 6

# Le château de Falaise: bilan de 150 ans de restaurations dans plus de 1000 ans d'histoire

*Charlotte Lapiche et Benoît Panozzo*

## Summary

*As early as the late 10th century, Falaise Castle was protected by stone fortifications and perched atop a rocky outcrop that acted as a natural defence. It was regularly strengthened during the 12th and 15th centuries so as to follow the evolution of architectural defence. It was later abandoned during the 16th century as it lost both its effectiveness and usefulness in terms of protection. It was only during the 19th century that the site was brought back to life in a context of renewed interest in the medieval period, when the concept of ancient monuments finally emerged. It was listed as an historic building in 1840 as it was of prime interest in terms of heritage, but also because of its grave state of disrepair. The castle benefitted from these early national measures of protection as well as through the associated funding. A lengthy period of restoration work began. Following the damage incurred during the World War Two, new campaigns of work followed repairs by previous architects. After centuries of neglect, the castle progressively recovered its lost identity. More restoration campaigns continued under chief architects for historical monuments, who all intervened in a contemporary way, rebuilding, recreating and recalling lost elements. These interventions are now fully part of the castle's history.*

## Introduction

### *Présentation générale du site*

À 30km au sud de Caen, Falaise et son château sont situés à la jonction de deux régions naturelles: au nord, une plaine sédimentaire calcaire fertile qui s'étend jusqu'à la mer et inclut la plaine de Caen; au sud, la limite orientale du massif armoricain dont l'escarpement de grès et de schistes sert de socle au château et à sa ville intra-muros (Figure 6.1).

À l'époque médiévale, ville et château sont au carrefour de grandes routes commerciales et de pèlerinage. Cette situation privilégiée au sud du duché entre Bretagne et Ile de France recueille la faveur des ducs de Normandie pour l'implantation d'une place forte. La cité verra naître en 1027 le plus célèbre d'entre eux: Guillaume de Normandie.

Le château se présente aujourd'hui sous la forme d'une enceinte orientée sud-est nord-ouest au tracé irrégulier imposé par la topographie. Il est bordé de part et d'autre par les vallées de deux rivières, l'Ante et le Marescot. Le rempart, flanqué d'une quinzaine de tours semi-circulaires, enserre un espace d'un hectare et demi environ, séparé par un fossé en une haute et une basse cour. L'ensemble est dominé au nord-ouest par la masse de trois donjons: deux tours-résidences quadrangulaires du XIIe siècle – dites Grand et Petit Donjon, et une tour maîtresse cylindrique de modèle philippien, dite Tour Talbot, attribuable au début du XIIIe siècle.[1] La ville fortifiée qui s'est développée aux pieds du château a conservé plus de deux kilomètres de remparts et une trentaine de tours d'enceinte (Figure 6.2).

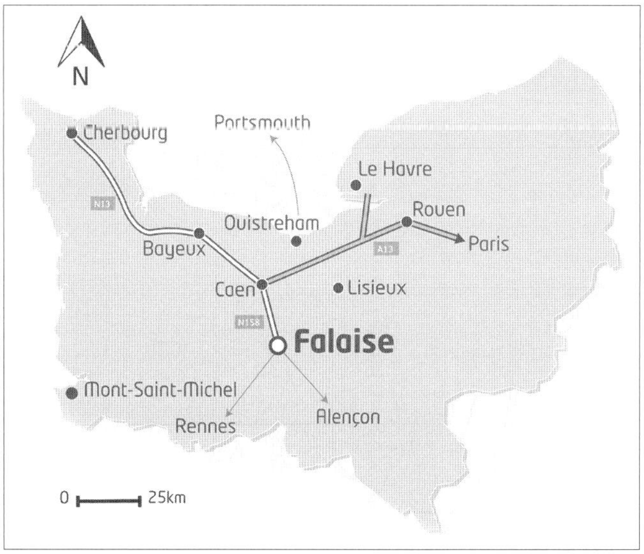


*Figure 6.1. Carte de la Normandie.*

### *Brève histoire du site: (Figure 6.3)*

Le tracé de l'enceinte actuelle remonte pour ses pans les plus anciens à la fin du Xe siècle ou au tout début du XIe siècle. À cette époque, il est probable que le château soit déjà constitué d'une haute cour et d'une basse cour sans doute séparées par un fossé, cet ensemble étant peut être déjà commandé par un donjon de pierre.

Le site aujourd'hui, bien qu'appuyé sur ces vestiges plus anciens, est profondément marqué par les campagnes de fortification menées par les héritiers de Guillaume le Conquérant durant la période anglo-normande, et par le roi de France de retour sur ses terres en 1204. C'est le roi Philippe Auguste ou ses successeurs du XIIIe siècle qui achèvent de donner au site sa silhouette actuelle: extension de l'enceinte vers l'ouest, édification de la tour Talbot, construction de poternes et du châtelet d'entrée de la haute cour, création de nouvelles tours de flanquement.

Aux XIVe et XVe siècles, le château s'adapte aux nouvelles techniques de la guerre: les ouvertures de tirs de certaines tours sont modifiées et des terrasses d'artillerie sont créées pour intégrer l'emploi du canon au système défensif (Figure 6.4). Autre témoin des remaniements de cette époque, certaines baies autrefois utilisées pour la défense sont remaniées pour répondre à des finalités résidentielles (Figure 6.5). Mais ces travaux restent mineurs et n'ont pas d'impact significatif sur la physionomie du site.

Pendant toute la période médiévale et durant les Guerres de Religion, le château de Falaise connaît de nombreux sièges dont les occupants sortiront rarement vainqueurs. Cette histoire mouvementée s'achève au début du XVIIe siècle, lorsque le site – au même titre que d'autres châteaux ayant comme lui perdu de leur intérêt militaire – est déclassé.

Commence alors une longue période de désintérêt et d'abandon qui va durer jusqu'au XIXe siècle. Elle s'accompagne chez les Falaisiens d'une perte de vue progressive de l'identité du monument: la basse cour, vide de tout bâti médiéval à l'exception du chœur de la chapelle Saint-Nicolas, devient peu à peu synonyme de parc public, les donjons seuls étant dès lors identifiés comme constituant 'le château'.

## Les campagnes de restaurations du XIXe siècle: renaissance du site

Symbole de l'Ancien Régime et de la féodalité, le château de Falaise échappe de peu aux destructions de la Révolution. La municipalité révolutionnaire songe à vendre les donjons comme carrière de matériaux avant d'y renoncer faute d'acheteur, et les divers projets de réutilisation des donjons – fonderie de plomb, gendarmerie, maison d'arrêt – ne sont qu'envisagés. En 1803, cependant, la ville décide d'implanter un collège dans l'enceinte castrale (Figure 6.6). Les bâtiments de l'établissement sont adossés contre le rempart nord, à l'emplacement de l'ancien logis des vicomtes puis gouverneurs de Falaise. Ils intègrent certains éléments architecturaux de la période médiévale.[2] La basse cour, quant à elle, est aménagée en jardins. La présence du collège entraîne un relatif entretien des remparts, mais les donjons, déjà dégradés par des décennies d'abandon, sont délaissés.[3]

Les premiers véritables travaux de conservation et de restauration du château débutent dans les années 1840. Ils s'inscrivent dans un contexte de forte prise de conscience de la nécessité de sauvegarder les monuments historiques.[4] En 1840, Le château de Falaise est inscrit sur la première 'liste des monuments pour lesquels des secours ont été demandés'.[5] Le monument va bénéficier des premières mesures de protection nationale et des subsides qui y sont liés. La longue période de restaurations commence: elle ne s'arrêtera quasiment pas jusqu'à aujourd'hui.

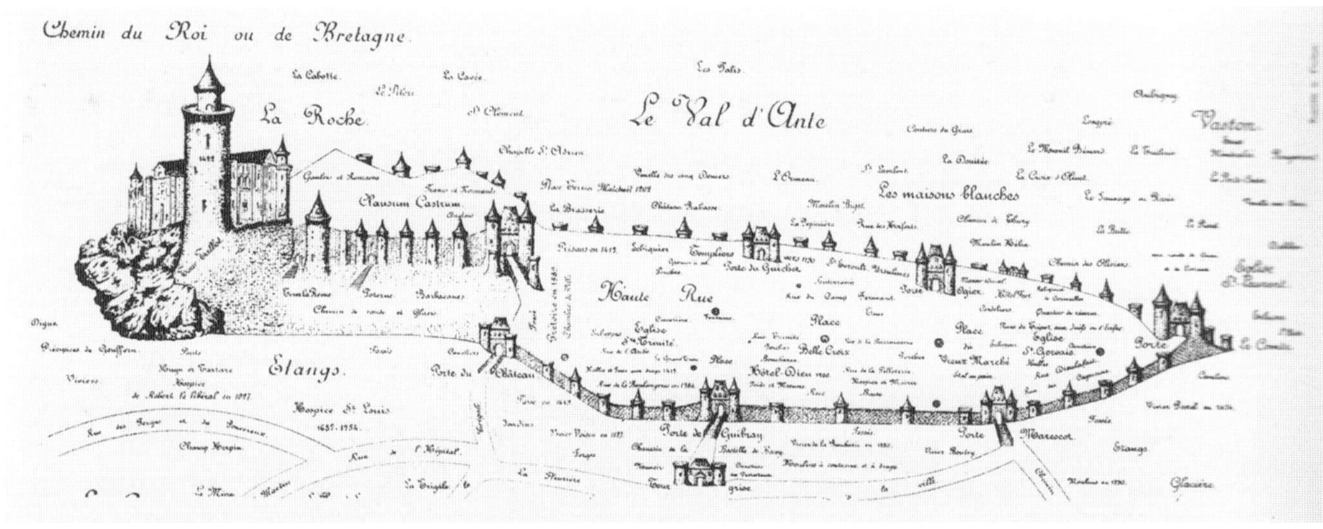


*Figure 6.2. Dessin d'Amédée Mériel daté de 1889 présentant le château et l'enceinte urbaine de Falaise (Collection de la Médiathèque du Pays de Falaise).*

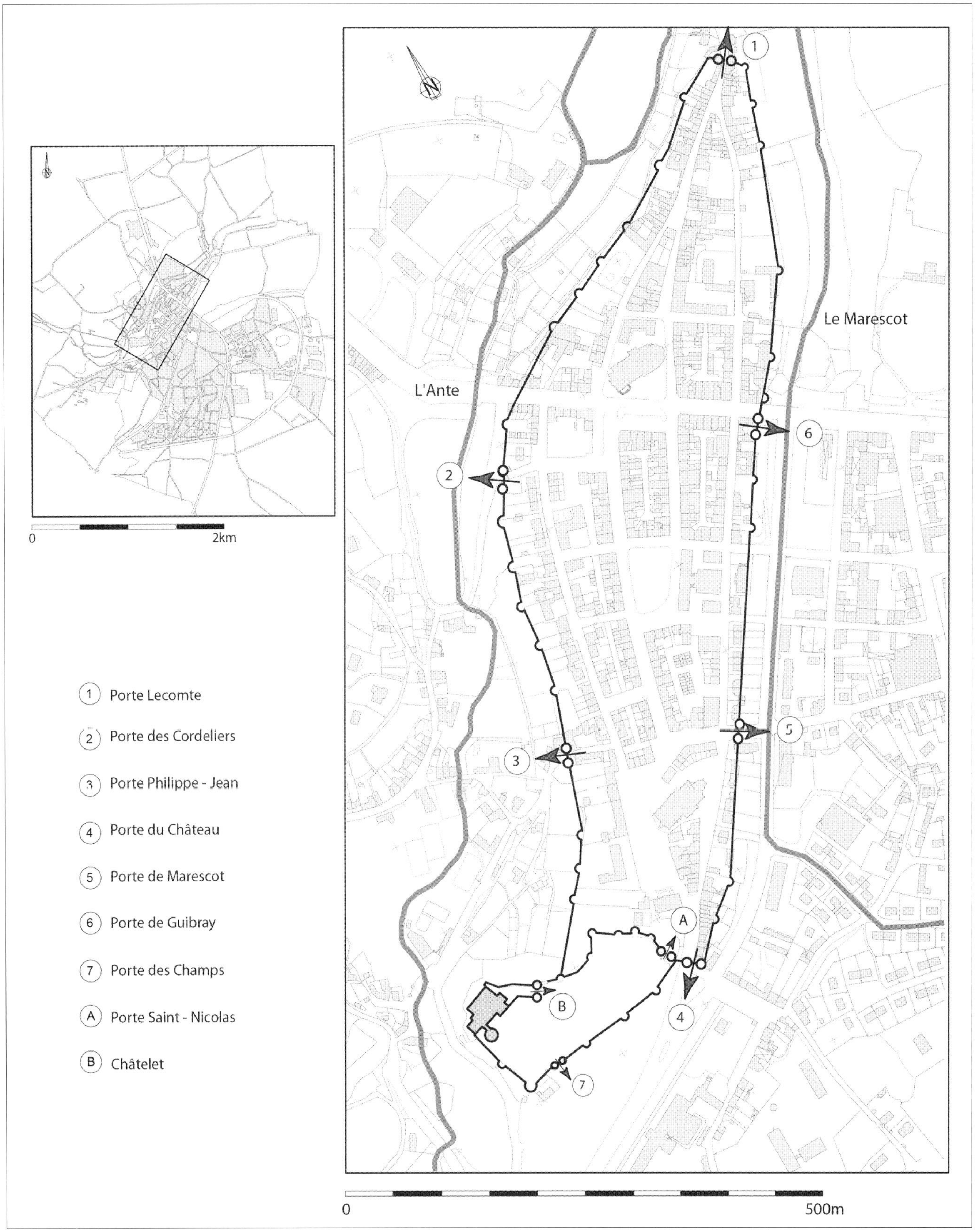


*Figure 6.3. Plan de la ville de Falaise et de la double enceinte castrale et urbaine.*

*Figure 6.4. Canonnière de tour d'enceinte. 1ère moitié du XVe siècle (Ville de Falaise).*

*Figure 6.5. Baie à meneaux de la tour philipienne. 1ère moitié du XVe siècle (Ville de Falaise).*

## Les interventions des XIXe et XXe siècles (Figure 6.7)

L'aspect de l'édifice avant intervention des architectes s'apparente à celui d'une belle ruine romantique. En 1843, un premier architecte, Jean-Charles Danjoy, est mandaté par la commission des monuments historiques pour intervenir

*Figure 6.6. Façade sud du collège construit dans la basse cour du château en 1803 (carte postale, Collection de la Médiathèque du Pays de Falaise).*

au château. Il décrit dans son rapport préliminaire le grand état de délabrement du site, notamment des donjons.[6] Il réalise les premiers relevés précis du monument et fournit des devis pour la réalisation de travaux d'urgence. Les interventions qu'il envisage concernent surtout la Tour Talbot et le Grand Donjon – élimination de la végétation minant les maçonneries, reprise des murs abimés à la base du Grand Donjon et en élévation, restitution d'une des baies géminées détruite sur le modèle de celles encore existantes, mise hors-d'eau des murs, rétablissement ou restauration des voûtes des baies, des escaliers et de la chapelle palatine. Il propose aussi, après réfection des murs et parapets, de 'rendre à la tour [Talbot] son toit en charpente couvert d'ardoises, ce serait un moyen d'abri plus sûr et plus historique'.[7] Pour cette restitution, il croit pouvoir se baser sur les vestiges de charpente encore visibles au sommet de l'édifice et sur une gravure du début du XVIIIe siècle. Le Petit Donjon, considéré comme une simple annexe du Grand, doit être simplement consolidé. Les remparts et les bâtiments de l'enceinte sont laissés sous la responsabilité de la municipalité et du collège. Si son jugement est parfois peu sûr, faisant la part belle à l'imagination et à l'interprétation gratuite – il n'identifie pas la chapelle du Grand Donjon qu'il interprète comme un 'arsenal' et date très approximativement l'édifice 'du Xe ou du XIe siècle', il établit des mesures claires pour prévenir l'effondrement imminent des donjons. Seule une petite partie des travaux projetés sera réalisée: la Tour Talbot et le Petit Donjon n'ont pas été traités, le Grand Donjon ne l'a été que partiellement. Les parties basses des deux donjons romans restent encombrées par les débris des toitures, des planchers et de maçonneries qui s'y sont effondrés. Ils exercent une poussée dangereuse sur la base des murs et menacent la survie même des deux édifices. On le voit, cette première intervention programmée au château présente donc un bilan contrasté[8] (Figure 6.8).

La nomination de l'architecte Victor Ruprich-Robert par la commission des Monuments historiques va changer la donne de ces interventions.[9] Il mène une étude historique et architecturale rigoureuse du monument avant de proposer un projet de réhabilitation complète des trois donjons qui va guider les travaux de restauration jusqu'au début du XXe siècle.[10] Son approche des monuments est basée sur un examen attentif de la mise en œuvre des maçonneries et un travail de comparaison stylistique avec des édifices mieux connus. Les datations qu'il propose pour le château sont souvent pertinentes. Ainsi, il est le premier à attribuer avec certitude le Grand Donjon au XIIe siècle.

De 1864 à 1870, cet homme réalise une campagne de conservation et de restauration du monument. Les travaux

*Figure 6.7. Gravure du début du XIXe siècle d'Olliamson représentant les donjons vus depuis la basse cour du château (Collection Ville de Falaise).*

*Figure 6.8. Projet de restauration des toitures de la Tour Talbot et relevé des donjons par l'architecte Danjoy (photo: RMN. Jean-Luc Paillé).*

vont préserver durablement le Grand Donjon roman qui reste malgré tout une coquille vide, l'architecte n'ayant restitué ni planchers, ni toitures. Une galerie en bois avec balustrade est installée le long des murs intérieurs du premier étage. Elle permet d'accéder aux baies, à la chapelle et d'observer les salles basses de l'édifice. La création de ces passerelles prend en compte la volonté de la ville de capter les visiteurs d'un tourisme monumental naissant.

En 1869, une vive querelle oppose Victor Ruprich-Robert et la municipalité. L'aumônier et les élèves du collège du château entreprennent une restauration du chœur de la chapelle Saint-Nicolas (XIIe siècle) située dans l'enceinte castrale, sans consultation des monuments historiques. L'architecte reproche la création indue d'une voûte qui risque selon lui de détruire les murs du chœur seulement destinés à l'origine à supporter une charpente. La municipalité se défend en arguant du fait que la chapelle ne fait pas partie du château et donc de la responsabilité de l'architecte en chef. Ruprich-Robert réaffirme que la chapelle appartient bien au château et relève de sa compétence. Il tient la ville et la direction du collège comme responsables de toute dégradation future qu'occasionnerait ces travaux et fait ordonner leur destruction. Mais cette demande ne sera jamais suivie d'effet. Cette anecdote montre que les élus de la Ville, pourtant propriétaire du lieu, considèrent que les donjons seuls constituent le château et que l'enceinte n'en fait pas partie. Cette confusion est encore fréquente aujourd'hui chez nombre de visiteurs mais aussi de Falaisiens.[11]

*Figure 6.9. Intervention du XIXe siècle dans le Grand Donjon (carte postale, Collection de la Médiathèque du Pays de Falaise).*

Les travaux prévus par Victor Ruprich-Robert pour le Grand Donjon se poursuivent après sa mort survenue en 1887. Ces interventions complémentaires s'étalent de 1892 à 1895: création d'un dallage au niveau inférieur pour l'écoulement des eaux pluviales, relèvement du mur de refend jusqu'au niveau du premier étage, remplacement de la galerie de circulation intérieure en bois du premier étage par des corniches maçonnées plus solides et plus sûres (Figure 6.9).

Au début du XXe siècle, le Petit Donjon et la Tour Talbot attendent toujours leur rénovation. Celle-ci a lieu de 1905 à 1913, sous la direction de l'architecte des monuments historiques Gabriel Ruprich-Robert, fils et élève de Victor Ruprich-Robert. Les travaux comprennent une réfection et une stabilisation durable des maçonneries du Petit Donjon et de la Tour Talbot, la mise hors d'eau de ces murs par pose d'un dallage à leur sommet, la restauration des aménagements intérieurs du niveau résidentiel du Petit Donjon – reprise des encadrements et des remplages des baies, restitution d'une cheminée dont seul subsistait le contre-cœur. Une galerie de circulation maçonnée est installée à l'étage du Petit Donjon, sur le même modèle que celle établie dans le Grand Donjon.

Le projet de restauration est défini par l'architecte en chef. Le suivi d'opération est confié à un architecte falaisien, Trolonge, qui est aussi architecte ordinaire des monuments historiques.[12] Suite à ces interventions, les murs des donjons sont sauvés, mais la physionomie du site est profondément modifiée. Bien que l'enceinte se dessine toujours clairement dans le paysage, seule la chapelle rappelle encore la forte densité du bâti dans la basse cour au Moyen Âge. Après-guerre, les restaurations effectuées au siècle précédent sont à reprendre. Les bombardements de 1944 ont peu touché les donjons mais les remparts est et sud sont endommagés. Le collège est presque entièrement détruit. Le chœur de la chapelle castrale a été soufflé par les bombes (Figure 6.10).

C'est dans ce contexte, en 1948, que la première fouille archéologique est menée sur le site. Elle est conduite par le Docteur Raoul Doranlo.[13] Chargé de fouiller la haute cour, devant la façade du Grand Donjon, il découvre les fondations d'un petit bâtiment rectangulaire qu'il identifie comme un 'avant-corps' dont la fonction était de défendre l'accès au donjon (Figure 6.11). Cette découverte ne conduira à aucun aménagement immédiat et le château ne subira pas de transformations notables avant les années 1980, moment où la Ville initie un projet de restauration d'envergure.

*Figure 6.10. Ruines du collège après les bombardements de 1944.*

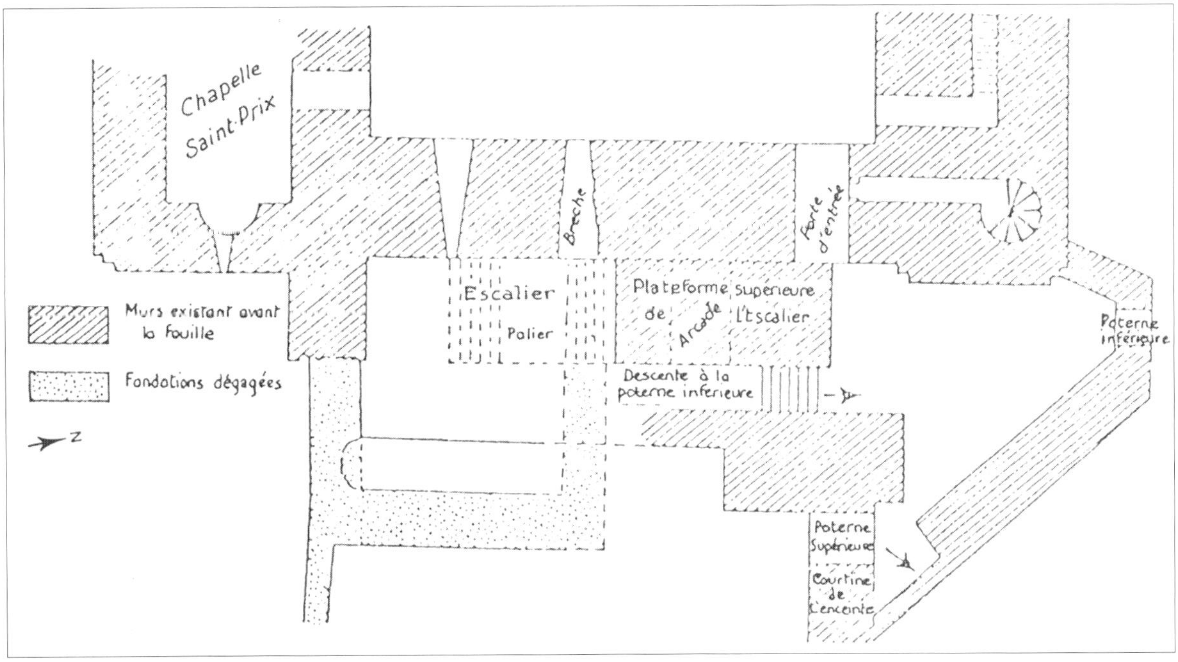


*Figure 6.11. Plan du bâtiment mis au jour en façade du Grand Donjon en 1948 (fouille du Dr Doranlo).*

La Ville met en place, en parallèle du programme de reconstruction de la cité endommagée à 80% le déblaiement de l'enceinte et des donjons. Les vestiges des bâtiments du collège encore debout, jugés sans valeur architecturale ou historique, sont abattus, le mur médiéval de l'ancien logis réapparait dans les décombres, les brèches dans les remparts sont réparées.

Les travaux sont réalisés entre 1945 et 1958 par deux architectes Maurice Berry puis Jean Merlet, ce dernier ayant assuré le suivi de la reconstruction de la Porte Saint-Nicolas qui s'est partiellement effondrée en 1958.

## La restauration de Bruno Decaris 1986–1996

En 1986, l'architecte entame une première réflexion visant à réhabiliter les donjons. Les murs porteurs sont intacts mais l'ensemble est peu compréhensible et en mauvais état. Toitures et planchers sont toujours manquants et les circulations intérieures sont tronquées.

S'appuyant sur les relevés des architectes précédents et les recherches documentaires existantes, Bruno Decaris ne peut proposer de restauration à l'identique. Ce constat le conduit à marquer clairement ses interventions. Là où il ne reste aucune trace des installations anciennes, il utilise des matériaux modernes ou détournés de leur emploi classique comme le plomb et le verre pour les sols. Son objectif est d'évoquer les parties disparues sans faux-semblant, et de restituer au monument sa lisibilité.

Le traitement de ces restitutions répond aux règles de conservation énoncées en 1964 dans la 'charte de Venise' proposée par l'Unesco et adoptées par la France.[14] Elle précise clairement qu'il ne faut pas créer de confusions entre 'l'ancien' et le 'faux ancien' comme cela a pu l'être auparavant dans certains monuments. Elle oblige par ailleurs à procéder à des interventions architecturales 'réversibles'.

*Figure 6.12. Restauration de la Tour Talbot (Ville de Falaise).*

Si il est indéniable que l'architecte a procédé au croisement de toutes les sources disponibles on peut toutefois déplorer l'absence d'une étude archéologique complète préalable au projet de restauration.

Les restaurations commencent par la Tour Talbot (Figure 6.12). Exemple majeur de l'architecture philipienne, cette tour est mieux préservée que les donjons normands. Mais bien que conservé sur toute sa hauteur, le donjon a perdu à l'intérieur certains de ses planchers de bois et de ses voûtes de pierres. C'est l'objet principal de cette intervention, avec le traitement du couronnement disparu. Les matériaux choisis pour cette restauration sont la pierre, le métal et la feuille de plomb pour les toitures. Les travaux sur les donjons quadrangulaires sont menés de 1992 à 1996. Le Grand Donjon attribué à Henri Ier Beauclerc est daté de 1123. C'est une tour résidence dont le premier étage abrite un ensemble palatial tripartite *aula*, *camera* et *capella*, disposition classique à l'époque dans les logis nobles. Les interventions portent sur le rétablissement des niveaux de sols, la restitution des volumes et des circulations intérieurs et sur la création de toitures.

Pour le traitement des sols, l'architecte opte dans la *aula*, espace particulièrement emblématique du statut aristocratique du lieu, pour un dallage de plomb et de verre: matériaux nobles qui rappellent la dimension ostentatoire de la pièce (Figure 6.13). La camera est revêtue de dalles de plomb et la *capella* (chapelle palatine) bénéficie d'un traitement en dallage de pierres (Figure 6.14). Le type de couverture et les dimensions des toitures d'origines sont inconnus, des hypothèses existent mais ne peuvent être vérifiées. Mis à part pour la chapelle dont les voûtes d'arêtes peuvent être restituées, le traitement des couvertures de la salle publique et de la salle privée est plus difficile à appréhender. La présence du mur de refend, l'épaisseur des murs, sont des indicateurs de la portée et de l'orientation des charpentes. Mais les éléments sont jugés trop minces pour entreprendre une restitution. Le choix de l'architecte se porte alors sur une toiture de toile en téflon tendue sur une charpente métallique.

Le Petit Donjon, situé sur le côté ouest de l'éperon rocheux est de dimensions plus modestes. Daté de la seconde moitié du XIIe siècle, son étage résidentiel se compose d'une salle dont les fenêtres ont été remaniées au XVe siècle avec l'ajout de baies gothiques pourvues en partie basse de canonnières (Figure 6.15). Les sols du Petit Donjon sont identiques à ceux proposés dans la *camera*, les baies sont restaurées, un escalier métallique évoque celui disparu et les murs intérieurs sont recouverts d'un enduit de chaux, comme dans le Grand Donjon (Figure 6.16).

La réflexion sur « l'avant-corps » intervient à la toute fin du chantier. Absente du projet initial, elle se fonde sur plusieurs éléments dont l'étude et la fouille menées en 1948

*Figure 6.13. Aula du Grand Donjon restaurée (Ville de Falaise).*

*Figure 6.14. Camera du Grand Donjon (Ville de Falaise).*

*Figure 6.15. Fenêtre du Petit Donjon après restauration (Ville de Falaise).*

*Figure 6.16. Petit Donjon après restauration (Ville de Falaise).*

par le Docteur Raoul Doranlo au pied du Grand Donjon et sur l'analogie avec d'autres édifices normands situés de part et d'autre de la Manche. L'analyse notamment de l'avant-corps du donjon de Castle Rising s'est avérée précieuse. L'avant-corps proposé reprend l'emprise au sol du bâtiment mis au jour à l'occasion de la fouille mais les données sont lacunaires et l'architecte opte, une fois de plus, pour une évocation des volumes disparus. Les matériaux choisis, le béton et le métal, soulignent sa fonction défensive (Figure 6.17).

Suite à cette campagne, les donjons rouvrent leurs portes mais le projet falaisien n'est pas terminé. Porté par la municipalité et soutenu financièrement par le Conseil général du Calvados, le Conseil régional de Basse-Normandie et l'Etat via le ministère de la Culture et la Direction régionale des affaires culturelles, il se poursuit. L'objectif étant une restauration complète du site.

## Les restaurations de Daniel Lefèvre 1998–2014

### *Le projet de la haute cour 1998–2003*

Ainsi, à la fin des années 1990, un nouveau programme de restauration visant à restituer les éléments défensifs de la haute cour au Moyen Âge commence. La maîtrise d'œuvre est confiée à Daniel Lefèvre, successeur de Bruno Decaris comme architecte en chef des monuments historiques du Calvados, qui s'adjoint les compétences des archéologues et d'une archiviste, Isabelle Chave, à qui il commande une étude exhaustive.[15]

Pour bâtir le projet il fait appel à une équipe d'archéologues et bénéficie dans son approche des premières analyses de Pascal Couanon lequel pense identifier dans le fossé dès 1986, les arases d'une tour ayant pu appartenir à un châtelet à deux tours.[16] cette hypothèse est confirmée par la fouille menée par François Delahaye en 1998, lequel met au jour les fondations de la tour sud du châtelet; sa jumelle, bien que très dégradée, étant encore visible dans le rempart nord.[17]

L'architecte propose une restitution la plus proche possible des dispositions d'origine; mais toute la courtine sud le long du fossé a disparu et son tracé est difficile à définir. Comme Bruno Decaris avant lui, Daniel Lefèvre choisit de marquer les parties disparues avec un traitement moderne: les murs de pierres sont élevés et enfermés dans des gabions de métal, leurs lignes sont interrompues et marquées à intervalles irréguliers par des garde-corps métalliques (Figure 6.18). Pour le franchissement du fossé, il choisit de poser une passerelle suspendue, faute d'avoir pu identifier de manière formelle les piles de l'ancien pont sur lesquelles il aurait pu appuyer sa construction.

### *Le projet 'remparts' 2007–2015*

Dernier volet et en conclusion des campagnes de restaurations menées depuis presque vingt ans en vue d'une exploitation touristique du site naît en 2005 le projet

*Figure 6.17. Evocation de l'avant corps disparu (Ville de Falaise).*

'Remparts'. Il concerne le traitement de l'enceinte castrale et vise également par l'aménagement des abords et des cheminements intérieurs à rétablir, autant que possible, le caractère défensif du site. Le vocabulaire architectural retenu pour ce projet reste simple et se résume à quelques matériaux, pierre, bois, inox et béton pour l'évocation des niveaux de sols des tours. Il ne vise pas – sauf pour le front ouest – à restituer des volumes disparus mais tend à consolider des vestiges en place. Par la création de cheminements le long des murs intérieurs, il invite les visiteurs à découvrir les courtines, les ouvertures de tirs et les tours d'enceinte. Ce programme mené là encore par Daniel Lefèvre se décompose en quatre phases.

La première phase de restauration est la plus audacieuse du projet, elle consiste à restaurer l'accès au château en creusant le talus artificiel situé au pied de la Porte Saint-Nicolas et à poser une passerelle pour rétablir le franchissement du fossé. Dès les premières interventions, l'équipe d'archéologues en charge du suivi de chantier met au jour les vestiges de l'avant-cour, espace fortifié renseigné par les quittances médiévales mais jamais identifié. Le projet est alors modifié en conséquence afin d'intégrer ces vestiges datés des XIVe et XVe siècles.

Les phases suivantes vont traiter successivement des remparts est, sud et ouest:

A l'est, les murs de courtines et les tours sont restaurés, les niveaux perdus des chambres de tirs sont restitués et le Bastion fait l'objet d'une fouille exhaustive. A l'intérieur de la basse cour, le long des remparts, un cheminement en pierres posées de chant est proposé afin de guider les visiteurs vers ces espaces nouvellement restaurés.

L'intégration des données archéologiques est essentielle et contribue à chaque étape à modifier le projet initial. Dans cette phase les vestiges du rempart primitif conduisent l'architecte à abandonner le projet de salle d'interprétation au profit d'un espace à ciel ouvert. Autre exemple des apports de l'archéologie: les datations des courtines apportées par les archéologues ont été rendues visibles dans la restauration par l'emploi de joints de parements de teintes différentes. Les couleurs ocres rouges sont utilisés pour les parties les plus anciennes (antérieures au XIIIe siècle) et les ocres clairs pour les parties XIIIe siècle et postérieures.

Au sud, les maçonneries extérieures sont très endommagées et les reprises seront importantes, l'analyse des parements et les datations par carbone 14 vont là encore changer la chronologie admise de ce rempart: il s'avère plus ancien qu'on ne le supposait. Attribué jusqu'alors au XIIIe siècle, une grande partie de son tracé remonterait en fait à la charnière des Xe–XIe siècles. Certaines de ses tours de flanquement quant à elles seraient attribuables à la période Plantagenêt.

La dernière phase de restauration concerne le secteur sud-ouest de la cour dite de la Reine. Cette zone est difficile à appréhender par l'architecte, lequel découvre rapidement que l'extension de la cour vers l'ouest est artificielle et

*Figure 6.18. Haute cour après restauration (Ville de Falaise).*

*Figure 6.19. Intervention sur le rempart ouest (Ville de Falaise).*

se compose de remblais rapportés, uniquement retenus par le rempart lui-même. La nature instable du sol étant peut-être à l'origine de l'effondrement de la courtine ouest dès le XVIe siècle. En préalable à toute intervention de maçonnerie, l'architecte apporte une solution technique adaptée pour assurer la pérennité du rempart à reconstituer. Un système de micro-pieux ancrés dans le talus est mis en place pour constituer une structure porteuse sur laquelle le mur maçonné viendra s'adosser en la masquant totalement (Figure 6.19). La tour Ravenel dont il ne reste que l'arase sera remontée sur la base de quelques assises.

## Conclusion

Les différentes campagnes de restaurations menées depuis le XIXe siècle, pour certaines d'entre elles éclairées par un suivi archéologique systématique, ont totalement renouvelé notre connaissance de l'histoire du château de Falaise. Un important travail d'étude reste à mener sur ce site et les inconnues sont encore nombreuses mais notre vision globale de cet exemple majeur de l'architecture médiévale en Normandie s'affine un peu plus chaque jour.

Les restaurations menées depuis presque 150 ans maintenant sur le site, que l'on juge certaines d'entre elles contestables ou pas, composent le début d'un nouveau chapitre passionnant dans la longue existence de ce monument remarquable.

C'est cette identité dans toute sa pluralité qui doit être considérée dans tout projet à venir.

## Notes

1 Sa datation autour de 1207, donc immédiatement après le retour de la Normandie dans le domaine royal, fait aujourd'hui consensus. Régnier, pp. 478–80; *Recueil des historiens des Gaules et de la France* T. 24 (1904) (Paris), p. 56.
2 Notamment les baies à coussièges visibles aujourd'hui dans le bâtiment d'accueil.
3 Si l'on excepte la réfection de la voûte du sommet de la Tour Talbot réalisée en 1834 par la municipalité, avec le concours financier du conseil général du Calvados et du gouvernement. Mais le calcaire employé pour les travaux s'avère d'une qualité très insuffisante. En outre, la nouvelle voûte est laissée sans couverture, exposée aux intempéries. L'intervention n'arrête pas les infiltrations d'eau qui continuent à détériorer les murs.
4 Création du poste d'inspecteur des monuments historiques en 1830 et de la commission des monuments historiques en 1837.
5 La liste de 1840 comporte 1082 monuments – dont 932 édifices – requérant des mesures urgentes de conservation en raison de leur intérêt patrimonial. Elle a été dressée à l'instigation de Prosper Mérimée, alors inspecteur des monuments historiques. Les édifices retenus sont en majorité médiévaux.
6 *Rapport au ministre de l'intérieur sur l'état actuel et les réparations à faire au château de Falaise* du 28 avril 1843.
7 *Ibidem.*
8 Jean-Charles Danjoy était considéré par sa hiérarchie comme un bon architecte, excellent dessinateur – les relevés qu'il a dressés du château le prouvent assez, mais fantaisiste. Ses relations avec les autorités centrales et locales sont souvent difficiles et placent son administration dans l'embarras. C'est semble-t-il le cas à Falaise où il cesse d'honorer sa mission dès 1845, sans avoir achevé ses travaux. Jusqu'en 1854 au moins, l'inspection des monuments historiques continue de solliciter l'architecte pour avis, lequel ne répond pas.
9 La création d'un véritable statut d'architecte en chef des monuments historique (ACMH) a lieu avec la mise en place d'un concours de recrutement en 1893, suivie en 1907 par un décret qui institue en corps les architectes en chef, faisant d'eux des agents de la fonction publique. Avant cela, les restaurations sont confiées à des architectes locaux, rapidement remplacés par des architectes parisiens ayant étudié l'architecture du Moyen Âge.
10 Victor Ruprich-Robert, *Rapport sur le château de Falaise (Calvados) à son excellence Monsieur le Ministre de la Maison de l'Empereur et des Beaux-arts*, 1 septembre 1863.
11 À ce sujet, et plus généralement pour ce qui concerne la chapelle Saint-Nicolas du château de Falaise, voir l'article très complet d'Isabelle Chave (Chave 2005).
12 Créés en 1897, les architectes ordinaires sont les relais locaux des architectes en chef. Ce sont des architectes libéraux nommés dans leur département. Ils assurent le suivi des restaurations et l'entretien des édifices classés au titre des monuments historiques. Ils sont remplacés en 1946 par les Architectes des bâtiments de France (ABF), aux compétences nettement élargies.
13 Médecin et archéologue, membre de la Société des antiquaires de Normandie.
14 Charte internationale sur la conservation et la restauration des monuments et des sites, dite Charte de Venise. Proposée par l'IIe Congrès international des architectes et des techniciens des monuments historiques, réunis à Venise en mai 1964. Ce traité pose un cadre international pour la préservation des édifices anciens validé en 1965 par l'ICOMOS (International Council on Monuments and Sites), organisation non gouvernementale agissant comme organe consultatif de l'Unesco pour l'application de la convention. Adoptée par la France, elle oriente depuis lors les interventions sur les monuments patrimoniaux.
15 Chave 1999.
16 Couanon 1987.
17 Delahaye 1998.

## Bibliographie


Boüard, M. de (1984) *Guillaume le Conquérant* (Paris, Fayard).

Brown, R. (2008) 'Falaise, Le château – Bastion nord-est', *Bilan Scientifique de la région Basse-Normandie*, pp. 43–4.

Carré, G. avec la collaboration de Fauq, B. (2003) *Étude préliminaire des parements extérieurs de l'enceinte castrale et sondages archéologiques (10 février/21 mars 2003)*, rapport dactylographié, DRAC BN–SRA 1648 (Caen).

Chave, I. (1999) *Le château de Falaise (Calvados) au Moyen Age à nos jours. Etude archéologique et documentaire*, 3 volumes, dactylographiés, DRAC–SRA 1226 (Caen).

Chave, I. (2002) *Château de Falaise (Calvados). L'enceinte castrale et ses abords (XIe–XXe s.). Étude archéologique et documentaire*, rapport dactylographié, DRAC BN–CRMH (Caen).

Chave, I. (2005) 'Des sources comptables au service de l'archéologie: essai de reconstruction documentaire de la chapelle dite Saint-Nicolas du château de Falaise (Calvados), XIIe–XVe Siècles', *Tabularia* 'Études' 5, 14 décembre 2005, pp. 75–124.

Couanon, P. (1987) *Le château de Falaise (Calvados) 1985–1986, Fouilles de sauvetage dans l'enceinte castrale*, rapport dactylographié, DRAC BN–SRA 57.

Decaëns, J. (1997) 'Le château de Falaise', dans M. Bayle, sous la dir., *L'architecture normande au Moyen Age*, Vol. 2, pp. 305–9.

Decaris, B. (1988) *Le Château de Falaise*, Monuments historiques 159.

Delahaye, F. (1998) Château de Falaise (Calvados), rampe d'accès aux donjons, DFS de sauvetage, AFAN. DRAC BN–SRA 1126.

Delahaye, F. (2001) *Falaise (Calvados). Le château. Bâtiment d'accueil. DFS de sauvetage*. AFAN, DRAC BN–SRA1382.

Delahaye, F. (2005) *Falaise (Basse-Normandie – Calvados). Le château, Bastion nord-est. Rapport de diagnostic archéologique*, INRAP, DRAC BN–SRA 1728.

Doranlo, R. (1946–1948) 'les fouilles de 1948 dans le château de Falaise', *Bulletin de la Société des Antiquaires de Normandie* L, pp. 496–501.

Doranlo, R. (1954) 'Le château de Falaise', *Congrès archéologique de France*, XI, session tenue dans l'Orne en 1953, pp. 181–200.

German, P. (1994) (éd. définitive) *Histoire de Falaise* (Condé-sur-Noireau, Éditions Charles Corlet).

Hurel, J-M. (1880) *Le château de Falaise, étude historique* (Falaise, Imprimerie de Mlle E. Trolonge).

Langevin, P-G. (1814) *Recherches historiques sur Falaise* (Falaise, Imprimeur-Libraire Brée l'aîné).

Lefèvre, D. (2003) *Château de Falaise. Etude préalable à la restauration et à la mise en valeur de l'ensemble des remparts et de leurs abords (hormis le front nord-ouest)*, dossier d'étude rendu par l'architecte en chef des monuments historiques, CRMH – DRAC BN.

Mastrolorenzo, J. (2009) *Falaise (Calvados) Le château, Sondages,* rapport, DRAC BN–SRA.

Mastrolorenzo, J. (2009) *Note sur les résultats d'analyse par le Radiocarbone des prélèvements de charbon de bois effectués sur le front est de l'enceinte du château de Falaise (14)*, rapport dactylographié, DRAC – SRA.

Mastrolorenzo, J. (2010b) *Falaise (Calvados), Le château, Front est, côté extérieur*, rapport en 2 volumes, DRAC BN–SRA.

Mastrolorenzo, J. (2010c) *Falaise (Calvados), Le château, Front est, Etude des élévations*, rapport à en cours.

Mériel, A. (1889) *Histoire de Falaise: antiquité, gouvernement militaire, fortifications,* Falaise.

Régnier, L. (1907) 'L'âge de la Tour Talbot du château de Falaise', dans *Annuaire des cinq départements de la Normandie* 74e année (Caen et Rouen).

# 7

# Le château de Caen[1]

*Jean-Marie Levesque et Pascal Leroux*

**Summary**

*Caen Castle was built under William the Conqueror around 1060. It bears the unusual distinction of having been built from scratch, at the heart of a new town, Caen, which would go on to be the second capital of the duchy of Normandy.*

*This dynastic creation – William and Matilda chose their burial place in the two abbeys built at the same time – came about at a time when the duke had defeated his internal enemies and secured the borders. He was now in a position to turn his attentions to conquering England. In 1066, Caen almost certainly served as a support base for the army assembled at the Dives estuary, although there is no documentary evidence of this. Caen Castle was an important building in the Norman duchy but does not have a particularly dramatic history. Few major events are reported as having taken place there and the fortress was never really threatened. Therefore, we have painstaking archaeology to thank for our knowledge of the site's history, enabling us to reconstruct the ramparts and the lost keep, the Exchequer Hall, courtyard life and the castle's living and working spaces.*

*Archaeological research and interpretation are thus at the heart of the current efforts to educate the public about this building's place in Anglo-Norman history.*

Châteaux, abbayes et cathédrales: c'est, passé le temps des batailles, dans la perspective de ces chantiers gigantesques qu'on se représente volontiers la construction de l'espace anglo-normand. Caen, avec ses deux abbayes et son château est sans doute une ville emblématique de cette vision de la puissance normande. Sans négliger d'autres grandes fondations ou rénovations à l'initiative du duc Guillaume à travers toute la Normandie, on peut observer à Caen, ville que Guillaume fait sienne, la mise en œuvre d'une ambition autant politique qu'architecturale par laquelle le prince affirme sa puissance. Le duc devenu roi, et les grands seigneurs qui se partagent le butin anglais, reproduiront dans le royaume conquis des entreprises comparables dans lesquelles l'imposition du pouvoir depuis le château, la prise de contrôle de la ville et du territoire, les fondations ou restaurations ecclésiastiques participent d'un même projet cohérent.

Les conditions de la prise du pouvoir, de sa conservation et de son imposition par la force conduisent à porter un regard particulier sur le château, qui apparaît bien, en tous cas dans ses formes nouvelles, comme le plus caractéristique de la période. En Normandie d'abord où les grandes tours apparaissent dès la fin du Xe siècle, en Angleterre ensuite, où, sous ces différents formes, ce nouveau type d'édifice frappe particulièrement les esprits. Dans l'espace anglo-normand en effet ce programme d'architecture militaire et aristocratique est caractérisé par son ampleur, tant en Normandie qu'en Angleterre, et par la volonté du prince d'en garder le contrôle. Symbole de l'éclatement et de l'anarchie dans d'autres principautés, le château dans le monde anglo-normand représente l'ordre – et même, dans le cas anglais, un ordre nouveau, étranger aux traditions locales. Pourtant Guillaume le Conquérant ne fut pas lui-même, en Normandie, un constructeur de châteaux sur une échelle comparable aux moyens déployés en Angleterre. Il bénéficia sur ce point de l'œuvre de ses prédécesseurs et son apport consista surtout à reprendre en main des fortifications existantes. Les textes et l'archéologie nous apprennent qu'il employa déjà à cette œuvre des types de fortifications temporaires comme les mottes de siège élevées pour réduire la forteresse d'Arques. A l'inverse, il dut aussi démanteler quelques fortifications rebelles et ajouta à son dispositif des positions de frontière importantes à Breteuil-sur-Iton, Ambrières, Saint-James-de-Beuvron et Vernon. De ce point de vue, Caen, sa fondation la plus emblématique, vient aussi compléter un vide stratégique en même temps qu'elle offre au duc l'occasion d'affirmer une dimension véritablement dynastique (Figure 7.1).

On fixe habituellement la construction du château de Caen vers 1060 et, pour reprendre la comparaison avec ce qui se passera en Angleterre, cette initiative fait suite également à un épisode militaire majeur. En 1047, Guillaume le Conquérant a vaincu en bataille rangée ses vassaux du Bessin et du Cotentin alliés aux intrigants de sa cour qui lui disputaient encore la légitimité de la succession. La bataille du Val-ès-Dunes marque la prise de possession complète par Guillaume de son duché et elle sera suivie d'autres opérations militaires et diplomatiques, comme le mariage avec Mathilde de Flandre vers 1051, la conquête du Maine en 1062–3, les derniers affrontements avec le roi de France et le comte d'Anjou (Mortemer 1054; Varaville 1057), et jusqu'à l'expédition de Bretagne à laquelle participe Harold Godwinson en 1064, qui établissent définitivement le pouvoir de Guillaume et le rendent disponible pour envisager l'aventure de la conquête de l'Angleterre.

A cette époque, le réseau des fortifications des ducs de Normandie est déjà solidement établi. Des châteaux existent dans la capitale, Rouen, et dans les résidences régulières et privilégiées des ducs de Normandie (Fécamp, Falaise, Valognes...). D'autres places connues comme Bonneville-sur-Touques posent plus de problèmes quant à la datation des premières fortifications, mais le duc utilise aussi le réseau des anciennes enceintes urbaines renforcées de tours maîtresses (c'est encore l'exemple de Rouen, mais aussi de Bayeux, d'Avranches…) tandis que les bases des comtés confiés aux familles les plus proches de la dynastie s'appuient aussi sur des châteaux autorisés par le duc (Arques, Eu, Ivry). La situation est plus floue sur les frontières exposées aux rébellions de quelques puissantes dynasties qu'il faudra soumettre (les Bellême, à Alençon, Sées, Mortagne), tandis que des garnisons sont déployées surtout face aux positions françaises du Vexin qui restera du XIe au XIIe siècle la ligne la plus fortifiée du duché (Figure 7.2). Une multitude de sites fortifiés,[2] enceintes, mottes castrales, maisons fortes, bases d'une noblesse de second rang, vient compléter sans doute le dispositif, mais ils doivent en temps normal se plier à la loi du duc qui rappelle régulièrement l'interdiction de creuser des fossés et de lever des palissades sans son autorisation. C'est donc dans les périodes de troubles que l'on voit proliférer ce qu'on appelle les châteaux adultérins, essentiellement les fameux châteaux à mottes dressées à l'occasion d'un conflit, au cœur du fief où s'affirme un pouvoir, en frontière des territoires rivaux ou sur une ligne de front des défrichements.

*Figure 7.1. Vue aérienne du château de Caen, vers 2000 – avant les travaux de restauration (document: Ville de Caen).*

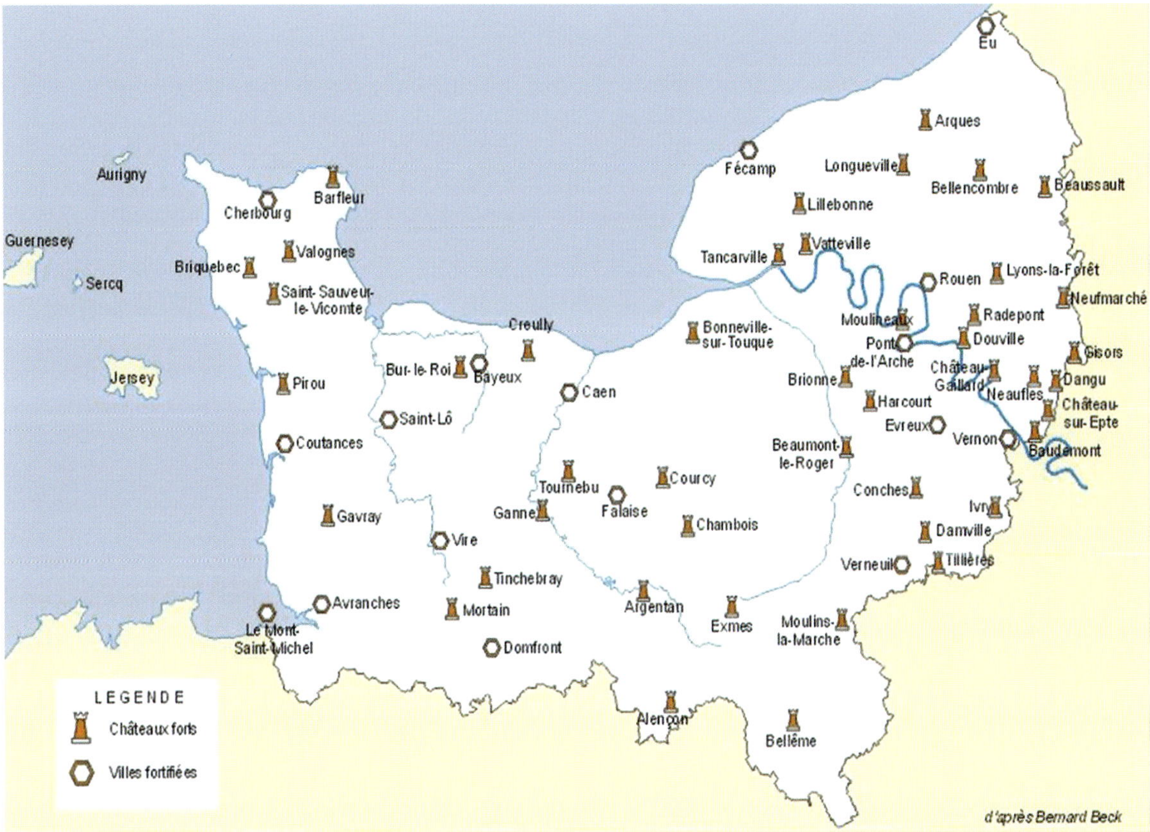


*Figure 7.2. Les principaux châteaux et places fortifiées aux XIe-XIIe siècles (document: Musée de Normandie, d'après Bernard Beck).*

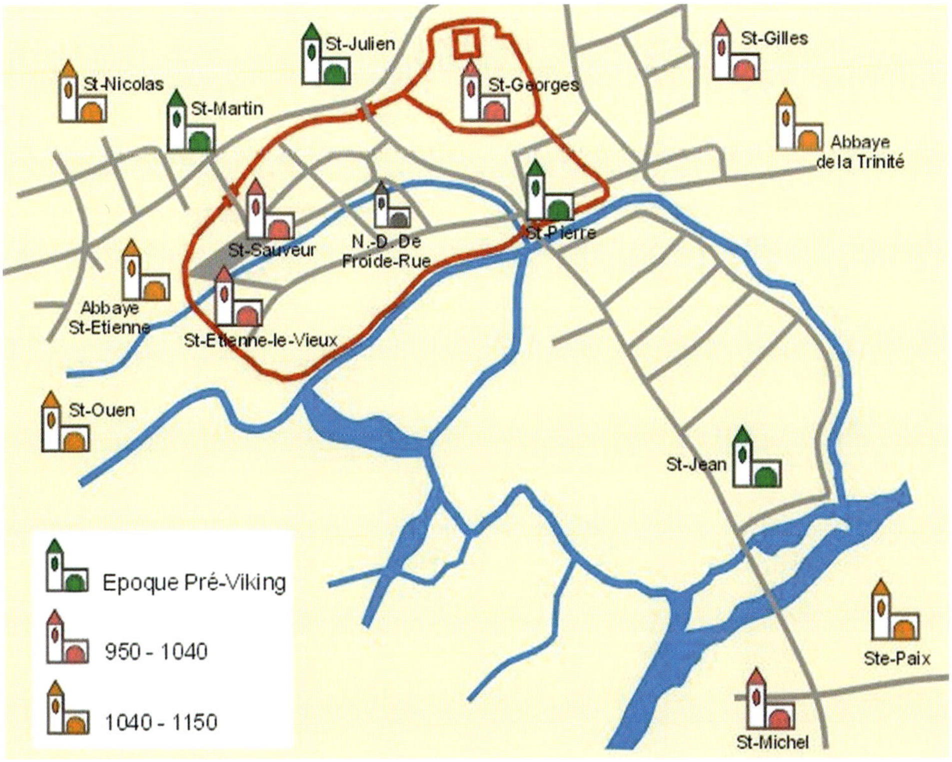


*Figure 7.3. Les paroisses et les fortifications de Caen, shéma simplifié de l'évolution de la ville médiévale (document: Musée de Normandie).*

C'est précisément ce qui vient de se passer pendant la minorité de Guillaume et les premières années de son règne. La construction du château de Caen vient donc renforcer le dispositif des forteresses ducales et combler une lacune dans une zone où la basse vallée de l'Orne et son carrefour de communications sont sans protection tandis que la ville de Bayeux, compromise dans la rébellion de 1047, est placée dès 1049 sous le contrôle d'Odon, demi-frère du duc. Tout le dispositif mis en place entre l'Orne et la Dives[3] pour la concentration des moyens d'invasion en 1066, le rôle des abbayes caennaises dans l'organisation du terroir, le fort investissement des familles les plus proches du pouvoir, comme celle des Montgommeri autour du site voisin de Troarn, donnent a posteriori raison à ce choix qui referme le triangle Falaise / Bayeux / Lisieux et assure le contrôle d'un carrefour routier, fluvial et maritime. Le choix de Caen n'est donc pas isolé, c'est toute une région qui est l'objet de l'investissement du pouvoir ducal. Ce n'est évidemment pas un hasard si c'est au cœur de ce territoire ou dans sa proximité immédiate qu'on trouve les deux champs de batailles sur lesquels le pouvoir de Guillaume est parvenu à maturité: Val-ès-Dunes, en 1047, Varaville en 1057.

## Aux origines de la ville de Caen

Malgré l'importance stratégique de cette fondation il ne faut pas chercher beaucoup d'informations dans les récits contemporains. Toutefois, le recoupement exhaustif des sources historiques et archéologiques a confirmé de solides éléments soumis à un nouvel examen dans une thèse récente.[4] Caen n'est pas l'héritière d'une cité épiscopale remontant à la période gallo-romaine, comme Bayeux ou Lisieux, et elle est loin d'avoir avant le XIe siècle l'importance de bourgades plus anciennes devenues éventuellement des chefs-lieux de vicomtés comme Falaise. Très discret dans les textes le site n'est surtout connu que par l'archéologie qui identifie plusieurs habitats et équipements, un vicus (implantation artisanale) gallo-romain dans le secteur où sera édifiée l'Abbaye aux Hommes, et déjà des paroisses et des cimetières d'époques mérovingienne et carolingienne. Le site de Caen n'est pas signalé dans la chronologie des raids vikings alors que Rollon brulait et pillait Bayeux vers 886/890, et s'emparait, pour l'épouser 'à la manière des Danois', de la fille du comte carolingien. Les traces nordiques ou scandinaves à Caen se réduisent à la microtoponymie, bien difficile à interpréter. Le nom du site de Darnetal, au pied du château, est d'origine germanique, mais peut bien davantage être saxon que scandinave (Caen se situe dans la proximité des colonies saxonnes identifiées dans le Bessin du VIe siècle à l'époque carolingienne).

La ville de Caen entre vraiment dans l'histoire au début du XIe siècle: des actes des ducs de Normandie (Richard II, Richard III, Robert le Magnifique) et de l'évêque de Bayeux, en faveur d'abbayes normandes (Fécamp, Cerisy, Saint-Wandrille), ou hors de Normandie (Chartres) font apparaître des maisons, des églises, des terres, des foires dans un site en grande partie sous l'autorité du duc lui-même ou de l'évêque de Bayeux. Des hypothèses ont été émises sur la possibilité d'identifier à Caen une résidence fortifiée du duc de Normandie dont l'évocation manquante dans les textes viendrait compléter logiquement l'énumération des autres éléments listés parmi les biens énumérés en 1025 dans un acte de Richard II pour le douaire de son épouse Adèle: une villa (c'est-à-dire un grand domaine rural), un port, des marchés, des moulins, des revenus fiscaux, et peut être déjà un bourg dans un ensemble auquel il ne manquerait plus alors que le 'castrum'. Sa présence sous la forme d'une grande enceinte positionnée sur l'éperon rocheux dominant l'Orne n'aurait rien d'invraisemblable. D'autres exemples de ce type de fortifications sont attestés au IX/Xe siècle[5] et à Falaise les fouilles récentes de murailles du château ont identifié des maçonneries d'époque carolingienne. Mais ce castrum caennais manque en effet aussi bien dans les textes que dans les vestiges archéologiques et, faute d'arguments plus définitifs, il faut en rester aux constats de la recherche et retenir l'époque de Guillaume le Conquérant pour voir s'élever les murailles du château de Caen (Figure 7.3).

Le premier récit à évoquer les fortifications de Caen nous dit justement qu'elles n'existent pas encore ! Wace, dans le 'Roman de Rou', situe à Caen le passage de l'Orne par les troupes du roi de France en marche vers le marais de Varaville en 1057. L'armée royale peut manœuvrer sans rencontrer nulle résistance: Caen n'a pas de fortifications pour lui barrer la route et pas de château à partir duquel organiser une contre-attaque du raid français.[6] Certes Wace écrit un siècle après les faits, et on peut toujours suspecter les informations tirées d'œuvres de courtisans qui ont d'autres objectifs que d'établir des chronologies détaillées. Aucun autre récit, aucun autre document ne viennent le contredire, et peut-être est-il quand même possible de retenir la valeur d'un témoin assez attaché à la ville pour en bien connaître la tradition historique par des récits de la précédente génération. On situe donc les travaux de fortification à Caen dans une période contemporaine du début des autres grands chantiers de la ville, l'édification de l'abbaye aux Dames (dès 1059–60) et de l'abbaye aux Hommes (vers 1063).

Caen illustre bien un cas de figure qu'on voit également beaucoup en Angleterre, dans des modalités certes différentes: l'importance de la fondation, ou de la re-fondation ecclésiastique associée à la mise en place de la forteresse, pour l'organisation et le contrôle d'une ville ou d'un territoire. Guillaume construit le château pour y abriter son palais, et les abbayes pour y élire sépulture, pour lui et son épouse. Si on peut relativiser le statut de capitale pour la ville de Caen, dans le contexte d'une cour sans cesse nomade, il s'agit bien d'une fondation dynastique dans un déplacement des symboles du pouvoir, de Rouen,

*Figure 7.4. Vue aérienne du château de Caen, vers 2000 – avant les travaux de restauration (document: Ville de Caen).*

sépulture de Rollon et Guillaume Longue Epée, à Fécamp, sépulture de Richard I et Richard II, puis à Caen sépulture de Guillaume, sa ville et son palais. Rouen toutefois garde la prééminence du siège archiépiscopal, de la richesse et de la tradition l'attachant aux origines de la dynastie des rollonides.

## Le château dans la ville des duc-rois

### *Les remparts*

Pour construire son château Guillaume le Conquérant utilise l'aplomb d'un éperon rocheux qui domine la vallée de l'Orne (Figure 7.4). Au nord, la protection des lieux est assurée par un profond fossé creusé pour barrer le plateau calcaire. C'est là que se situe l'accès principal au château qui restera longtemps en limite d'une campagne ouverte, la croissance de la ville se développant sur ses flancs sud, est et ouest. Le pont qui enjambe le fossé débouche sur une solide tour-porte en pierre, que l'on doit passer sous la surveillance des gardes. Les vestiges de cette construction ont été découverts lors des fouilles réalisées au cours des années 60 par Michel de Boüard qui cite en exemple la tour-porte de Rougemont Castle à Exeter. La voie empierrée qui traversait le passage couvert comporte de profondes ornières maintes fois comblées, creusées par les passages répétés des roues de charrette. Au sud, un autre accès au château est attesté de façon certaine dès le XIe siècle. Toutefois, la pente du chemin qui y accède depuis la ville est trop forte pour qu'aucun convoi n'ait pu l'emprunter. Cet accès était certainement destiné aux seuls piétons qui pouvaient ainsi aller et venir du château à la ville. Aucune protection particulière n'assurait la défense de cette poterne, c'est sans doute l'indice d'un projet conçu dès le départ dans la complémentarité des murailles du château et des fortifications urbaines et abbatiales. Le quartier de la ville qui s'étend au sud et à l'ouest du château, le Bourg le Duc, est entouré d'un rempart ouvert par des portes fortifiées. Cette poterne sud du château facilement condamnable permettait certes d'ouvrir le refuge du château aux habitants du bourg mais aussi de limiter les communications avec une population éventuellement rebelle. De fait, il arrivera plusieurs fois dans l'histoire, que le château et la ville ne soient pas dans le même camp, mais rien de tel du temps du Conquérant.

Ce vaste espace de cinq hectares est enclos par un premier rempart qui a dû être construit progressivement en maçonnerie de pierre utilisant directement le matériau de construction extrait des fossés. On ignore tout de la conduite de ce premier chantier, mais il serait logique que les moines de Lanfranc, premier abbé de Saint-Etienne de Caen, y aient pris leur part. Les travaux de l'abbaye aux Dames et de l'abbaye aux Hommes commencent dans les mêmes années. Et on peut observer que Guillaume en Angleterre se fait accompagner de maîtres dans l'art de bâtir dont certains ont pu faire leur apprentissage à Caen dans les années 1060. Prenons l'exemple de Gundulf, né en 1024, formé à Rouen, pendant la période de construction de la cathédrale romane. On le retrouve au Bec en 1057, d'où il suit Lanfranc à Caen (1063), puis en Angleterre (1070). Il est cité pour son rôle sur les chantiers de la Tour de Londres et de Colchester, et il devient évêque de Rochester en 1077, où un château et une cathédrale sont à construire.[7] Chaque station de cet itinéraire est en effet celle d'un grand chantier. Il est sans doute un bon exemple de ces bâtisseurs ou administrateurs que Guillaume a emmenés en Angleterre. Avec les spécialistes sont aussi passés les matériaux: à Caen, les travaux des abbayes et du château ont aussi lancé le commerce transmanche de la pierre dans lequel les abbayes caennaises sont d'importants opérateurs.

L'archéologie ne permet pas de connaître ce premier état du rempart et ce n'est que très récemment dans les travaux de restauration des années 2004/2005[8] qu'une étude d'archéologie du bâti a apporté des informations sur le rempart nord et montré à contrario l'importance des recherches qui restent à faire sur l'histoire de la muraille. Aucune information n'émerge toutefois pour le XIe siècle. Le rempart en pierre visible de nos jours a maintes fois été réparé mais les parties visibles les plus anciennes semblent pouvoir être datées du premier tiers du XIIe siècle, contemporaines des travaux commandés par Henri 1er Beauclerc, pour le donjon. Le circuit des remparts est aujourd'hui ponctué de 13 tours. Elles n'existaient pas non plus à l'époque du Conquérant et les archéologues discutent de leur datation entre le règne de Henri Ier et celui d'Henri II. Les deux tours rondes qui renforcent la muraille là où la fortification de la ville rejoignait celle du château sont attribuables aux travaux commandés par Philippe Auguste au début du XIIIe siècle.

## *Le Palais de Guillaume*

C'est au cœur de l'enceinte fortifiée qu'il vient de créer vers 1060 que le duc Guillaume aménage son palais, à l'abri de la tour-porte. Organisé selon l'ordonnancement habituel: *aula, camera, capella*, il nous est principalement connu par les fouilles.[9] Construit à proximité de la tour-porte, à l'ouest de celle-ci, il a perduré jusqu'au XVe siècle, englobé dans un ensemble de constructions postérieures et disparates. Parmi les éléments du XIe siècle, la chapelle palatine Saint-Georges a survécu en partie jusqu'en 1944, où elle a été détruite par les bombardements. Seules quelques assises des murs latéraux sont conservées sous une importante végétation. Le hall de Guillaume, dont les vestiges sont visibles perpendiculairement à la salle de l'Echiquier, était une salle mesurant intérieurement 16m de long pour 8m de largeur, les murs étaient épais de 0.80m et le sol était en terre battue. Une cheminée murale était appuyée sur le mur nord du bâtiment et l'âtre s'étendait largement dans la pièce. Il n'est pas certain que ce rez-de-chaussée était l'étage noble car les vestiges d'un escalier à vis ont été découverts dans l'angle sud-ouest du bâtiment. (Ce détail nous introduit à un autre débat sur les dispositions du second hall du château, la salle de l'Echiquier, dont il sera question plus loin.) Dans le prolongement est du hall de Guillaume ont été également découverts les vestiges d'un sol en terre battue qui appartenait vraisemblablement à une pièce annexe accolée à la grande salle de réception.

Du palais construit au XIe siècle, il ne reste rien en élévation aujourd'hui. Les rares vestiges visibles sont soit des assises de murs témoignant de l'état du XVe siècle soit une reconstitution, après les fouilles, du pavage daté également du XVe siècle.

## *La salle de l'Echiquier*

Henri 1er Beauclerc, vers 1120/1123, aménage dans le château deux nouvelles constructions importantes: le donjon et la grande salle de réception. Ce nouveau hall vient s'ajouter au palais de Guillaume qui est conservé et sans doute réorganisé.[10] Le grand hall porte le nom de Salle de l'Echiquier depuis la publication des *Magni Rotuli Scaccarii*[11] par Thomas Stapleton, à Londres en 1840. L'auteur choisit d'illustrer son ouvrage d'une lithographie représentant la grande salle du château de Caen – la première image de l'intérieur du bâtiment qui nous soit connue – introduisant ainsi l'idée qu'elle fut le lieu privilégié des séances des cours de justice et des comptes du duc de Normandie, même s'il y a plus d'attestations de ces séances dans la chapelle que dans le hall.

Le nouveau bâtiment mesure intérieurement 30.70m sur 11m. Profondément remanié au cours des siècles et plus spécialement entre le milieu du XIXe et 1944 par les militaires de la caserne Lefebvre il a eu, lui aussi, à souffrir des bombardements de 1944. Il a été fouillé sur les faibles parties restées vierges et restauré consécutivement à ces fouilles. Les transformations successives ont effacé la plupart des aménagements d'origine.

La salle présente une façade harmonique, à contreforts plats, typique de l'architecture normande. Elle est ouverte par une porte en façade surmontée d'un tympan sculpté de motifs géométriques, éclairée par une baie en façade, au-dessus de la porte et 12 fenêtres de même taille, en six travées alternant avec des contreforts plats sur chaque mur gouttereau. Il s'agit d'arcatures en plein cintre, à double archivolte, colonnettes et chapiteaux sculptés qui donnent à l'édifice l'allure d'une église avec laquelle le grand public le confond souvent.

En son état actuel, la salle de l'Echiquier a été plus recréée que restaurée en 1962 avec un beau dallage et une magnifique charpente. Mais l'observation de la salle aujourd'hui, ne laisse pas envisager que les militaires, au XVIIIe et XIXe siècle, en avaient fait une écurie, avec râteliers à foin et boxes, et qu'ils avaient aménagé un plancher sur une partie de la salle. Les photographies anciennes et les plans du Génie sont heureusement là pour en témoigner. La reconstitution du dispositif des origines pose des problèmes encore plus difficiles.[12]

Quoi qu'il en soit, La salle de l'Echiquier reste un des rares exemples d'architecture civile romane conservé sur le continent et sa monumentalité est un indice de l'importance donnée au château par le séjour régulier du duc-roi et de sa cour.

### *Le donjon*

Il n'y a pas d'information archéologique ou historique sur la présence d'une grande tour à Caen à l'époque de Guillaume le Conquérant. Le seul point haut de la muraille est la tour-porte qui contrôle l'entrée nord. Elle ne ressemble en rien aux donjons qui ont commencé à se multiplier dans la France du Nord à partir du Xe siècle. On sait que dès le début de son règne en Angleterre Guillaume commence l'édification de cet impressionnant donjon qu'est la Tour de Londres (vers 1067/1068, achevée en plusieurs phases vers 1100[13]). Des modèles normands, préexistant à la construction du château de Caen, sont cités comme exemples de la Tour[14]: les donjons d'Ivry-la-Bataille et Avranches – sur lesquels on peut faire d'utiles comparaisons – ceux de Bayeux et de Rouen – qui n'ont laissé aucune trace archéologique (mais que Robert de Torigni compare, pour ce dernier, construit sous Richard I, à celui qu'il verra s'élever plus tard à Caen). Mais Guillaume ne semble pas avoir obéi pour Caen à la règle de ce siècle selon laquelle '*les grands hommes font de grandes tours*' (E. Impey). Règle dont il pouvait pourtant s'inspirer à partir des exemples des comtes de Blois et d'Anjou, à ses frontières, ou des donjons d'Île de France, de l'Amiennois ou de Champagne, qui forment déjà une solide tradition architecturale développée entre 950 et 1050, et sans doute même avant (Doué-la-Fontaine et Mayenne dans le Maine, Ivry-la-Bataille en Normandie). Mais surtout, il aurait pu reprendre l'exemple des constructions de ces aïeux à Rouen et à Bayeux. Il l'a fait en Angleterre. Pas en Normandie. Pas à Caen.

Cette absence étonne et fait du château de Guillaume un dispositif finalement assez faible: un palais et une paroisse dans une large enceinte pleine de vide, défendue seulement par le relief et des murailles sans tours identifiées par l'archéologie pour cette époque; une seule entrée fortifiée mais pas non plus de traces d'avant-poste. On a plus l'impression d'une grande cour close de murs que d'un château fort. Un débat peut alors s'engager sur la présence de constructions disparues sous les remaniements successifs. On en est réduit aux conjectures et aux comparaisons théoriques. Les indices matériels restent à découvrir.

Il faut donc attendre le règne de Henri Ier et la période des troubles des années 1118–9, pour proposer des jalons dans la chronologie de l'édification du donjon car on suit ici, traditionnellement, Robert de Torigni qui place plusieurs interventions du roi Henri dans les châteaux normands après cette période d'instabilité.

Construit en même temps que la salle de l'Echiquier[15] et à quelques mètres à l'est de la tour-porte, le donjon n'a pas survécu aux siècles. Seules les fouilles ont permis la redécouverte de sa base large de 27.40m sur 24m. D'une hauteur supposée comprise entre 25 et 30m, il n'en subsiste pas plus de 1.50m aujourd'hui. Les vestiges des murs larges de 4.40m permettent de se représenter la masse de la construction. Une visite à Rochester, Colchester ou Norwich donne seule l'impression de puissance dont nous sommes aujourd'hui privés dans le château de Caen.

*Figure 7.5. Vue du Château de Caen en 1702 (Fonds Gaignères, BNF, Paris).*

Il est difficile de projeter sur ces bases une reconstitution en élévation assez précise. D'autant moins que les deux seules gravures connues avant la destruction commencée en 1793, donnent une idée de la masse énorme de l'édifice, mais peu d'informations sur son organisation intérieure (Figure 7.5). En se basant sur les modèles classiques il n'est pas difficile de proposer un premier niveau sans aucune ouverture renfermant un puits attesté par l'archéologie et abritant peut-être une cuisine (il n'y a pas de traces de foyer) et des magasins de vivres. Cet étage est partagé par un mur de refend qui devait tenir sur toute la hauteur et aider à supporter, au dernier étage, les charpentes attestées au XVIe siècle au moment où elles sont remplacées par une plate-forme de tir pour les canons. Au-dessus du premier niveau existait un étage accessible par l'avant-corps dont les traces sont observées sur le mur sud, mais entre ces deux premiers niveaux et la charpente, on ne sait pas s'il y avait un ou deux étages.

Sur cette question, le seul indice exploitable est un texte d'inspection des ingénieurs du roi daté de 1700. Il est donc largement postérieur aux destructions des charpentes pour l'installation d'une terrasse à canons et des modifications consécutives du ou des étages supérieurs; le texte identifie un niveau inférieur sous plancher, semi-enterré dans les remblais modernes, et un volume d'un seul tenant au-dessus de ce plancher sous la voûte construite pour porter la plateforme d'artillerie. Le document indique donc en première analyse un donjon à deux étages si on admet que le voûte et la plateforme succèdent à la charpente du XIIe siècle et au couronnement du rempart qui la protégeait, mais il n'exclut pas une construction à trois étages qui n'est pas incompatible avec les élévations subsistantes?[16]

L'absence d'informations sur les équipements du donjon (disposition des ouvertures, cheminées, cuisines, latrines…) ne permets pas d'identifier quel niveau de confort pouvait être atteint et à qui pouvait être destiné le bâtiment.

Au XIIIe et XIVe siècle des bâtiments sont ajoutés dans la cour du donjon pour les fonctions résidentielles réservées au capitaine du château, mais cela ne signifie pas que ces fonctions n'existaient pas avant, dans les étages du donjon ou déjà dans des bâtiments annexes. On peut aussi retenir pour discuter l'organisation du donjon du château de Caen au XIIe siècle selon la trilogie aula/camera/capella, observée dans le château de Falaise, que Caen possède déjà deux halls au XIIe siècle: le palais de Guillaume et la salle de l'Echiquier. Il est impossible de savoir comment tous ces bâtiments fonctionnaient ensemble.

Après 1204, le donjon est séparé du château en raison de la construction de la chemise et des tours qui l'entourent, et le creusement d'un profond fossé. A partir de ce moment le commandement militaire du château est clairement replié dans le donjon, tandis que les fonctions civiles, celles de représentation du roi, se déploient dans le reste de l'enceinte, où sera construit le logis du Gouverneur, attesté en 1338, et où est installé aujourd'hui le Musée de Normandie.

On ne connait pas la répartition précise des lieux de pouvoir dans le château avant cette époque.

Comment fonctionnaient en l'absence du duc ou en sa présence, le donjon, l'ancien palais de Guillaume, la salle de l'Echiquier? Qui hébergeaient-ils? Où logeaient vraiment le duc et ses invités prestigieux en dehors des cérémonies du pouvoir? On voit assez souvent des informations sur la présence du duc à Caen, et après 1204, du roi de France. Mais il n'est pas toujours évident que le château soit le véritable lieu de résidence. Il n'est jamais décrit en détail, le donjon moins encore, ses aménagements intérieurs pas du tout.

Enfin, il ne faut pas oublier la dimension fortement symbolique de la construction de cette tour, affirmation du pouvoir ducal. Philippe-Auguste qui la fait enfermer dans sa muraille à quatre tours ne s'y trompe pas.

## *L'église Saint-Georges*

Curieusement, saint Georges qui est devenu un saint plus anglais que français, est très présent dans l'histoire du château de Caen. On a mentionné dans le palais ducal, une chapelle dédiée à saint Georges. Elle a disparu et ne doit pas être confondue avec l'église paroissiale qui demeure. Depuis ses débuts en effet, le château abrite un quartier de la ville dont les habitations semblent concentrées à proximité des portes. Ce quartier est constitué en paroisse pour le service de la garnison, des personnels des communs assurant des fonctions d'intendance, certainement aussi une population d'artisans et de boutiquiers nécessaires à la vie animée par la présence itinérante du duc et de sa cour, et le séjour régulier de ses représentants, enfin, quelques privilégiés qui possèdent des maisons dans la cour du château. Des maisons, des jardins, des vignes passent de main en main dans les actes conservés concernant le château, comme dans n'importe quel quartier de la ville. Cette situation va traverser les siècles et ne semble vraiment perdre de l'importance qu'avec l'occupation anglaise en raison de la méfiance envers les Caennais. Mais on continue à baptiser et, sur la fin, surtout à célébrer des funérailles, dans cette paroisse jusqu'en 1789. Pour ces fonctions il faut une église et un cimetière, qui sont bien là en effet.

Si on ne sait rien d'une hypothétique église paroissiale antérieure à 1100, les textes nous indiquent qu'en 1080, la reine Mathilde en racheta les droits au chapitre de Bayeux pour les confier peu après à l'Abbaye aux Dames. Cette anecdote qui semble indiquer que le duc ne possède pas tous les droits sur le territoire du château au moment de sa construction, plaide pour l'existence d'une paroisse avant le XIe siècle. Elle n'a laissé aucune trace archéologique.

Si l'édifice a été profondément remanié au XVe et au XVIe siècle, d'importants vestiges pouvant être datés de la fin du XIe siècle ou du début du XIIe sont encore visibles. La nef est romane et on peut y observer plusieurs fenêtres en plein cintre à fort ébrasement intérieur dont certaines ont été bouchées lors d'une période de travaux du XVe siècle. De magnifiques modillons représentant des musiciens sont en place à la base du toit, certains d'entre eux, qui comptent parmi les mieux conservés, sont maintenant à l'intérieur de l'église englobés dans la construction d'une chapelle au XVIe siècle. Le chœur actuel est du XVIe siècle, mais la fouille a permis la redécouverte de l'abside semi-circulaire romane. Si les vestiges n'ont pu être conservés en l'état, un traçage sur le pavage en conserve le souvenir. L'élément le plus remarquable d'époque romane est sans conteste l'arc triomphal en plein cintre entre la nef et le chœur. Ses bandeaux d'archivoltes qui retombent sur des chapiteaux reconstitués d'après un seul fragment conservé, sont décorés d'une succession d'étoiles en creux à quatre branches qui surmontent des claveaux décorés de bâtons brisés.

## Le château à travers l'histoire

Rempart, palais, donjon, paroisse et lieu de vie, voici les éléments constitutifs du château de Caen et de son histoire. Nous avons évoqué les principales transformations de ces différentes parties du château au moment de les présenter l'une après l'autre. La datation de ces évolutions est souvent approximative car il n'est pas facile de placer l'histoire du château de Caen dans le contexte d'évènement précis. On a vu qu'on ne pouvait dater sa fondation avec plus de certitude que vers 1060. On ne sait pas quel pouvait être l'état d'avancement des travaux en 1066 quand l'armée de Guillaume est rassemblée pour le départ en Angleterre et que celui-ci en profite pour faire consacrer l'église de l'Abbaye aux Dames. Le château a t'il pu déjà servir de base arrière dans ce dispositif ? Quelles ont été exactement les étapes de la construction du rempart en maçonneries appareillées depuis les années 1060 jusqu'à 1120, date de la datation traditionnelle de la seconde phase de grands travaux?

Après la mort de Guillaume et à travers les batailles que se livrent Robert Courteheuse, Guillaume le Roux et Henri Ier Beauclerc, il y a peu de mentions d'épisodes militaires majeurs à Caen. Au contraire c'est une assemblée de réconciliation qui se tient dans la ville en 1091 et en 1105, c'est Bayeux qui est brûlée par Henri Ier. Caen ne cherche pas à résister à la progression d'Henri contre Robert. Le vainqueur séjourne à Caen après sa victoire à Tinchebray en 1106 et à plusieurs reprises. Par la suite Henri passe régulièrement par Caen lors de ses traversées de la mer. Une dame de la ville au moins peut en témoigner, puisqu'elle lui donne un fils illégitime promis à un grand avenir: Robert de Caen (Robert de Gloucester). Mais c'est seulement vers 1120 qu'Henri entreprend de grands travaux dans le château.

Après sa mort le château de Caen est d'ailleurs tenu par Robert de Gloucester, non pas en raison de sa naissance mais en raison de son mariage avec la fille des Hamon, riches seigneurs du Bessin qui ont la garde des châteaux de Creully et de Caen. Henri a doté richement Robert en Angleterre et en Normandie – sur les terres qui furent les siennes quand Henri était encore en lutte contre ses frères. Robert 'Fitzroy' est après la mort de Guillaume Adelin dans le naufrage de la Blanche Nef, le fils préféré et il sera un des acteurs clefs de la guerre entre Mathilde et Etienne. Seigneur de premier plan, immensément riche, bon capitaine et grand mécène, il est pourtant d'un temps où les bâtards ne peuvent plus prétendre à la succession.

Robert ouvre 'sa' ville de Caen et son château à Geoffroy d'Anjou en 1138. Là non plus aucune bataille n'a été nécessaire. Par la suite le château de Caen est mentionné dans quelques épisodes secondaires. On n'entend pas beaucoup plus parler du château de Caen dans la chronique des Plantagenêt. On sait pourtant qu'en 1170, Margueritte de France séjourne au château de Caen sous la garde l'Aliénor d'Aquitaine, manière de l'éloigner du couronnement de Henri le Jeune qui a lieu à Westminster. En 1174, Henri II fait enfermer dans le château quelques-uns des révoltés les plus notoires du soulèvement de 1173/1174, dont Guillaume le Lion, roi d'Ecosse capturé à Alnwick (Northumberland) par Renouf de Glanville, et transféré à Falaise. Mais ce n'est pas cette maigre chronique des personnalités qui nous en apprend davantage sur le château de Caen mieux connu toutefois sous les souverains Plantagenêt grâce à des archives administratives plus fournies.

On sait ainsi qu'en 1176, la cour de l'Echiquier s'est effectivement réunie dans le hall du château de Caen. On a quelques indications sur la fonction de connétable qui a la garde du château au nom du roi, et sur le trésor sans doute abrité dans le donjon sous Henri II (Henri Ier le faisait garder à Falaise). A proximité des ports d'embarquement vers l'Angleterre, à l'Ouest de la Normandie (Barfleur, Ouistreham, Dives...), Caen est un séjour régulier des ducrois et des événements solennels s'y déroulent comme l'assemblée de l'enquête de chevalerie de 1172 et la grande cour de Noël en 1182, où plus de mille chevaliers se rassemblent dans la ville. On trouve donc surtout Caen et son château dans des fonctions curiales, car en 1204, la ville et le château ne résistent pas plus qu'en 1105 au nouveau pouvoir. Cette fois ce n'est plus un descendant de Guillaume, mais le patient adversaire des Plantagenêt, le roi de France Philippe-Auguste.

## Les transformations du château du XIIIe siècle au XVIe siècle

Après les grands travaux de l'Echiquier et du donjon, sous Henri Ier, et peut être des aménagements non datés sur la muraille et sur les tours, sous les Plantagenêt, il faut donc attendre 1204, et la commise de la Normandie par Philippe Auguste pour que de nouveaux aménagements importants soient réalisés. On a mentionné la chemise du donjon et le transfert des fonctions du bailli dans le logis identifié dès

1338 et transformé en 1682 pour le gouverneur. Parmi les maisons et installations qui se développent dans le 'bayle', dans la paroisse Saint-Georges, il faut placer la maison et les installations artisanales fouillées depuis 2005 dans le secteur nord-ouest.[17] A cet endroit, les premières traces d'occupation remontent aux origines du château. Les travaux archéologiques menés ont récemment révélé ce passé resté inconnu du château. On ne sait d'ailleurs pas très bien s'il faut situer ces découvertes dans le 'bayle' ou dans le palais… La salle de l'Echiquier et le secteur nord du château – le secteur palatial – étaient-ils séparés du reste du château par un mur d'enceinte, même symbolique, après que le donjon ait été enfermé dans sa chemise? L'étaient-ils d'ailleurs avant?

L'aménagement de la chemise du donjon entraîne la destruction de la tour-porte primitive. Un autre accès est alors créé à l'est de l'enceinte. Il s'agit de la porte des Champs, flanquée dès sa création sinon d'une barbacane – trop proche en son état actuel du modèle de la barbacane de la Porte Saint-Pierre pour n'avoir pas été aussi modifiée au XVe siècle – du moins nécessairement d'un avant poste chargé d'en garder l'approche.

C'est aussi à cette époque que deux tours rondes, évidemment mieux adaptées aux défenses d'angles, sont ajoutées au rempart, là où les fortifications de la ville (Bourg le Roi) joignent celles du château.

Au siècle suivant, commence la guerre de Cent Ans. La Normandie, par sa situation géographique y joue un rôle majeur. En juillet 1346, après avoir débarqué à Saint-Vaast-la-Hougue, les troupes anglaises menées par Edouard III assiègent Caen. La ville ne peut résister longtemps en raison de fortifications vétustes et inadaptées. Rendus maîtres de la ville, les Anglais ignorent le château, préférant continuer leur chevauchée, et seule une poignée de leurs soldats stationne en ville pour y maintenir l'ordre. Les troupes françaises enfermées dans la forteresse font alors une sortie et chassent sans difficulté les occupants.

C'est en 1417 que les Anglais attaquent de nouveau Caen. Les fortifications de la ville pourtant améliorées pendant les années précédentes ne résistent pas davantage et le 4 septembre, les Anglais lancent une attaque décisive. Une fois encore ils délaissent le château dont les occupants se rendent sans combattre le 21 septembre, après avoir perdu l'espoir de recevoir des renforts extérieurs.

Les Anglais qui occupent le château se préoccupent peu de son entretien avant 1435 et le début de la reconquête française. Pendant les trois années qui suivent, ils aménagent une barbacane en avant de la porte Saint-Pierre (Figure 7.6) par crainte d'un soulèvement des Caennais. C'est l'occasion de signaler la présence à Caen d'un personnage appelé à la notoriété sous un autre avatar que celui de capitaine du château de Caen: Sir John Falstof, dont Shakespeare fera

*Figure 7.6. Le château depuis le clocher de l'église Saint-Pierre (photo: Pascal Leroux, Musée de Normandie).*

son Falstaff! On doit à cette période la transformation de la nef de l'église Saint-Georges en style gothique et, selon la tradition, la belle charpente lambrissée que l'on y voit encore. L'occupation anglaise prend fin le 1er juillet 1450 avec l'entrée en ville des troupes de Charles VII. Le château de Caen redevient français après 33 ans de présence anglaise.

La paix revenue, l'église Saint-Georges est de nouveau l'objet de travaux à la fin du XVe siècle où Jacques de Silly, alors bailli, fait reconstruire en style gothique le chœur de l'église probablement endommagé pendant les combats de 1450. La clef de voûte porte ses armes. Son fils François qui lui succède dans ses fonctions, se préoccupe quant à lui du renforcement du rempart que les progrès récents de l'artillerie ont affaibli. D'énormes talus de pierre et de terre sont appliqués le long des murailles à l'intérieur du château pour en augmenter l'épaisseur. Il fait également aménager des terrasses à canons dans l'enceinte du château, la première dans l'angle nord-ouest de l'enceinte, la seconde au sommet du donjon.

Ces travaux font sortir le château de Caen du moyen-âge. Palais ducal de 1060 à 1204, forteresse royale ensuite (Figure 7.7), il va connaitre le destin d'une caserne mal entretenue car ne convenant plus aux exigences de la guerre moderne, puis progressivement mais totalement transformée pour l'installation d'un régiment d'infanterie, envoyé à Caen à partir de 1875, dernier épisode de l'histoire militaire du site.

Les remblais du XVIe siècle ont fait disparaitre des constructions antérieures, notamment les ateliers et la maison situés dans le secteur nord-ouest du rempart et le bâtiment dont la fouille se poursuit en 2012 et 2013. La conclusion de ces travaux posera sans doute de manière très nouvelle la question de l'organisation du secteur palatial du château de Caen. Jusqu'à l'ouverture de ce chantier en effet le regard s'était porté sur l'étude et la restauration des éléments détruits après la promulgation de l'édit révolutionnaire ordonnant la destruction du donjon, l'occultation du site par la construction des casernes du XIXe siècle et les ravages des bombardements de 1944. Les fouilles de Michel de Boüard après guerre s'étaient ainsi concentrées sur le donjon, le palais de Guillaume et l'Echiquier. Les travaux de restauration du rempart et d'aménagement des salles du Musée de Normandie de 2004 à 2008 ont eu pour conséquence de relancer la recherche archéologique aujourd'hui menée dans le cadre d'une coopération européenne associant les châteaux de Caen, Falaise, Hastings, Rochester, Colchester et Norwich. Les journées de Norwich en mai 2012, qui sont l'occasion de la publication de cet ouvrage, ont été la première présentation publique des acquis de ces recherches. Un centre d'interprétation inauguré dans l'église Saint-Georges du Château de Caen les restituera au grand public en cohérence avec les démarches similaires accomplies sur les sites des partenaires de ce projet. C'est la prochaine étape de la redécouverte de l'histoire du château de Caen (Figure 7.8).

*Figure 7.7. Les fortifications de Caen sur le sceau de la Ville au XIIIe siècle (Archives nationales).*

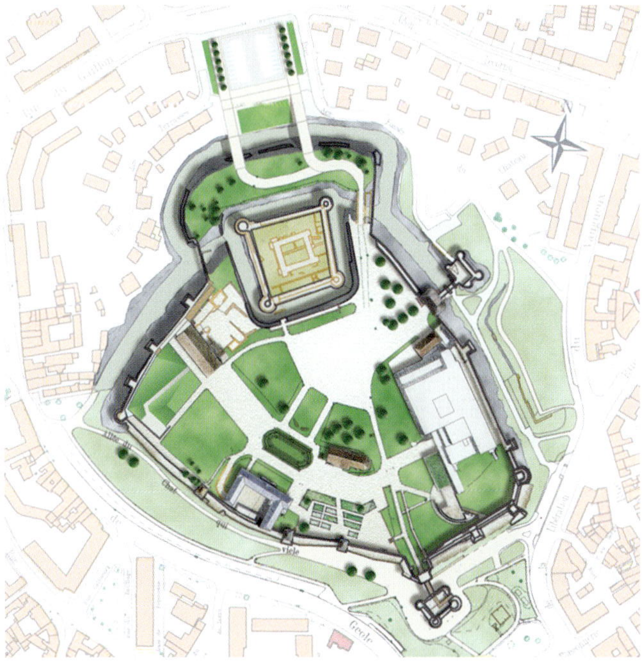

*Figure 7.8. Le château de Caen – plan général (document: Hervé Chéri pour le Musée de Normandie, Ville de Caen).*

## Notes

1. L'ouvrage fondamental sur l'histoire du château de Caen reste la publication des fouilles de Michel de Boüard: Boüard, M. de (1979) *Le Château de Caen* (Caen, Centre de Recherche d'Archéologie Médiévale), complété de *Mémoires du château de Caen*, catalogue d'exposition sous la direction de Levesque, J-M. et Marin, J-Y. (2000), Musée de Normandie (Caen, Editions Skira) et de *Le château de Caen, mille ans d'une forteresse dans la ville*, ouvrage collectif sous la direction de Decaëns, J. et Dubois, A. (2009) (Caen, Publications du CRAHM, Université de Caen).

   La relation du château avec la ville est étudiée dans Jean-Marie, L. (2000) *Caen aux XIe et XIIe siècles. Espace urbain, pouvoirs et société* (Caen, Editions La Mandragore).

   Un guide de visite du château a été publié en 2011 par Leroux, P. *Le château de Caen, un monument à visiter* (Editions OREP); la documentation sur les fouilles archéologiques est conservée au CRAHAM, Université de Caen et au Musée de Normandie.

   Les travaux les plus récents sont de: Guillot, B. (2006) *Le château, abords de l'enceinte* (Calvados, 14), rapport final de fouille, Direction Interrégionale Grand Ouest, Vol. III (Cesson-Sévigné, INRAP); Leon, C. 'La forge du château de Caen au Moyen-âge d'après les sources écrites (XIV–XVe siècles)', *Annales de Normandie*, 57e année, 3–4 novembre 2007, pp. 231–48; Carre, G. 'Le rempart nord-ouest du château de Caen (XIe–XVIe siècles). L'apport récent de l'archéologie du bâti', *Annales de Normandie*, 59e année, n° 2, juillet décembre 2009, pp. 3–25.
2. On consultera parmi les articles de cet ouvrage le texte de la conférence présentée par François Fichet de Clairfontaine pour une approche typologique et statistique très détaillée de ces sites pour la seule Normandie occidentale.
3. Sur l'organisation de cet espace dans la longue durée et le rôle de Guillaume le Conquérant dans l'organisation de ce territoire proche de Caen voir: Carpentier, V. (2011) *Guillaume le Conquérant et l'estuaire de la Dives*, Cahiers d'Auge, 3 (Lisieux, Les Editions de l'Association le Pays d'Auge).
4. Jean-Marie, L. (2000) *Caen aux XIe et XIIe siècles. Espace urbain, pouvoirs et société* (Caen, Editions La Mandragore).
5. Voir dans ce volume l'article de François Fichet de Clairfontaine.
6. 'e a Caen Ogne passerent / encore est Caen sainz chastel / n'i aveit fait mur ne kernel' (*sic*), Wace, 'Roman de Rou, III-5170/5173', dans *Le Roman de Rou de Wace*, publié par Holden, A. J. (1071) Tome III (Paris, Picard), p. 79 (traduction anglaise: Burgess, G. S., ed. (2004) *The History of the Norman people, Wace's Roman de Rou*, (Woodbridge, Boydell Press), p. 148).
7. Harris, R. B. (2008) 'The Structural History of the White Tower', dans E. Impey, ed., *The White Tower* (New Haven et London, Yale University Press), pp. 43–5.
8. Voir à ce sujet et sur d'autres enseignements des travaux récents l'article de Bénédicte Guillot, archéologue en charge des fouilles du château de Caen.
9. Boüard, M. de (1979) *Le Château de Caen.*
10. Un débat ancien et des recherches récentes questionnent la chronologie et l'organisation de ces constructions. On a repris ici les conclusions des fouilles de Michel de Boüard publiées en 1979. Voir sur ce sujet l'article d'Edward Impey et John McNeill publié dans ce volume, les contradictions qu'il apporte à cette thèse et ses propres conclusions.
11. Stapleton, T. (1840) *Magni rotuli Scaccarii Normanniae sub regibus Angliae*, Proceedings of the Society of Antiquaries of London (London).
12. Voir les éléments du débat repris par Edward Impey.
13. Harris, R. B. (2008) 'The Structural History of the White Tower', dans E. Impey, ed., *The White Tower* (New Haven et London, Yale University Press), pp. 29–93.
14. Impey, E. (2008) 'The Ancestry of the White Tower', dans E. Impey, ed., *The White Tower* (New Haven et London, Yale University Press), pp. 227–42.
15. Voir, contre cette hypothèse, le travail d'Edward Impey, notamment dans le présent ouvrage.
16. '… il y a une grosse tour eslevée deprès de 60 pieds dont la voute a 10 pieds d'espaisseur terminée par le haut par une belle plateforme de pierre de taille qui a 8 th(oises) en quarré. Cette tour est divisé en deux estages celui d'en bas a environ 20 pieds d'exhaussement sous le plncher et celuy d'en haut 30 pieds sous la voute' (*sic*), dans *Embouchures de la Touque, de la Dives, de la Horne, et Caen*, Lepeltier, le 30 août 1700. Signalé par Pascal Leroux dans un rapport manuscrit conservé au Service historique de l'Armée de Terre, Vincennes (SHAT, article 4, section 2, chapitre 2). Recensement effectué en 1999/2000 par Florence Mazzella pour le Musée de Normandie. Sur le contexte de ce recensement: Chapelot, J. et Mazzella, F. (2000) 'Les sources de l'histoire du château de Caen', dans *Mémoires du château de Caen*, catalogue d'exposition sous la direction de J-M. Levesque et J-Y. Marin, Musée de Normandie (Caen, Editions Skira), pp. 93–7.
17. Ces recherches qui se poursuivent en 2011, 2012, 2013 et 2014 dans le cadre du programme INTERREG 'Norman Connections' ont profondément renouvelé le dossier archéologique du château de Caen, indiquant notamment une occupation beaucoup plus dense dans le secteur palatial. Voir dans ce volume la contribution de Bénédicte Guillot.

# 8

# The Great Hall of the Dukes of Normandy in the castle at Caen

*Edward Impey and John McNeill*

**Résumé**

*Bien qu'elle ait été fortement endommagée en 1944, la grande salle de l'Échiquier, à Caen, est le mieux préservé des bâtiments séculiers de statut élevé et à fonction non-défensive de la Normandie romane. Élevée dans la partie nord-ouest de la basse-cour du château, elle mesure 13,16m sur 32,90m, l'entrée se faisant par le pignon et des fenêtres étant placées dans la partie supérieure des murs latéraux. A la fin du XIIe siècle, on ajouta un petit bâtiment sur sa face orientale, et, au XIVe siècle une cheminée murale et une annexe au nord. D'autres modifications furent apportées au bâtiment après qu'il ait été relégué au rang d'édifice à vocation militaire, au cours du XVIe siècle ou d'une période antérieure; les transformations les plus importantes datent de 1881, mais elles furent supprimées lors de la restauration menée en 1960. Les données que l'on peut retirer de l'étude des structures, des documents picturaux et de la comparaison avec d'autres bâtiments similaires montrent cependant qu'il était, à l'origine (et c'est aussi le cas aujourd'hui), constitué d'un seul volume, ouvert du sol à la charpente, sans étage, comme on le croit depuis les années 1960. On attribue traditionnellement cette grande salle à Henri I, mais, selon nous, sa conception générale et sa décoration le placent à la fin du XIe siècle, et nous sommes d'avis qu'elle fut créée par Guillaume Rufus, afin de servir à certaines cérémonies. Nous supposons enfin que sa construction marqua l'introduction (ou la réintroduction) en Normandie des grandes salles hors normes, isolées des autres bâtiments et pourvues d'une architecture distincte, et qu'elle encouragea l'aristocratie normande à l'adopter au siècle suivant.*

## Introduction

On the north side of the vast bailey of the castle at Caen stands the best-preserved, the largest and earliest Romanesque hall to survive in Normandy, known since 1840 as 'The Hall of the Exchequer' or *l'Echiquier*.[1] The building was studied by Professor Michel de Boüard, historian and pioneer of French medieval archaeology, and his excavations of 1949–66 in the castle and of the Echiquier's interior in 1960–1 remain the basis for all further research.[2] His accounts of the building published in 1962, 1965 and 1979, definitively identify it as a secular building, as part of the ducal and royal palace, and as an occasional seat of the Norman Exchequer.[3] None of this is disputed. There are, however, good reasons for challenging De Boüard's view that the building contained an upper floor, an interpretation that has had considerable influence on that of other Norman buildings since:[4] it is argued here that in its original form it contained a single volume (i.e. open from floor to roof), significantly altering its implications for the history of medieval domestic architecture in Normandy. In addition, a close analysis of the architectural and sculptural detail – itself deserving of more attention than so far received – challenges the building's long-accepted attribution to the 'reign of Henry I', and even more so to 'about the year 1120'.[5]

Now that the castle is undergoing the most substantial programme of research, conservation and re-display since the 1950s and '60s, and the reinsertion of a first floor is once again proposed, it is an appropriate moment for reassessment.[6] Based on a new measured survey of the building made in 2009,[7] and taking into account developments since the 1960s in the study of medieval domestic planning, Romanesque architecture and sculpture, this article offers a detailed description of the building, its structural history, and original form, and considers its architectural and art-historical context, date, attribution, and its place in the development of the 'great hall' in 11th- and 12th-century Normandy.

## Town, castle and palace

At the opening of Duke William's rule his most important cities were Rouen and Bayeux, both of Roman origin and the seats of bishoprics, ducal palaces and strongholds since the reign of Richard I (943–96). Caen, by contrast, is first known from references to the *burgus* and *villa* of *Cathim* from 1021–5 and 1026–7, and although levying tolls and boasting a port, a market place and fairs, remained obscure until the 1060s:[8] its emergence in the later 11th century as the second town of Normandy owed entirely to its selection by Duke William as the site of his new power base in Lower Normandy.[9]

*Figure 8.1. Detail from an MS* plan cavalier *of the castle of about 1650, looking north. The Echiquier is to the left, labelled 'Salle des munitions'. Attached and extending to the right is the 'Palais', by then a many-period complex but which incorporated and overlay parts of De Boüard's 'palais de Guillaume' (reproduced by kind permission of the Service Historique de la Défense (SHD Bibliothèque CF Atlas 2, France, Tome III, f. 60).*

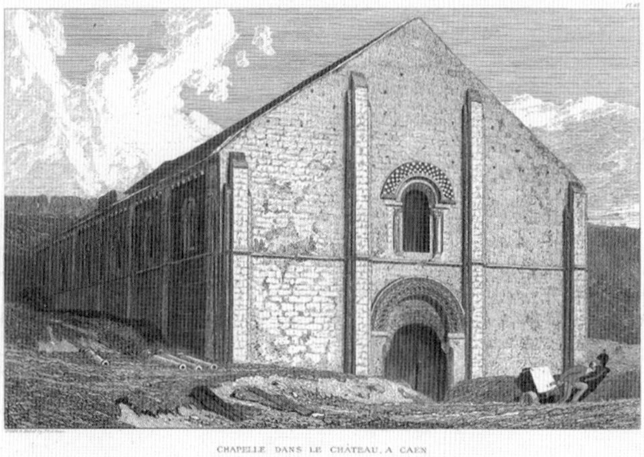


*Figure 8.2. Engraving of the Echiquier based on a drawing made on 18 August 1818 by John Sell Cotman (1782–1842), and published in Cotman and T. H. Turner's* Architectural Antiquities of Normandy *of 1822 (reproduced by kind permission of the Musée de Normandie).*

William's best-known legacy to Caen is the abbeys of La Trinité and St Etienne, founded in 1059–60 and 1063 respectively.[10] He also fortified and added to the town, but it was the castle that fitted it for the political and military role he had in mind: that William was its founder is stated in a 14th-century chronicle[11] and indicated by archaeology,[12] but near-proven by Wace's statement that Caen was '*encore … sainz chastel*' at the time of Varaville (1057),[13] and reference to its '*castellum*' and '*castrum*' in charters of 1080–2 and 1082;[14] De Boüard's considered that work began soon after, '*c.* 1060'.[15] The site was a flat-topped promontory overlooking the Orne valley, steep-sided except where joining higher ground to the north, already part-occupied, perhaps, with houses and a church.[16] Of the early defences, the ditch across the neck of the promontory, the footings of a gate-tower facing it and masonry in the north-west sector of the ramparts have been identified archaeologically,[17] but the walls (if probably towerless) must largely have followed their existing course. The use of stone is suggested by its availability and implied by two chroniclers' claims that the walls were 'heightened' by Henry I.[18] The perimeter provided the only defences and enclosed a vast area – at least 5 hectares (12.355 acres) – an arrangement which, in serving both governmental and defensive purposes, resembled that of *oppida* such as at Fécamp (2.5 hectares: 6.1 acres) more than the compact castles of more familiar type.[19]

Within the defences, close to the north-western rampart and immediately to the east of the Echiquier, stood a substantial stone-built residence,[20] excavated by De Boüard in 1962–3. This he dated to the second half of the 11th century on the basis of structural technique and coin evidence, and identified as the ducal palace, for reasons including the label '*Viel Palais*' attached to the complex on this site in the 17th century, the nature of what he found and, at least implicitly, its proximity to the Echiquier.[21] The footings remain exposed, although understanding the excavator's interpretation requires very careful reading of his 1979 text and plan, the fullest source available. Essentially, they represent a building containing a single room at ground level of 16 × 8m with a flagged floor and fireplace, and (at least as indicated in his reconstruction drawing), an upper floor. Accompanying this were service buildings and a clearly-identified chapel. The whole, he concluded, '*constituait très vraisemblablement l'aula et la camera du prince et leurs dépendences immédiates*'.[22] Whilst a nagging doubt must remain as to whether this really was the Duke's main residence at Caen – or all of it – its most striking characteristic is its meanness. By contrast, the scale and dignity of the Echiquier, befitting any princely residence of the period, suggests not simply an improvement but a step-change in the status and purpose of the ducal palace.

## The Echiquier: sources, layout and phasing

### *Sources*

Most important to understanding the original form and structural history of the Echiquier is the fabric itself, roughly 60% of which survived the 1944 bombardment (below), supplemented by the results of De Boüard's excavations. Other sources add to this in varying degrees. Medieval administrative material is confined to references to repairs to the halls *aulae* of the castle in 1180 and the '*grant sale … appelée le Tynel*' (almost unquestionably the Echiquier) in 1356;[23] repairs were again urged in 1662 and 1759, the military written records being of little value thereafter.[24] The 'epistle' *Ad Robertum* written by Ralph Tortaire in the early 12th century describes the town's 'high buildings shining like Parian marble', but does not, as has sometimes been claimed, mention the palace.[25] Graphic sources are of more help, the earliest useful representations being a detailed *plan cavalier* of the castle and immediate surroundings drawn (*c.* 1650) for the *Atlas Louis XIII* [26] and one of the town, surveyed at about the same time by Jacques Gomboust but engraved in 1672 (Figure 8.1).[27] The building's footprint is also shown on the numerous small-scale plans of the castle in the military archives at Vincennes and elsewhere, dating from 1699 onwards.[28] More informative is J. S. Cotman's exterior view engraved for his *Architectural Antiquities of Normandy*, published with Dawson Turner in 1822, based on his (lost) original of 1818[29] (Figure 8.2), and the interior view in Thomas Stapleton's *Magni Rotuli Scaccarii Normanniae* of 1840 (Figure 8.4). Two sketches by J. C. Buckler of 1836 also survive – one the original on which Stapleton's engraving is precariously based, and the other a view from the south, accompanied by details of the doorway and window above (Figure 8.3).[30] Equally important are a number of later 19th-century proposal drawings, a frustratingly partial record by Lucien Sallez of 1904,[31] surveys prepared by the army, a few pre-1944 photographs and others showing the building after bombardment and under restoration.[32] The drawings prepared by the office of Jean Merlet, post-war Architecte en Chef des Monuments Historiques for L'Eure and Calvados, are also of importance. Antiquarian writing, meanwhile, is disappointing. Neither Charles de Bras (1588)

*Figure 8.3. Sketch of the Echiquier and various details made by John Chessell Buckler (1793–1894) in 1836 (The British Library Board).*

nor Pierre-Daniel Huet (1706 and 1726) make any reference to the building, and Ducarel (1767) only to 'an arsenal called LE BESLE' – probably but not necessarily the Echiquier.[33] In the 1820s De Joliment and De La Rue identified it as a church (and so worthy of a brief description), but leave no useful observations.[34] Stapleton admired the '… ancient edifice which still stands undefaced…now used as a storehouse', but his text is little help.[35] The great Arcisse de Caumont, who might have said so much, fails to mention the Echiquier at all.[36]

*Figure 8.4. Interior of the Echiquier looking east, engraved by James Basire and printed as the frontispiece to Vol. I of Thomas Stapleton's* Magni Rotuli Scacciarii Normanniae *of 1840. It was taken from a sketch made by Buckler in 1836. The roof was a 17th-century replacement and the door had been widened, but otherwise the interior remained much as built. Thanks to the restoration of the 1960s it looks much the same today (reproduced by kind permission of the Society of Antiquaries of London).*

*Figure 8.5. The Echiquier after July 1944, showing the remains of the floor inserted at the south end in the 19th century, and the upper and lower openings in the south wall. The north end of the building was more severely damaged (reproduced by kind permission of the Ministère de la Culture – France – Médiatheque de l'architecture et du patrimoine).*

## *Layout*

Twenty years after its devastation in 1944, the building was restored to what was, as then understood, its late-medieval, single-volume form – owing, ironically, to the lack of detailed evidence for the form of its 'original' upper floor[37] (Figures 8.5 and 8.6). As a result, it in fact regained, it is argued below, a close approximation of its primary form. This is superbly simple: a rectangle, orientated north-west by south-east, with the main entrance and a window in the south-east gable and windows in the upper register of the side walls, and a single interior open from floor to rafters. Externally it measures (on average) 13.16m × 32.90m and internally 30.70m × 11.02m, giving it a floor area of just over 338m².[38] Inside, the walls are interrupted only by a string course, chamfered at its lower edge, at the sill-level of the windows. Externally, the elevations are articulated by pilaster buttresses (except the north), plinth, string course, and (side walls) with a corbel-table.

## *Phasing*

Alterations to the primary building (*Period I*) fall into three periods. *Period II*, dating to the later 12th century, saw a structure attached to the south end of the north-east side, consisting of or including the surviving single-storey vaulted room. *Period III*, dated from finds to about 1310–40 and inferred from documentary evidence to pre-date 1344, saw the building re-roofed, the ground floor flagged, a fireplace built into west wall, a building attached to the east side (with a chimney cut into its exterior wall)[39] and, according to the excavator, the removal of the original first floor. At or about this time a vaulted storage room was built against the north wall.

The building then remained substantially unchanged until 1881, with the insertion of a first floor over the southern half of the building, a series of forges, ground-floor windows, and new doors at two levels in the south gable. (*Period IV*).[40] The fifth period (i.e. its current state) dates from restoration in the early 1960s, following the destruction of most of the three northern bays of both side walls and of the north (gable) wall down to string-course level in July 1944.[41]

## Detailed description

The four elevations (internally and externally) are described in clockwise order, beginning with the entrance front, and the bays numbered consecutively. The true orientation of the building's main axis is north-west south-east (Figure 8.7),

*Figure 8.6. The Echiquier from the east, overlooking the site of the* 'palais de Guillaume'. *All but the upper part of the three bays to the right is largely original, although there are traces of medieval alterations, notably the remains of a fireplace inserted to serve an attached building in the 14th century. The 1960s structure to the left conceals a vaulted room added in the 12th century.*

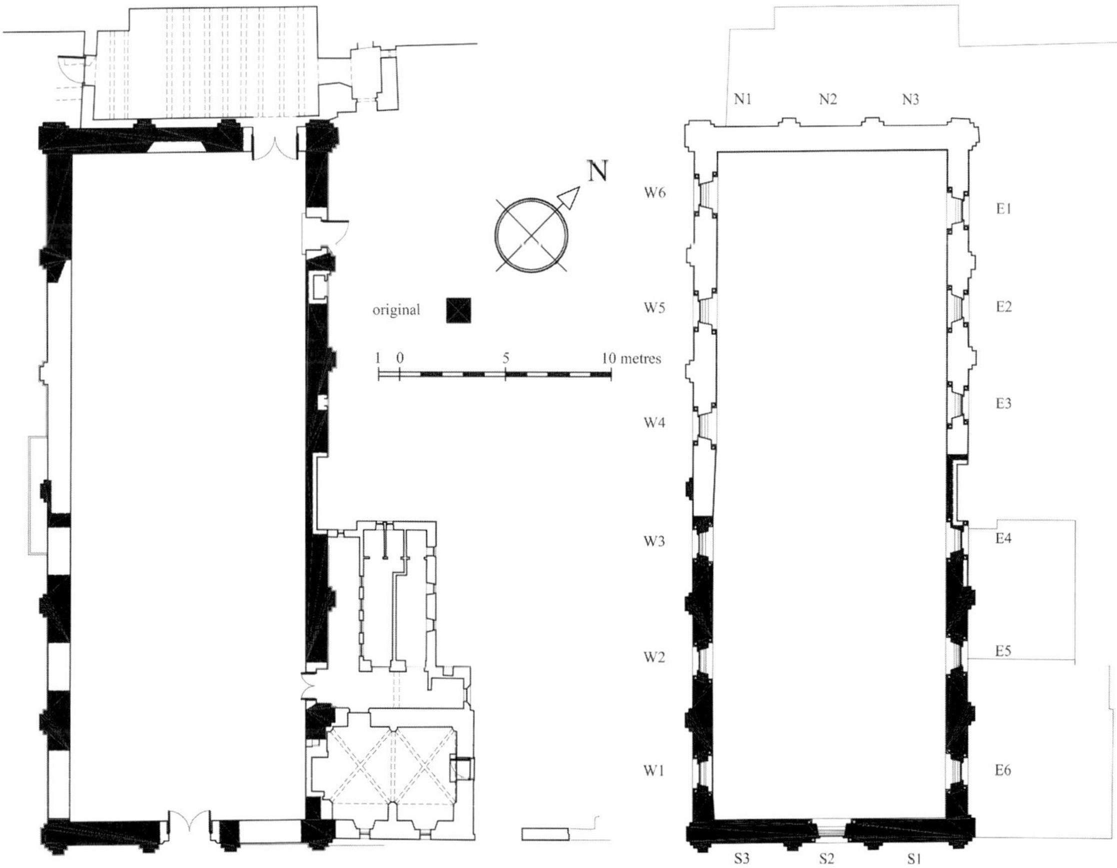


*Figure 8.7. Plans at entrance level and upper level (left, right).*

but for present purposes this is simplified to north to south. The description concentrates on the physical form of the building and its phasing: its art-historical context and the implications of architectural form and sculptural decoration are considered below.

### *South (entrance) front*

The entrance front survived 1944 intact (Figure 8.8). The elevation is of three bays (S.1–3), defined by buttresses at the corners rising to the eaves and two others, rising almost the full height of the elevation, defining the central bay. As throughout, the buttresses have dosserets, tabled summits, and rise from plain chamfered plinths; the top eight courses of the extreme left-hand buttress differ in omitting the dosseret and broadening out to form a single rectangular block (Figure 8.9). The string course, plain-chamfered to head and base and stepping across the buttresses, runs across the whole elevation at approximately mid-height.

The central bay (S.2) contains the building's main entrance (198cm wide; height from existing sill to soffit of segmental arch 293cm). The doorway has two orders of jambs – the outer one chamfered, the inner square, supporting a tympanum with a segmental arch to its underside, the whole tympanum surface being decorated by chip-carved saltires (see Figure 8.14). This is in turn framed by an order of chevron, composed (using Rachel Moss's classification and terminology) of two rows of lateral centrifugal chevron with a cogwheel inner edge,[42] i.e.:

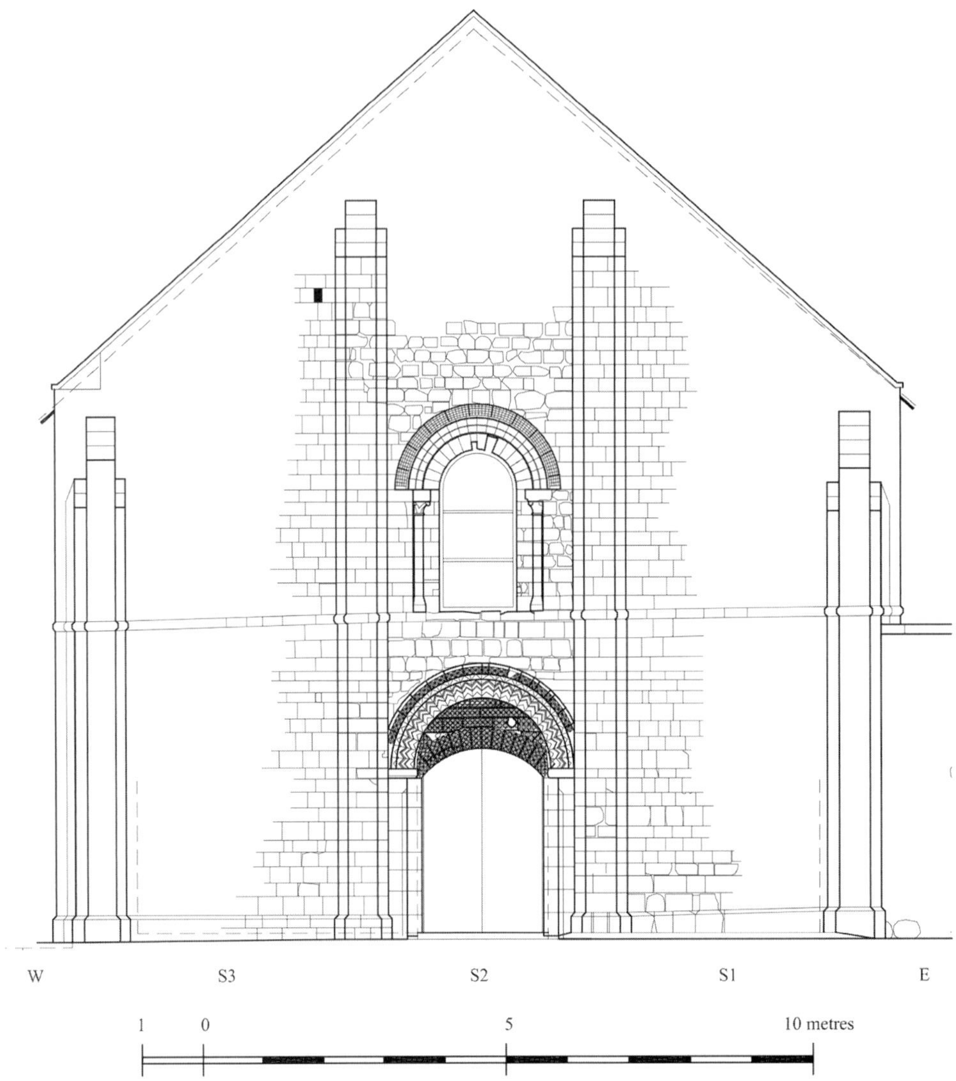


*Figure 8.8. Elevation, south, showing detail.*

1. The chevrons lie in the same plane as the wall (lateral);
2. The points facing outwards at the centre of the individual voussoirs into which they are cut face outwards (centrifugal);
3. The spaces between the chevron points at the inner edge are occupied by wedges, projecting at right-angles to the plane of the wall ('cogwheel edge').

Framing the chevron orders, and dying into the sides of the buttresses to either side, is a hood mould embellished with a geometric design beneath a plain upper border (14 voussoirs). Minute examination, and comparison with pre-restoration photographs, reveals no indication that any of the chip-carved and chevron-decorated masonry has been replaced, nor that, as De Boüard has argued, the chip-carved hoodmould (and thus the whole doorway) has been re-set;[43] the structural basis of his argument – that the hood-mould 'dies' into the flank of the adjacent buttress – being a common feature of Romanesque design, displayed locally, for example, on the lateral doors to the west front of St Etienne and the westernmost bays of the nave at La Trinité.[44]

The 14 voussoirs of the segmental arch, crudely cut back by 1818,[45] all largely survive *in situ*, although all but the left-hand springer were skilfully repaired with pieced-in stone to re-create the segmental soffit, in or shortly after 1962.[46] Both abaci survive in damaged condition, although the right-hand one bears traces of quirk and chamfer.[47] Beneath these there may, as in the case of the window above (and as Merlet assumed) have been capitals and colonnettes: if so the right-hand jamb, certainly pre-1944, must be a replacement, as it leaves insufficient width (14cm) to accommodate the capital under the abacus. The inner reveals, jambs, rere-arch and soffit, however, as evident from the fabric and Jean Merlet's 1963 specification, are modern.[48] The curious 'trefoiled' appearance of the rere-arch as shown in the Buckler sketch and the Stapleton engraving (Figure 8.3) was the result of widening and heightening at some stage before 1818.

Above the stringcourse, directly over the doorway, is an original window, formed of a round-arched single light has an unchamfered surround, flanked by colonnettes, coursed with the ashlars to the wall. The bases and capitals survive, although badly weathered and better understood with reference to the Cotman view: the left capital is of volute broadleaf form, the right one similar but with straps running to the volutes and crossing on the face; the abaci have been cut back flush with the wall, but were similar to those of the door. The head of the window opening itself is formed of voussoirs with chip-carved saltire decoration. Surrounding this a roll-moulding, hollow, and a broad order of multiple billet decoration.

At various stages other openings have been made in this elevation. The 1650 *Atlas Louis XIII* (Figure 8.1) shows upper openings in the side bays (S.1 and S.3), but the fact that neither the Cotman or Buckler views, any other image, or the surviving fabric either show or hint at traces of openings suggests they were the draughtsman's invention. In the 19th century (Period IV), however, a ground-floor opening and another directly above (its sill below the string

*Figure 8.9. The Echiquier from the south-west.*

course), were inserted in the right-hand bay, the latter giving access to a half-length mezzanine for munitions storage.[49] By 1889 the sill and lintel of the lower door had been raised and the upper opening blocked.[50] Both openings were skilfully made good with re-used ashlars in the 1960s.[51]

### West

The west elevation is of six bays, articulated by buttresses, plinth, string-course and corbel-table, with a single window to each bay above the string course. The spacing/setting out of the bays is (unlike on the east elevation) regular. Numerous photographs show that the three northern bays (W4, 5, 6), except for the lower part of bay 6, were completely destroyed in 1944.

*W1:* Both the external and internal facing is largely original, including the surround and detailing to the window: outside a single, round-headed light is surrounded by plain un-chamfered ashlars, flanked by colonnettes, with second un-chamfered arch over; inside is a similar overall arrangement, with a three-stepped sill, the basic form shared by all other side windows in the building. Externally, the well-preserved capital to the left has crude volutes and beaded strapwork (*entrelacs perlés*) crossing on the face: the right-hand capital is original (Figure 8.9) but badly eroded, as are both interior capitals. In 1881 a square-headed window with splayed reveals was cut through the lower register, as also in bays W2 and W3, all carefully blocked with re-used ashlars in the 1960s. Here as in the adjoining bays (W2, W3), but nowhere else, the corbels are original, as shown by their appearance, condition, and known survival in 1944.[52] These are as follows (right to left):

1. No surviving motifs
2. Head, much damaged
3. Crude, low relief face on roundel, neck below
4. Pig's head and forequarters, round flat-ended snout, large ears.
5. Horizontal cylinders (roll mouldings), the lower one split into two sections;
6. Damaged, probably a head.

*W2:* The window form and 19th- and 20th-century alterations below are as per W1. The left-hand external capital is of the strapworked form, similar to but that of W1; the right-hand capital is badly eroded. Inside, both capitals are original but all detail is lost. Corbels as follows (right to left):

1. Damaged, perhaps a head
2. Bracket form, concave underside
3. Monkey (?)
4. Head, damaged
5. Owl (?)
6. Bracket form, concave underside, central rib presenting T-shaped elevation at top

*W3:* The original fabric of the upper register largely survives. Externally, the right-hand capital right, has volutes and diagonal straps across the face. The left-hand capital is a 1960s replacement. Inside, left, badly eroded; right, crude volutes.

1 Three animal heads arranged as triangle – two above, one (centred) below
2. Chevron to the top; head or ball hanging from centre
3. Head, face intact
4. No surviving motifs
5. Two figures embracing (or fighting?)
6. Post-medieval replacement

Substantial alterations were made to bays W3 and W4 in Period III, which could be fully explained only with the aid of a large-scale phased drawing. De Boüard's excavation showed that a fireplace had been inserted in the wall straddling the two central bays, 4m wide, at least as deep as the wall thickness (1.05m) and with a paved hearth projecting 75cm into the interior.[53] This accounts for the mass of ashlar, 5.48m long and 91cm deep and four courses high, which survives – thanks to its burial as the ground-level rose – on the outside, clearly built to house the fireplace opening and form the base of its stack. The stack base is carefully scribed and bonded with the original masonry, but faced with larger, better finished and finely jointed blocks. A hollow chamfer to the top of the plinth supports De Boüard's late medieval dating. The presence of a chimney also explains the protrusion atop the side wall in Cotman's view (Figure 8.2). The date of its removal is unknown, although, taken literally, the *Atlas* view would place it before *c.* 1650, in keeping with the legend '*Salle des munitions*', in which a fireplace would have been both useless and dangerous. Certainly it had gone by 1818.[54] The careful re-facing (some of which survived the 1881 and 1960s work), however, suggests the continued high-status use of the interior, perhaps associated with the display of weaponry as much as with storage.

*W4:* Post-1944 photographs show the destruction of this bay to ground level, up to the north (left) flank of the buttress.

*W5:* Entirely 1960s.

*W6:* The original fabric of at least 22 courses (i.e. to approximately string-course level) of the clasping buttress at the north-west corner, and a substantial area of adjacent walling to bay W6 survive intact. The buttress has no plinth.

### North

The photographic record shows that in 1944 the north wall was destroyed to within 20 courses of the ground, most of the internal facing to within 12 and a short section at the centre to its foundations.[55] The exterior is buttressed as on the east (entrance) front, although without a string-course. The upper parts dating from the 1960s, and the lower parts concealed (below). The existing doorway in the eastern bay (N3) is entirely modern, pierced through intact Romanesque masonry. The Sallez plan, however, appears to show a ground-level doorway in the central bay (N2), not incompatible with photographic evidence mentioned above, but of which no trace survives. Built against the north wall is a ground-level cellar, apparently undamaged in 1944. The interior measures 10.62m east-west by 4.94m and is spanned by a 12-bay barrel vault with broad-chamfered ribs, suggesting a 14th- or 15th-century origin.

### East

The upper parts of the three northern bays were destroyed in 1944, but the three to the south left largely intact. On this side of the building, the post-Period I structural history is complicated by buildings placed against it in the 12th and 14th centuries (Periods II and III), alterations to them known from 17th- and early 20th-century documents but for which the physical evidence is absent or confused, and the selective consolidation of the 1960s.

*E1:* Whether the doorway is an entirely post-1944 insertion or replaces an earlier and perhaps Period I original is unclear: on the inside is a square embrasure and semicircular head, all in 1960s stonework; on the outside, although apparently contemporary with the post-1944 re-facing, it has a segmental head of ostensibly post-medieval form, perhaps wholly or partly re-used. The jambs are modern. No door here is shown on the 1881 plan, although a walled-up opening could have been ignored or omitted.[56] The Sallez plan of 1905 shows an opening in this bay but is unclear as to whether this was at ground-floor level or above. [57]

*E2*: The lower (*c.* 14–17) courses of the external facing appear to be original. Cut through it towards the right-hand side of the bay is a cupboard of late-medieval design, 61cm deep and 71cm wide, with stone ledges to support three shelves, rebated for shutters, with a segmental head. This shows that, when inserted, this bay faced an interior. Opposite this, *c.* 3.70m from the wall face, is the top step of a straight flight of 28–29 steps descending at right-angles to the wall to a cellar under the Echiquier. This consists of a central barrel-vaulted passage (2.11m wide), faced by two barrel-vaulted recesses (153m wide, up to 2.00m deep), and originally by at least one more on each side to the south-west (concealed by modern blocking). A narrow vertical shaft led to the floor of the Echiquier. The cellar is of typical French 13th-century to late medieval form, similar to examples surviving at the Manoir d'Agnès Sorel (Seine-Maritime, *c.* 1300), Ailly (Eure, *c.* 1275), Chauvincourt (Eure, *c.* 1220):[58] together with the only detailing (chamfered segmental head to below-ground doorway) this supports De Boüard's attribution to the 14th century (Period III). At some stage, possibly from its creation, it was linked by steps and a narrow passage to the cistern described below. The upper part of the wall, from below string-course level, belongs to the 1960s.

*E3*: In the lower part of the exterior face is a small square-headed niche, with sides rebated for doors., cut into the Phase I wall in Phase III. As with the similar feature in the bay adjoining, it must have faced an interior. The upper parts are work of the 1960s.

*E3–4*: Of interest with regard to the original form of the building is the distance between the windows, substantially greater than between the others (Figure 8.10). This could be explained by the presence of an original mural fireplace at this point, the moving of the windows to make space for the hood of the fireplace placed against the outside in Period III, or an error in setting out. Given the inadequacies of the structural evidence, all three are possible, but it would be curious if an original fireplace was destroyed in the 14th century to be replaced by another on the opposite wall. The left capital to the window is original, although probably re-set (and not necessarily from this position). In good condition although missing the projecting corner, it has volutes with interlaced straps across the face.

The most prominent feature, however, is the vast later-medieval (and probably Period III) fireplace cut into the original exterior, 3.33m wide and 49cm deep (Figures 8.9–8.11). The stone hood of the fireplace rose to the corbel-table, carried by stone corbels 70cm by 29cm in section, propped by subsidiary corbels with round-chamfered lower edges, all now cut off flush with the wall. The width and relatively shallow depth of the fireplace and the absence of associated ovens etc suggest that this was not a kitchen fireplace, and so not the '*cuisine de tinel*' mentioned in 1344, but a habitable room. [59] The creation of the fireplace obliterated the buttress between bays E3 and E4 and the associated building may or may not have obscured the windows, depending on its orientation and the arrangement of its roof. The absence of any traces of attachment suggests that the building was timber-framed.

*E5:* The window had been blocked since at least 1881, but survived the bombardment largely intact, although its head and the wall above fell or were subsequently removed. Inside, the left-hand capital, much damaged, may be the original re-inserted; the right-hand example is modern, as are both capitals on the outside and the corbels above. At ground-floor level a doorway, cut through in the 1960s, leads into the adjoining multi-phase annexe (below).

*E6*: The window had been blocked at least since the placing of a chimney flue against the other side of the wall in the 17th century (below) and was reopened only in the 1960s. Inside, the left-hand capital is original but has lost all detail but is perhaps original; the right-hand example is modern.

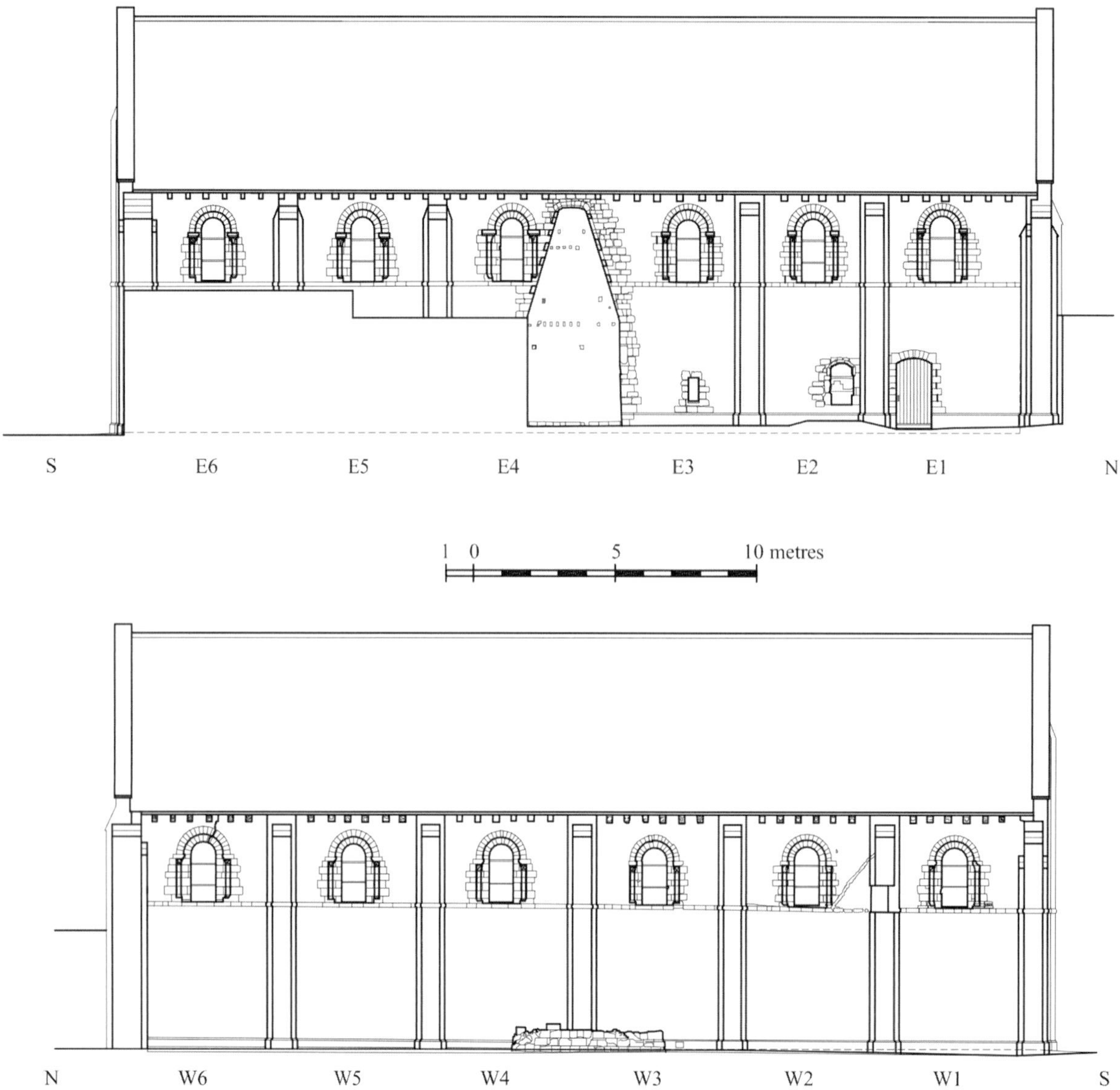


*Figure 8.10. Elevations: east (above), west (below).*

*E5–6, attached building:* The lower part of both bays is today obscured by a single-storey structure: the main part, built against NE6, is a vaulted chamber originally measuring 5.95m from south-west to north-east and 3.65m across, spanned by two bays of quadripartite vaulting. A doorway in the north-east wall is probably original; the other, to the north-west, may be too. The square-sectioned, plain-chamfered ribs and the faceted piers with battered capitals, similar (for example) to those in the chamber-block undercroft at Fontaine-Henry, or the ribs to the undercroft at Creully, imply a date in the later 12th century.[60] In the 17th century a fireplace and oven were built into the side wall of the Echiquier, creating a kitchen for, or later used by, the '*Major*' (1729) and his successors.[61] To the north of this is a 1960s lavatory block, but details shown on the 1905 plan and one slender, hollow chamfered vaulting-rib show that the 12th-century building was added to in the later middle ages, presumably contemporary with the building of the Period III fireplace and associated building.

De Boüard identified the vaulted room as the '*cuisine du Tinel*' (above), and argued that it replaced the original kitchen in the ground floor of the Echiquier;[62] more probably the room became a kitchen only in the 17th century with the insertion of the existing fireplace. Meanwhile the general form and appearance of the vaulted interior is reminiscent of those carrying external first-floor landings to the 12th-century chamber-blocks at Creully and Fontaine-Henry: as such it would, on the face of it, fit De Boüard's 'first floor' interpretation very neatly, but must in fact have served a room to the north-east.

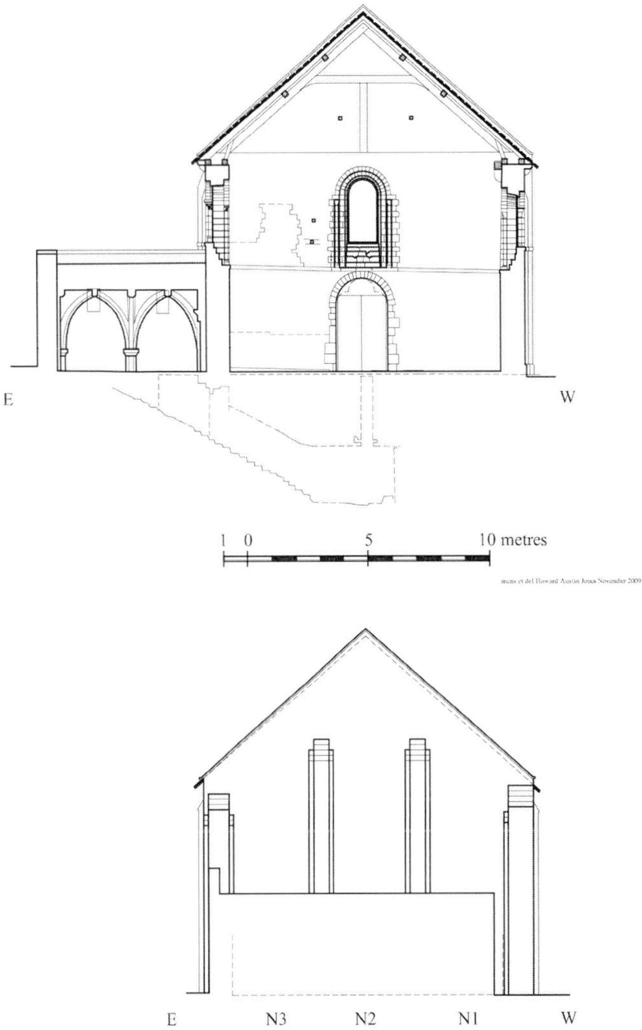


*Figure 8.11. Cross-section, facing south and north elevation.*

### *Internal features – the cistern*

Under the south-west corner of the Echiquier is a stone-lined void, excavated and left empty in September 1961 (accessible from the later medieval cellar to the north: below). The interior is *c.* 2.30m north–south by 1.97m, and its floor is 4.50m below the 1961 ground-level. It is partly lined with plain ashlar of late 11th–12th-century type: on the east by plain walling, on the west side reinforced by four buttress-like projections, on the north by a short stretch of wall and another buttress. The south wall is formed by natural bedrock, but reinforced by a pier carrying, at the top, a stone water-spout linked to a channel conveying water from the roof. The space is spanned by a barrel-vault, reinforced by square-section ribs (springing from well behind the face of the wall). De Boüard identified the feature as a cistern, used from the 13th century as a rubbish pit, and suggests that the vault replaced a flagged covering. Water could only have been extracted through a trap-door.[63]

## Original form

### *An upper floor?*

A-propos its original form, the main question is whether it was, as De Boüard insisted, two-storeyed, an interpretation supported (with the occasional acknowledgement of debate), by all French authors[64] except Jean Mesqui (1993, 1997 and 2008):[65] the 'single-volume' interpretation, put forward by Impey in the 1980s and in print in 1993, has found more favour (if indeed ever doubted), in England.[66] De Boüard's reasons and the counter-arguments can be summarised as follows.

1. *The absence of flagged paving (*dallage*) to the original floor and the presence of pits containing food remains.*[67] The original floor was of blackened beaten earth, 2–4cm thick, its uneven surface pierced by at least nine pits (7–70cm deep) filled with household waste.[68] De Boüard equates the absence of paving with low-status use, notes that similar pits and contents are known in medieval kitchens, and infers the presence of a ground-floor kitchen and services: the implication is that the grand interior of this manifestly high-status building must have been at an upper level. However, floors of beaten earth are not unknown in high-status medieval buildings, both secular and ecclesiastical (and floors of chalk or plaster were very common): examples include Westminster Hall.[69] The absence of paving does not therefore imply low-status use, still less the presence of an upper floor.
2. *The placing of the existing windows* high up in the walls, which, along with their small size, would have made them inadequate for lighting a room open to the full height of the building.[70] However, Romanesque interiors, most obviously churches, but also secular halls and monastic refectories, were routinely lit by relatively small windows in the upper register of the wall, largely because this was the most effective way of lighting the interior. Indeed, when it comes to Romanesque single volume spaces, low windows are an exception. This is true at both a small and a large scale, exemplified in Normandy in the aisleless naves of the parish churches of Tollevast (Manche) or St-Céneri-le-Geréi (Orne).[71] However, since no Romanesque unaisled great churches survive in elevation in Normandy, and were anyway rare, the point is best made by looking south, particularly to the Loire valley, where aisleless naves were the preferred Romanesque form. Eleventh century examples include Cravant-les-Coteaux (Indre-et-Loire), Le Lion d'Angers (Maine-et-Loire) and Villevêque (Maine-et-Loire), while a number of major 12th-century churches updated the format to include a tall internal dado arcade, most

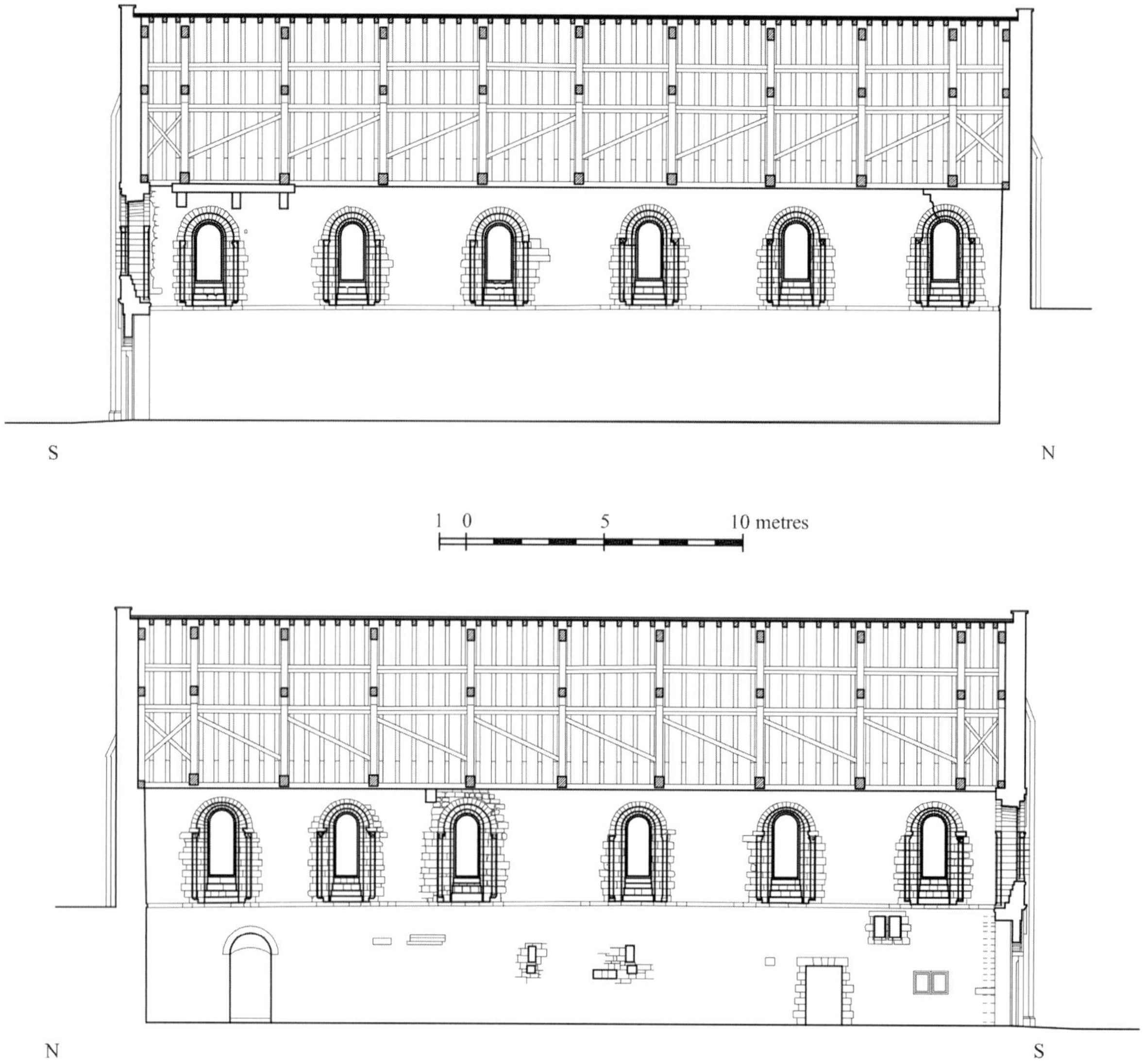


*Figure 8.12. Long sections, facing east (top) and facing west.*

spectacularly at Fontevraud and Angers cathedral, where the sills of the nave windows are set around 9m above pavement level.[72] The Romanesque preference for high-level fenestration extends to aisles also, where windows are invariably arranged in the upper part of the wall, a tradition taken to an extreme in the tall aisles of hall churches.[73]

3. *That the windows originally had stepped sills*, the inference being that this would have been a more suitable arrangement, with sills so close to floor-level, than the usual *glacis*.[74] In fact, stepped sills are frequently found well above floor level, a local example being provided by the church of St Nicholas at Caen. De Boüard argues that the steps were mortared over to make a *glacis* only when the floor was removed, to improve the lighting of the space below. In fact, as laying mortar over square-cut ashlars is easier than cutting them at an angle, this was (as elsewhere) probably the arrangement from the start.
4. *That, as a storeyed building, it conformed to 'one of the best known types of domestic architecture of the 12th century'.*[75] While De Boüard's understanding that a storeyed arrangement was normal for high-status halls was not the basis of his interpretation, he clearly saw it as an important endorsement. Given what he knew of such buildings in France,[76] and that halls were then thought, in England, to have normally been at first-floor level, this is understandable.[77] However, work since the 1970s has shown that not only are high-status ground-floor halls known in France before 1100 (such as the spectacular example at Angers, perhaps as early

as the late 10th century),[78] but more importantly that the 'first-floor hall' model of the 1960s was based on a misunderstanding.[79] Furthermore, the single volume, un-aisled, high-windowed form of the Echiquier is common to a number of halls in England, most obviously Westminster, now believed to have been roofed by a single span.[80] At a slightly less ambitious level the aislesless hall range at Sherborne Castle (Dorset) was clearly a single-volume space, and traces of a string-course where the west wall of the hall abutted the keep, along with standing evidence for the ground plan and doorways, suggest high-set windows and a single-span roof. The hall of the courtyard house at Old Sarum castle, also built by Roger of Caen (*aka* Roger of Sarum, d. 1139), was almost certainly similarly arranged as a single-volume, high-windowed aisleless space.[81] Still more exact analogies can be found among monastic refectories, from which it has been suggested that the type derives.[82] These include the late 11th-century refectory at Westminster Abbey,[83] the refectory or hall at Minster Court (Kent: *c.* 1120), a rural residence of St Augustine's abbey, and perhaps most strikingly similar of all, the refectory of Dover Priory of the 1130s (Figure 8.13).[84]

5. In addition, although not cited in his published reports but recorded in his notes, De Boüard considered the *interior string course to be a late insertion*, and so, given that it would have been pointless in a two-storeyed building, took it as a further indication of its original storeyed form.[85] Subsequent authors, although not De Boüard himself, cite the under floor cistern as further evidence or proof of the menial function of the ground floor, inferring, in such an imposing building, the presence of an *étage noble* above. [86]

Moreover, it is worth noting that the *absence* of a floor would immediately provide better answers than De Boüard's to some of his own residual questions. He asks, for example, how the smoke would have escaped from the ground floor, responding that holes must have been provided in the walls.[87] As for how the ground floor would have been lit, he concludes that all traces of such 'inelegant' openings were obliterated with the removal of the floor.[88] Considering how the upper floor might have been supported, he postulates a line of props, all traces of which, he suggests, were lost when this arrangement was replicated in the 19th century.[89] The height of the rere-arch to the south doorway, rising well above the postulated upper floor level, is explained by its identification as a 14th-century insertion, removed from its original first-floor position to replace a much smaller original – a proposition roundly refuted by the fabric.[90] Finally, he can provide no suggestion at all as to the site of the original upper doorway. Overall, the inescapable conclusion must be that the Echiquier was, as built, a single-storey structure.

*Figure 8.13. The south side of the 12th-century refectory at the priory of St Mary and St Martin at Dover (Kent), viewed from the south. It shows the elevational treatment found at the Echiquier (high windows, buttresses, string course and corbel table) applied to a building which indisputably housed a 'double-height' interior, open from floor to rafters.*

### *Other features*

The span of the hall, at 11.02m (36ft) would not have required posts to support the roof, nor would posts be easily compatible with the gabled ends and the central position of the south door.[91] This was, however, an era when wide-span roof design was seriously flawed, and the major repairs to the building required in the 1330s may have owed to the roof's structural failure. Although there could have been a fireplace in the east wall (between the widely-spaced windows in E3 and E4), a central hearth, no doubt nearer the northern than southern end, is more likely. The most important problem remains the position of any secondary doorways, which, for practical reasons, must have supplemented the southern entrance. Any such opening or openings must have been to the east, the most likely position being that of the existing doorway towards the north end (Bay E1).

## Date and art-historical context

### *Dating: the received view*

De Boüard was cautious in dating the Echiquier. In 1962 he placed it simply 'in the 12th century', and only in 1965 and 1979 to the reign of Henry I.[92] In the two later publications he placed it on stylistic grounds only in 'in the first half of the 12th century',[93] although in a general article on the Norman Romanesque he noted the habit of mixing the archaic with the novel and observed that 'entrelacs perlés' (as found at the Echiquier) can be of 11th-century date.[94] His attribution to Henry I (i.e. from 1106–35) was based, his text implies, on the king's documented building of the donjon.[95] Lucien Musset agreed, although implied an early initiative on the King's part, noting that 'its austere façade displays the same purely geometric decoration' as the churches of the early 12th century.[96] Eric Carlson, in his study of St Etienne, accepts its attribution 'in large part … to the reign of Henry'.[97] Other authors have followed their lead, some offering greater precision:[98] Jean Mesqui places it in the 1120s (as do the new visitor information boards in the adjoining museum).[99] Only Maylis Baylé demurs, placing the Echiquier, if without explanation, 'vers 1100'.[100] All this is understandable. On the face of it Henry I is a good candidate: he was a frequent visitor to Normandy and did business in Caen in 1118, 1120, 1124, 1130–1, and twice between 1133 and 1135, although he did so at Rouen at least 45 times.[101] He was also a well-known architectural patron and his brother's hall at Westminster could have served as a model and incentive. Such a project could have been a fitting signal of his swift assertion of authority after Tinchebrai.[102] Nevertheless, on the evidence presented to date, a firm attribution to the either the 12th century or Henry, let alone 'the 1120s', could not be justified. In fact, at least two scraps of historical and archaeological evidence may specifically suggest otherwise, the first (*pace* De Boüard) being the *absence* of the Echiquier from de Torigni's detailed enumeration of his works there and elsewhere, which included a 'fittingly royal house' (*mansio*) at Rouen.[103] The second – the larger blocks and narrower joints used in facing the donjon – implies that the donjon and the Echiquier were not built as part of the same campaign.[104] The best evidence for the building's date, however, lies in its design and decorative detailing. Although considered by De Boüard, Musset, Baylé and others, this remains to be properly explored, and tells a rather different story.

### *Architectural and art-historical context*

#### *Form and articulation*

In considering the date and art-historical context of the Echiquier, the first point that should be made is that there is nothing in the essential form of the building (rectangular, single-volume with high windows) that either indicates or precludes a date anywhere between the early 11th and the mid-12th century. This obvious, basic arrangement was used at Westminster Hall, the great hall at Angers and in any number of aisleless churches scattered across western France. Nor can one confine the elevational format to a narrow chronological span. High windows resting on a string-course, pilaster buttresses, and corbel-tables were a standard arrangement from the second half of the 11th century to the advent of Gothic: locally, these elements are found at the church of St Nicholas in Caen (aisles), begun perhaps *c.* 1080–82,[105] Lessay (eastern parts) by 1098,[106] the west front of St Etienne as completed by 1087, and at Gournay-en-Bray (south nave aisle), placed by John James *et al. c.* 1075–85.[107] The same is true of the three-bay gable end, with central doorway and window above flanked by pilasters, the whole fronting an unaisled interior, as at Restigné (Maine et Loire), Tennie and Malicorne-sur-Sarthe (Sarthe) and Chambois (Orne).

Examined at a more detailed level, however, there are indications of an earlier date. The articulation of the windows with two un-moulded arches, a lower string-course, and coursed nook shafts inside and out supporting capitals and abaci, has no precise local parallels, but is a variation on a repertoire well established by 1100. String-courses were being applied in Normandy in the last quarter of the 11th century, internally and externally, as at St Nicholas, Caen, Cerisy-la-Forêt and the presbytery and apse at Lessay. Unmoulded window arches in two orders are paralleled by the clerestory of St Nicholas, Caen, and the west front of St Etienne, while coursed angle shafts supporting capitals and unmoulded arches in two orders are used in the presbytery clerestorey of Notre-Dame-sur-l'Eau at Domfront (Orne). Precise Norman parallels for the Echiquier windows are rare simply because ambitious late 11th-century Romanesque churches in Normandy are aisled as a matter of course, and from St Etienne onwards employ thick walls and clerestorey wall passages. The relatively thin walls of the Echiquier rule out wall passages, and although nave aisle windows are frequently in two orders with angle shafts and capitals, by the early 12th century the angle shafts were more often monolithic colonnettes, and the outer arch was usually moulded. The sole feature potentially indicative of a later date is the segmental arch over the south doorway, yet pre-1100 examples do exist, including in the presbytery of La Trinité, probably finished by 1066.[108] Others, at Catenoy, Saint-Vaast-Lès-Mello and Thiverny (Oise), have been placed between 1080 and 1105.[109] Most important, however, is the decorative detail.

### *Sculpture: bases and capitals*

Less than a fifth of the original capitals survive and these are mostly badly weathered. As far as can be judged the bases were varied, though the mouldings themselves seem to have been shallow, amounting to little more that undulations on the surface of an architectural element designed to meet the horizontal stringcourse at an angle of around 120°.[110] The capitals are characterised by prominent volutes and plain rear grounds, the latter sometimes cut to suggest a broadleaf support. The surface of this ground is embellished by tendrils or ribbons, some of them thin and rounded, like stalks, others shallow and grooved, like plaits. Two of the capitals (exterior W1 east and exterior W3 west) carry a loosely symmetrical design, in which the ribbons cross to make a saltire (Figures 8.16 and 8.17). The majority of the capitals carry asymmetrical designs, however, in which the stalks are entangled or intersect. The effect of weathering makes it difficult to judge the original depth of carving, but they were probably fairly shallow (certainly more so than their modern companions), a point worth making in that the designs have a freedom and a linear quality associated with painted capitals, such as those at Blyth (Nottinghamshire) or St-Jean-d'Abbetot (Seine-Maritime).[111] There is little else like them that survives in Caen, and while there are sites within easy reach with capitals of broadly similar type and shape – as at Lion-sur-Mer, Beaumais, Cerisy-la-Forêt and Falaise (Notre-Dame-du-Guibray), none of these are strikingly close.[112] Given the existing state of knowledge the best parallels seem to be with work further south, in the Passais, particularly with Lonlay-l'Abbaye and Notre-Dame-sur-l'Eau at Domfront, and although neither church is documented and therefore of use in establishing a date for the Echiquier, they point to the same geographical origin as that suggested by the south façade.[113]

### *Sculpture: the south façade*

The south façade is self evidently the great decorative set-piece of the Echiquier, handled with a consistency and

*Figure 8.14. South doorway. The main arch is carved with chevron ornament, while the hood-mould carries a design based on intersecting circles. Beneath this one can be seen the segmental arch and tympanum embellished with étoiles en creux.*

*Figure 8.15. South doorway: detail.*

*Figure 8.16. Exterior capitals (W2, north and south). Though weathered the freely drawn carved plaits of the left-hand capital are still clearly visible.*

*Figure 8.17. W3: exterior window capitals: both capitals illustrate the tendency of the Echiquier sculptors to eschew geometrically well-defined compositions in favour of looser asymmetrical designs. The capital on the left is particularly notable in using a broad-leaf support as a rear ground.*

precision at odds with the freer detailing of the capitals and investing the entrance with an impressive sense of ceremonial purpose (Figures 8.9 and 8.14). Excepting the window capitals, the major decorative elements are geometric, and from bottom to top consist of diaper (*étoiles en creux et découpées en biseau*), chevron, a pattern based on intersecting circles (above the doorway), diaper (*étoiles en creux et découpées en biseau* – this time applied across rectangular ashlars), mouldings (an angle roll and hollow), and multiple-billet (above the window). The façade has usually been dated on the basis of the appearance of chevron, but this is simply one of several geometric forms, all of which require examination (Figures 8.14 and 8.15). From an Anglo-Norman perspective, the *étoiles en creux et découpées en biseau* are typologically the earliest form, appearing on the transept arches of La Trinité as early as *c.* 1059–66,[114] over the doorway to the Great Tower at Chepstow (Monmouth), and in the chapel at Durham Castle, probably both built before *c.* 1090.[115] By the late 1080s and 1090s, *étoiles en creux* were beginning to be used more widely in Normandy, appearing in Caen at Sainte-Paix, in the south at Notre-Dame-sur-l'Eau and Goult (Orne), and in the Seine valley by *c.* 1090 at Graville-Sainte-Honorine (Seine-Maritime).[116] It is at its most prolific in the parish churches of the Bessin and the Orne valley, buildings which are notoriously difficult to date, but a distribution which probably owes to an origin and early development in high-status buildings in Caen.[117] In the case of the Echiquier, the *étoiles en creux* of the tympanum and segmental arch are of the simplest and most common form: four-pointed stars, bevel-edged and inscribed within squares, arranged with only minor variations in scale (most noticeable on the radial voussoirs). If the intention was to create the illusion of a shimmering surface the result must be counted as a great success.

The tympanum in turn is framed by an arch made up of two rows of lateral centrifugal chevron with a cogwheel inner edge, a type among the most widely used and long lived in the Anglo-Norman repertoire. The problem with dating this, however, is not its ubiquity or longevity, but that its origins are so little understood. The reason for this is partly historical. Since Alan Borg first attempted to classify chevron in 1967, the south transept vaulting campaign at Durham of *c.* 1110 was taken as the earliest instance of chevron.[118] A result of this is that those quietly composed lists of possible late 11th-century candidates – the nave aisle portals at Le Mans cathedral of the late 1080s, the apse arch at Cerisy-la-Forêt of about the same date, the south aisle of Great Malvern Priory (*c.* 1085–1100), Anselm's choir at Canterbury (as begun *c.* 1096) – have only recently gained wide acceptance.[119] However, the major reason why our grasp of the origin of chevron is imperfect is formal. It has taken a long time for it to be realised that the simplest forms of chevron are based on mouldings, and that conceptually chevron is simply a chopped and recomposed moulding.[120] What follows is that chevron is most likely to have been invented in a region where masons were experimenting with elaborate and varied arch forms, and above all where there was an interest in combining mouldings with geometric forms with patterns. In late 11th-century France this points to the Loire Valley and Aquitaine, areas with an established tradition of applying elaborate geometric patterns to arches, and where, from the third quarter of the 11th century, one can detect a growing interest in breaking, deconstructing and re-ordering mouldings to feed an appetite for highly varied arch designs. Multiple-billet is an outcome of this, albeit one already used by ivory carvers in the 1050s.[121] More unexpected are those designs in which mouldings were arranged radially, or were even broken and recomposed in section, appearing as a series of discs that run back into the wall as tubes.[122] By the 1080s western French masons had also begun inserting geometric forms into the hollows of moulded arches, as in the upper storey of the choir of St-Eutrope at Saintes of 1083–96, the upper stages of the belfry at Cunault (Maine-et-Loire) of before 1091 and the west front of Le Mans cathedral.[123] Experiments with pattern and moulding were raised to an extraordinary pitch in western France in the last quarter of the 11th century, and resulted in an astonishing number of arch and voussoir designs. One of these is likely to have been chevron. Indeed, as things stand the earliest surviving examples of chevron are almost certainly the nave aisle portals at Le Mans, datable to the early part of the episcopacy of Bishop Hoel (1085–96), and used in a building which sits squarely within a western French architectural tradition (Figure 8.18).[124] That chevron was subsequently rarely used in the Loire valley and Aquitaine should not blind us to the likelihood that it was developed there. Whether the Echiquier was the first building in Normandy to take up chevron is more difficult to determine. The profile of the arch is close to that of Le Mans, though the Echiquier has dropped the angled fillet between the two rolls and added a cogwheel edge. But it is certainly much closer to Le Mans than to the apse arch at Cerisy, the only other 11th-century candidate to survive in the duchy.

The last element of the portal to be discussed – the hood mould – employs a pattern likely to have come from the same stable of designs that produced the chevron. The design itself is best described as a sequence of circles, which contain a square with concave sides, a pattern which is based on intersecting circles. The simplest way to illustrate this is to take a late antique pavement design, such as the 6th-century tessellated pavement from Porec (Croatia), and visually isolate a row of circles (Figure 8.19).[125] Reticulated designs based on intersecting circles were a commonplace of Roman and late Antique pavements, and survive in significant numbers, particularly at ecclesiastical sites in

*Figure 8.18. Le Mans Cathedral, south nave aisle portal. The type of chevron used on the outer arch at Le Mans is typologically close to that of the Echiquier. The lower stages of the west front at Le Mans date from the episcopacy of Bishop Hoel (1085–1096).*

*Figure 8.19. Poreč (Croatia), detail of mosaic pavement from the 6th-century Euphrasian basilica (the south hall of the cathedral complex). The design was popular throughout Late Antique Europe, and is based on a pattern of intersecting circles.*

*Figure 8.20. St-Jean-de-Montierneuf, Poitiers, west front detail. The fragments of geometric ornament illustrated were re-set in the present west front after its 11th-century predecessor was destroyed in the 17th century. The left-hand pattern is very similar to the design of the hood-mould above the south portal of the Echiquier. The original position of these fragments is uncertain, but it is likely that they were used as string-courses and date from* c. *1087–*c. *1096.*

4th–7th-century Italy. As early as the 2nd century, Roman designers had started to isolate and reconfigure the individual motifs created by intersecting circles,[126] but although the individual elements were widely used in the Roman and late Antique periods they do not seem to have been among the early wave of geometric motifs revived and used in decorative masonry patterns in the Poitou and Loire valley in the course of the 11th century. This seems to change in the last quarter of the 11th century, when bands or friezes of encircled concave-sided lozenges were used on the west front of the new Cluniac priory of St-Jean-de-Montierneuf at Poitiers in 1086–96 (Figure 8.20).[127] Thereafter the form is used on relief panels, string courses and arches (particularly hood moulds) becoming notably popular in England, where its earliest dateable use is probably on the inner elevation of the crossing tower of Winchester cathedral as rebuilt after the tower collapse of 1107.[128]

## Implications and dating

The portal is obviously the key to understanding and dating the ornamental repertoire.

Individual ornamental elements alone cannot date a building, but the prominence given to the juxtaposition of chevron and encircled concave-sided squares, both of which had been brought into use in the late 1080s or early 1090s at Le Mans and Poitiers respectively, argue for a date in the 1090s for the Echiquier. They are the geometrically precocious elements within an otherwise well-established repertoire, alongside which the coursed angle-shafts, unmoulded arches, and shallowly carved plaits of the capitals look positively conservative. On balance, it is a repertoire far more likely to have come together just before 1100 rather than significantly later.

The use of these forms also raises the question of the provenance of the masons responsible for the carved stonework. The importance given to the *étoiles en creux* probably rule out a western French workshop, or at least one with a free hand. The form is so closely associated with the visual culture of the Anglo-Norman world to either side of 1100 that a western French workshop would only have included the form if instructed to do so. Since the capitals suggest a southern Norman origin, and any workshop from this area would be well positioned to familiarise itself with the latest trends in western French architectural ornament, this would seem the most likely area from which this workshop was recruited. Whether they had worked in Caen previously it is now impossible to say, though the nature and prestige of the Echiquier make it an obvious candidate for being the building in which the type of enriched portal so familiar from the 12th century first came together in Normandy.

## Historical context and 'attribution'

If a creation of the 1090s, then the Echiquier was built under the rule either of Robert Curthose or William Rufus (respectively as Duke of Normandy and as ruler in Robert's absence from 1096–1100), and, as part of the ducal palace, in their knowledge. Of the two, Robert is the less promising candidate, partly as there were only two brief periods when it could be argued that he had both a reason and the resources to improve the palace at Caen. The first followed the 'inquest', jointly conducted by Robert and Rufus at Caen in July 1091, which produced the *Consuetudines et iusticie*:[129] in affirming the importance of the *curia*, this would have underlined the need for a fitting venue at Caen, which the Echiquier could, as it later did, have provided. However, the rapid descent into chaos which followed, suggests otherwise. The second occasion was in 1100, on his return from Crusade, rich, promising peace, and where Caen was his first destination following a visit to Mont-St-Michel.[130] However, whilst allowance must be made for Orderic's undoubted bias, further chaos, his immediate relapse into 'sloth and idleness',[131] coupled with the absence of any single building project attributable to Robert (including the Orne canal that bears his name) all count against him.[132] Nor are Robert's chronic insecurity, poverty, lamentable administration and inattention to formal process easily to reconcile with authorship of a major piece of governmental and ceremonial infrastructure.[133]

Rufus's candidature, whilst ruler of Normandy in Robert's absence (1096–1100) is more promising on several grounds. First, he was frequently resident, including for the Christmases of 1096, 1097 and 1098.[134] These may have been held at Rouen or elsewhere in Normandy, but his recognition at least of Caen's importance is underlined by its retention when ceding the county of Bayeux (in which it lies), and the cities of Bayeux and Coutances, to Henry in 1096.[135] Secondly, William was famously interested in building, and the originator, most significantly, of Westminster Hall, not only put up in precisely this period (1097–9) but having important structural affinities with the Echiquier.[136] Thirdly, and most interestingly, are the implications of Rufus's long-term intentions with regard to Normandy and his behaviour whilst in control. Rufus's position from 1096 was as temporary ruler of the duchy, to whom it had been consigned or 'pledged', awaiting redemption by his brother on his return. [137] However, Rufus was not only Robert's heir as Duke, but must have doubted that Robert would return, and, it has been suggested, 'would have held it against him if he did', both of which would have encouraged him to take a long-term view.[138] This is not the place to elaborate on Rufus's (or his father's) interpretation and representation of royal status when in, and pertaining to, the French Duchy of Normandy.[139] But whilst there is evidence that the Conqueror was wary of trading on his royal status in Normandy,[140] William of Poitiers asserts that in his master's youth Normandy was 'almost a kingdom', and certainly the Conqueror's grandiose gestures in founding two dynastic mausolea were on a more than kingly scale. [141] Rufus would not have been short of precedent as to how regally the King of England could behave in the Duchy. Moreover, as a king but not the duke – a title Robert seems to have maintained until his death – Rufus may have had both more reason and more leeway to emphasise his royal status, 'unencumbered with ambiguities that had surrounded the Conqueror's status in Normandy'.[142] In this context it is of interest that, between summer 1096 and January 1098, Rufus purchased from the monks of St Etienne a set of royal regalia including 'the crown he [the Conqueror] wore on the festivals, his sceptre and rod'.[143] Why should he have done so? No reason is given in the relevant charter (surviving as a 15th-century *vidimus*), but it seems likely that he intended to use the regalia to replicate, in Normandy, the 'crown-wearing' ceremonies that he and his father held at the great festivals of the church in England;[144] the charter's reference to their use by William I 'on festivals', implicitly in the duchy, may indicate that had he too had used it there to express his status as King *in* Normandy.[145] This would be consistent with Rufus's constitutional position, his robust interpretation of 'acting' authority (as shown for example by his attitude to Maine), and the sheer 'pleasure that he took in the royal title and dignity'.[146] However, such occasions required a fitting setting, such as the great halls inherited (and perhaps created) by William I in England and in particular Westminster Hall, intended, it has been argued, for this very purpose, and underway by 1097.[147] Whilst provided for at Rouen, at Caen, if De Boüard is correct, Rufus had no such facility – a problem to which the Echiquier, dwarfing the cramped buildings of his father, would have been a spectacular solution.[148]

## The *Echiquier* and the great hall in Normandy

### *Halls in Normandy* c. *930–1100*

The monumental, free-standing status, architectural qualities, and above all the sheer and unrivalled scale of the Echiquier set it apart from all other Romanesque domestic buildings in Normandy. Yet according to what we know so far, its form, in Normandy, has no obvious precursors or prototypes and no immediate successors. This prompts a number of questions. First, what *do* we know of the form and function of halls of ducal and near-ducal status in Normandy before *c.* 1100? What does this suggest about the development and traditions of their design and use? Can it be argued that the Echiquier was a new departure, and if so, what may have prompted it? Finally, can the Echiquier be said to have influenced the form of later halls, or the status and siting of the hall in 12th-century Norman houses?

'Halls' defined in the loosest functional sense as rooms serving domestic but communal functions, and at the highest social level ceremonial, celebratory, judicial and administrative purposes, were a standard feature of seigneurial residences and palaces in northern Europe throughout the Middle Ages.[149] Normandy was no exception, as is clear in the first instance from references to occasions and customs which required large and impressive interiors: an early 11th-century account, for example, describes William Longsword (925–42) 'feasting in splendour from golden vessels and cups; hedged about by a multifarious gathering of servants, both noble and unfree … zealous in applying the laws and decrees of his orthodox fathers'.[150] Reminiscent of post-Conquest and Anglo-Saxon royal custom in England and Normandy,[151] we are also told that William '… celebrated Easter at Bayeux that same year and assembled the chief men of the lands of Brittany and Normandy', staying until after Pentecost.[152] A 12th-century source implies that Richard II (996–1026) usually had Easter at Fécamp,[153] and by 1024 it seems Rouen and Fécamp were used alternately for the celebration of the two main festivals.[154] It was with a great feast ('*coenaculum ingens*') that William the Conqueror sealed his celebration of Easter at Fécamp on his triumphal return to Normandy in 1067.[155] On this basis we can be fairly confident that by *c.* 1100 the dukes' important bases, rural and urban (and whether *palatii* or *castri*, or always directly in their hands),[156] amongst them being those at Bayeux, Bonneville-sur-Touques, Cherbourg, Eu, Falaise, Fécamp, Lillebonne, Lisieux, Rouen, and latterly at Caen – were equipped to hold substantial gatherings.[157] The bishoprics, the *comtés* established in the 10th century under ducal relatives, and the *vicomtés* ruled by lesser men in the 11th, must have had theirs too.[158]

What we know of the actual buildings at such places, however, is very limited. Some hints are to be found in the obvious written sources, for the period up to *c.* 1025 confined largely to Dudo of St Quentin's work, known since the 17th century as *De Moribus et Actis Primorum Normanniae Ducum*, written *c.* 1015–26 and covering the period from the early 10th century until the death of Richard II.[159] For the later ducal period the main chronicle sources are the *Gesta Normannorum Ducum*, finished *c.* 1070, which takes up the story where Dudo left off, and William of Poitiers' *Gesta Guilelmi Ducis Normannorum et Regis Anglorum*, of *c.* 1077. The pre-1066 comital/ducal charters assembled by Marie Fauroux also offer a handful of incidental hints. The main 12th-century chronicle source extensively covering the period before 1100 is Orderic's *Historia Ecclesiastica*, but which must, as with the other sources, be used with caution when it refers to events of earlier periods. A comprehensive trawl of other chronicle, hagiographic and literary sources touching on Normandy, and of published and unpublished non-ducal charters would certainly make a further contribution.[160] In exploiting these sources an obvious starting point is their use of the word *aula* in contexts where (although carrying no connotations of a particular layout or type) it indicates a familiarity with the 'hall' either as a venue for important events or as the *raison d'être* of an eponymous household institution: thus Raoul de Tancarville appears as William II's *magister auleque et camera*,[161] and Dudo refers to 'royal halls' (and metaphorical, heavenly ones) in ways that suggest that 'halls' were familiar features of the architectural landscape and recognised adjuncts to the exercise of power;[162] in three instances the *aula* at Fécamp is referred to as 'of the seat' (*sedes*), suggesting (although 'palace' may have been intended), that the hall was distinct entity within the overall complex.[163] In several instances the word *palatium*, when referring not to the whole complex but a part of it, was also, it seems, used to identify a 'hall', as it certainly was in non-Norman contexts.[164] The value of such references is enhanced by ducal Normandy's apparent orthodoxy in making use of the 'chamber'– part of the oft-touted 'trilogy' of '*aula, camera et capella*' which formed the core of the grand medieval house. This is indicated partly by the existence of the *camera* as an administrative entity from the reign of Richard II (996–1026) and of chamberlain ('*camerarius*') as a post from *c.* 1050, although the naming of the function after a room was not of Norman origin:[165] literal references to the *camera* as a place, such as that to the '*camera Guilelmi ducis*' at Bayeux in 1066, are admittedly much rarer;[166] *solarium* makes rare appearances in contexts that imply domestic use and, in at least one case, an elevated position.[167] In no single instance, however, can a room identifiable through terminology or context as a hall (still less a chamber) in a near-contemporary source, be incontestably identified with a structure known from standing fabric or from excavation. What we do have are part-surviving or excavated structures to which, or to part of which, a 'hall' function can be attributed, and references to specific but long-lost *aulae* accompanied by some information about their form.

Taking these in approximately chronological order, the earliest buildings to which ducal use can be attributed appear at Fécamp (Seine-Maritime), most frequented of the comital/ducal bases from the time of Richard I (942–96) until 1087, and exhaustively studied by Annie Renoux.[168] Here, the earliest structure (Building 6), attributed to the reign of William Longsword (932–42) or shortly after *c.* 950 under Richard I (942–96) was timber-built, 16.5m long and 5.00m–5.80m wide, containing a kitchen (6m long) and a '*salle à manger*' (10m long).[169] Its grooved-plank earth-fast construction shows similarities to buildings at Yeavering and elsewhere, and 'bow-sided' plan broadly speaking places it within a well-known, widespread and long-lived Norse-Germanic tradition;[170] as subsequently rebuilt (Period 2), the walls were straightened and fitted to a sill-beam.[171] Renoux acknowledges that the building belonged to the '*catégorie inférieure des bâtiments de grand taille qui agrémentent les résidences des grands au Xe siècle*', but is in no doubt that this was where the great gatherings of the Counts were held.[172] In the second half of the 10th century, whilst Building 6 still stood, another structure (Building I) was put up within 15m to the east, constructed of mortared flint, 20m long and 5m wide, housing a ground floor of menial purpose, and, according to the excavator, a '*salle noble*' above, perhaps extending over the full length of the wing.[173] If it was from this building (rather than a successor) that the Duke famously looked down on church from an upper window or landing, observing the relative meanness of the church, it must have been built by its consecration in 990.[174] Although, once again, modest in size compared to the halls of greater princes, Renoux sees this as the building in which, at Fécamp, Richard '*réunit les grands lors des festivités pascales*'.[175]

A very different sort of building is also credited to Richard I at Rouen – the *turris* in that Robert of Torigni tells us that 'Richard, first Duke of the Normans, had built in his palace'.[176] That this was literally a tower is clear from Robert's mention that Henry I had built one 'no less tall in the Castle at Caen', a building known to have been at least 24m high.[177] What this building contained is unknown, but it clearly had several floors, and its inclusion of a hall is suggested by comparable buildings (below), and the reference to the *aula turris*, in which a charter was witnessed in 1074.[178]

The reign of Richard II (996–1026) saw further activity at Fécamp. Although there is some ambiguity in Renoux's account, on balance it seems that this included a new hall, on the strength of a reference in 1215 to the '*aula* of Count Richard of pious memory' and the identification of the Count as Richard II, restorer of the abbey.[179] Little can be said about its form except that it was impressive or useful enough to survive not only until 1215 but to the end of the century, and that it may have been of more than one storey:[180] Benoît de St Maure offers a eulogistic description of the palace (*palais*), noting its height, painted decoration, vaulted and panelled rooms, and its masonry construction, although his literal reliability is doubtful.[181]

Of around the period 1000, the earliest part-surviving structure may be the Great Tower at Ivry-la-Bataille (Eure), built for Raoul d'Ivry, a member of the ducal family. Possibly the prototype for the great four-square double-pile great towers of the later 11th and 12th centuries, this remarkable building contained a first-floor room measuring 11.15m × 26.70m, probably with a mural fireplace:[182] if there was a 'hall' in the building it was surely this. At Avranches a building of comparable dimensions, probably dating from the early 11th century, and perhaps attributable to Richard, first Count of Avranches, contained a first-floor room measuring 14.00m wide, and at least 21.25m but perhaps as much as 30m in length.[183]

Completely different but in every way as remarkable is the complex unearthed by Jacques Le Maho at Notre-Dame de Gravenchon (Seine-Maritime), attributable to Robert, son of Richard I and Archbishop of Rouen 989–1037. Here, matching storeyed ranges, 6m wide and 35m long (north–south), linked at the north end by a cross-range, faced each other across a courtyard. The western wing contained a kitchen at ground-floor level with the '*aula*' or '*grande salle*' above, up to 35m long. The north wing contained a second large room (also labelled by Le Maho '*grande salle*'), and the west wing the services. A freestanding latrine tower, and three further storeyed blocks, part free-standing but linked to main ranges, lay to the north, west and south-east. All the main rooms had stone-built mural fireplaces, probably at both levels, and were framed around massive earth-fast posts, the walls between them formed of timber uprights fitted to slender sill-beams. The complex remained in use until burnt *c.* 1100.[184]

Finally, from later in the century we have (to use the excavator's terms), the '*Palais de Guillaume*' at Caen, comprising a number of modest structures grouped informally around a two-storey '*aula*' measuring 16m × 8m.[185]

A handful of other buildings, lower down the social scale, contribute to the overall picture of high-status building in the ducal period. From the written sources we learn, for example, of the *aula* of a private house in a charter of 1063–5, and that of the castle at Brionne (Eure) in the context of an event in the aftermath of Val-és-Dunes (1047).[186] Prominent and earliest among these is the precursor, at Notre-Dame de Gravenchon, to the building described above, measuring 22m by 6m, single-storeyed and similarly constructed around earth-fast posts: it was built in the second half of the 10th century and can be attributed to Turstin le Riche, the powerful descendant of an early Norman settler.[187] At

Grimbosq (Calvados) the '*grand bâtiment résidentiel*', dated to the early 11th century, was interpreted by Joseph Decaëns as a storeyed building, *c.* 10m × 11m inside.[188] Excavations in the 1960s at Plessis-Grimoult (Calvados), revealed vestiges of a pre-1047 seigneurial residence, part wood, part stone, of which the largest building may have may have measured 6.50m × *c.* 12m.[189] At Mirville (Seine Maritime), the late 11th- or early 12th-century seigneurial residence was centred on a 'boat-shaped' building of earth-fast timbers, containing several subdivisions, one identified by the excavator as '*un petit hall*'.[190] Once again a systematic survey, this time of the published and 'grey' literature, would no doubt reveal others.

### *The place of the Echiquier*

Taken together, the sources hint at the existence, at least after the mid-10th century, of two parallel traditions, loosely reflecting the Normans' double inheritance of, or deference to, Carolingian and Norse traditions, both social and architectural.[191] The first to appear belongs to the vernacular, northern European type represented in Building 6 at Fécamp (both phases), and persisting, lower down the social scale, until at least the early 12th century:[192] the early building at Notre-Dame de Gravenchon may also be placed in this category. Alongside this, however, from the construction of Building I at Fécamp but best exemplified at Notre-Dame de Gravenchon, we see the appearance of sophisticated multi-storeyed structures (of stone or timber), containing rooms which could undoubtedly have served as halls. Allied to these are the great towers at Ivry, Rouen and Avranches, part of a tradition then proliferating across northern France.[193]

Where does this leave the Echiquier? Certainly, there may have been comparable buildings in Normandy from which it took a cue: arguing for the *absence* of a form or building type before a certain date would be a mistake. On the face of it, however, it was something of a new departure, firstly, with a floor area of 338m², in scale, as its closest known rival, at Avranches, could have covered a maximum of 297m². Second, and more important is its free-standing status, distinct, monumental in its own right, and very significantly larger than any building associated with it. But if this was new departure in Normandy, what architectural precedents elsewhere and why might the new departure have been useful or desirable? Certainly there were comparable buildings outside Normandy – most obviously the great hall in the castle at Angers, and the products of Carolingian '*gigantisme*' survived elsewhere.[194] For the immediate precedents, however, it is tempting to look across the channel to the buildings that William I and Rufus built or inherited: these can be assumed to have included a hall at Gloucester (at Kingsholm), apparently still adequate for use in the 13th century, at Cheddar, at York, the Confessor's hall at Westminster, the old hall at Winchester and new *aula* which the Conqueror built 'in handsome fashion' ('*honorifice*') as part of his '*palatium*', and most obviously to Rufus's own creation at Westminster.[195]

But why the precedent of highly sophisticated, integrated, multi-roomed and '*polyvalent*' buildings such as at Avranches, Ivry, Notre-Dame de Gravenchon and Rouen, should be discarded, in this instance, for the simplicity of the *Echiquier* requires some explanation. The answer may lie in the particular purpose for which it was intended, specifically its *royal* as opposed to 'merely' ducal function and associations: simply put, as king, Rufus (and it has to be said, Henry I) may have felt the need for something suitable for great ceremonies and which had architectural associations with royalty and stood apart from the buildings of the counts and dukes. In this context it is interesting that the blessing payer *Prospice*, included in the coronation liturgy as used by the Conqueror, appears to accept the royal hall as a potent, central signal and embodiment of royal status: it asks that God:

> Grant that the glorious dignity of the royal hall [*palatium*] may shine before the eyes of all with the greatest splendour of kingly power and that it may glow with the brightest rays and to glitter as if suffused by illumination of the utmost brilliance.[196]

An emphasis, then, specifically on the magnificence and distinctive identity of the royal hall, would have been understandable – and could have been better served by the *Echiquier* than by a room housed amongst others in a more complex structure. In short, the use of this architectural form may derive from the building's peculiarly royal and propagandist function. Certainly, we can agree that then as today, in the words of Lucien Musset, that '*Sobre et nue, mais grandiose, elle exprime, mieux qu'aucun edifice sur la rive méridionale de la Manche, l'esprit de la monarchie anglo-normande*'.[197]

### *Halls in Normandy in the 12th century: the legacy of the Echiquier*

Domestic architecture in Normandy in the 12th century deserves a new and comprehensive study: what follows is a brief comment on the impact Echiquier may have had on the form and status of the hall, as a component of great houses, in this period. The first point to make concerns the evidence. More documentary material is of course available than from or covering the 11th century; *aula* and *camera* are abundantly used – in respect, for example, of 19 and nine places in the fragmentary Norman exchequer rolls alone.[198] But there are no Norman resources of the value in this respect (for example) of the St Paul's Cathedral leases,[199] and what there is remains to be comprehensively examined with architectural issues in mind. And while the archaeological record and surviving stuctures have been more thoroughly studied, the evidence from the second half of the century is much better than from the first.

What is evident is that the tradition of building integrated, multi-storeyed structures, housing a hall or halls along with other rooms, continued and gained in importance throughout the century: examples include Château Ganne (Calvados), *c.* 1000,[200] Vatteville-la-Rue (Calvados), *c.* 1124–55,[201] Rubercy (1150–1204),[202] and the extraordinary early 12th-century complex at Longeuil, which combined a tower, attached ground-floor chapel and services.[203] The domestic buildings in the castle at Lillebonne (Seine-Maritime), recently and plausibly attributed to Henry II (*c.* 1150–70),[204] and the vast '*château rectangulaire*' (46m × 24m) at Fécamp, may also fall into this category.[205] Use of the storeyed arrangement was reinforced towards the end of the century, as evidenced, for example, at Chauvincourt (Eure, *c.* 1190), and became the norm in the next.[206] The allied tradition of the great tower – or the complex variant that plausibly included all essential high-status accommodation – of course continued too, a tradition re-invigorated in Normandy by Henry I, first as Count of the Cotentin at Domfront (Orne, after 1092),[207] and as Duke probably at Alençon, Ambrières, Argentan, Arques, Coutances, Exmes, Falaise, Gavrai, Gisors and Vernon.[208] Of these Arques, Caen, Domfront, Falaise, and very probably those at Evreux and Alençon, were of the complex type, although the status and functions of hall-like rooms in great towers relative to halls at their feet followed no set pattern: at Caen, Henry built a tower to accompany an existing hall (the Echiquier) and at Rouen a *mansio* to accompany the tower; at Caen, Phillip-Augustus seems to have added (what was later called) the '*Salle à la Royne*' within his new *chemise*.[209] On the whole however, the later great towers diverged from their 'storeyed house' ancestry, retaining symbolic and defensive purpose but ceding domestic functions to buildings of various forms in the bailey.

Although they may have existed earlier, buildings and domestic planning of markedly different form, however, appear in the second half the century, and it is on this tradition that, in Normandy, the Echiquier may have had a bearing. The best examples are those at Beaumont-le-Richard and Creully (both in Calvados) and at Bricquebec and the 'Grand Doyenné' at Avranches (both in Manche).[210] Partially understood buildings at Grosley-sur-Risle (Eure)[211] and Saint-Vaast-sur-Seulles (Calvados)[212] may have been very similar, and the existence of at least four others dating from before 1200 is inferred by known or surviving chamber-blocks.[213] These – or certainly the first three – are distinguished from the 'integrated' arrangement by the size and near-independence of the halls (all, as it happens, single-aisled). In addition, these halls were also ground-floor rooms occupying the full volume of the building, though the important point is functional not structural, in that (unlike in at least the later integrated structures), their purpose was not replicated or rivalled by another 'hall' beneath.[214] It could therefore be argued that the builders of these houses – all members of the highest aristocracy – took as a cue the outsize ground-floor hall in the ducal castle. In so doing they would have imitated not just its form, but presumably have adopted and perpetuated associated traditions of communal and ceremonial use which made that form useful and the investment worthwhile.

These sites belong to a tradition described elsewhere as the 'hall and chamber block' tradition – a very specific structural response to the requirement for a hall, chamber/s and other offices, and it may be that with the building of the Echiquier, the complex at Caen conformed to this type: if so, Caen may have been instrumental in the adoption, at Beaumont-le-Richard and its analogues, not only of the outsize hall, but of a more comprehensive approach to domestic planning. Here much depends on the purpose, form and date of the building measuring 24.65m by 13.65m, ashlar-faced inside and out and with walls 80–95cm thick, excavated in 2011–13 about 45m to the south-west of the Echiquier. If, as the excavator argues on stratigraphic grounds, it dates from *c.* 1200, it could be interpreted as a vast chamber-block, akin in function to the 'Lesser Hall' at Westminster – resulting in a 'hall and chamber-block' arrangement formed of larger buildings, but not earlier than, the examples described above.[215] If, however, as the upright blocks and wide joints of the masonry suggest, the second building was contemporary with the Echiquier, or roughly so, then the resulting complex would have been the earliest known example, and perhaps even the prototype, of this arrangement in Normandy. In either case, it remains probable that the endorsement of halls of this type with the building of the Echiquier was instrumental in their introduction, or re-introduction, to Normandy in the 12th century.

## Acknowledgements

The preparation and writing of this article has depended on the help from a large number of people and organisations. Thanks are due to Howard Jones for his survey of the building, and Jean-Marie Levesque, Pascal Leroux and their colleagues for repeated access to the Echiquier and other parts of the castle, De Boüard's archive and much else. In addition, I am grateful for the help of Martin Biddle, John Blair, Jean-Paul Corbasson, David Bates, Philip Dixon, Bénédicte Guillot, Hugh Doherty, Eric Fernie, Pierre Garrigou-Grandchamp, Lindy Grant, Karen Impey, Michael Jones, Yves and Elisabeth Lescroart, Gwyn Meirion-Jones and Tim Tatton-Brown.

## Glossary

Aisle; *bas-côté*; or, if equal height to accompanying vessels, *collatérale*
Ashlar; *pierre de taille*
Bailey, of castle; *basse cour*
Barrel vault; *voûte en berceau*
Bay; *travée*
Beaded strapwork; *entrelacs perlés*
Beaten earth; *terre battue*
Billet; *baton*
Billet moulding; *moulure à batons brisés; billettes*
'Bow-sided walls'; *flancs arqués; murs flanc arqués; à murs incurvés*
Broad-leaf; water-leaf; *feuille d'eau*
Buttress; *contrefort*
Chamfer/chamfered; *chanfrein, chanfreiné*
Chevron; *chevron*; *bâtons rompus*
Chip-carved; *sculpture méplate*
Colonnette; *colonnette*
Corbel; *corbeau* or probably better *modillon* (e.g. *modillon à tête humaine/d'animal* etc.)
Corbel table; *tablette de pierre en saillie portée par des corbeaux;* or probably better, *corniche à modillons*
Crossing tower; *tour de croisée*
Dado arcade; *arcature aveugle*
Diaper [as used here]; *étoiles en creux*
Dosseret; *dosseret*
Earthfast post; *poteau planté*
Exchequer Rolls; *rôles de l'Echiquier*
Facing; *parement*
Fillet, Angled fillet; *filet*
Gable wall; *mur pignon/pignon*
Grooved-plank (construction); *planches bouvetées*
Hood (of fireplace); *hotte*
Hoodmould; *archivolte*
Jamb; *jambage, piédroit*
Moulding; *moulure*
Nave; *nef*
Nook-shaft; coursed nook-shaft; *colonnette apareillé [check]*
Nook shaft, monolithic; *colonette en délit*
'Open from floor to rafters'; '*ouvert du sol jusqu'a la charpente*'
Order (as in 'two orders of moulding'; *rouleau; à double rouleau*
Panel, panelling; *lambris, lambrissage*
Pilaster buttress; *contrefort plat*
Plinth; *socle*
Post; *poteau*
Register (as in 'upper register'); *niveau, deuxième niveau*
Rere-arch; *arrière voussure*
Rib, vaulting rib; *nervure*
Roll-moulding; *boudin, tore*
Rosace; *rosace*
Round-arched; *en plein cintre*
Saltire; *croix décussée, sautoir*
Segmental arch; *arc surbaissé*
Service buildings, service rooms; *pièces de service*
Side wall; *mur gouttereau*
Sill, stepped; *gradins*
Sill beam; *sablière basse*
Soffit; *intrados*
Springer; *sommier*
Strapwork; *entrelacs*
String course; *bandeau*
Trefoiled arch; *arc treflé*
Unmoulded; *à simple rouleau*
Vaulting, quadripartite; *voûte quadripartite*
Volute; *volute*
Voussoir; *claveau*
Wing; *aile*

## Notes

1 The name was first applied by Thomas Stapleton (1840, p. xxix), based on his partly correct assumption that it was used by the Norman Exchequer (Stapleton 1840, pp. xxvii and xxxi; De Boüard 1979, p. 67). The name was popularised by Eugène de Beaurepaire in 1896 (p. 47) and endorsed by the architect Lucien Sallez in 1904 (Archives des Monuments Historiques 12852), and again in 1908 (*Congrès Archéologique de France*. 75, p. 1, plan facing p. 110).

2 Professor at Faculté des Lettres from 1940–79 at the University of Caen. See obituary by Arnold Taylor (*Archéologie Médiévale* 19 (1989), pp. IX–X). On the excavation see Leroux 2000.

3 'La Salle dite L'Echiquier, au Château de Caen', *Medieval Archaeology* IX (1965), pp. 64–81; *Le Château de Caen*, Centre de Recherches Archéologiques Medievales.

4 Decaëns 1981, p. 176; Flambard Héricher 1998b, p. 132; Renoux 1991, p. 38.

5 See below.

6 Marino 2000, pp. 107 and 111; Lefèvre 2000, p. 116.

7 The survey was commissioned from Howard Jones RIBA by the author and carried out in November 2009. For reasons of cost the brief was not to produce a full, minutely phased, stone-by-stone archaeological survey, but a dimensionally accurate record of the building to aid its interpretation, present it to the reader, and identify the original (Period I) fabric. The survey could, however, be used as the starting point for a much more detailed record and analysis.

8 Jean-Marie 2000, p. 31; De Boüard 1979, pp. 9–10; for the charters see Fauroux 1961, nos 34 and 58.

9 Bates 1981, pp. 13, 152 and 178–9.

10 Jean-Marie 2000, p. 35.

11 Chantel, ed. 1892, *Chronicarum Anonymi Cadomensi*, p. 138.

12 Carré 2009, p. 12.

13 Burgess and Holden 2002, p. 22, lines 5170–71.

14 Musset 1967, no. 6, p. 69: by which in 1080–82 the Conqueror granted to La Trinité a house '…*in castello Cadomi*'; and *ibid*, no. 8, p. 85, also of 1082, which mentions the '*ecclesia Sancti Georgii de Castro Cadomi*'.

15 De Boüard 1979, p. 11; Burgess and Holden 2002, lines 5170 and 5171: '*encore ert Caen sainz chastel/ni aveit fait mur ne kernel*'. The passage sets the context for the battle of Varaville, usually placed in 1057.

16 As considered by De Boüard 1979, p. 9 and Marin 1986, p. 117. Lucien Musset disagreed (1971, p. 44). On this debate see Jean-Marie 2000, p. 323.

17 De Boüard 1979: for the absence of traces of the ramparts, p. 39; for the 11th-century ditch, p. 40; ditch for the gate-tower, pp. 44–5; Carré 2009, p. 12.

18 Chantel, ed. 1892, *Chronicarum Anonymi Cadomensi*, p. 149; Robert of Torigni, Howlett, ed. 1889, p. 106. Carré emphasises the lack of evidence for earthwork defences (*op. cit.* p. 12).

19 De Boüard 1979, pp. 9–11; Renoux 1991, p. 307; Impey 'Before the White Tower: London's early castles and the context of their creation', in Impey, ed. 2008, *The White Tower*, pp. 13–26.

20 De Boüard 1979, pp. 64–7 and p. 82, facing 22.

21 De Boüard 1979, p. 9. De Boüard considered the mention of the 'Le Palais' at the beginning of the 15th century to be a reference to this complex (*ibid.*, p. 21 and note 35).

22 De Boüard 1979, pp. 63–7; p. 31, fig. 3. See also p. 10.

23 Moss, ed. 2004, p. 41: '*In operationibus domorum turris et castri et cappelle parve et aule…*'; De Boüard 1979, p. 68, note 15, citing Bibliothèque National Ms Fr. 26002, no. 754.

24 De Boüard 1979, p. 68, note 13, citing Archives Municipales de Caen, EE 29, 2 Août 1662; SHAD, and Art 8, Section 1, carton 1, no. 21.

25 De Certain, ed. 1855, p. 512. De Joliment (1825, p. 8) writes of the castle '*…et l'on y chercherat inutilement aujourd'hui des vestiges du palais des anciens ducs, tout revetu de marbre precieux*', citing Tortaire. De Beaurepaire assumes that Tortaire was describing the castle (1896, p. 46). Tortaire wrote:
*Ac primum Cadomi sublimia tecta subivi,*
*Quae tanquam Pario marmore tota nitent*

26 SHAD Bibliothèque CF Atlas2, France, Tome III, f. 60.

27 The complete view from the *Atlas* is reproduced e.g. by Marin and Levesque 2000, p. 112, and Decaëns and Dubois 2009, p. 123. Huet (1726, p. 145) explains how the plan came to be engraved so long after the survey was made.

28 SHAD IV H.490, cartons 1 and 2 (1699–1821). See also for example ADC CPL 660 (plan of 1882).

29 Rajnai 1975, p. 20. The drawing was made on 18 August.

30 BL Add Ms 36422 f. 50 and f. 61. The attribution of the view to Buckler is confirmed by Stapleton (1840, p. xxvii).

31 Archives des Monuments Historiques 12852.

32 DRAC, Caen, MH 14, nos 110–26.

33 De Bourgeville 1588 (the castle is described in some detail at pp. 19–21); Huet (1726, p. 41) describes the castle but ignores the Echiquier. Ducarel's description (1767, p. 49). Ducarel's may have mistakenly attached the name 'Le Besle', described by Huet (much used by Ducarel) as the parade ground, to the Echiquier. However, by 1767, the principal arsenal was the Echiquier, and it seems likely that Ducarel was referring to it.

34 De Joliment 1825, p. 9; La Rue 1820, pp. 83–4.

35 Stapleton 1840, Vol. I, p. xxvii.

36 Either in his *Cours d'Antiquités Monumentales* (Caen is covered in part V, 1835, p. 232) or in the *Statistique Monumental de Calvados* (the castle is otherwise described in Vol. 1, pp. 52–3).

37 De Boüard 1979, p. 70: '*…faute de témoins suffisants d'un état plus ancien*'.

38 Internally at ground level the long sides each measures 30,860mm, but while the SE entrance gable wall is 11,180mm wide, the NW end gable is 130mm narrower.

39 De Boüard 1979, for the TAQ of 1344 see p. 79: accounts for 1344 mention the '*cuisine du Tinel*', i.e. the kitchen of the hall, which De Boüard identified as this building. As he assumed the kitchen to have previously occupied the ground floor of the hall, he assumed the creation of the 'new' kitchen and the destruction of the old by the removal of the first floor, were part of the same campaign.

40 The date of 1881 is given in the legend of a plan of the castle of 1882 (ADC CPL 660): '*étage construit en 1881. Salle de harnachement.*' A drawing showing this as proposed or after completion, undated, but bearing the legend 'PROJET D'ETABLISSEMENT D'UNE SALLE D'ARMES DANS LE BATIMENT', is published by De Boüard (1979, p. 89, fig. 31). The original can not now be located. See also a number of post-war photographs. The new masonry in the positions of those on the eastern three bays shows clearly in Merlet's photograph of 25 February 1963.

41 The main damage, including the crater mentioned by De Boüard (1979, p. 71) was probably done on the 16th, although more may have followed before the last bombardment on 15 August (Poirier 1944, pp. 30 and 68).

42 Moss 2009, pp. 3–4.

43 Compare existing stonework to that shown in photographs of the damaged but un-restored building (De Boüard 1979, p. 92, fig. 34).

44 De Boüard 1979, p. 79 and p. 97, caption to fig. 42.

45 i.e. the date of Cotman's original drawing (Rajni 1975, p. 20).

46 As shown in Jean Merlet's drawing of 6 October 1962 (DRAC MH 14 no. 115).

47 Much eroded since 1944; see De Boüard 1979, p. 92, fig. 34.

48 Salle de l'Echiquier, Porte Principale, J. Merlet 14 April 1963. Copies kindly supplied by the Conservation Régionale des Monuments Historiques de Basse Normandie.

49 De Boüard 1979, p. 89, fig. 31.

50 Photograph of 1889 (Archives des Monuments Historiques, MH00 12/62).

51 Photograph of *c.* 1930 (De Boüard 1979, p. 86, fig. 28).

52 Lord Methuen 1952, p. 201; photographs, including Archives des Monuments Historiques MH0181004.

53 De Boüard 1979, pp. 78 and 97, fig. 41 and caption.

54 Marin and Levesque 2000, p. 124.

55 See photograph reproduced in De Boüard 1979, p. 92, fig. 34.

56 De Boüard 1979, p. 89, fig. 31.

57 Archives des Monuments Historiques 12825.

58 All studied and recorded by the author.

59 De Boüard 1979, p. 79, note 57.

60 Impey 1995, plan opposite p. 13; 1999, p. 53; p. 55, fig. 8 and p. 65, fig. 18 (no. 17).

61 Vincennes… Art. 8. section I, carton 1, no. 9.

62 De Boüard 1979, p. 79, note 57.

63 Visited 2 March 2011; De Boüard 1979, p. 73, and De Boüard, Cahier des Fouilles, September 1961.

64 Jean-Marie 2000, p. 79; Renoux 1994, p. 32 (although recognising that this is a matter of debate) Decaëns 2000, p. 20; Leroux 2000, p. 86; Decaëns and Dubois 2009, pp. 42–5 (although acknowledging uncertainty, p. 42).

65 Mesqui 1991–3, II, pp. 81–2; 1997, p. 86; 2008, p. 90.

66 Impey 1993, pp. 84–5.

67 De Boüard 1979, p. 70, para. 1, and p. 71, para. 3.

68 De Boüard 1979, p. 71, para. 3. The number of pits is suggested by Decaëns and Dubois 2009, p. 42.

69 Westminster, see Smirke 1836, p. 407; Harris and Crook 'Reconstructing Westminster Hall'. See examples given by Wood (1964, pp. 389–93) and Salzman (1952, p. 147).

70 De Boüard 1979, p. 70, para. 1.

71 Musset *Normandie Romane*, I, pp. 163–7 and 216–221.

72 On the earlier examples see Mallet 1984, pp. 15–21 and 2003, pp. 52–65.

73 See for example the late 11th-century hall naves of Le Ronceray, Angers (Maine-et-Loire), St-Jouin-de-Marnes (Deux-Sèvres), Airvault (Deux-Sèvres), or St-Savin-sur-Gartempe (Vienne).

74 De Boüard 1979, p. 70, para. 1: '*que les fenêtres furent primitivement muni des gradins*'; p. 74, para. 3.

75 De Boüard 1962, pp. 17–8; 1979, p. 70, para. 2: '*… notre bâtiment se rattache à l'un des types les mieux connus de l'architecture civile du XIIe siècle*'.

76 De Boüard cites the hall of the Counts of Nevers at Druyes (Yonne), of the bishops of Limoges at Castelnau de Bretenoux (Lot et Garonne) and of the Bishops' Palace at Angers (Maine et Loire).

77 Faulkner 1958, pp. 151 and 163–4; Wood 1964, pp. 14–34.

78 Mesqui 2001, pp. 36–7; Brodeur, Chevet and Mastrolenzo 1998, p. 107, fig. 4.

79 Blair 1993, *passim*.

80 On the 11th-century roof Wilson 1987, p. 43; p. 280, note 46, and Harris and Crook (forthcoming). Wilson also points out the similarity between Westminster and the Echiquier (*ibid.*).

81 On Roger of Caen (Sarum) see Kealey 1972; for Sherborne Castle see RCHME 1952, pp. 64–6. For the courtyard house at Old Sarum and its relationship with Roger's work at Sherborne see Ashbee 2006, pp. 73–7, and for a general assessment of Roger's patronage see Stalley 1971.

82 Blair 1993, p. 13

83 Tim Tatton-Brown, pers.com

84 Kipps 1929; Impey (unpublished doctoral thesis) 1991, Vol. 3, pp. 177–203; Turner and Parker, I, 1877 (2nd ed.), pp. 43–5 and intervening view and plan. The hall or refectory at Minster measured (internally) *c.* 8m × 19m; the Dover refectory 30.48 × 8.22m.

85 Cahiers de Fouilles, 24 March 1964.

86 Decaëns 2000, p. 19; Renoux 1997, I, p. 214.

87 De Boüard 1979, pp. 72–3.

88 *ibid.*, p. 72, para. 2.

89 *ibid.*, p. 71, last para.

90 *ibid.*, p. 79, para 1.

91 Roofs over undivided spaces in 11th-century churches can significantly exceed this, as for example at Angers cathedral, where it can be deduced that the early 11th-century nave was around 14.4m wide (Mallet 1984, Planche VII). The nave of York Minster, as built for Thomas of Bayeux after 1070, was 13.77m wide (see Phillips 1977, pp. 212–3)

92 In 1962 De Boüard dated it just to the 12th century; in 1965 (p. 67) and 1979 to Henry I (pp. 12 and 69)

93 De Boüard 1965, p. 67; 1979, p. 69.

94 De Boüard 1961, p. 112.

95 De Boüard 1979, p. 12, citing Robert of Torigni ('*Chronica*', Howlett, ed., Vol. IV, p. 106).

96 Musset 1985, Vol. 1, p. 50: '*... sa façade austère presente le même décor purement géometrique que les églises du temps*'.

97 Carlson 1968, p. 88.

98 Neveux 1998, p. 399; Decaëns 1997, p. 300; Decaëns 2000, p. 19; Decaëns and Dubois 2009, p. 40.

99 Mesqui 2008, p. 90.

100 Baylé 1992, pp. 29 and 104. Lord Methuen, although he would not have regarded his opinion as expert, placed it in the 'late 11th century' (1952, p. 201).

101 Haskins 1918, Appendix G, pp. 309–20.

102 Aird 2008, p. 245.

103 '*Turrem nihilominus excelsam fecit in castello Cadomensi, et murum ipsius castelli, quem pater suus fecerat, in altum crevit*'. (Robert of Torigni 1889, '*Chronica*', *Chronicles of the Reigns of Stephen, Henry II., and Richard I*, Howlett, ed., Vol. IV, p. 106 ('*...et aedificia as mansionem regiam congrua infra eundem murum [curtain wall] parat*'.

104 The original facing of the *donjon* survives on the west side, where it includes an original buttress (De Boüard 1979, p. 103; p. 127, fig. 45).

105 Baylé 2001, p. 62.

106 Musset 1987, Vol. I, p. 171. The founder's son was buried in the middle of the choir in February 1098.

107 James 2006, part B, Vol. 3, p. 323.

108 La Trinité was heavily restored in 1860s (Baylé 1979, pp. 25–31). The western of the two on the north side retains enough (apparently) 11th-century fabric to give confidence in the restoration.

109 James *et al.* 2006, Part B, Vol. 3, pp. 160, 648 and 680.

110 See Baylé 1992, p. 419 for a selection of 11th-century base moulding profiles. The Echiquier is not included, but the tendency of the later 11th-century buildings to avoid deep hollows or rolls in favour of the shallow ridges and cavities used at the Echiquier is clear, and particularly evident in Caen, Cerisy and Falaise.

111 For St-Jean-d'Abbetot see Baylé 1992, p. 390, fig. 607.

112 For good illustrations of capitals from all four sites see Baylé 1992.

113 The most convenient illustrations of the granite capitals at Lonlay and Domfront are again those gathered together in Baylé 1992, at figs 585–95. Although seemingly unrepresented in Caen before the Echiquier the very free and often linear detailing of the surface of the capital evident there probably lies behind the later development of these forms in the Cotentin, most splendidly at Ste-Marie-du-Mont. See Baylé 2001, Vol. 2, pp. 105–7.

114 Baylé 1979, p. 57; 1993, p. 102.

115 Turner 2002, pp. 5–8 and 27–30; Leyland 1984, pp. 413–4; Goodall 2011, pp. 86–7.

116 Musset 1987, pp. 295–6, pl. 117.

117 Whether it was used in Odo's 11th-century cathedral in Bayeux is unknown. Of the parish churches, Secqueville-en-Bessin is likely to be among the earliest, and stylistically fits most comfortably in the 1090s. For a broader discussion of the *étoile en creux* in the development of sculpturally enriched Anglo-Norman architecture *c.* 1100, see Baylé 1993, pp. 102–5.

118 Borg 1967.

119 For Le Mans see below. For Cerisy-la-Forêt see Baylé 1992, p. 102, who was among the first to recognise the significance of the apse arch at Cerisy when exposed in the 1980s. For a list of potentially early English examples see Fernie 2000, p. 276. Rachel Moss unambiguously places the introduction of chevron in the last quarter of the 11th century and ascribes a bracket of *c.* 1080–*c.* 1240 for its widespread use in Anglo-Norman architecture (2009, pp. 4–5).

120 An excellent example of this is the west front at Le Mans, where the section of the chevron of the nave aisle portals is identical, move for move, to the moulding profiles used on the upper façade (see Tcherikover 1989, esp. pp. 51–4). On the relationship between mouldings and chevron see Moss 2009, pp. 12–6.

121 Multiple billet can be seen on the reliquary casket of St John the Baptist and St Pelagius in the treasury of San Isidoro Leon, given in 1059. For an illustration see Lasko 1972, p. 148, plate 150. Architecturally it is widely used in western France, as at St-Jouin-des-Marnes (Deux-Sèvres), *c.* 1060–70.

122 As at Aivault (Deux-Sèvres), St Pierre at Melle and St Hilaire-le-Grand, Poitiers (Vienne). These later designs seem to have been particularly popular in northern Poitou. The paired discs used for the inner orders of the aisle portals at Le Mans cathedral are also best understood as mouldings sliced in section.

123 Tcherikover 1988, pp. 348–71.

124 The dating has been much discussed (e.g. Mussat 1981, pp. 31–2; Salet 1961, p. 34). The attribution of the west front to Hoel, who could only have had the means and opportunity to build it between 1085 and 1090 (Mussat, pp. 23–4) stems from the 12th-century *Gesta Domni Hoelli Episcopi*, which says that he '*... exteriores etiam parietes,*

*quos alas vocant, per circuitum consummavit*'. Busson and Ledru, 1901, chapter xxxiv, p. 383.

125 Sintès 1996, pp. 104–6.

126 See the encircled concave-sided squares in the late 4th-century pavement of the north hall of the cathedral at Aquileia, for example, or the seemingly-precocious 1st- or 2nd-century funerary stela of Lucius Furius Lucii from Aulnay, now in the Musée Archéologique at Saintes (Charente).

127 The nave and west front of St-Jean-de-Montierneuf were rebuilt in 1643–4 following the partial collapse of the crossing. A number of carved stones from the earlier west front were then re-used in this reconstruction, consisting for the most part of shallowly-carved geometric designs on voussoirs or ashlar blocks that were probably originally arranged as string-courses and spandrel decoration. The variety of geometric forms in use at Montierneuf was clearly considerable and their position, on the west front of the most important building to be created in the last quarter of the 11th century in Poitiers, lends them a peculiar significance. The west front campaign can be closely dated, and will have been undertaken between the reburial of Duke Guy-Geoffroi-Guillaume immediately in front of the altar of the Holy Cross in 1087, and the consecration of one of the two altars in the choir by Pope Urban II on 22 January 1096. The nave and the west front are likely to have been finished some time before the papal consecration. See Favreau 1996, pp. 18–23 and 26–29; Camus 1992, pp. 191–4.

128 If the restoration of the tympanum at Beaumais (Orne) was accurate, it may be that there was a direct connection with St-Jean-de-Montierneuf at Poitiers, with which it shares a number of motifs. See Baylé 1992, fig. 339.

129 Haskins 1918, pp. 277–84; Barlow 1983, p. 283. Aird (2008, p. 146) that the 1091 date is not proven, and that these events could perhaps have taken place on 1096.

130 Visit to Mont-St-Michel, Orderic Vitalis, *Ecclesiastical History*, Chibnall, ed., Vol. V, p. 301; visit to Caen, hinted at by Wace (Burgess and Holden, ed. 2002, *The Roman de Rou*, p. 304, lines 9691–9698); David 1920, p. 124; Aird 2008, pp. 199 and 201.

131 Aird p. 246; Orderic Vitalis, Chibnall, ed., Vol. VI p. 96: '*Nam ex quo dux de Ierusalem rediit, et ducatum Normanniae recepit, torpori et ignaviae nimis subiacuit* …'.

132 Holden, ed., Vol. 2, p. 289; Jean-Marie 2000, pp. 9–101.

133 On Robert's government see; Orderic Vitalis, Chibnall, ed., Vol. V, p. 25; Vol. VI, pp. 86 and 96.

134 Whitelock, ed., *Anglo-Saxon Chronicle*, pp. 174–5.

135 Barlow 1983, p. 364; Green 2009, p. 36; Howlett, ed. 1889, Robert of Torigni, 'Chronica', p. 54.

136 Respectively for the start and end dates see *Anglo-Saxon Chronicle*, Whitelocke, ed. 1961, p. 175, and Henry of Huntingdon (Greenway, ed. and trans. 1996, *Historia Anglorum*, pp. 444–7).

137 David 1920, p. 91; Barlow 1983, p. 369; Green 2009, p. 36; Aird 2008, p. 162. The sources include Hugh of Flavigny (*Chronicon*, col. 354) and Eadmer (*Historia Novorum*, p. 74, both of whom used the word *tradere*. Orderic Vitalis (Chibnall, ed., Vol. V, p. 26) simply says that Rufus 'received' (*recepit*) Normandy. Robert of Torigni (*Gesta Normannorum Ducum*, 2, p. 204), *Regesta* ii, 377, refers to a '*concordia*' and Wace (Burgess and Holden, ed. 2002, line 9671 ('*gage*')).

138 Warren Hollister 1976, p. 213. See Barlow 1983, p. 365: 'No official record of the treaty of 1096 between Robert and William has survived'.

139 English 1991, p. 234. Le Patourel asserts that '…there is a good deal of evidence to confirm the idea contained in the phrase used by the author of the *Gesta Stephani*, that the Norman kings were kings "in" Normandy as well as in England' (1976, p. 238). The words of the *Gesta* (Potter, ed. 1955, p. 8) are as follows: '… *regem eum in Angliam et Normanniam … sacravit et iniunxit*'. On the Conqueror's adoption and use of the royal title in preference to that of *dux*, see Warren Hollister 1976, p. 206.

140 Nelson 1981, p. 131; Warren Hollister 1976, pp. 207–8.

141 William of Poitiers, *Gesta Guillelmi*, Davis and Chibnall, ed. 1998, pp. 44–5); Warren Hollister 1976, p. 208; Douglas 1964, pp. 263–4; Nelson 1981, p. 131.

142 Warren Hollister 1976, p. 213.

143 Barlow 1983, p. 368; *Neustria Pia*, p. 638; Musset 1967, no. 24, pp. 132–4. *Vidimus* of 1424. William, seeing death approaching, gave to St Etienne '*coronam, qua in celebrioribus festivitatibus inter sacra missarum sollempnia, coronabatur, cum sceptro et virga et praetiosi lapidis, calice aureisque candelabras et caeteris ad coronam pertinentibus, regalium insignium*'.

144 Barlow 1983, p. 368; Biddle 1985; Nelson 1981, pp. 130–1, note 143.

145 William could perhaps have worn it at Caen, where he may have spent the Christmases of 1080 and perhaps 1068 (Bates 1998, p. 84).

146 Barlow 1983, pp. 99–100; *Oxford Dictionary of National Biography*, online edition (2004–11) 'William Rufus'.

147 Wilson 1997, p. 34.

148 Although it is possible that William had another residence within the precincts of St Etienne. A tradition to this effect is recorded by Huet (1727, p. 180), and buildings which could have served such a function for later Dukes or royalty stood there until the mid-19th century.

149 See for example Thompson 1995.

150 Christiansen, ed. 1998; Lair 1865, p. 196: '… *aureis vasis poculisque splendide epulatur, vernarumque nobilium atque servorum multimoda exxageratione circumseptus, exercet iura decretaque orthodoxorum Patrum sedulus*'.

151 Biddle 1985, p. 52; Hare 1997, pp. 44–52. When in Normandy, the Conqueror routinely spent the great festivals at one of his residences (Bates 1998, pp. 75–84).

152 Dudo of St Quentin .Christiansen 1998, p. 98; Lair 1865, p. 222: '… *Pascha ipsius anni Baiocas celebravit, coadunatis optimatibus Britannicae Northmannicaeque regionis*'.

153 Renoux 1991, p. 245; Van Houts, ed., Robert of Torigni, *Interpolations*, p. 288: '*Ibi* [Fécamp] *etiam erat solitus fere omni tempore suam curiam in paschali solennitate tenere*'.

154 Renoux 1991, p. 245.

155 William of Poitiers, *Gesta Guillelmi*, Davis and Chibnall, ed. 1998, p. 180); Nelson 1981, p. 128.

156 On *palatii* and *castri* see Renoux 1998.

157 Richard I had a *palatium* and *arx* at Bayeux ('*Translatio secunda Sancti Audoeni*', in Bollandus, *et al.*, *Acta Sanctorum* (Augusti), Vol. 4, col. 823).

158 Bates 1982, p. 99 and 116–7.

159 Christiansen, ed. 1998; Lair 1865.

160 For a brief summary of the sources see (e.g.) Bates 1982, pp. xiii-xiv.

161 Fauroux no. 197, p. 382.

162 Lair, pp. 145 and 290; Christiansen, ed., pp. 29 and 165.

163 Lair, pp. 927 and 218.

164 See e.g. Wilson 1997, p. 275, no. 8, for the unambiguous use of 'palatium' for Westminster Hall.
165 Fauroux 1961, no. 197, p. 382; no. 123, p. 293 for *camerarius*; *ibid.*, no. 34, p. 130, and no. 86, p. 227, for *camera* as treasury/office of state. See also Bates 1981, p. 154.
166 Fauroux 1961, no. 227, p. 437; see also no. 165, p. 356.
167 Fauroux 1961, no. 165, p. 356; Orderic Vitalis, *Historia*, Chibnall, ed., Vol. IV, p. 224.
168 Renoux 1991*, passim.*
169 Renoux 1991, p. 361; on the dating, *ibid.*, pp. 374–5.
170 Renoux 1991, pp. 348. On all this see Chapelot and Fossier 1980, pp. 79–135; James, Marshall and Millett 1984, *passim.*
171 Renoux 1991, pp. 359–60.
172 Renoux 1991, pp. 338 and 369.
173 Renoux 1991, p. 381.
174 On the ambiguity, see Renoux 1991, p. 382; for the incident, see Dudo of St Quentin, p. 290 and *Libellus de Revelatione*, *PL* cli, col. 716.
175 Renoux 1991, pp. 381–2.
176 Howlett, ed., Vol. 4, p. 106: '… *turrem Rothomagi quam aedificavit primus Ricardus dux Normannorum, in palatium sibi*'.
177 Howlett, ed., Vol. 4, p. 106: '*Turrem nihilominus excelsam fecit in castello Cadomensi*'; De Boüard, M., 1979, p. 103; see also Orderic Vitalis (Chibnall, ed., Vol. VI, pp. 224 and 226) for further evidence of the building's height.
178 *Antiquus Cartularius Ecclesiae Baiocensis* (Bourienne, ed., Vol. 1, no. ii, p. 3); Bates 1998, no. 26, pp. 174–5.
179 See Renoux 1991, p. 382, where Building I is firmly attributed to Richard I while following Dudo in attributing a second hall to Richard II; see also p. 339. But at p. 342, it is claimed that the sumptuous palace known in the 12th century was centred on a hall built by Richard I before 990. Renoux 1991, p. 338, note 198, citing B. M. Rouen, Y 51, f. 46 r: '*iuxta muros aulae piae memoriae comitis Ricardi*'. That the reference is to Richard II*, ibid.*, p. 339.
180 Renoux 1991, p. 580.
181 Renoux 1991, p. 340; Fahlin, ed. 1951 and 1954, *Benoît de St Maure*, Vol. II, pp. 187–192:
*En ses palaiz riches e hauz,*
*De quarreiaus tailliez e de chauz*
*Celez e vouctz en lanbruschez,*
*Od colors peinz e deboissiez.*
*Haut sor les murs li ploct munter*
*Por veeir la terre e la mer.*
182 Impey 2002. Mesqui (2011, p. 236, note 215) indicates the absence of evidence for an upper floor in the 'tower' as originally built. However, not only do the windows at this level have all the hallmarks of basement windows (small, low-set) but by far the best explanation of the exceptionally broad buttress towards the southern end of the west wall is that it carried a hearth at an upper level.
183 Impey 2002, pp. 255–6.
184 Le Maho 2004, pp. 192 and 194–8.
185 De Boüard 1979, pp. 63–7.
186 Fauroux, no. 165, p. 356; William of Poitiers, *Gesta Guillelmi*, Davis and Chibnall, ed. 1998, p. 10 ('*Nam praetor alia firmamenta … aulam habet lapideam arcis usum pugnantibus praebentem*'.
187 Le Maho 2004, pp. 192 and 194.
188 Decaëns 1981, p. 176; p. 194, fig. 2. Decaëns acknowledges that the uprights could have carried a roof ('les entraits du toit'), but cites the irregularity of the ground, and the supposed arrangement of the Echiquier, as evidence of an upper floor.
189 Zadora-Rio 1970, p. 235.
190 Le Maho 1984, p. 19.
191 Renoux 1991, pp. 305 and 369.
192 Le Maho 1984, *passim.*
193 On *turres*, see Impey, ed. 2008, pp. 227–41.
194 Renoux 1991, pp. 295–97.
195 Colvin, ed. 1963, pp. 43–5; Barlow 1983, pp. 132–3, note 174; *Hyde Register*, pp. 2–3; Hurst 1985, pp. 18–20.
196 Wilson 1997, pp. 33–4, for context and translation. *Palatium* is the word used, but Wilson convincingly argues for his translation as hall. For the text see Legg 1901, p. 92: '*Tribue … sit in regno et dignitas gloriosa regalis palacii maximo splendore regie potestatis oculis omnium fulgeat: luce clarissima choruscare atque splendescere quasi splendidissima fulgura: maximo perfusa lumine videatur*'.
197 Musset 1971, pp. 56–7.
198 Renoux 1991, p. 578, note 124.
199 Blair 1993; Hale, ed. 1858.
200 Flambard Héricher 2008, pp. 31–9.
201 *Ibid.*
202 Lorren 1977a.
203 Coutan and Quenedey 1931; Le Maho 1997.
204 Mesqui 2008, p. 90. The buildings were demolished in 1827.
205 Renoux 1991, pp. 543–87; esp. pp. 579–80 and fig. 141.
206 Impey 1993, pp. 105–7.
207 Dixon 2008, p. 261.
208 Robert of Torigni, Howlett, ed. 1889, pp. 106–7 and 162 ('… *turris Ebroicarum, turris Alentionis, turris Constantiarum*'). Otherwise towers are specifically mentioned only at Arques ('… *castellum, quod vocatur Archas, turre et moenibus mirabiliter firmavit*') and Caen, but the King is described as having done the same thing at the others ('*Sic etiam fecit* …'). For an 18th-century plan and view of the tower at Alençon see Chave 1998, pp. 113–4, figs 4 and 7.
209 De Boüard 1979, p. 115. The 'salle' measured 6.17m × 25–30m.
210 On Beaumont-le-Richard, Creully and Bricquebec see Impey 1999a; on the Grand Doyenné see Nicholas-Méry 2004.
211 Lemaitre 1990, pp. 134–7.
212 Burnouf and Decaëns 1985.
213 Impey 1999, pp. 64–5, fig. 18.
214 Impey 1993, pp. 111–3.
215 I am grateful to Bénédicte Guillot for a tour and discussion of the site in 2013. For an interim excavation report see Guillot 2011, pp. 24–35.

## Bibliography

### *Published Primary Sources (ordered by author or, in the case of modern compilations etc., by editor)*


Anon (1735) 'Translatio Secunda Sancti Audoeni', in *Acta Sanctorum* (Augusti), Bollandus *et al.*, ed., Vol. 4 (Antwerp).

Bar, F. (1938) *Les Epitres latines de Raoul le Tourtier (1065?–1114?)* (Paris).

Bates, D. (1998) *Regesta Regum Anglo-Normannorum: The Acta of William I (1066–1087)* (Oxford, Clarendon Press).

Benoît de Saint Maure *Chronique des ducs de Normandie*, C. Fahlin, ed., 2 vols (1951 and 1954) (Uppsala).

Birch, W. de G. (1892) *Hyde Register* (Winchester, Hampshire Record Society).

Busson, G. and Ledru, A. and Busson, G. (1901) *Actus Pontificum Cenomannis in Urbe Degentium, Société des Archives Historiques du Maine*, Vol. 2 (Le Mans). The *Gesta Domni Hoelli Episcopi* is at pp. 382–97.

Chatel, E., ed. (1892) *Chronicarum Anonymi Cadomensi*, M.S.A.N., p. 138.
De Certain, E. (1855) 'Raoul Tortaire', *Bibliothèque de l'école des chartes*, Vol. 16, no. 1, pp. 489–521.
Dudo of St Quentin, *De Moribus et Actis Primorum Normanniae Ducum*, J. Lair, ed., (1865) (Caen).
Dudo of St Quentin, *History of the Normans*, E. Christiansen, trans. (1998) (Woodbridge).
Du Monstier, A. (1663) *Neustria Pia seu de Omnibus et Singulis Abbatiis et Prioratibus Totius Normanniae* (Rouen).
Eadmer (1884) *Historia Novorum in Anglia*, M. Rule., ed., Rolls Series (London).
Earle, J. and Plummer, C., ed. (1952) (2nd ed.) *Two of the Anglo-Saxon Chronicles Parallel*, (London).
Fauroux, M. (1961) *Recueil des actes des ducs de Normandie (911–1066), Mémoires de la Société des Antiquaires de Normandie*, XXXVI (Caen).
Henry of Huntingdon, *Historia Anglorum (The History of the English People)*, D. E. Greenway, ed. and trans. (1996) (Oxford, Oxford Medieval Texts).
Hugh of Flavigny, *Chronicon*, in J. Migne, ed., *Patrologia Latina*, cliv, cols. 21–404.
*Libellus de Revelatione*, in J. Migne, ed., *Patrologia Latina*, cliv, cols 701–24.
Moss, V., ed. (2004) *Pipe Rolls of the Exchequer of Normandy for the Reign of Henry II, 1180–1184*, Pipe Roll Society Vol. 91, New Series Vol. 53 (London).
Musset, L. (1967) *Les actes de Guillaume le Conquérant et de la reine Mathilde pour les abbayes caennaises, Mémoires de la Société des Antiquaires de Normandie*, XXXVII (Caen).
Orderic Vitalis, *The Ecclesiastical History*, M. Chibnall, ed. (1969–80), 6 vols (Oxford).
Robert of Torigni, 'Chronica', in *Chronicles of the Reign of Stephen, Henry II and Richard I*, R. Howlett, ed., Vol. 4, pp. 81–315.
Roger of Howden, *Chronica Magistri Rogeri de Hovedene,* W. Stubbs, ed., 4 vols, RS, 1868–71 (London).
Stapleton, T. (1840), *Magni Rotuli Scacciarii Normanniae*, 2 vols (London).
Wace, *The Roman de Rou*, G. S. Burgess and A. J. Holden, ed. (2002) (St Helier).
William of Jumièges, *The Gesta Normannorum Ducum of William of Jumièges, Orderic Vitalis and Robert of Torigni*, Van Houts, ed. and trans., E.M.C., 2 vols (1992 and 1995) (Oxford, Oxford Medieval Texts).
William of Malmesbury, *Gesta Regum Anglorum*, R. A. B. Mynors, R. M. Thomson, and M. Winterbottom, ed. (1998) (Oxford).
William of Poitiers, *Gesta Guillelmi Ducis Normannorum et Regis Anglorum*, R. H. C. Davis and M. Chibnall, ed. and trans. (1998) (Oxford).

## Secondary Sources

Aberg, F. A. and Brown, A. E. (1981) *Medieval Moated Sites in North-West Europe*, British Archaeological Report International Series 121 (Oxford).
Aird, W. M. (2008) *Robert Curthose, Duke of Normandy (c.1050–1134)* (Woodbridge, Boydell & Brewer).
Ashbee, J. (2006) 'Cloisters in English palaces in the twelfth and thirteenth centuries', *Journal of the British Archaeological Association* 159, pp. 71–90.
Aubert, M. (1961) *L'Art Roman en France* (Paris, Picard).
Barlow, F. (1983) *William Rufus* (London, Methuen).
Bates, D. (1982) *Normandy Before 1066* (London and New York, Longmans).
Baylé, M. (1979) *La Trinité de Caen: Sa place dans l'histoire de l'Architecture et du Décor Romans* (Geneva, Arts et Métiers graphiques).
Baylé, M., ed. (2001) (2nd rev. ed.) *L'architecture normande au Moyen Age*, 2 vols (Caen, Presses universitaires de Caen).
Baylé, M. (1992) *Les Origines et les Premiers Développements de la Sculpture Romane en Normandie, Caen*, Art de Basse Normandie 100.
Beaurepaire, E. de (1896) *Caen Illustré. Son histoire, ses Monuments* (Caen).
Beaurepaire, F. de and Chaline, J-P., ed. (2000) *La Normandie vers l'An Mil* (Rouen, Société de l'Histoire de Normandie).
Beresford, G. (1987) *Goltho: the Development of an Early Medieval Manor, c. 850–1150*, English Heritage Archaeological Report 4 (London, English Heritage).
Biddle, M. (1985) 'Seasonal festivals and residence: Winchester, Westminster and Gloucester in the tenth to twelfth centuries', *Anglo-Norman Studies* 8, pp. 51–72.
Blair, J. (1993) 'Hall and chamber: English domestic planning 1000–1250', in G. Meirion-Jones, and M. Jones, ed., pp. 1–21.
Borg, A. (1967) 'The development of chevron ornament', *Journal of the British Archaeological Association* 120, pp. 122–40.
Boüard, M. de (1961) 'L'art Roman en Normandie et en Bretagne', in M. Aubert, ed., pp. 69–128.
Boüard, M. de (1962) 'Le Château de Caen', *Le Mois à Caen* 9, November 1962.
Boüard, M. de (1965) 'La Salle dite l'Echiquier, au Château de Caen', *Medieval Archaeology* 9, pp. 64–81.
Boüard, M. de (1978) 'Le Château de Caen', *Congrès Archéologique de France* 132, pp. 9–21.
Boüard, M. de (1979) *Le Château de Caen* (Caen, CRAHM).
Bourgeville, C. de (1588) *Les Recherches et Antiquitez de la Province de Neustrie, à present, Duché de Normendie, comme des villes remarquable d'icelles: mais plus speciallement de la Ville et Université de Caen* (Caen).
Brodeur, J. Chevet, P. and Mastrolenzo, J. (1998) 'Construction sur le site du château d'Angers d'après les fouilles récentes', in D. Prigent and Y. Tonnerre, pp. 101–12.
Burnouf, J. and Decaëns, J. (1985) 'La fin du château de Saint-Vaast-sur-Seulles (Calvados)', *Château Gaillard* 12, pp. 23–37.
Camus, M-T. (1992) *Sculpture Romane de Poitou: Les grands chantiers du XIe siècle* (Paris, Edition a. and J. Pacard).
Carlson, E. J. (1968) *The Abbey Church of St Etienne at Caen in the 11th and early 12th centuries* (unpublished PhD thesis, Yale University).
Carré, G. (2009) 'Le rempart nord-ouest du château de Caen (XIe–XVIe siècles). L'apport récent de l'archéologie du bâti', *Annales de Normandie* 59(2) (July–December), pp. 3–25.
Caumont, A. de (1830–35) *Cours d'Antiquités Monumentales*, 6 parts (Paris).
Caumont, A. de (1846–59) *Statistique Monumentale de Calvados*, 4 vols (Caen).
Chapelot, J. and Fossier, R. (1980) *La village et la Maison au Moyen Age* (Paris, Hachette).
Chapman, H., Coppack, G. and Drewett, P. (1975) *Excavations at the Bishop's Palace, Lincoln*, Occasional Papers in Lincolnshire History and Archaeology I (Lincoln).
Chave, I. (1998) 'Guillaume Milles dit le Tailleur, maître des oeuvres du roi en la vicomté d'Alençon, actif de 1431 à 1447', in B. Fajal, ed., pp. 87–130.
Clapham, A. (1936) *Romanesque Architecture in Western Europe* (Oxford, Clarendon).
Cotman, J. S. and Turner, T. H. (1822) *Architectural Antiquities of Normandy*, 2 vols (London).
Coutan, F. and Quenedey, R. (1931) 'Le Château de Longeuil', *Bulletin Monumental*, pp. 249–69.
Crook, J. and Harris, R. H. (forthcoming) *Reconstructing Westminster Hall.*
Cunliffe, B. (1976) *Excavations at Portchester Castle*, Vol. II: Saxon (London, Society of Antiquaries).
David, C. W. (1920), *Robert Curthose, Duke of Normandy* (Cambridge MA, Harvard University Press).

Decaëns, J. (1981) 'La motte d'Olivet à Grimbosq (Calvados), résidence seigneuriale du XI siècle', *Archéologie Médiévale* 11, pp. 167–201.

Decaëns, J. (2000) [re Caen] 'Le premier Château, de Guillaume le Conquérant à Richard Coeur de Lion (XIe–XIIe siècles)', in J-M. Levesque and J-Y. Marin, pp. 15–21.

Decaëns, J. and Dubois, A. (2009) *Le Château de Caen. Mille ans d'une forteresse dans la ville* (Caen, CRAHM).

Dixon, P. (2008) 'The influence of the White Tower on the Great Towers of the 12th century', in E. Impey, ed., pp. 243–73.

Douglas, D. (1964) *William the Conqueror. The Norman Impact upon England* (London, Yale English Monarchs Series).

Ducarel, A. C. (1767) (2nd ed.) *Anglo-Norman Antiquities Considered in a Tour through part of Normandy* (London).

Emery, A. (2006) *Greater Medieval Houses of England and Wales*, Vol. 3 (Cambridge, University Press).

English, B. (1991) 'William the Conqueror and the Anglo-Norman succession', *Bulletin of the Institute of Historical Research*, pp. 221–36.

Fage, R. (1909) 'La décoration géometrique dans 'l'école romane de Normandie', *Congrès Archéologique de France*, 75th session, Vol. 2, pp. 615–33.

Fajal, B., ed. (1998) *Autour du Château médiéval,* Société Historique et Archéologique de l'Orne, Mémoires et documents 1 (Alençon).

Faulkner, P. A. (1958) 'Domestic planning from the twelfth to the fourteenth centuries', *Archaeological Journal* 105, pp. 150–83.

Favreau, R. (1996) *Poitiers: Saint-Jean-de-Montierneuf* (Poitiers, Association pour le neuvième centenaire de Montierneuf).

Fernie, E (2000) *The Architecture of Norman England* (Oxford, Univeristy Press).

Flambard-Héricher, A-M. (1998a) 'La construction dans la basse vallée de la Seine: l'exemple du château de Vatteville-la-Rue', *Château Gaillard* 18, pp. 93–102.

Flambard-Héricher, A-M. (1998b) 'La cuisine du logis seigneurial du "Vieux Château" de Vatteville-la-Rue (Seine-Maritime), in B. Fajal, ed. (1998), pp. 131–45.

Flambard-Héricher, A-M. (2008) *Le Château Ganne* (Caen, CRAHM).

Goodall, J. (2000) 'The medieval palace of Westminster', in C. Riding and J. Riding, pp. 49–68.

Goodall, J. (2001) *Richmond Castle and Easby Abbey*, English Heritage Guidebook (London, English Heritage).

Goodall, J. (2011) *The English Castle* (Newhaven and London, Yale University Press).

Gordon, D. Monnas, L. and Elam, C., ed. (1997) *The Regal Image of Richard II and the Wilton Diptych* (London, Harvey Miller).

Grant, L. (2005) *Architecture and Society in Normandy*, 1120–1270 (London, Yale University Press).

Green, J. (2009) *Henry I* (Cambridge, University Press).

Guillot, B. (2011) 'Un édifice à étage de l'ensemble palatial', *Institut National de Recherches Archéologiques Préventives* (December 2011).

Haines, C. R. (1910) *Dover Priory: a History of the Priory of St Mary the Virgin and St Martin of the New Work* (Cambridge).

Halbout, P. and Le Maho, J., ed. (1990) *De la Gaule a la Normandie* (Rouen, CRAHM).

Hallam, E. M. (1980) 'The king and the princes in 11th-century France', *Bulletin of the Institute of Historical Research* 53, pp. 153–4.

Hare, M. (1997) 'Kings, crowns and festivals; the origins of Gloucester as a Royal ceremonial centre', *Transactions of the Bristol and Gloucestershire Archaeological Society* 115, pp. 41–78.

Haskins, C. H. (1918) *Norman Institutions* (Harvard).

Huet, P-D. (1726) (2nd ed.) *Les origines de la ville de Caen, revues, corrigées, augmentées* (Rouen).

Hurst, H. (1985) *Kingsholm* (Cambridge, University Press).

Impey, E. (1993) 'Seigneurial domestic architecture in Normandy, 1050–1350', in G. Meirion-Jones and M. Jones, ed., pp. 82–120.

Impey, E. (1995) *Le Château de Creully* (Cabourg, des Cahiers du Temps).

Impey, E. (1999a) 'The seigneurial residence in Normandy, 1125–1225: an Anglo-Norman tradition', *Medieval Archaeology* XLIII, pp. 45–73.

Impey, E. (1999b) 'Le Manoir de Chauvincourt (Eure): une résidence seigneuriale du XIII siècle', *Bulletin Monumental* 157, pp. 63–70.

Impey, E. (2002a) 'The *donjon* at Avranches, Normandy', *Archaeological Journal* 159, pp. 249–257.

Impey, E. (2002b) 'The *turris famosa* at Ivry-la-Bataille, Normandy', in G. Meirion-Jones, E. Impey and M. Jones, ed., pp. 189–210.

Impey, E. ed. (2008) *The White Tower* (London, Yale University Press).

James, J. (2006) *The Ark of God*, Part B, Vol. 3 (Woodbridge, Boydell).

James, S., Marshall, A. and Millett, M. (1984) 'An early medieval building tradition', *Archaeological Journal* 141, pp. 182–215.

Jean-Marie, L. (2000) *Caen aux XIe et XIIe siècles. Espace urbain, pouvoirs et société* (Caen, Editions La Mandragore).

Joliment, T. de (1825) *Description historique et critique et vues des monuments religieux et civils les plus remarquables du Département du Calvados* (Caen).

Kealey, E. J. (1972) *Roger of Salisbury, Viceroy of England* (Berkeley, Los Angeles and London, University of California Press).

Kipps, P. K. (1929) Minster Court, Thanet, *Archaeological Journal* 86, pp. 213–23.

La Rue, G. (1820) *Essais historiques sur la ville de Caen et son Arrondissement* (Caen).

Lasko, P. (1972) *Ars Sacra 800–1200* (Harmondsworth, Pelican).

Lefèvre, D. (2000) 'L'avenir du Château de Caen: schéma directeur de conservation et de mise en valeur', in J-M. Levesque and J-Y. Marin, pp. 113–7.

Legg, L. G. W. (1901) *English Coronation Records* (London).

Le Maho, J. (1984) *La Motte Seigneuriale de Mirville (XIe–XIIe s.)* (Rouen, CRAHM).

Le Maho, J. (1997) 'Remarques sur la construction de bois en Haute-Normandie au XIe et XIIe siècles', in M. Baylé, ed., vol. 1, pp. 243–68.

Le Maho, J. (1998) 'Notes de Castellologie Haut-Normande: châteaux à motte, enceintes et églises fortifiées (XIe–XIIe s.)', in B. Fajal, pp. 219–43.

Le Maho, J. (2000) 'La Tour-de-Rouen, palais du duc Ricard Ier', in F. de Beaurepaire and J-P. Chaline, pp. 73–6.

Le Maho, J. (2004) 'Un grand château de terre et bois aux environs de l'an mil: l'enceinte fortifiée de Notre Dame de Gravenchon (Haute Normandie), *Château Gaillard* 21, pp. 191–201.

Lemaitre, P. (1990) 'Grosley-sur-Risle (Eure), résidence seigneuriale fortifiée (XIe–XIIIe siècle) et village deserté', in P. Halbout and J. Le Maho, pp. 134–7.

Le Patourel, J. (1976) *The Norman Empire* (Oxford, Clarendon).

Leroux, P. (2000) 'Un chantier archéologique pionnier (1956–66)', in J-M. Levesque and J-Y. Marin, 2000, pp. 83–7.

Levesque, J-M. and Marin, J-Y. (2000) *Mémoires du Château de Caen* (Caen, CRAHM).

Leyland, M. (1994) 'The origin and development of Durham Castle', in *Anglo-Norman Durham 1093–1193*, D. Rollason, M. Harvey and M. Prestwich, ed. (Woodbridge, Boydell), pp. 407–24.

Lorren, C. (1977a) 'La demeure seigneuriale de Rubercy (Calvados), étude de la demeure principale', *Archéologie Médiévale* 7, pp. 109–78.

Lorren, C. (1977b) 'La demeure seigneurial de Rubercy (milieu du XIIe – début XIIIe siècle), *Château Gaillard* 8, pp. 185–92.

Lorren, C. (1981) 'The castle of Rubercy (Calvados) (*c.* 1150–1204), in F. A. Aberg, and A. E. Brown, *Medieval Moated Sites in North-West*

*Europe*, pp. 103–25, British Archaeological Report International Series 121 (Oxford).

Mallet, J. (1984) *L'art roman de l'ancien Poitou* (Paris, Picard).

Mallet, J. (2003) 'La nef unique dans l'art religieux angevin', in J. McNeill and D. Prigent, ed., *Anjou: Medieval Art, Architecture and Archaeology*, British Archaeological Association Conference Transactions 26 (Leeds), pp. 52–65.

Marino, L. (2000) 'Le château de Caen: nouveaux relevés des structures architectoniques et contributions à la restauration et à la mise en valeur', in J-M. Levesque and J-Y. Marin, pp. 105–11.

Mason, E. (2005) *William II. Rufus, the Red King* (Stroud, Tempus).

Meirion-Jones, G. and Jones, M., ed. (1993) *Manorial Domestic Buildings in England and Northern France*, Society of Antiquaries Occasional Paper 15 (London).

Meirion-Jones, G., Impey, E. and Jones, M., ed. (2002) *The Seigneurial Residence in western Europe AD* c. *800–1600,* British Archaeological Report International series 1088 (Oxford).

Mesqui, J. (1993) *Châteaux et enceintes de la France médiévale. De la défense à la résidence* (1991–3), 2 vols (Paris, Picard).

Mesqui, J. (1997) *Châteaux forts et fortifications en France* (Paris, Flammarion).

Mesqui, J. (2008) *Le Château de Lillebonne des Ducs de Normandie aux Ducs d'Harcourt,* Mémoire de la Société des Antiquaires de Normandie 42.

Mesqui, J. *Le Château d'Angers* (Paris, Editions du Patrimoine).

Mesqui, J. (2011) *Les seigneurs d'Ivry, Bréval et Anet aux XIe et XIIe siècles. Châteaux et familles à la frontière normande* (Caen, Mémoire de la Société des Antiquaires de Normandie 46).

Methuen, P. (1952) *Normandy diary: being a record of survivals and losses of historical monuments in north-western France, together with those in the island of Walcheren, and in that part of Belgium traversed by 21st Army Group in 1944–45* (London, Robert Hale).

Moss, R. (2009) *Romanesque Chevron Ornament. The Language of British, Norman and Irish Sculpture in the Twelfth Century*, British Archaeological Report International Series 1908 (Oxford).

Mussat, A. (1981) *La Cathédrale de Mans* (Paris, Berger-Levrault).

Musset, L. (1971) *Caen: Ville d'Art* (Colmar-Ingersheim, SAEP).

Musset, L. (1985) (2nd ed.) *Normandie Romane*, Vol. 2 (La Pierre qui Vire, Zodiaque).

Musset, L. (1987) (3rd ed.) *Normandie Romane*, Vol. 1 (La Pierre qui Vire, Zodiaque).

Nelson, L. (1981) 'The rites of the Conqueror', *Proceedings of the Battle Conference on Anglo-Norman Studies* IV (Woodbridge, Boydell), pp. 117–32.

Neveux, F. (1997) *La Normandie des Ducs aux Rois, Xe-XIIe siècle* (Rennes, CRAHM).

Nicholas-Méry, D. (2002) 'Le donjon d'Avranches: redécouverte d'un monument médiéval', *Revue de l'Avranchin et du pays de Granville* 79, fasc. 391 (June 2002), pp. 87–150.

Nicholas-Méry, D. (2004) 'Le Grand Doyenné à Avranches, résidence urbaine des seigneurs de Subligny', *Revue de l'Avranchin et du Pays de Granville* 81, pp. 134–71.

Phillips, D. (1985) *The Cathedral of Archbishop Thomas of Bayeux: Excavations at York Minster Vol. 2.* (London, RCHME).

Poirier, J. (1944) *La Bataille de Caen* (Caen, CRAHM).

Prigent, D. and Tonnerre, N-Y. (1998,) *La Construction en Anjou au Moyen Age, Actes de la Table ronde d'Angers des 29 et 30 mars 1996* (Angers).

Quenedey, R. (1927) 'Château de Longeuil', *Bulletin de la Commission Départementale des Antiquités de la Seine-Inférieure*, séance du 15 Juin 1927, pp. 57–8.

Quenedey, R. and Coutan (Dr) (1931) 'Le château de Longeuil', *Bulletin Monumental*, p. 253.

Rahtz, P. (1979) *The Saxon and Medieval Palaces at Cheddar, Excavations 1960–62*, British Archaeological Report British Series 65 (Oxford).

Rajnai, M. (1975) *John Sell Cotman. Drawings of Normandy in Norwich Castle Museum* (Norwich).

RCHME (1952) *Dorset*, Vol. 1, West (London, RCHME).

RCHME (1980) *City of Salisbury*, Vol. 1 (London, RCHME).

Renoux, A. (1991) *Fécamp. Du Palais ducal au Palais de Dieu* (Paris, CNRS).

Renoux, A., ed. (1994a) *Palais Médiévaux (France Belgique) 25 ans d'archéologie* (Le Mans, Actes du colloque du Mans).

Renoux, A. (1994b) 'Caen, Calvados. Château et résidence des Ducs de Normandie', in A. Renoux, pp. 31–3.

Renoux, A., ed. (1996a) *Palais Royaux et Princiers au Moyen Age* (Le Mans, Actes du colloque du Mans).

Renoux, A. (1996b) 'Espaces et lieux de pouvoirs royaux et princiers en France (fin IXe-début XIIIe siècle): changement et continuité', in A. Renoux, pp. 17–42.

Renoux, A. (2002) '*Palatium* et *castrum* en France du Nord (fin IXe – début XIIIe siècle), in G. Meirion-Jones, E. Impey and M. Jones, ed., pp. 15–25.

Riding, C. and Riding, J., ed. (2000) *The Houses of Parliament: History and Architecture* (London, Merrell).

Salet, F. (1961) 'La Cathédrale du Mans', *Congrès Archéologique de France*, 119th session, pp. 18–99.

Salzman, L. F. (1952) *Building in England Down to 1540. A Documentary History* (Oxford, Clarendon).

Schofield, J. (1993) *The Building of London from the Conquest to the Great Fire* (London, British Museum Press).

Sintès, C., ed. (1996) *Musée de l'Arles antique: collections archéologiques d'Arles* (Arles, Actes Sud).

Smirke, S. (1836) 'Remarks on the architectural history of Westminster Hall', *Archaeologia* 26, pp. 406–14.

Stalley, R. (1971) 'A twelfth-century patron of architecture. A study of the buildings erected by Roger, Bishop of Salisbury 1102–1139', *Journal of the British Archaeological Association* 34, pp. 62–83.

Stanley, A. (1890) *Historical Memorials of Westminster Abbey* (London).

Stratford, N., ed. (1987) *Romanesque and Gothic Essays for George Zarnecki* (Woodbridge, Boydell).

Taylor, A. (1989) *Archéologie Médiévale* 19, pp. IX–X (obituary of Michel de Boüard).

Tcherikover, A. (1988) 'Anjou or Aquitaine? The case of Saint-Eutrope at Saintes', *Zeitschrift für Kunstgeschichte* 51, pp. 348–71.

Tcherikover, A. (1989) 'Romanesque sculpted archivolts in western France: Forms and techniques', *Arte Médiévale* 3, pp. 49–75.

Tcherikover, A. (1997) *High Romanesque Sculpture in the Duchy of Aquitaine c. 1090–1140* (Oxford, Clarendon).

Thompson, M. W. (1995) *The Medieval Hall. The Basis of Secular Domestic Life, 600–1600 AD* (Aldershoy, Scolar Press).

Thurlby, M. (2006) *Romanesque Architecture and Sculpture in Wales* (Woonton Aimeley, Little Logaston).

Turner, T. H. (1877) *Some Account of Domestic Architecture in England from the Conquest to the end of the Thirteenth Century* (Oxford and London).

Turner, R. (2002) *Chepstow Castle Guidebook* (Cardiff, CADW).

Warren Hollister, C. (1976) 'Normandy, France and the Anglo-Norman *Regnum*', *Speculum* 51(2), pp. 202–42.

Wilson, C. (1997) 'Rulers, artificers and shoppers: Richard II's remodelling of Westminster Hall, 1393–99', in D. Gordon, L. Monnas and C. Elam, pp. 33–59.

Wood, M. E. (1965) *The English Medieval House* (London, Phoenix).

Zadora-Rio, E. (1970) 'L'enceinte fortifiée du Plessis-Grimoult, résidence seigneuriale du XIe siècle', *Château Gaillard* V, pp. 227–40.

Zarnecki, G. (1966) '1066 and architectural sculpture', *Proceedings of the British Academy* 52, 87–104.

Zarnecki, G. (1979a) 'Romanesque sculpture in Normandy and England in the eleventh century', *Proceedings of the Battle Conference, 1978* (London), pp. 200–21.

Zarnecki, G. (1979b) *Studies in Romanesque Sculpture* (London, Dorian).

# Part II

# The Castles in Context

# 9

# Châteaux et résidences princières dans la *Tapisserie de Bayeux*

*Pierre Bouet*


## Summary

*The Bayeux Tapestry features around 30 monuments that have been the object of numerous studies, particularly by art historians. These buildings (castles, ceremonial halls, churches, pavilions, towers and country houses) are represented according to iconographic conventions of the time, for which we find numerous examples in sculpture as well as illustrations from manuscripts, particularly ones copied in Kent.*

*When closely examining these representations of timber or stone monuments, we can sometimes make uncanny analogies with reality, apparent from excavations and archaeological studies. It therefore seemed interesting to study the castles and princely houses represented in the Bayeux Tapestry to see how artists of this embroidery succeeded, beyond the iconographic conventions that they had inherited, to paint these architectural realities. This research on castles and princely houses has been driven by findings from archaeological excavations that show how the designers and draftsmen of the Bayeux Embroidery had precise knowledge of these Norman and English buildings.*


## Introduction

La *Tapisserie de Bayeux* présente une trentaine de monuments qui ont fait l'objet de nombreuses études. C'est donc une véritable gageure de ma part de reprendre un dossier aussi complexe et aussi discuté, mais je le fais en m'appuyant principalement sur les travaux publiés par les archéologues comme Michel de Boüard, Richard Gem, Brian Hope-Taylor, Anne-Marie Flambard Héricher.[1] Il importe en premier lieu de tenir compte de la spécificité du document et des conventions artistiques qui expliquent en partie certaines particularités de la représentation iconographique.

## La *Tapisserie*, une œuvre anglo-normande

Il y a désormais un accord entre la plupart des spécialistes de la *Tapisserie* pour reconnaître qu'elle fut réalisée en Angleterre, vraisemblablement dans la région du Kent, à la demande de l'évêque de Bayeux, Odon de Conteville, peu de temps après la bataille. Lors du colloque international de Cerisy-la-Salle en 1999, nous avions mis en évidence le fait que la *Broderie de Bayeux* avait été conçue et réalisée par une équipe comprenant à la fois des Normands et des Anglais.[2] La présence de termes comme *caballi* (à la place d'*equi*) et de *parabolant* (à la place de *loquebantur*) ne pouvait émaner que d'artistes continentaux s'exprimant en langue française: *parabolant* est à l'origine du verbe « parler » et *caballi* à celle du mot 'cheval'. A l'inverse, les termes *Bagias*, *Gyrth* (avec le D barré) et *ceastra* (avec la graphie anglo-saxonne *ce-* pour noter la palatalisation de la gutturale [k] devant [e] ou [i]) attestent la présence d'artistes anglo-saxons. La mise en valeur du personnage d'Harold dans la majorité des scènes et l'absence de qualificatifs dépréciatifs, tels que *perjurus, impurus, vesanus, tyrannus, perfidus* qui se rencontrent dans les chroniques latines postérieures à 1070 montrent clairement que la *Tapisserie de Bayeux* est un monument qui, tout en justifiant la conquête de l'Angleterre par le duc de Normandie, présente Harold comme un personnage éminent et héroïque. L'un des messages de la *Tapisserie de Bayeux* c'est d'affirmer conjointement la légitimité de Guillaume de Normandie et la dignité d'Harold. Ces constatations nous avaient alors conduit à estimer que la *Tapisserie de Bayeux* avait été conçue et réalisée peu après la bataille, durant une courte période, entre fin 1066 et 1070, où Guillaume de Normandie avait cru possible une réconciliation des deux peuples ennemis et avait agi fermement en ce sens en se présentant comme le protecteur du peuple anglais et de ses coutumes. Après 1070 et les massacres d'York, une telle œuvre de réconciliation, conçue et réalisée par une équipe d'artistes anglais et normands, n'était plus envisageable. C'est à cette même datation que Barbara English était arrivée en analysant la scène du couronnement d'Harold, lors de ce même colloque à Cerisy-la-Salle.

## Les conventions iconographiques

Avant d'examiner les châteaux et les palais princiers de la *Tapisserie*, il convient de rappeler que les représentations des divers bâtiments répondent à des critères esthétiques qu'il importe de préciser. Tout d'abord l'édifice n'est pas toujours présenté vu de l'extérieur, comme le sont les châteaux de Rennes, d'Hastings et de Rouen (Figure 9.1, scène 12). La plupart du temps, on propose aux visiteurs des coupes transversales des bâtiments, comme s'ils se trouvaient à l'intérieur de la construction et participaient en témoins à la scène (Figure 9.2, scène 14). Ensuite, les artistes qui ont eu en charge les cartons de la *Tapisserie* avaient à leur disposition les nombreux modèles existant aussi bien dans la sculpture que dans l'enluminure. Les travaux de Francis Wormald, de Charles Dodwell, de Cyril Hart et plus récemment de Michael Lewis[3] ont mis en évidence les ressemblances saisissantes qui rattachent la *Broderie de Bayeux* à plusieurs manuscrits anglo-saxons, dont certains sont originaires de Cantorbéry, un des lieux, où aurait pu être confectionnée cette œuvre d'art.

*Figure 9.1. Château de Rouen: scène 12 (Ville de Bayeux).*

Le *Psautier d'Utrecht* (Utrecht Universiteits-bibliotheek, ms 32), daté du IXe siècle, a exercé, avec d'autres ouvrages disparus, une influence considérable sur l'enluminure anglo-saxonne. En témoignent le *Psautier Harley* 603 (British Library, Harley 603) et le Cotton Caligula A.XV de la British Library. Une parenté plus étroite encore rattache la *Broderie* à certains manuscrits copiés et enluminés à Cantorbéry: *l'Old English Hexateuch* de la moitié du XIe siècle (British Library, Cotton Claudius B. IV) et la *Caedmon Genesis / Junius manuscript* du début du XIe siècle (Oxford, Bodleian Library, Junius 11). À titre d'exemples, évoquons les ressemblances dans la façon originale de représenter les arbres, qui constituent des ponctuations entre les scènes dans la bible d'Alcuin (datée de 843), dans le calendrier hymnaire de la British Library Cotton Julius A VI et sur la *Tapisserie de Bayeux* (Figure 9.3) ou d'enrouler les rideaux autour des montants du lit dans *l'Old English Hexateuch* et dans la scène de la mort d'Édouard le Confesseur (Figures 9.4 et 9.5).

*Figure 9.2. Aula du palais ducal de Rouen: scène 14 (Ville de Bayeux).*

*Figure 9.3. Arbre stylisé séparant deux scènes: scène 9–10 (Ville de Bayeux).*

Dès lors quels jugements peut-on porter sur les représentations de bâtiments que nous retrouvons dans des illustrations antérieures, qui souvent ont vu le jour dans la région où, pense-t-on, la *Broderie* a été confectionnée. Faut-il aller jusqu'à la position extrême de Wolfgang Grappe et considérer que 'les villes et leurs portes, les forteresses et leurs salles sont dénuées de toute réalité et qu'elles n'ont d'autres fonctions que de symboliser les différents lieux de l'action'.[4]

En examinant minutieusement ces représentations de monuments de bois ou de pierre, on constate parfois des analogies troublantes avec la réalité, telle qu'elle se révèle dans les fouilles et les études archéologiques. Le chercheur ne peut se contenter de découvrir les modèles qui, directement ou indirectement, ont pu inspirer les concepteurs de la *Broderie*, mais il doit se demander comment les artistes de la *Broderie* ont réussi à peindre les réalités contemporaines à travers leurs modèles iconographiques et leurs conventions esthétiques.

## Les châteaux

Examinons d'abord les cinq châteaux à motte de la *Broderie de Bayeux*, ceux de Dinan, de Dol, de Rennes, de Bayeux et d'Hastings. Il faut avoir présent à l'esprit que les concepteurs et dessinateurs de la *Broderie de Bayeux* avaient, comme nous venons de le dire, à leur disposition de nombreux modèles de constructions architecturales dont nous trouvons des exemples dans certains manuscrits des IXe, Xe et XIe siècles et qui sont repris parfois tels quels sur la *Broderie de Bayeux*. C'est le cas des kiosques de la scène 11 et de

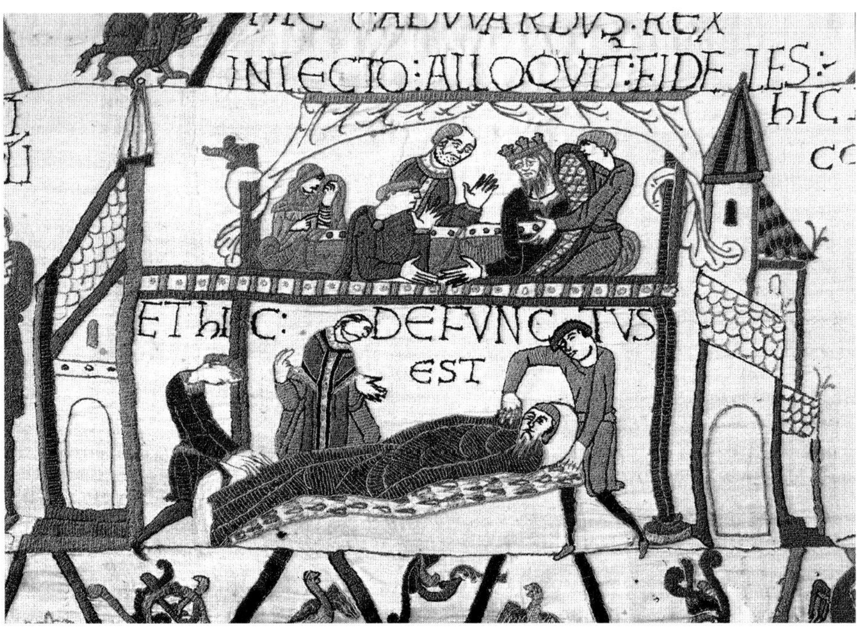


*Figure 9.4. Rideaux du lit d'Édouard le Confesseur: scène 27 (Ville de Bayeux).*

*Figure 9.5. Rideaux de lit dans le manuscrit Old English Hexateuch (fig. 33 de l'article de Cyril Hart, Anglo-Norman Studies 22 (2000), p. 164).*

*Figure 9.6. Kiosque: scène 10–11 (Ville de Bayeux).*

*Figure 9.7. a) Kiosques du Psautier d'Utrecht* (c. *820) et b) de Harley Psalter (c. 1000) (fig. 7 de l'article de Cyril Hart, Anglo-Norman Studies 22 (2000), p. 136).*

la scène 36 qui, comme l'a montré Cyril Hart, sont des reprises fidèles du *Psautier d'Utrecht*, daté des années 820 et du *Psautier Harley* des premières années du XIe siècle (Figures 9.6 et 9.7). Mais l'étude des représentations de ces châteaux fait apparaître de nombreux détails révélant la volonté des dessinateurs de s'inspirer de la réalité par le biais des traditions iconographiques.

Le monticule sur lequel est édifiée la structure défensive n'a jamais la même configuration. Il est impossible de savoir si ce tertre est naturel ou artificiel. La présence d'un fossé peut suggérer que le monticule a été vraisemblablement réalisé par l'accumulation de la terre retirée lors du creusement du fossé tout autour de la motte. La comparaison de la colline du Mont Saint-Michel, représentée couverte de verdure comme un site naturel (Figure 9.8), avec les tertres des autres châteaux, militerait en faveur de l'existence de sites artificiels (Figure 9.9). Celui de Rennes (Figure 9.10) semble même recouvert de plaques de pierre ou de schiste. En Calabre, A-M. Flambard Héricher a trouvé des monticules recouverts de dalles de pierre, alors que M. Biddle avait mis en évidence la présence à Therfield de planches de bois en couverture de la motte. La scène 45 (Figure 9.11) évoque la construction de la motte d'Hastings : on y voit des terrassiers avec des pelles chargées de cailloux qui s'activent. Les bandes horizontales, que certains ont interprété comme un élément purement décoratif, peuvent être un indice du mode de terrassement par une succession de niveaux de terre, de cailloux, de sable, entre lesquels on disposait des bandes de gazon afin de consolider l'ensemble. Ce genre d'aménagement des mottes permettait d'installer très vite et de façon stable une structure en bois ou en pierre au sommet de la motte. En outre, comme il existait une coutume consistant à prendre appui sur un bâtiment préexistant, il n'est pas interdit de penser que la structure en bois figurant sur la *Borderie* ait pu être édifiée préalablement à l'emmottement de l'ensemble, ce qui avait l'avantage de rendre opérationnelle immédiatement la tour de guet.

Au sommet de la plate-forme se trouvait généralement une construction de bois, soit une simple tour comme à Dol, à Hastings et Bayeux (Figures 9.9 et 9.11), soit une tour protégée par une palissade, comme à Dinan et à Rennes (Figure 9.10). De nombreuses fouilles en Normandie et en Angleterre ont révélé des trous de poteaux qui nous aident à reconstituer les dispositifs défensifs en bois, très proches de ceux que l'on aperçoit sur la *Broderie de Bayeux*. Lorsque le sommet de la motte avait une surface réduite, la tour en bois n'était pas entourée de palissade: c'est ce qu'a montré, par exemple, les fouilles de Joseph Decaëns à la motte d'Olivet à Grimbosq (Figure 9.12). Telle est la structure représentée à Dol et à Hastings. En revanche, lorsque la

*Figure 9.8. Le Mont Saint Michel: scène 17 (Ville de Bayeux).*

*Figure 9.9. Château de Dol: scène 18 (Ville de Bayeux).*

*Figure 9.10. Château de Rennes: scène 18–19 (Ville de Bayeux).*

*Figure 9.11. La motte castrale de Hastings: scène 45 (Ville de Bayeux).*

*Figure 9.12. La Motte d'Olivet à Grimbosq (dessin: A. Letort).*

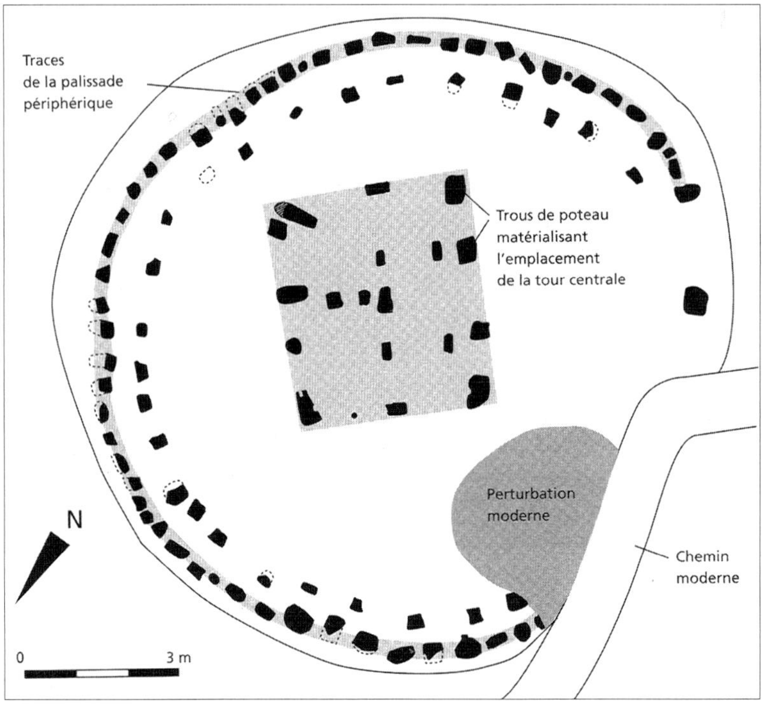


*Figure 9.13. Plan du sommet de la motte d'Abinger (A-M. Flambard Héricher d'après B. Hope-Harper, dans P. Bouet, B. Levy et F. Neveux, éd., La Tapisserie de Bayeux: L'art de broder l'Histoire, p. 265).*

plate-forme sommitale était suffisamment importante, on édifiait une tour en bois plus imposante ainsi qu'une palissade périphérique sur laquelle prenait appui un chemin de ronde: les fouilles de B. Hope-Taylor à Abinger en Surrey met bien évidence, d'une part, les trous de poteaux du donjon (mesurant environ 4m sur 5m) et, d'autre part, une double rangée de trous de poteaux encerclant le donjon et correspondant à la palissade proprement dite et à son chemin de ronde (Figure 9.13). C'est ainsi que l'on peut analyser la motte de Dinan (14), qu'elle corresponde ou non à la réalité de cette ville. La tour pouvait se terminer en terrasse, comme le suggère la représentation de Dol, ou par une toiture de forme circulaire ou rectangulaire, comme à Dinan et Rennes (Figures 9.14 et 9.10).

Pour accéder au sommet de la motte, on se servait de deux dispositifs différents si l'on fait confiance à la *Broderie de Bayeux*. A Rennes, où il n'y a pas de fossé, on montait par une rampe comportant des barres de bois horizontales pour empêcher les hommes et les animaux de glisser. Cette rampe prenait appui totalement sur le flanc de la colline. A Dol, à Dinan et à Bayeux (Figures 9.9, 9.14 et 9.15), où la motte était entourée d'un fossé et d'un rempart de terre, c'est une passerelle (sans doute mobile) qui était utilisée pour les franchir et pour parvenir au sommet. Cette passerelle pouvait

*Figure 9.14. Château de Dinan: scène 19 (Ville de Bayeux).*

être ou non munie de barres horizontales antidérapantes : on les aperçoit bien à Dol, mais pas à Dinan. Il n'y a que dans cette dernière cité qu'est figurée une sorte de châtelet d'accès à la passerelle. En outre, à Dol et à Bayeux, la passerelle se termine par une porte protégeant l'entrée dans la forteresse (Figures 9.9 et 9.15). Le dessinateur a eu également le souci de faire figurer les poteaux de bois qui supportaient la passerelle, comme on peut le constater dans de nombreux sites archéologiques, comme à la motte d'Olivet à Grimbosq (Figure 9.12). Il reste encore à signaler que le château de Rennes se distingue de ceux de Dol et de Dinan. On constate, d'une part, la présence d'un mur de pierre qui pourrait entourer le bas de la colline et suggérer l'existence d'une muraille de pierre cernant la cité et, d'autre part, la nature de la construction située à l'intérieur de la palissade. Le dessin de la tour n'évoque pas le bois comme l'étaient les donjons, représentés par des bandes verticales de couleurs différentes: le donjon de Rennes a les caractéristiques d'une construction en pierre, avec contreforts, fenêtres à l'étage et couverture en tuiles vernissées ou avec des essentes de bois peintes. La même constatation peut être faite pour la forteresse de Bayeux: la tour semble surmontée d'une coupole et d'un hourd dont on aperçoit la partie en saillie.

Notre intention n'est pas d'affirmer que chacun de ces châteaux correspond fidèlement à la réalité historique. Aucune comparaison n'est possible puisque de telles constructions ont disparu, pour être remplacées très tôt par des forteresses plus efficaces. Nous avons voulu montrer que la plupart des éléments figurés sur ces représentations de châteaux trouvaient confirmation et justification dans les nombreuses fouilles archéologiques effectuées dans le monde anglo-normand sur des châteaux à mottes de la fin du XIe siècle. Les concepteurs et dessinateurs de la *Broderie de Bayeux* ont puisé autant dans la réalité quotidienne que dans les modèles que leur offrait la tradition iconographique. Seule, peut-être, la représentation du château de Bayeux (Figure 9.15) doit davantage à l'imagination des dessinateurs qu'à un souci de vérité, car la configuration du terrain semble indiquer que le château, édifié à la fin du règne du duc Richard 1er, ne pouvait pas avoir été construit sur un tertre.

*Figure 9.15. Château de Bayeux: scène 22 (Ville de Bayeux).*

La ville de Rouen, qui n'est pas nommée à la différence des autres châteaux, est présentée sous la forme soit d'une tour, soit d'une porte de la cité (Figure 9.1). R. Allen Brown et Lucien Musset y voient la fameuse tour de Rouen, un grand donjon de pierre élevé au début du XIe siècle par Richard II, dont la grandeur impressionna tellement les Normands qu'elle passa en proverbe. C'était à la fois la résidence du duc, un centre militaire et administratif et une prison que le roi Philippe Auguste fit raser en 1203. A côté de cette tour s'élevait un édifice palatial qui est représenté quelques scènes plus loin. Les dessinateurs ont pris grand soin à mettre en évidence les pierres de la forteresse qui se termine par un chemin de ronde avec un mur à créneaux et deux tourelles d'angle. On aperçoit à l'intérieur ou à l'arrière de la tour un édifice avec trois arcades et une couverture en coupole que L. Musset identifie avec l'une des chapelles du palais tout proche. Mais, comme le suggère David Wilson, la fortification peut aussi bien s'interpréter comme la ville de Rouen entourée de ses murs, voire comme une porte de la cité par où Guillaume est sorti pour aller à la rencontre de Guy de Ponthieu et d'Harold.

## Les résidences princières

Avant d'évoquer les résidences princières, il convient d'évoquer le souci de précision qu'ont eu les dessinateurs dans la représentation de l'église de Bosham (Figure 9.16) et dans celle des abbatiales du Mont Saint-Michel et de Westminster (Figures 9.8 et 9.17). La majorité des historiens de l'art et des archéologues ont constaté que la représentation en coupe de l'abbatiale de Westminster devait s'inspirer de la réalité: les fouilles et les travaux de Richard Gem ont, en effet, prouvé que cet édifice était comparable à celui de Jumièges. Or la comparaison avec les vestiges de l'abbatiale de Jumièges montre la parti pris de l'artiste d'avoir voulu représenter toutes les parties d'un grand édifice roman : nef, tour de croisée, transept, tourelles et chœur.

L'étude des résidences princières se révèle aussi délicate que celle des châteaux. Le manoir de Bosham possède deux niveaux (Figure 9.18) : au rez-de-chaussée, trois grandes arcades en plein cintre reposent sur des chapiteaux bien marqués. Au premier étage une table occupe toute la longueur de la salle, où ont été déposés vases et coupes pour un repas. On accède à cet étage par un escalier extérieur. L'édifice est couvert d'une toiture aux tuiles ou aux essentes de couleurs variées disposées symétriquement. Lucien Musset y voit un édifice souvent mentionné au haut Moyen Âge, la *laubia* avec un rez-de-chaussée largement ouvert et un étage noble (*solarium*). David Wilson et A-M. Flambard Héricher admettent que le manoir de Bosham représente aussi bien pour l'Angleterre saxonne que pour la Normandie un type d'édifice avec salle d'apparat à l'étage. Cette disposition rappelle des constructions contemporaines ou de peu postérieures. A-M. Flambard Héricher a retrouvé ce type de bâtiment avec salle d'apparat à l'étage à Vatteville-la-Rue (Figure 9.19) où le rez-de-chaussée était occupé par des cuisines et des celliers ; l'étage noble auquel on accédait de l'extérieur par un escalier de bois était soutenu par des poteaux dont on a retrouvé les traces. En outre, si l'on prend en considération la gravure que J. S. Cotman a dessinée de l'*aula* de Lillebonne (Figure 9.20), où aurait été prise la décision de revendiquer le trône d'Angleterre, on remarque au rez-de-chaussée de grandes arcatures aveugles en plein cintre, comme à Bosham, et une salle de réception à l'étage éclairée par de larges baies: on y accédait par un escalier extérieur (sans doute en bois) qui a disparu, mais la porte sur le pignon occidental atteste bien l'existence de cette entrée à l'étage. La toiture était soit recouverte de bois, d'ardoises, voire de tuiles vernissées, puisque tout récemment sur la charpente de la cathédrale de Lisieux on a découvert la présence de tuiles de ce genre.

*Figure 9.16. Eglise de Bosham: scène 3 (Ville de Bayeux).*

*Figure 9.17. Abbatiale de Westminster: scène 26 (Ville de Bayeux).*

*Figure 9.18. Manoir de Bosham: scène 4 (Ville de Bayeux).*

*Figure 9.19. Vatteville-la-Rue: logis des comtes de Maulan (A-M. Flambard Héricher, dans P. Bouet, B. Levy et F. Neveux, éd., La Tapisserie de Bayeux: l'art de broder l'Histoire, p. 271).*

*Figure 9.20. Aula du château de Lillebonne d'après J. S. Cotman.*

Tout différent est la salle d'apparat où Guillaume accueille Harold dans le palais de Rouen (Figure 9.2). Il s'agit d'une *aula* sans étage, comme semble l'avoir été l'échiquier du château de Caen, avec un éclairage se faisant uniquement par les fenêtres hautes. Cette salle d'apparat ressemble bien à Westminster Hall que Guillaume Le Roux fit édifier vers 1090: la lumière pénétrait par les seules fenêtres hautes. Les Anglo-Saxons disposaient également de ces grandes salles sans étage comme le manoir royal de Cheddar édifié au début du XIe siècle, même s'il avait été édifié en bois.

Les autres édifices de la *Broderie de Bayeux* sont d'interprétation plus difficile dans la mesure où les dessinateurs présentent parfois en même temps l'extérieur et l'intérieur des bâtiments. C'est le cas du palais d'Édouard le Confesseur, que celui-ci se situe à Westminster ou à Winchester (Figure 9.21). Édouard se trouve dans une salle intime du palais avec la présence d'une tenture qui abrite le roi et ses deux interlocuteurs. Juste avant cette scène, nous apercevons l'entrée du palais encadré de deux tours à plusieurs étages. La partie centrale entre ces deux tours évoque un édifice à deux niveaux : celui de la porte

*Figure 9.21. Palais de Winchester ou de Westminster: scène 1 (Ville de Bayeux).*

*Figure 9.22. Palais de Westminster: scène 25 (Ville de Bayeux).*

à laquelle on accède par trois marches et celui des trois arcades surmontées de petites fenêtres. Les dessins en formes de losanges, que l'on retrouve aux scènes 24 et 30, peuvent aussi bien être des peaux tendues sur des parois de bois ou un décor de carreaux vernissés intercalés dans l'*opus reticulatum*, comme ceux que Richard Gem a découvert à Westminster Abbey dans l'ancien réfectoire.

Sur la plupart des édifices la polychromie des toitures et des parements de murs supposent soit l'usage de tuiles ou carreaux vernissés, dont l'existence a bien été confirmée par l'archéologie, soit l'emploi de bardeaux de bois peints, sans exclure l'hypothèse d'un dessin purement figuratif. Entre les scènes 24 et 35, la *Broderie de Bayeux* fait figurer à plusieurs reprises des salles du palais de Westminster: salle où Édouard reçoit le rapport d'Harold (Figure 9.22), salle où meurt le roi (Figure 9.4), salles où Harold siège au moment de son couronnement (Figure 9.23). Ces représentations contiennent des éléments identiques: la salle est encadrée par des tours plus ou moins imposantes, certaines parties des murs et les toitures sont décorées soit d'essentes de bois (naturelles ou peintes) se recouvrant à la manière d'écailles, soit de carreaux bichromes. Au-dessus des toitures on aperçoit de petites tourelles qui font partie du bâtiment, comme dans la scène du couronnement (Figure 9.23, scène 30), ou qui semblent figurer un arrière plan du palais ou de la cité, comme dans la scène 25 (Figure 9.22).

Comme dans notre étude des châteaux, il nous est impossible de dire si les représentations du palais de Bosham, de Westminster ou de Winchester correspondent fidèlement à la réalité, faute d'édifices de références. Cependant, de nombreux éléments qui figurent sur ces dessins ont reçu des confirmations archéologiques qui nous incitent à conclure que les concepteurs et dessinateurs de la *Broderie* se sont servis des *realia* normandes et anglaises pour donner une crédibilité plus grande à leur ouvrage. Chaque fois que cela était possible, les artistes de la *Broderie* ont modifié les modèles iconographiques que leur avait

*Figure 9.23. Palais de Westminster: scène 30 (Ville de Bayeux).*

transmis la tradition par fidélité à la réalité. Ils se servent de ces modèles pour choisir une technique particulière ou des éléments précis. Cela devrait nous inciter à adopter une attitude moins idéologique à l'égard de ce chef d'œuvre fruit de la collaboration des Anglais et des Normands. En continuant à affirmer que les décors de la *Tapisserie de Bayeux* ne sont que des créations purement imaginaires ou des imitations fidèles de modèles fournis par la tradition, on prend le risque de recevoir régulièrement des démentis sévères, chaque fois que l'archéologie prouvera le contraire.

## Remerciements

Toutes les images de la Tapisserie ont été reproduites avec l'aimable autorisation des Musées de Bayeux.

## Notes

1 Boüard, M. de (1975) *Le château de Caen* (Caen, CRAHM); Gem, R. (1981) 'The Romanesque rebuilding of Westminster Abbey', *Anglo-Norman Studies* III, pp. 33–60; Hope-Taylor, B. (1956) 'The Norman motte at Abinger (Surrey) and its wooden castle', *Recent Archaeological Excavations in Britain*, pp. 223–49 (London, Routledge and Keagan Paul); Flambard Héricher, A-M. (2004) 'La Tapisserie de Bayeux et l'archéologie', dans P. Bouet, B. Levy et F. Neveux, éd., *La Tapisserie de Bayeux: l'art de broder l'Histoire, actes du colloque international de Cerisy-la-Salle, 1999* pp. 261–88 (Caen, Presses universitaires de Caen).

2 Lewis, M. J., Owen, G. R. et Terkla, D., éd. (2011) *The Bayeux Tapestry. New Approaches* (Oxford, Oxbow Books).

3 Wormald, F. (1962) 'An English eleventh-century Psalter with pictures: British Library, Cotton MS Tiberius C. VI', *Walpole Society* 38, pp. 1–13 ; Dodwell, C. R. et Clemoes, P. (1974) 'The Old English Illustrated Hexateuch', *Early English Manuscripts in Facsimile* 18 (Copenhagen, Roskilde and Bagger); Hart, C. (2000) 'The Bayeux Tapestry and schools of illumination at Canterbury', *Anglo-Norman Studies* 22, pp. 117–67; Lewis, M. (2011) 'The Bayeux Tapestry and Oxford Bodleian Library Junius 11', dans M. Lewis, G. R. Owen-Crocker et D. Terkla, éd., pp. 105–11.

4 Grappe, W. (1994) *La Tapisserie de Bayeux*, p. 27 (Munich et New York, Prestel).

## Annexe 1: Inventaire des 33 monuments figurant sur la Broderie de Bayeux

| | |
|---|---|
| 1. Villes (ou parties de ville) | sc. 12: Rouen<br>sc. 22: Bayeux |
| 2. Châteaux | sc.18: Dol<br>sc. 18/19: Rennes<br>sc. 19: Dinan<br>sc. 45/46: Hastings |
| 3. Palais | sc.1: Westminster ou Winchester<br>sc.3/4: Bosham<br>sc.9: Beaurain<br>sc. 14/15: Rouen<br>sc. 25: Westminster<br>sc.27/28: Westminster<br>sc. 30: Westminster<br>sc. 31: Westminster<br>sc. 33: Westminster<br>sc. 35: Rouen |
| 4. Autres demeures | sc. 44: Hastings<br>sc. 47: Hastings |
| 5. Eglises | sc 3: Bosham<br>sc. 18/17: Mont-Saint-Michel<br>sc. 26: Westminster |
| 6. Maisons rurales | sc. 41: trois maisons de paysan<br>sc. 47: maison incendiée |
| 7. Tours isolées | sc. 14<br>sc. 15<br>sc. 17<br>sc. 24/25 |
| 8. Kiosque | sc. 10/11<br>sc. 36/37 |
| 9. Villa de bord de mer | sc. 24: villa de la côte anglaise |
| 10. Portique | sc. 15: Aelfgiva et le clerc |

10

# Visible from afar? The setting of the Anglo-Norman donjon

*Jon Gregory and Robert Liddiard*

**Résumé**

*Cet article examine la situation du donjon anglo-normand, en se rapportant plus particulièrement à la grande tour comme marqueur visible de l'autorité seigneuriale. La relation visuelle entre le donjon et son plus large environnement était importante, que l'on considère le regard porté par les occupants vers l'extérieur ou celui des spectateurs contemplant le château dans son paysage. Les indices provenant des bâtiments survivants suggèrent que la vue vers l'extérieur depuis le donjon était un enjeu important, soit dans un contexte cérémonial, ou pour la contemplation du paysage. De même, la vue du donjon, pour ceux qui vivaient à l'extérieur, était également importante et il existe des preuves qui montrent que les visiteurs ne pouvaient s'approcher du donjon que par des chemins bien précis qui le montraient à son avantage. L'organisation spatiale du donjon faisait souvent référence à ces structures environnantes: l'espace le plus public que constituait la grande salle avait tendance à être ouvert sur la cour du château tandis que la chambre donnait sur l'espace plus privé du parc. Il semble indéniable que la visibilité comptait beaucoup pour les constructeurs du donjon, évaluer l'importance relative de la visibilité comme facteur d'organisation des paysages du château reste difficile. Des potentialités de progrès résident dans l'utilisation des systèmes d'information géographique (SIG) qui permettent une évaluation plus rigoureuse de la visibilité d'un château. La visualisation SIG suggère que, alors que si les grandes tours dominent bien, visuellement, leurs arrière-pays, il ne s'agissait pas uniquement d'une question de construction sur le site le mieux exposé; mais au contraire, de la recherche de modalités spécifiques d'inter-visibilité, comme par exemple le fait qu'un visiteur puisse garder le château en vue aussi longtemps que possible. Dans une certaine mesure, toutefois, la position exacte du donjon avait peu d'importance parce que l'échelle de la construction signifiait en général que, où qu'elle soit placée, la tour serait résolument visible. On a plus de profit à débattre de l'idée d'une prééminence du château, plutôt que de sa simple visibilité.*

## Introduction

In a volume that chiefly deals with the physical fabric of the Anglo-Norman donjon, it should be stated at the start that this piece is not primarily concerned with the towers themselves, but rather with their surrounding structures and settings. This contribution hopes to serve as a reminder, if any were needed, that the study of what are, at least for castellated architecture, the signature buildings of the period, cannot be divorced from their wider environments. The importance of donjons, not just in themselves, but also for broader debates within castle studies is reflected in the considerable body of work that has done much to re-interpret them from a 'place of last resort' in the event of siege, to buildings that were variously residences, the spiritual home of the lord, symbols of lordship, and the arena for ceremony and ritual (Heslop 1991; Marshall 2002a; Turner 2004; Impey 2008). While any discussion of donjons as a group inevitably imposes a false unity to a diverse range of structures (Dixon 2002), the role of the tower as an expression of 'peaceable power', albeit in many forms, has been a theme common to the majority of recent studies (Coulson 2001).

It is important to appreciate that work on settings has reinforced and complemented the conclusions of architectural analysis. For landscape historians and archaeologists the emphasis has also been on the iconography of lordship, but rather how it was articulated beyond the castle walls. The distinctive archaeological footprint of structures such as monastic houses, deer parks, warrens and fishponds that were placed adjacent to castles are, of course, well-known, but scholars are increasingly sympathetic to the idea that their spatial arrangement may not simply be a utilitarian response to the economic demands of lordly subsistence, but rather a result of careful planning, in part engineered in order to heighten the visual appearance of castle within its immediate environs (Taylor 2000). The existence of an 'ideal approach' to the castle, which often involved an approach over water, through a borough and with the buildings set off with a sylvan backdrop of a deer park is well-attested in Romance literature of the period, but has now been shown to have been a physical reality (Creighton 2009). The Anglo-Norman period has already been identified as important: this is the first time when there is widespread documentary and field evidence for the form of castle landscapes and their study can potentially contribute much to our understanding of the cultural aspirations of aristocrats in northern Europe during the 11th and 12th centuries (Casset 2007).

## The setting of the donjon

Given the diversity of buildings that could be described as a donjon and the variety of forms that the castle of which it formed a part could take, it follows that settings could be equally diverse. At a general level, the difference between those donjons placed in urban castles and those in the rural countryside seems an obvious point of contrast, but such a straightforward division works best only at the extremes. While there is clearly a major difference, for example, between the setting of the White Tower and a tower such as that at Prudhoe in Northumberland, in reality landscape contexts defy simplistic categorisation just as much as donjons themselves. Those castles at the centre of rural estates were often provided with proto-urban settlements and markets, while more 'rural' appurtenances such as deer parks and hunting grounds could often be found in close proximity to urban castles. An additional layer of complexity is that arrangements on the ground often reflected distinctly local conditions. Castles in general tended to 'mirror' the morphology of their local settlement patterns, inasmuch as isolated castles are often found in areas of dispersed settlement and associated with villages in areas of nucleation (Creighton 2002, pp. 193–222). In turn, so the structures surrounding the donjon could also relate closely to these distinctly regional landscapes (Liddiard 2006). It is therefore more profitable to discuss settings according to a more general set of issues, such as how the donjon projected power in its own particular locality, its spatial relationship with the rest of its castle, how it was accessed by different social groups and how it might be viewed from outside the castle walls.

Crucial to all these questions is the issue of visibility, be it from the donjon looking outwards, or from outside the building looking in, or the visual impression of a donjon when viewed in its original setting. It is worth emphasising at the outset that there is nothing inherently strange or implausible about the idea that Anglo-Norman builders took an interest in the benefits of both viewing the wider landscape from their donjons or the visual impression that donjons could make on those looking at them from a distance. There is plenty of evidence, be it architectural, historical or literary that both were desirable attributes. The long-held explanation that the prospect to be gained from a donjon allowed the occupants to see their enemies approaching and buy time to prepare a defence has now to be set alongside the duller, but probably just as significant, requirement to survey the economic workings of estates (Creighton 2012). The greatest testament to the importance attached to the visibility of the donjon by onlookers is the buildings themselves. It is difficult, if not impossible, to find an example of a great tower being sited discreetly and the architectural elaboration of doorways, windows and elevations can only make sense if they were intended not just to be seen, but conspicuously displayed. The provisions made for dummy upper stories in buildings such as Castle Hedingham seal the issue; here the intention can have only have been to give the impression of a further story of functional rooms for those looking at the building from outside.

## The view looking out

Architectural historians have long argued that there was a relationship between height and status in the arrangement of space in towers, with the lordliest areas located towards the top of the buildings (Mesqui 1991). It follows that the view to be gained from high places might have had similar exclusivity. From the 13th century, the provision for window seats in upper chambers in castles makes it clear that looking out from the principal buildings was routine. The investment involved in the creation of seating arrangements and elaborate fenestration also suggests that this purpose was not altogether secondary; rather, it indicates that looking out was integral to the functional use of the rooms (Creighton 2009). As Tom McNeill has pointed out, there is considerable evidence from *c.* 1200 onwards of restricted access to roof spaces from private chambers, which suggests that the view from the tallest buildings was not only considered desirable, but worth limiting to privileged individuals or groups (McNeill 2006). Such arrangements are likely to have their origin at least as far back as the 10th century and probably draw on Carolingian practice. Pamela Marshall in particular has drawn attention to the existence of evidence for a viewing gallery at the donjon at Loches, which represents an early 11th-century example of provision for those inside the building to look out, or to be observed from those below (Marshall 2002b). At Langeais the donjon dating to about 1000 also shows evidence for a wooden gallery at the upper levels, which probably served some kind of function as a viewing platform (Impey and Lorans 1998).

Evidence for galleries or balconies is also found in post-Conquest donjons (Marshall 2002a, *passim*). While it would be unwise to ascribe a single purpose or function for such features at this early date, lordly display is probably a common element and bears comparison with castle gate and pre-Conquest burh-geat towers, which Renn has suggested were analogous to the balcony at Buckingham palace (Renn 1994). This seems to have been the case at Norwich, where a probable gallery on the western side of the donjon overlooked the Norman market place (Dixon and Marshall 2002). This seems an ideal location for dignitaries to show themselves to the urban population below and it is tempting to see the Christmas visit by Henry I to the city in 1121 as the kind of occasion when any balcony facility would actually have been used. In other cases the view out would seem to have been more private. At Castle Rising in Norfolk, the probable gallery on the western side of the donjon would have overlooked an enclosed bailey that is the most likely location of the documented garden.

The architectural evidence for viewing galleries needs to be set alongside historical accounts that suggest that there was also a relationship between viewing the landscape and a tangible sense of power. Such a connection is revealed by Orderic Vitalis in his account of the death of Conan of Brittany. After Conan's capture following an unsuccessful rebellion, the future Henry I led Conan through the 'turris' whereupon he pointed out the countryside that the rebels had being trying to take, amongst other things the urban landscape of Rouen and the ducal hunting landscape. This was all, however, a 'bitter jest' on the part of Henry, who then threw Conan out of the window to his death (Chibnall 1973, pp. 224–7). Of course, the irony to this story is that such a situation would normally have been a moment of satisfaction, an occasion of boastful congratulation, but the event provides a valuable indication that for contemporaries there was a tangible relationship between the exercise of political authority and viewing the landscape from principal buildings.

If there were clearly benefits to be gained by the view from the donjon, then it follows that some features may have commanded more attention than others. What exactly Anglo-Norman aristocrats wanted to see from their towers is an area that requires greater investigation and the present state of research only allows some preliminary observations, but work that has taken place is suggestive of a concern to have a line of sight to specific landscape elements. At Peveril, for example, the two windows of the tower chamber appear to have been arranged with different views in mind: one facing the Iron Age hillfort at Mam Tor, the older seat of power in the immediate landscape, while the second was aligned on the church in the castle borough (Barnwell 2007). Arrangements such as these are now attracting widespread interest from scholars, but only a body of case studies will show whether such ordering represents the manifestation of a common set of principles or were the fortuitous by-product of other factors. One general observation that can be made, however, is there appears to be a tendency in those square donjons with crosswalls for the more 'public' space of the hall to face the castle settlement, while the more 'private' space of the chamber faced the castle deer park. This is seen very clearly at some East Anglian donjons, such as Rising and Mileham and was also probably the case at Devizes and is echoed in the more elaborate 13th-century Launceston, which is one of the best examples of what seems to be a purpose-built display tower to overlook the park (Herring 2003; Saunders 2006). Occasionally there is evidence for the idea that such arrangements were not necessarily the result of piecemeal addition of landscape elements over time, but part of a wider scheme from the start. The foundation charter of Kenilworth priory in Warwickshire is a case in point, where in the 1120s Geoffrey de Clinton stated which areas of ground had been reserved for the forthcoming priory, castle and park, implying a clear understanding of how the whole ensemble would look on the ground (Thompson 1991, pp. 141–2).

## The view looking in

If the view out of the donjon was important, then how the building appeared from beyond the castle walls, and how much access a visitor was permitted, was just as significant. Again, much of the recent work by landscape archaeologists dovetails neatly with the conclusions from architectural analysis, which suggests a concern on the part of donjon builders to structure and manipulate the approach route into castle buildings. As Philip Dixon has demonstrated, there is considerable evidence in the design of donjons for something akin to choreography in the access arrangements to the lord in residence. This chiefly took the form of an intimidating approach whereby the visitor was kept constantly at a spatial disadvantage by being made to negotiate a series of separate spaces and then probably be kept waiting before being granted access to the lord. When the meeting did take place, the arrangement of fenestration and fireplaces often kept the visitor at a psychological disadvantage while at the same time giving the host a preferential position (Dixon 1990, 1998).

This manipulation of the visitor did not, however, begin once they had entered the donjon; rather it extended into the outer curtilage and in turn the wider landscape. The entry into and between particular areas of the castle was, to judge from contemporary accounts, clearly of some substance. Benoit of Ste-Maure, writing in about 1150 recounted the seduction by Duke Robert the Magnificent of Arlette the tanner's daughter who, when realising that she was pregnant, requested that in future she enter Falaise castle by the main entrance as a legitimate wife, rather than a subsidiary entrance as a mistress (Hicks 2009). It remains unclear if Benoit's comments relate more to the social milieu and etiquette of the mid-12th century rather than the early 11th-century events it purports to describe, but in any event reflects the close relationship between entering the castle and social rank.

If the entry, exit and circulation around a donjon was important, then the same applied to the visual impression of the castle within its broader landscape. In the late 12th century Gerald of Wales famously penned an idealised portrait of the castle of his birth at Manorbier in Pembrokeshire that was, among other things, 'visible from afar because of its turrets and crenellations' (Thorpe 1978, p. 150). In Romance literature, a consistent feature of the perfect castle was that it was conspicuous in its surroundings. In *Le Conte de Floire et Blancheflor* (*c.* 1150), for example, the tower was remarkable because 'when one sees it from twenty miles away, it would seem only one mile away' (Liddiard 2005, p. 123). There was also a sense in which travelling to a castle and seeing it within its surroundings could be an event of some significance. The clearest evidence to this effect relates to the story of the death of Ranulf the Chancellor in 1123 who, when travelling with Henry I to Berkhamsted Castle in Hertfordshire, 'and had reached the very spot from which his castle could be seen, in his exultation of mind, he fell from his horse and a monk ran over him' (Greenway 1996, p. 471). Clearly a moral point was being made here – the accident was seen by Huntingdon as a just comeuppance for Ranulf's activities in office – but the significance for castle landscapes is obvious: that as early as the 12th century the idea that a castle in its setting should draw praise when viewed from some distance away was already of some currency.

Although it is altogether more difficult to prove, there is some evidence that castle-builders took a more active role in the visual promotion of their residences and in some cases the external appearance of the donjon took account of the principal direction of approach. At Norwich, for example, the most architecturally elaborate blind arcading on the southern exterior faced the main approach route into the city from London (Heslop 1994). Norwich also seems a particularly clear example where the spatial hierarchy of the baileys was reflected in the overall visual composition that the visitor would have encountered on their arrival in the city. Here the donjon was effectively on the highest level, with its subordinate series of baileys all on lower ground in something that resembled a series of terraces (Shepherd Popescu 2009). At Launceston, the natural geography of the castle site lent itself to a similar hierarchy, with the castle crowned by the donjon at the summit of the motte (Saunders 2006). At Castle Acre in Norfolk it is possible that a Roman road was diverted in order to provide a more stage-managed approach to the castle in which the visual juxtaposition of priory, settlement and castle were centre stage (Liddiard 2000a). In such cases, the height of the curtain wall, position and relative height of mural towers and the placement of the donjon appear to have been intended to raise the visual impression of the whole ensemble. At Trim in County Meath, the main approach from Dublin was marked out by a trophy gatehouse which would have led the eye across the curtain wall and towards the donjon in something of a set piece view (McNeill 2000). A similar situation is seen at Dover (Figure 10.1), where on the main approach from the north, a combination of gatehouses, mural towers and donjon were arranged in order to create an impression that was almost crown-like, perhaps appropriate for a castle that, at least by the 13th century, was used as a showpiece building to give a suitable impression to visiting dignitaries (Coulson 1979; Goodall 2011, pp. 140–2).

Once within the castle walls, the approach and then entry into the donjon was usually convoluted and rarely straightforward, almost always it was longer than purely functional requirements allow and was characterised by numerous turning points. A common device seems to have been making the visitor travel around the donjon before gaining entry. Earlier generations interpreted such arrangements as a response to the requirements of siege warfare, but the demands of display and the demonstration of lordship through residential magnificence are now preferred as an explanatory factor. The key point here is that the donjon usually reveals itself gradually, it is a visible landmark when seen from far away and always stays in view, but thereafter does not give up the details of its materials, external decoration and spatial arrangement until the visitor has gained full access. Here the study of donjons dovetails with broader interpretations about how medieval men and women perceived their environment, in particular the apparent merits of seeing great buildings and environments revealing themselves sequentially (Howes 2002).

Such discussions inevitably invite consideration of the wider symbolism of the donjon in medieval society, remindful as they are of a metaphor that relates the difficulty of gaining admission to a castle to the courtly seduction of a woman, where entering the tower is the ultimate prize. Although such notions might sound far-fetched, there is evidence from the Anglo-Norman period which is suggestive at the least. In Romance literature the long descriptions often given of castles can be related to the perceived qualities of the female form, chiefly elegance, favourable proportions and impregnable to all except God and the ideal knight. It is also probably significant in this context that, in the later Middle Ages at least, the donjon could stand as a metaphor for the female genitalia (Croll 2005, p. 115). Such evidence also needs to be set aside the possible association of donjons with young women; Norwich for example, appears to have attracted the appellation of 'Blaunchefiour' at an early date (Shepherd Popescu 2009, p. 376). The image of the female body was one of only a number of meanings that towers (and castles

*Fig. 10.1. Dover Castle, Kent. The main approach to the castle was from the north, where the viewer was presented with something of a set piece view, in which the combination of donjon, mural towers and entrances was centre stage (Photo: Robert Liddiard).*

more generally) could sustain during the Middle Ages, but they do offer a valuable evidence that in settings, just as much as buildings there was castles of the mind, as well as of stone.

## Visibility and viewshed analysis

As the above discussion makes clear, there is a good deal of evidence pointing to the fact that visibility, both from within and from outside the building, was a significant element in the wider setting of the donjon. What is unclear, however, is to what extent this represented a priority for builders and was a determinant of siting: were donjons located in positions that maximised their visibility? Any attempt by a castle builder to raise the visual effect of their tower in the wider landscape is, needless to say, difficult to measure; postcard images of sites such as Corfe in Dorset seem to encapsulate the ideal (Figure 10.2), but it is altogether more problematic to judge whether such locations were an attempt to exploit the undoubted visual advantages, or were simply an attractive by-product of other factors. One method of shedding light on this problem – and one until recently untried in castle studies – is the GIS technique of 'viewshed analysis', which can calculate the visibility between points and, within tolerable limits, give a more empirical basis to the study of a donjon's visual relationship with its landscape (Chapman 2006, pp. 101–3; Wheatley and Gillings 2000).

A major viewshed survey of the first generation of masonry castles in Anglo-Norman Ireland shows the advantages that such technology can offer and points the way forward for future research (McManama-Kearin 2013). Here, the evidence suggests the existence of a 'one kilometre zone' around the castle site where the idea that a building could visually control its immediate landscape became a reality. While the castle was visible beyond this distance, it was the domination of the immediate hinterland that seems to have been of importance to the builder. Significantly, it is only when the visitor is within the one kilometre zone that it becomes possible to meaningfully 'read' the building and draw comment about the constituent elements and arrangement of individual structures. Such observations seem to ring true when placed against the literary evidence for approach routes, particularly on those occasions where the visitors appear to stop and spend some time looking at the building. Viewshed analysis therefore seems to confirm that donjons did 'dominate the landscape', but also offers some potential to understanding to what extent visibility was a priority for builders.

## Castle Rising

A case in point is Castle Rising in Norfolk. Here a manorial site was substantially re-developed in the 1140s by William d'Albini II, following his marriage to the royal widow, Alice of Louvain. The centrepiece of the new castle was its

*Fig. 10.2. Corfe Castle, Dorset. One of the best examples of a donjon being visible in its landscape setting (Photo: Robert Liddiard).*

donjon, which in its design and internal spatial arrangements was a smaller version of that at Norwich – at that date the only royal castle in East Anglia. The donjon stands on the false crest of the southern slope of the valley of the river Babingley, which makes the tower more visible from the north. This could only have been heightened by the fact that as originally built, the donjon's surrounding ringwork was less than half its present size; the massive earthworks extant today being the result of a later phase of construction (Morley and Gurney 1997).

The construction of the castle took place hand in hand with a re-designing of its surrounding landscape, including a planned settlement with market place and church, leper hospital and deer park (Liddiard 2000b). The placing of these elements seems to have been undertaken with a certain degree of concern for the appearance of the castle both in the wider landscape and on its approach by the visitor; the site obeys the 'rules' inasmuch as the castle is skylined when observed from the north (Figure 10.3) and is approached via the settlement with attendant religious house, church, market place and grid-plan. This would have always been the main approach to the castle as the position of the deer park to the south effectively channelled visitors in this direction (Figure 10.4). During the 12th century the estuary of the Babingley was extensive and an approach to Rising by boat via the northerly route seems to be the most likely approach route for high-status guests.

His marriage to Alice and subsequent elevation to the peerage catapulted William into the highest ranks of the Anglo-Norman aristocracy and this meteoric rise drew derisive comment from the Waltham chronicler who commented that 'as a result he became arrogant and inordinately conceited so that he could not bear anyone being his equal, and anything that our world possessed that was special, apart from the king, was worthless in his eyes' (Watkiss and Chibnall 1994, pp. 76–9). The social circumstances surrounding the building of the castle are suggestive of a certain flamboyance and perhaps a case where visibility might seem particularly desirable for the builder. The location of the false crest and the arrangement of the archaeology would seem favourable to an interpretation where visibility seems high on the builder's list of priorities and this has been argued in the past (Liddiard 2000b).

Viewshed analysis, however, would suggest that the issue of visibility is more involved (Figure 10.5 and 10.6). As would be expected, the donjon is highly visible to the north and it visually dominates the whole of the Babingley valley. To the north-west towards the Wash the only factors that could obscure a view of the donjon while at sea would be the weather and the limitations of the human eye. What complicates this rather neat analysis is the fact that viewshed suggests that the donjon would have had a *different* visibility pattern had it been placed on the higher ground to the south. This location would not only retain the visual dominance of the Babingley valley, but also open up visible points to the east and west: when measured in totality, it does in fact have an overall greater visibility 'score'. Perhaps crucially, such a position would, however, have negated the castle's visibility from the southern slope of the valley, meaning that it would have passed out of sight in the journey up from the river. While the donjon is, therefore, a highly visible monument within its landscape, if visibility was the crucial factor determining siting, other locations were perhaps more favourable. But in terms of guaranteeing a line of sight from out at sea to entering the gate, its location was second to none.

## Castle Acre

Castle Acre in Norfolk was the regional *caput* of the Warennes, a major magnatial family which dominated East Anglian politics for the whole of the Anglo-Norman period. William of Warenne I, a companion of the Conqueror, founded the castle at Acre during the 1070s, which was almost certainly on the site of the manorial hall of the king's

*Fig. 10.3. Castle Rising Castle, Norfolk, from the main approach from the north. The location of the castle on the skyline enhances visibility from this direction and ensures that the visitor would always have the castle in their line of sight as they approached (Photo: Robert Liddiard).*

*Fig. 10.4. Castle Rising Castle from the south. This is the view of the donjon from the castle deer park, showing the castle situated on the sloping ground of the Babingley valley. Such a view would have been more exclusive and reserved for those granted access to the park.*

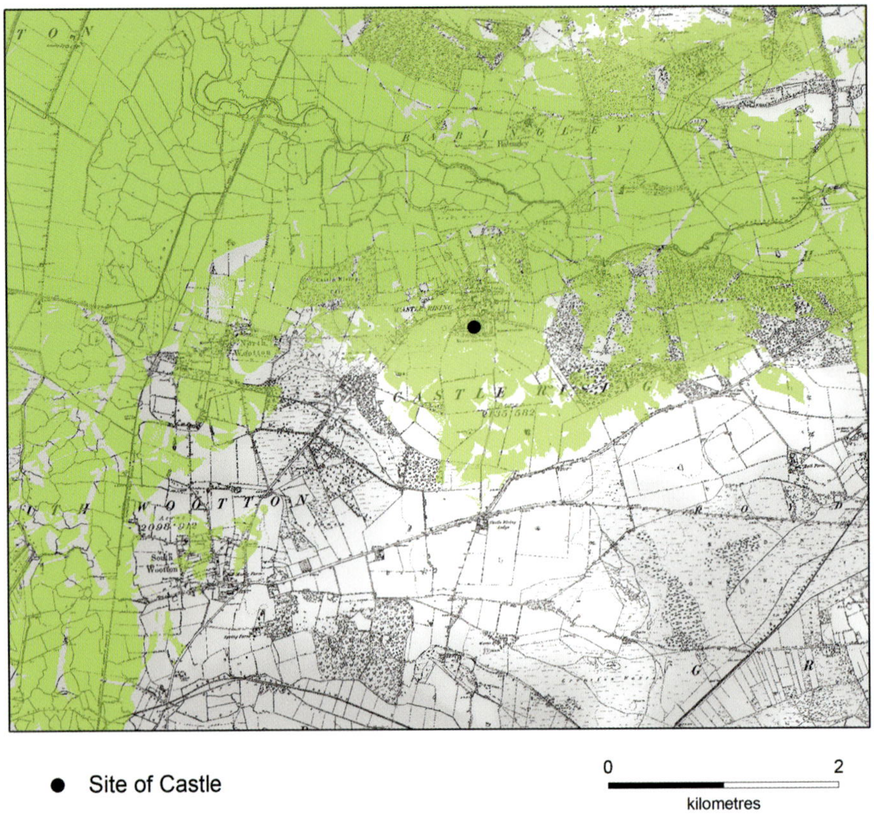


*Fig. 10.5. Viewshed analysis for the donjon at Castle Rising, with visible points shown in green. The visual dominance to the north over the valley and estuary of the Babingley is clear, but the view to the south over the park is more restricted. (Jon Gregory).*

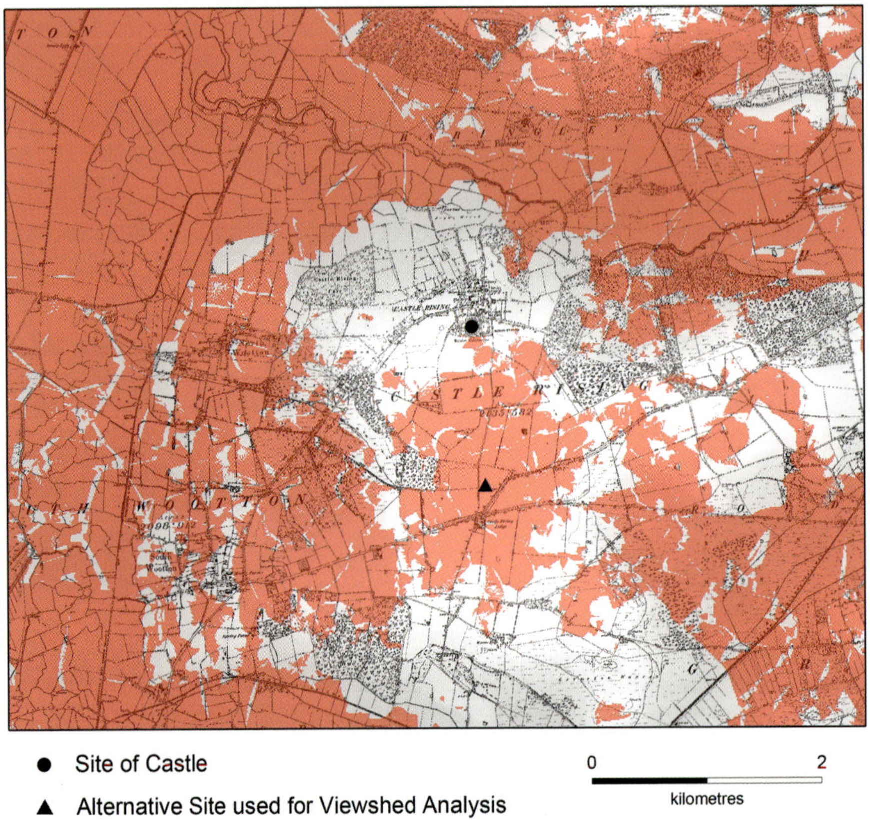


*Figure 10.6. Alternative viewshed showing the visibility of the donjon at Rising had it been constructed on the highest point of the landscape to the south. Here the visibility over the Babingley was also extensive and exceeds that of the actual site to the east and west. Such a location would have left a considerable blind spot on the southern slope of the Babingley valley, however, which would have meant that the castle would have passed out of view had a visitor approach from this direction. (Jon Gregory).*

thegn Toki, himself a major landowner in pre-Conquest East Anglia (Liddiard 2000a). The excavation of the castle in the 1970s contributed much to the study of donjons, showing as it did the complex development of the site from relatively unfortified 'country house' of the 1070s to the altogether more ambitious scheme of the 1140s and later 12th century (Coad and Streeton 1982).

Castle Acre is a well-known example of the effect of the Norman Conquest on the English landscape, with the castle, attendant settlement and Priory here occupying the northern side of the shallow valley of the river Nar. The castle occupies a textbook location, straddling two major communication routes, the river Nar and the Peddars Way, the former an important east–west communication route linking the interior of west Norfolk with the Wash and beyond, and the latter a north–south Roman road that was the principal routeway through the west of the county (Figure 10.7).

Viewshed analysis of Castle Acre shows a similar result to that seen at Rising (Figure 10.8 and 10.9). Taking the likely height of the donjon after the mid-12th-century re-building, the tower does indeed dominate its visual surroundings. The location on the false crest of the Nar ensures that visibility along the valley and towards the south is maximised, whereas that to the north is restricted. Castle Acre, then, to take Michael Thompson's phrase effectively 'nails the valley' (Thompson 1991, p. 23); it is a tangible symbol of lordship that was an unmistakable landmark in a local context. But once again, however, a more visually favourable site exists a short distance away, some 500m to the north, which would open up additional views, not just in this direction, but also further down the valley. Once again, however, such a location would have compromised the line of sight from the castle from the valley bottom.

## Discussion

The results of viewshed analysis undertaken on these two sites are similar to those obtained for other East Anglian donjons, such as Norwich, Thetford, Castle Hedingham and Orford (Butler 2007). The unifying factor is that, while all are highly visible monuments in their landscapes, this is not something exclusive to their location; better placed sites with greater overall visibility (albeit often not dramatically so), can normally be found in close proximity. This conclusion suggests that, at least in these cases, lords were not deliberately seeking out the *most* visible location upon which to build, but might have been keen to exploit places that offered particular *kinds* of visual opportunities: the domination of the immediate surroundings and a direct line of sight to the castle for any visitor for as long as possible.

The results of viewshed analysis suggest a number of possibilities, not all of which need be mutually exclusive. Firstly, it might be that any such visibility that such sites commanded was incidental to lords, who chose to locate their castle according to different set of priorities. As already discussed with reference to both Rising and Acre, the choice of location reflected an earlier pattern of seigneurial significance and evidence from across the region suggests that this may have been the decisive factor in siting (Liddiard

*Fig. 10.7. Castle Acre castle, Norfolk, from the west showing its siting on the slopes of the Nar valley, a location that increased its visibility: 'nailing the valley' (Photo: Robert Liddiard).*

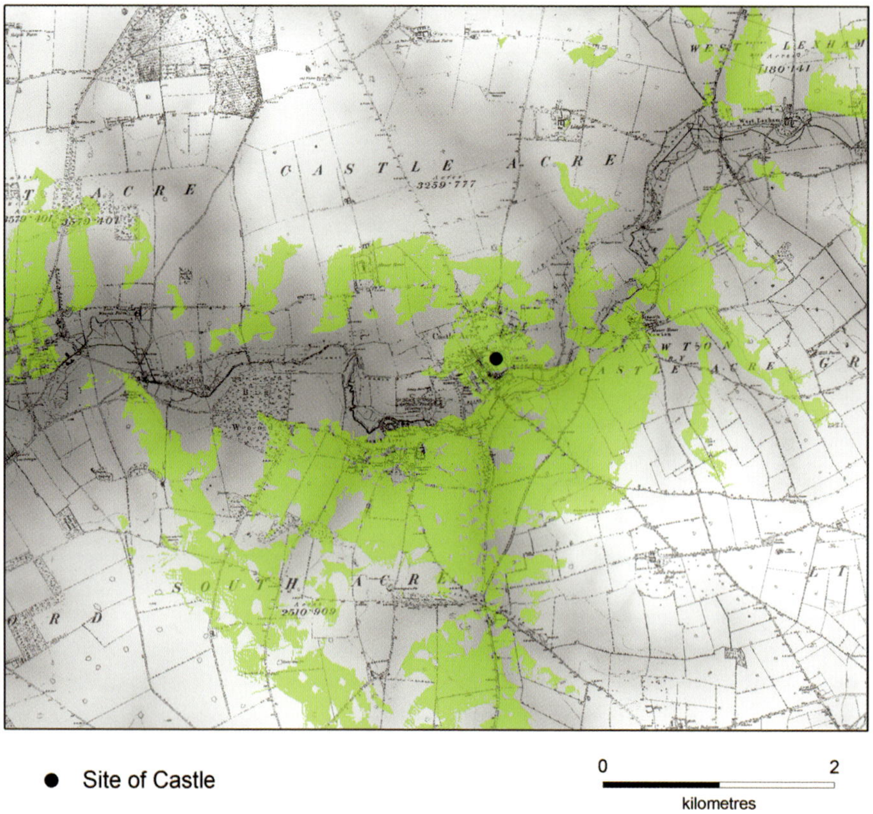


*Fig. 10.8. Viewshed of Castle Acre castle, taken with the estimated height of the donjon in the late 12th century. The castle has extensive visibility in all directions but particularly from the south, which was the likely direction of approach by visitors. (Jon Gregory).*

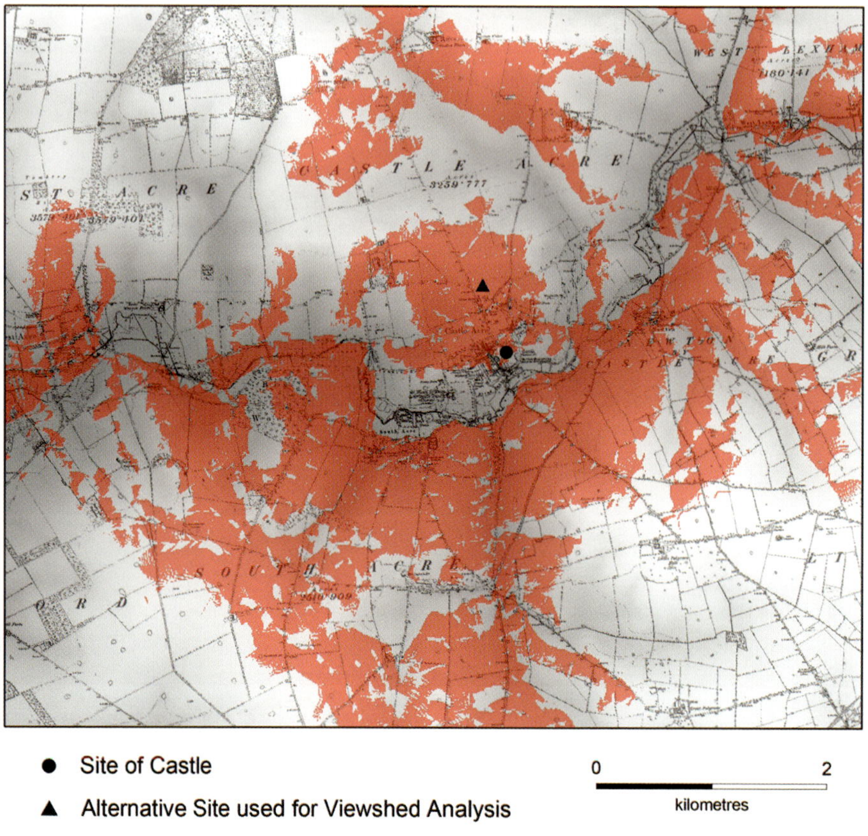


*Fig. 10.9. Alternative viewshed showing the visibility of the donjon had it been built on slightly higher ground to the north. This would have made the castle more visible overall, but only at the expense of anyone trying to look at the castle from the bottom of the Nar valley. (Jon Gregory).*

2000a). A second factor might be that any latent visibility that a site offered may have been exploited by lords both before and after the Conquest. Pre-Conquest lords might have wished to 'nail' their valleys just as much as their post-Conquest counterparts and it is worth noting in passing that one of the many attributes of Hrothgar's hall in *Beowulf* was that it was visible in its setting. Thirdly, especially when the building of a donjon was being considered, choosing a particularly visible site was irrelevant as the scale of the enterprise usually meant that it was going to dominate its immediate hinterland (and possibly beyond) regardless of location.

This last observation might be closest to the mark, which is not to say that castle-builders did not care about the visual impact of their residences; rather, the raising of a donjon on any scale necessarily meant that it would appear monumental in its local landscape and would be seen from a suitable distance away. This did not, of course, prevent the development of the castle site with a degree of care as to the placing of elements around the donjon, or attempting to manipulate the visitor on the main approach. It is important to bear in mind the difference here between visibility and prominence. While it is the case that donjons such as that at Rising could, it seems, have been placed almost anywhere in its landscape and been *visible*, this is not to say that it would have been *prominent*. The latter is usually an undeniable attribute of a donjon, great or small. At a castle like Rising, the prominence of the donjon was certainly foregrounded by the location on a false crest and the imparking of the neighbouring higher ground, which meant that the castle was experienced from its most commanding position.

A discussion of prominence takes the discussion of visibility full circle as it almost defies standards of proof – it is not immediately obvious how it can be measured. In archaeological discussions, particularly concerning phenomenological approaches to landscapes, intervisibility often features conspicuously as evidence, but it is in fact rather an indiscriminate judge of whether something is prominent (Tilley 1994). To see a round barrow some miles away as a speck on the horizon, even though it might be visible, is not to be confronted with the donjon of Corfe as a traveler traversed the Purbeck hills or Rochester as they crossed the Medway.

## Conclusion

This consideration of the landscape settings of the donjon has hopefully highlighted two principles that, while well-known, deserve repetition. Firstly, that donjons were not just closely related to the other castle buildings in their immediate vicinity, but also to their wider landscapes. Secondly, work on settings cannot take place independently of the study of the buildings themselves. Attempting to analyse the function of the donjon as a visible marker of lordly authority is a case in point as it not only shows the connection between towers and landscapes, but how a greater understanding of one is a prerequisite for the other. Close co-operation between those in the fields of architectural and landscape history is undoubtedly the way forward. Much work has been completed by both in recent years, but a holistic picture of the setting of the donjon in the Norman cross-channel empire (and beyond) remains elusive. Comparative work is undoubtedly key and this volume serves as a reminder of how connectivity can help to make the view a little clearer.

## Bibliography


Barnwell, P. S. (2007) 'The power of Peak castle: cultural contacts and changing perceptions', *Journal of the British Archaeological Association* 160, pp. 20–38.

Butler, J. (2007) *The Application of GIS in Studying the Placement and Visibility of Castles in East Anglia* (unpublished MA dissertation, University of East Anglia).

Casset, M. (2007) *Les Évêques aux Champs. Châteaux et Manoirs des Évêques Normands au Moyen Âge (XI–XV siècles)* (Caen, Presses universitaires de Caen).

Chapman, H. (2006) *Landscape Archaeology and GIS* (Stroud, Tempus).

Chibnall, M. (1973) *The Ecclesiastical History of Orderic Vitalis* Vol. 4 (Oxford, University Press).

Coad, J. G. and Streeton, A. D. F. (1982) 'Excavations at Castle Acre Castle, Norfolk, 1972–1977', *Archaeological Journal* 89, pp. 138–301.

Coulson, C (1979) 'Structural symbolism in medieval castle architecture', *Journal of the British Archaeological Association* 132, pp. 73–90.

Coulson, C. (2001) 'Peaceable power in Norman castles', *Anglo-Norman Studies* 23, pp. 69–95.

Creighton, O. H. (2002) *Castles and Landscapes* (London, Continuum).

Creighton, O. H. (2009) *Designs upon the Land: Elite Landscapes of the Middle Ages* (Woodbridge, Boydell).

Creighton, O. H. (2012) *Early European Castles. Aristocracy and Authority, AD 800–1200* (London, Bloomsbury).

Croll, L. (2005) *Francois Villon: Gender, Psychoanalysis and Metaphor in the Middle Ages* (Durham theses, Durham University). Available at Durham E-Theses Online: http://etheses.dur.ac.uk/3005/.

Dixon, P. (1990) 'The donjon of Knaresborough: the castle as theatre', *Château Gaillard* 14, pp. 121–39.

Dixon, P. (1998) 'Design in castle-building: the control of access to the lord', *Château Gaillard* 18, pp. 47–57.

Dixon, P. (2002) 'The myth of the keep', in G. Meirion-Jones. E. Impey and M. Jones, ed., *The Seigneurial Residence in Western Europe, AD* c. *800–1600*, pp. 9–13, British Archaeological Report International Series 1088 (Oxford).

Dixon, P. and Marshall P. (1993) 'The great tower at Hedingham castle: a reassessment', *Fortress* 18, pp. 16–23. Reprinted in R. Liddiard (2003) *Anglo-Norman Castles*, pp. 297–306 (Woodbridge, Boydell).

Dixon, P. and Marshall, P. (2002) 'Norwich castle and its analogues', in G. Meirion-Jones. E. Impey and M. Jones, ed., *The Seigneurial Residence in Western Europe, AD* c. *800*–1600, British Archaeological Report International Series 1088, pp. 235–39 (Oxford).

Goodall, J. (2011) *The English Castle* (London, Yale University Press).

Henry of Huntingdon, *Historia Anglorum (The History of the English People)*, D. E. Greenway, ed. and trans. (1996) (Oxford, Oxford Medieval Texts).

Herring, P. (2003) 'Cornish medieval deer parks', in R. Wilson-North, ed., *The Lie of the Land: Aspects of the Archaeology and History of Designed Landscapes in the South West of England*, pp. 34–50 (Exeter, Devon Gardens Trust).

Heslop, T. A. (1991) 'Orford Castle, nostalgia and sophisticated living', *Architectural History*, pp. 34 and 36–58.

Heslop, T. A. (1994) *Norwich Castle Keep: Romanesque Architecture and Social Context* (Norwich, Centre of East Anglian Studies).

Hicks, L. (2009) 'Magnificent entrances and undignified exits: chronicling the symbolism of castle space in Normandy', *Journal of Medieval History* 35, pp. 52–69.

Howes, L. L. (2002) 'Narrative time and literary landscapes in Middle English poetry', in J. Howe and M. Wolfe, ed., *Inventing Medieval Landscapes: Senses of Place in Western Europe*, pp. 192–207 (Gainesville, University Press of Florida).

Impey, E. and Lorans, E. (1998) 'Langeais, Indre-et-Loire. An archaeological and historical study of the early donjon and its environs', *Journal of the British Archaeological Association* 151, pp. 43–106.

Impey, E., ed. (2008) *The White Tower* (London, Yale University Press).

Liddiard, R. (2000a) *Landscapes of Lordship: Norman Castles and the Countryside in Medieval Norfolk, 1066–1200*, British Archaeological Report 309 (Oxford).

Liddiard, R. (2000b) 'Castle Rising, Norfolk: a 'Landscape of Lordship'?' *Anglo-Norman Studies* 22, pp. 169–86.

Liddiard, R. (2005) *Castles in Context: Power, Symbolism and Landscape, 1066–1500* (Macclesfield, Windgather).

Liddiard, R. (2006) 'Early castles in the medieval landscape of East Anglia', *Château Gaillard* 22, pp. 243–50.

Marshall, P. (2002a) 'The great tower as residence in the territories of the Norman and Angevin kings of England', in G. Meirion-Jones. E. Impey and M. Jones, ed., *The Seigneurial Residence in Western Europe, AD* c. *800–1600*, pp. 27–44, British Archaeological Report International Series 1088 (Oxford).

Marshall, P. (2002b) The ceremonial function of the donjon in the twelfth century, *Château Gaillard* 20, pp. 141–51.

Mesqui, J. (1991) *Châteaux et enceintes de la France médiévale*, Vol. 1 (Paris, Picard).

McManama-Kearin, L. (2013) *The use of GIS in Determining the Role of Visibility in the Siting of Early Anglo-Norman Stone Castles in Ireland*, British Archaeological Report 575 (Oxford).

McNeill, T. (2000) *Irish Castles: Feudal Power in a Gaelic World* (London, Routledge).

McNeill, T. (2006) 'The view from the top', in J. De Meulemeester, ed., *Mélanges d'archéologie médiévale : liber amicorum en hommage à André Matthys*, pp. 122–7 (Namur, Les Cahiers de l'Urbanisme).

Morley, B and Gurney, D. (1997) *Castle Rising Castle, Norfolk*, East Anglian Archaeology 81 (Dereham).

Renn, D. (1994) 'Burhgeat and gonfanon: two sidelights from the Bayeux Tapestry', *Anglo-Norman Studies* 16, pp. 177–99. Reprinted in R. Liddiard (2003) *Anglo-Norman Castles*, pp. 69–90 (Woodbridge, Boydell).

Saunders, A. (2006) *Excavations at Launceston Castle, Cornwall* (Leeds, Society for Medieval Archaeology).

Shepherd Popescu, E. (2009) *Norwich Castle. Excavations and Historical Survey, 1987–98*, East Anglian Archaeology 132 (Dereham).

Taylor, C. (2000) 'Medieval ornamental landscapes', *Landscapes* 1, pp. 38–55.

Thompson, M. W. (1991) *The Rise of the Castle* (Cambridge, University Press).

Thorpe, L. ed. (1978) *Gerald of Wales: The Journey through Wales and the Description of Wales* (London, Penguin).

Tilley, C. (1994) *A Phenomenology of Landscape* (Oxford, Berg).

Turner, R. C. (2004) 'The great tower, Chepstow castle, Wales', *Antiquaries Journal* 84, pp. 233–316.

Watkiss, L. and Chibnall, M., ed. (1994) *The Waltham Chronicle* (Oxford, University Press).

Wheatley, D. and Gillings, M. (2000), 'Vision, perception and GIS: developing enriched approaches to the study of archaeological visibility, in G. Lock, ed., *Beyond the Map: Archaeology and Spatial Technologies*, pp. 1–27 (Amsterdam, IOS Press).

# 11

# Some thoughts on the use of the Anglo-Norman donjon

*Pamela Marshall*

**Résumé**

*Considérant la fréquente référence aux donjons dans les articles de ce volume, laquelle traduit la persistance du donjon à travers toute la période anglo-normande, et tenant compte des dépenses engagées pour ces chantiers, cet article se penche sur l'importance évidente prise par ce type de construction dans l'architecture de châteaux des XIe et XIIe siècles. Il traite des difficultés d'interprétation sur l'utilisation des donjons et des tentatives de classification, en fonction des variations considérables d'échelle et de forme. A l'aide d'un certain nombre d'exemples, ce document examine dans quelle mesure les sources documentaires et picturales sont des facteurs déterminants et utiles, mais conclut que le manque de preuves directes conduit à un recours prédominant à l'analyse des vestiges architecturaux. Il passe en revue diverses caractéristiques, de la place dans le paysage aux traits architecturaux d'ordre général ou plus spécifiques, et examine en quoi ces détails peuvent nous informer sur l'usage des bâtiments. L'article évoque les fonctions défensives, domestiques, administratives, protocolaires et symboliques et conclut à postuler une variation des usages dans une plus ou moins grande combinaison de ces fonctions déduite des caractéristiques propres à chaque bâtiment. Alors que les variations constatées dans l'aspect des constructions ne permettent que des sous-classifications d'ordre très général, l'article conclut néanmoins que le donjon anglo-normand reste un type de bâtiment fortement reconnaissable et identifié à la volonté des commanditaires d'incarner et d'afficher le concept de la seigneurie.*

From the late 11th century to the opening years of the 13th the landscape of Britain was irrevocably imprinted with high-status buildings borne of a powerful ruling authority rooted on both sides of the English Channel. The papers in this volume present a remarkably comprehensive overview of this legacy and its origins. The aesthetics of the buildings, the motivation of the builders, the documentation that illuminates their history, the below-ground, above-ground and landscape archaeology that throw light on their form, surroundings and environment – all these aspects are examined in the wake of emerging study. In most of the papers a particular type of building is at least mentioned and often figures prominently: the Anglo-Norman *donjon* – used here in the sense of a 'great tower' (*magna turris*) or 'keep'.[1] This is not surprising, for the care taken over their design and the expense lavished on their execution is sufficient evidence that these were considered very important structures. Often the donjon is the only building to survive above ground from earlier periods of castle construction, or to survive in better condition than other contemporary structures. It became a defining element in the western European castle and had achieved a polished form by the mid-11th century.[2] Castles and their donjons were built as an adjunct of conquest and accumulated studies over recent decades have underlined the symbolic role of the donjon in representing the embodiment of their owners' power.[3] Thus the donjon provides a vital key to understanding the aspiration of Anglo-Norman builders and the role of castle architecture in the social order that was imposed on the British Isles.

This key, however, is not easy to turn. It would certainly be illuminating to know exactly how these prominent and extravagant buildings were used, but I have to confess at the outset that we are unlikely to find a single and provable, let alone certain and definitive, answer to this question. In our quest to interpret the architecture of the donjon there are elements that the modern mind may struggle to comprehend. Conditioned by centuries of refining and defining specific use for space, we must be reminded that private rooms were rare and the multifunctional use of space a more pronounced characteristic of medieval living. From the modern perspective, laying out great expense for something that will result in little use is difficult to comprehend. Even where building accounts are lacking, the physical remains show that enormous sums were lavished on donjons, yet their owners held extensive and diverse estates, often on both sides of the English Channel, and their castles were left in the hands of caretakers for most of the time. In addition to this, strong formal and ceremonial overtones in the architecture of many larger donjons suggest that they are likely to have been used infrequently even if the lord was in residence, or possibly even built for use on a specific occasion.[4] Their design rarely makes defence or military advantage the chief priority in this expenditure,[5] which seems puzzling in an architecture viewed as primarily martial in nature. Lastly, the variation in their form, ranging from lookout towers to much more palatial buildings, is one of their more bewildering factors, practically defying classification.[6] There is a distinction between *tours beffrois* that lack accommodation, their emphasis more purely landscape markers and perhaps lookout towers, and *tours maîtresses,* more substantial donjons characterised by personal attachment to their owners and providing a degree of accommodation.[7] One may go on to distinguish between towers large enough to contain a hall and those too small to do so, or between towers requiring a spine wall,[8] but one is still left with many deviations in individual plans.

So, what can we draw on to build up a picture of the use of the donjon at this period? Contemporary depictions are rare: in the Bayeux Tapestry the small, timber, motte-top donjons at Dinan, Rennes and Dol and the building of a motte with a tower at Hastings are shown in the context of military action (see Figures 9.9–9.11). Yet, even allowing for artistic licence, there is an architectural elaboration in the depiction of the French towers, for example that at Bayeux, which counters the feeling that they were seen as single-purpose military buildings (see Figure 9.15). Contemporary documentation sometimes informs us about the cost of building – in England, most obviously, royal expenditure accounted for in the Pipe Rolls. But these are concerned with the nuts and bolts of administration and give little or no insight into the form, let alone use, of the buildings in question. Apart from the bare bones of administration and transactions or property grants recorded in charters, writing was reserved for chronicles, romances and eulogies. As contemporaries were perfectly *au fait* with court and household customs and practices, any references to the actual use of buildings tend to be slipped in. Chronicles were concerned with warfare and war-like deeds, so references to donjons tend to underpin their traditional interpretation as a defensive building of 'last resort'.[9] Marc Morris's paper in this volume illustrates this in relation to the great tower at Rochester and its prominent role in the great siege of 1215. But the fact remains that if one wanted to design a tower primarily to withstand a siege one would not have designed the tower at Rochester: one look at the central arcade on the second floor is all you need to be convinced of that (Figure 11.1). Similarly, the external decoration at Norwich and Castle Rising, or even surviving external detailing on the small (although royal) and much stone-robbed tower at Peveril, do not suggest their designers saw them as targets. Under battlefield conditions any substantial building will be pressed into action and the availability of a strong tower would certainly be used.[10] This does not mean it did not serve other functions, much less that it was primarily conceived to fulfil that role. The donjon at Ivry-la-Bataille (Eure), finished by 1020, had an unbarred exterior doorway at ground level.[11] The lack of internal security often found in large donjons seems only to reinforce the conclusion that their owners did not expect trouble to find its way inside. Castles were the product of a militaristic society and castle building was a necessary adjunct of conquest, so strength was essential and the greater this impression the better. In practice the majority of castles saw proportionately little action during the course of their, usually long, lifespans and some saw none at all: that might be seen as a mark of success on the part of their architects.

We have only one written description of any length that tells of normal day to day life within a donjon. Found in a chronicle written to glorify the life of Arnold II, Count of Ardres, who flourished in the Pas de Calais in the opening decades of the 12th century, and written late in the same century, its author saw fit to include what he clearly considered to be Count Arnold's most prestigious building project: a timber donjon, built around 1120 on the motte at Ardres.[12] This Arnold was not in the same league as the builders of the grand stone donjons described towards the end of this paper and the chronicler might have indulged in some exaggeration, but it is the only account we have of what can be dubbed 'normal' life within a donjon. Most noticeably, the accent is on domesticity, showing a very unusual preoccupation with women and children. Although watchmen and guards are mentioned in relation to the top floor, catering activities, with attendant storage (even of livestock) and cooking facilities, are given more prominent attention. Specific reference is made to the lord and lady sleeping in a great chamber on the first floor with a nearby warm and cosy room for nursemaids and small children, while sleeping accommodation was provided for older sons and daughters on the top floor. Stairs and corridors that linked the different living spaces are mentioned and much is made of a *logium*, used as a parlour, and a fine chapel located 'in a convenient place overlooking all else from high up on the eastern side'.[13] There are tenets in the description that are instantly recognisable from surviving stone examples: within the stacking of storeys (here three), specific mention is made of social distinction, with service at ground level, the best residential accommodation on the first floor and the top floor given over to sleeping and the watch. However, the description of the donjon at Ardres is nearly unique,[14] so for the most part there is no avoiding our need to rely on the architecture of the buildings themselves to interpret

*Figure 11.1. Part of the magnificent arcade that stands instead of a spine wall on the second floor at Rochester (A. Edwards).*

how they might have been used in practice. As well as plans and detailing of the donjons themselves, their general setting and any knowledge of nearby associated buildings should be taken into account. Donjons did not stand alone and in most cases it seems likely that the usual range of domestic buildings on their doorstep – hall, kitchen, chapel and chamber block – remained the main focus of the household.

One thing donjons all have in common is visual impact and one can argue that this is their chief identifying factor. Their designers had in mind the embodiment of power and were so successful in its realisation that it remains tangible even today. Thus a prestigious donjon at Chepstow was built in the vanguard of William I's advance into South Wales,[15] while the White Tower in London was a supreme demonstration of the permanent nature of the new regime.[16] In post-Conquest Britain the novelty of the architectural form and the use of stone in a secular context would have increased the psychological impact of the donjon. The ruling class, familiar with the concept, made a natural association between social advancement and raising a donjon. Aubrey de Vere's tower at Hedingham, for example, coincides with his elevation to the title of first earl of Oxford.[17] A 'noble tower' is recorded as having been built at Rochester in 1127 when Henry I granted the constableship of the castle to William de Corbeil and his successors in perpetuity.[18] The donjon at Richmond was begun by Conan IV, earl of Richmond (1146–71), to mark his becoming Duke of Brittany in 1164, although finished by Henry II between 1172–87 after Conan's death and the marriage of his heiress to Prince Geoffrey.[19] Countess Lucy of Chester built a motte with a tower at Lincoln on her acquisition of the constableship of that castle, although the king already had a tower on another motte there. There are numerous examples where shared lordship also resulted in double or additional donjons being built.[20]

We might deduce that the primary use of a donjon was to be seen and advertise a message of feudal domination, serving as a permanent reminder that the lord's absence, though frequent, was temporary and that his authority remained (Figure 11.2).[21] In this context it should come as no surprise that the landscape setting of the castle and its donjon should also be well managed, as Robert Liddiard and Jon Gregory's paper in this volume clearly emphasises (see Figure 10.1). Research on a series of sample castles in Ireland has shown that the siting of the castle allowed it to come into full view at an average distance of one kilometre; it is perhaps significant that this is also the point at which architectural detail becomes observable.[22] It follows that

*Figure 11.2. Seen from a distance, the great tower at Richmond dominates the town and the surrounding country (P. Marshall).*

*Figure 11.3. At Hedingham the decorative treatment of the topmost windows is the most elaborate, despite these openings having given only on to the gutters.*

care was taken over the external appearance of the donjon to make the best impression. Raising a very high parapet and so creating a false 'storey' around a countersunk roof to make towers look taller was a common ploy: it is noted at the White Tower and Rochester (both featured in this volume), but is found in other donjons too numerous to mention. It is at this false level at Hedingham (Essex) that the best external window decoration is applied (Figure 11.3). At first glance the elaboration of the external treatment of the windows seems to be associated with social progression: loops in the basement, plainer openings to the lower hall, nook-shafts and roll-moulded heads to the upper hall and the same treatment but with double lights to the gallery overlooking the upper hall. On arriving at the top 'storey', however, the theory appears to break down. Here the most elaborately treated openings are found, with nook-shafts, attached jamb-shafts and zigzag decorated headings, yet these 'windows' pierced the dummy wall that masked the leads. Until the roof was raised in the late medieval period to insert an extra storey, they looked out only from the gutters.[23] Nevertheless, these were the openings that would have been most readily seen from a distance and, significantly, rising above the ramparts in the angle of view from the settlement, while onlookers would have been ignorant of the nature of the space behind them.[24]

Donjons were designed for elite use: few people entering the wider confines of the castle would have had occasion to pass through its doors. Nevertheless, and perhaps because of this, there seems to have been a desire to convey outwardly some sense of the grandeur of its interior, as if the donjon were conveying a message about the very nature of lordship and aiming to broadcast it as widely as possible. String courses are frequently used to delineate internal floor divisions, so it is clear from the outside how many storeys there are and where levels change on the inside. While a string course will help to throw off rainwater, there is more to it than this practical application, for at Norwich the string course varies in height, externally indicating the placement of the mezzanine floor at the west end. Exterior decorative treatment generally indicates the location of superior internal spaces, even if this was occasionally disingenuous, as we have seen at Hedingham. The application of decorative arcading across the external elevations was superb at Norwich (see Figure 2.8). But the ground floor was left with a rough rubble surface on two counts: the space at this level was lowly, used only for storage, and in any case it would not have been seen behind the palisade encircling the motte.[25] Conversely, while the attention of the general population might have been drawn to the castle and its donjon, there is a growing body of evidence suggesting that castle builders were not entirely insensitive to the perception and appreciation of their landholdings, arranging viewpoints not only from battlements but from windows, doorways and balconies deliberately engineered to give good views of 'potent seigneurial markers' such as planned town, marketplace, abbey, bridge, parish church, forest and parkland.[26]

Turning to interiors, the interpretation of spaces depends on their attributes. For example, a space interpreted as a hall might be expected to be large and readily accessible because its envisaged use was the reception of many, rather than fewer, people and accessibility to service facilities or connection with cellarage would only reinforce this interpretation. Conversely, rooms where access is convoluted or restricted, perhaps by the need to pass through other rooms or by climbing more stairs, can be seen as more private, their entry more controlled, perhaps confined to personal or élite use. As well as access and size, provision of facilities in individual rooms and their ornamentation have some bearing on their planned function. Ornament is an important indication of status and a room's relative importance, although we should be aware that while carved stone embellishment is more likely to survive than plastered and painted ornament, the latter might have been quite impressive. Obvious features relating to litany indicate a chapel, its size indicating how many people it could house or whether it was a personal oratory. Other diagnostic features can help piece together possible use: whether a room was heated; had wall-cupboards; had access to one or more garderobes, or none; to a water supply; or a sink. The deliberate disposition of features helps to determine the arrangement of the room and its intended focus: the placing of a fireplace; the arrangement of the windows; the position of doors; the provision of a wall niche or recess for a chair or a place where a guard might stand; even a length of wall left blank for the placing of a table or a dais. Architectural pointers can also indicate the intended progression though a building: the placing of staircases and differences in their design and dimensions; the disposition and treatment of doorways, whose headings or jamb decoration can sometimes be seen as indicators of admissible or restricted spaces and/or of status.

So who might have entered these donjons and what might they have experienced inside? Clearly we would expect the lord, his family, members of his household and servants, but there must have been occasions when people outside the castle community attended. The description of the donjon at Ardres, with its 'nursemaids and weaned children' warming themselves by the fire and its gatherings in the parlour for conversation and recreation, paints a very domestic picture, down to the lord's daughters being obliged to sleep in their upper chamber, although the boys could please themselves whether they came home at night. Some donjons are exquisitely built, as we are told Ardres was, but incorporate far less accommodation. The small donjon at Goodrich (Herefordshire) was probably built by Richard 'Strongbow' de Clare in the mid-12th century and is likely to have provided private apartments for its owner to withdraw to with immediate family or special guests.[27] It only had two compact rooms stacked over the basement, the first floor room entered directly and a second reached by a narrow vice, and there are no fireplaces, although it could have been heated with braziers. However, it has already been noted that privacy was a rare commodity in the medieval period and it commanded a great premium. Use for the transaction of feudal affairs by representatives of the lord, at least from time to time, may also be mooted. Henry II's castle of Peveril in the Peak District of Derbyshire controlled the lucrative local lead-mining industry and administered its revenue.[28] Representing the king's authority, the donjon occupies a prominent position and one can see that, despite virulent stone-robbing at a later date, it was beautifully detailed externally. Regular visits by the king were not to be expected and the interior had only one room over the basement, with no surviving element of internal decoration and no heating other than by brazier.

Turning to donjons designed to cope with a larger body of people, we find a sophisticated and manipulative architecture. The cement that held together feudal society was the bond of loyalty between vassal and lord, lord and king. The ruthless management of family ties, the clever manipulation and deployment of vassals and the exercise of influence and control over monastic foundations, with their valuable fiscal rights, played as important a part in keeping political equilibrium as did physical force. The bond between leader and led is highlighted graphically in the Bayeux Tapestry, including a social element underpinned by feasting and giving gifts as well as ceremonial acts. There was a need to receive vassals, to whom the lord wished to emphasise his authority or whose loyalty he wished to keep on board, or peers invited for social reasons, or with whom negotiations were in train. At Christmas, Easter and Whitsun, Norman kings publicly wore their crowns amid feasts, council gatherings and religious celebrations and we also know the importance set upon acts of homage. We know little enough detail about these practices but the imposing mass of the great tower provided a worthy backdrop for diplomatic negotiation, the renewal of allegiance and official business such as charter-signing. This would explain the need for a donjon upon gaining social promotion noted above. In numerous donjons ceremonial use best accounts for the architectural layout and devices.[29] The donjon gave a psychological advantage to the owner in entertaining; not only on his own ground, but in a building that was designed to embody his personal power and the architecture was engineered to instil a sense of intimidation. Entry through a forebuilding provided a prolonged and stately stair route to the main doorway, acting also as a vehicle for show and some conspicuous defence along the way (Figure 11.4 and 11.5). Waiting rooms are a common feature: very practical in one sense, they might also give an opportunity to admire a magnificent doorway while reflecting upon one's own place in the world, on the forthcoming encounter with the lord's representative, or even the great presence himself.[30] Norwich, Castle Rising and Rochester are good examples. Once inside, one can detect a planned and controlled progression within the building, often by means of a hall or waiting room, but often with the facility to by-pass these and 'fast-track' chosen people more directly to higher-status spaces. Dual-tiered sets of reception rooms imply social discrimination, with more

*Figure 11.4. External decoration over the entrance to the forebuilding at Castle Rising.*

*Figure 11.5. On entering the forebuilding at Castle Rising this wide and imposing staircase led to a waiting room before one entered the main body of the donjon. There was a magnificently decorated doorway into the Hall for those waiting to contemplate.*

prestigious spaces often found on the second floor.[31] This was not a matter of defence, but a question of establishing a distinction between classes of visitor. Some donjons had a completely separate and more direct outer door designed for the lord's private use; if present, these avoid prescribed routes and provide short-cuts to main reception rooms. One is present at Loches (Indre-et-Loire), a donjon built during the lifetime of Fulk Nerra, Count of Anjou (died 1040),[32] in the contemporary donjon at Beaugency (Loiret) at Colchester and, possibly originally, at Norwich and its derivative at Falaise (Calvados).

The division of formal reception spaces into two social levels could work in two ways: the 'lower' social level could be used by the lord's representatives for business, but when there was a formal or ceremonial occasion with a large attendance further social division could take place with preferment of the élite to the 'upper' level. 'Upper' and 'lower' are used here in a social sense, because donjons like Norwich, Falaise, Castle Rising and Colchester worked horizontally, with dual social division on a single floor, but in many examples the 'upper' and 'lower' descriptions can also be taken literally in tall donjons such as Loches, Beaugency, Richmond (Yorkshire), Rochester (Kent), Hedingham and the White Tower. The upper hall in the 12th-century bishop's palace at Angers (*Salle Synodale*) bears an inscription apparently making it clear that one should know one's place: 'the priest and knight may come in, but the lower orders must go elsewhere, for this fine room is suitable for the former and the humble downstairs room for the latter'.[33] The inscription is quite possibly an intellectual clerical joke,[34] but even so it must be at the expense of received social practice.

To be included in these ceremonial occasions must have been a great privilege. Donjon architecture often incorporated a way of including a wider class of people who did not qualify for admission, but to whom some sense of the procedure was relayed as they stood outside. Derek Renn first highlighted the phenomenon of upper external doorways for 'the display of people or relics' in the towers of Saxon and Norman churches, gatehouses, town gates and a handful of Norman keeps.[35] My own research into Romanesque donjons across the Angevin Empire has thrown up many instances of these, dubbed appearance doorways. Many gave on to galleries or balconies, but both the nature of the doorways and the galleries distinguish them from hourding galleries. They seem to have facilitated a formal appearance to people gathered in an enclosed ward of the castle, or to a much wider set of spectators in the township, sometimes to both.[36] At Scarborough the parapets of the forebuilding could be accessed from the upper audience chamber and in other cases, such as at Loches, Beaugency and Colchester (Essex), the lord's private entry commanded the castle bailey. Rick Turner has suggested that the most elaborate doorway at Chepstow, which commanded the castle ward, was possibly an appearance doorway rather than an entry.[37] Richmond had three large openings overlooking the market-place, the heart of the township and another commanding the castle ward from a small lobby outside the upper floor audience chamber. Here the polite route through the tower proceeds from this room to the battlements, suggesting that in some instances these might also have been used for a larger party to be seen by a crowd.[38] At Norwich an external doorway in the anteroom to the great chamber overlooked the economic hub of the city (marked 'to balcony or private entrance' on Figure 11.13).[39] This doorway is well preserved on the interior but was blocked probably not long after the building was completed, for the blocking shows typical 12th-century masonry and tooling. It may have been used by Henry I when he wore his crown at Norwich shortly after his marriage to Adeliza of Louvain, after which it was considered redundant. Allowing the largest number of people to see the protagonists involved in a formal event such as a homage ceremony, a charter-signing or a crown-wearing may simply have been a hangover from half-remembered Carolingian imperial practice and was as close as they could aspire to the diplomatic handshake on international news channels today.[40]

The ceremonial nature of impressive single-hall great towers like Chepstow, which had niches for formal seats and the capacity to receive a large number of people, can be understood as audience chambers where the intention was to receive homage. Its three differing doorways, which I have interpreted as a place to enter, a place to make an appearance and a place to survey, appreciate and show off one's domain, add sophistication to a deceptively simple plan.[41] The first phase of the less well-preserved and less spectacular great tower at Norham (Northumberland) belongs to the same genre,[42] as does Richmond but on two floors.[43] Here, entry level can be interpreted as the lower of its two-tier reception or as a large waiting room, particularly draughty, for it is here that the three large appearance openings that overlook the market-place are located. The donjon's entry lobby allowed an alternative route directly to an audience chamber on the second floor, via a small waiting lobby with an appearance doorway commanding the castle ward. Richmond had some small mural chambers and probably some garderobes, but none of these donjons make any pretence at comfort. At Hedingham we find a similar format to that at Richmond, but with heating and an extraordinary standard of embellishment. Here both reception halls, with their diaphragm arches, are impressive, but the upper chamber is stunning, and very high with an additional storey occupied by a gallery (Figure 11.6). The jambs of the gallery doorways imply a prescribed route was to be taken through it (Figure 11.7–11.8). One rises into the upper apartment by a straight stair, so that the magnificence of the apartment comes into view in a sedate manner. All of these features are the stuff of ceremony and there is no serious hint of domesticity. The whole comes across as a vehicle for the display and presentation of the person of Aubrey de Vere.[44] In very large donjons rooms proliferate, with the addition of chambers, chapels, even occasionally kitchens. The grouping of an anteroom, a room we might see as a great chamber or audience chamber and a chapel is frequently found, not surprising given the weight placed upon the close partnership between church and state. We find a magnificent version on the second floor suite at Rochester, all overlooked by an internal gallery. The principle of the two-cell tall donjon with a central support for the roof had been realised at Beaugency between 1020 and 1040,[45] in contrast to the larger donjons of Fulk Nerra, which were typically L-shaped.[46] The influence of Beaugency, which had three storeys above the basement and used superimposed arcades instead of a central spine, can be detected at Rochester.[47] The question is raised whether these 'palace'[48] donjons might have served as residences. It is difficult to reconcile the very large interior spaces with comfortable or 'normal' living, while the layouts more readily lend themselves to ceremonial use.[49]

Jeremy Ashbee has debated this with reference to the White Tower.[50] The tower originally had a forebuilding from which one entered by rising a few steps through a lobby into a hall the full length of the building (see Figure 12.5). This works as a first tier reception room, heated and with two sets of garderobes: it could have hosted feasts, or acted as a huge waiting room. Beyond the spine wall there was a room we might interpret as an audience chamber, with three large niches in the west wall, a throne-sized recess in the south wall and a secure room beyond that, perhaps for robing, with a large mural cupboard. One had to pass through both the hall and the north end of the chamber to reach the stair that leads to the upper tier of apartments, and that was quite unusual (see Figure 12.6). On the upper floor the first room encountered might have worked as an antechamber, for it had a garderobe, but Ashbee argues for a timber partition that formed a corridor leading the visitor directly into the room in the western half of the tower, as large as the hall below, making that another huge antechamber. From there one might be ushered into the eastern room, interpreted as the king's chamber. Each of these upper rooms had independent access into the chapel, which had another large recess at its west end, probably to

*Figure 11.6. The upper floor at Hedingham. The diaphragm arch is as great as some cathedral chancel arches (P. Marshall).*

*Figure 11.7. Contrasting decorative treatment of the gallery doorways at Hedingham suggest the entrance (jamb detail – Figure 11.8) and the plainer exit. (Note that the roll moulding here is only on the approach side).*

accommodate the king's chair. The large western chamber also had a stair leading up to a mural gallery in the wall thickness above the leads, which in turn led to the chapel triforium (see Figure 12.7). The passage had a series of special double-light windows on the south elevation, externally highlighting the last part of the passage. None of this looks as if it was designed for everyday use of the type we read about in the donjon at Ardres.

Colchester is often regarded as a parallel for the White Tower, but while it may have been initially conceived as a version of the White Tower, the spaces were even more immense because of the deliberate decision to build it on the podium of the Roman temple of Claudius.[51] The form that Colchester finally took may be endlessly debated,[52] but I am using here a proposed reconstruction that works with the available evidence.[53] The architectural difficulties involved in such a large structure may well account for a

*Figure 11.8. Jamb detail at Hedingham (P. Marshall).*

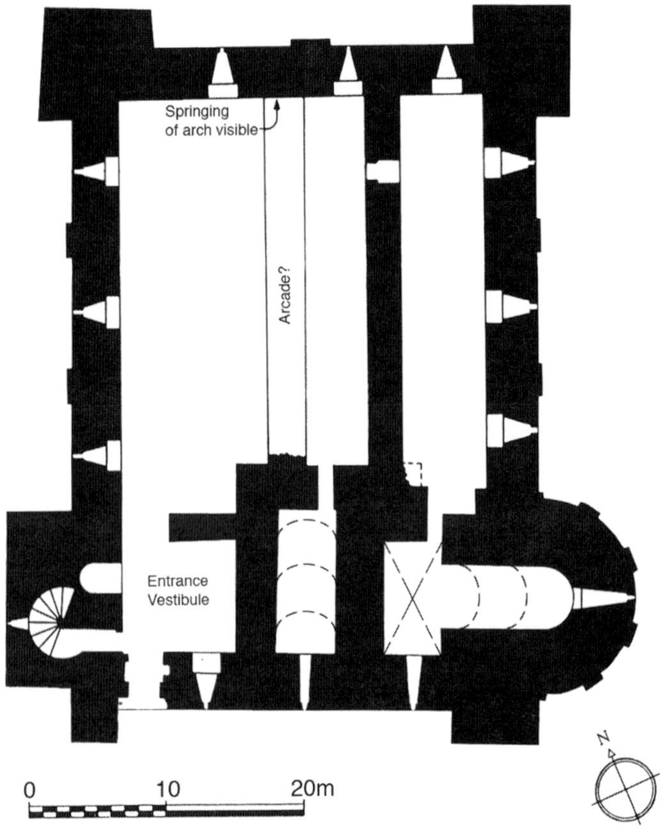


*Fig. 11.9. Suggested reconstructed floor plan of the basement level of the great tower at Colchester after its completion during the reign of Henry I (P. Marshall).*

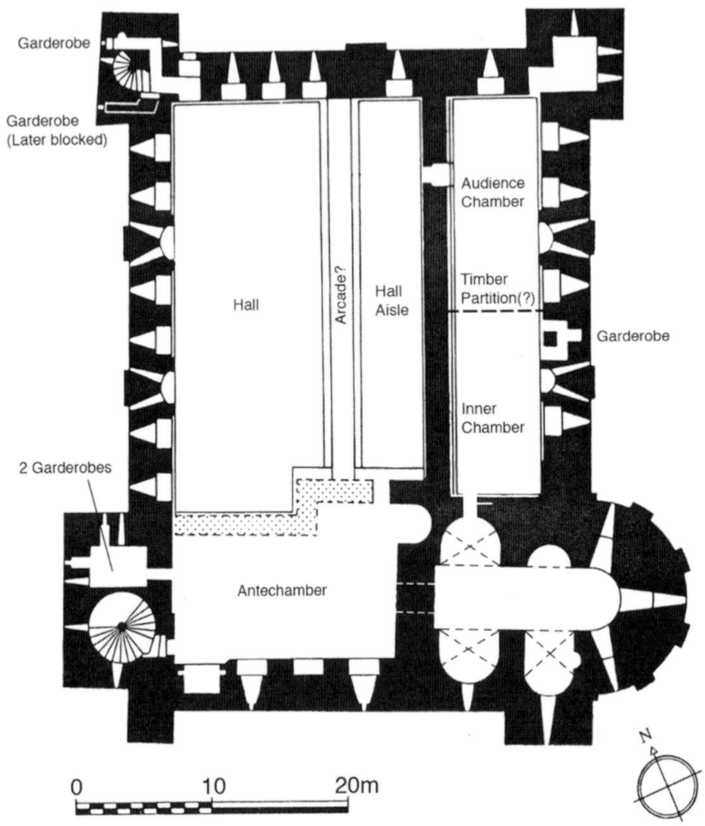


*Fig. 11.10. Suggested reconstructed floor plan of the first floor level of the great tower at Colchester after its completion during the reign of Henry I (P. Marshall).*

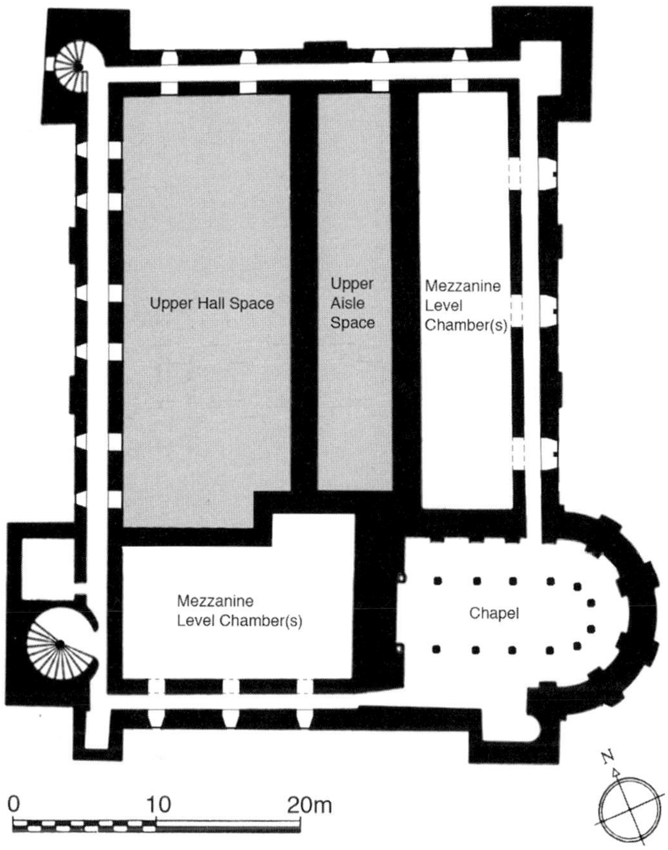


*Fig. 11.11. Suggested reconstructed floor plan of the second floor level of the great tower at Colchester after its completion during the reign of Henry I (P. Marshall).*

very long building break between ground and first floor levels and for a second floor, although originally envisaged, never being realised in full.[54] The donjon needed to be triple-piled because of its huge size, so using an arcade to create an aisled hall on the first floor helped solve this problem (Figures 11.9–11.11). Entry was at basement level, although this was already raised above ground level by the temple platform. A very wide vice took the visitor up to a waiting room or antechamber, with a niche for a guard to stand, before entering the hall, which was enormous and warranted two fireplaces. In order to keep any sense of proportion it must have risen through two stories, although it is possible the height of the aisle was lower. (This formed the central and narrowest section of the triple-piled roof). Beyond this were two chambers on the east side of the tower, where the disposition of the windows, fireplaces, a garderobe and some remaining evidence of a housing on the west wall all suggest the position of a timber partition. These did not require the height of the hall and it is likely there were chambers above. At parapet level there is some remaining evidence for a mural gallery, like that at the White Tower, giving access to a chapel. (At Norwich, Rochester, Hedingham and later at Newcastle, a gallery was brought inside as part of the plan.) The chapel and possibly the upper chambers were all that was built of an originally intended second floor at Colchester. The chapel undercroft is well preserved on the first floor and there is evidence for a doorway connecting it with the adjoining chamber, as at the White Tower. The whole first floor arrangement is reminiscent of the White Tower but much expanded, to the point of getting out of hand. The height required to keep the hall in proportion destroyed the viability of a full second floor. But the principle of a single floor of magnificent rooms with mezzanine-level chambers at one end might have cross-fertilised with the works at Norwich under Henry I, where the plan is more refined (Figure 11.12). Strong echoes of the plan at Norwich have long been recognised at Falaise and Castle Rising.[55] Colchester may form the link between very tall donjons and these squatter plans.[56]

At Norwich, with only one and a half storeys of polite accommodation, the social division was horizontal rather than vertical. As at the White Tower, we find a sequence of hall with great chamber beyond, both with direct access to a chapel. A waiting area in the forebuilding and the hall form the first tier of reception: that the hall was designed to be actually used for feasting is perhaps underlined by the ample provision of 16 garderobes and the decision to

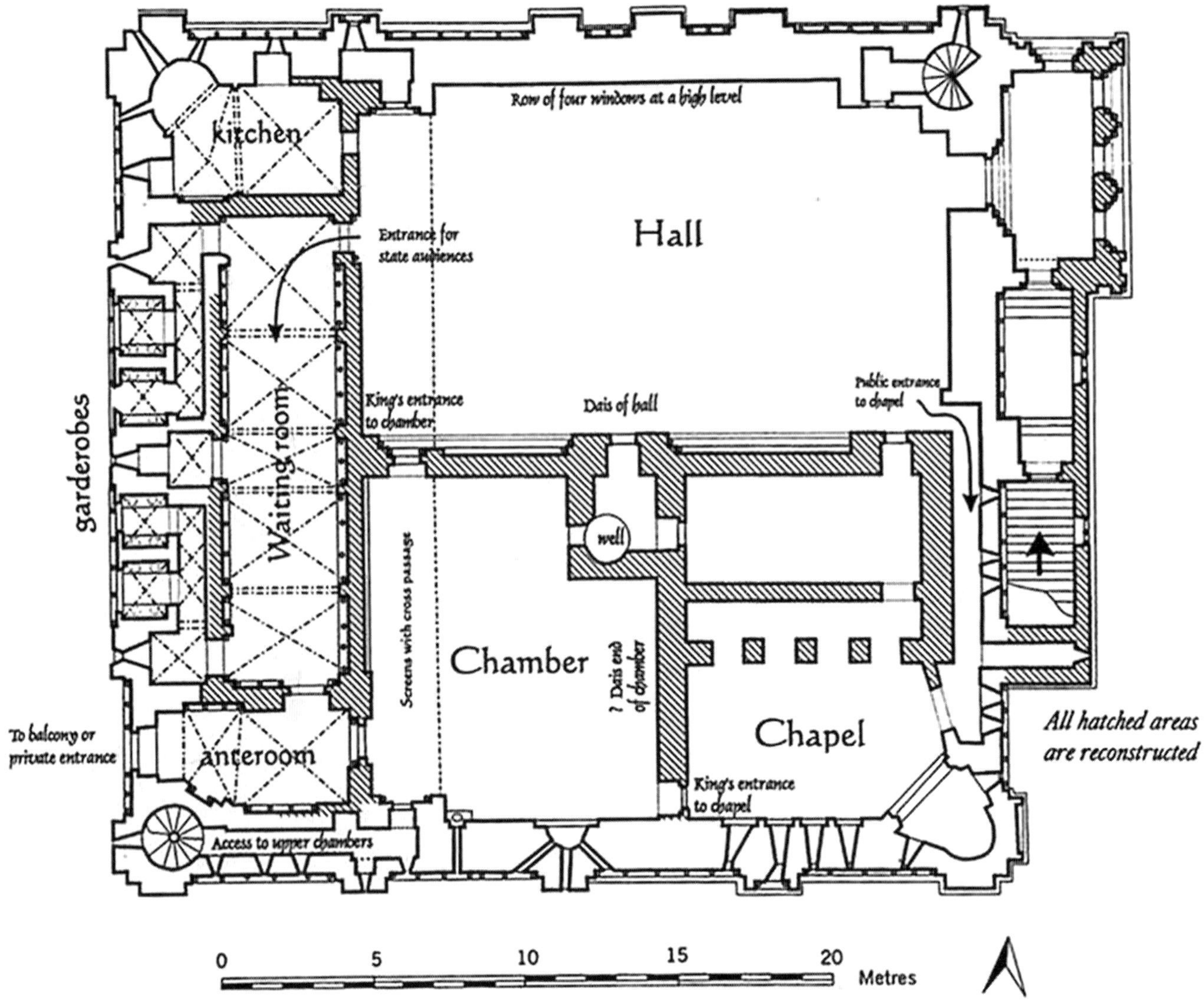


*Figure 11.12. Suggested reconstructed plan of the main floor at Norwich after its completion under Henry I (P. Dixon and P. Marshall).*

exchange a staircase for a kitchen. Even if inadequate to cope with large-scale catering, this could have served to re-heat food or prepare small dishes for the king's chamber. A second tier of reception is represented by another waiting room at the west end of the hall and an anteroom linking this with the great chamber.[57] It was in this anteroom that the appearance doorway had its short existence. Mezzanine-level chambers over the vaulted waiting room and antechamber below were gained by a doorway off the great chamber, by a short passage, a spiral stair and an upper mural passage, all furnished with places for guards to be stationed; a privileged and secure access that indicates royal use. The existence of this mezzanine level, it will be remembered, was highlighted to the outside world by the decorative composition on the exterior.

Jeremy Ashbee has discussed in some detail the surviving documentary evidence for the actual use of the White Tower in the years following its completion, and has noted a certain reluctance on the part of the Norman kings to take advantage of its accommodation on their own behalf. William Rufus was too preoccupied with the new palace of Westminster to stay in the Tower and Henry I used it to confine high status prisoners: Rannulf Flambard, Bishop of Durham, seems to have enjoyed a decent standard of living when he was imprisoned, probably in the Tower, in 1100 and 1101.[58] It may be that neither of these kings ever envisaged the Tower as a residence except in the most symbolic sense, and that the empty building being put to another use did not detract from its main purpose. That there is no documentary evidence for the ceremonial usage implied by the architecture, although frustrating, does not invalidate what the architecture appears to be telling us. The meticulous interior planning of the larger donjons shows that they were meant to be seen inside as well as out, so they were certainly designed to be used: how often may be a different matter. None of the elaborate ceremonial spaces that we find in donjons suggests permanent, or even frequent, habitation. Some, like Norwich, might have hosted feasts more conveniently than others, although not very conveniently. With its king's chamber, chapel, privy kitchen and mezzanine-level chambers it is possible to imagine the king actually staying in the donjon with a host of followers during one of his rare sojourns, but one suspects an official rather than a practical residence. We may have to come to terms with a psyche that was prepared to spend a huge amount of money on a building that was used infrequently, perhaps only once, or even not at all: Turner has suggested that the Norman phase of the donjon at Chepstow was barely used or was even redundant by the time it was finished.[59] Yet builders were happy to do this because the building remained a permanent, conspicuous and tangible embodiment of their authority and the success of their house. The subsequent development of the great tower at Chepstow by later generations into a kind of *gloriette* only confirms this.

At the lower end of the scale the donjon might have made a useful watch-tower, a private refuge from the more public rooms of the castle, or even – perhaps more rarely – a fully-equipped house like that at Ardres. One can imagine a reasonable domestic existence in Henry II's donjon at Orford while struggling to do so in his great tower at Dover, where he had a 'king's house' just outside. At Ardres the top floor was for sleeping while at Hedingham it was the best and most outrageously appointed reception room. We cannot lay down rules and suggest that every donjon worked by them: there were different agendas.

In conclusion, we cannot speak of the donjon with one model in mind and we must accept that within its manifestations there are many shades of grey when it comes to useage. What we can say with some confidence is that the imposing nature and quality of their build, their height and their careful siting in the landscape were all designed to impress a dual message on human consciousness. On the one hand it flagged up the owner's authority and issued a warning not even to think of meddling with it, while it also extended an invitation to admire and stand in awe. In the first instance, then, the donjon worked at arm's length, and for the most part this was enough. It served as a permanent reminder of the authority of a frequently absent lord. We might expect that a connection with the lord might be strengthened if he was actually seen to use the building. This may simply be a modern perception and expectation, but flagging up the king's apartments at Norwich and the incorporation of appearance doorways and galleries suggests otherwise. We will never know whether Richard 'Strongbow' de Clare retired into the tower at Goodrich and sat around a brazier before sleeping there with his wife, his daughters safely ensconced in the upper room; or whether they chose to stay by the fireside in their chambers in the bailey. In a sense it does not matter. Strongbow and the chambers are long gone, but the donjon is still there. Retained through a massive 14th-century rebuild of the rest of the castle, it stands out as a defiant blob of pink amidst a sea of mustard yellow on English Heritage's phased plan.[60] That says a great deal about the medieval perception and the purpose of the donjon.

## Notes

1 For an etymological discussion of 'donjon', see *Castle Studies Group Newsletter* 2001–2, p. 15. For the derivation of 'keep', see Kenyon and Thompson 1994. 'Donjon' was also used synonymously with 'motte' and, especially in the 13th century, to refer to a whole inner ward. See Ashbee 2008, p. 125, note 2. In French it means a great tower.

2 See Impey 2008, pp. 227–33.

3 Allen Brown 1976, p. 32; Thompson 1991, p. 23; Mesqui 1992, pp. 138–261; Ashbee 2008, p. 139; Impey 2008, pp. 235–6; Marshall 2014.

4 Dixon and Marshall 1993ii with regard to Hedingham.

5 McNeill 1990; Heslop 1991; Mesqui 1992, pp. 106–38; Dixon and Marshall 1993i and ii; Impey and Lorans 1998; Mesqui 1998; Goodall 1999i and ii; Dixon 2002, pp. 9–10; Marshall 2002i, p. 27 and 2002ii; Ashbee 2008, pp. 136–9; Impey 2008, p. 235.

6 Dixon 2002, p. 12; Marshall 2002i. Thompson 1992; Goodall 2011, pp. 118–9; Dixon 2008, p. 243; Marshall 2014.

7 Mesqui 1992.

8 Thompson 1992; Goodall 2011, pp. 118–19.

9 Impey 2008, p. 235.

10 Dixon 2002, p. 9; Purton 2002–3, pp. 86–8; 2009, pp. 311–8; Ashbee 2008, p. 235.

11 For a detailed survey and discussion of the history of Ivry see Impey 2002.

12 *Chronique de Lambert d'Ardres*, Mortet, ed. 1911, p. 182. See discussions in Higham & Barker 2004, pp. 115–16, and Ashbee 2008, p. 136, each with differing translations.

13 Dixon interpreted the last two apartments as formal ceremonial spaces detached from the tower itself: 2008, pp. 244–5.

14 Two late 11th-century descriptions are much shorter. A timber tower at Le Cour Marigny (Loiret) had 'an upper floor in which Seguinus and his household lived, conversed, dined and slept at night': Impey and Lorans 1998, pp. 74–6. A tower at Castelpers (Aveyron) had three storeys: an unlit basement; reception rooms on the first floor; sleeping accommodation on the top floor, one of which was occupied by the owner: Mortet and Deschamps 1911–29, pp. 49–50.

15 For a summary of the various historical interpretations of the early history of the castle and the building of the great tower see Turner 2004, pp. 251–4. For comparison with Langeais and further discussion on Chepstow see Marshall 2014.

16 Ashbee 2008, pp. 138–9 and Harris's paper in this volume. William Fitz Stephen's late 12th-century use of the term *arx palatina*,

usually interpreted as 'fortified palace' with reference only to the donjon has been reinterpreted by Ashbee as 'palatine citadel', referring to the whole castle. While the difference is relevant to academic discussion about how far the donjon was perceived by contemporaries as a palace or as a fortress, one suspects the Normans might have been content with either reaction.

17 The promotion actually took place in July 1141: Barrow 1990, p. 176. Allen Brown first suggested that Hedingham might have been built by Aubrey de Vere *c.* 1141 for this reason: 1976, p. 69. The date accords with the decorative styles employed on the tower and the occasion accords with the ceremonial style of the architecture: Dixon and Marshall 1993ii, p. 306.

18 Gervase of Canterbury quoted in Allen Brown 1986, p. 8.

19 The sums recorded in the Pipe Rolls represent relatively minor royal expenditure and can only show completion of work that was well advanced. See Allen Brown, Colvin and Taylor 1963, II, p. 806, notes 2 and 3; Allen Brown 1955, p. 391.

20 Marshall 2004, p. 63.

21 Marshall 2002i, p. 35.

22 McManama-Kearin 2013, p. 130 has proposed the 'one-kilometre' rule using GIS 'viewsheds' – that is the range and distance in a landscape over which a building has observational command.

23 Dixon and Marshall 1993ii, p. 306.

24 The castle stands on high ground to the NE of the town and the tower was built within an earlier ringwork that was encircled by a palisade or curtain wall. RCHME 1916, p. 51; it is not clear whether the curtain was contemporary with the donjon, but one would expect a timber palisade, at least.

25 For a detailed account of the external treatment of the building see Heslop 1994, chapter 2.

26 See Liddiard and Gregory's paper in this volume. Creighton 2010; McManama-Kearin 2012; Marshall 2012; on this subject see also Marshall 2014 with regard to Langeais and Chepstow.

27 Ashbee 2005, p. 17.

28 Eales 2006, p. 21. Goodall 2011, p. 139, also draws our attention to the siting of the donjon over a cave redolent with folklore, but that leads to a discussion of donjon symbolism that falls outside the scope of this article.

29 Marshall 2002ii.

30 On this subject see Dixon 1998. On theatricality in the 14th-century donjon at Knaresborough see Dixon 1990.

31 Mesqui 1992, p. 115.

32 Despite its early date this meticulously planned building incorporates all the features of the ceremonial donjon discussed in this paper. For a comprehensive survey of the building and its history see Mesqui 1998. For the dendrochronology see Dormoy 1998. For its use see also Marshall 2002i, pp. 28–9; 2002ii, pp. 143–5; 2014.

33 Mesqui 1991–2, Vol. 2, p. 85.

34 Ashbee 2008, p. 138 and note 38.

35 Renn 1993.

36 Marshall 2012.

37 Turner 2004, p. 257.

38 Marshall 2014.

39 Dixon and Marshall 2002, p. 215. See also Drury 2002, fig. 2.

40 Marshall 2012, p. 240.

41 Marshall 2014.

42 Dixon and Marshall 1993i.

43 Renn 1993; Goodall 2001; Marshall 2002ii and 2012; Dixon 2008.

44 Dixon and Marshall 1993i; Marshall 2014; Dixon 2008, p. 167.

45 For Beaugency see Valery-Radot 1930 and Mataouchek 2004; Impey 2008, pp. 230–1; Marshall 2014.

46 This was the arrangement at Tours, known from excavation: Galinié 1977 and at Montbazon: Marshall 2014ii.

47 For Rochester see also Goodall 2006; Marshall 2002ii, pp. 145–9; Dixon 2008, pp. 265–7.

48 The term derives from William Fitz Stephen's late 12th-century reference to the White Tower as *arx palatina*, but see note 15 above.

49 Marshall 2002i; 2002ii; Impey 2008, pp. 233–5.

50 Ashbee 2008, pp. 129–39.

51 The symbolic implication is discussed by Wheatley 2004, p.41.

52 See Allen Brown, Colvin and Taylor 1963; Drury 1982; Dixon 2008, pp. 245–7.

53 Marshall 2010.

54 Henry I granted the castle by charter to his steward Eudo, who had close personal connections with Colchester. He may have overseen the earlier phase of building on behalf of William I and probably completed the unfinished work on his own account. On his death in 1120 the castle returned to royal ownership. See Allen Brown, Colvin and Taylor 1963, I, p. 31; Drury 1982, pp. 399–400.

55 Allen Brown, Colvin and Taylor 1963, I, p. 38; Allen Brown 1976, p. 67.

56 Marshall 2010, p. 188.

57 This interpretation is based on Dixon and Marshall 2002; for variations see Drury 2002 and Heslop 1994.

58 Ashbee 2008, pp. 137–9.

59 Turner 2004, p. 260.

60 Ashbee 2005, p. 49.

## Bibliography

Allen Brown, R. (1955) 'Royal Castle-Building in England, 1154–1216', *English Historical Review* 70, pp. 353–98.

Allen Brown, R., Colvin, H. M. and Taylor, A. J., ed. (1963) *The History of The King's Works*, Vols I and II (London, HMSO).

Allen Brown, R. (1976) *English Castles* (Woodbridge, Boydell).

Allen Brown, R. (1986) *Rochester Castle* (London, English Heritage).

Ashbee, J. (2005) *Goodrich Castle* (London, English Heritage).

Ashbee, J. (2008) 'The function of the White Tower under the Normans', in E. Impey, ed., *The White Tower*, pp. 125–39 (New Haven and London, Yale University Press).

Bachrach, B. S. (1993) *Fulk Nerra, the Neo-Roman Consul, 987–1040: A Political Biography of the Angevin Count* (Berkeley, Los Angeles and London, University of California Press).

Barrow, J. (1990) 'A Twelfth-Century Bishop and Literary Patron: William de Vere', *Viator*, pp. 176–89.

Castle Studies Group (2001–2) *Newsletter*.

Creighton, O. (2010) 'Room with a view: framing castle landscapes', *Château Gaillard* 24 (Caen), pp. 37–49.

Dixon, P. W. (1990) 'The donjon of Knaresborough: the castle as theatre', *Château Gaillard* 16, pp. 121–39.

Dixon, P. W. (1998), 'Design in castle building: the controlling of access to the lord', *Château Gaillard* 18, pp. 47–56.

Dixon, P. W. (2002) 'The myth of the keep', in G. Meirion-Jones, E. Impey and M. Jones, ed., *The Seigneurial Residence in Europe, AD c 800-1600*, British Archaeological Report International Series 1088, pp. 9–13 (Oxford).

Dixon, P. W. (2008) 'The influence of the White Tower on the Great Towers of the Twelfth Century', in E. Impey, ed., *The White Tower* (New Haven and London, Yale University Press), pp. 243–75.

Dixon, P. W. and Marshall, P. E. (1993i) 'The Great Tower in the 12th century: the case of Norham Castle', *Archaeological Journal* 150, pp. 410–32.

Dixon, P. W. and Marshall, P. E. (1993ii) 'The Great Tower at Hedingham Castle: a Reassessment', in R. Liddiard, ed. (2003) *Anglo-Norman Castles*, pp. 297–306 (Woodbridge, Boydell). Reprinted from *Fortress* 18 (1993), pp. 16–23.

Dixon, P. W. and Marshall, P. E. (2002) 'Norwich Castle and its analogues', in G. Meirion-Jones, E. Impey and M. Jones, ed., *The Seigneurial Residence in Europe, AD c 800-1600*, British Archaeological Report International Series 1088, pp. 235–43 (Oxford).

Dormoy, C. (1998) 'L'expertise dendrochronologique du donjon de Loches (Indre-et-Loire): Des données fondamentales pour sa datation', *Archéologie Médiévale* 27, pp. 73–89.

Drury, P. J. (1982) 'Aspects of the origins and development of Colchester Castle', *Archaeological Journal* 139, pp. 302–419.

Drury, P. J. (2002) 'Norwich Castle keep', in G. Meirion-Jones, E. Impey and M. Jones, ed., *The Seigneurial Residence in Europe, AD c. 800-1600*, British Archaeological Report International Series 1088, pp. 211–34 (Oxford).

Durand, P. (1996) 'Les conséquences de la datation dendrochronologique du donjon de Loches pour la castellologie', *Bulletin Monumental* 154, pp. 224–8.

Eales, R. (2006), *Peveril Castle*, (London, English Heritage).

Galinié, H. (1977) 'La Résidence des comptes d'Anjou à Tours', *Archéologie Médiévale* 7, pp. 95–108.

Goodall, J. A. A. (2001) *Richmond Castle* (London, English Heritage).

Goodall, J. A. A. (2006) 'The Great Tower of Rochester Castle', in T. Ayers and T. Tatton-Brown, ed., 'Medieval art, architecture and archaeology of Rochester', *British Archaeological Association* 28, pp. 265–99, (Leeds, Maney Publishing).

Goodall, J. (2011) *The English Castle* (New Haven and London, Yale University Press).

Heslop, T. A. (1991) 'Orford Castle, nostalgia and sophisticated living', *Architectural History* 34, pp. 36–58.

Heslop, T. A. (1994) *Norwich Castle Keep: Romanesque Architecture and Social Context* (Norwich, Centre of East Anglian Studies).

Higham, R. and Barker, P. (2004) *Timber Castles* (Exeter, University Press). Reprint of original 1992 publication (London, Batsford).

Impey, E. (2002) 'The turris famosa at Ivry-la-Bataille, Normandy', in G. Meirion-Jones, E. Impey and M. Jones, ed., *The Seigneurial Residence in Europe, AD c 800-1600*, British Archaeological Report International Series 1088, pp. 189–210 (Oxford).

Impey, E. (2008) 'The Ancestry of the White Tower', in E. Impey, ed., *The White Tower*, pp. 227–41 (New Haven and London, Yale University Press).

Impey, E. and Lorans, E. (1998) 'Le donjon de Langeais et son environnement', *Deux donjons construits autour l'an mil en Touraine*, pp. 9–59 (Paris, Société Française d'Archéologie).

Impey, E. and Lorans, E. (1998) 'Langeais, Indre-et-Loire: An Archaeological and Historical Study of the Early Donjon and it Environs', *Journal of the British Archaeological Association* 151, pp. 43–106.

Kenyon, J. and Thompson, M. (1994) 'The origin of the word 'keep', *Medieval Archaeology* 38, pp. 175–6.

Marshall, P. (2002i) 'The Great Tower as Residence', in G. Meirion-Jones, E. Impey and M. Jones, ed., *The Seigneurial Residence in Europe, AD c. 800-1600*, British Archaeological Report International Series 1088, pp. 27–44 (Oxford).

Marshall, P. (2002ii) 'The ceremonial function of the Donjon', *Château Gaillard* 20, pp. 141–51.

Marshall, P. (2004) 'Lincoln Castle: the architectural context of the medieval defences', in P. Lindley, ed., *The Early History of Lincoln Castle*, pp. 53–65, Society for Lincolnshire History and Archaeology Occasional Papers 12 (Lincoln).

Marshall, P. (2010) 'The internal arrangement of the donjon at Colchester in Essex: a reconsideration', *Castle Studies Group Journal* 23, pp. 178–90.

Marshall, P. (2012) 'Making an appearance: some thoughts on the phenomenon of multiple doorways and large upper openings in Romanesque donjons in western France and Britain', *Château Gaillard* 25, pp. 233–41.

Marshall, P. (2015) 'The Angevin donjon and its legacy in post-Conquest Britain', in R. Oram, ed., *A House That Thieves Might Knock At*, pp. 198–213, Tower Studies 1: Proceedings of the 2010 Stirling and 2011 Dundee Conferences on 'The Tower and Lordly Residence' and 'The Tower and the Household' (Donington, Shaun Tyas).

Marshall, P. (forthcoming) 'The Romanesque donjon at Montbazon (Indre-et-Loire): a reassessment', in B. Murtagh, ed., *Papers in Honour of David Johnson.*

Mataouchek, V. (2004) 'Beaugency, la Tour César', in *Lumières de l'an mil en Orléanais*, pp. 403–6 (Brepols, Turnhout).

McManama-Kearin, K. (2012) 'Forced focus: a room with viewshed', *Château Gaillard* 25, pp. 233–41.

McManama-Kearin, K. (2013) *The use of GIS in Determining the Role of Visibility in the Siting of Early Anglo-Norman Stone Castles in Ireland*, British Archaeological Report 575 (Oxford).

McNeill, T. E. (1990) 'Trim Castle, Co. Meath; the first three generations', *Archaeological Journal* 147, pp. 308–36.

Mesqui, J. (1991–3) *Châteaux et enceintes de la France médiévale*, 2 vols (Paris, Picard).

Mesqui, J. (1998) 'La tour maitresse du donjon de Loches', in *Deux donjons construits autour l'an mil en Touraine*, pp. 65–125 (Paris, Société Française d'Archéologie).

Mortet, V., ed. (1911) Chronique de Lambert d'Ardres, in Mortet, V. and Deschamps, P., ed., *Recueil des textes relatifs à l'histoire de l'architecture en France*, Vol. I, p. 182 (Paris).

Mortet, V. and Deschamps, P., ed. (1911–29) *Receuil des textes relatifs à l'histoire de l'architecture et à la condition des architectes en France au moyen âge, XIe–XIIe siècles,* Vol. I (Paris).

Purton, P. (2002–2003) 'Donjons: some heretical thoughts', *Castle Studies Group Newsletter* 16, pp. 86–8.

Purton, P. (2009) *A History of the Early Medieval Siege,* c. *450–1200* (Woodbridge, Boydell).

Renn, D. F. (1993) 'Burhgeat and gonfanon: two sidelights from the Bayeux Tapestry', *Anglo-Norman Studies* 16, pp. 177–98.

RCHME (1916) *The County of Essex* (London, Royal Commission on Historic Monuments).

Stubbs, W., ed. (1889) William of Malmesbury, *De gestis regum Anglorum* (London).

Thompson, M. W. (1991) *The Rise of the Castle* (Cambridge, University Press).

Thompson, M. W. (1992) 'A suggested dual origin for keeps', *Fortress* 15, pp. 3–15.

Turner, R. C. (2004) 'The Great Tower, Chepstow Castle, Wales', *Antiquaries Journal* 84, pp. 223–318.

Vallery-Radot, J. (1930) 'Beaugency – le donjon', *Congrés* 93, pp. 341–51.

Wheatley, A. (2004) *The Idea of the Castle in Medieval England* (York, Medieval Press).

# Part III

# Recent Archaeological Research

# 12

# Recent research on the White Tower: reconstructing and dating the Norman building

*Roland B. Harris*

**Résumé**

*La Tour Blanche est le monument central de la Tour de Londres, à laquelle elle a donné son nom dès 1100: c'est le palais le plus complet conservé de l'Europe du XIe siècle. Les travaux de conservation et la réorganisation interne en 1996–8 et 2008–11 ont permis de procéder à des recherches archéologiques. Cette analyse récente a donné trois résultats importants, qui ont trait à la construction primitive de la tour romane, examinés dans cet article. Tout d'abord, la forme actuelle de la Tour Blanche, comme le démontre sa maçonnerie, n'est pas seulement, dans une large mesure, celle de son état à sa date d'achèvement vers 1100, mais bien celle qui avait été conçue dès l'origine: cette remarque concerne les murs, les contreforts, quatre tourelles et l'abside en saillie. Ensuite, la principale modification durablement apportée au bâtiment comprend le relèvement des toitures des salles est et ouest par l'ajout d'un étage, créant ainsi des salles supplémentaires dont le plancher se situe au niveau des assises de la charpente et des gouttières de la toiture d'origine. Il n'existe aucune preuve de cette surélévation de la toiture avant environ 1490 et, auparavant, les charpentes des salles est et ouest étaient divisées par les murs du deuxième étage de la Tour Blanche. Troisième remarque: il y eut une pause assez longue dans la construction primitive, alors que seule la moitié du premier étage était construite (l'étage de la chapelle). Cette pause se reconnaît par les changements dans les matériaux et de technique et - d'une plus grande importance pour l'étude de l'architecture de la fin du XIe siècle – dans le détail sculpté de la chapelle Saint-Jean. L'identification d'une pause majeure dans la construction est intimement liée à une réévaluation de la date de construction de la Tour Blanche, qui a pendant tant d'années été donnée, en toute certitude, aux environs de 1078: un ensemble de preuves scientifiques, documentaires et architecturales suggère que la construction primitive de la Tour Blanche commença autour de 1075–9 pour se terminer en 1100, la longue coupure dans la construction commençant aux alentours de 1079 83 (et plus probablement vers 1080) pour se terminer aux alentours de 1090–3.*

## Introduction

The White Tower (Figure 12.1 and 12.2) is the centrepiece of the Tower of London – one of the best-known castles in the world – to which it had given its name by 1100: it is the most complete 11th-century palace in Europe, and the best example of the great tower or *donjon* of this period. Opportunities for the first systematic investigation of much of the building were provided in 1996–8, when the building was emptied for installation of new displays and conservation works were carried out on the external south elevation. The archaeological recording and analysis was accompanied by a programme of dendrochronological sampling (which included additional work on the well in 2005), petrographic survey and documentary research. The results were published in a substantial multi-authored monograph (Impey 2008b). In 2008–11 cleaning and conservation of the north, east and west elevations, and the turrets allowed continuation of the earlier research to the rest of the exterior, with the archaeological recording again integrated with a detailed petrographic survey. This second phase of analysis supported the findings of the 1996–8, with some minor modifications, and usefully expanded our understanding of the building, especially in relation to extent, form and dating of the post-medieval alterations and repairs. This paper presents a summary of the primary construction of the Romanesque tower, based on both the recent investigations.

Prior to these recent investigations, it had long been accepted that the White Tower was a building surviving largely intact from the late 11th century, albeit with post-medieval modifications that included the replacement of quoins and architraves with Portland stone, the insertion of brick vaults

*Figure 12.1. View of the White Tower from the south-west, across the River Thames (Photo: Roland Harris).*

in the basement, and the addition of a floor at the level of an original gallery (e.g. Allen Brown, Colvin and Taylor 1963, pp. 29–32). Other interpretations have been advanced over the years, with the theory that the basic form of the building evolved – rather than was conceived from the outset – reappearing in a more compelling manner: it has been proposed that the White Tower was initially built a storey lower, except for the chapel, and that, shortly after, this gabled structure was heightened by the addition of the mural passage (Parnell 1998).

The investigations of 1996–8 and 2008–11 show that the structural history of the White Tower is neither as simple as the traditional interpretation nor as complex as the evolutionists would have it. There were three important findings of the analysis, which are explored in this paper and, insofar as they are relevant to St John's chapel, in the paper elsewhere in this volume by John Crook. First, the present form of the White Tower as expressed by its masonry is not only largely that achieved by completion *c.* 1100, but as conceived from the outset: this includes the walls, buttresses, four turrets and the projecting apse. Second, the one lasting major alteration made to the building comprised the raising of the roofs of the east and west rooms by a storey, with a new floor added where previously there were rafter feet and roof drains, creating additional rooms. There is no evidence of this higher roof before *c.* 1490 and, previously, the roofs of the east and west rooms were screened by the second-floor walls of the White Tower. Third, there was a substantial pause in the primary construction, midway through the building of the first floor (i.e. that with the chapel). This break is reflected by changes in material and technique and, most importantly for the study of late 11th-century architecture, in the sculptural detail of St John's chapel. The identification of a major building break is intimately bound up with a re-assessment of the date of the White Tower, for so long confidently cited as *c.* 1078: a combination of scientific, documentary, and architectural evidence suggests that the primary construction of the White Tower began around 1075–9 and was completed by 1100, with the long building break beginning *c.* 1079–83 and ending *c.* 1090–3.

## Form of the 11th-century building

### *Introduction*

As built by 1100, the White Tower comprised three floors, each with a larger and smaller pair of oblong rooms (those above basement level having fireplaces and garderobes), separated by a spine wall, with the south-east corner of the tower occupied by a room that had an apsidal projection. At first-floor level this apsidal room formed the barrel-vaulted chapel of St John. The chapel rose through two storeys and, thus, projected above the level of the adjacent rooms: the chapel gallery connected to mural passages that linked the embrasures of the false windows in the walls that screened the roofs of the east and west rooms. The western basement room contained a well. Access to the three floors was possible via the circular north-east turret, with the main entrance on the middle floor, on the south face (i.e. the main entrance used today).

### *Foundations, basement and plinth*

As with all levels of the White Tower, the basement comprises three spaces: a room measuring 25.91m × 10.75m occupies the whole of the western half, while the eastern half is occupied by another room measuring 20.47m × 8.16m and, to the south, a smaller barrel-vaulted space with a projecting apse measuring 14.12m × 4.32m (Figures 12.3 and 12.4). The insertion of brick vaults in the larger two rooms in 1733 considerably altered the appearance of the basement floor. This resulted in the loss of most of the original fenestration, although the rear-arch of a primary loop remains intact in the south wall of the west room and, remarkably, the dolomitized Chalk window sill has now been identified on the external elevation. Similar windows are recorded in pre-1733 plans (TNA, Work 31/84 and

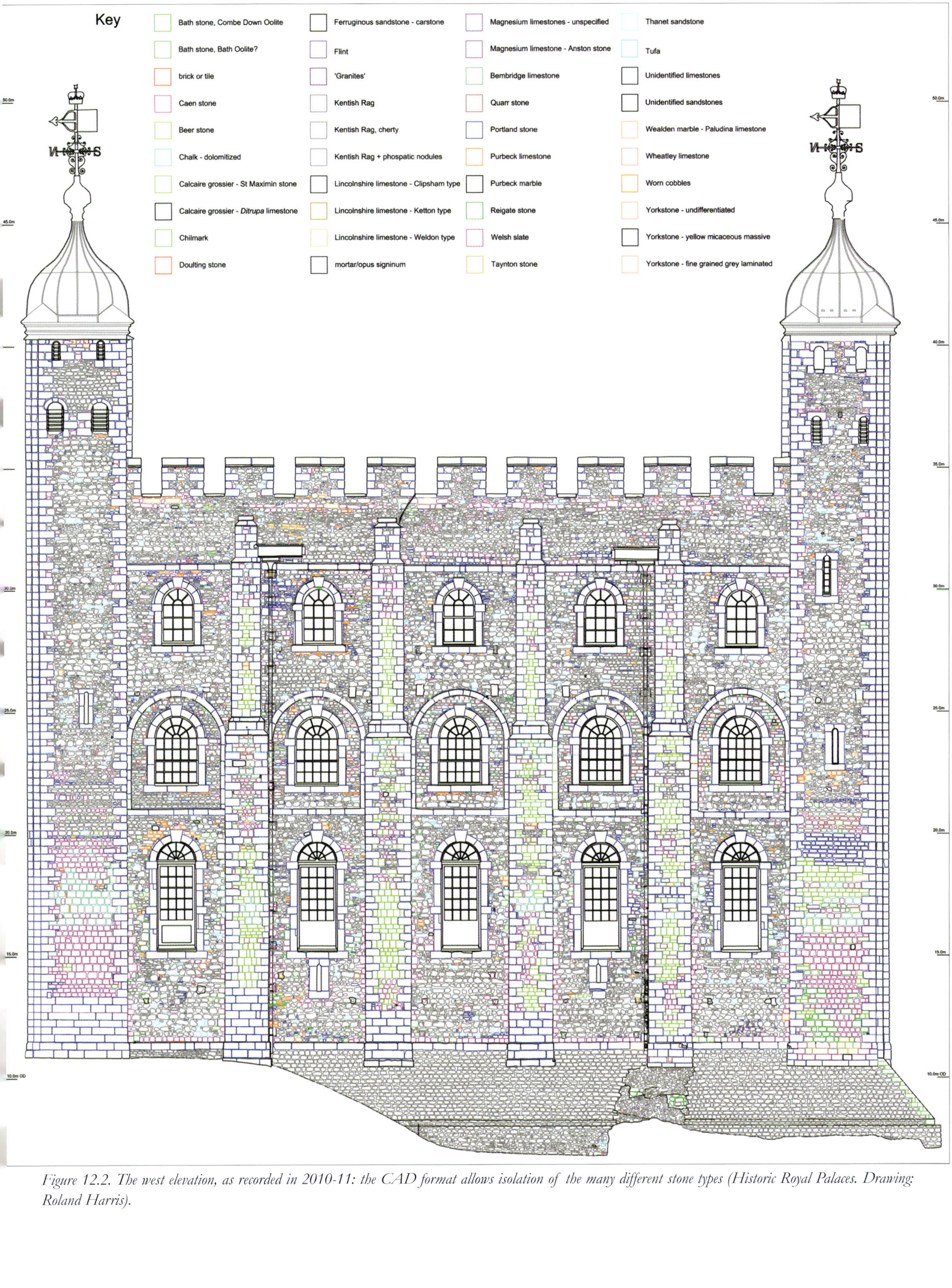


*Figure 12.2. The west elevation, as recorded in 2010-11: the CAD format allows isolation of the many different stone types (Historic Royal Palaces. Drawing: Roland Harris).*

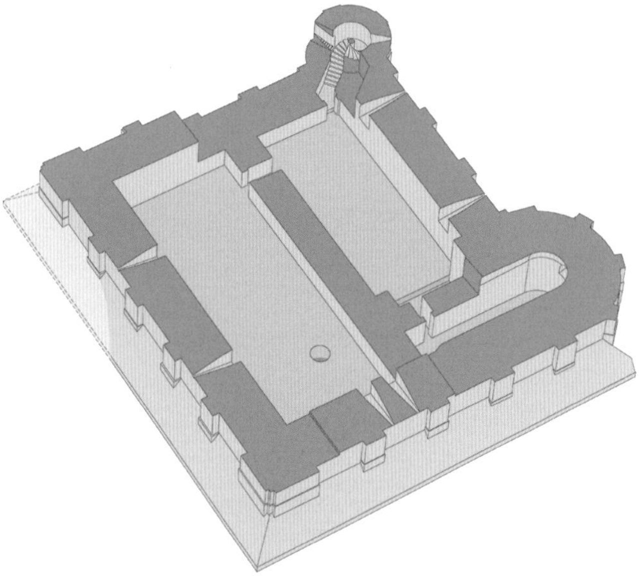

*Figure 12.3. Basement: three-dimensional reconstruction of the primary form (Historic Royal Palaces. Drawing: Helen Jones).*

*Figure 12.4. View of the apse from the south-east (Photo: Roland Harris).*

31/86). The three 11th-century internal doorways survive. That at the north end of the spine wall and that between the apsidal and east rooms were modified in the 14th century to allow replacement of flush-mounted doors by rebated doors at the other ends of the doorway passages. The north-east doorway is better preserved, and provided the only primary access to this storey, via the spiral stair turret in the north-east corner. All three doorways preserve evidence of drawbar sockets, with that of the spine wall doorway having a primary 25mm (1") thick lining plank intact: dendrochronological analysis has produced a felling date of after 1068. Another dendrochronological date was forthcoming – in this case of after 1082 – from the well in the west room. This came from the beech template located at the bottom of the ashlar-lined well, over 12m deep, during its draining for investigation in 2005.

The most misunderstood element of the basement level of the White Tower has been the apsidal projection at the south-eastern corner. Something of a tradition has emerged in which it is supposed that it was added to the White Tower after the construction of both the foundations and the lowest storey (e.g. Parnell 1993, p. 20). The origins of this idea lie in the fact that previous scholars were unaware of the existence of square great towers with apsidal projections other than at Colchester Castle and the Tower of London: it was accepted, on minimal and questionable evidence, that the former owed its existence to underlying Roman remains, yet the White Tower appeared to have been begun earlier and, thus, was easier to explain if its plan was achieved by subsequent modification inspired by Colchester. However, the great tower at Ivry-la-Bataille is now known to have established a similarly scaled double-pile plan with an east-facing apsidal projection much earlier in the 11th century, and, moreover, the evidence for the supposed fortuitous adoption of the plan at Colchester has not stood up to close scrutiny (Impey 2008a, pp. 239–41). Turning to the structural evidence of the White Tower itself, it is clear that to date the only indication that the apse could be secondary is a minor discontinuity at the junction of the foundations of the apse and east wall, recorded in a photograph of 1955–6 (Harris 2008, fig. 38). That this relates to the lowest levels of the east and apse walls that otherwise show remarkable consistency in their banding of rubble and in their lack of plinths suggests that this anomaly does not indicate two separate phases of construction. Indeed, the primary nature of the apse is positively supported by the facts that, first, the short length of plinth running north from the south-east corner of the White Tower terminates against the wall of the apse; second, the neatly mitred corner of this plinth lies a substantial 1.7m too far to the east to align with the east wall; and, third, archaeological excavation of the interior of the apsidal basement room in 1965 revealed no evidence of any discontinuity in the fabric, but, rather, a 390mm wide offset running around the entire room at the primary floor level.[1]

Likewise, the identification of distinctive and unusual shelly mortar (unique to the pre-break construction) elsewhere in the basement as low as 8.40m OD and as low as 7.09m OD on the plinth of the south wall, means that there is a strong case for rapid and continuous construction from foundations to the first-floor building break. Finally, when the design implications of adding an apse are considered fully in terms of both the external bay divisions of the White Tower and the precise and related geometry of the first-floor chapel (Harris 2008, pp. 90–3), it is even more apparent that the idea of the apse being added to the White Tower has no basis in structural analysis.

## Entrance floor

Other than the main entrance, the internal arrangement of the entrance storey replicates that of the basement, although the spine wall has a doorway at the southern end in addition to that at the north. Offsets at floor joist level mean that the east and west rooms are slightly larger than below, at 20.81m × 8.74m and 27.63m × 11.32m respectively. As at basement level, the east room is distinguished by a recess at its southern end, although on the entrance floor it is shallower (1.80m) and wider (6.12m) (Figure 12.5). The barrel-vaulted apsidal room is also larger than that below (15.34m × 4.23m), mainly due to a 1.42m-deep recess in the west wall. The increased sophistication of this room compared to its counterpart in the basement is also seen in the treatment of the apse, with its more extensive use of ashlar, in the fenestration that is extended to include three windows on the south side, and the small unlit room (3.37m × 2.56m) that opens off the north wall. Unlike their basement equivalents, the east and west rooms have preserved something of their primary internal arrangement in that they have timber arcades, with the posts supporting the wide span of the floors: the surviving posts, however, are post-medieval and it remains a matter of pure conjecture as to whether any primary supports took the form of single or, as now exists, double arcades. Although the barrel-vaulted window embrasures survive largely intact, the 11th-century windows themselves have been replaced, mostly in 1638–40, and then again in 1715 (the east and west rooms) and 1881–2 (the apsidal room). The steps in the floors of the embrasures in the apsidal room suggest that the windows here were smaller than in the other rooms, but there is no accurate record of the original fenestration. The spine wall on the entrance floor differs from the solid wall below in that it is penetrated by three wide plain openings and two doorways at the extremities. The soffits and reveals indicate that the plain openings were formerly blocked on the western side, and this is corroborated by the complete absence of Romanesque quoins and voussoirs on this side: confusingly, even recently published plans show the recesses on the wrong side (e.g. Parnell 1993, fig. 9, p. 21). Both east and west rooms have fireplaces. That in the east room has been restored, while the other is in a less doctored but more ruinous state. The wall over the latter slightly projects, raising the possibility of a more subtle version of the conical hoods found at Loches (Mesqui 1998), but the evidence is far from conclusive and there may have been no more than an arch spanning the fireplace on the plane of the wall. The provision for garderobes on the entrance floor comprised two at the northern end of the west room only. The eastern of these was mostly obliterated during the construction of the splayed opening to the north doorway in the 16th century, but enough survives to show that it was a mirror-image of its dog-legged western counterpart, which is better preserved.

While no longer the only entrance to the White Tower, the doorway in the westernmost bay of the south elevation at this level provided the only known primary external entrance, raised roughly 6.4m above the external ground, as it is today. The location of the entrance on the south side probably reflected the greater importance attached to the elevation facing the river, and would have opened into the larger part of the bailey, which is known to have surrounded the building. The position of the doorway in the westernmost bay implies that the external stair ran eastward, parallel to the façade. Perhaps we can assume that this was still the case in the later 12th century, when the south forebuilding that protected the top of this stair was almost certainly in existence (Harris 2008, pp. 86–90). Significantly, similar arrangements are found in the square keeps at Canterbury, Corfe, Norwich, Rochester, and Castle Rising. Although not ornamented, the doorway passage is given special treatment in that it is of ashlar (here mostly comprising dolomitized Chalk), with the exception of the rubble vault. Moreover, in the side walls there are niches,

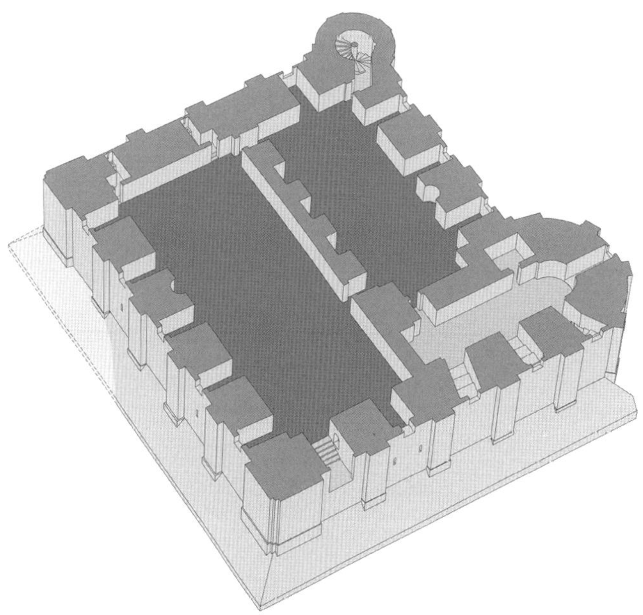

*Figure 12.5. Entrance floor: three-dimensional reconstruction of the primary form (Historic Royal Palaces. Drawing: Helen Jones).*

which although now rectangular in form, preserve evidence of their original roundheaded arches and bear comparison with the single example at Colchester Castle.

## First floor

The first floor replicates the three volumes of the two floors below (Figure 12.6), although the progressive offsets mean that at this level the east and west rooms are larger, at 19.69m × 9.29m and 29.20m × 12.04m respectively. Lateral fireplaces in both east and west rooms (the latter is blocked) duplicate those below and intercommunication follows the pattern of the entrance floor. Minor differences are to be found in the absence of a recess at the southern end of the east room, an additional doorway linking the apsidal room to the western room, and in the distribution of the garderobes, with both rooms in this case provided with a pair. More significant differences are to be found in the greater number of windows, and in the provision of staircases in the north-west and south-west corners. Although the east and west rooms now have post-medieval timber arcades, in this case supporting the floors above, the absence of a second floor in the original building strongly suggests that these rooms contrasted from those below in that they were uncluttered by posts: it is possible, however, that the primary roofs utilized mid-span supports. The third, apsidal, room has the greatest difference to its entrance-floor equivalent, for at this level the aisled chapel of St John rises up through two storeys to include a gallery and a stone barrel-vault. Although, it went out of ecclesiastical use by the early 14th century and was thereafter adapted for a variety of other functions – notably a store for records – the chapel remained largely intact. As a result, the restoration by Salvin in 1864 involved little more than removal of a spiral stair from the ambulatory, replacement of aisle respond abaci lost to shelving, and replacement of 17th-century Portland stone windows with what he considered more appropriate designs (Keay and Harris 2008, pp. 209–12). The form of the chapel, its famous capitals, and its art historical context were studied anew in the course of the recent investigations (Crook 2008), and the findings are summarized elsewhere in this volume in John Crook's paper.

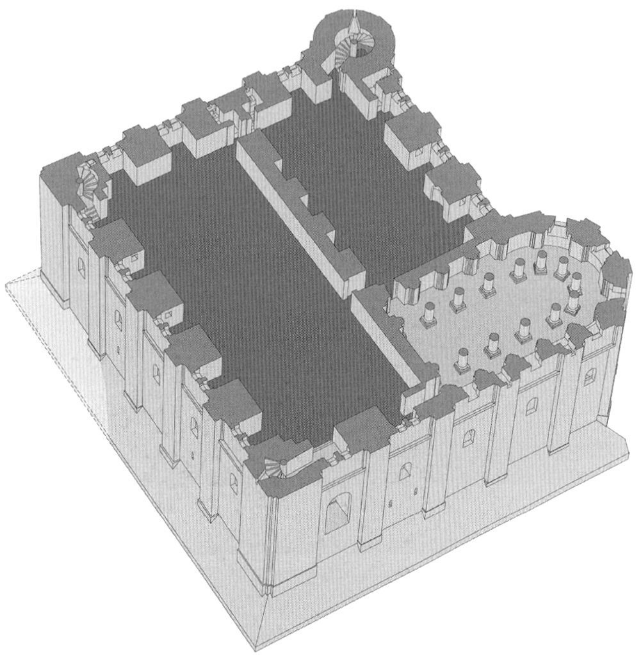

*Figure 12.6. First-floor: three-dimensional reconstruction of the primary form (Historic Royal Palaces. Drawing: Helen Jones).*

The exterior of the first floor is more elaborate than that of the other levels, which, together with the location of the chapel here, strongly suggests pre-eminence of this storey. The main embellishment is the blind arcading, in which wide arches surround the windows and span the bay widths between the buttresses. Examination of the south elevation in 1996–8 confirmed that the blind arches were a primary feature, not on the basis of the arches themselves – which are entirely of 17th-century and later Portland stone – but on the basis that the rubble walling (which is essentially primary) is offset at the arch by up to 200mm. Portland stone (as well as other more recent) replacement of the voussoirs and the angle order from which the arches spring is evident in the apsidal, east, north and west elevations too, but the 2008–11 investigation showed that it is less complete and that primary ashlar (comprising Quarr stone, Bembridge limestone and Caen stone) survives, most of which is *in situ*, in the angle orders.

The large windows within these arches date from 1805, replacing smaller double-windows of 1638–9. As with most of William Mills's 17th-century repairs at the White Tower, these double-windows exactly perpetuated the 11th-century arrangement and dimensions: this is evident from the intact Romanesque rear arches in the second bay from the west in the north wall at this level. Externally, the recent investigations have identified other survivals from the primary first-floor windows, comprising an *in situ* jamb in the south elevation, together with four *ex situ* primary voussoirs found at first-floor level in masonry in the north and west elevations, reset during the 1638–40 repairs. Two of the voussoirs were of Quarr stone (a stone that ceased to be used outside the immediate hinterland of the quarries on the Isle of Wight from *c.* 1120), with the others comprising Bembridge stone and Reigate stone (both key primary ashlar types at the White Tower). All four were from arches of *c.* 650–80mm diameter, which corresponds precisely with the narrow double-windows at this level as rebuilt in 1638–9 (*c.* 660mm). These four voussoirs suggest that the Romanesque double-windows were of simple form, lacking mouldings. This plainness is confirmed by the part-surviving jamb in the western bay of the south elevation, in which the quoins have no outer moulding and run back into the wall (i.e. there is no return which would have allowed for a nook shaft). Internally, the Romanesque barrel-vaulted embrasures survive largely intact, again lacking any evidence for stepped floors. Uniquely, the embrasures on each side of the fireplaces in the two main rooms at this level have small square cupboards. They have plain timber lintels, two of which have produced dendrochronological dates (felling date ranges of 1055–87 and 1072–1104) linking them to the primary construction.

### *Second floor, roof and turrets*

Today the second floor of the White Tower differs from the other storeys in matters of detail only. With the first-floor chapel rising through two storeys, there is, of course, no self-contained apsidal room at this level, but a barrel-vaulted gallery instead (Figure 12.7). The chapel gallery forms part of a mural passage that makes a complete circuit of the White Tower, cutting through window embrasures that are otherwise similar to those below. The east and west rooms are present again, and are also separated by a massive spine wall: offsets at floor level make these rooms a little larger than those below at 29.23m × 12.36m and 19.74m × 9.36m.[2] Some elements of the floors below are missing, however, for the second floor has no garderobes or fireplaces. Moreover, the details are less sophisticated. For example, the voussoirs of the embrasures and spine wall openings (the latter were never only recesses here) are of rubble, not ashlar. The north-east, south-west, and north-west stairs reach this level and continue further up the corner turrets, which then break free of the building. In the chapel roof space a fourth turret rises from the top of the barrel vaults of the chapel, giving the White Tower a degree of symmetry it would otherwise lack. The irregular plan of this turret does not imply that it is secondary, but rather responds to its position above the ambulatory of the chapel: the east face of the turret is precisely angled so that it loads onto the piers of the gallery and main arcades of the chapel below. Despite this general consistency with the storeys below, the second floor of the White Tower has been viewed for many years as a substantial modification of the original design. The most consistently presented view of the primary form has been one in which the first-floor east and west rooms rose through two storeys in the manner of the chapel (e.g. Armitage 1912, p. 225, no. 2; Allen Brown 1984, pp. 30–2; Parnell 1993, pp. 20–2). The second-floor mural passage then becomes akin to a clerestory passage, overlooking the principal rooms. Such a model explains the absence of garderobes and fireplaces, and, indeed, the need for a mural passage. More recently, it has been suggested that the primary form of the White Tower was gabled, with the rest of the north and south walls and the east and west mural passages added later (Parnell 1998). The recent investigations have shown that the reality was rather different.

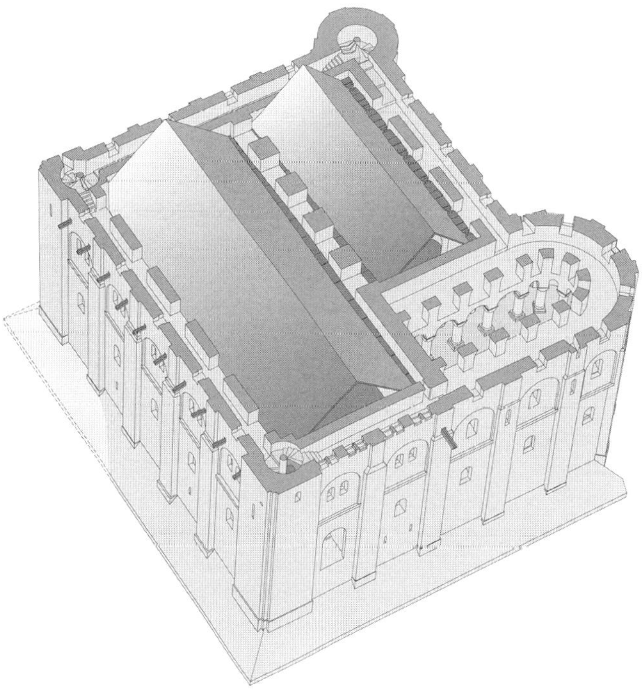

*Figure 12.7. Second floor: three-dimensional reconstruction of the primary form (Historic Royal Palaces. Drawing: Helen Jones).*

*Figure 12.8. Primary roof scupper, or drain, unblocked in the northern bay of the east elevation in 2008, showing lead lining over disintegrating timber channel (Photo: Roland Harris).*

The most important element of the primary roof was that it was a storey lower than that surviving today, which, on the basis of dendrochronology, has been dated to *c.* 1490. The evidence for the lower and more steeply-pitched roof comprises a soot imprint of the roof in the south wall of the east room (first recorded in 1966), scars of similar roof abutments in the north and south walls of the west room, and a series of scuppers, or roof drains, below the east and west mural passages (Figure 12.8). Many of the latter were excavated in 1996, with others investigated externally in 2008–11, showing survival of wooden drains with lead coverings: these presumably continued as spouts projecting clear of the building. Although now finished to look like the other scuppers, the squared hole in the west face of the south-west turret was examined in 2010 and found to be a putlog hole. That the lower roof was surrounded by the walls essentially as they survive today, rather than having gables, is clear from the homogeneity of the fabric of the closely studied south and north elevations, the stairs, the turrets, the mural passages, and, above all, the end walls of the two rooms. The spine wall is also tied into the primary fabric at both ends, and, uniquely at this level, exhibits a dramatic taper in plan. Given that it rose above the primary roofs and was necessarily flanked by gutters, or roof valleys, it is likely that the tapering was designed to increase the width of the long drains of the enclosed roof at their narrowest points. The original boxed-in roof form of the White Tower was something of a norm and existed, for example, at Norwich, Montrichard, Portchester, Richmond, Rochester, and the south-west gatehouse at Sherborne Old Castle. That the walls rising above the eaves of an enclosed roof could be given false fenestration is also seen at Hedingham.

## Dating the primary construction

### *Documentary evidence*

The earliest unambiguous reference to the Tower of London makes it plain that the White Tower was in existence or well advanced: in the course of an explanation of how the cathedral church of Rochester came to possess several London properties from Eadmer the Cripple, the *Textus Roffensis*[3] relates that 'Gundulf, by command of King William the Great, was supervising the work of the great tower of London' (*Textus Roffensis*, Hearne 1720, p. 212). As Gundulf was appointed to the see of Rochester on 19 March 1077, it has become something of a tradition to date the construction of the White Tower to 1078, or *c.* 1080. However, the *Textus Roffensis* does not imply that the bishop

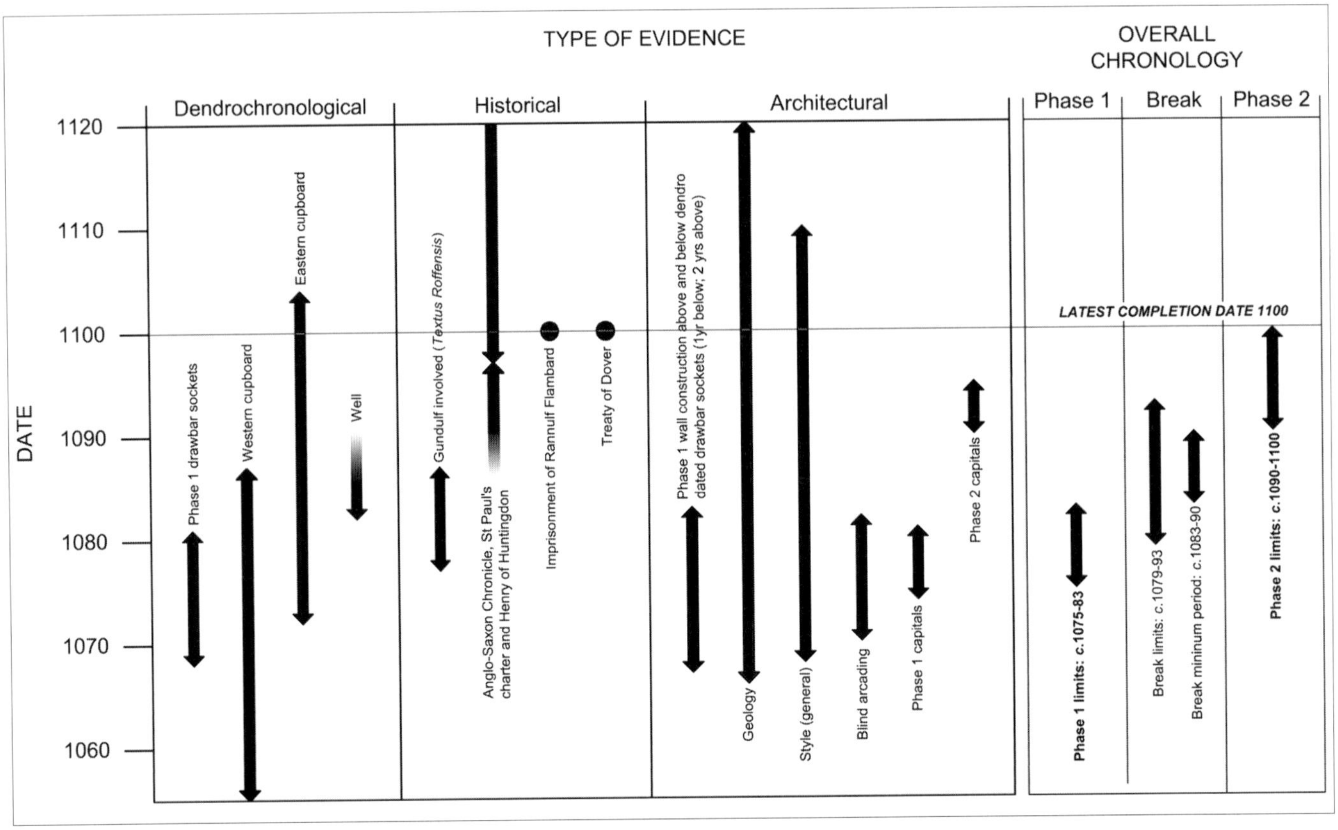


*Figure 12.9. Summary of the diverse evidence for the chronology of the primary construction of the White Tower (Diagram: Roland Harris).*

initiated the works, or that they were in progress immediately after his appointment, but simply that Gundulf was involved with the building of the White Tower sometime between becoming bishop in 1077 and the death of William I on 9 September 1087.

That the building was well under way by 1097 is clear from the *Anglo-Saxon Chronicle* entry which records that in that year many shires whose labour was due at London were hard pressed because of the wall that they built about the Tower [*túr*], and because of the bridge [i.e. London Bridge] that was nearly all carried away by a flood, and because of the work on the king's hall, that was being built at Westminster, and many a man was oppressed thereby (Whitelock 1961, p. 175).[4] Together with a charter of 1093–7 by which William II confirmed exemption of St Paul's demesne from work on the 'castle of London, the wall, the bridge and the bailey, as the writ of my father ordered' (Gibbs 1939, Charter No. 13, p. 15), these sources confirm that the castle was still under construction in the 1090s, with the implication that the White Tower itself was complete, or well advanced, by 1097 and that work on an enclosing wall was in progress.

The completion of the White Tower is also implied by the accounts in the *Anglo-Saxon Chronicle* and by Orderic Vitalis of the famous escape from the castle by William Rufus's chief minister, Rannulf Flambard, in 1101 (Whitelock 1961, p. 177; Chibnall 1975, pp. 310–2). The *Anglo-Saxon Chronicle* records the prison as the *ture on Lunden* while Orderic uses the term *arce Lundoniensi*: both almost certainly refer to the White Tower. Additionally, Orderic recounts how Rannulf organized a great feast and then, while the guards slumbered drunkenly, escaped down a rope tied to a shaft in the middle of a window. Orderic's references to the building imply that the White Tower was complete and this concurs with the more general inference that can be drawn from Rannulf's imprisonment: that the building was fit for use as a prison and for feasting. It is unlikely that a half-completed building, let alone an active building site, would have provided secure or suitable accommodation. If it is to be accepted that Rannulf was imprisoned in a great tower that was near, if not wholly, complete, then the dating of his escape at Candlemas (2 February) 1101 means that the building was finished by or in 1100: an 1101 building season would not have begun as early in the year as Candlemas. Moreover, as Rannulf Flambard was sent to the Tower by Henry I in August or early September 1100, this would imply that works were completed by that date. The condition of Henry I's treaty with Robert Curthose of 1101 that, should he break it, hostages would be imprisoned in the Tower of London (*Turri London'*) supports this, in addition to being the earliest date by which the White Tower is known to have given its name to the whole castle (Chaplais 1964, no. 1).

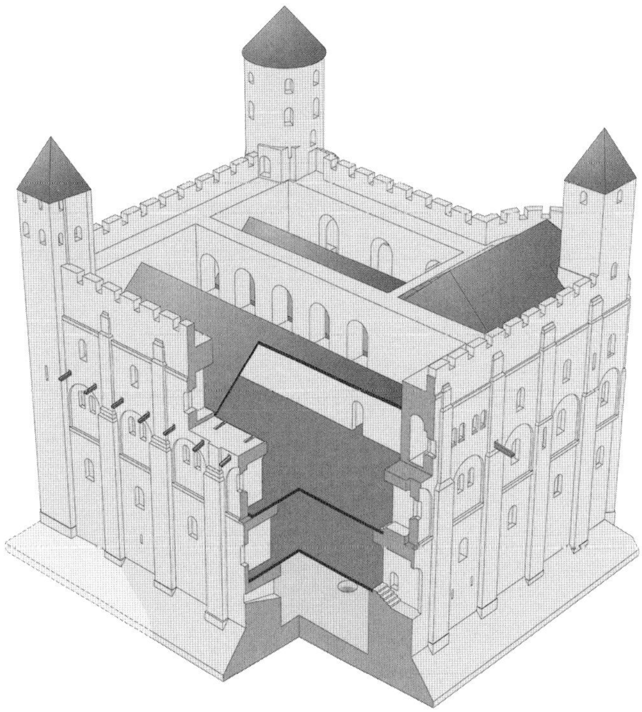

*Figure 12.10. Three-dimensional cut-away reconstruction from the south-west (Historic Royal Palaces. Drawing: Helen Jones).*

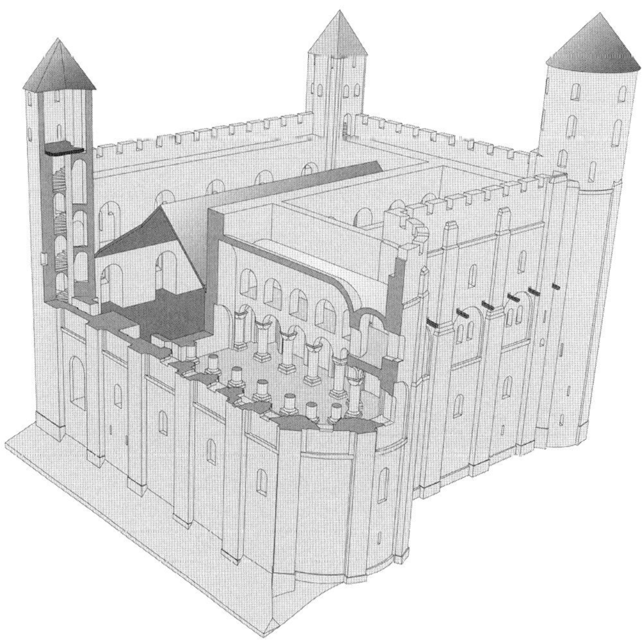

*Figure 12.11. Three-dimensional cut-away reconstruction from the south-east (Historic Royal Palaces. Drawing: Helen Jones).*

### *Architectural evidence*

The chronology indicated by the architecture of the White Tower is typically broad, reflecting the long currency of aspects of the design, workmanship and materials, especially given the simple and robust nature of many of the details. For example the overall design – a combination of a tower of double-pile construction with multiple storeys and a projecting apsidal chapel – is known from Ivry-la-Bataille in Normandy in the early 11th century, as well as from at least two other examples from northern France in the 12th century (Impey 2002, 2008a). Specific features at the White Tower that can be identified simply as symptomatic of Norman construction prior to the early to mid-12th century include the vaulting in the two rooms below the chapel, the garderobes, and mural passages; the pilaster buttresses, of which we know only the general form; the fireplaces, which have lost their hoods; the plain non-rebated doorways; the plain windows; and the spiral stairs with rubble vaults rather than structural steps.

Several other features are unusual, but no more closely datable: into this category must go the recesses in the spine wall on the entrance and first floors, and the round-headed niches in the side walls of the entrance. There are also features for which dated parallels can be found but which, it must be suspected, are insufficiently distinctive to be used as grounds for dating the White Tower: an example is the double-course of ashlar immediately above the junction of plinth and wall, which is found at the castles of Canterbury (*c.* 1100–20) and Colchester (probably 1080s), but which probably represents a more widely used feature in buildings mainly of rubble construction.

More distinctive is the use of blind arcading on the first floor of all four external elevations and the chapel apse, which finds its closest parallels in the blind arcading that encloses the gallery windows at St Etienne, Caen (begun in the early 1060s and well advanced by 1070; Figure 12.12), and at Lanfranc's Canterbury Cathedral (1071–7) where sufficient fragments survive to show that arches enclosed the clerestory and, very probably, the gallery windows. The more sophisticated architecture of the chapel of St John, however, provides the best scope for stylistic dating. Here, study of the bases, capitals, and responds of the arcade, and the side aisle abaci confirms that construction of the chapel was indeed interrupted by a significant building break (Figure 12.13). Inevitably, it is the capitals that have proved most datable, and they have been the subject of a thorough re-examination in the course of the recent investigations. A detailed analysis of the sculpture has been undertaken by

*Figure 12.12. St Etienne, Caen, south side of nave showing arcading surrounding the gallery-level windows (Photo: Roland Harris).*

*Figure 12.13. St John's chapel: view looking south-east (Photo: Roland Harris).*

John Crook (Crook 2008) and is summarized in his paper in this volume. The eight chamfered block capitals and the single free standing volute capital are best paralleled by other examples from the mid to late 1070s. This is in contrast to the remaining capitals, for which the closest parallels date from the early 1090s.

### *Dendrochonology*

The recent investigations included dendrochronology that, while inevitably concentrated on the predominant later medieval and, especially, post-medieval carpentry, included the few surviving primary timbers. Felling dates have been determined for boards lining drawbar sockets for doorways in the basement (after 1068), the main entrance (after 1050), and elsewhere on the entrance floor (two samples, one dating to after 1052 and the other, with a heartwood-sapwood boundary, giving the only precise range of the series, to 1049–81). The linings to the drawbar sockets were so constructed that they must have been placed in position as the wall around them was being built. The lintel of a first-floor cupboard in the west room produced a heartwood-sapwood boundary at 1046, giving a felling date range of 1055–87, while a counterpart from the east room produced a heartwood-sapwood boundary at 1063, giving a felling date range of 1072–1104. A dendrochronological match was achieved for one of the wooden drains at the primary eaves level on the east side, but this had no heartwood-sapwood boundary and thus the timber simply dates from after 1101: given that it came from a simple board *c.*100mm (4") wide, in contrast with the carefully channelled drains surviving in the west wall and, as discovered in 2008, elsewhere in the east wall, it must be suspected that this relates to an early repair. More securely primary is the beech template at the bottom of the well, which dated its construction to after 1082.

### *The building break and a new chronology for the building of the White Tower*

The combining of this diverse evidence for the dating of the construction of the White Tower needs to accommodate the evidence discovered during the recent investigations for a hitherto unsuspected building break. This break was first suspected during the analysis of St John's Chapel, where John Crook identified various anomalies in the construction, and where the two groups of capitals suggest quite different dates. The subsequent survey programme identified more widely distributed and clearer evidence that includes a fundamental change in the bedding mortar type from one with a very high concentration of small bivalve shells to one with little or no such shell, but with large pieces of unburnt chalk: this change was observed on the interior and exterior around sill height on the first floor. The change in mortar type that marks the building break is echoed in the geological variation of the building stones. Although successive banding of different types of ashlar is no evidence of a break in itself, the overall difference in distribution is consistent with it and it is noteworthy that the top of the band of Quarr stone marks the level of the break as indicated by the change in mortar. More tangible evidence for a building break is seen in the abrupt reduction in the use of ashlar. This is especially clear in the three spiral stairs where the ashlar lining gives way to rubble: in the case of the north-west and south-west turrets this is particularly striking as they only begin to rise from first-floor level, so that the ashlar to rubble transition is almost immediate. The reduced use of ashlar is also visible externally in the bays between the buttresses where there are ashlar quoins to the internal, or re-entrant, angles at the lower two storeys only: the additional angle order of the blind arcading of the first floor means that the break is obscured, but the second floor has no ashlar quoins. More obvious still is the change from ashlar to rubble on the faces of the three full-height corner turrets and the wide north-west buttress of the chapel apse.

While no significant modifications to the design are apparent following the building break, the changes in technique, mortar type and stone supply, and the remarkably horizontal level of the break across the whole building, suggest that the pause in construction was more than a normal seasonal break. At near-contemporary Colchester Castle a pause in construction just above the level of the existing first floor was sufficiently substantial for the building to be battlemented at this lower level and justifies doubt as to whether the putative final three-storey height of Colchester was originally intended. There is no such evidence for use of the White Tower on the completion of Phase 1, and the level of the break midway through a storey, but too high for battlements, positively suggests this was not the case. Furthermore, the fact that the first floor, with its two-storey chapel and the north-west and south-west stairs, was begun before the break reveals that the Phase 2 fabric was not in any sense an afterthought, but fully part of the original design.

The early documentary references strongly suggest that work was completed by 1100, but do not provide such a convincing *terminus post quem*. If the connection between Gundulf and the Tower is accepted, it is still not immediately clear when he was involved, or indeed whether he inherited responsibility for an existing construction project. In this light, the date range for the building of the lower part of the White Tower (Phase 1) provided by dendrochronology has particular significance, since it gives a more precise outer limit for the start of construction: 1068 minus perhaps one year to allow for the foundations, giving *c.* 1067. The dendrochronological dating of the lower part of the White Tower also provides us with the latest likely date for the building break: 1081 plus perhaps two years to allow for the 6.63m of Phase 1 walling above the highest dated drawbar socket, giving *c.* 1083. The dated lintel in the western room around the level of the break means that at the very latest Phase 1 was completed by 1087, although this would represent improbably slow construction of the walling above the entrance-floor drawbar sockets, or, even, the storage of timber prior to use. Stylistic dating provides some evidence for Phase 1 belonging to the 1070s, with the chamfered block capitals and the free-standing volute capital in the chapel having closest parallels in the mid to late 1070s. Such comparative dating of sculptural detail is more precise as a means of dating the Phase 2 capitals in St John's Chapel to the early 1090s. On reasonable structural grounds, the upper part of the White Tower must have been finished soon after, and this accords well with the latest completion date of 1100 suggested by the documentary sources. Thus ranges of *c.* 1067–83 and *c.* 1090–1100 almost certainly contained the two primary construction phases of the White Tower.

Needless to say, this does not imply that construction in Phase 1 lasted fully 17 years or that Phase 2 lasted fully 11 years. Studies agree that the rate of tower or keep construction during this period was typically 10–12ft (3.1–3.7m) per year (Renn 1960, pp. 1–2; Harvey 1950, p. 17) so it might be expected that Phase 1 lasted as little as five years. Phase 2 involved more complex architectural detail, inherently more laborious work at height, and more complex carpentry and roofing, and may be supposed to have taken a little longer. Evidence for the rapidity of progress in Phase 2 (especially the lack of ashlar) may mean that even this phase was also as short as five years. Possible corroboration of the rate of construction in Phase 2 is provided by what appear to be annual building breaks visible on the interior of the upper part of the north-east turret, which suggest 2.8m for one year. Placing an actual building campaign within the broad date limits of *c.* 1067–83 of Phase 1 is helped by the oft-quoted *Textus Roffensis*, which, thus, assumes a new significance. If Gundulf was involved in supervision of the construction of the White Tower after his appointment as bishop and before the death of William I, then Phase 1 must have been still underway at some point within the period 1077–87. As we have seen, dendrochronology provides the basis for a probable end date of *c.* 1083 for Phase 1 and thus permits the refinement of the chronological limits of Gundulf's work for the Conqueror at the White Tower to 1077–83. Furthermore, for Gundulf to be so firmly associated with the works in the time of William I, whilst Bishop of Rochester, it is fair to assume that Phase 1 extended into this period by a year or two at the very least, suggesting that Phase 1 could hardly have finished prior to, say, 1079. The shorter date limits of *c.* 1090–1100 mean that there is less uncertainty for Phase 2. On the basis of the dating of the later capitals of St John's Chapel, which must have been amongst the first work when construction resumed, any shorter period of actual construction is most likely to have started in the early 1090s, but not before *c.*1090. This accords well with those documentary references that seem to imply that the White Tower itself was complete by 1097. Therefore, while lacking the robustness of our more general chronological framework – which dictates that construction of the White Tower began no earlier than *c.* 1067, had finished by 1100, and saw a major pause in construction in at least the years between *c.* 1083 and *c.* 1090 – there are good grounds to suppose that we can achieve something very near to the actual chronology of the construction programme. Such diverse evidence as we can draw upon suggests that the somewhat extended period of primary construction at the White Tower began around 1075–9, was completed by 1100, with a break probably beginning *c.* 1079–83 (and most probably *c.* 1080) and ending *c.* 1090–3. The break, then, is unlikely to have been less than 7 years in duration and may have been as much as 14 years.

## Notes

1 A north–south wall or revetment was also exposed in the 1965 excavation, which appeared to be part of the primary construction: it is too far to the west to be identified as the surviving eastern wall prior to the addition of the apse.

2 The width measurements are minimums since the spine wall tapers (see below, p. 184).

3 The *Textus Roffensis* is a term used since the 16th century for a cartulary of Rochester Cathedral compiled in the 1120s that was bound together with another manuscript, possibly in the 13th century and certainly by the 14th century: Flight 1977, pp. 17–18.

4 The building of the wall surrounding the Tower (*turrim Londonie*) in 1097 is also mentioned by Henry of Huntingdon, writing in the 1120s (Henry of Huntingdon, ed., Greenway 1996, pp. 444–5).

## Bibliography

### Primary Sources and Documents in Print

Chaplais, P., ed. (1964) Diplomatic Documents preserved in the Public Record Office, Vol. 1 (1101–1272) (London, HMSO).

Gibbs, M., ed. (1939) *Early Charters of the Cathedral Church of St Paul, London*, Camden Society, 3rd Series, LVIII (London).

Henry of Huntingdon, *Historia Anglorum: The History of the English People*, D. E. Greenway, ed. and trans. (1996) (Oxford).

*Orderic Vitalis, Ecclesiastical History*, M. Chibnall, ed., Vol. V (1975) (Oxford).

Plummer, C. A. and Earle, J. (1892) *Two of the Saxon Chronicles parallel*, Vol. 1 (Oxford).

*Textus Roffensis*, T. Hearne, ed. (1720) (Oxford).

The National Archives (TNA), Work 31/84 and 31/86.

Whitelock, D. (1961) *The Anglo-Saxon Chronicle, a Revised Translation* (London).

### Secondary Sources

Allen Brown, R., Colvin, H. M. and Taylor, A. J. (1963) *The History of The King's Works. Vol. I: The Middle Ages* (London, HMSO).

Allen Brown, R. (1984) *The Architecture of Castles* (London, Batsford).

Armitage, E. S. (1912) *The Early Norman Castles of the British Isles* (London, J. Murray).

Crook, J. (2008) *St John's Chapel*, in E. Impey, ed., pp. 95–123.

Fernie, E. (2000) *The Architecture of Norman England* (Oxford, University Press).

Flight, C. (1977) *The Bishops and Monks of Rochester 1076–1214* (Canterbury, Kent Archaeological Society Monograph VI).

Harris, R. B. (2008) *The Structural History of the White Tower, 1066–1200*, in E. Impey, ed., pp. 29–93.

Harvey, J. (1950) *The Gothic World 1100–1600* (London, Batsford).

Impey, E. (2002) 'The Turris Famosa at Ivry-la-Bataille, Normandy', in G. Meirion-Jones, E. Impey and M. Jones, ed., *The Seigneurial Residence in Western Europe, AD* c. *800–1600*, British Archaeological Reports International Series 1088, pp. 189–203 (Oxford).

Impey, E. (2008a) *The Ancestry of the White Tower*, in E. Impey, ed., pp. 227–41.

Impey, E., ed. (2008b) *The White Tower* (New Haven and London, Yale University Press).

Keay, A. and Harris, R. B. (2008) *The White Tower, 1855–2000*, in E. Impey, ed., pp. 209–24.

Mesqui, J. (1998) 'La Tour Maîtresse du donjon de Loches', *Bulletin Monumental* 156, pp. 65 125.

Parnell, G., Butcher, S. A., Cameron, F. J., Curnow, P. E. and Gilyard-Beer, R. (1982) 'The excavation of the Roman city wall at the Tower of London and Tower Hill, 1954–76', *Transactions of the London and Middlesex Archaeological Society* 33, pp. 85–133.

Parnell, G. (1993) *The Tower of London* (London, English Heritage).

Parnell, G. (1998) 'The White Tower, The Tower of London', *Country Life* (9 July 1998), pp. 86–9.

Renn, D. F. (1960) 'The Anglo-Norman keep 1066–1138', *Journal of the British Archaeological Association* 23, pp. 1–23.

# 13

# Castle heritage (10th–13th centuries) in Lower Normandy and the current state of archaeological research

*François Fichet de Clairfontaine*


## Résumé

*Avec près de 800 sites fortifiés recensés dans la 'carte archéologique', la Basse Normandie semble bien être terre de 'castels'. Au delà des problèmes posés par la nature exacte de ces ensembles et de leur état originel, ce riche inventaire offre une image complexe et variée, voire difficile à classer, d'un phénomène architectural et d'un patrimoine qui constituent l'un des traits originaux de la région. Il associe de puissants châteaux de pierre, châteaux princiers ou de la grande aristocratie normande, à des fortifications de terre et de bois parfois à l'origine d'autres ensembles fortifiés, des enceintes urbaines ou monastiques, des maisons fortes devenues souvent des manoirs de plaisance quand ces derniers ne les ont pas imitées, et enfin, bien que très anecdotiques dans notre propos, des jardins et des églises fortifiés. La fortification médiévale en Basse-Normandie, parce qu'elle fut en constante évolution, offre un potentiel scientifique, historique et architectural de grande valeur que démontrent les fouilles et études archéologiques conduites récemment à Caen, Bretoncelles, Falaise et Chambois.*


Since the beginning of the 19th century there has been a regular series of inventories and studies of medieval earthworks and stone castles in Lower Normandy, through the work of scholars including de Gerville (1825–30), de Caumont (1846–67) and R. Doranlo (1914) (Figure 13.1). This programme of study was developed further during the 1950s under the aegis of Professor Michel de Boüard and the medieval archaeological research centre he created (now CRAHAM – UMR 6273 CNRS/UCBN) located at the University of Caen. The work of M. Fixot, M Daliphard, F. Delacampagne, J. Decaëns, Ch. Pilet, M. Fixot (1968), M. Daliphard (1980), F. Delacampagne (1982), J. Decaëns (1998), Ph. Siguret (1960), J. Yver (1955–8), I. Chave (2003), G. Louise (1984), to mention only the principal contributors, together with recent studies of texts related to archaeological data, have created a corpus of over 800 fortified sites of the 10th–12th centuries. This number is impressive, suggesting the existence of a fortified site every 25km$^2$. It will be shown here that this ratio was much higher in reality.

The study of Normandy's castle heritage poses questions to the archaeologist and historian alike. Our understanding of these recorded sites remains fragmentary and incomplete, despite the numerous studies. The state of preservation of the sites varies significantly among the different classes of monument. Also, in the past, attention was mainly focused on their physical appearance.

## A complex and varied castle heritage

### *What is the reality behind the inventories?*

Almost 800 sites have been identified, mostly dating from the 10th–13th centuries. Undoubtedly the list is not exhaustive. It does not include many sites of the Perche, Cotentin and Pays d'Auge regions, where we lack precise knowledge of their origins, particularly in relation to their possible defensive roles. It is more often the noble, residential houses and fortified mansions, like Aunou-le-Faucon (Chave 2003, pp. 230–1), or fortified houses such as Rubercy (Calvados), erected towards the middle of the 12th century (Lorren 1977), that they are classified as *fort, forteresses* or *chastel.* Some houses have been classified as *domus fortis* but as they fall between the castle and the non fortified residence in structural terms, this definition remains hypothetical. For the Perche region, a defensive function is undeniable for houses such as the Ventrouze (Orne), which were developed within a ringwork and accessed by a gatehouse. The example of Aunou-le-Faucon (Orne), dated to *c.* 1350, was probably built within a primitive ringwork.

There is often insufficient evidence to conclusively link a monument to the medieval period or to prove a military usage. We must remain cautious when considering the significance of a fragment of a rampart or a half-filled moat, which may be features of ostentatious architecture of a much later origin, suggesting a fortress but in fact representing a show of status by a much later noble family. Other examples may just be follies, such as that within the historic moat behind the castle of Masle (Orne), where a mound was created during the early 19th century for recreational purposes. Also, a number of mounds that have been called *mottes* can turn out to be remnants of warrens, mills, moated platforms or ice houses.

Other sites surveyed in forest areas (such as around Tourouvre in the Perche area, Orne) or in the marshes of Cotentin (Manche) or Bessin and Dives (Calvados)[1] remain enigmatic due to lack of archaeological fieldwork and because vegetation often limits full study. Aerial surveys covering marshy areas have also produced anomalies. In many cases fortified houses, such as Rubercy and Ruppaley, discovered along the marshes of Isigny-sur-Mer (Calvados) (Figure 13.2) or Boutemont in Taillebois (Orne), are in the form of small quadrangular mounds, which are sometimes referred to as *motte* and surrounded by a moat (Litoux and Carré 2008, 81). To this group, which are also called *moated sites*, can be added the Herbage in Thibaut Angerville (Daliphard 1980, p. 186) where field walking has provided artefacts dating to the 13th and 14th centuries. This was previously considered a castle motte. Last but not least, the inventory includes a particular type of fortification known as the *urban enclosure*. These sites are often overlooked (for example in the cases of Caen and Falaise). They are seldom studied[2] and surviving evidence may be restricted to a few short stretches of rampart. Urban enclosures comprise the association of a village or town and its

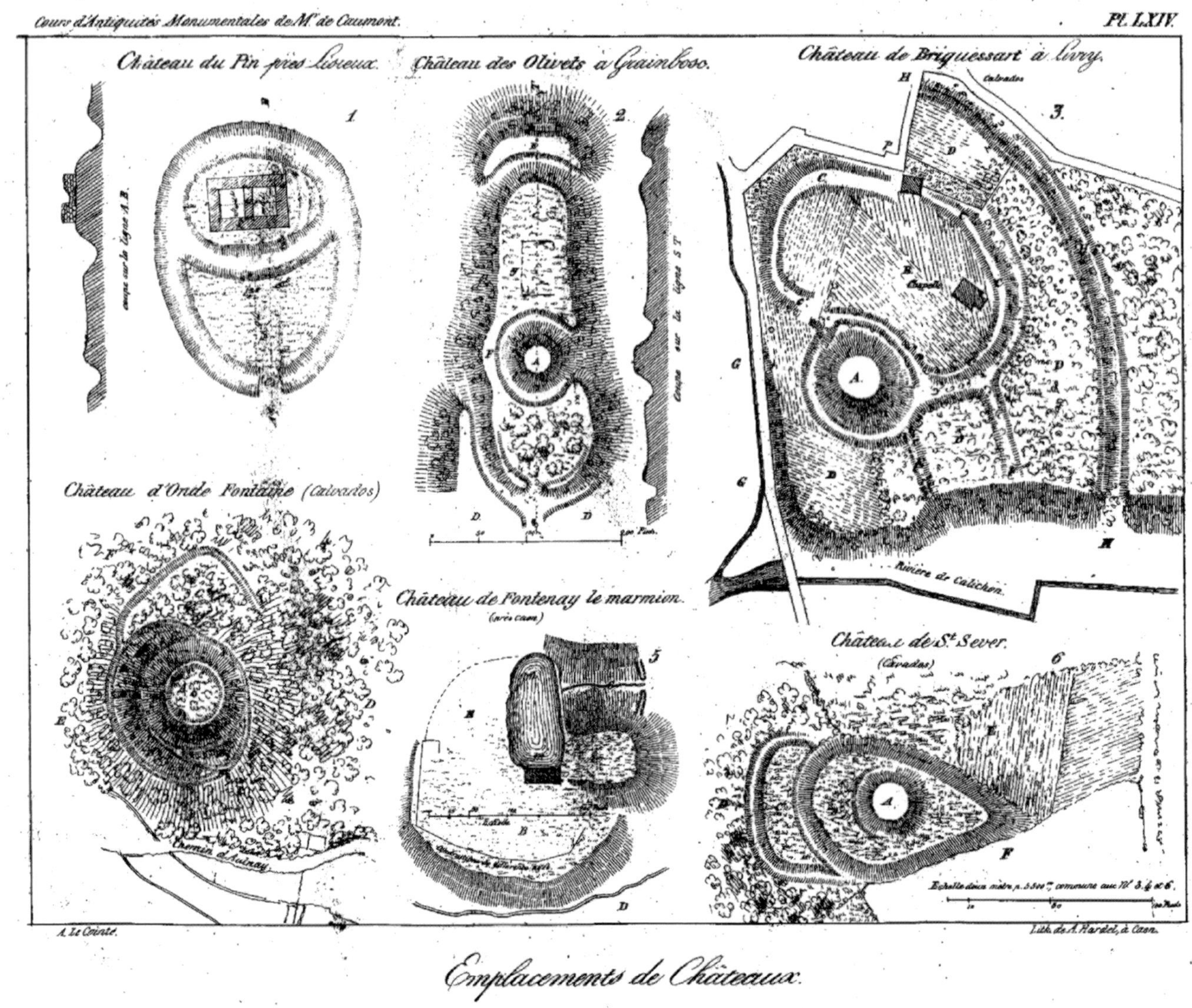


*Figure 13.1. Castle mottes and ringworks in Calvados from 'Les cours d'antiquités monumentales de M de Caumont', pl. lxiv, 5ème partie, Paris 1835.*

*Figure 13.2. Ruppaley in Isigny-sur Mer (Calvados): a moated site? (photo: G. Hulin).*

castle and they form a large group. They can be seen as both symbolic and protection for the *ville forte*, *ville close* or *ville fermée* (as Argentan is described at the end of the 14th century). Some were of early origin, such as at Cherbourg and Bayeux. Others were created during the 12th century. With the emergence of urban spaces, these town walls have undergone significant changes since the second half of the 14th century, particularly in the context of the conflict between the crowns of France and England. Most cities of any size in Normandy feature a fortified enclosure, which was modified or completed at the end of the medieval period.

So, the 800 listed sites reflect the developing state of our knowledge but, although they provide a useful distribution map of castles, the situation is far more complex than has been assumed. Among the 800 sites 195 entries are identified as *fortified buildings*, but there are only 28 mentions of fortified houses3, the number of which was nevertheless significant in the second half of the 12th century and throughout the late medieval period.

## Earthworks castles: ringworks and mottes

Earthworks account for a strong majority of the entries, with nearly 424 sites identified. Ringworks represent a very small proportion, with only 57 (Figure 13.3). It is often assumed that the ringwork was constructed prior to the castle motte (Colloque Caen 1981). The examples of Mirville (Seine-Maritime) and Sébécourt (Eure) (Colloque Caen 1981, pp. 48 and 59) are often cited as examples. The creation of early ringworks is also observed in Plessis Grimoult and in Blay (Calvados) where the recent excavation of the castle site suggests that this Carolingian court (of the 9th–10th centuries) was replaced towards the end of the 10th century by a ringwork, bounded by a substantial ditch, with the backfill used to create a motte (Delahaye 2008). We can include several fortifications that were occupied later such as at Chapelle Colbert (Decaëns 1968, pp. 131–51), Saint-Gatien (13th–14th centuries), the Audrieu ringwork (12th–14th centuries) and Saint-Vaast-sur-Seulles, which was besieged by the English troops in 1356 (Decaëns 1999b).

In Normandy we note the presence of very large ringworks, some of which seem to have been created or reused during the medieval period. They include the Bierre Camp in Merri (Calvados), which is a reoccupied fortified Iron Age site, where the ramparts were consolidated and restored by the 10th century. This site might be related to that of Mont Castre in Montebourg (Manche), although we have no chronological evidence to confirm this. In both cases, the sites may have become a refuge, occupied or redeveloped during the Viking invasions. The Iron Age camp at Péran (Côtes d'Armor), occupied during the 10th century, is also worth noting. Elsewhere, it is likely that Exmes (Orne) and Saint-Lô (Manche) were built on Iron

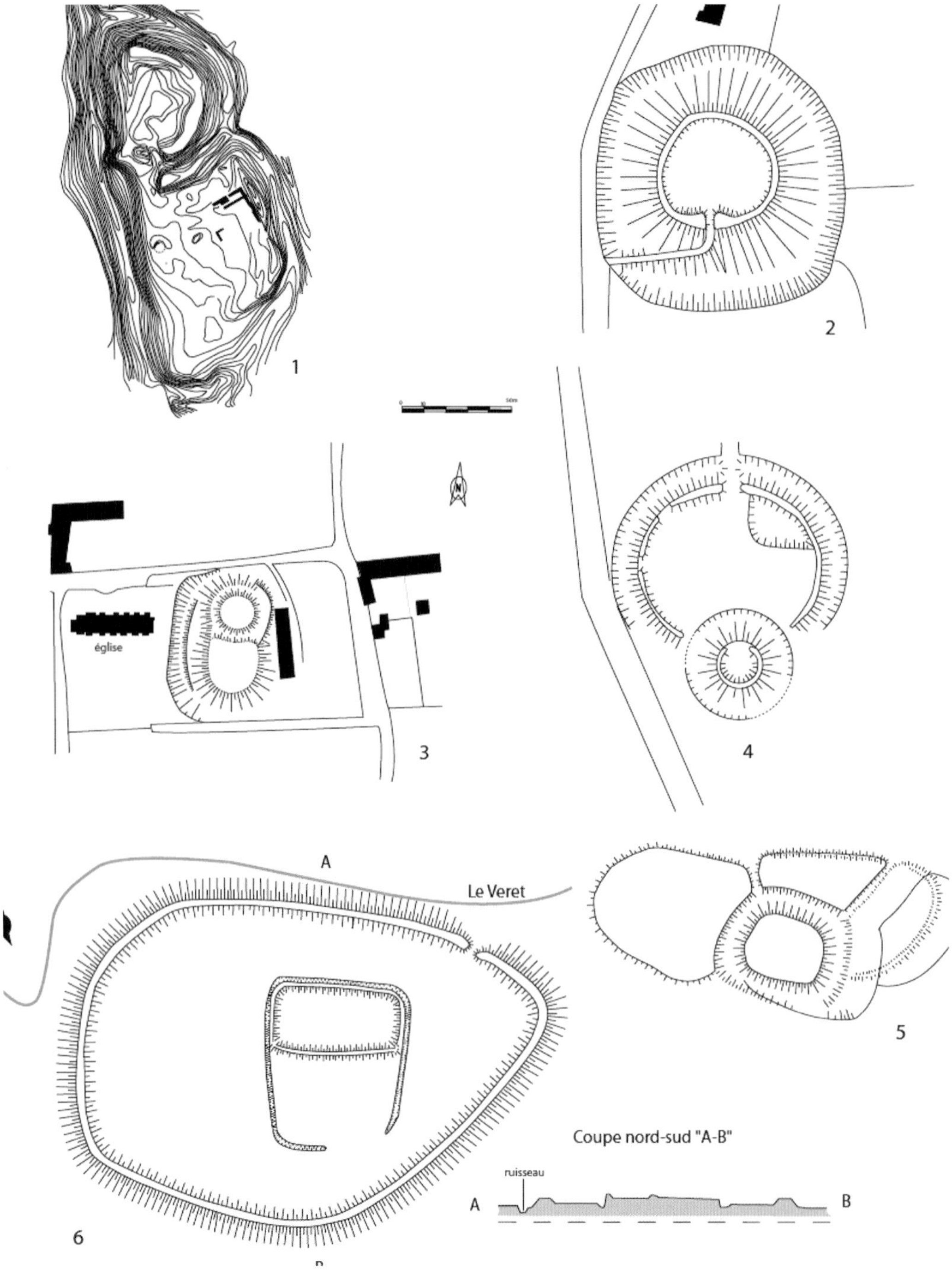


*Figure 13.3. Enclosures: 1) Saint-Vaast-sur-Seulles (Calvados) and 2) Saint-Germain-de-Montgommery (Manche); castle mottes: 3) Curcy-sur-Orne (Calvados) and 4) Silly-en-Gouffern (Orne); Moated sites or fortified houses: 4) Cricqueville-en-Bessin (Calvados) and 5) Angerville. Information from the land registry and orthomap except Saint-Vaast-sur-Seulles (SRA F. Fichet de Clairfontaine).*

Age fortified sites. These became the temporary seats of bishoprics in the 6th century during periods of instability, and then became fortified enclosures in the early medieval period. In relation to Saint-Lô, the history of Saint-Vaast mentions the siege that the castle underwent in 889 (Yver 1955–8, p. 35). Other castle sites comprised large enclosures, whose defenses were strengthened at an early date by the introduction of the use of stone, during the end of the 10th or 11th century at the latest. It seems that the castles of Caen and Falaise initially belonged to the category of large enclosures, which occupied a high topographic position on a plateau or spur.

A second group consists of ringworks of medium size (of between 50m and 100m in diameter). They are represented by Plessis-Grimoult, Blay, Lingèvres, Audrieu, Château- Ganne in La Pommeraye (Calvados), la Couillardière in Ranes (Orne), the 'Vieux Bourg' in Buais, Brix which is mentioned in the dowry of Adele in 1027 and La Fière at Sainte-Maire-Eglise (Manche). These are often located at the edge of a plateau as in Saint-Germain Montgomery (Manche), on promontories (Château-Ganne in La Pommeraye), earthworks at the end of spurs such as at Montanel (Manche), or alongside a river in a low valley (Sainte-Mère-Eglise with the Merderet). If an enclosure is at the same altitude as the surrounding land, the interior was often elevated significantly, as at the *Vieux Château* in Audrieu (Renoux 1972), Villers-Canivet (Calvados), *le Castel* in Blay or at the ringwork of Saint-Germain Montgomery (Figure 13.3). This internal 'emmotement' may explain the confusion or uncertainty that led some authors to attribute a particular group of enclosures to the category of mottes. A third category of sites must be distinguished here and then put to one side. It is that of the small enclosure, with an average diameter of 30m, surrounded by a low rampart and a smaller ditch. The examples of Urville and Bretteville-sur-Laize (Decaëns 1968) (Calvados), which were studied by J. Decaëns, are worth mentioning. He considered that these small farms have an almost non-existent military character.

The castle motte, as shown on the Bayeux Tapestry, is particularly well represented in Normandy (Figure 13.4). These sites are identified almost everywhere, whether on the plains, in areas of woodland, or on river terraces near crossing points. Various studies and surveys led Decaëns to suggest that the number of castle mottes could exceed 1000 (Decaëns 1997, p. 273). He showed that these fortifications could belong to great families such as that of Belleme.[4] They were situated to protect borders along communication routes (Buré in Orne, Angoville) or to control river crossings, sometimes alongside clearings or at the edge of marshes (Le Plessis Lastelle in Manche) or forests (Silly-en-Gouffern and Tourouvre in Orne, Saint-Martin de Sallen in Calvados). They were instruments of power, ensuring control over land expansion. Overall, there is a high density of mottes in the Calvados (Figures 13.5

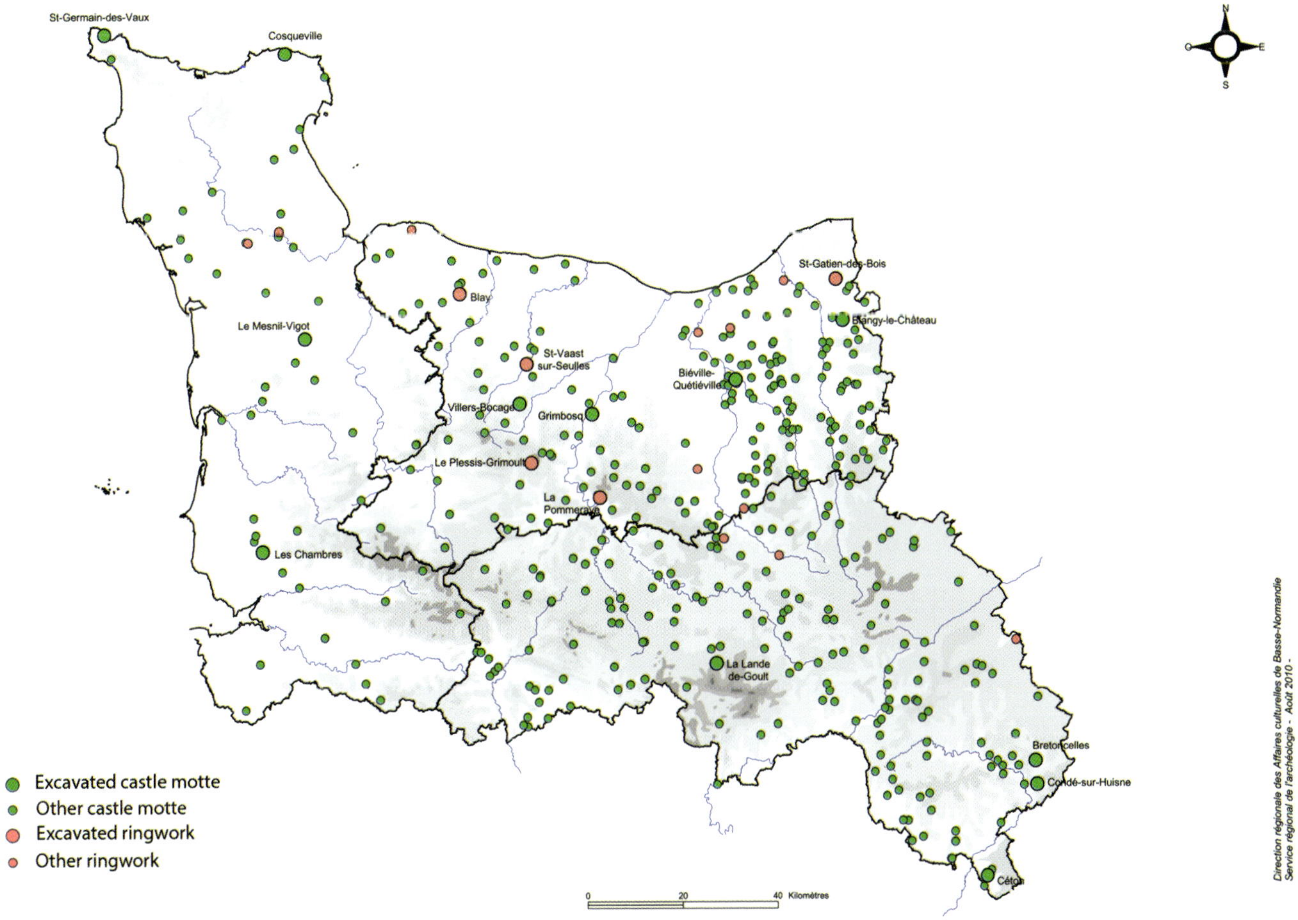


*Figure 13.4. Distribution map of castle mottes in Lower Normandy (SRA Caen).*

and 13.6) and Orne departments, especially in the bocage area, but less in the Manche department where the ducal power had probably asserted its control more firmly. If some mottes are now in isolated locations, several are to be found in the heart of towns or villages, as at Bonsmoulins and Sept-Forges in Orne, Saint-Honorine la Guillaume, Blangy-le-Chateau in Calvados, Bricquebec in Manche. We may consider that the keep is later than the motte, as in Argentan where the shell-keep formed a ring wall surrounding the mound (Chave *et al.* 2008, p. 138). One of the most iconic examples is represented by the castle mound of Saint-Pierre at Sees, which dominates the heart of the city of Saint-Pierre, of Merovingian origin. This great motte created by the family of Belleme in the 11th century, probably led to the development of the *Bourg neuf* or *Bourg le Comte* which faced the Episcopal city of Sées.

*Figure 13.5. Saint Germain du Pert (Calvados): castle motte (photo: G. Hulin).*

*Figure 13.6. Saint-Désir de Lisieux (Calvados): castle motte (photo: Ch. Maneuvrier).*

Site plans indicate a variety of forms, mainly involving a mound with one or two baileys and often reflecting an adaptation of the fortress relating to topographical conditions, as at Saint-Ceneri-le-Gerei (Orne) or Aunay-sur-Odon (Calvados). Some mottes do not seem associated with a bailey (some enclose a courtyard, as at Tourouvre and Bellou-sur-Huisne, Orne)._However, the baileys could have been defined by means other than an earthen rampart. Elsewhere, subsequent agricultural practices or development may have truncated remains (Saint-Denis-sur-Huisne, Orne and Angoville, Manche). Some sites may combine several mounds, like the exceptional *buttes* in Buré (Orne). This fortification (Hanachi 2006, pp. 69–75), on the summit of a natural hill, contains no less than four aligned mounds, separated from each other by ditches. Recent excavations at Bretoncelles (Orne) revealed the form and nature of the buildings occupying the bailey and on the top of the mound, which were lined with stone. In some cases, the pointed form of the mound does not suggest anything other than the existence of a small watchtower; at least a lightweight construction. In other cases, we note the development of the upper part of the mound, which can be greatly expanded like in Aunay-sur-Odon (where the platform is around 50m), or at Curcy-sur-Orne (Calvados) where masonry remains were mentioned in the 19th century (Hanachi 2005, pp. 25–32). At Blangy-le-Château, the motte seems to have been raised in the 12th century to host a quadrangular tower, which had two levels (Delahaye 2006). The castle of Pin (Calvados), near Lisieux, had a similar development. Its tower has a very similar form to quadrangular keeps.

### *Princely or aristocratic strongholds (Figure 13.7)*

Lower-Normandy has a relatively high number of imposing fortresses wrongly called *castles* which are characterised by strong stone curtain walls flanked by towers and sometimes dominated by a main keep. Some of these sites result from the transformation of castle mottes (Argentan and Briquebec), or large ringworks. The castle distribution map projects a fairly dense pattern of fortified sites, but a different picture emerges when chronological phases are distinguished, indicating the evolution of their strategic importance, the movement of borders during periods of conflict and the level of control of ducal power. The original morphology of many castles still eludes us, as at Hambye (Manche) which was destroyed around 1832. And what would we know about Gavray[5] (Manche), the 'most beautiful castle of Normandy' (according to Froissart), without the contribution of archaeology?
fig 13.7 and 13.8

Lower Normandy offers a huge variety of stone fortresses,[6] which reflect complex and varied power struggles. They combine fortresses which are as dissimilar

*Figure 13.7. Distribution map of medieval strongholds in Lower Normandy (SRA Caen).*

as the castles of Caen, and Courcy (Calvados), the latter consisting of an enclosure flanked by nine cylindrical towers (late 12th century), Briquebec or Chambois (Orne) (Figure 13.8). Several categories can be distinguished. First are the princely castles of the late 10th and early 11th centuries belonging to the phase of creation and consolidation of the Norman ducal territory. These are the great ducal castles of Caen, a large enclosure defined (possibly from the beginning) by a rampart of stone resting on a stony slope, and Falaise, created on a rocky spur, provided with a stone wall and originally devoid of towers. Ongoing studies suggest that Falaise was built at the end of the 10th century, at the earliest. Related sites are Bonneville-sur-Touques (Calvados), Valognes, Cherbourg, Bayeux and Exmes. Several castles were created to protect the borders of the duchy, before being falling into the hands of powerful families. That was probably the case for Alençon, Domfront, Argentan, Coutances, Avranches or Bellême, where almost nothing remains of the two later fortresses which were built towards the end of the10th or during the first third of the 11th century.

Other castles were built with or without ducal permission. Essay (Orne) was probably built between 1005 and 1035, and referred to as *fortissimum castellum* in 1088 (Chave 2003, 214). The crises experienced during the 12th century led to the strengthening of certain fortresses, whilst others were destroyed. At the beginning of the 12th century this almost uninterrupted period of structural work is characterised by the development of keeps. Quadrangular Anglo-Norman buildings were erected at Caen, Domfront, Vire, Pin, Falaise, Alençon, Avranches, Blangy-le-Château, Saint-Sauveur-le-Vicomte, and probably also at Bellême and Gavray,

*Fig. 13.8. View of the walls and mural towers of Courcy (Calvados), end of 12th century (photo: J. Turquety, STAP, Calvados).*

where a massive tower of square plan is placed against the rampart with irregular flanking. In the second half of the 12th century, ramparts were strengthened (including towers and crenellations at Caen and Falaise) and there was the development of the first gatehouse tower at Falaise. It was also during this period that Courcy Castle (Calvados) was provided with a keep flanked by round towers with slope-shaped bases.

Quadrangular keeps were also built at Bonneville-sur-Touques, Falaise (with the *little keep* in 1180) and Chambois (Orne), which is the best preserved of all the Anglo-Norman main keeps (Figure 13.9) (Decaëns 1997). It is perhaps at this point that we can place the construction of the first floor level of the polygonal keep of Briquebec (Roulley 2007, pp. 166–92) (Figure 13.10). This feature, of the Plantagenet period, can be found both at the entrance gate of the high bailey of Falaise Castle and at the keep at Argentan. Current research suggests the importance of building work conducted by the Plantagenets, whose architectural 'trademark' seems more prevalent today than that of Philip Augustus. The first decades of the 13th century saw the transformation of fortified sites, with the introduction of the large circular tower keep at Tournebu (Calvados) and Falaise (Talbot tower), and by the building of large, more massive flanking towers, enforcing the protection of donjons, and with the construction of the stone fortified shirt of Caen.

It has been suggested that, from the 14th century onwards, the large rectangular keep was reintroduced at sites including Regnéville-sur-Mer, La Haye-du Puits, Hambye (Manche), Creully (Calvados), Ranes and perhaps at Carrouges (Orne). At Hambye, a 19th-century engraving shows a large compact tower with flat buttresses (MSAN 1825). It is also considered that the main keep of Saint-

*Figure 13.9. Anglo-Norman keep of Chambois: Orne (photo: F. Fichet de Clairfontaine).*

*Fig. 13.10. The polygonal main keep of Bricquebec: Manche (Photo: F. Fichet de Clairfontaine).*

*Fig. 13.11. Main keep of Saint-Sauveur-le-Vicomte (Manche): possibly late Middle Ages or 12th century (Photo: F. Fichet de Clairfontaine).*

Sauveur-le-Vicomte was built at this time (Figure 13.11). Architectural features at the keeps of Hambye and Saint-Sauveur suggest that they were built in the 12th century, before being modified during the late medieval period (as is the case at Chambois which is adorned with turrets of that date, as at Alençon). The same sequence probably occurred with the first Bricquebec keep; a low massive tower which was raised in the course of the 14th century. The later reintroduction of quadrangular towers remains an outstanding question, in which the dating of the original mortars of these buildings may help.

### *Urban and religious enclosures (Figure 13.12)*

There are 22 early urban or religious enclosures listed in Lower Normandy. These sites provide a rich overview of military architecture from the 12th to the early 16th century. Generally speaking, most large or medium sized towns in Normandy have partially preserved ramparts, but their current form derives from building work dating to the late medieval period (usually to the Hundred Years' War or just after). What was the extent of the Norman origin of these enclosures? These fortified sites are mostly urban (Caen, Lisieux, Falaise, Argentan, Domfront, Sees, Avranches, Coutances, Cherbourg, Alençon, Mortagne au Perche and Bayeux). There are also religious enclosures, including the Caen abbeys, the abbey of Saint-Martin at Sées. Later examples (of the 14th–15th centuries) include the fort at Saint-Gervais in Sées, Lisieux and insular enclosures, such as Tombelaine.

Some village enclosures have limited defenses remaining (including Saint-Pierre-de-Semilly, Manche). An unusual example is the village of Mont-Saint-Michel, the importance of which is linked to the abbey dominating the site.

Several towns of Gallo-Roman origin have a rampart dating to the 3rd century, or to the beginning of late antiquity. For example, Cherbourg, Bayeux and Lisieux were provided with no additional protection until the end of the late medieval period. There are no indications of such defenses for the Gallo-Roman towns of Avranches and Sees. With the emergence of towns, it may be that new ramparts were built in the 12th century, or shortly before, at Rouen, and perhaps even earlier in Argentan (Chave *et al.* 2008). We can attribute the first rampart of the village of Mont-Saint-Michel to the 13th century, even if earlier stone or wooden fortifications probably existed under Jean Lackland, at least shortly before 1204 (Fichet de Clairfontaine 1999). The medieval town of Caen was also surrounded by a wall during this period (Neveux 1997), as was probably Falaise (Figure 13.13), Bellême, and certainly Argentan. It may be that the first line of fortifications often took the form of a palisaded enclosure which was possibly preceded by ditches that have left no visible traces. The 14th and 15th centuries were a period when cities needed protection. Building work was carried out on their walls, as at Domfront (late 13th and early 14th century), and Cherbourg (Plaisse 1999), reflecting the establishment of a true policy. The ramparts of Caen were restructured and strengthened in 1356, and it was after the British occupation in 1435 that the barbicans defending the Saint-Pierre and the Fields gates were built. The main enclosure at the walled town of Argentan saw major works during the years 1370–1410 (Chave 2003, pp. 88–96) (Figure 13.15).

### *Fortified houses (Figures 13.3 and 13.14)*

This survey would not be complete without dealing with the issue of the fortified house which, with so many variations, cannot be classified under a single and somewhat vague term. There are 219 entries within this group, which are also sometimes called *strong houses*. It can be extremely difficult to distinguish between castles and fortified houses. The castle named Tarennière in Préaux-du-Perche (Orne) with its high walls and towers, must be mentioned in this respect, as well as Bonvouloirs in Juvigny-on-Andaine (Orne) with a very strange, 26m high guard tower.

There is an even finer division between fortified houses and mansions. There are a very large number of manors renovated from the 15th century, which preserve or contain elements borrowed from 12th- or 13th-century military

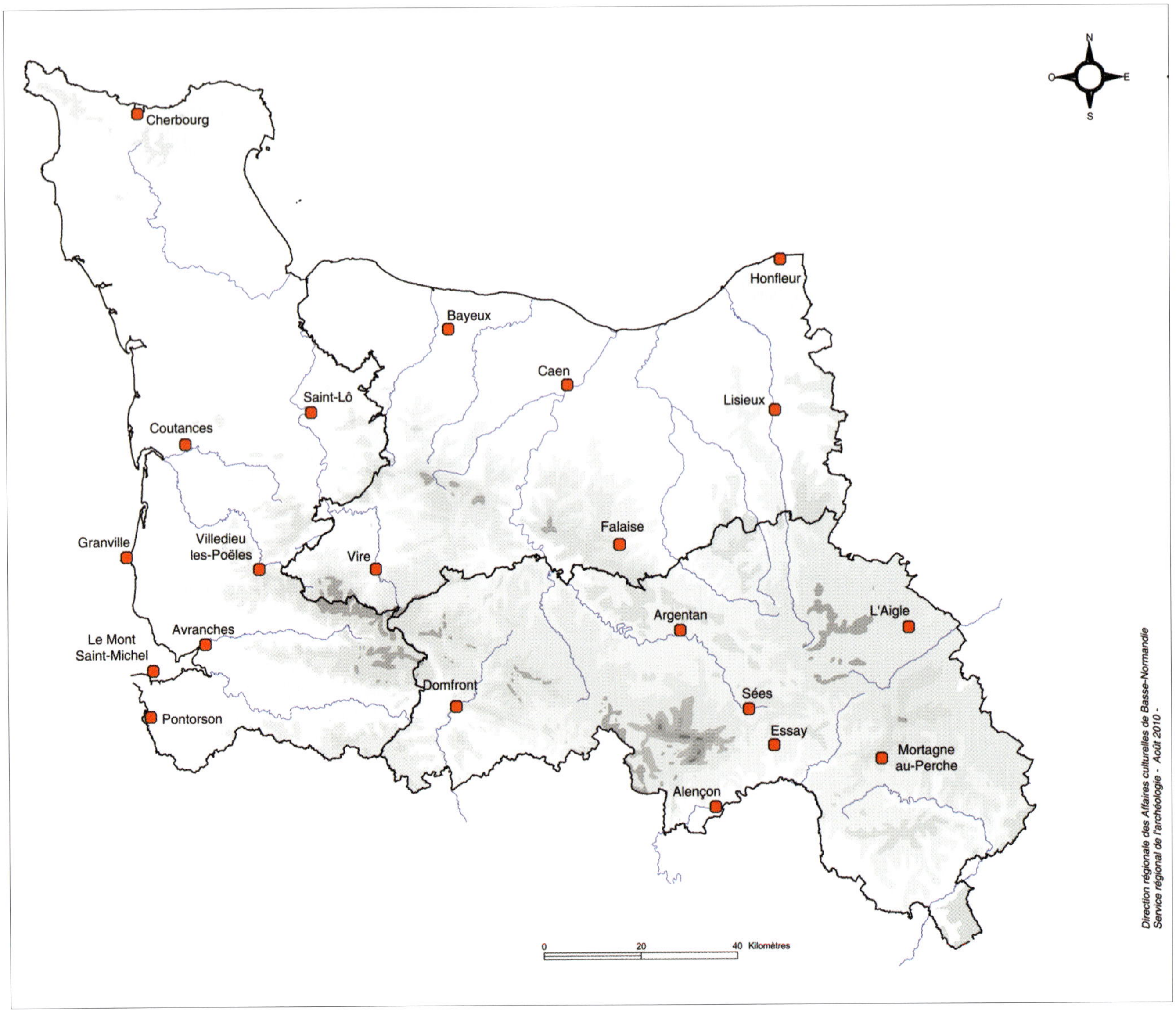


*Fig. 13.12. Urban and religious enclosures in Lower Normandy (SRA Caen).*

*Fig. 13.13. Urban enclosure in Falaise, Calvados (Photo: F. Fichet de Clairfontaine).*

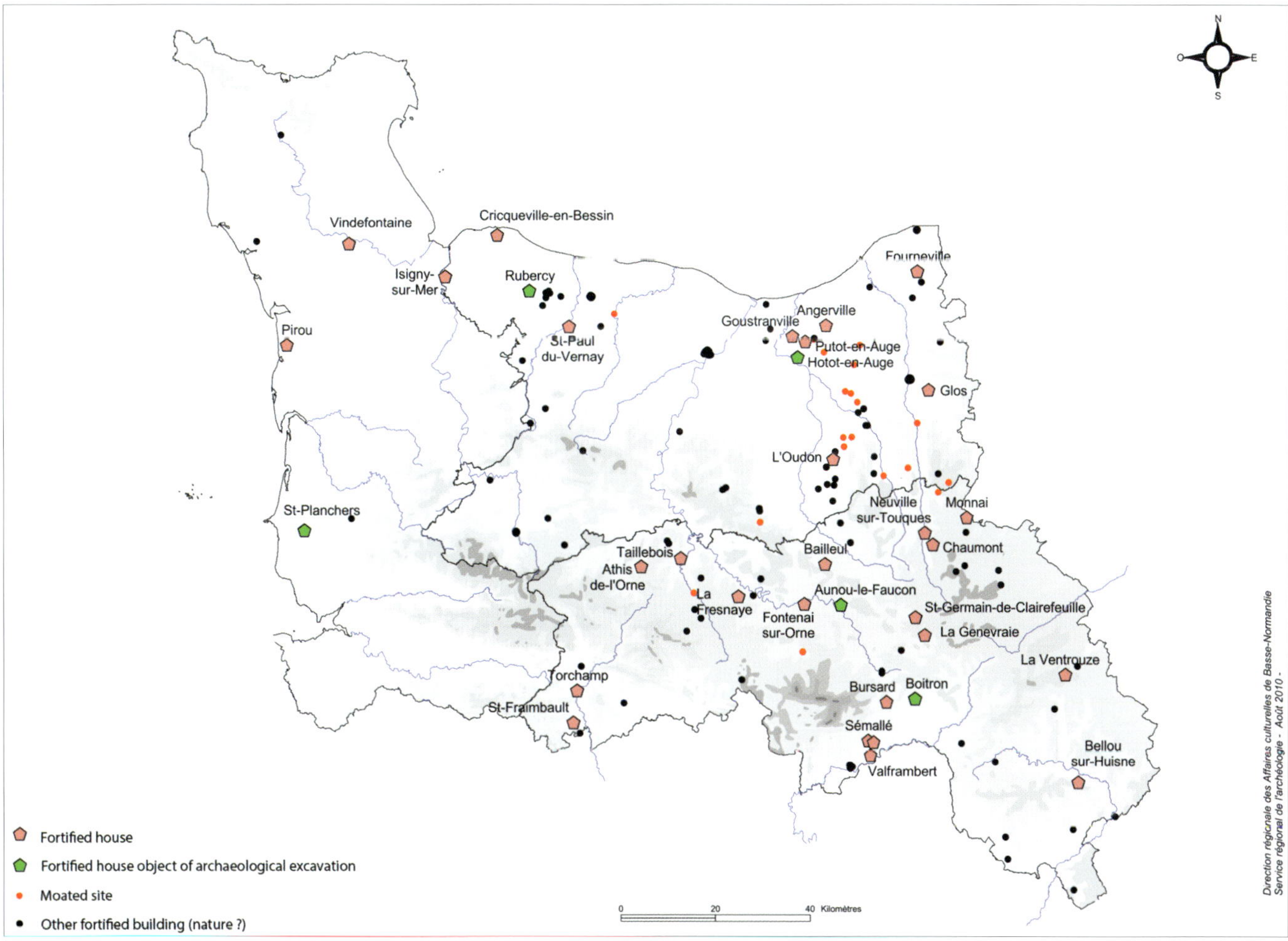


*Fig. 13.14. Distribution map of fortified houses in Lower Normandy (SRA Caen).*

style, sometimes substantially altered by recent restorations. In the words of J-M. Pesez 'changeante dans ses structures, d'une province à l'autre, diverse aussi dans ses dimensions, traversée par la hiérarchie des pouvoirs' (Pesez 1986).

The fourth group of fortified houses includes *moated sites*, of which Rubercy Castle, excavated in 1977, is the prominent example. These sites were often built in a square-shaped piece of ground, at the bottom of a valley, near floodplains or alongside a river. They were constructed with a low mound and defended by a large ditch. Examples include Ruppaley in Isigny sur Mer, Boutemont in Taillebois (Orne), Goustranville, Ham in Hotot-en-Auge (Calvados), (Carpentier 2008) and Herbage-Thibaut in Angerville (Calvados) which is unique in having two baileys. Another example is the site of Jumilli at Torchamp (Orne) established in a meander of the Varenne (Hanachi 2006, pp. 120–5). The *old Castel* in Cricqueville en Bessin (Calvados) was mentioned in the investigation about the fortresses of the Bailiwick of Caen. The recently discovered 'Les Fresneau', situated on the edge of the Orne in Fontenai-sur-Orne, is a 12th-century moated site, morphologically very close to a ringwork (Carpentier 2010). Castle Pirou (Manche) was built in a harbour on a small rocky island. This fortress, built in the late 12th century, was originally located within an enclosure protected by three concentric ditches. The austere and compact construction consists of a huge rampart defended by a circular crenellated parapet, dominated by polygonal turrets (Figure 13.15). The entrance is defended by a square tower with a drawbridge. Its defensive system has no equivalent. Despite its military style architecture, Castle Pirou would not actually have been able to resist a long siege. This site is an early example of a fortified house, characterised somewhere between a castle and a fortified house.

## The current state of research

Castle heritage has been and still is a topic of active and ongoing archaeological study in Normandy. While Caen Castle was the focus of modern medieval archaeology in the early 1950s, research has since then mainly focused on earthwork fortifications. An ambitious programme considers issues including their role in relation to seigniorial policy. Ringworks and castle mottes have been investigated at Audrieu (1971),[7] Grimbosq (1975), Le Plesssis-Grimoult (1971), Les Chambres (1978), Saint-Vaast-sur-Seulles (1979–86), Biéville-Quietteville (1980), Villers-Bocage (1989), Ceton (1993), Rivray in Condé-sur-Huisne (1989–91), Bretoncelles (1992–2001), Blay (2006), Blangy-le-Château (2006 ) and Chateau Ganne at La Pommeraye (since 2004). After a particularly active period, escalating in the early 1970s, research reached its climax in 1980 with the Caen Conference 'Earthen Fortifications in Western Europe from the 10th to 12th centuries' (Colloque Caen 1981). It then stalled until the early 1990s, when it was re-launched through important studies on Condé-sur-Huisne, Bretoncelles (Orne) and La Pommeraye.

Fortified houses have also been the subject of research, at such places as Rubercy (1970–7), Aunou-le-Faucon (2000), Boitron (1997), L'Oiselière in Saint-Planchers (2000), Ham in Hotot-en-Auge (1983–4) and more recently at Les Fresneaux in Fontenai-sur-Orne (2007–8).

Research into large fortresses is certainly less active but this area remains pertinent. Highlight excavations include the polygonal main keep of Argentan (1999–2000), surveys and standing building studies of Saint-Sauveur-le-Vicomte (2002–4), Regnéville-sur-Mer (1991–4) and Alençon (1990). There have also been larger excavations at Gavray (1985–9), Domfront (mainly on the priory church of Saint-Symphorien) (1990–2), Falaise (1985–11) and Caen (2005–12). Overall, 117 interventions (including surveys, excavations and standing building studies) were authorised from the early 1970s until today, averaging nearly three operations per year. The statistics show a diversification of research since the early 2000s. It has addressed the issues of feudal mounds (Bretoncelles, Blangy-le-Château), enclosures (Château-Ganne in Pommeraye, Blay), fortified houses (Fontenai-sur-Orne), stone-built princely castles (Falaise, Caen, Chambois), and urban sites (Lisieux, Avranches and particularly the Mont-Saint-Michel). Emphasis has also recently been placed on the study of both urban and religious sites through standing building studies, related to restoration or site enhancement projects. Thus all the ramparts of Mont-Saint-Michel have benefitted from a comprehensive analysis of their elevations (Delahaye 2008). A similarly exhaustive 3 year study has been carried out on Falaise Castle. An initial study has also been started at Caen Castle (Decaëns and Dubois 2009).

With regard to the protection of this particularly fragile and threatened aspect of our heritage, it should be noted that the situation is very mixed. With nearly 1800 monuments listed or registered as historic monuments, Lower Normandy (17,568km$^2$ and 1812 communes) is probably one of the pre-eminent regions in France for protected built heritage (Figure 13.16). Among these protected buildings, 818 monuments (45.5%) constitute the rich group of enclosures, castles and fortified houses. In terms of protection, it has been possible to include the most important fortresses and enclosures of medieval origin through their classification as historical monuments. For a long time, only buildings with preserved elevations were subject to legal protection. Evolving legal criteria have helped to include more sites. However, the situation is still not good for castle mottes. A recent report shows that only five mottes and earthen ringworks are protected in Calvados, three in Manche and ten in the Orne Department. We are far from where we need to be. The situation is even more worrying because earthwork fortifications are subject to ongoing intentional and unintentional destruction, such as ditch filling and land levelling.

*Figure 13.15. A strange castle on the coast in Lower Normandy, end of 12th century, Pirou, Manche (Photo: F. Fichet de Clairfontaine).*

*Figure 13.16. The stone ringwork (12th century) of Crevecoeur-en-Auge, Calvados (Photo: F. Fichet de Clairfontaine).*

## Conclusion

Lower Normandy has a rich heritage of medieval castles. It is important that the inventory of these sites is continued, but in future this work should be directed more towards thematic studies whilst better methods for the analysis of standing buildings are developed, as well as promoting closer collaboration between historians and archaeologists. We should prioritise a study of the existing archaeological database and classify the exact nature of the sites listed. This is a long-term project and will also require new fieldwork. A survey of fortified houses and a review of the better-known fortified buildings would also be helpful. In addition, it is now essential that scientific work on the urban ramparts of Normandy should be supported, whether in

Lisieux, Bayeux (the Gallo-Roman city walls), or in Falaise, Domfront and Avranches. At the same time, it is important to promote research into the origin and morphology of the first castles, dating to the 10th and 11th centuries, and further analyses into the function of the bailey and into Plantagenet architecture in Normandy.

These proposals support work towards the enhancement of this part of our heritage, for which restoration projects are currently being completed at Mont-Saint-Michel, Caen and Falaise Castles and the main keep of St. Sauveur le Vicomte. Other similar projects are being planned for the future, including the keeps of Briquebec and Regnéville-sur-Mer. There is also currently a marked interest in the protection of fortifications made of earth and timber, for example through the purchase of the motte of Sées and the enhancement of the mounds of Saint-Sever-Calvados and Silly-en-Gouffern (Orne). Such an approach must be supported in order to save these fragile monuments, which are so often forgotten and are now threatened by the changes within our countryside.

## Notes

1 See, however, the work of Carpentier (2008).

2 It should be noted that they are barely described or referred to in books of Norman architecture of the medieval period, and only through textual sources. See Neveux (1997).

3 G. Louise has listed 13 in Orne (1984). The Sausserie is identified as a manor house and not as a fortified house on the archaeological map.

4 One charter of 1092 about the new Castle Belleme refers to the powerful lordship of Montgomery-Belleme, created by Guy de Bellême at the beginning of the 11th century. It mentions *terrale turris* which A. Renoux suggests to be a wooden dungeon or an earth motte (Colloque Caen 1981, pp. 31–2; Chave 2003, pp. 146–7).

5 In addition to the notices published in the journal *Archéologie Médiévale* (1983–91), see Leparmentier 2004.

6 The archaeological map identifies 233 castles but many are late or uncertain.

7 The date of the excavation.

## Bibliography


Barbaroux, J. (1979) *130 châteaux de la Manche centre et sud* (Bayeux, Heimdal).

Beck, B. (1986) *Châteaux forts de Normandie* (Rennes, Ouest France).

Boüard, M. de (1979) *Le château de Caen* (Caen, CHRAM).

Carpentier, V. (2008) 'Les seigneurs du Marais. Regard sur l'encadrement des hommes au bord des marais de la Dives (Calvados): châteaux, maisons fortes, manoirs et prieurés, XIe–XVIIIe siècle', in *Des Châteaux et des sources. Archéologie et histoire dans la Normande Médiévale. Mélanges en l'honneur d'Anne-Marie Flambard-Héricher*, pp. 223–53 (Rennes, Publications des Universités de Rouen et du Havre).

Carpentier, V. (2010) *Petite fortification et habitat médiéval au bord de l'Orne. Fontenai sur Orne (Orne), Les Fresneaux, A88 Caen-Sées*, excavation report (INRAP).

Caumont de A. (1846–67) *Statistique monumentale du Calvados*, 5 vols (Paris and Caen).

Chave, I. (2003) *Les châteaux de l'apanage d'Alençon (1350–1450)*, Société Historique et Archéologique de l'Orne, Mémoires et documents4.

Chave, I., Corvisier, C.H. and Desloges, J. (2008) 'Le château d'Argentan (XIe–XVe siècle): du castrum roman à la résidence princière', in M-A. Moulin, I. Chave, B. Fajal and J. P. Foucher, dir., *Argentan et ses environs au Moyen-Âge. Approche historique et archéologique*, pp. 115–206, Conseil général de l'Orne.

Colloque Caen (1981) 'Les fortifications en terre en Europe occidentale du Xe au XIIe siècle', *Archéologie Médiévale* XI, pp. 5–124.

Daliphard, M. (1980) *Seigneurs et châteaux dans le pays d'Auge aux XIe et XIIe siècles. Introduction à une étude archéologique de l'habitat seigneurial fortifié* (Thèse de l'École des Chartes, Vol. 1).

Decaëns, J. (1968) *Les enceintes circulaires d'origine médiévale en Normandie. Contribution aux recherches sur l'habitat fortifié* (doctoral thesis, Université de Caen).

Decaëns, J. (1982) 'L'enceinte de la Chapelle-Colbert dans la forêt de St-Gatien, près du Vieux-Bourg (Calvados)', in *Mélanges d'archéologie et d'histoire médiévales en l'honneur du Doyen Michel de Boüard*, pp. 91–104. Mémoires et documents publiés par la société de l'Ecole des Chartes, XXVII (Genève).

Decaëns, J. (1998) 'Les châteaux du XIe au XIIIe s'., dans l'actuel département de l'Orne, essai d'inventaire et de classement, in B. Fajal, éd., *Autour du château médiéval*, pp. 25–35 (Alençon, des Rencontres Historiques et Archéologiques de l'Orne).

Decaëns, J. (1999a) 'Le château et la ville de Caen pendant la guerre de Cent Ans', in Marin, J-Y., dir., *La Normandie durant la Guerre de Cent Ans, 1346–1450*, pp. 18–21 (Milan, Editions Skira).

Decaëns, J. (1999b) 'Le château de Saint-Vaast sur Seulles dans la guerre de Cent Ans', in Marin, J-Y., dir., *La Normandie durant la Guerre de Cent Ans, 1346–1450*, pp. 116–9 (Milan, Editions Skira).

Decaëns, J. and Dubois, A., dir. (2009) *Le château de Caen. Mille ans d'une forteresse dans la ville* (Caen, CRAHM).

Delacampagne, F. (1982) 'Seigneurs, fiefs et mottes du Cotentin (Xe–XIIe siècles)', *Archéologie Médiévale* XII, Etude historique et topographique, pp. 175–207.

Delahaye, F. (2008) 'Blay, le Castel', *Bulletin Scientifique régional de Basse-Normandie* (Caen), pp. 30–1.

Doranlo, R. (1914) 'Camps, enceintes, mottes et fortifications antiques du Calvados', *Bulletin de la Société des Antiquaires de Normandie* XXIX, pp. 219–50.

Fichet de Clairfontaine, F., Flambard-Hericher, A-M. and Fajal, B. (2007) 'Témoins du Moyen-Age – l'Orne médiévale', in F. Delrieu and J. Desloges with S. Quevillon, dir., *ArchéoOrne, 250 ans d'archéologie dans l'Orne*, exhibition catalogue for 'Alençon-Flers et Saint-Cyr-la-Rosière', pp. 127–34 (Les Cahiers du Temps).

Fixot, M. (1968) *Les Fortifications de Terre et la Naissance de la Féodalité dans le Cinglais* (Caen, Centre de recherches archéologiques médiévales).

Flambard-Hericher, A-M. (2004) 'Fonctions et répartition de l'espace dans la basse-cour d'une fortification des frontière: Bretoncelles (Orne), XIe–XVe siècle', *Château-Gaillard*, pp. 79–97.

Gerville de, M. (1825–30) 'Mémoires sur les anciens châteaux du département de la Manche', *Mémoires de la Société des Antiquaires de Normandie,* I, pp. 177–367; II, pp. 183–338 ; IV, pp. 59–196 and V, pp. 187–319.

Hanachi, S. (2005) *Fortifications de terre médiévales de Basse-Normandie susceptibles de faire l'objet d'une protection au titre des Monuments Historiques.*

*Tranche 1, Manche et Calvados Occidental*, Rapport SRA 1713 (Caen, CRAHM and SRA).

Hanachi, S. (2006) *Fortifications de terre médiévales de Basse-Normandie susceptibles de faire l'objet d'uen protection au titre des Monuments Historiques. Tranche 2 – Calvados oriental et Orne,* Rapport SRA 1861 (Caen, CRAHM et SRA).

Impey, E. (1996) *Le château de Creully* (Caen, CRAHM).

Leparmentier, J. (2004) *Le château de Gavray. Histoire et visite du site archéologique* (Rouen, Edition L'Echo des Vagues).

Litoux, E. and Carre, G. (2008) *Manoirs médiévaux. Maisons habitées, maisons fortifiées* (Rempart, Patrimoine vivant).

Lorren, Cl. (1977) 'Le château de Rubercy: Etude de la maison principale (*c.*1150–1204)'. *Archéologie Médiévale* VII, pp. 109–78.

Louise, G. (1984) 'Les maisons fortes du bocage normand (XIIe–XVe siècle)', in M. Bur, dir., *La maison forte au moyen Age*, pp. 31–41, Pont-à-Mousson 31 mai–3 juin 1984, (Paris, Editions du CNRS).

Louise, G. (1990–1) *La seigneurie de Bellême (XIe–XIIe siècle)* (Alençon, Le Pays Bas-Normand).

Neveux, F. (1997) 'L'urbanisme au Moyen-Age dans quelques villes de Normandie', in M. Bayle, dir., *L'architecture normande au Moyen Age, 1, Regards sur l'art de bâtir*, pp. 271–287, Actes du Colloque de Cerisy la Salle (Moisiney, Editions Gaud).

Pesez, J-M. (1986) 'Maison forte, manoir, bastide, tour, motte, enceinte, moated-site, wasserburg, ou les ensembles en archéologie', in Bur, M. (dir.), *La maison forte au moyen Age*, Pont-à-Mousson 31 mai–3 juin 1984, pp. 331–9 (Paris, Editions du CNRS).

Plaisse, A. (1999) 'Cherbourg durant la guerre de Cent Ans', in Marin, J-Y., dir., *La Normandie durant la Guerre de Cent Ans, 1346–1450*, pp. 23–29 (Milan, Editions Skira).

Renoux, A. (1972) 'L'enceinte fortifiée d'Audrieu (Calvados), (XIIe–XIVe siècles)'. *Archéologie Médiévale* II, pp. 1–88.

Renoux, A. (1989) 'Châteaux et résidences fortifiées des ducs de Normandie aux Xe et XIe s.', in *Les Mondes normands (VIIIe–XIIe s.), Actes du IIe congrès international d'archéologie médiévale*, pp. 113–24 (Caen, CRAHM).

Renoux, A. (1997) 'Résidences et châteaux ducaux normands au XIIe siècle. L'apport des sources comptables et des données archéologiques', in M. Bayle, dir., *L'architecture normande au Moyen Age, 1, Regards sur l'art de bâtir,* pp. 197–217, Actes du Colloque de Cerisy la Salle (Moisiney, Editions Gaud).

Renoux, A. (2010) 'Châteaux, palais et habitats aristocratiques fortifiés et semi-fortifiés', in J. Chapelot, dir., *Trente ans d'archéologie médiévale en France. Un Bilan pour un avenir*, pp. 239–56, IXe congrès international de la Société d'Archéologie médiévale, Vincennes 16–18 juin 2006 (Caen, CRAHM).

Roulley, S. (2007) *Etude monumentale du vieux château de Bricquebec (Manche)*, Mémoire de Master I recherche en histoire de l'art sous la direction de N. Faucherre (Université de Nantes).

Siguret, Ph. (1960) *Les manoirs du Perche* (Amis du Perche).

Yver, J. (1955–8) 'Les châteaux forts en Normandie jusqu'au milieu du XIIe siècle', contribution à l'étude du pouvoir ducal, *Bulletin de la Société des Antiquaires de Normandie* 53, pp. 28–115.

Zadora-Rio, E. (1973–4) 'L'enceinte fortifiée du Plessis-Grimoult (Calvados)', contribution à l'étude historique et archéologique de l'habitat seigneurial au XIe siècle, *Archéologie Médiévale* III–IV, pp. 111–243.

# 14

# Recent excavations at Caen Castle (2005–2014): medieval forges and renaissance stable

*Bénédicte Guillot*

*Translated by Angela Riley*

## Résumé

*Cet article reprend les résultats de la fouille archéologique de l'angle nord-ouest du château de Caen qui a eu lieu en 2005 et les premières données d'une fouille programmée qui s'est terminé en 2014. L'occupation du secteur est continue entre le XIIe et le XVIe siècle et se caractérise, outre l'aspect militaire, par des activités techniques et de l'habitat, ces deux fonctions étant sans doute intimement mêlées. Au XIIIe siècle émerge ce qui constituera l'activité spécifique de ce secteur du château: le travail du fer. Trois forges successives ont été étudiées dont la deuxième est un édifice important et imposant représentant près de cinq fois la surface des deux autres ateliers (160m² contre 33m²) et dont la construction au XIVe siècle est probablement liée à la Guerre de Cent Ans. L'étude paléo-métallurgique montre une grande similitude dans le travail du fer entre le XIIIe siècle et le XVIe siècle. Il s'agit de petites chauffes marquant la fin d'un travail et d'une forge d'ajustement, ce qui est le cas, entre autre choses, pour la ferrure équestre avec en particulier la mise en forme finale du fer, ou pour le façonnage d'un fer de trait par exemple.*

*La fonction résidentielle est représentée par un grand édifice du XIIe siècle, auquel s'accole au XIVe siècle une annexe conservée sur deux niveaux. Le rez-de-chaussée peut être assimilé à un cellier communiquant avec une cave installée dans des chambres d'extraction d'une ancienne carrière de pierre.*

*Au XVIe siècle, le grand édifice est démoli et son annexe devient une maison indépendante comprenant une cuisine avec une grande cheminée dans l'étage bas. Durant la même période, la grande forge perd sa destination première et est transformée en écurie d'apparat par le gouverneur du château, Jean de Feschal. Ses murs sont alors recouverts d'enduits, dont une partie fut peint selon un motif en quinconce, un monogramme étant intercalé avec un dessin de mors de chevaux.*

## Introduction

This article examines the findings of archaeological excavations carried out in the north-west corner of Caen Castle since 2005, between the hall called the 'Echiquier' (Exchequer Hall) and the round 'Puchot' tower (Figure 14.1).

The excavations were part of a conservation and castle development programme launched by the City of Caen in 1998. The archaeological operation of 2005, at the site of a new exhibition hall, covered a surface area of nearly 900m², and took place at the same time as restoration of the ramparts and a building study by G. Carré. A scheduled dig began in 2011 and was completed during 2014. Its results enable the study of a large building situated outside the boundaries of the 2005 excavations. I want to thank all the excavators and the many specialists who worked on the ground and on the excavation data.[1]

The studied area has revealed a tangle of buildings and circulation zones; with each reorganisation being a clearly defined phase of work (Figure 14.2).

## The exploitation of stone

No activity dating to the period of the construction of the castle in the 11th century, or even to before the castle walls, has been discovered. It was not until the 12th century that this area of the castle seems to have been in use. Although we cannot date them precisely, we know that some quarries were being mined here thanks to the bedrock geology that shows regular sloping in a westerly direction. The entrances to the underground quarries must therefore have been located in the west. Quarrymen mined the best layers of Creully limestone before extracting very fractured limestone, useful only in the production of rubble, rubble stone or

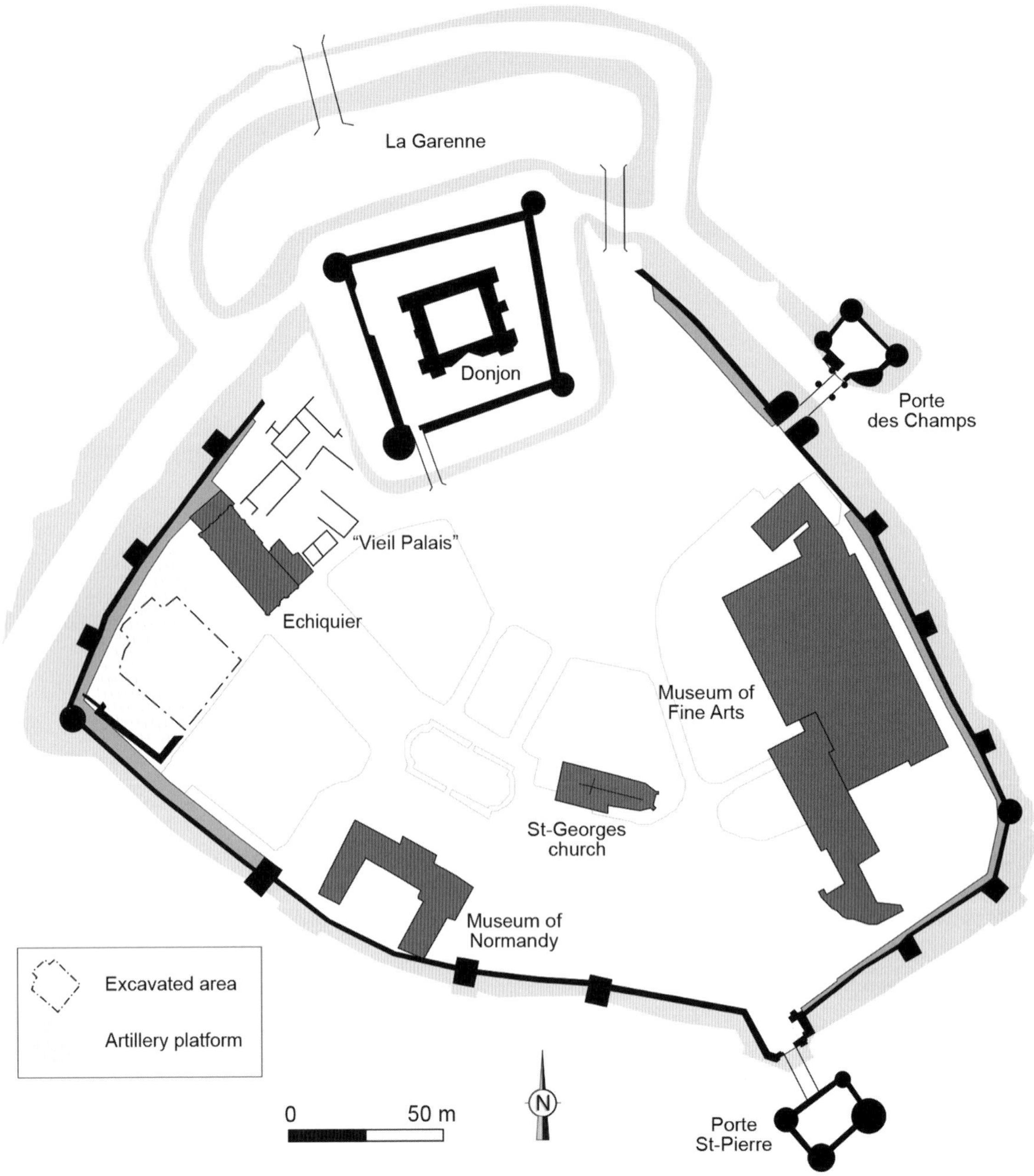


*Figure 14.1. Plan of Caen Castle with the 2005 excavation area (B. Guillot).*

lime. The discovery of a possible lifting implement in the north of the main quarry leads us to think that, as well as access in the west, there could also have been one or more mineshafts for lifting the primary material.

The first known activity in this area was therefore associated with the exploitation of an underground stone quarry. Stone production had become quite considerable after the establishment of the town of Caen. Quarrymen therefore began mining the sides of the natural slopes in search of building stone. The ditches and steep slopes of the castle were created by extracting large quantities of stone that were probably used on-site, through opencast mining. Three quarries were studied by Laurent Dujardin in 2005 and 2006 during construction of the new exhibition hall. They are of the type called 'chambres avec piliers de roche laissées en place' (chambers with pillars of rock left in place) (Figure 14.3). We noticed that the roof of the underground cavity was very thin (1–2m in parts); the quarrymen went as far as they could and would not have been able to continue much further before striking a significant layer of clay.

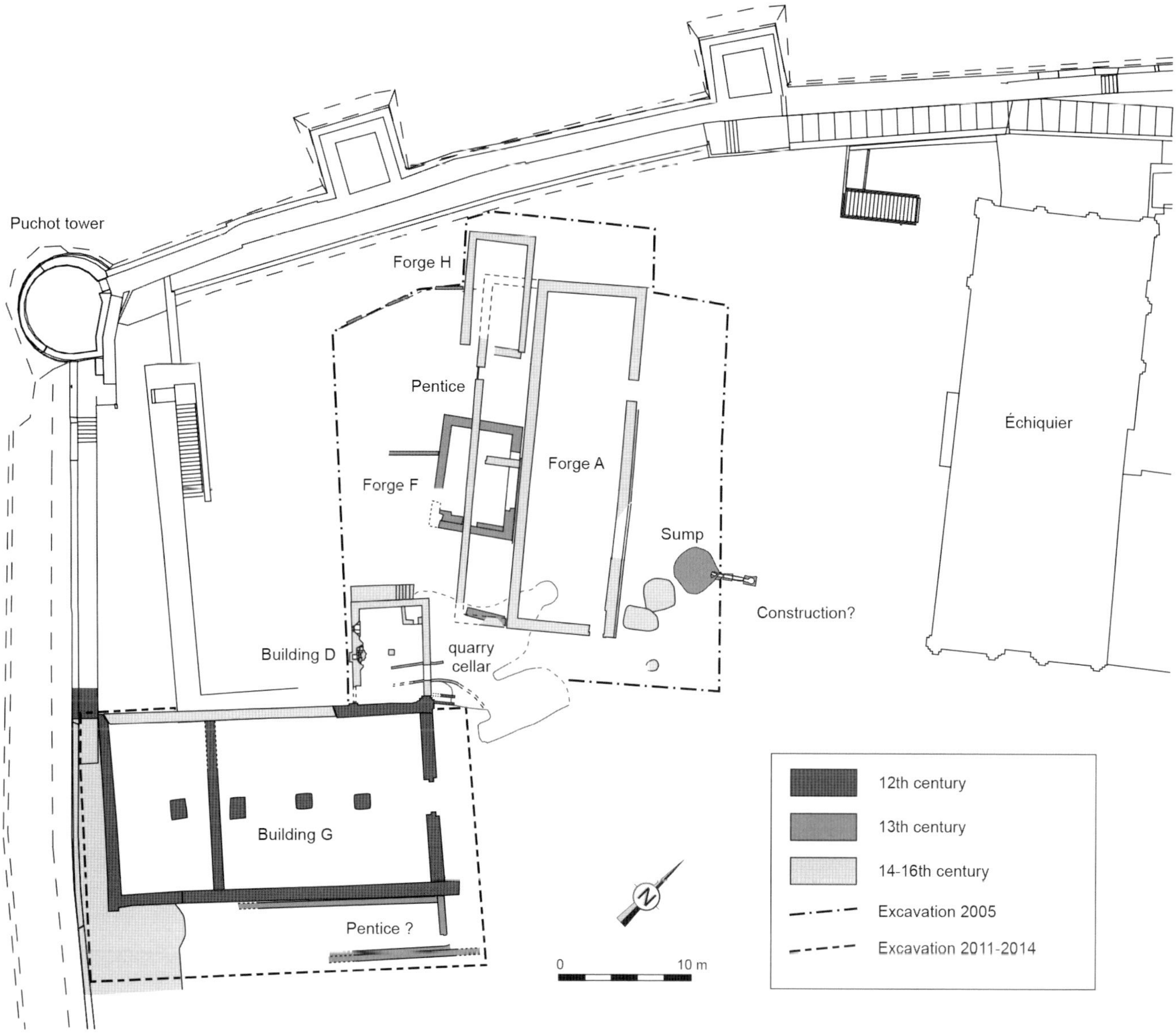


*Figure 14.2. General plan of the excavations (B. Guillot).*

It seems that during the 13th century these quarries ceased to be used and became inaccessible. To date, they are the only known underground quarries mined within material that is also degraded.

## Late 12th-century to early 13th-century large ceremonial building

During the exploitation of these quarries, or possibly more likely after their abandonment, a large building with flat buttresses was constructed in freestone (Figure 14.2). Built against the west curtain wall, according to primary sources, it opened onto a terraced garden in the south. Although still under excavation (at the time of writing), it can be dated to the end of the 12th to the beginning of the 13th century. Its layout and building technique make it one of several ceremonial and prestigious castle buildings. Sited at least 50m south-west of the Exchequer Hall, the *aula* of the dukes of Normandy from the 12th century, this building is part of a series of palatial structures that cover at least the northern part of the castle. The building measures 24m long by about 13m wide, using large masonry blocks of 0.80m to 0.95m and a principal entrance in the centre of the east gable wall. Its surface area (more than 300m$^2$) makes it one of the most imposing castle buildings. By comparison, this structure is as wide as the Echiquier but shorter (24m compared to 32m). The position of floor joists in the west gable enables us to reconstruct a building on two floors.

*Figure 14.3. View of the main quarry during survey work in 2006; to the right is the drain of the large building (B. Guillot).*

The ground between this large building and the Echiquier began to be fully occupied from the 13th century onwards.

## Construction of the first forge (F) in the 13th century

The first forge was built during the 13th century, between the two prestigious structures that are the Echiquier and the large building under recent excavation (Figure 14.4). The activity of ironworking then emerged and became the main activity of this area of the castle.

The decision in the 13th century to introduce a forge in an open space (possibly a garden?) between these two buildings could have been connected to the conquest of Normandy by Philip Augustus. A former capital of the Plantagenet Empire, Caen was incorporated into the kingdom of France, its political and administrative role becoming less important.

The new construction was timber frame on a stone floor but freestone was no longer used. Its surface area (30m$^2$) contrasts with that of the Echiquier (close to 450m$^2$) and the large building under recent excavation. The dimensions of this forge are amongst the largest known metallurgic workshops, making Caen Castle one of the greatest fortresses in Northern France. We must note that the entrance to the new forge faces west and towards the curtain wall, and not east and the Echiquier.

Sampling of earthen floors on each occupied level was carried out in 25cm$^2$ squares, in order to count metal particles (i.e. slag and hammer scales – fragments of metal removed under the impact of the forge hammer). The analysis of these samples by N. Zaour has enabled us to distinguish two probable locations for the anvil. The first forge originally contained a principal fireplace, covering an area of little more than 2m$^2$, with two work-posts positioned near the anvils (Figure 14.5). There is a bench against the south wall and graffiti representing a game of 'grande merelle' (nine men's morris) on one of the stones. There are three squares, one inside the other, connected by four lines in the middle that end at the perimeter of the smallest square or slightly past it. The game is played with two players and nine pieces, the winner being the first to line up three pieces at the intersecting points. The stone is positioned vertically; therefore one would not have played the game here. The graffiti must have been done before the construction of the forge, maybe when the stone was cut. An alignment of post holes enables us to reconstruct a palisade and suggests that the charcoal stockpile needed for the day-to-day running of the forge was placed here.

*Figure 14.4. General phasing of the excavations (B. Guillot).*

In the area surrounding the large building, a low wall marks out a separation between the metallurgical working area in the north and residential part in the south, with a well-maintained bailey. We note that graffiti of a boat was found on one of the stones in the low wall (Figure 14.6, no. 1). Engravings of boats are very common in Normandy and there is a rich bibliography of the different types of boats represented up to the present day. The drawing of the ship is quite simple. It is composed of a crescent featuring the hull, a line in the middle for the mast and two diagonal lines that link the ends of the crescent and form the shape of a shroud. It is a stereotypical drawing of which we find numerous examples in Normandy. But what is interesting is that it also features seven characters on two levels, two on the left of the mast and five on the right. These characters are identical: a long rectangle open at the bottom where two small lines depict the feet. The rectangle is closed by a horizontal line in the upper quarter with a hole inside this space. The rest of the drawing is a less distinctive square pattern. The whole thing makes one think of men in armour with helmets and chainmail. They do not seem to have arms except maybe the two characters on the higher level, to the right of the mast, which are linked by two horizontal lines. This depiction of the characters is very rare and it has not been possible to find comparisons for the graffiti.

*Figure 14.5. Reconstruction of Forge F based on archaeological and paleo-metallurgical evidence (S. Le Maho, INRAP).*

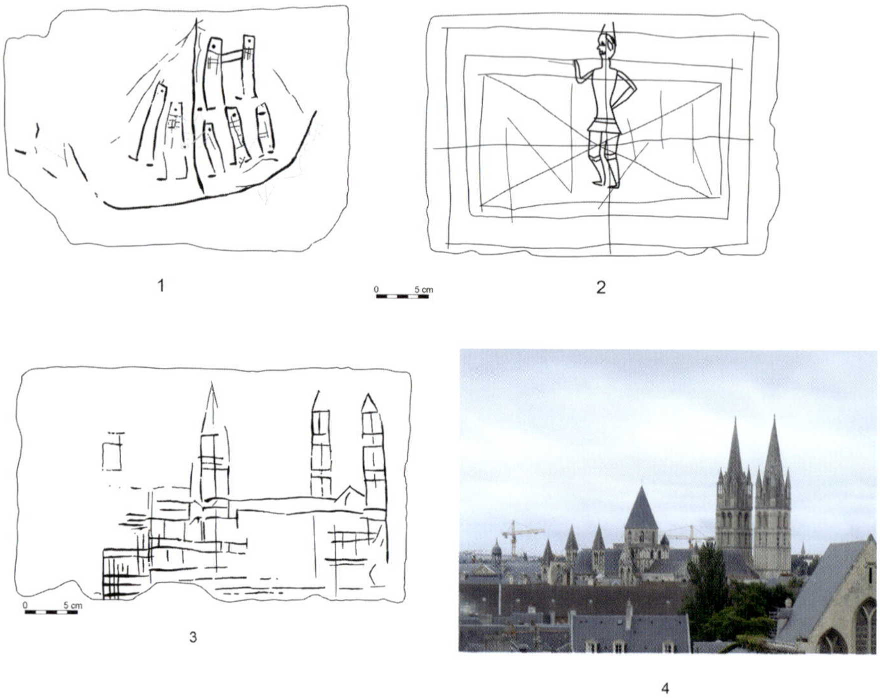


*Figure 14.6. Graffitied blocks of limestone: (1) boat with characters engraved on a low wall from the 13th century (drawing: S. Le Maho); (2) game of Nine Men's Morris with a character on foot in the centre, on the wall of Annexe D (drawing: B. Guillot); (3) a building on a wall from Building A (drawing: S. Le Maho); (4) abbatial church of Saint-Etienne viewed from the top of the castle ramparts (photo: B. Guillot).*

Finally, we may turn to the disposal of waste in the occupied area. We have only been able to find very few remains in the surrounding area that are associated with the forge. Scrap waste must therefore have been taken elsewhere within the castle or it could have been used, for example, as material in the construction of floors. This implies a strict organisation of waste until the definitive abandonment of the forge, except during the 15th century where we note a reduction in use (*cf. infra*).

It is therefore significant that after digging a large pit between Forge F and the Echiquier, a pit later transformed into a sump, we find no slag amongst the waste of the first layer dating to the second half of the 13th century. Interpreted as remains from the preparation of an aristocratic feast (*cf. infra*), this waste relates to a specific event in daily castle life and not to metallurgical activity. The allotted use for this area seems to have been clearly defined and does not extend into the more prestigious buildings.

## A pit, evidence of a building and two aristocratic meals

The pit, dug 13m away from the Echiquier, measures 3.40m in diameter and about 3m deep (Figure 14.4). It seems that there was an aborted attempt to dig a well or an access point to a quarry here. In-fill enables us to distinguish four phases that correspond to its very distinct uses through time (Figure 14.7). First of all, it served as a rubbish pit and is very rich in ceramic artefacts and bones (688). It was then transformed into a sump. A basin and then a stone pipe collected used water and rainwater and transported it to the pit. In order for the liquid to flow well, there was a layer of rubble but it was not packed down. Amongst the rubble, we uncovered a lot of waste from the quarries and fragments of stone mortar. This suggests the existence of a building, of which there is no longer a trace, in close proximity to the Echiquier.

At the end of a fairly short period of time it seems that subsidence took place in the pit, forcing one part of the

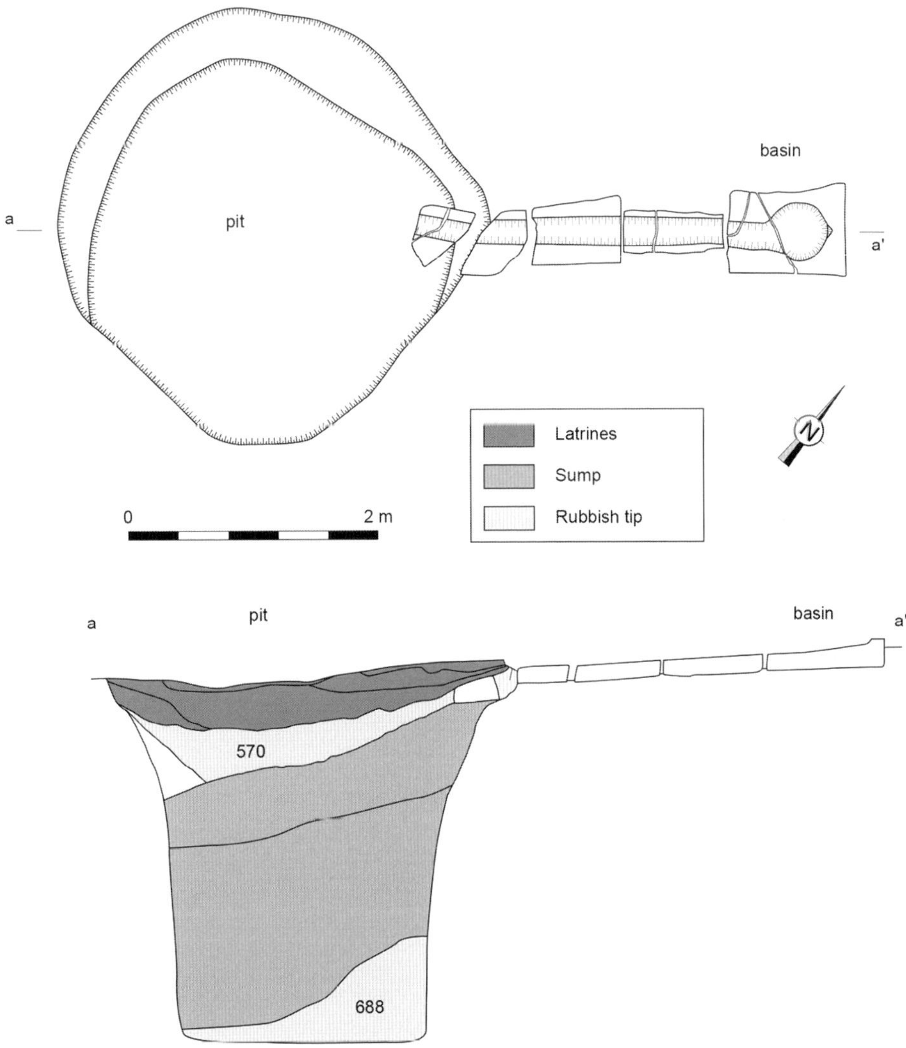


*Figure 14.7. Plan and cross-section of pit F386 (B. Guillot).*

drainage pipe to collapse. The drainage system was therefore abandoned and it was used as a new rubbish pit (570). It was definitively filled with latrine waste.

The pit was dug in the second half of the 13th century, judging by the ceramic artefacts, and it seems to have been filled a final time during the first half of the 14th century. This *terminus post quem* rests primarily on the dating of a *denier tournois* coin of Philip IV 'Le Bel', struck in the first decade of the 14th century. Significant wear leads us to think that it was in circulation for quite a long time before being lost. This coinage, studied by J-C. Moesgaard, was circulated in large numbers until the middle of the 14th century. The dating is also backed-up by the presence of a seal-like impression of a type of *denier tournois* on a pitcher-jug, and finally by the study of ceramics that demonstrates slow but evident chronological progression. Typology and technical categories vary between the first (688) and second (570) rubbish pits but remain characteristic of the second half of the 13th century, according to a ceramic study carried out by S. Dervin. They do not seem to appear in the next phase (middle of the 14th century).

The composition of the levels before and just after the drainage pit (688 and 570 respectively), and analysis of their artefacts, makes us consider the events leading to the production of such waste. A low number of small artefacts make the variety of pottery and bone remains found all the more remarkable and stand out in these two rubbish pits.

Pitcher-jugs represent more than half of the ceramic vessels (of which 20–25% are very decorative ceramics), as well as two bottles and an aquamanile; the rest are essentially cooking pots. The large quantity of reassembled pottery and the presence of complete or archaeologically complete pots enable us to say that these two types of deposits are in prime positions within the pit. We must point out an overrepresentation of vessels used for liquids, of which a large proportion are decorative ceramics (Figure 14.8).

The two levels, already extraordinary in terms of the ceramic artefacts they contain, also contained prolific bone material, evident from both the quantity and variety of species represented. B. Clavel notes that there are very few differences between these two levels of fill, with the same types of artefacts or parts of the body being found in both. The diversity only varies a little but may be due to the method of sampling (there is more material in 688 compared to 570). The determining of close to 70 species of animals – a large proportion being poultry, the presence of three *cervidae* (deer, roe deer and stag), a good 20 species of wild birds and the highest proportion being fish products (marine or fresh water) – suggest an exceptional diet. The range of animals eaten supports this idea with the following, amongst others, being found: sturgeon, salmon, swan, pheasant, peacock, crane and dolphin. The latter is, for example, considered the 'roi des poissons' (king of the fish) in the 'ravitaillement' chapter of the work 'Du fait de cuysine' published by Maistre Chiquart in 1420: *'Et pour tant que le daulphin est roy des autres poyssons de mer il se mectré premierement'*.[2]

Various indications, such as the large homogeneity of bone remains, the remains of birds' legs – of a variety of species – all cut as a single joint, a significant number of fish scales (62,500 in rubbish pit 688 alone), a very low number of bite marks from a carnivore (dogs or wild animals) and well preserved bones of young birds etc., enable the identification of each of the two levels of fill as the discarded remains of a single meal that can only have been from an aristocratic environment.

The presence of a high quantity of stone mortar in the material making up the drainage pit, a pit that was rapidly cut after the first rubbish pit, has led G. Verbrugghe to question the origin of the mortar. Although from two stratigraphically different groups, it remains possible that it comes from the same source: the preparation of a feast. If this is this case, they would have been put to one side and would have been used, in the same way as remains from the limestone quarries, to build the drainage pit.

One question remains unanswered regarding the composition of two groups, associating ceramic vessels classified as 'table vessels' (as well as some glasses in the second rubbish pit 570) with bone remains from cooking. These two groups, in prime position and mixed up, are both from the same event. It could therefore be the case that these pitcher-jugs were not used as table vessels but were used to carry water, wine or verjuice,[3] or contain oil. All these liquids were used in culinary preparation and would have been at the disposal of the cooks. In a kitchen scene in the famous illuminated manuscript the Luttrell Psalter in England, which dates from the 14th century, we can see a character on the right filling a small dish with liquid (probably a sauce) contained in a clearly distinguished pitcher.[4] Pitchers could therefore also have been used for measuring ingredients to ensure certain quantities were achieved.[5]

This would explain the homogeneity of pottery production. The products are all from the same geographical area, purchased locally (?), and there is absence (in the first rubbish pit) and rarity (in the second) of glassware. Moreover, we can say that at such a banquet, the tables would have displayed remarkable pieces of earthenware and a number of items in pewter and silver; such magnificent precious vessels are shown in representations of festive aristocratic meals.

This pit therefore reveals precious evidence of the first items of rubbish from the preparation of two different meals held at the castle during large celebrations. The importance and the quality of animals consumed, of which there is no comparable example in France to date, lead us to consider what these uncommon events were in a fortified town were; possibly feasts held on the occasion of the arrival of great princes, or even the king of France.

During the period between the second half of the 13th century and the first half of the 14th century, we could be talking about Louis IX 'Louis le Saint' (1226–70) who visited Caen on two occasions, in 1256 and 1269, Philip IV 'Le Bel' who made a passing visit to Caen Castle in 1307, or the future John II 'Jean le Bon', duke of Normandy between 1332 and 1350.

## Large reorganisations during the 14th and 15th centuries

### *An annexe (D) to the north of the large building*

A structure, utilising the wall with flat buttresses of the large building, was built in the north[6] (Figures 14.2 and 14.4). Constructed in stone, it contained at least two floors and is in an exceptional preserved state, with an average height of 3.40m and a floor area of $34m^2$. It was built at the point of a change of ground incline, so the first floor is level with the bailey in the east and the ground floor is at street

*Figure 14.8. Pottery recovered from the large pit (Photo: P. Leroux, Musée de Normandie).*

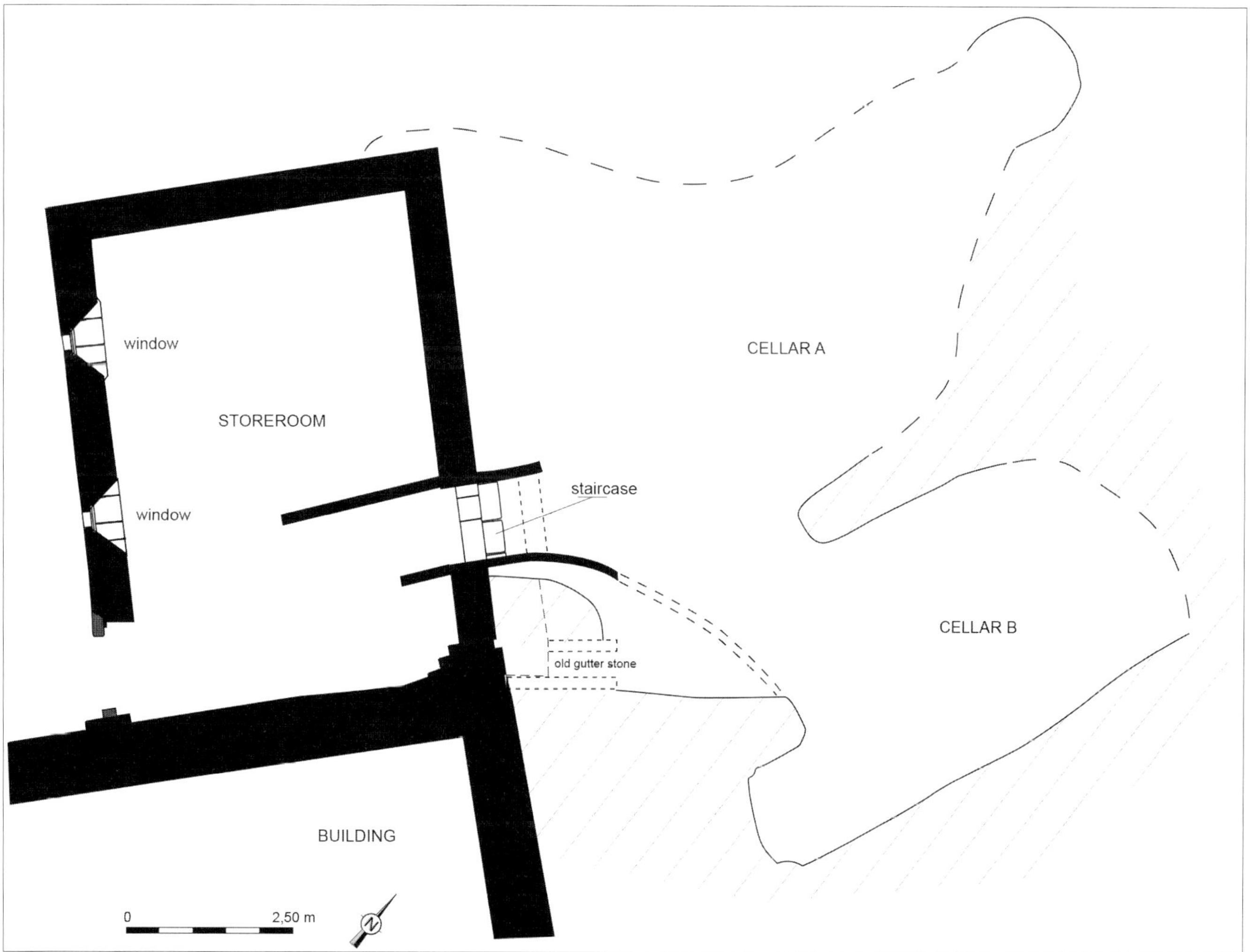


*Figure 14.9. Plan of the lower level of Annexe D (first floor) (B. Guillot).*

*Figure 14.10. View of the exterior of the south window on the lower level of Annexe D; it is blocked during a reorganisation of the building in the 16th century (B. Guillot).*

level in the west. The latter is fully preserved (Figure 14.9) and measures 1.90m in height. On the west wall, we find a door and two very narrow windows (Figure 14.10). In the east, a door has been fitted in order to access ancient quarry chambers that are transformed into cellars. This enables us to propose the existence of a connecting storeroom that contained provisions. The roof was composed of beams with eaves supported by corbels and then joists. There is no longer any indication of the type of floor – it could have been wooden, tiled etc.

On the top floor of the annexe, we have been able to reconstruct two doors, an evacuation duct for a sink and the remains of a fireplace; all of which suggest the arrangement of a kitchen (Figure 14.11). Amongst the graffiti observed, we found a variation of '*petite merelle*'. As well as this game, the side view of a person on foot is engraved (Figure 14.6, no. 2). He seems to be wearing tall headdress, breeches and hose but not shoes, and a tailored doublet with a fairly low belt. The left arm is at the waist, whereas the right is raised.

### *Construction of an imposing forge in the second half of the 14th century*

The start of the Hundred Years' War, and the cavalcade of Edward III in the middle of the 14th century, resulted in a reorganisation of the area (Figure 14.4). The first forge F was demolished and replaced with a large building of 160m² (A), equipped with a pentice 3.40m wide (E) (Figure 14.12). Situated between the Echiquier and the large building, the new forge was built from new, entirely in limestone and measuring at least 3m high. On the exterior wall there is graffiti of a building, probably a church, which bares strong

*Figure 14.11. Internal facing of the north wall of Annexe D with spaces for beams to support the upper level ; bottom left is a recess; top right is a chimney (B. Guillot).*

resemblances to the abbatial Saint-Etienne visible from the top of the curtain wall (Figure 14.6, nos 3 and 4).

As for the pentice, it is constructed in timber and cob on a stone floor. The walls were plastered and its roof was made from slate in a green and blue/grey colour. The whole of the new construction covered an area of nearly 320m², close to the dimensions of the large building, which is located at least 10m south-west. Even if the military threat of the English drove the development of metal-working activity, it would not have necessitated the building of such a large forge that cannot be compared to any other known workshop in Europe. The desire to construct a new building, in stone, between the Echiquier and the large building, must have been a personal choice. During the 14th century we also find textual references to the dwelling of the governor, now the Museum of Normandy, which is situated around 55m south of the large building, completing the collection of large stone buildings all of a size that demonstrate the political, military and administrative power of the castle.

The large forge was built in a way that allowed for all stages of the production of objects. The hearths were in the north and north-east and were mostly positioned against the side gutter wall to make the most of the masonry for storing and diffusing heat (Figure 14.13).

The paleo-metallurgic study by N. Zaour shows a strong similarity between ironwork in the 13th century in the first forge, and the 14th century in the new workshop. They are both finishing forges for the final stage of producing ironwork. There are very few mill scales and metal fragments in the slag, which indicates that the blacksmith did little work with heat and did not strike much (or very little). This is characteristic of small fire-chambers used in the final stage of work and in bespoke forges. This provides a case, amongst others, for horseshoeing taking place, particularly the final production of the shoe, or possibly the shaping of iron arrows. The new forge, with its five hearths, was therefore able to produce large quantities of objects that had already been shaped in the previous stage. As Edward III approached the castle in 1346, the garrison increased to 700–800 armed men, 500 archers and 3,000 militiamen (Prentout 1904, p. 28). The need for ironwork must therefore have been very important and required an enlargement of the existing forge.

We can directly access this part of the forge through a door situated in the north-east. A second door, that was used more, is found on the south gable. It brings us into a partitioned area where we find the actual smithy. It is a well-maintained domestic space, where there was evidence of plant bedding that has been trampled on. It was occupied by a large herbivore, probably a horse, evidenced by coprolites observed here. Irène Béguier also discovered micro fragments of skin and heated horn, and micro-scraps of the mill scale type that would have come from the forge.

*Figure 14.12. To the right is a general view of Forge A; bottom left is Forge F in the 13th century; top left is Forge H from the second half of the 15th century (M. Dupuis, INRAP).*

All of this enables us to determine the existence of at least one stable and a dedicated space for the smithy (Figure 14.13) in the south part of the large forge. It therefore seems probable that one type of work carried out by this large forge was the shaping of iron horseshoes before they were fitted to the hoof of the animal. The micro-morphological study carried out by I. Béguier shows that the area in the south also served as a domestic space.

As well as horseshoeing, the workshop may also have been used for making weapons and wheel rings for horse carts. The pentice provided storage space for primary materials and other items necessary for the efficient running of the forge.

## *English occupation of the castle during the first half of the 15th century*

The siege of the castle by the English during the first half of the 15th century did not really affect the forge but its activity evolved a little. The southern partition remained in place, possibly the smithy too, and there were still many

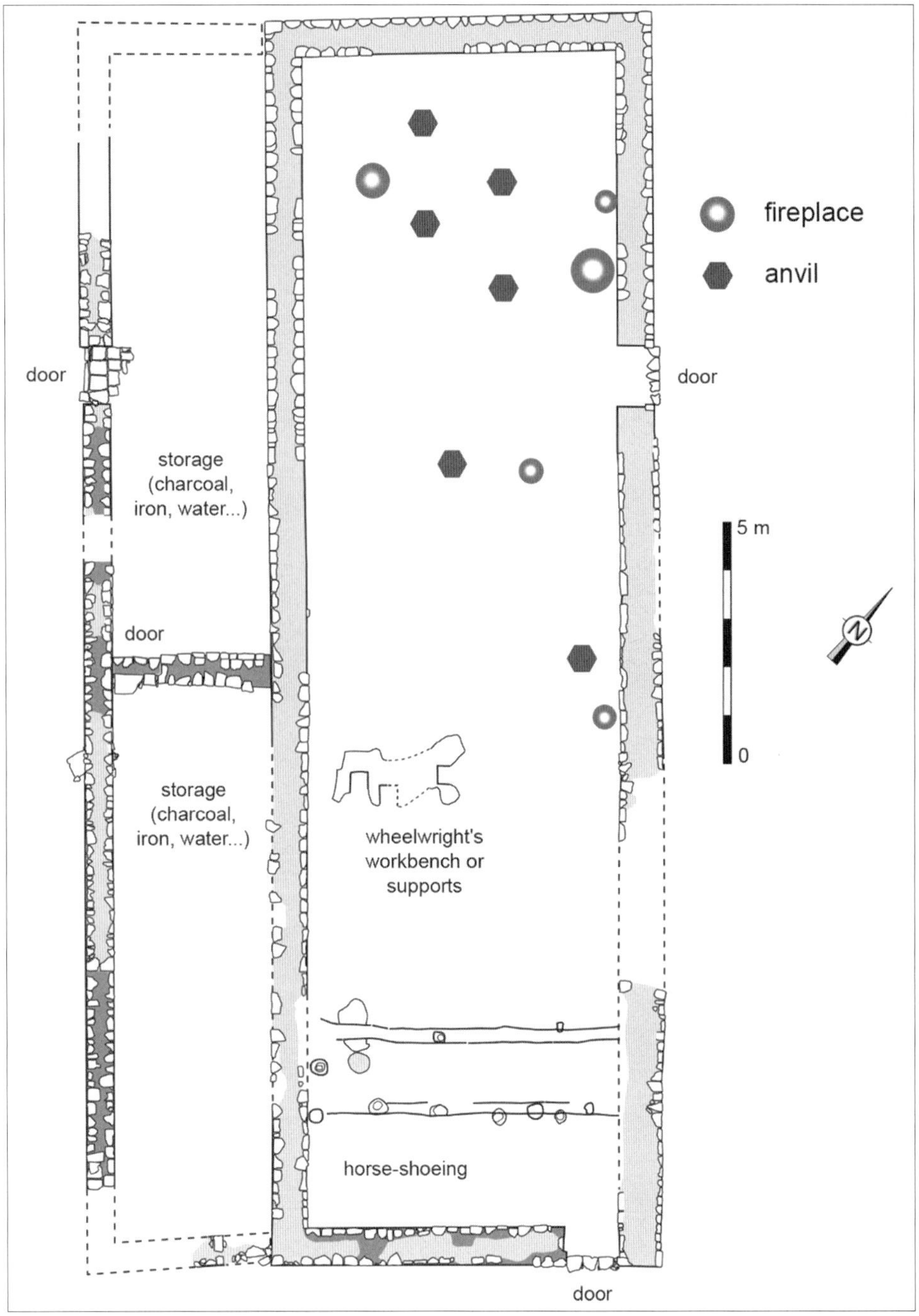


*Figure 14.13. Plan of the large Forge A and pentice E in the 14th century (B. Guillot).*

hearths along the wall in the north but access in the eastern side gutter wall was blocked. All that remained was therefore the south door. Two other hearths were built in the centre of the building and seem to have been used for working with iron as well as cuprous alloys. One of the biggest differences concerns metal scrap; it was no longer discarded outside the area but is found in spreads within a section of the building or as in-fill for the pits.

The pentice was demolished by bombardment, possibly that by Henry V in 1417 (a fragment of a stone cannonball was discovered *in situ* in the middle of the collapsed roof (Figure 14.14)) and it was not reconstructed. Debris was simply spread around and the area remained abandoned. The only place where we have noted much activity is along the north curtain wall, which is easily explained.

Apart from some rebuilding of the floor, we do not note many big changes to the annexe of the large building. The first half of the 15th century does not therefore seem to be a period of much activity in this area. The study of texts and the composition of the garrison confirm this relative loss of interest in the castle. It is therefore likely that the civic population had deserted, or been evicted from the fortress.

### *A new forge in the second half of the 15th century (Figure 14.4)*

It is not until the end of the 15th century that there was a resumption of activity in this part of the castle. A large forge was no longer needed and a new building was constructed on fallow land in the north-west (Figure 14.12). This new forge has more 'classic' dimensions (33m²). It was still one of the most important castle workshops. The hearth of the forge was paved in limestone, with a tiled fire-back (Figure 14.15). Another hearth, in clay, was probably used for culinary purposes (indicated by an absence of mill scale in the surrounding area). Half-timbered, and built in cob on a stone floor, its internal walls were covered in lime mortar. Traces of paintings, forming bands of red or green colours, were found on fragments of this plaster but it is not possible to recreate the design.

The earlier large forge was then reconverted into housing with internal compartmentalisation. In the south we find the more domestic part with hearths and rubbish pits; in

*Figure 14.14. View of the roof in the south section of the pentice. Its collapse is probably due to a cannonball, a fragment of which is visible in the centre (D. Corde, INRAP).*

*Figure 14.15. Principal fireplace of Forge H (X. Perrin, INRAP).*

the north, and especially in the north-west, the ground was better managed and it must therefore have formed a more residential section. Between the annexe of the large building and this housing area, a path was created giving access to the fortifications and round Puchot tower.

This phase does not seem to have lasted very long and the new forge was abandoned at the turn of the 15th and 16th centuries. The large building recommenced its principal activity as a forge. Some new hearths were positioned along the side gutter wall, reassuming the layout of the 14th-century forge but the compartmentalisation in the south no longer existed.

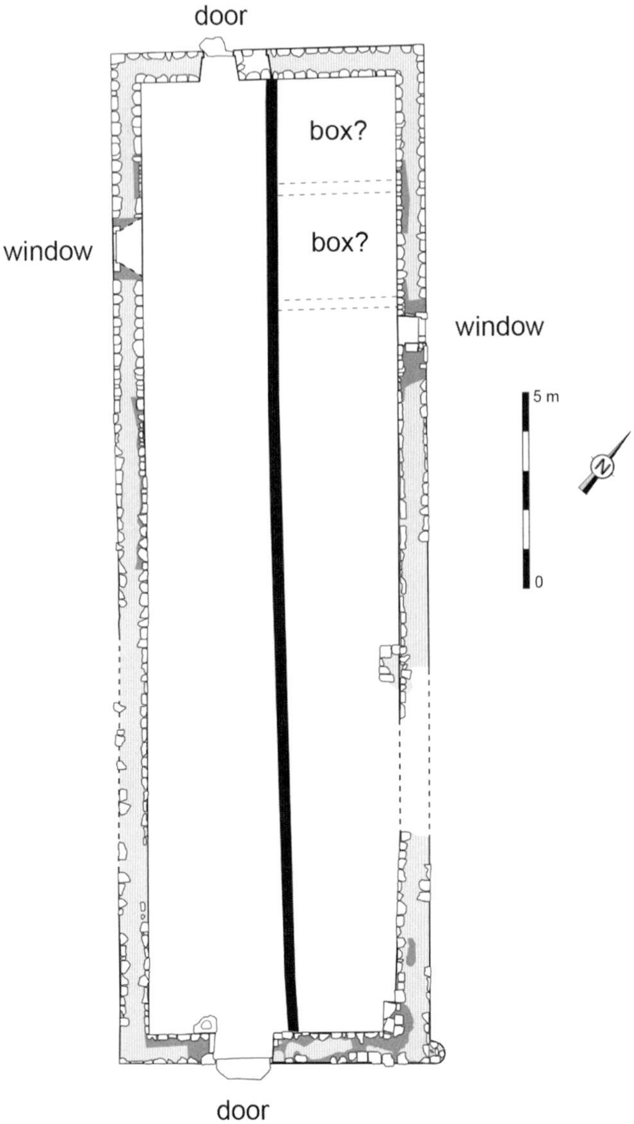


*Figure 14.16. Plan of the stable at the beginning of the 16th century (B. Guillot).*

## *A prestigious stable at the beginning of the 16th century*

At the very beginning of the 16th century, the large forge was reconstructed a final time. The metallurgical work must therefore have been carried out in another part of the castle, probably in a smaller building. The governor of the castle, Jean de Feschal, converted the large building into a prestigious stable in the decorative style of the early Renaissance period (Figure 14.16). A large part of the interior facing was redone; the hearths having greatly damaged the stone. The remains of a thick layer of limestone enable us to re-establish the ancient floors of the forge. Two large doors, facing each other, opened out to the north and south, and there were also windows to complete the arrangement (Figure 14.17). A large string-piece beam crossed the building from north to south, dividing it into two distinct areas. It formed a space in the west where there were the only two access points to the building (measuring between 3.30m long in the north and 3.60m in the south), and a smaller space in the east (between 3.12m in the north and 2.60m in the south) where we can reconstruct the stables.

The walls were then refaced in plaster, and the western part was painted with a repeated motif in staggered rows representing a monogram interpolated in a drawing of horse bits (Figure 14.18). The design, which starts about 1.20m above ground, is visible on at least four rows. We can infer from the preserved plaster that the building would have displayed around 140 drawings of horse bits. The free-hand painting of each motif and the evident differences between each preserved horse bit show how unique the decoration is, representing the results of a complete programme of work.

The monograms are all the same size, which implies the use of a stencil. The motif is distinctive as it is identical if you turn it upside down. We note in passing that there is research into the use of polychrome in monograms. These monograms were alternately in black or blue. As for the bits, some were heavily highlighted in grey-green, which was undoubtedly in order to make them stand out more, but the large majority were monochrome, having been drawn simply.

The horse bits, which are all different, have been drawn to a scale of 1:1 (0.35m in height by 0.24m long). We assume the alternating of the monogram in the motifs is a decorative choice; however, it is not the most decorated part of a horse bit that is highlighted but rather the technical part, the bridle. [The latter is made up of three principal parts: the mouthpiece or the bit (commonly known as the canon), the curb chain and the shank. There are two types of the latter featured on the painted plaster. No rosette (raised ornament fixed to the two ends of the canon) is represented, even though this is part of the decoration of a bridle bit. These different canons therefore demonstrate the originality of the wall paintings.]

*Figure 14.17. Detail of the new south door, with a large stone for the doorstep; top right, a large limestone block with a hole (D. Flotté, INRAP).*

*Figure 14.18. General view of the painted plaster on the north gable wall to the west of the door (S. Le Maho, INRAP).*

A study of these bits has been carried out by Vincent Juhel who has compared them to drawings from a book written by Jean de Feschal, governor of Caen Castle at the beginning of the 16th century. The book is a manuscript on parchment, called 'traité d'hippiatrie et d'embouchure'. It is made up of two treatises. The first, the *mouthpiece treatise*, contains 160 ink drawings of horse bits; the second is the *Hippiatrica treatise*, which contains 36 formulae for the care of horses and is not illustrated. Of the 13 drawings of horse bits that are sufficiently complete that they can be identified, 12 are definitely linked to the manuscript by Jean de Feschal (Figure 14.19). The 13th does not exactly draw any parallels with the *mouthpiece treatise* but does bare resemblance to at least two drawings.

This type of decoration illustrates a revival of horse art because each type of bridle bit is detailed according to

C

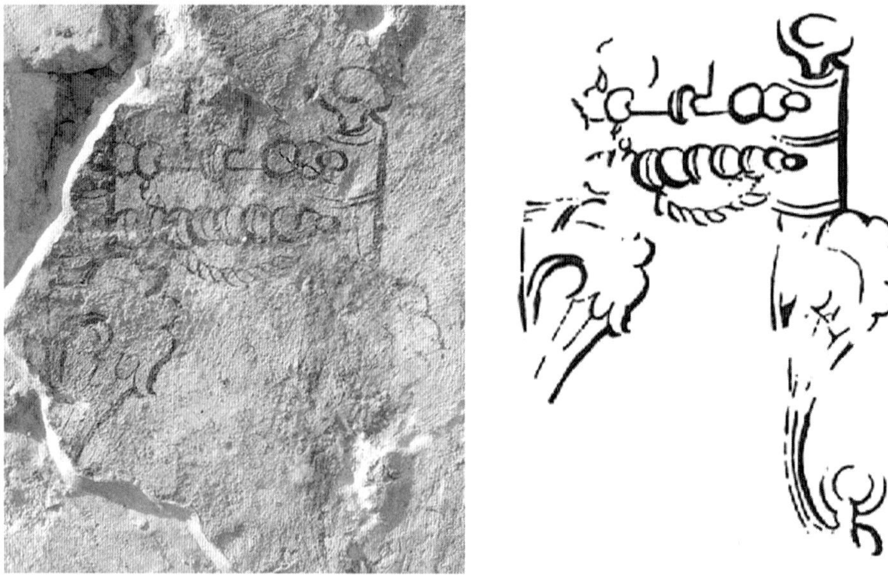

Pl. XIX, « A cheval qui lieve la teste et aulcunement ait la bouche dure »

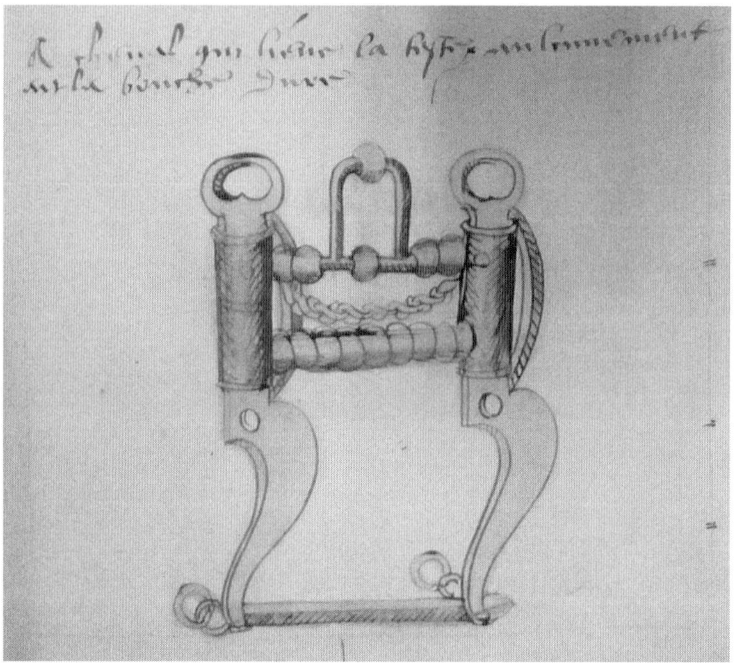

*Figure 14.19. Comparison between bridle bit C (image and drawing: S. Le Maho) and the manuscript by Jean de Feschal (photo: Musée de Normandie).*

the nature of the horse and the size of its mouth, with a reference to its character or flaws needing correcting. Each bit corresponds with a very distinctive type of horse.

The importance of the relationship between the manuscript of Jean de Feschal and the preserved paintings enable us to see the decoration as a painted copy of the manuscript. The decoration would therefore date to between 1504 and 1516 when Jean de Feschal was governor of the castle, as confirmed by stylistic and archaeological evidence. The monogram is not always identified but it is very probably two letters merged together. The first letter is without doubt an I (or a J), the second is almost identical but the diagonal joins the two from bottom to top – the reverse of an ordinary downstroke. It could equally be a symbol used by Jean de Feschal to mark his horses. An important point from the treatise is the way in which it

*Figure 14.20. View of the cellar door blocked by masonry (D. Corde).*

*Figure 14.21. Detail of the chimney installed in the west wall of House D (D. Corde).*

mentions one of his predecessors, Alain Gouyon, who also worked on bridal bits but in a more technical and experimental way. One appealing hypothesis, which cannot be confirmed, is that Alain Gouyon, as governor of the castle, used the large forge for experimenting with various horse bits from the end of the 15th century through to its final use.

After the departure of Jean de Feschal as governor in 1516, the stables were possibly reorganised a final time. The string-piece beam was taken out and the north door was blocked and replaced with a smaller access situated in the north-east corner. Nothing suggests the new use of this building; it possibly simply served as a warehouse, as was the case with the neighbouring Exchequer Hall.

## The ancient annexe becomes a detached house

It was during the same period that the large building in the south area was demolished. The annexe therefore became detached (Figure 14.4). The cellar was abandoned and used as a rubbish tip before the collapsing of the roof caused it to be completely abandoned. We can tell that rubbish continued to be thrown from the door of the cellar through to the last moment. Access was blocked by large pieces of limestone (Figure 14.20). The storeroom, which became half-buried, was transformed into a kitchen with the addition of a large chimney wall (Figure 14.21). A staircase was fitted to enable continued use of the entrance. One window was converted into a basement window, the second being blocked by the construction of the chimney. The first floor probably served as a living room with a chimney and large window opening onto the west bailey. A stone staircase was built, providing access to a third floor along the north wall.

During restoration work on the house we discovered a large coat of arms in bas-relief, representing the Dauphin arms, on the second step of the staircase. The date of this plaque is difficult to ascertain because, from the second half of the 14th century, all Dauphins had the same arms (that of Charles V). The re-use of such a coat of arms on the step of a staircase in the 16th century still remains unexplained.

## Conclusion

In conclusion, the excavations in the north-west part of Caen Castle have enabled us to broach questions relating to the origins of the site, the specialisation of ironworking

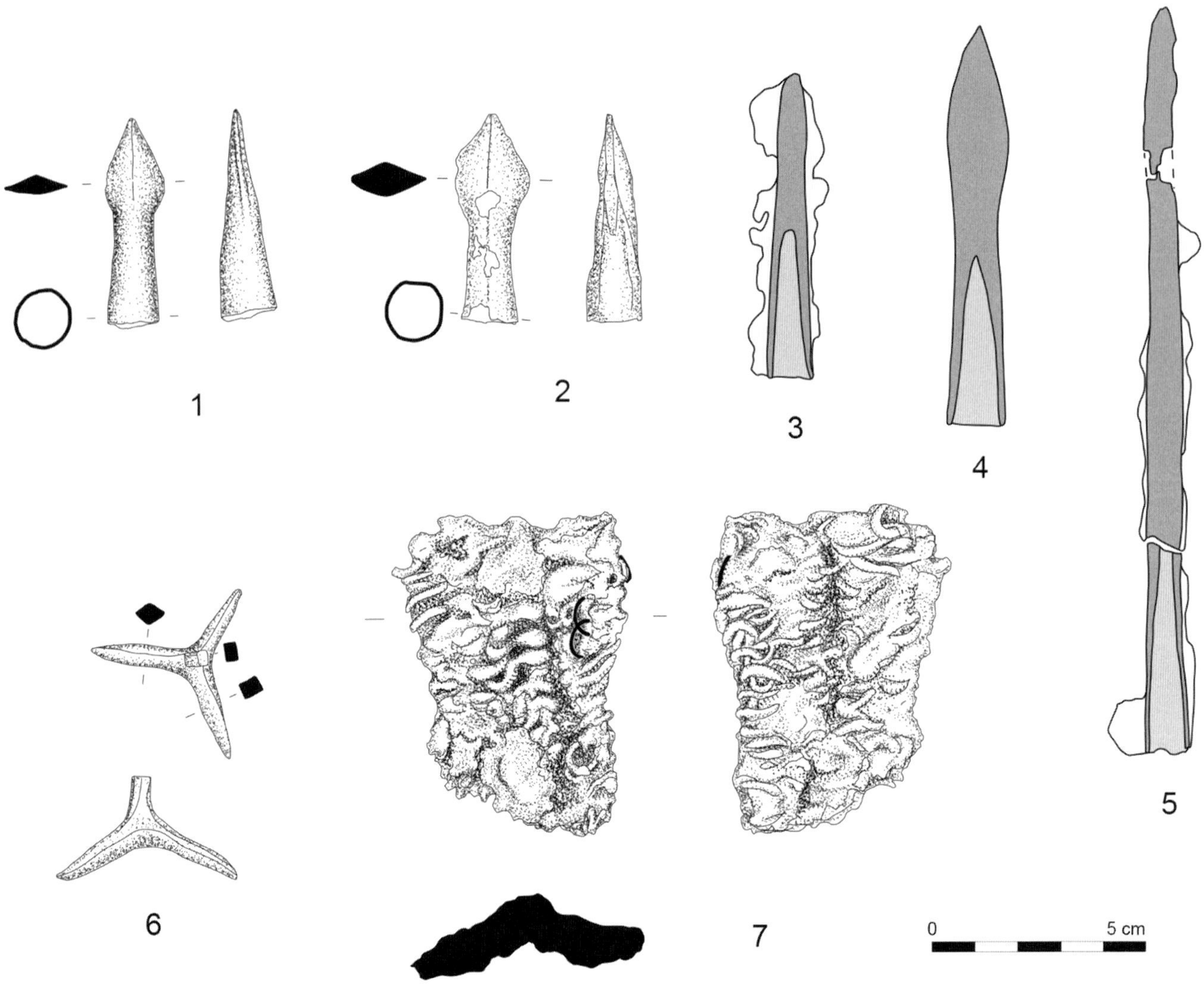


*Figure 14.22. Military objects (N. Zaour) (drawings 1, 2, 6 and 7: S. Le Maho; Computer aided drawings 3–5: B. Guillot, based on drawings by N. Zaour from x-ray photography).*

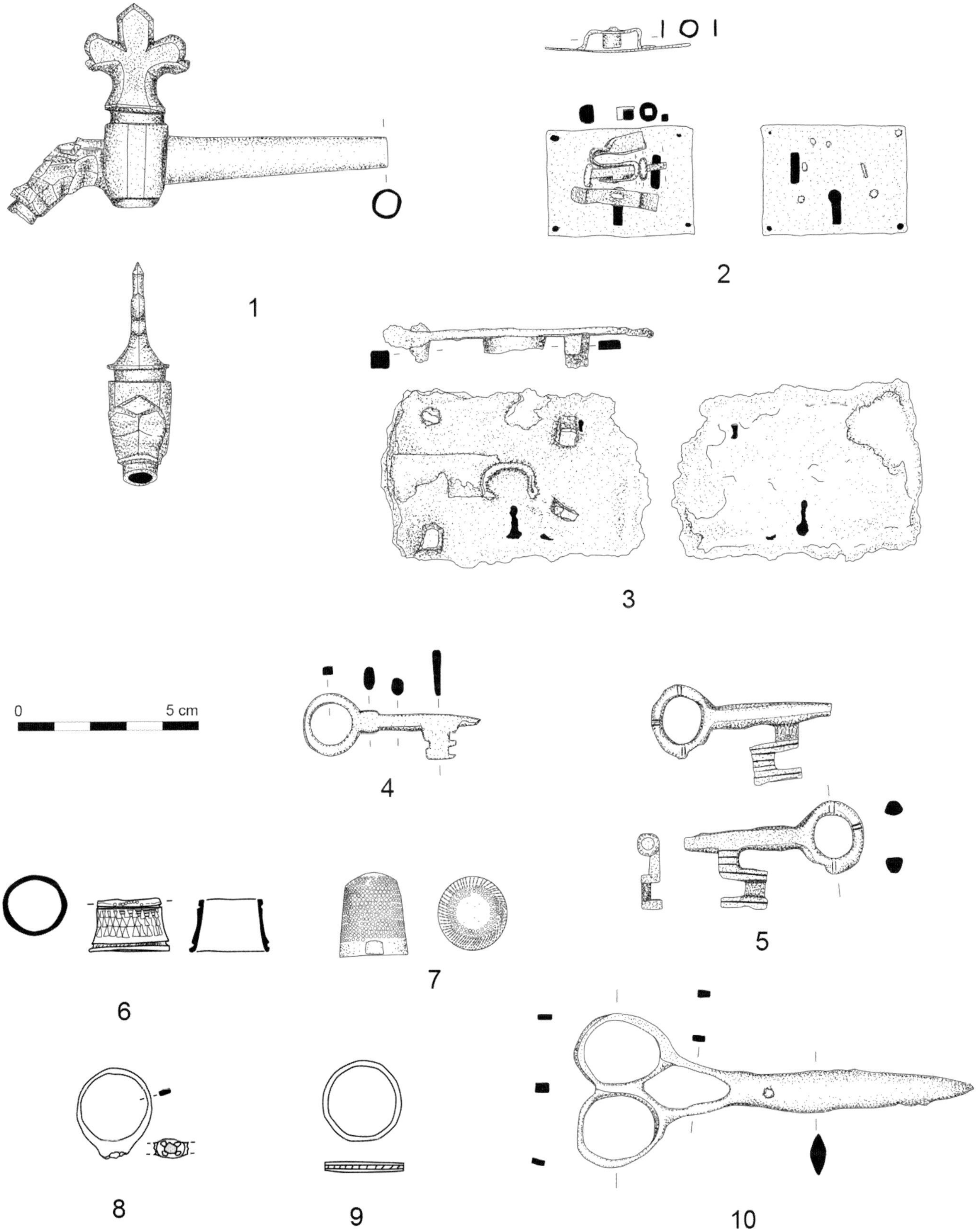


*Figure 14.23. Daily life objects in copper alloy (except No. 5 in iron) (N. Zaour) (drawings: S. Le Maho).*

in this section of the castle, and also in daily life, close to a ducal and later royal palace. Throughout the 16th century, this area of the castle fell gradually into disuse, and only the house seems to have retained a specific purpose. The introduction of an artillery platform to the castle, in response to new military developments, fundamentally changed the appearance of the fortress. For the first time since at least the 12th century, the north-west corner of the castle became an unoccupied space. Only the Exchequer Hall, although reorganised and used as an arsenal, remains as evidence of the large stone buildings that once filled this section in the Middle Ages.

The construction of the so-called 'Salle du Rempart', and the excavations that were undertaken there, provide a new dimension to our understanding of the north-west corner of the castle.

## Notes

1 A monograph on the findings of the 2005 excavations is in preparation with Publications du CRAHM. I summarise the findings of the following specialists in this paper: Irène Béguier (micromorphologist), Anne Bocquet-Liénard (archaeometrist, CRAHAM), Benoît Clavel (archaeozoologist, CNRS), Stéphanie Dervin (ceramologist, INRAP), Laurent Dujardin (study of stone quarries, CRAHAM), Vincent Juhel (study of wall paintings, Société des Antiquaires de Normandie), Guillaume Lemaître (historian), Jean-Marie Levesque (chief curator, Musée de Normandie), Jens-Christian Moesgaard (numismatist, Nationalmuseet, Copenhagen), François Neveux (historian), Geert Verbrugghe (study of stone mortar, INRAP), Nolwenn Zaour (paleo-metallurgist, INRAP).

2 Chiquart, *Du fait de cuisine*, in Scully, ed. 1985, 16r and 16v. Text and French translation available at: http://www.diachronie.be/lexique/textes/15e/chiquart/1420-chiquart-01.html

3 'Suc acide que l'on extrait d'un gros raisin qui mûrit imparfaitement ou de tout autre raisin cueilli avant maturité, employé autrefois dans les sauces, dans la fabrication de sirops et aujourd'hui dans la préparation de la moutarde'. French definition available at: http://www.cnrtl.fr/definition/verjus. Consultation, June 2012.

4 Luttrell Psalter (London, British Library, Add. MS 42130, fol. 207v°). This illuminated manuscript is, for example, on the cover of the work directed by Ravoire and Dietrich (Ravoire and Dietrich 2009).

5 Proposed by F. Blary to partly explain the feeble representation of pitchers, bowls and small dishes found at Château-Thierry (Blary 2009, p. 378).

6 The excavation programme of summer 2012 in the south has enabled us to find evidence of a second annexe leaning against the large building.

## Appendix 1: Objects of military equipment

### *Figure 14.22*

1. Crossbow bolt, traces of copper alloy (rubbish tip in the second half of the 15th century).
2. Crossbow bolt (fill of a pit in the second half of the 15th century).
3. Iron arrow (abandoned level of the pentice from the beginning of the 15th century).
4. Complete iron arrow (final layer of fill of House D from the second half of the 16th century).
5. Large iron arrow, which seems complete (pocket of ash in Forge A from the beginning of the 16th century).
6. Caltrop made up of four parts forming a tetrahedron shape (fill from a rut in the path leading to the Puchot tower in the 16th century).
7. Fragment of chainmail comprised of an assembly of iron rings and three copper alloy rings (layer of soil of Building A from the 16th century).

## Appendix 2: Objects of daily life in copper alloy (except no. 5 in iron)

### *Figure 14.23*

1. Complete tap, knob in the shape of a cross (fill from floor of House D from the 16th century).
2. Latch lock case with the locking mechanism behind and holes in the four corners for fixing to the closing support. In the centre of the metal plate, and on the side, is the hole for the key, enabling the key holder to insert and turn it (fill of a pit in the first half of the 14th century).
3. Rectangular door latch with a rivet in the centre of the metal plate on which there is a hole enabling a key to be inserted (fill from the chimney flue of House D during the second half of the 16th century).
4. 'Bénarde' key (a primitive key) comprising a circular bow and flat key bit with two longitudinal wards at the bottom and one longitudinal ward at the top between the other two (rubbish in the path leading to the Puchot tower from the 16th century).
5. Small plain key shank with a circular bow and a ward in the shape of an 'S' with multiple projecting parts covered with regular incisions on both sides (backfill of subsidence from the 14th century).
6. Open-ended thimble for sewing, the paunch is engraved with three rows of triangular bodkins; the knurling possibly showing needlework marks (fill from floor of House D in the 16th century).
7. Thimble for sewing, with a concave top and knurling engraved in staggered rows (soil from Building A used as a house in the second half of the 15th century).
8. Ring with a rectangular section of a band with rounded corners. The stone is undetermined, round and fixed to the centre of the bezel using the four-prong setting technique (fill from a pit during the demolition of House D in the 16th century).
9. Circular ring, a rectangular section with rounded corners. The ring comprises a central raised band decorated with ridges, traces of gilding on the outer side and traces of

red on the inner side (fill of a gutter along House D from the 15th century).

10. Complete pair of scissors (fill from floor of House D in the 16th century).

## Bibliography

Blary, F. (2009) 'Les grandes cuisines seigneuriales et les principaux ustensiles culinaires en terre cuite de Château-Thierry des XIVe et XVe siècles', in F. Ravoire and A. Dietrich, dir. (2009) pp. 365–82.

Boüard, M. de (1979) *Le château de Caen* (Caen, Editions du CRAHM).

Guillot, B. (2005) *Caen, le château. Abords de l'enceinte nord. Fouilles de 2005.* Excavation report submitted to the Service Régional de l'Archéologie de Basse-Normandie in Caen, 3 vols (INRAP).

Marin, J-Y. and Lévesque, J-M., dir. (2000) *Mémoires du château de Caen*, exhibition catalogue for 'Redécouvrir le château de Caen. Mille ans de vie et d'architecture', held at the Museum of Normandy 24 June–31 December 2000. (Milan, Editions Skira).

Prentout, H. (1904) 'Étude critique sur la prise de Caen par Édouard III en 1346', in *Mémoires de l'Académie national des sciences, arts et belles lettres de Caen* (Caen, Delesques).

Ravoire, F. and Dietrich, A., dir. (2009) *La cuisine de la table dans la France de la fin du Moyen Age* (Caen, CRAHM).

Scully, T., ed. (1985) 'Du Fait de Cuisine par Maistre Chiquart, 1420', *Vallesia* 40, pp. 101–231.

# Part IV

# Presenting the Sites

# 15

# Le château de Falaise (Calvados): état des connaissances sur l'évolution du site castral du dixième au treizième siècle

*François Fichet de Clairfontaine, Joseph Mastrolorenzo et Richard Brown*

**Summary**

*Falaise Castle is one of the principal medieval fortresses in Lower Normandy. Its history can be traced back to the end of the 10th century, and is associated with the early ducal period and also the birth of William the Conqueror. It is closely linked to the vicissitudes of Normandy in the 12th century and beginning of the 13th century. Its history is not only illustrated by textual sources, but a major part of it also comes from numerous construction phases implemented since the origins of the castle. A great archaeological and architectural location; the fortified site is a prime location from which to study ducal Normandy.*

Depuis 1987, de manière quasi continue, le château de Falaise (Calvados) est l'objet de campagnes de restauration et de valorisation (Figure 15.1). Jusqu'en 1996,[1] aucune observation ou surveillance archéologique n'a pourtant été réalisée que ce soit sur les donjons ou leurs sous-sols, ces derniers étant déblayés sans contrôle. Ces premières campagnes de restauration ont culminé avec la construction d'un avant-corps en béton adossé au grand donjon. Le scandale qui en suivit, donna alors lieu à une véritable prise de conscience. En 1997, une fouille était conduite sur 400m$^2$ par F. Delahaye sur la haute-cour et s'accompagnait de la mise au jour d'un fossé la ceinturant initialement.[2] En 1999 puis 2002, I. Chave conduisait une recension et analyse des sources textuelles et iconographiques, proposant à l'issue de celles-ci de restituer l'évolution de l'enceinte castrale et de ses abords. Entre temps en 2001, sur 170m$^2$, l'emplacement du futur bâtiment d'accueil adossé au mur nord du logis vicomtal faisait l'objet d'une fouille préventive par F. Delahaye.[3] Depuis cette date, avec l'aide de la commune de Falaise, les études archéologiques ne se sont quasiment plus interrompues. En 2003, une première étude du bâti a été conduite par G. Carré[4] sur les courtines et tours de l'enceinte du château, complétée par des sondages auprès de la porte des Champs. Dans le cadre d'un projet d'aménagement, un diagnostic était réalisé en 2005 sur le bastion nord-est, par F. Delahaye.[5] L'intervention a été complétée fin 2008–début 2009, par une fouille préventive menée par R. Brown d'Oxford Archaeology. Enfin de 2007 à 2012, un programme d'étude du bâti a été mené par J. Mastrolorenzo[6] et S. Hanachi sur les courtines du château.

Il est évident que l'ensemble de ces recherches a fortement renouvelé nos connaissances sur la genèse, la morphologie et l'évolution du site castral classé Monument Historique. en 1840. Le colloque de mai 2012 nous a donné l'occasion de revenir sur les principaux acquis tout en nous intéressant au premier chef à la période des Xe–XIIIe siècles.

## Le château de Falaise – Présentation

A la fin des années 1990, le site castral présente une physionomie bien éloignée de celle qu'il avait à la période médiévale. La haute cour forme un simple pointement rocheux dominé par un arbre et les donjons. On y accède directement par une longue pente (appelée souvent rampe d'accès aux donjons) depuis la basse-cour aux formes estompées. Celle-ci affecte davantage la forme d'un parc romantique que d'un espace castral austère et clos. Une longue terrasse rectangulaire de 35m de longueur et de fonction énigmatique sépare la cour dite de la Reine du reste de la basse-cour. Tout cet ensemble a été endommagé durant les bombardements de 1944, lesquels ont détruit une grande partie du collège impérial implanté en 1803 ainsi qu'une chapelle castrale romane[7] que l'on finira d'araser lors du nettoyage du site.

Edifié sur un éperon rocheux de grès armoricain dominant les petites vallées de l'Ante et du Marescot, le château se situe à l'extrémité ouest de la ville close de Falaise (Figure 15.2). La forteresse de plan grossièrement trapézoïdal s'est adaptée à la topographie des lieux. Elle est à la fin du XVe siècle défendue par une courtine longue de 600m ponctuée de 11m

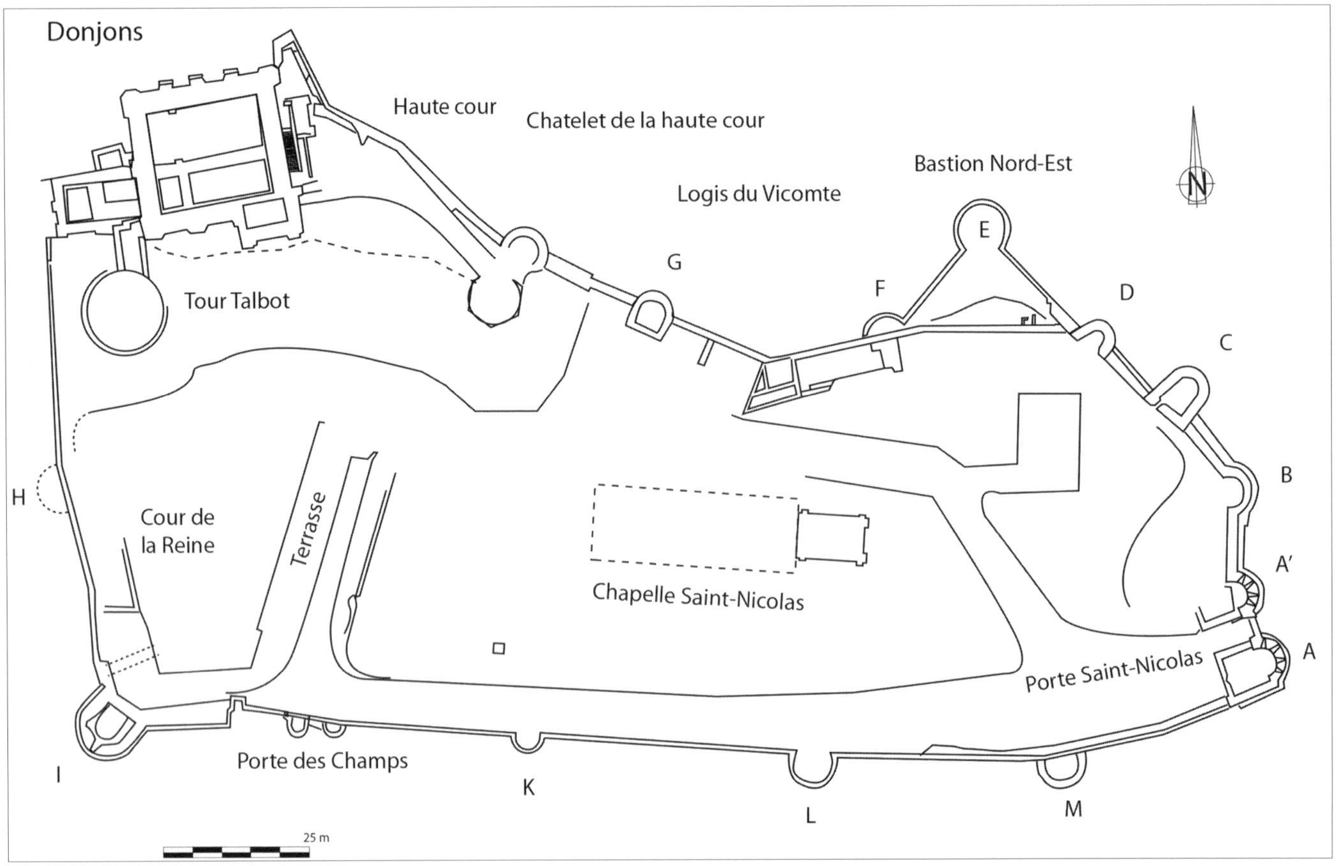


*Figure 15.1. Plan du château de Falaise et localisation des tours, portes et principales zones étudiées (DAO: SRA, B. Fauq).*

tours de flanquement hémi-circulaires, le plus souvent à archères plongeantes à ébrasement simple et fente de tir étroite. Deux châtelets d'entrée (porte Saint-Nicolas, porte des Champs) complètent cet ensemble qui encadre une grande basse-cour d'une superficie de 1,5 hectares environ, séparée en deux partie d'inégales superficies par une terrasse allongée. Cet ensemble est dominé par une haute cour accessible depuis un châtelet d'entrée et à l'extrémité de laquelle s'élèvent deux donjons quadrangulaires du XIIe siècle accolés d'une tour cylindrique (ou tour Talbot) probablement élevée au début du XIIIe siècle (Figure 15.3). Pour M. de Boüard, le site castral aurait été au début du XIe siècle protégé par 'une vaste enceinte palissadée, ou plus probablement, maçonnée, avec une porte fortifiée', 'un mur de pierre sans tour de flanquement' pour J. Decaëns.[8] On suppose ainsi que le site devait être puissamment fortifié pour nécessiter l'emploi de béliers et d'engins lanceurs lors de son siège par Richard III en 1027.[9] Les donjons sont attribués à Henri Ier Beauclerc pour le plus grand et Henry II Plantagenêt pour le second,[10] la tour Talbot à Philippe Auguste, tout comme l'enceinte qui aurait été renforcée et pourvue de ses tours de flanquements. Quant au bastion nord-est qui forme une excroissance, il a été longtemps considéré qu'il datait de la guerre de Cent Ans, période à laquelle on attribue aussi les travaux transformant les meurtrières pour les adapter aux armes à feu.

## 1997–2012: Le site castral des origines au XIIIe siècle

### *La genèse d'un site castral (fin Xe siècle au début XIe siècle)*

La question demeure de savoir si le premier château de Falaise n'a pas disposé d'une haute-cour couronnée d'un donjon en pierre dès la fin du Xe sinon au XIe siècle, et implantée sur la pointe de l'éperon, peut-être déjà barré d'un fossé. Plusieurs éléments militent pour cette hypothèse. En 1997, sur la haute-cour une maçonnerie épaisse de 3m et longue d'autant a été mise au jour sur 0,80m de hauteur. Montée de blocs de grès liés au mortier grossier, elle est recouverte par la base du grand donjon du début XIIe siècle comme par la courtine qui est liée à ce dernier. Cette maçonnerie est associée à des niveaux qui ont livré du mobilier céramique caractéristique de la fin du Xe et du XIe siècle, ainsi que des nodules de mortier

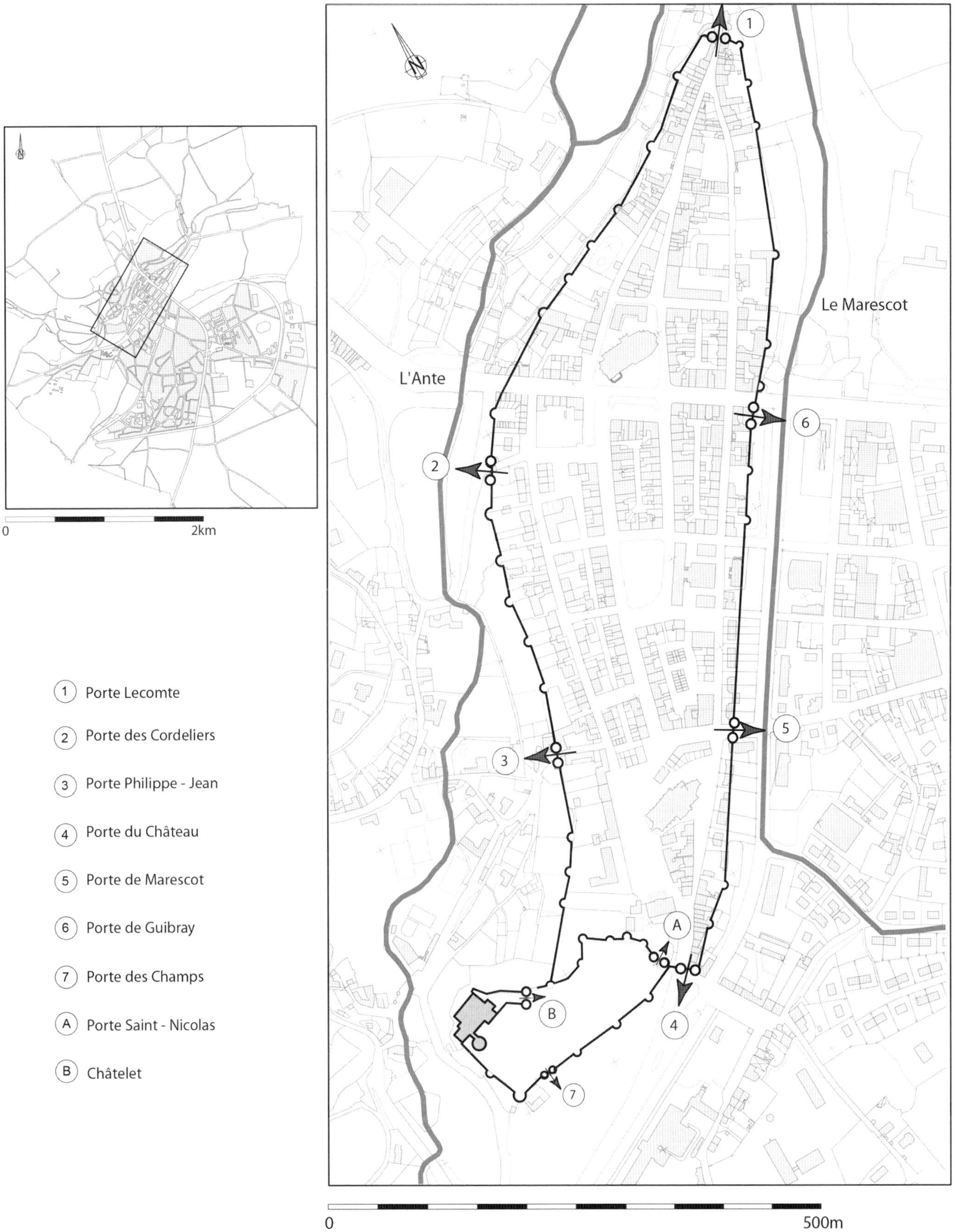


*Figure 15.2. Le bourg fortifié de Falaise et le château (DAO: J. Mastrolorenzo).*

*Figure 15.3. Vue aérienne du château (cliché: J. P. Nivelet).*

de chaux attestant l'existence d'élévations maçonnées à proximité (Figure 15.4, Phase 1). Tout proche mais dans un niveau du XIIIe siècle a été recueilli un denier de Richard 1er frappé entre 950 et 960. Il nous rappelle le texte de Robert de Thorigny[11] qui signale l'existence d'un château vers ces mêmes dates. C'est aussi sous le grand donjon qu'une maçonnerie au tracé légèrement désaxé et à l'appareillage plus grossier a été mise au jour lors des travaux de restauration. Sa position stratigraphique suggère qu'elle est antérieure au monument du XIIe siècle, sa localisation démontre qu'elle a pu appartenir à une construction différente d'une courtine, probablement une tour ou un premier donjon résidentiel.[12]

Les données récentes (que soutiennent les textes) suggèrent la mise en place au pied de la haute-cour, d'une grande enceinte maçonnée au plus tôt dans les dernières années du Xe siècle ou au cours des deux premières décennies du XIe siècle. Les éléments les plus probants sont des portions de courtines de 5m à 9m de hauteur observées sur les fronts est et sud, (Figure 15.5) et derrière le bastion nord-est. A l'est et au nord, elles ont été observées entre les tours B et C (Figure 15.6), à la base de la courtine séparant les tours C et D et enfin derrière le bastion nord-est, entre D et F.[13] La courtine BC a livré deux dates radiocarbone à partir de charbons de bois recueillis dans son mortier.[14] Les datations 14c calibrées donnent 987–1030 pour la première et 995–1040 pour la seconde. Nous pourrions avec prudence y voir la confirmation des propos d'Orderic Vital selon lequel Richard II aurait augmenté les défenses du castrum de Falaise, entre 996 et 1020.[15] Plus récemment une datation obtenue avec un prélèvement effectué au cœur de la courtine A'B a livré la fourchette 889–1015 confirmant que les courtines au parement remanié peuvent intégrer à cœur des parties plus anciennes. Sur le front sud, les maçonneries les plus anciennes ont été observées en plusieurs endroits. Les datations radiocarbones suggèrent aussi la fin du Xe siècle ou le début du XIe siècle. Sur ce flanc, les courtines primitives sont montées en moellons de grès et de quartzite, par endroit appareillés en opus spicatum. Formant une muraille discontinue passant derrière les tours K et L plus tardives, elles vont de la porte Saint-Nicolas jusqu'à un coup de sabre situé un peu avant la Porte des Champs (courtine JK). Il s'agit probablement ici de l'angle sud-ouest du rempart primitif.

Ainsi, la première forteresse est sans doute déjà constituée d'une haute-cour très saillante probablement couronnée d'un premier donjon de pierre,[16] comme défendue par un puissant fossé la séparant de la basse-cour. Cette dernière, d'une surface plus restreinte, avoisinant toutefois 1,20 hectares environ, est protégée par une muraille sans flanquement et à défense passive, essentiellement sommitale. Peu de vestiges caractéristiques de l'habitat ont été encore reconnus pour cette période. L'exemple le plus probant, outre la présence de niveaux détritiques dans la haute-cour,[17] nous semble celui offert par un grand four banal de 4,64m de diamètre qui stratigraphiquement apparaît antérieur à des niveaux de remblais épais de 1,10m et datés des XIe–XIIe siècles tout comme à la tranchée de fondation de la courtine élevée au

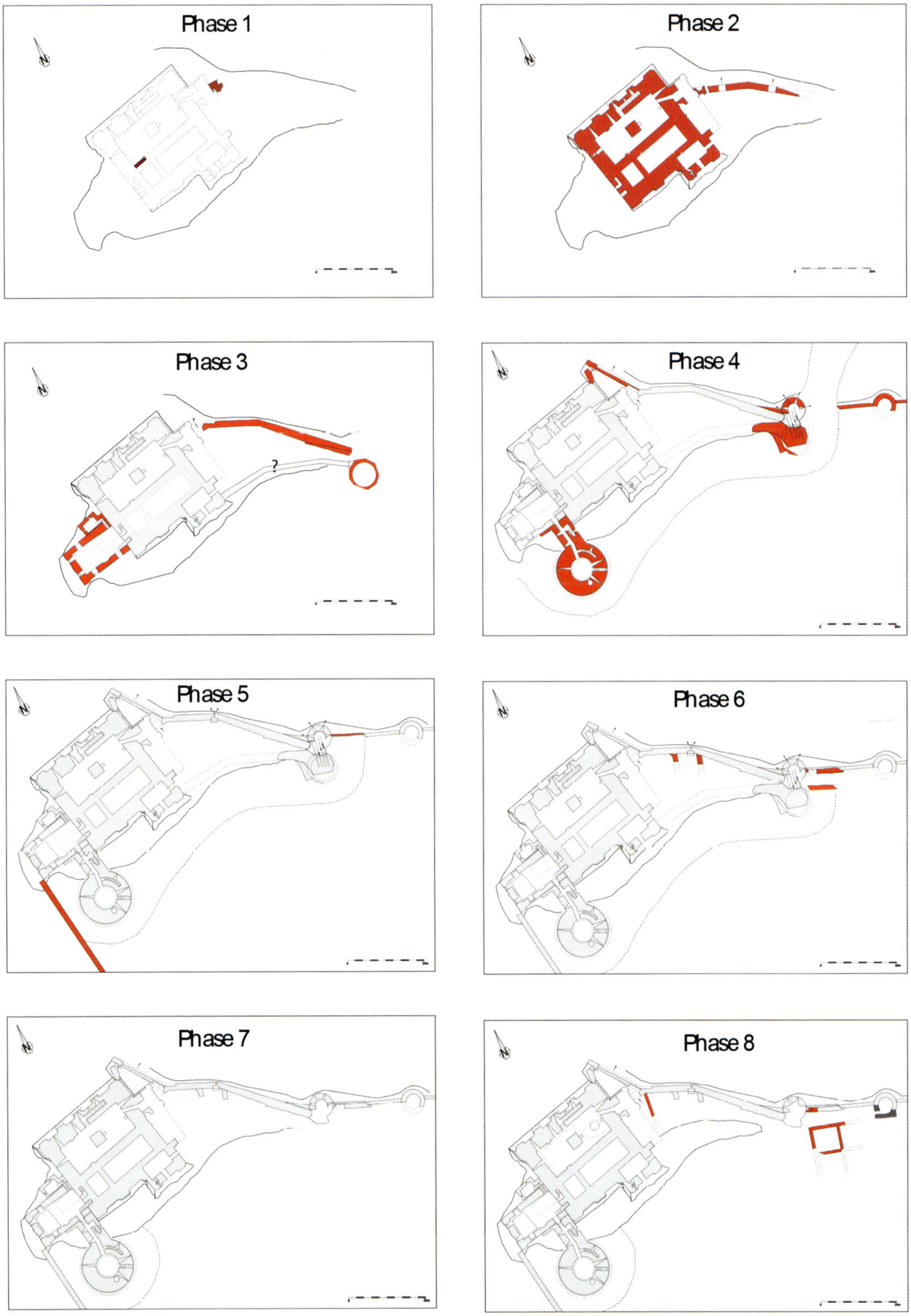


*Figure 15.4. Evolution de la haute-cour: Phase 1 (Xe–XIe siècle); Phase 2 (vers 1120); Phase 3 (2e moitié du XIIe siècle); Phase 4 (début du XIIIe siècle); Phase 5 (vers 1393); Phase 6 (fin moyen-Age); Phase 7 (période moderne); Phase 8 (collège, XIXe–XXe siècle), (DAO: J. Mastrolorenzo).*

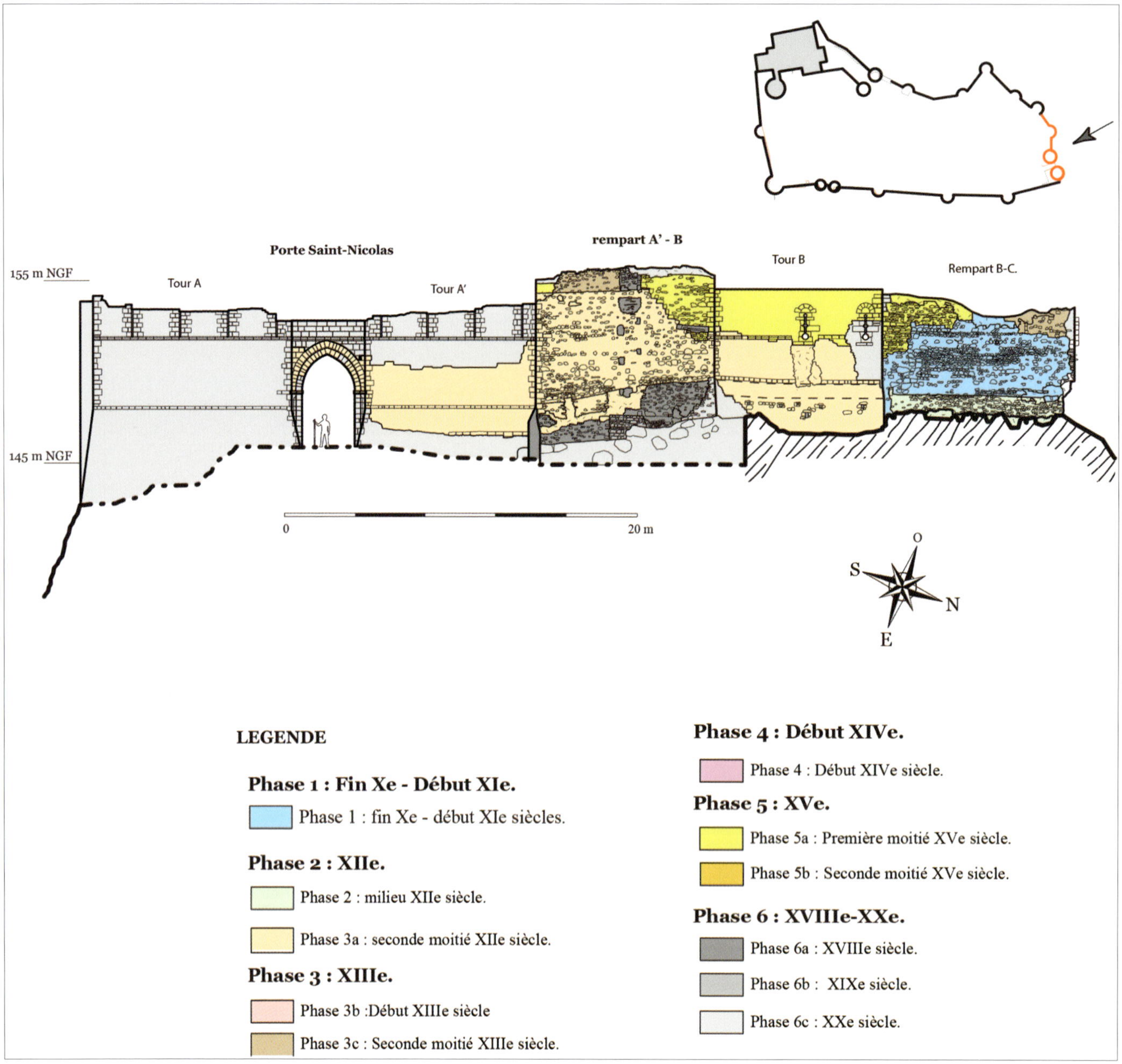


*Figure 15.5. Relevé en élévation du bâti sur le front est. Face externe (relevé, étude et mise en forme J. Mastrolorenzo et S. Hanachi).*

début du XIIe siècle (Figure 15.7). On pourra lui adjoindre des maçonneries partiellement mises au jour en 1986 sous la chapelle Saint-Nicolas.[18] Tout cela fait bien peu!

Durant le XIe siècle, des travaux vont venir compléter ou renforcer la défense du site en une ou plusieurs fois. Le front ouest est reculé d'environ 20m, au-delà de la future porte des Champs qui sera élevée au XIIe siècle. Une datation radiocarbone a livré la fourchette 980–1038 ap.et suggère ainsi une rapide extension de la surface protégée de la basse-cour. On constate aussi un rehaussement de la courtine sud, lequel peut être supérieur à 2m. Une datation radiocarbone (fourchette 1031–1180) pourrait venir confirmer qu'il s'agit de travaux réalisés par Guillaume le Conquérant. Sur les flancs est et nord, ont été individualisées plusieurs portions de courtines qui pourraient confirmer l'importance du programme militaire vers le milieu du XIe sinon la seconde moitié de ce siècle. Celui-ci concernerait aussi l'élévation de la courtine située entre la tour de l'Echiquier (Tour G) et celle F, et des travaux effectués sur les courtines FD et BC, ainsi que CD. Des charbons de bois prélevés dans le mortier du reparement interne de la courtine BC[19] ont fourni la date calibrée 1021–1161, la datation probable de la restauration

Figure 15.6. Vue de la courtine BC (cliché: SRA, F. Fichet de Clairfontaine).

Figure 15.7. Vue du four circulaire, fin Xe–début XIe siècle (?) (cliché: F. Delahaye).

*Figure 15.8. Photographie du grand donjon du début du XIIe siècle (cliché: Ville de Falaise).*

nous situant entre 1041 et 1108. Rien ne s'oppose certes à une contemporanéité avec le programme de Henri Ier Beauclerc au début XIIe siècle, mais on peut aussi retenir la réalisation de travaux par Guillaume le Conquérant à la suite du siège de 1041.[20] Selon Wace et surtout Guillaume de Jumièges (vers 1070), ce dernier aurait fait renforcer *Falisae castellum* après le siège mené contre Toutain Goz en 1041. L'hypothèse est alléchante, qui suggère au-demeurant une quasi contemporanéité de ces travaux avec ceux de l'enceinte du château de Caen. Ainsi dans les deux cas nous pourrions nous situer soit durant les troubles de la minorité du duc, soit à la phase d'affermissement de son pouvoir.

## D'importants travaux au début du XIIe siècle

Le site castral a bénéficié d'une importante campagne de travaux sur ses défenses au début du XIIe siècle, date suggérée par les textes, le mobilier céramique caractéristique de cette période ainsi que par des datations radiocarbones. La forteresse se situe au cœur des intérêts du pouvoir et on rappellera le texte d'Orderic Vital citant un discours d'Henri Ier Beauclerc à ses soldats en 1106, leur évoquant la '*firmissimum munitionem*' de Falaise.[21] Le château se dote d'un grand (et nouveau?) donjon quadrangulaire de 26,60m par 22,80m élevé à la pointe du promontoire, étayé par de puissants contreforts et accolé d'un avant-corps hors-œuvre (Figure 15.8). Cette construction qui intègre un cadre résidentiel et que l'on date communément de 1123 est liée à une courtine enserrant la haute-cour. Suivie sur près de 28m le long du flanc nord, elle présente un parement de grès et de calcaire monté en *opus spicatum* et est haute de 1m et (Figure 15.4, Phase 2). Elle est contemporaine de niveaux mêlant des pierres rubéfiées à des foyers et des céramiques

*Figure 15.9. Photographie du petit donjon fin XIIe siècle (cliché: Ville de Falaise).*

des XIe–XIIe siècles. La haute-cour dont l'accès demeure inconnu (une tour-porche?), était protégée par un large fossé dont les flancs seront chemisés de pierre à une date encore imprécise que nous situons toutefois avant la fin du XIIe siècle,[22] lorsque le fossé est élargi pour l'élévation de la tour à base polygonale.

On a par ailleurs suggéré que la première moitié du XIIe siècle soit contemporaine de l'élévation des premières tours de flanquement, tours pleines semi-circulaires et dépourvues de fentes de tir, la défense se faisant en partie sommitale. La première étude conduite en 2003 le supposait pour les tours K et D que l'on considérait élevées vers le milieu du XIIe siècle.[23] Les récentes datations radiocarbones posent toutefois davantage de problèmes qu'elles n'apportent de certitudes et ainsi ces tours sont depuis apparues plus tardives. Les fouilles conduites par R. Brown sur le bastion nord-est semblent y avoir localisé la plus ancienne tour du site, probablement datable de la première moitié ou du milieu du XIIe siècle. Adossés perpendiculairement à la courtine du XIe siècle, deux massifs de maçonnerie d'un peu plus de 1m de large ont été reconnus (Figure 15.12, US 1142). On a d'abord supposé qu'il pouvait s'agir d'un escalier accédant à un espace extérieur au site. Cela semble improbable et incongru pour la défense de la forteresse.

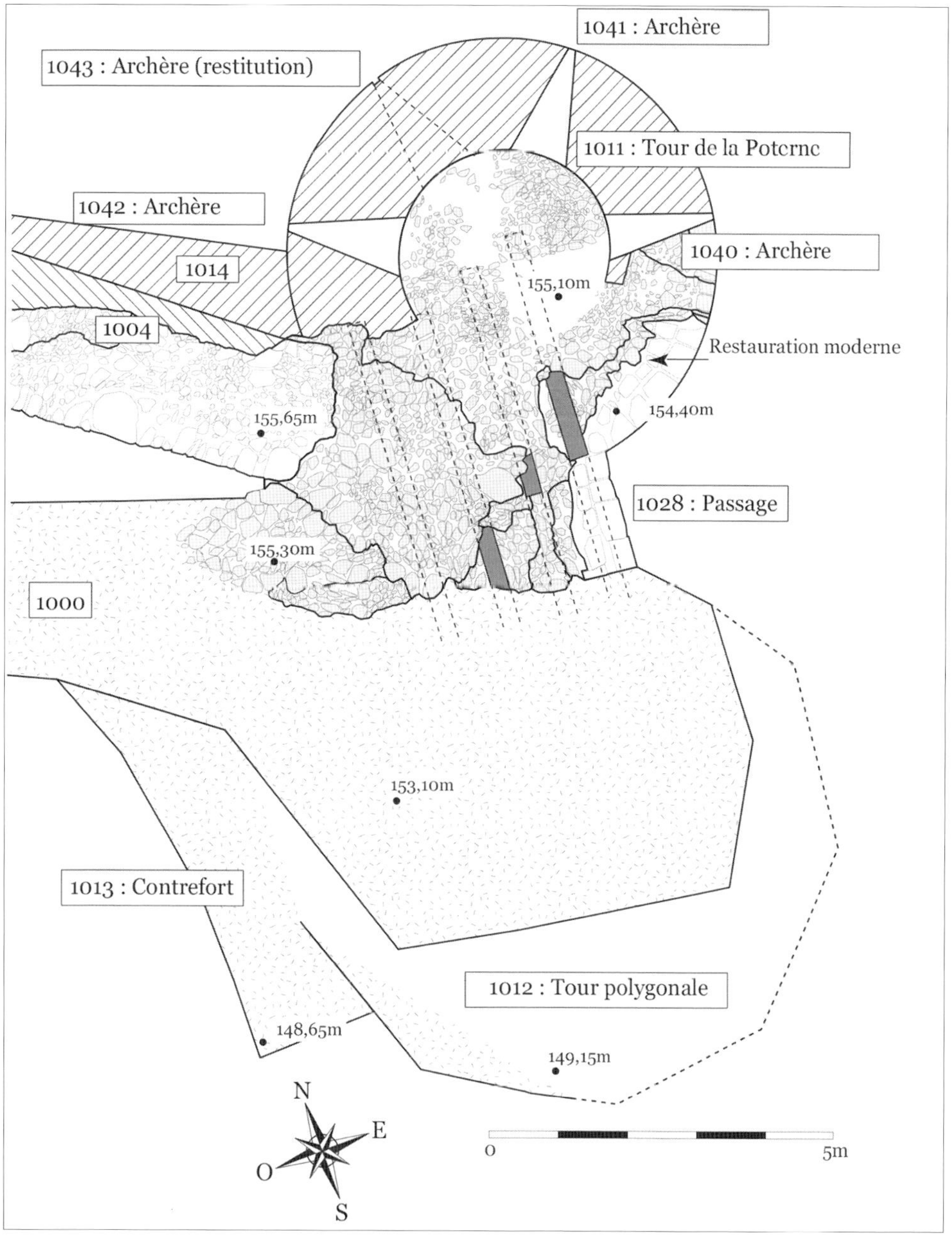


*Figure 15.10. Relevé en plan du châtelet de la haute-cour: 1004 et 1012 – Courtine et tour polygonale de la fin du XIIe siècle; 1011 – Tour cylindrique du début du XIIIe siècle; 1040 – Archère bouchée vers 1394 (relevé et mise en forme: J. Mastrolorenzo).*

*Figure 15.11. Relevé en plan phasé des vestiges de l'espace du bastion nord-est (relevé: Oxford Archaeology).*

*Figure 15.12. Porte des Champs (cliché: Ville de Falaise).*

Nous suggérons qu'il s'agit des vestiges d'une petite tour d'au moins 5m de largeur, proche et contemporaine de celles reconnues par A-M. Flambard-Héricher sur le site castral de Château-Ganne à la Pommeraye (Falaise). La construction de cet élément de flanquement viendrait ici renforcer un des angles fragiles de la défense du site.

La basse-cour dont la superficie demeure identique à celle de la fin du XIe siècle n'intègre pas l'espace de la cour de la Reine qui n'a pas livré de vestiges antérieurs au milieu du XIIIe siècle, ni celui du bastion nord-est. Il est par ailleurs possible, qu'à l'entrée du site, une tour porche ait existé au XIIe siècle (peut-être dès le début de ce siècle), mais en avant de la porte Saint-Nicolas actuelle, là où un massif de maçonnerie a été reconnu partiellement par G. Carré en 2003,[24] puis revu en 2010 par J. Mastrolorenzo.[25] On notera enfin que la douve protégeant le site castral sur ses flancs est et nord a pu être creusée dès le XIIe, voire le XIe siècle. La douve séparant le château de la ville close est large de près de 20m et profonde de 11m, avec un fond plat de 7m de large. Les sondages réalisés à son emplacement par J. Mastrolorenzo ont permis de démontrer qu'elle est parementée au moins sur le front est. L'escarpe et la contrescarpe sont déjà maçonnées au XIIIe siècle, mais rien nous empêche de suggérer qu'elles le soient déjà auparavant à l'exemple du fossé de la haute-cour, dès le XIIe siècle. Du reste, l'étude conduite sur l'avant-cour précédant la porte Saint-Nicolas démontre qu'elle comportait une première escarpe maçonnée antérieure à la tour carrée dominant le fossé au XIIIe siècle[26] (Figure 15.13).

Au sein de la basse-cour, un édifice antérieur au logis du vicomte, adossé à la courtine du début du XIIe siècle, à l'est de la tour de l'Echiquier (G), est suggéré à partir d'une anomalie repérée sur le tracé du parement de cette courtine.[27] Elle s'accompagne d'une différence de mise en œuvre des moellons et plus à l'est d'une assise de dalles calcaire conservée sur 5,56m. Ces dernières semblent appartenir au dallage d'un édifice de plan inconnu qui aurait pu former un premier logis seigneurial au XIIe siècle, sous ce qui deviendra plus tard au XIIIe siècle, le logis du Vicomte (Figure 15.25). On ignore la morphologie des autres constructions qui se sont élevées sur la basse-cour, excepté pour la chapelle castrale Saint-Nicolas implantée à l'est du premier logis et entièrement détruite en 1944. Cet édifice religieux à nef rectangulaire et chevet plat est mentionné pour la première fois en 1200 comme dépendance de l'abbaye Saint-Jean de Falaise.[28] Seul le chœur formé d'une seule nef à deux travées terminée par un chevet plat et aux murs épaulés de contreforts plats (11,90 × 7,60m) a été dégagé lors de sondages réalisés en 1985–6. I. Chave a depuis démontré que la nef, qui aurait pu représenter trois fois la surface du chœur, a été détruite en 1772. La chapelle constituait donc un édifice très imposant ce que les textes confirment.[29] Son chevet percé d'un triplet couvert d'arcs en plein cintre et les rares descriptions de l'ornementation dont celle des chapiteaux à palmette suggèrent une datation vers le milieu du XIIe siècle. Quoiqu'il en soit cet édifice se situe dans l'espace nord de la basse-cour qui semble avoir été privilégié pour l'implantation des constructions 'nobles'. Les sondages réalisés dans l'autre moitié sud en 1985–6 puis en 2003 n'ont jusqu'alors livré, outre un puits, que des vestiges d'édifices à architecture de terre et bois et des traces de foyers, reconnus entre 1,50m et 1,80m de profondeur. Le nivelé atteint même près de 4m entre

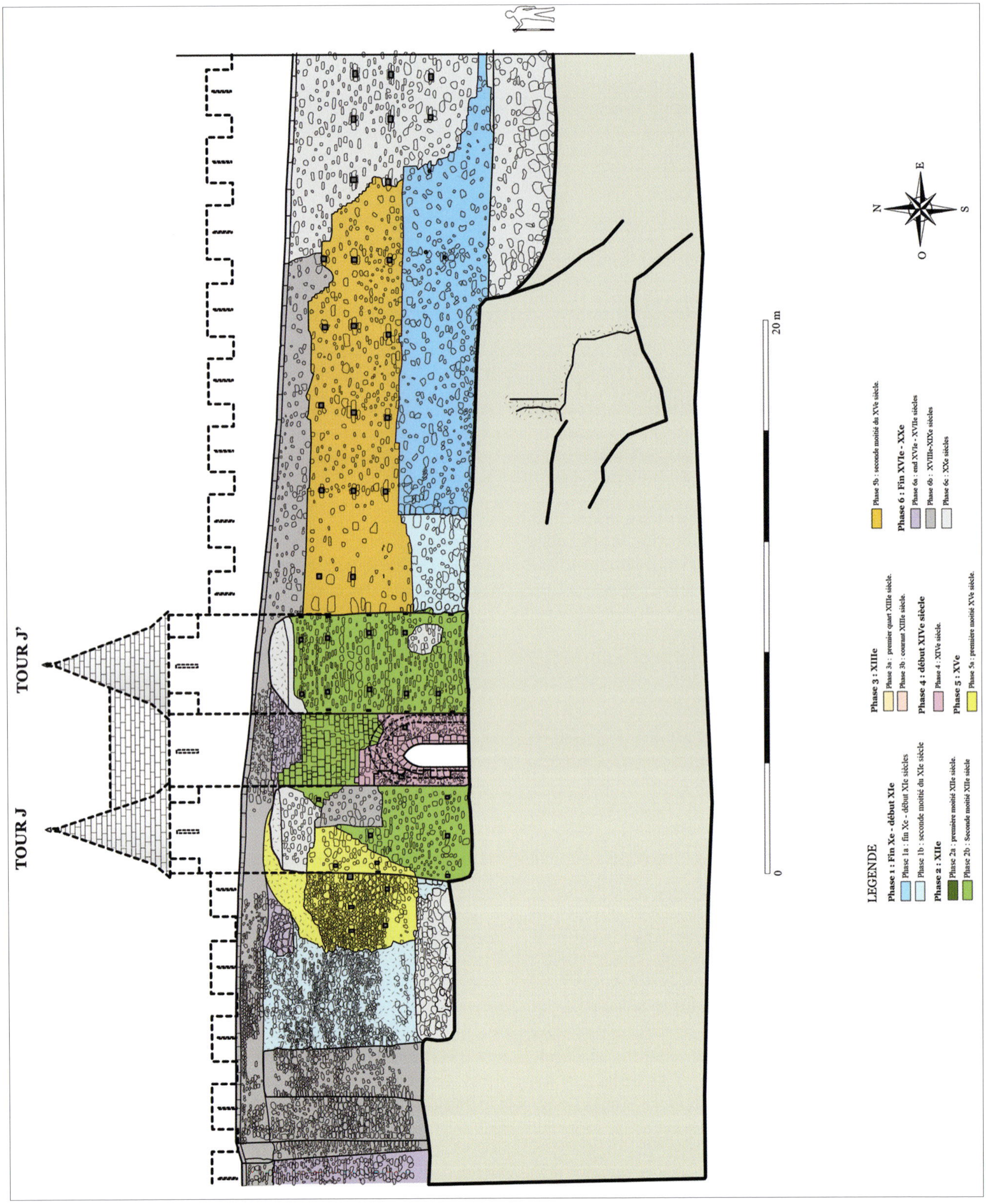


*Figure 15.13. Relevé en plan phasé du front est (étude et mise en forme: J. Mastrolorenzo et S. Hanachi).*

*Figure 15.14. Vue de la tour D (cliché: SRA, F. Fichet de Clairfontaine).*

*Figure 15.15. Vue de la tour K (cliché: Ville de Falaise).*

le logis du vicomte et les niveaux reconnus au pied de la courtine KL. Il est ainsi probable que ce secteur bas à la topographie plus marquée qu'aujourd'hui ait été davantage dédié aux activités domestiques et artisanales. C'est dans cette zone, non loin de la porte Saint-Nicolas, que l'on situe ultérieurement, au milieu du XIVe siècle, une forge ainsi que plus tard des 'estables'.[30] Les données recueillies suggèrent donc une partition fonctionnelle de la basse-cour au XIIe siècle au plus tard, avec des espaces hiérarchisés aménagés en terrasse ou profitant du dénivelé, 'nobles' à architecture de pierre au nord, domestiques et artisanaux au sud.

### *Une nouvelle et importante phase de fortification dans la seconde moitié du XIIe siècle jusque 1204*

Les recherches suggèrent que toute la seconde moitié du XIIe siècle et le premier tiers du XIIIe siècle ont représenté une période quasi continue de travaux. On a pu croire que l'essentiel s'est inscrit d'une part sous le règne de Henri II Plantegenêt auquel on doit sans aucun doute l'élévation du petit donjon vers 1180[31] (Figure 15.9), et Philippe-Auguste avec par exemple l'élévation de la Tour Talbot. Toutefois, pour I. Chave, le coût des travaux conduits sous Richard Coeur de Lion ou Jean sans Terre (selon le rôle de 1203) est très important, bien supérieur à celui engagé par Henri II Plantegenêt.[32] Nombre de constructions ont donc pu s'élever durant une courte période cernant l'orée du XIIIe siècle. Mais les dates radiocarbones nous placent sur une phase 'plateau' et offrent des fourchettes d'estimation bien larges. Il est souvent difficile de savoir à qui attribuer un programme de construction On notera du reste que ces travaux se sont souvent surimposés aux constructions déjà existantes, ce qui ne facilite guère la tache.

Sur et auprès de la haute-cour, plusieurs phases de construction semblent se succéder rapidement. La première comprend l'érection du petit donjon accolé au premier vers 1180 (Figure 15.4, Phase 3), ceci afin d'augmenter la surface résidentielle comme probablement de mieux surveiller l'extrémité de l'éperon. Lui est contemporaine la construction d'une nouvelle courtine, reconnue sur 40m de longueur au nord et destinée à protéger toute la haute-cour. Elle est légèrement décalée par rapport à celle du début du XIIe siècle et montée de blocs de grès liés à un mortier de chaux friable et blanchâtre. Ce décalage est peut-être lié à un programme de travaux visant à agrandir la surface de la haute-cour ou à adapter ses défenses avec l'aménagement ou le réaménagement de son accès. Nous supposons en tout cas que cette haute-cour est alors entièrement cernée d'une maçonnerie, dont les fondations au sud recouvrent du reste une couche livrant du mobilier des XIe–XIIe siècles. La nouvelle courtine nord devait probablement venir buter contre une tour dont subsiste la base polygonale de la tour sud du châtelet d'entrée (Figure 15.10, US 1012). Elle présente la morphologie d'un modèle bien connu dans le monde anglais[33] et a été reprise au début du XIIIe siècle lors de la construction du châtelet d'entrée, dans un programme de travaux qui inclura aussi l'élévation de la Tour Talbot.

Sur le flanc nord-est de la basse-cour, entre les tours F et D, la courtine primitive et la petite tour semblent avoir été endommagées soit par un siège (1138?) soit en raison de défauts structurels? Elles seront protégées par une nouvelle construction (Figure 15.11, US 1150) présentant un léger fruit et distante au maximum de 5m vers le nord (Figures 15.11 et 15.12). Celle-ci se compose d'une grande majorité de moellons calcaire de petit appareil, posés à plat en assises à peu près régulières.[34] Il peut s'agir d'une nouvelle courtine ou plutôt d'une sorte de fausse-braie venant reprendre et renforcer cette partie fragile du dispositif de défense en assurant une protection rapprochée. Il peut aussi s'agir d'une terrasse venant simplement raidir la base de la courtine d'origine (mur de soutènement) pour lutter contre la sape et la pose d'échelle par les assaillants. Dans tous les cas de figure, l'hypothèse de la fausse-braie ayant ici notre préférence, cette construction ne semble pas s'être élevée plus haut que la courtine primitive. Nous supposons que cet aménagement, dont la couche de démolition sera recouverte par le niveau de construction du bastion, date de la seconde moitié du XIIe siècle et qu'il pourrait ainsi être contemporain des premières tours D et peut-être F (?) ou encore K sur le flanc sud.

Sur le flanc est, les travaux successifs n'aident guère à la compréhension claire d'une chronologie des aménagements. La réfection de la base de la courtine BC a été datée des années 1057–1267 (à 95% de confiance), intervalle très large, le pic de probabilité à prendre avec prudence nous situant dans la période 1150–1213. Rien ne s'oppose donc à inscrire ces travaux dans une période comprise entre le règne de Henri II et celui de Jean Saint-Terre.

C'est à la seconde moitié du XIIe siècle et sans doute dans les toutes dernières décennies de ce siècle que nous attribuons actuellement l'élévation des premières tours de flanquement, K, D, peut-être F, voire B, les portes d'entrée (Saint-Nicolas et des Champs) (Figure 15.11), enfin l'élévation de la tour-porche à base polygonale de la haute-cour (Figure 15.4, Phase 3). Le contexte architectural semble bien celui du monde Plantagenêt dont on notera que l'architecture fut inventive, offrant des tours de plans carrés (Caen), circulaires pleines ou non à Loches, Chinon, Gisors ou Château-Gaillard et même en amende.[35] Les différents sondages ont montré que la reprise des courtines DF et CD, marquée notamment par un amincissement des murs, était contemporaine de l'édification de la tour D. Morphologiquement, cette tour cylindrique à base épaissie dans le tiers inférieur de l'élévation apparaît précoce (Figures 15.13–15.15). D'un diamètre moindre que les tours voisines, présentant un parement plus grossier, elle est postérieure à la courtine du XIe siècle mais stratigraphiquement antérieure au bastion nord-est du XIIIe siècle. De plus, ses meurtrières ne sont pas contemporaines de sa phase primitive (tour pleine) et ont sans doute été créées après l'élévation du bastion. Une datation radiocarbone sur un charbon prélevé à la base de la tour D a donné la date de 1161–1265.[36] Le bastion nord-est aurait été lui élevé vers 1030–1210 (95,4% de confiance pour l'intervalle) ou 1029–1212 (95,1%),[37] ces deux dernières dates radiocarbones provenant de niveaux immédiatement antérieurs à la nouvelle fortification. Stratigraphiquement, rien ne s'oppose donc à ce que la tour D ait été construite entre 1180 et 1203 et nous suggérons que la construction des premières tours a pu correspondre à la nécessité de flanquer les angles extrêmes de l'enceinte primitive.

Sur le flanc sud, l'analyse de la tour K a démontré qu'elle venait s'adosser à la courtine du XIe siècle. Elle repose sur le ressaut de fondation de l'enceinte primitive et recouvre son parement sans aucune forme de chaînage. Elle est de plus plaquée contre le parement d'une reprise de la courtine que l'on attribue à la seconde moitié du XIe siècle. Une datation radiocarbone sur un charbon de bois recueilli à la base de la tour K a donné la fourchette 1036–1211 (95% de confiance), ce qui suggère une contemporanéité avec la tour D. D'autres tours ont pu être élevées ailleurs et on restera étonné de l'absence d'une construction similaire, adossée à la courtine, entre la tour K et la porte Saint-Nicolas. Si aucune trace n'a été reconnue par l'archéologie, l'hypothèse vaut pourtant d'être avancée.[38]

Les deux châtelets d'entrée longtemps datés du XIIIe siècle doivent aujourd'hui être rattachés à la phase Plantagenêt. La morphologie originelle de la porte principale d'accès au site castral, devenue la porte Saint-Nicolas au XIIIe siècle (Figures 15.5, 15.13 and 15.16), a été analysée. Ce châtelet d'entrée a été quasi entièrement reconstruit au cours des années 1960 après s'être effondré en 1958. Des élévations originelles, l'étude du bâti révèle qu'il ne subsiste plus qu'une partie du passage couvert d'un arc ogival et les bases de la tour semi-circulaire nord (A'). Les maçonneries médiévales présentent un mortier similaire à ceux de la courtine A'B et de la base de la tour B et sont bien chaînées entre elles. Les constructions semblent présenter les caractéristiques architecturales du style philippien (tours à base talutée en glacis, archères simples plongeantes à niche voûtée en plein cintre légèrement brisée). Toutefois, nous n'avons pu observer aucune archère d'origine! La tour B a entièrement été remontée en partie haute tandis que les archères visibles sur la porte Saint-Nicolas datent de l'architecte Merlet. Nous ne savons pas si ce dernier s'est basé sur des vestiges existants Cela paraît peu probable, car les cartes postales du début du XXe siècle montrent que les tours A et A' étaient alors entièrement arasées. Au final seule la morphologie globale du châtelet, dont l'entrée présente un passage couvert d'un arc brisé et est encadrée de deux tours hémi-circulaires, a suggéré jusqu'alors une datation au début du XIIIe siècle. Deux dates radiocarbone remettent en question le premier schéma chronologique attribuant à Philippe-Auguste l'élévation du châtelet. Le premier prélèvement réalisé sur la fondation de la tour A' a donné la fourchette 1031–1214 avec un pic de probabilité vers 1156 et le second prélèvement dans un mortier blanc de cette même tour a livré 1033–1214 avec un pic de probabilité de 1157. Ces dates peuvent être tout à fait cohérentes avec les travaux initiés par Henri II Plantagenêt et ses suiveurs immédiats à qui on attribue la mise en place des tours de flanquement circulaires pleines sur l'ensemble du domaine angevin.[39] Nous suggérons aujourd'hui d'attribuer à la seconde moitié du XIIe siècle l'élévation du châtelet d'entrée dont les tours seront probablement fortement remaniées dans leurs parties supérieures au siècle suivant. Ce châtelet était précédé d'une avant-cour dont l'emprise et la forme ne peuvent être clairement restituées, seuls quelques vestiges d'une escarpe maçonnée ayant été reconnus.[40]

*Figure 15.16. Vue de la porte Saint-Nicolas et de la tour B à droite (cliché: SRA, F. Fichet de Clairfontaine).*

La petite porte des Champs encadrée de deux tours pleines cylindriques présente des traits qui la rapproche de la tour K (absence de glacis et de fenêtres de tir.). Accessible depuis l'extérieur par une rampe maçonnée, ce châtelet d'entrée présente une morphologie qui le rattache aussi au programme de travaux du XIIe siècle.

La physionomie du château à la veille de son siège par les troupes de Philippe-Auguste nous livre donc l'image d'un site puissamment fortifié, en phase avec les évolutions architecturales et défensives innovantes de son époque, marqué par l'architecture Plantagenêt nourrie de multiples influences dont celle anglaise. L'enceinte percée d'un châtelet d'entrée côté ville (notre hypothèse actuelle) et d'une petite poterne encadrée de deux tours pleines côté étang semble avoir été davantage réparée ou surélevée que reconstruite, sauf sur le flanc nord-est où elle a été « doublée » par une construction basse permettant une défense rapprochée, du moins venant renforcer un angle trop fragile du dispositif architectural. Elle est dotée de ses premières tours de flanquement[41] et dominée par une haute cour ornée des grands donjons résidentiels, protégés par un fossé aux flancs chemisés de pierre et accessibles depuis une tour-porche à base polygonale.

### *Le château au début du XIIIe siècle et programme de Philippe Auguste*

Alors que le château semble s'être rendu sans dommage à Philippe Auguste, le début du XIIIe siècle est marqué par un vaste et imposant programme de construction et de renforcement des défenses. Il n'est pas le seul à en profiter et l'exemple proche du château de Caen et de son donjon roman ceint d'une chemise flanquée de tours d'angle vaut d'être cité. Pour Falaise, il se peut que l'on ait voulu simplement adapter le site aux exigences architecturales et militaires du principe philippien. Mais sans doute les travaux sont-ils liés à la nécessité de restaurer une forteresse beaucoup plus endommagée que ne le laissait croire Guillaume le Breton, panégyriste de Philippe-Auguste, lequel évoquait pourtant une reddition sans heurt du site castral?

*Figure 15.17. Tour Talbot (cliché: SRA, F. Fichet de Clairfontaine).*

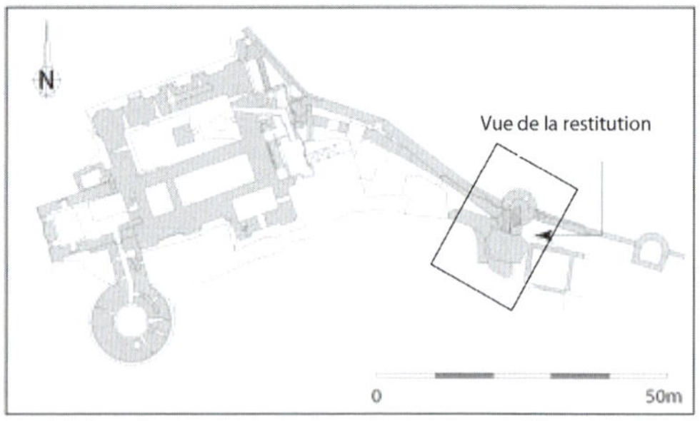


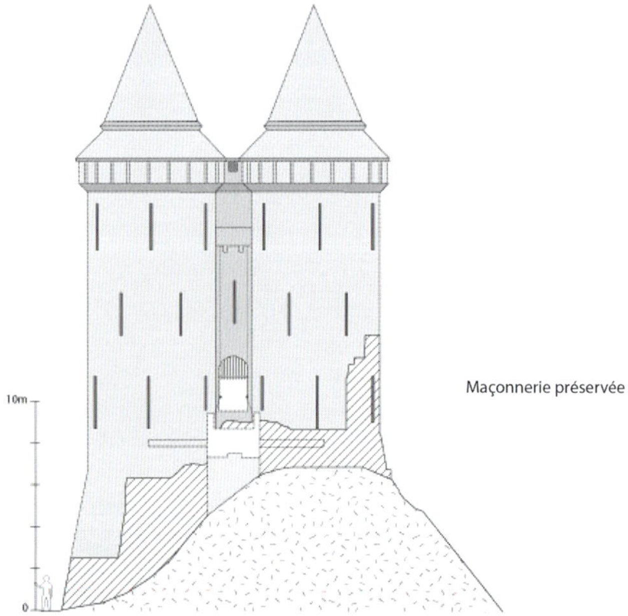


*Figure 15.18. Restitution en élévation du châtelet d'entrée de la haute-cour – début XIIIe siècle (relevé, étude et mise en forme: J. Mastrolorenzo et F. Delahaye).*

La haute-cour et son système de donjons romans s'adjoignent une grande tour cylindrique à base talutée. Appelé Tour Talbot du nom d'un gouverneur du site durant l'occupation anglaise de la guerre de Cent Ans, cette construction massive de 13m de diamètre et de près de 30m de hauteur est éclairée de grandes fentes verticales à plongée (Figure 15.17). Elle est reliée au petit donjon par un couloir qui a nécessité l'agrandissement d'une baie romane éclairant originellement le flanc sud de la tour résidentielle. Une autre porte permet elle l'accès au grand donjon. La nouvelle tour, dont les parements sont traités avec une grande qualité, présente une allure élancée et plus militaire que les donjons résidentiels. Elle marque fortement le site tout en se situant à l'extrémité ouest de la haute-cour et à sa base, s'élevant ainsi depuis le fond du fossé. On peut considérer qu'elle est venue compléter le système défensif de ce secteur en se plaçant ainsi en avancée. La haute- cour est aussi concernée par la construction d'un châtelet d'entrée dont les deux tours encadreront un étroit passage de 1,70m (Figure 15.4, Phase 4 et Figures 15.10 et 15.18). La tour polygonale sud est reprise et liaisonnée avec une seconde tour nord circulaire (tour de la Poterne de 6m de diamètre) à l'aide de poutres de près de 8,60m de long. Cette tour bien que très restaurée en 1393 après un incendie,[42] présente une morphologie similaire à la tour de l'Echiquier (G) qui lui semble bien contemporaine. Elle a livré en 1997 une archère simple à forte plongée et fente étroite, bouchée à la fin XIVe siècle, d'un type proche de ceux de la Reine ou du Bastion nord comme de la tour C et de la tour de l'Echiquier. Sa datation au XIIIe siècle peut ainsi être proposée. En ce qui concerne le liaisonnage, loin d'être inédit ce mode de construction à l'aide d'une poutraison destinée à consolider et lier les maçonneries entre elles se retrouve sur d'autres sites dont par exemple les châteaux d'Aubigné et de Saint-Aubin du Cormier (Ille-et-Vilaine) où il est daté du XIIIe siècle.[43] Cet aménagement s'est accompagné de la construction d'une portion d'enceinte qui est venue s'accrocher à celle du XIIe siècle dont le parement sud avait été en partie démonté pour insérer la tour nord à la pointe de l'éperon.[44] La question reste posée de savoir de quand date la cour de la Reine, créée de manière à compléter la défense du flanc ouest ? Elle pourrait se situer à la fin de la phase de remaniement, peut-être vers le milieu du XIIIe siècle et être ainsi postérieure à l'élévation de la tour Talbot. Peu d'éléments soutiennent cette proposition : des sondages réalisés en 1985–6 ont livré un mobilier céramique plus caractéristique du milieu du XIIIe siècle dans les premiers niveaux d'occupation[45] de la cour de la Reine. D'autre part, tout comme la tour C (Figures 15.13, 15.19 et 15.20), la tour d'angle à plan en U presque en fer à cheval dite de la Reine semble constituer l'aboutissement de l'évolution morphologique des tours du château (Figure 15.21). Quoiqu'il en soit, la basse-cour initialement limitée au tracé de la grande terrasse, est étendue de près de 22m vers l'ouest pour couvrir dorénavant près de 1,5 hectares et une nouvelle courtine est élevée avec la construction de deux tours, celle dite de la Reine (I) qui ne sera mentionnée qu'en 1359, tout comme la tour Ravenel (H) qui est aujourd'hui effondrée (en raison du siège de

*Figure 15.19. Vue de la tour C (cliché: SRA, F. Fichet de Clairfontaine).*

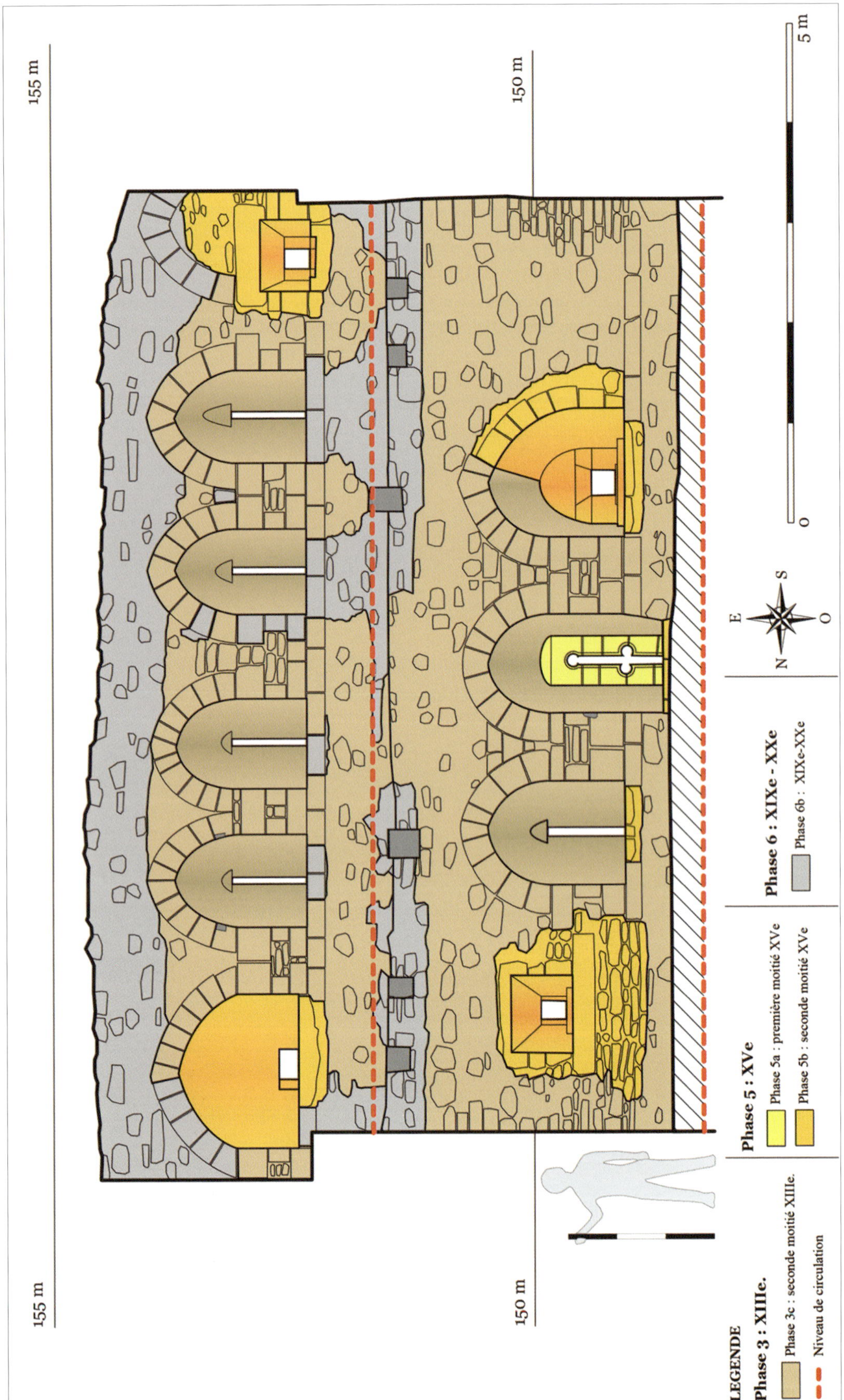


*Figure 15.20. Développé phasé de la face interne de la tour C (relevé, étude et mise en forme: J. Mastrolorenzo).*

*Figure 15.21. Vue de la tour de la Reine (cliché: SRA, F. Fichet de Clairfontaine).*

*Figure 15.22. Vue de la tour E du bastion nord-est (cliché: SRA, F. Fichet de Clairfontaine).*

1579?). La tour Ravenel devait venir initialement protéger l'entrée du fossé ceinturant la haute-cour, comme la tour dite de l'Echiquier (G). De ses vestiges encore visibles, on peut observer la base d'une archère à fente étroite et un pan de mur qui paraît bien lié à la maçonnerie de la courtine, ce qui suggère une contemporanéité de leur construction. La tour d'angle dite de la Reine (I) bien qu'ayant fait l'objet de remaniements structurels importants et de restaurations au XXe siècle conserve dans sa moitié inférieure des maçonneries originelles. A base élargie et de plan en U profond de près de 10m, montée de plaquettes de calcaires, elle conserve trois archères à fente étroite dont les embrasures sont couvertes d'une voussure au tracé brisé et possèdent une plongée inférieure. Elles sont d'un même modèle que celles reconnues sur la tour C. Fait remarquable, cette tour abrite même la seule archère double connue pour l'ensemble du site.

Sur le flanc nord-est, les changements sont tout aussi spectaculaires ou presque. Longtemps daté de la Guerre de Cent ans, le bastion nord-est (Figures 15.11, 15.22–15.24) s'est vu en 2003 attribué au début du XIIIe siècle.[46] Il pourrait appartenir à la première phase des travaux auxquels nous lions aussi la tour Talbot, sans doute du fait de nécessités de défense. La fausse-braie de la seconde moitié du XIIe siècle

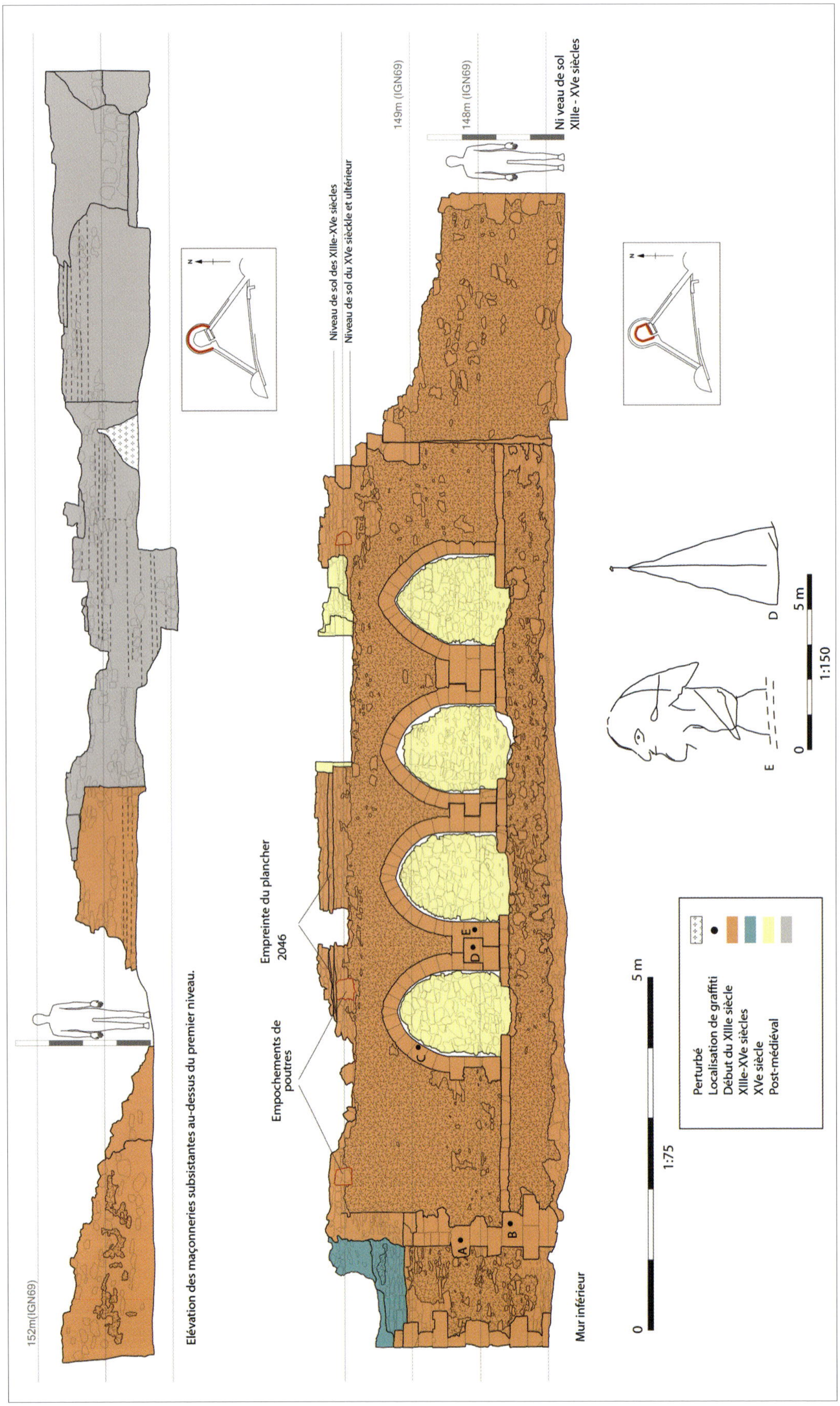


*Figure 15.23. Relevé développé de l'élévation interne de la tour E (relevé: Oxford Archaeology).*

semble en effet ruinée ou détruite. Ses liens avec les tours F et D sont coupés par la construction du nouvel ensemble qui forme une extension en avancée de quelques 400m². Le bastion constitue une construction homogène à cour ouverte et de plan trapézoïdal à tour centrée (E). Il est relié aux tours D et F par deux portions de courtines, celle FE étant percée dès l'origine d'une petite poterne. La courtine DE comporte aussi une voire deux archères aménagées et il est possible qu'il en soit de même pour la courtine EF. La fouille conduite en 2008[47] a permis de suggérer l'existence de structures de bois, dont les éléments d'une galerie en encorbellement longeant intérieurement les courtines.[48] La tour E d'un diamètre circulaire un peu irrégulier de 8,70m, de morphologie philippienne (base talutée en glacis, archères à fente étroite), est à deux niveaux et présente la singularité d'être pourvue d'un escalier droit accédant au deuxième niveau. Notons que très rapidement, probablement dès la seconde moitié du XIIIe siècle, la courette interne au sol de mortier de chaux blanc sera remblayée de rejets domestiques.

Si on excepte la construction de nouvelles tours (L, M, G puis sans doute C), les flancs nord, est et sud semblent surtout l'objet de travaux de réparation des courtines, reprises ou par endroit surélevées. La porte des Champs est remaniée intérieurement avec l'aménagement de deux niveaux superposés, la porte étant rétrécie et couverte d'un arc brisé puis surmontée d'une salle voûtée. On y accède depuis l'intérieur de la basse-cour par une longue rampe parallèle à la terrasse. Enfin nous supposons que l'on modernise la porte Saint-Nicolas dont les tours seront dotées d'archères. Son avant-cour semble aussi faire l'objet de travaux de grande ampleur avec en premier lieu l'édification d'une tour carré protégeant le pont dormant qui sera reconstruit vers 1350.[49]

Au sein du site, dont les textes démontrent une forte densité d'occupation à la fin du Moyen Age,[50] l'étude du logis du Vicomte suggère que c'est aussi au cours du XIIIe siècle, plus probablement au début de ce siècle, que l'édifice est repris et agrandi pour atteindre une surface de 115m² au sol (Figures 15.25 et 15.26). Sa datation peut être confortée par l'élévation de la courtine percée de trois baies en plein cintre pourvues chacune de coussièges latéraux accessibles par un emmarchement. Pour E. Impey le plan, les proportions et les dispositions de l'édifice révèlent de

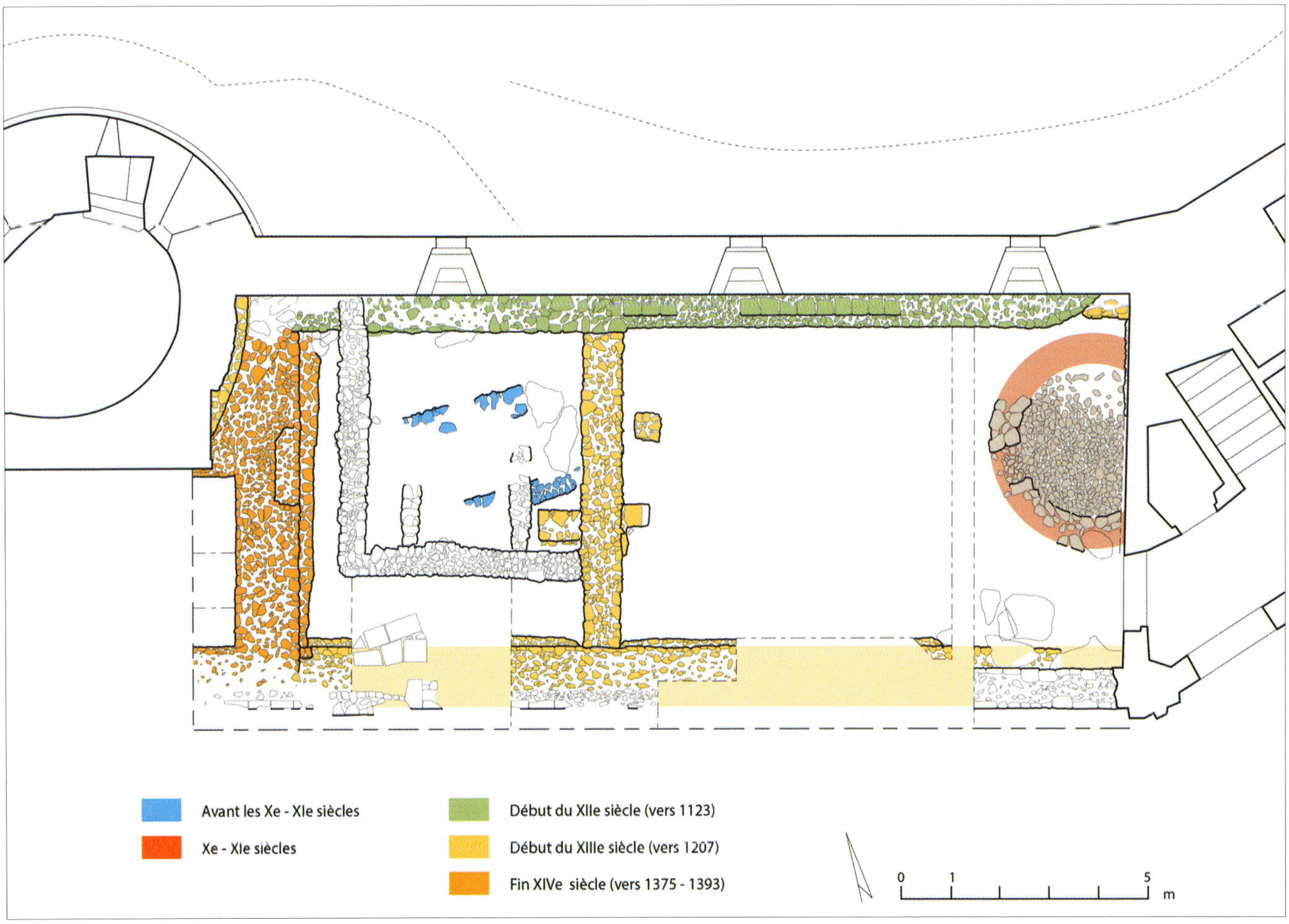


*Figure 15.24. Relevé en plan phasé du logis du Viccomte (relevé et étude: F. Delahaye-INRAP).*

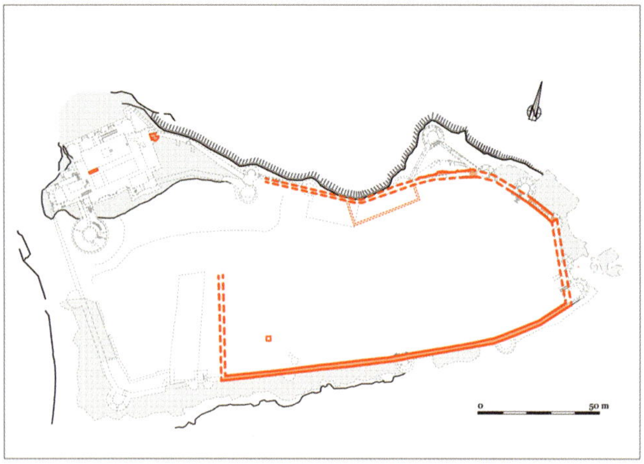


Fin du Xe siècle

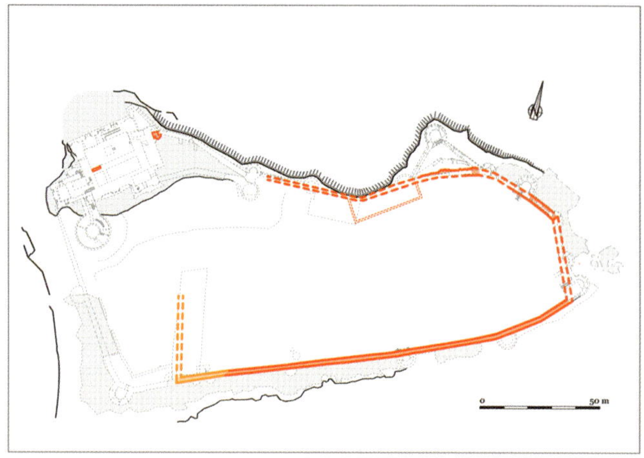


XIe siècle

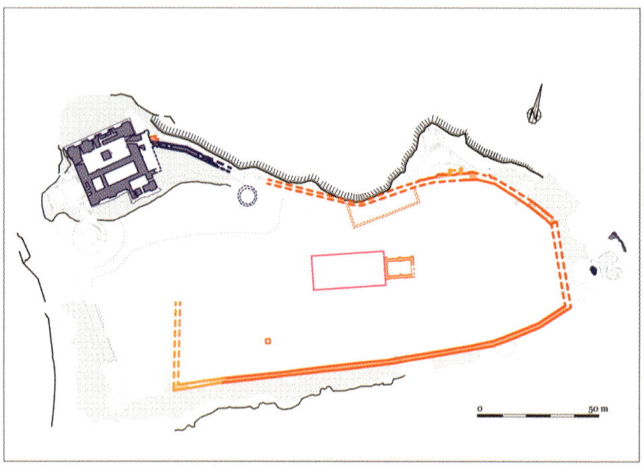


Début à milieu du XIIe siècle

Fin XIIe à début du XIIIe siècle

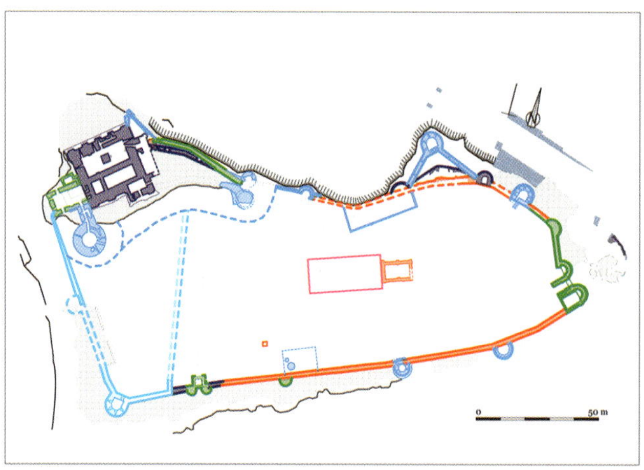


Première moitié - milieu du XIIIe siècle

*Figure 15.25. Evolution par phase du château de Falaise (étude: J. Mastrolorenzo).*

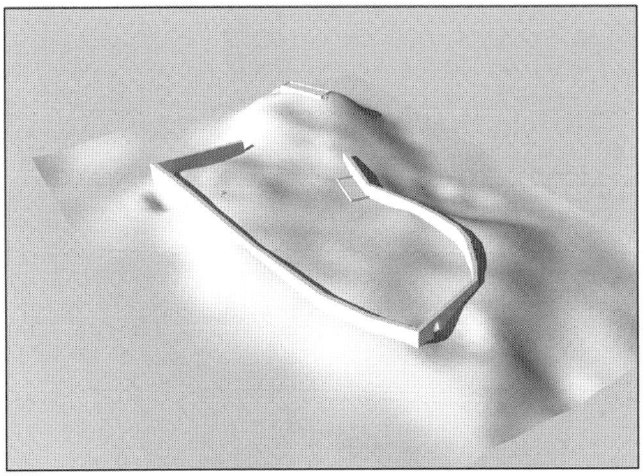

Phase 1a : fin Xe - début du XIe siècle

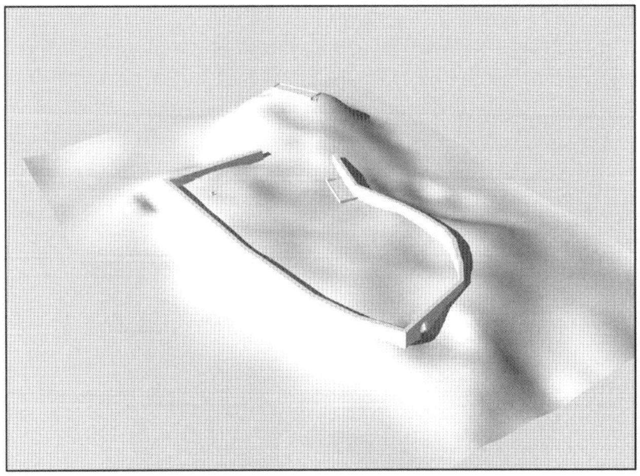

Phase 1b : seconde moitié du XIe siècle

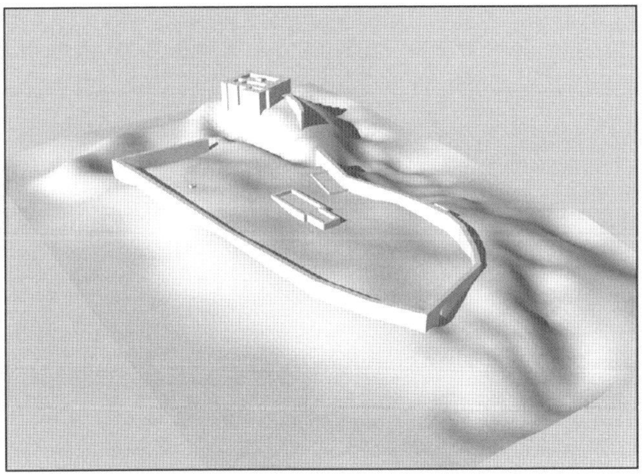

Phase 2a : première moitié du XIIe siècle

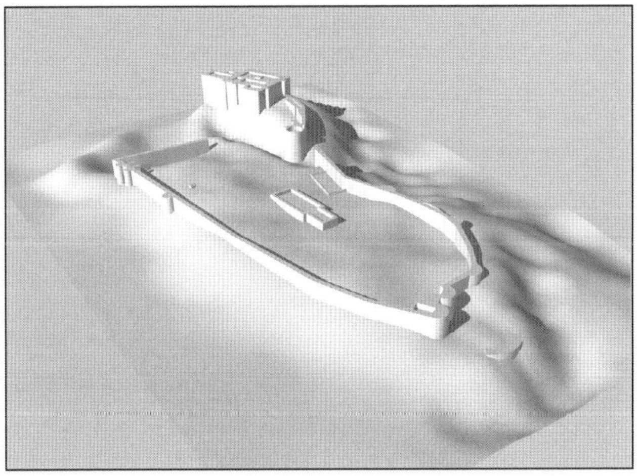

Phase 2b : fin du XIIe siècle

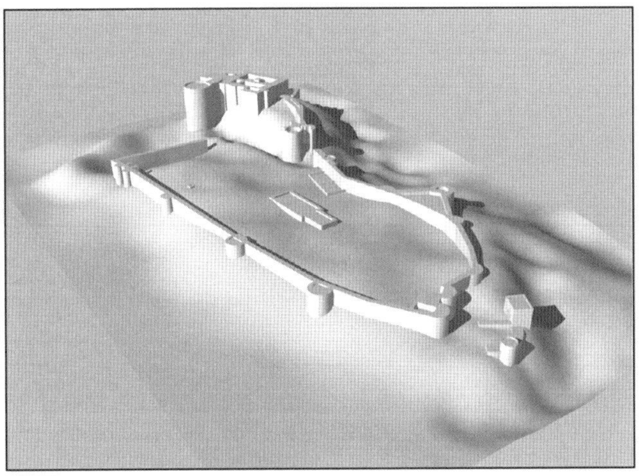

Phase 3a : début du XIIIe siècle

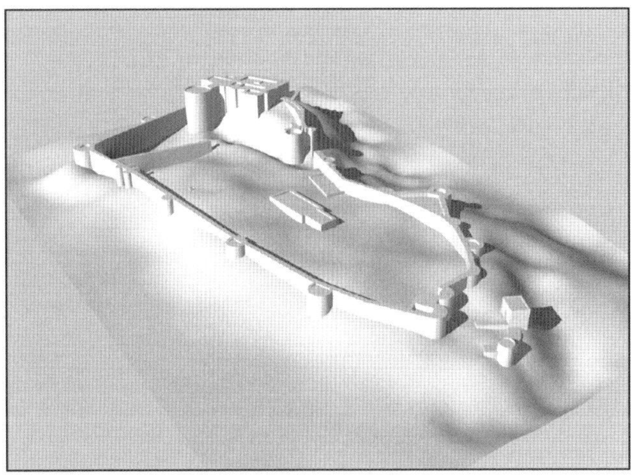

Phase 3b : milieu du XIIIe siècle

*Figure 15.26. Le château de Falaise de la fin du Xe siècle au milieu du XIIIe siècle.*

fortes similitudes avec les édifices nobles ou *chamber-block* de tradition anglo-normande, suggérant une datation peu avant la conquête de 1204.[51] Mentionné par les textes en 1340–50,[52] le bâtiment de 16,70m de long par 6,85m de large se compose de deux grandes pièces en rez-de-chaussée, une cuisine adossée à l'angle de la tour de l'Echiquier et à l'ouest une grande salle (*la salle du manoire au vicomte* citée en 1350) de quelques 60m$^2$, chacune pourvue d'une cheminée et communiquant par une porte en pleine cintre. Les textes du XIVe siècle indiquent qu'il ne comprenait qu'un seul étage (appartements privés et salle d'apparat?).

Comme on le constate aisément, le château de Falaise présente vers le milieu du XIIIe siècle une physionomie considérablement renouvelée avec la tour Talbot en point de mire. C'est une forteresse dont l'espace s'est étendu d'un peu plus de 2000m$^2$ et qui apparaît encore plus inexpugnable avec ses tours de flanquements, les modifications apportées aux châtelets d'entrée aux défenses 'modernisées', enfin les flancs ouest et nord-est, naguère sans doute médiocrement défendus, dorénavant renforcés par l'adjonction de nouvelles courtines et de tours. La chronologie des faits demeure imprécise et pour l'heure nous supposons que la tour Talbot et le bastion nord-est appartiennent à une première phase de travaux et sont antérieurs à la création de la tour de la Reine ou l'élévation de la tour C.

## En guise de conclusion pour l'avenir

Les travaux archéologiques consacrés principalement aux fortifications du château de Falaise ont modifié de manière importante notre perception de l'évolution du site castral en à peine 15 ans, bouleversant noter connaissance du site. Il est ainsi maintenant assuré qu'une fortification de pierre sans doute dépourvue de tours de flanquements s'élève sur le site dès le tout début du XIe siècle au plus tard et qu'elle est modifiée fortement au cours de trois grandes phases de travaux jusque la fin de la première moitié du XIIIe siècle. L'étude de la ceinture fortifiée du château de Falaise laisse sans doute quelques zones d'ombre et il est indéniable qu'il faudra affiner la datation des tours. Pour autant l'avenir doit être davantage celui d'un réexamen des élévations des donjons (l'existence d'un deuxième étage pour le grand donjon étant toujours discutée) et surtout de recherches à consacrer à l'analyse de l'occupation de la basse-cour, qui bien que documentée par les textes de la fin du Moyen-Age, nous demeure encore trop méconnue.

## Notes

1 En 1993 Edward Impey étudie toutefois le mur nord du logis vicomtal qu'il date vers 1200 et qu'il considère comme typique de l'architecture de tradition anglo-normande (Impey 1993).
2 Delahaye 1998.
3 Delahaye 2001.
4 Carré 2003.
5 Delahaye 2005.
6 Mastrolorenzo 2009, 2010a–c.
7 Elle abritait le laboratoire de chimie du collège, la salle du logis vicomtal servant de réfectoire.
8 De Boüard 1984, p. 73 ; Decaëns 1997.
9 Guillaume de Jumièges Vol. I, p. 99.
10 R. Doranlo démontre en 1948 que le grand donjon est accolé d'un avant-corps permettant d'accéder à la grande salle (Doranlo 1948 ;1954).
11 Robert de Torigni suggère l'existence d'un château (castrum) vers 960 sous Richard 1er dont il rappelle qu'il fit étendre le bourg et enclore le château de tours et de murs (Decaëns 1997 ; R. de Torigni, pp. 164 et 196).
12 Delahaye 1998, pp. 14 et 27.
13 Brown 2008.
14 Mastrolorenzo 2009.
15 Orderic Vital IV, pp. 35 et 39. La présence d'une défense maçonnée explique aussi sans doute le difficile siège du site par Richard III en 1027.
16 Au sein du grand donjon, il subsiste aussi une portion de maçonnerie qui lui est bien antérieur.
17 On peut aussi mentionner un denier normand émis entre 996 et 1027 recueilli sur la « rampe » mais dans des niveaux du XIIIe siècle (Couanon 1987).
18 Couanon 1987, fig. 59, pp. 82 et 87.
19 Mastrolorenzo 2009.
20 « ses castiaz fist fort renforcier, fossez parer, murs redrecier » Wace II, v.10294.
21 O. Vital, IV, p. 90.
22 Même si l'existence d'un fossé de défense est très probable dès l'origine, rien ne permet de le dater d'avant le XIIe siècle.
23 Carré 2003, p. 16 pour la tour K; pp. 26 et 36 pour la tour D.
24 Il a été suggéré en 2003 l'existence d'une maçonnerie antérieure à la tour A', peut-être un vestige d'une tour porche primitive (Carré 2003). Mais l'examen approfondi de cette anomalie a depuis démontré que cela correspond juste à l'utilisation d'un mortier différent en partie basse, le mortier blanc utilisé étant mêlé et chevauchant même le mortier jaune formant le corps de la Porte Saint Nicolas (Mastrolorenzo 2010).
25 Mastrolorenzo 2010a, II, fig. 7, M.604.
26 Mastrolorenzo 2010b.
27 Delahaye 2001, pp. 31–3.
28 Chave 2005, p. 76.
29 Chave 2005, p. 82.
30 Chave 1999, II, p. 13.
31 Ce qui est peu probable pour cette construction qui est à l'évidence surtout destinée à augmenter l'espace résidentiel.
32 Chave 1999, I, pp. 143–4.
33 Renn 2000. Voir aussi par exemple la tour à base octogonale du XIIe siècle de Richard's Castle (Kenyon 1996, p. 53). Pour la Normandie, on peut aussi mentionner la base polygonale du premier donjon de Bricquebec (Manche).
34 La mise en oeuvre est assez éloignée de celle du bastion même dont les maçonneries se composent uniquement de moellons et de blocs de grès rouges/bruns.
35 Voir en particulier Mesqui 1997 ; Mesqui 2000 et Baudry 2001.
36 Un intervalle de 95% de confiance avec un pic de probabilité vers 1218, à prendre avec prudence, sauf à considérer qu'il témoigne de travaux de reprises au début du XIIIe siècle.

37 Brown 2009.
38 Une datation radiocarbone de la tour L a livré la fourchette 1050–1217 (95% de confiance), mais la morphologie de la tour la distingue de celles du XIIe siècle et une construction au début du XIIIe siècle est pour l'heure privilégiée.
39 Baudry 2000 et voir aussi Mesqui 2000 qui pour la seconde moitié du XIIe siècle mentionne des tours circulaires et semi-circulaires à archères à Gisors (avec archères doubles), Château-Gaillard ou Boneville-sur-Touques etc. On peut aussi mentionner l'exemple très proche offert par les tours du château de Courcy (Calvados) élevé dans la seconde moitié du XIIe siècle.
40 Mastrolorenzo 2010b, I, pp. 29–30 et II, fig. 16.
41 Nous suggérons ici que la tour D et peut-être celle F qui n'a malheureusement pas été étudiée avant restauration ont été élevées peu après la « fausse-braie ».
42 Chave 1999, I, pp. 135–7 et BNF, fr 26026, n°1906.
43 Chave 1999, I, pp. 139–140 ; Cucarull et Leprêtre 1997.
44 Cette insertion évitant que la tour soit trop saillante sur le flanc nord nous semble confirmer l'antériorité de la tour à base polygonale.
45 Couanon 1986, pp. 108–14. Ces sondages nous suggèrent aussi que cet espace se situe hors les murs du château auparavant.
46 Carré 2003 et Delahaye 2005 qui confirme cette nouvelle datation.
47 Brown 2009.
48 Il est donc possible que l'on accédait d'abord à la tour E puis à la courette depuis son escalier, Du moins aucun autre aménagement n'a été reconnu permettant de restituer le mode d'accès au bastion depuis la basse-cour du site castral.
49 Mastrolorenzo 2010b.
50 Voir surtout Chave 1999, II.
51 Impey 1993, pp. 64–8.
52 Chave 1999, II, pp. 10–52.

## Bibliographie


Baudry, M-P., sous la dir. (2000) *Les fortifications dans les domaines Plantagenêt, XIIe–XIVe siècles,* Actes du colloque international tenu à Poitiers, 11–13 novembre 1994. Colloque conçu et organisé par M-P. Baudry, Ph. Durand, N Fauchère et J. Mesqui (Poitiers, Centre d'études supérieures de civilisation médiévale, Université de Poitiers).

Baudry, M-P. (2001) *Les fortifications des Plantagenêts en Poitou 1154–1242* (Paris, CTHS).

Boüard, M. de (1984) *Guillaume le Conquérant* (Paris, Fayard).

Brown, R. (2008) 'Falaise, Le château – Bastion nord-est', *Bilan Scientifique régional de Basse-Normandie*, pp. 43–4.

Carré, G. (2003) avec la collaboration de Fauq, B. *Etude préliminaire des parements extérieurs de l'enceinte castrale et sondages archéologiques (10 février/21 mars 2003)*, rapport dactylographié, DRAC BN–SRA, 1648 (Caen).

Chave, I. (1999) *Le château de Falaise (Calvados) au Moyen Age: étude documentaire et archéologique*, 3 vol. Dactylographiés, DRAC–SRA 1226 (Caen).

Chave, I. (2002) *Château de Falaise (Calvados). L'enceinte castrale et ses abords (XIe–XXe s.). Etude archéologique et documentaire*, Rapport dactylographié, DRAC BN–CRMH (Caen).

Chave, I. (2005) *'Des sources comptables au service de l'archéologie: essai de reconstruction documentaire de la chapelle dite Saint-Nicolas du château de Falaise (Calvados), XIIe–XVe Siècles'*, *Tabularia 'Études'* 5, 14 Décembre 2005, pp. 75–124.

Couanon, P. (1986) *Le château de Falaise (Calvados) 1985–1986, fouilles de sauvetage dans l'enceinte castrale*, rapport dactylographié, DRAC BN–SRA 57.

Cucarull, J. et Leprêtre, B. (1997) 'Organisation et évolution du château d'Aubigné (Ille-et-Vilaine) d'après l'analyse de ses vestiges', *Revue Archéologique de l'Ouest* 14, pp. 198–200.

Decaëns, J. (1997) 'Le château de Falaise', dans M. Bayle, sous la dir., *L'architecture normande au Moyen Age*, vol. 2, pp. 305–9.

Delahaye, F. (1998) Château de Falaise (Calvados), rampe d'accès aux donjons. DFS de sauvetage, AFAN. DRAC BN–SRA 1126.

Delahaye, F. (2001) *Falaise (Calvados). Le château. Bâtiment d'accueil. DFS de sauvetage.* AFAN, DRAC BN–SRA 1382.

Delahaye, F. (2005) *Falaise (Basse-Normandie – Calvados). Le château, Bastion nord-est. Rapport de diagnostic archéologique*, INRAP, DRAC BN–SRA 1728.

Doranlo, R. (1946–1948) 'les fouilles de 1948 dans le château de Falaise', *Bulletin de la Société des Antiquaires de Normandie* L, pp. 496–501.

Doranlo, R. (1954) 'Le château de Falaise', *Congrès archéologique de France*, XI, session tenue dans l'Orne en 1953, pp. 181–200.

Guillaume de Jumièges, *Gesta Normannorum ducum*, J. Marx, éd., 2 volumes (1914) (Rouen et Paris).

Impey, E. (1993) *L'architecture seigneuriale en Normandie (1050–1350)*, rapport de prospection thématique, DRAC–SRA (Caen).

Kenyon, J. R. (1996) *Medieval Fortifications* (London et New York, Leicester University Press).

Lefèvre, D. (2003) *Château de Falaise. Etude préalable à la restauration et à la mise en valeur de l'ensemble des remparts et de leurs abords (hormis le front nord-ouest)*, dossier d'étude rendu par l'architecte en chef des monuments historiques, CRMH–DRAC BN.

Mastrolorenzo, J. (2009) *Falaise (Calvados) Le château, Sondages,* rapport, DRAC BN–SRA.

Mastrolorenzo, J. (2009) *Note sur les résultats d'analyse par le Radiocarbone des prélèvements de charbon de bois effectués sur le front est de l'enceinte du château de Falaise (14)*, rapport dactylographié, DRAC–SRA.

Mastrolorenzo, J. (2010a) *Falaise (Calvados), Le château, Basse-cour, Tranchée technique du bâtiment d'accueil,* rapport en 2 volumes, DRAC BN–SRA.

Mastrolorenzo, J. (2010b) *Falaise (Calvados), Le château, Front est, côté extérieur,* rapport en 2 volumes, DRAC BN-SRA n°.

Mastrolorenzo, J. (2010c) *Falaise (Calvados), Le château, Front est, Etude des élévations,* rapport à en cours.

Mériel, A. (1889) *Histoire de Falaise: antiquité, gouvernement militaire, fortifications* (Falaise).

Mesqui, J. (2000) 'Les tours à archères dans le domaine Plantagenêt français 1160–1205', dans M-P. Baudry sous la dir., pp. 77–88.

Orderic Vital, *Historiae ecclesiasticae libri tredecim*, M. Chibnall, éd. (1980) (Oxford, University Press).

Renn, D. (2000) 'Plantagenêt castle-building in England in the second half of the twelfth century', dans M-P. Baudry, sous la dir., pp. 15–21.

Robert de Torigni, *Chronique de Robert de Torigni*, Vol. I (1872) (Rouen, Léopold Delisle).

Wace, R., ed. *Roman de Rou,* 2 volumes (1877–9) (Andresen, Heilbronn).

# 16

# The question of site enhancement in rural contexts: examples of projects managed by the Calvados Departmental Council (Conseil Général du Calvados), Lower Normandy

*Nicola Coulthard*

**Résumé**

*Le Conseil Général du Calvados met en œuvre une politique volontariste quant à la gestion et la valorisation de sites patrimoniaux publics et privés départementaux, d'une part à travers des conseils et des aides financières, d'autre part à travers la gestion directe d'un certain nombre de sites. Les dispositifs sont esquissés dans cet article, avec un focus sur l'action du service archéologie qui gère plusieurs sites, conduisant où gérant des projets de recherche, initiant les programmes de mise en valeur, et mettant en place des actions de médiation culturelle.*

*A travers quatre sites archéologiques datant de périodes chronologiques différentes et localisés dans des cadres géographiques distincts, les spécificités et difficultés de la valorisation de sites ruraux seront abordées.*

- *Le tumulus néolithique de Colombiers-sur-Seulles: Accès libre, mise en valeur simple dans le respect de l'environnement rural.*
- *Le village déserté 'Courtisigny' à Saint-Ursin, Courseulles-sur-Mer: En l'absence d'un projet de mise en valeur cohérent, protection et conservation des vestiges par rebouchage.*
- *Vieux-*Aregenua*, capital de la cité antique des Viducasses: Equipe de recherche permanente, création de l'entité 'Vieux-la-Romaine', musée de site récent, sites archéologiques restaurés, visites de fouilles en cours, actions pédagogiques.*
- *Le Château Ganne à La Pommeraye, localisé au sein d'un Espace Naturel et Sensible (ENS): Consolidation des vestiges, accès au public partiel et contrôlé.*

In France, a major decentralisation law passed in 1982 delegated clearly defined legal functions to the departmental councils (Conseils Généraux), the most important of which are social welfare and road infrastructures. Remaining a unitary state, with clear-cut distinctions between obligatory and voluntary functions within local government, the only cultural functions delegated were archives and library network management. Both departments and municipalities were nevertheless allowed to create their own cultural services, in the domains of the performing arts and/or heritage management, though national policy making, relayed by prefectural services in each region, remains the prerogative of central state government.

The Calvados Departmental or 'General' Council was one of the first in France to create specific cultural services, with a precursory organisation promoting performing arts in 1981[1] and an archaeological service in 1982. A Heritage Service,[2] the principal functions of which are to manage grants and give advice for the preservation of both historical buildings and art and antique objects, was later created in 1992.

The Archaeology Service differs somewhat as alongside the corresponding managerial and advisory role for archaeological sites, it also comprises a permanent fieldwork team. The service's functions are threefold: research, heritage management and cultural mediation, particularly at 'Vieux-la-Romaine, Museum & Sites'. These functions are not exclusive. The service endeavours to strike a balance between heritage preservation and the public's enjoyment thereof, conducting or coordinating research programmes and developer funded projects, carrying out consolidation or restoration work, and diffusing knowledge through a wide range of educational actions.

This paper focuses on site management, using four case studies, illustrating the particularities and problems of site enhancement in rural contexts. The sites are:

- a Neolithic long barrow;
- a Roman town;
- a deserted medieval village;
- a medieval castle.

None of these sites is the result of legacies or management responsibility transfers; they have all been acquired since the decentralisation laws and correspond to proactive policy. The criteria were chronological and geographical coherence, the educational value of each site, a promotion of a sense of place for the local population and for all but one of the four, the reinforcement and diversification of the Department's historical resources for touristic development.

The two medieval sites reflecting the Middle Age heritage omnipresent in Normandy are counterbalanced and set in a 'site timeline' by the prehistoric and Gallo-Roman sites. Historical/industrial archaeology should also soon become part of this departmental network, as the Council has recently acquired 19th-century limekilns,[3] as yet not accessible to the public. Situated between 12km and 40km from the Caen agglomeration, where a third of the Department's population lives, the sites are located in very different, complementary environmental settings with contrasting geological and geomorphological contexts, and different land use histories. This highlights the diversity and functional complementarity of the Calvados territory.

Both the chronological and geographical criteria reinforce perhaps the strongest incentive for the acquisition and enhancement of these sites, which is their educational value. The aim is to strike a balance between the charismatic, exceptional sites (Falaise Castle, the Bayeux Tapestry, the D-Day landing beaches) and lesser known sites representing the broader history of the Department's human occupation. The sites selected are representative examples of our material heritage, and as such are invaluable educational resources. Each of them represents a relatively coherent chronological timespan, quite easy for a neophyte public to relate to, with few reoccupations; the Neolithic tumulus presents a single funerary chamber, the medieval castle is a singularly fossilised example of a 12th-century fortification. These sites, within their environmental settings, represent chronological stepping stones and as such are designed to help people link with the passage of time on a regional scale while situating the phenomena (megalithism, the Roman occupation, castle building) within a global historical framework, advancing understanding, whilst promoting a sense of local identity.

Last but not least, the tourism criterion is not the easiest to reconcile with the others, as statistics clearly show the tendency of visitors to limit their stay in the Department to a few days, visiting a few World War II and William the Conqueror associated sites before moving on. With the exception of the Roman town, just a 15 minute drive from Caen, the sites are indeed 'off the beaten track'. However, the increasing demand for rural gîtes and the development of 'green tourism' give reasons to hope for an evolution of the current trends. Working more closely with the Calvados Tourist Board is an encouraging development.

## The Neolithic long barrow at Colombiers-sur-Seulles

Though somewhat overshadowed by the Megalithic phenomenon in neighbouring Brittany, the diversity of tombs in Lower Normandy led to several excavations in the late 1980s, in a programme to further knowledge of the Neolithic monumental tomb tradition. The Colombiers long barrow (Figure 16.1 and 16.2) was excavated in the 1980s by a Franco-British team.[4] The excavation of the trapezoidal monument revealed segmented internal architecture with wooden shuttering and contrasting fill. The single circular funerary chamber excavated was built however with orthostats, and was accessed by a short drystone entrance passage. Dated to 4200–4000 BC, the monument is the only example of this type in Lower Normandy, and as such is a key in the evolution of monumental funerary architecture. The excavation team, aware of the importance of the site and its educational potential, took early elementary steps to consolidate the monument as part of the fieldwork project. This foresight preserved the site while overtures to the Departmental Council regarding the acquisition and management of the monument were successfully made.

The nature of the site and its setting enabled a simple site enhancement project, comprising minimal consolidation, a small car park (large enough to accommodate a school bus however), and information panels (Figure 16.3). The consolidation of the monument itself was successfully carried out by an association dedicated to social and professional requirements, directed by an archaeologist. The vegetation surrounding the site was preserved as much as possible. Access is free for all in an environmentally friendly and peaceful site. School groups can be provided with specific documents to help prepare visits (including 'Discover the Palaeoenvironment'), or book an onsite 'Prehistory Workshop'. Occasional events such as Heritage Open Days are essential for involving the public and promoting a sense of place, but it was deemed neither necessary nor desirable to install permanent, durable, facilities for the public's convenience. This choice, prioritising the natural environment and tranquillity of the site, has its drawbacks however as groups of children, for example, have no real sheltered picnic area, and more problematically, no toilet facilities. Feedback from visitors highlights these problems, and ecologically friendly solutions must be found.

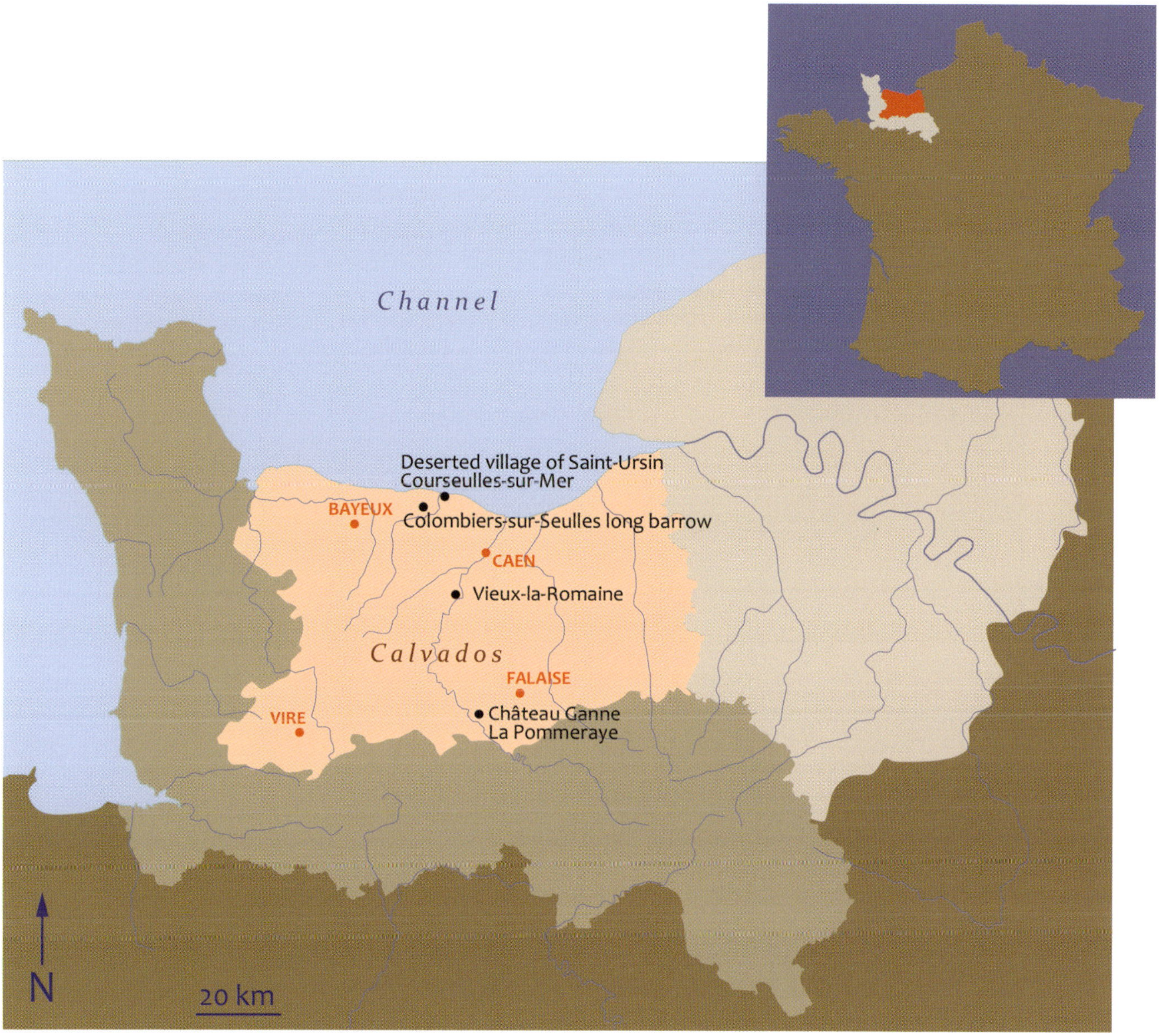


*Figure 16.1. Location map of the archaeological sites managed by the Departmental Council (Conseil Général du Calvados).*

## Vieux-*Aregenua*, Roman capital of the Viducasses territory

Vieux, a typical Norman village close to Caen, is a micro-territory where the Council's aims are most clearly expressed, and where the service can develop the full range of its functions.

Vieux, 2000 years ago, was the location of *Aregenua*, the Roman capital of the Viducasses tribe. This territory was actually one of the smallest in Gaul, and *Aregenua* was probably a fairly typical small capital. The current estimation of its surface area is around 40 hectares; the population between 4000 and 6000 (Figure 16.4). Considering that in Calvados there are also two other Roman capitals (Lisieux-*Noviomagus* and Bayeux-*Augustodurum*), why should there be an investment at the Vieux site? The difference between Vieux and the other capitals resides in the fact that it is both relatively well preserved, and accessible. Archaeologically distinguishable in the late 3rd- and 4th-century levels, *Aregenua* lost its political status to the benefit of *Augustodurum* in late antiquity, slowly declining to become a village during the early Middle Ages, and remaining so until today.[5] Both *Noviomagus* and *Augustodurum* developed into flourishing medieval and modern towns, covering earlier remains. At Vieux, with hardly any later development, the Roman town consequently lies protected, quite accessible, under between only 20cm and 40cm of topsoil.

*Figure 16.2. The Colombiers-sur-Seulles long barrow (Photo: F. Levalet).*

*Figure 16.3. Information panel at the Colombiers-sur-Seulles long barrow (Conseil Général du Calvados).*

Known since the 16th century, prominent excavations were carried out in the late 18th and 19th centuries, notably by the 'Société des Antiquaires de Normandie'.[6] In the 1980s, local politicians, aware of their well-preserved heritage and fully backed by community pride, convinced the Department to instigate a land acquisition programme, and to launch the excavation of a *domus*.

Since 1988 the Council has invested in an archaeological base with a permanent team pursuing research[7]. The first *domus* excavated, named the 'Grand Peristyle House' because of its mediterranean plan, has been restored and opened to visitors (Figure 16.5). The restoration of a more modest *domus,* named the 'U shaped Courtyard House', is being carried out as an educational programme under the public's eye. The major current excavation of the political and administrative buildings of the *forum* is the object of guided visits. Last but not least, a rich programme of events and activities is provided by a modern, dynamic, museum, which was opened in 2002 to present and protect the finds and to forward understanding. The museum and sites are identified as 'Vieux-la-Romaine' for the purposes of tourism.

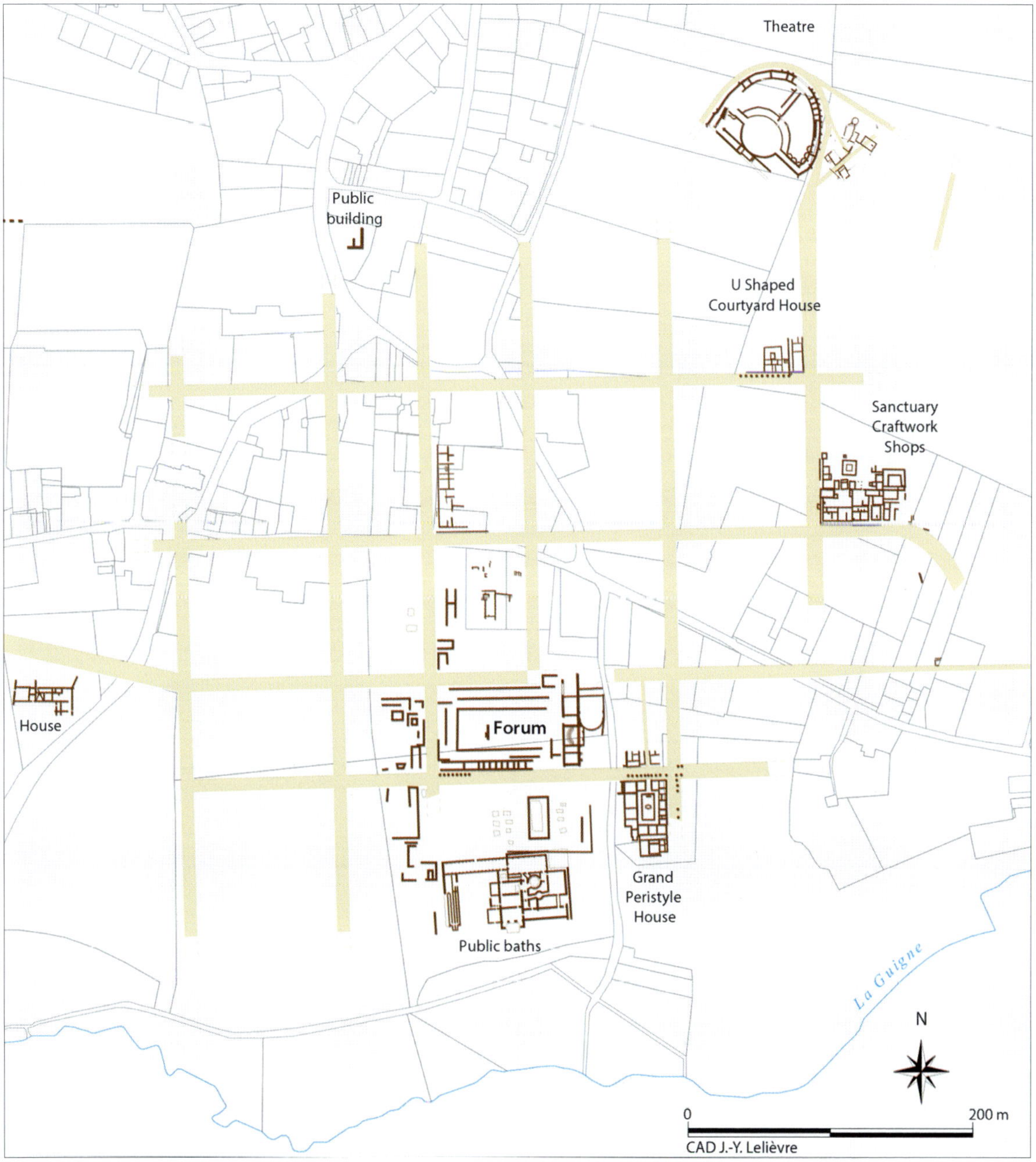


*Figure 16.4. Map of the known roman remains at Vieux-Aregenua (Conseil Général du Calvados).*

*Figure 16.5. The Grand Peristyle House, free access to visitors (Conseil Général du Calvados).*

*Figure 16.6. The U Shaped Courtyard House with the museum in the background (Conseil Général du Calvados).*

At Vieux the Archaeological Service's different functions are deployed and their centralised coordination is the key to success, but also requires a constant balancing of resources. Archaeological feedback and participation from the research team is crucial to maintaining the (essentially regional) visitor interest. In the first ten years of the museum's existence, 250,000 visitors, about half of which comprised school groups, came to Vieux-la-Romaine. These are good figures for a French site-based museum, but whereas a regularly renewed offer in terms of exhibitions and events is necessary to improve the non-scholar visit statistics and to attract visitors from further afield, a coherent educational programme is also necessary to maintain school visits, in keeping with the original site development criteria (educational value). The common denominator appears to be ongoing activities and public participation, and of course the 'raw material' - the archaeological sites themselves.

Different choices have been made concerning the enhancement of the three sites that can now be visited. The Grand Peristyle House, the large luxurious home of a Viducasse dignitary which opened to the public in 1991, makes use of an approach current at that time, as a '*jardin archéologique*'. The masonry remains of the house have been consolidated and partly restored with mainly original materials, to recreate an easily interpreted house plan, in a landscaped surrounding. The advantage of this type of restoration is to present a pleasant open air site that one can walk freely around. One disadvantage is that of creating a very false idea of the house's original environment; eradicating the urban context. However, it can be argued that the complementary data is provided by the information panels near the site and of course in the museum. More problematically, the main disadvantage is that of recurrent maintenance problems. In the Norman climate the masonry must be continually re-restored, slowly detracting from the site's authenticity, and incurring ever-increasing costs. The effects of natural weathering are also accentuated by tourist erosion; the price to pay for hundreds of school children scrambling around, playing discovery games, or filling in questionnaires. Because of these problems, and also because the second site the public can visit is of a more fragile nature, different site enhancement methods have been chosen elsewhere.

The U-shaped Courtyard House, situated close to the museum, is a fairly modest *domus* with external masonry walls and timber and earth internal partitions (Figure 16.6). At Vieux, it is part of our educational approach to present the *typical*, rather than the *spectacular*. We aim to explain what everyday life was really like in a Gallo-Roman town. The U-shaped Courtyard House shows that not everyone lived in a 'text book' type wealthy home, such as the Grand Peristyle House. This approach is also reflected in other areas of the museum presentations. In order to present fragile remains, such as stones comprising the base of long-since disappeared wattle and daub walls, walking on the actual remains is absolutely forbidden. The solution has been to protect the site with a roof, and to install a footbridge enabling visitors to observe the site from above (Figure 16.7). The restoration work is an educational project in itself, carried out by successive teams of young people learning building trades or groups within social and professional rehabilitation programmes, directed by an archaeologist.

The forum buildings undergoing excavation since 2007, including the curia with preserved graded seats, are monumental in scale and have necessitated immediate protection by the installation of a very specific scaffold and roof cover,[8] erected with no ground penetration (Figure 16.8 and 16.9). It is crucial to protect the remains from the elements during excavation, which is indeed proving to be

*Figure 16.7. Roof and footbridge to facilitate non destructive viewing of fragile remains (Conseil Général du Calvados).*

*Figure 16.8. Protective structure of the forum excavation (Conseil Général du Calvados).*

*Figure 16.9. The forum excavation under the protective scaffolding structure (Conseil Général du Calvados).*

a long-term project. The excavation has revealed an earlier monumental occupation phase – public baths. Permanently covering these buildings provides a valuable opportunity from which to evaluate the future enhancement project.

These three examples show how our approach to site management has evolved over time, with the integration of precautionary measures and the need to balance site preservation with public access; all being influenced by the nature of the remains themselves, and the first and foremost requirement of protecting them.

All of the projects at Vieux, whether excavations, restoration work or museum activities, are experienced by visitors, often involving local people. The ground roots initiative in the 1980s that led to the department's investment at Vieux has developed a deep sense of place, recently expressed, for example, by the naming of two roads in a new housing estate; the 'rue de l'Acqueduc' and 'rue des fours à chaux' ('Limekiln road'), following a developer-funded excavation. Indeed, a strong link exists between Vieux-la-Romaine and the local population.

## The 'Courtisigny' deserted village at Saint-Ursin, Couseulles-sur-Mer

The acquisition of two separate plots in 1998, which have topographically visible remains of a deserted medieval village, was motivated by two very different criteria. The first was as a means of preserving a site in danger of slow destruction due to inappropriate agricultural use. The second was to provide a geographically and administratively accessible site for a long-term university research project (ensuring educational value). The close relationship existing between the departmental Archaeology Service and Caen University,[9] more specifically the Centre de Recherches Archéologiques Médiévales (CRAM),[10] led to the establishment of the university's archaeological training excavation on this site from 1999 to 2008 (Figure 16.10), directed by a university teacher.[11]

Almost ten years of annual fieldwork seasons revealed a village clustered closely around a parish church occupied during the 13th and 14th centuries, which subsequently experienced a slow process of abandonment. The semi-sunken dwellings were built using limestone, extracted *in situ*, and then thatched. Temporary measures were taken to protect the fairly unstable stonework brought to light during the excavation, but in retrospect these now appear to have been insufficient. Following the excavation, taking into account the fragile nature of the dry stone remains, the intensive weathering processes due to the exposed locality of the site near the coast and the lack of means to ensure regular monitoring, preservation by backfilling was adopted (Figure 16.11).

The research programme is currently suspended, but as only one of the plots has been excavated (and this not entirely), the site remains a protected archaeological 'reserve'. Further study remains a possibility at a later date.

## The medieval castle 'Château Ganne' at La Pommeraye

Château Ganne is a fortified castle site dating from the 11th–13th centuries, situated on a rocky spur in a well preserved wooded environment, 40km south of Caen (Figure 16.12). The castle itself, a protected heritage site, includes two baileys, defined by well-preserved earthworks, and a circular high court accessed by a gatehouse, parallels for which are mainly English (Figure 16.13).[12] The combination of its ecological and heritage value motivated this acquisition in 2001, and the site was rapidly classed as a nature reserve. Château Ganne is located in 'Suisse Normand',[13] a part of Lower Normandy renowned for its rugged and lush landscape resembling the Swiss Alps, which is currently experiencing a notable development in green tourism. The initial management project thus included the integration of the site into nature-friendly tourist networks. Several different players are involved in the site management. Two services apply the Council's policies for site conservation, management, and enhancement in their respective domains

*Figure 16.10. Excavation at Saint-Ursin, Courseulles-sur-Mer (Conseil Général du Calvados).*

*Figure 16.11. Preservation by backfilling (Conseil Général du Calvados).*

(the Archaeology and Natural Environment Services), with delegated management for the maintenance of the site as a whole to the Suisse Normande 'communauté de communes'[14] (SNCC), according to guidelines allowing a partial opening of the site to visitors, while enforcing the protection of the site. Access to the castle itself, which presents risks to visitors from falling masonry and unprotected escarpments, as well as risks to the monument through misuse, is carefully controlled.

The Archaeology Service entrusted the study of the historical remains to a university professor[15] working with both Rouen and Caen universities, as a Rouen training school. They carried out extensive surveys of the well-preserved earthworks, and excavated the masonry buildings in the main bailey from 2003 to 2011. Prior to the excavation, full 3D laser scanning of the standing remains of the gatehouse[16] was carried out in order to record the monument with precision, before engaging transitory preservation and safety measures, comprising netting the stonework and supporting the damaged arches. The excavations have revealed the presence of masonry buildings backing onto the earthworks all around the main bailey, including a chapel and residential buildings. The 12th- and 13th-century remains are extensive and particularly informative, presenting a coherent layout with clear functions attributable to the different elements. These remains, however, are very fragile and have already deteriorated notably since being brought to light; the protection afforded to them not having been able to cope with several recent winters of particularly harsh freezing.

The enhancement project at this site has proved very difficult to achieve. The relatively poor state of preservation of the extensive remains and the question of security, both to visitors and the monument, on the one hand, need to be balanced against the strong educational value and tourism possibilities on the other. There is also another important factor. The site is much appreciated by the local population who organise medieval festivities, attracting hundreds of people annually, and who flock to the site on the occasional open days and guided tours. This population has fully understood the need to close the site while research and consolidation takes place, but would find the idea of protecting the site by backfilling – a feasible possibility at one point – unacceptable. Here, the term 'sense of place' is no abstract concept. The castle is considered to *belong* to the locality.

After much discussion between the different parties, a consensus has been reached, aided and validated by the Ministry of Culture – who exercise their legal control of protected monuments[17] – achieving financially acceptable investment, accessibility to the public, and respect of the environment. All of the buildings in the main bailey will be consolidated in a very measured manner, with the aim being to use them as educational and tourist resources.

*Figure 16.12. Arial view of Château Ganne by drone (François Monier).*

The gatehouse will also be the object of very necessary consolidation and repair work.

The public will not, however, have free access, as at the sites of Colombiers-sur-Seulles or Vieux. The remains must not be damaged by 'tourist erosion'. In relation to public safety, the installation of appropriate security features that would allow free groups of visitors within this historic and natural setting would be impossible. The public will nevertheless have access, but solely through guided visits and specific events, that will be organised by the SNCC and the local tourist office.

In conclusion, each site, considered within its own environmental setting, presents particular maintenance issues that need to be weighed against their value as historical and educational assets. Consequently, the four sites presented have been treated in different ways. One has been reburied. One will be consolidated for opening to the public in controlled ways. One is open to visitors at any time. One is open to the public as part of a 'museum and sites' package, with constant updating of the historical content and methods of interpretation. However, options for different policies remain open. Should financially and academically coherent projects be put forward in the future, it would be possible to further excavate the medieval sites and/or reconsider the question of their access. Facilities for the public's convenience could be installed alongside the long barrow, and there is virtually *no end* to site enhancement possibilities in a Roman town which is, as yet, only very partially investigated.

*Figure 16.13. Standing remains of the gatehouse (Conseil Général du Calvados).*

## Notes

1 ODACC, Office départemental d'action culturelle dans le Calvados.
2 Service patrimoine.
3 These limekilns, at Landes-sur-Ajon, Calvados, are currently managed by the HeritageService (Service patrimoine).
4 Antoine Chancerel, Circonscription des Antiquités de Basse-Normandie, Ministère de la Culture and Dr Ian Kinnes, British Museum.
5 The current population of Vieux is just under 600.
6 The 19th-century excavations were carried out by the 'Société des Antiquaires de Normandie', the first antiquarian society in France, created by Arcisse de Caumont, inspired by the London model.
7 Research themes include the urban network, the political and administrative organs, and the early medieval occupations and the transformation of the agglomeration to parishes (Christianisation).
8 This type of 'meccano' like protection is more commonly used in the restoration of historical monuments; to our knowledge, it has been used in France for the first time on a large archaeological excavation at Vieux.
9 Université de Caen Basse-Normandie (UCBN).
10 Now the 'Centre Michel de Boüard', Centre de recherches archéologiques et historiques anciennes et médiévales (CRAHAM).
11 Mme Claire Hanusse, Maître de conférences.
12 Gatehouses are very rare in France; strong similarities exist with Exeter Castle gatehouse.
13 'Norman Switzerland'.
14 A federation of municipalities (communes) forming a framework within which local tasks are carried out together.
15 Mme Anne-Marie Flambard-Héricher, Professeur Emeritus.
16 Plowman Craven Associates (PCA), in conjunction with the Museum of London Archaeology Service (MoLAS).
17 Ministère de la Culture, Direction des Affaires Culturelles de Basse-Normandie, le pôle patrimoines et architecture.

## Bibliography

Chancerel, A., Dron, J-L. and Kinnes, I. (1993) 'The Normandy Neolithic, excavations of tombs at Rots, Colombiers and Erne', *Current Archaeology* 133, pp. 28–31.

Coulthard, N. and Jardel, K. (2015) D'*Aregenua* à Vieux-la-Romaine, de la Recherche à la meditation culturelle, Gestion du patrimoine, Mise en valeur, Médiation culturelle', in Fleury, P., Jacquemard, C. and Madeleine, S. dir., *La technologie gréco-romaine*, Caen, PUC, pp. 129–48

Delacampagne, F. and Delaval, E. (2010) 'Fouilles, recherches et mise en valeur à Vieux (Calvados), antique *Aregenua*', in Delacampagne, F. and San Juan, G., dir., *La mise en valeur du patrimoine monumental antique en Normandie, Actes de la table-ronde de Eu (Seine-Maritime), 25–26 novembre 2004*, pp. 73–80 (Rouen, Publications des Universités de Rouen et du Havre).

Flambard-Héricher, A-M. (2008) *Le Château Ganne, Premiers résultats de la fouille archéologique* (Caen, CRAHM), p. 128.

Hincker, V. (2007) 'De la ville antique au village médiéval: déclin de la capitale de la cité des Viducasses Vieux (Calvados) du IVe siècle à l'an Mil', *Annales de Normandie* pp. 1–2 and 3–26.

Jardel, K. and Lelièvre J-Y. with collaboration from Mazure, P. (forthcoming) 'Découvertes anciennes et investigations récentes sur le *forum* d'*Aregenua* (Vieux – Calvados)', *Gallia.*

Vipard, P. (2002) *La cité d'Aregenua (Vieux, Calvados), chef-lieu des Viducasses : état des connaissances* (Paris, Exé Productions), p. 204.

# Part V

# Sculpture and Objects

# 17

# The evolution of capitals in early post-Conquest architecture as evidence for the completion date of the White Tower

*John Crook*

**Résumé**

*Les chapiteaux de la chapelle Saint Jean à la Tour de Londres ont souvent éveillé l'intérêt des historiens des édifices, mais il est difficile de les dater d'une manière assurée par les sources documentaires à notre disposition sur la Tour Blanche. Cependant, les différents types de chapiteaux trouvés dans la chapelle et leur pétrographie fournissent des preuves cruciales de la chronologie des phases de construction de la Tour dans son ensemble, et particulièrement de la durée d'une assez longue pause pendant la construction qui a été l'une des découvertes les plus décisives révélées par les études effectuées durant les travaux de restauration de la Tour au milieu des années 1990. Dans cet article les éléments 'quasi-sculptés' de la chapelle (chapiteaux, bases de colonnes, impostes) sont considérés dans le contexte du début de l'architecture anglo-normande, y compris la genèse des chapiteaux cubiques et de leurs dérivés, les chapiteaux à godrons.*

The Chapel of St John, located on the first floor of the White Tower, the principal building of the Tower of London, is rightly regarded as one of the most significant examples of early Romanesque architecture in England (Figure 17.1). Its long use as a repository for state documents caused only minor damage to the historic fabric – notably the removal of the projecting imposts of the aisle responds to allow presses to stand closer to the walls – and this was made good in the restoration directed by Anthony Salvin in 1862–3. The White Tower as a whole has been the subject of a recent study (Impey 2008), and in another paper in these conference proceedings Dr Roland Harris has traced the early history of the building.

The chapel is located in the south-east corner of the White Tower at main (first floor) level, rising up through the second storey. The architecture of the chapel has been more fully studied elsewhere (Crook 2008). Its length was determined by the Tower's spine wall; its width by the east-west wall that separates the southern third of the Tower from the rest of the building. In its plan (Figure 17.2) the chapel, comprising four straight bays terminating in a five-bay apse, resembles the choir of a Romanesque church of apse-and-ambulatory design, without radiating chapels. The exterior of the apse is a notable feature of the south end of the Tower's east wall.

The chapel is two-storeyed, with a continuous gallery but no clerestory. The main elevation comprises a main arcade of round-headed arches, supported on stout cylindrical columns of coursed masonry, and an upper tier of similar arches opening into a gallery. The elevation lacks any kind of vertical articulation, though this would not be expected in a nave with a tunnel vault, as there are no transverse arches. There is a simple chamfered string-course at gallery floor level, but the main vault springs directly from the head of the walls without an impost. The aisles are groin-vaulted, with transverse arches between each bay and the aisle wall is articulated by pilasters.

During detailed analysis of the masonry of the White Tower a major 'building break' was identified in St John's Chapel. There had clearly been a significant pause in the construction of the Tower, followed by stylistic and constructional changes when work resumed – this was more than the normal winter pause. The break, traceable around the chapel as a well-defined horizon (where not obscured by later render) was characterised by three main constructional features. Firstly there was a noticeable change in the type of mortar used. Below the horizon the mortar contained numerous bivalve fragments, often whole shells, suggesting that the sand and gravel used to make it had been brought from the Thames estuary, perhaps transported by water from a sandbank. Above the horizon a more conventional white lime mortar was observed. Secondly, there was an abrupt change in the petrography of the masonry, notably the responds of the aisle walls, where Bembridge limestone

*Figure 17.1. Eastward view in St John's Chapel (photo: John Crook).*

made its appearance for the first time. Finally, a general reduction in the proportion of worked stone blocks was noted; the internal walls above the building break tended to be formed of uncoursed rubble rather than coursed ashlars. All these features suggested that a new team of masons was employed after the break, and that when work resumed the principal concern was to complete the building as quickly as possible.

Dendrochronological analysis of timbers surviving on the lower floors has produced outer date limits between 1068 (the earliest possible felling date of timbers sampled at basement level) and 1081 (the latest possible date of a timber sampled at entrance level). Allowing four and two years respectively for construction from those levels to the break, limits of *c.* 1072–83 seem reasonable for the final year of the first phase, before work was interrupted. It is argued below that an indication of the date at which work resumed is best provided by stylistic analysis of the chapel's 14 finely carved capitals. There are 12 on the free-standing piers of the main arcade, and two on the western responds, and their distribution is shown in Figure 17.2.

Despite stylistic variations, all the capitals and bases in St John's Chapel share a unique geology, being of Taynton stone. This is a pale yellow oolitic limestone quarried near Burford (Oxfordshire). It is characterised by pronounced current-bedding and the presence of darker 'bars' where the deposits of calcite cemented shell fragments are particularly dense. The Taynton stone appears to have been brought to the Tower in a single consignment, uniquely for the capitals and bases, and was perhaps chosen because it was available in larger blocks than the other stones used at the Tower. Apart from its specific use in the chapel, Taynton occurs only in a few fragmentary stones in the upper part of the walls, and these could be waste material from the production of the capitals and bases, which were undoubtedly carved on site.

The use of Taynton stone is crucial in the use of the capitals as dating indicators. Most importantly, the bases of the western responds are of this stone, and the responds above them still form part of the first phase, before the building break. Likewise, the bases of the free-standing piers are of Taynton. As we shall see, some of the capitals on

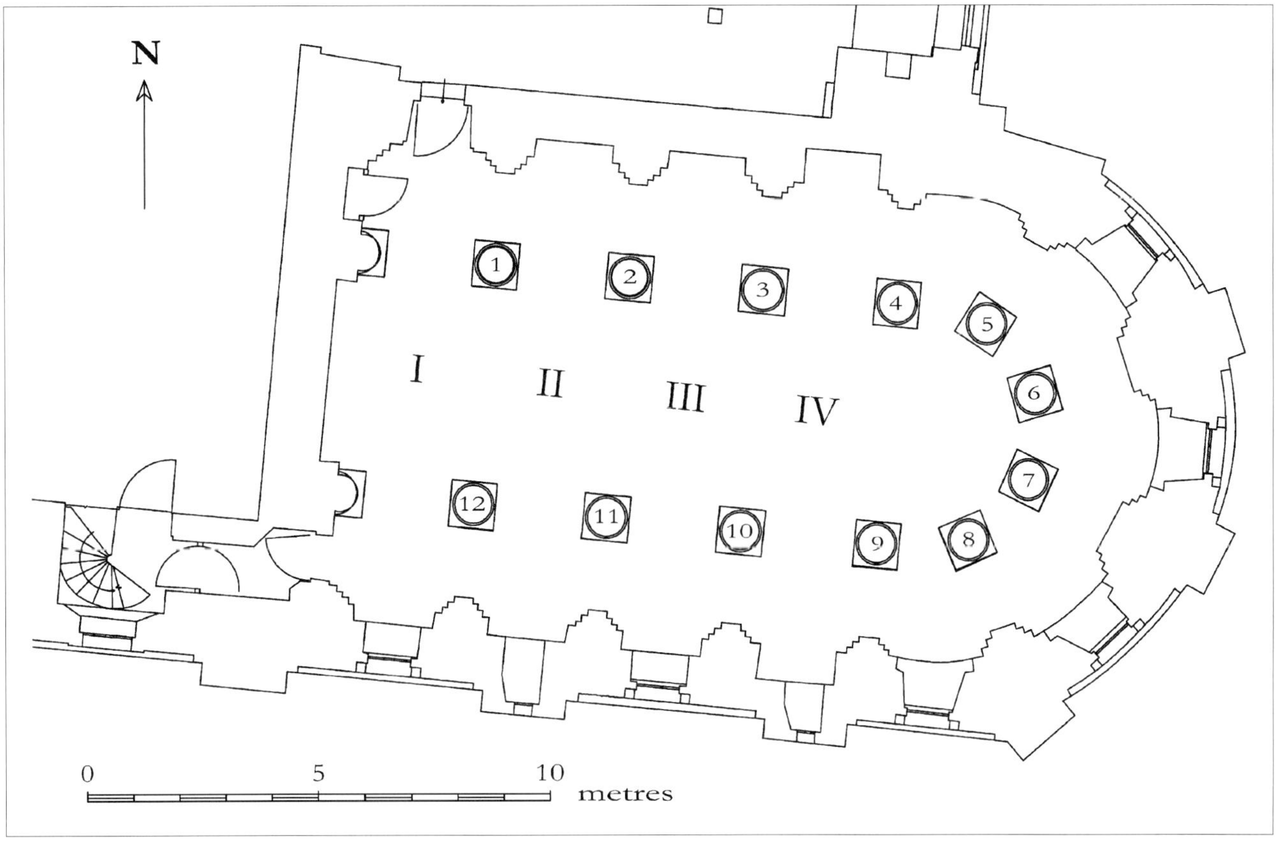


*Figure 17.2. Plan of St John's Chapel showing the location of the capitals discussed in this paper.*

these piers were almost certainly carved before the building break and were probably set in position; others are identified in this paper as forming part of the second phase and are stylistically different, though still using the same Taynton stone. This is why the analysis of the style of the second group of capitals is so important as dating evidence.

Four types of capital are found on the free-standing piers (Figure 17.3): eight chamfered block capitals with tau crosses (Piers 1–4, 6, 7, 9, 10); one volute capital with tau crosses (Pier 8); two double cushion ('proto-scallop') capitals (Piers 11, 12); and a single cushion capital with mitred corners, formed of several pieces of stone (Pier 5). In addition, the western responds are volute types with tau crosses.

## Analysis of the White Tower capitals and their likely date

The chamfered block capitals, which, with their tau crosses, are the chapel's most memorable sculptural features, are of a type with a long ancestry. The simplest way of achieving the transition between a cylindrical column and a square abacus is simply to chamfer off the lower parts of the corners of the block from which the capital is formed. For a post-Conquest building like the chapel, examples from mainland Normandy are clearly the most relevant. The capitals used in the reconstruction of the nave of Jumièges abbey church in the mid-1060s (Figure 17.4a) seem a particularly close parallel, though lacking the flat, leaf-like motifs on the corner chamfers.

The most distinctive feature of the White Tower's chamfered block capitals is their so-called 'tau crosses'. These appear to be a development of the tall, rectangular consoles that appear on the Jumièges nave capitals and which are also found in some of the capitals of the Conqueror's churches at Caen. Ultimately these consoles derive from antique prototypes, when they were usually decorated with rosettes or palmettes. Tau-cross capitals are, admittedly, found in more distant locations, such as the church of Saint Vicenzo in Prato in Milan (mid-11th century) but it is perhaps unlikely that there is a direct lineage.

The earliest known English examples are from the dorter range of Westminster Abbey (Figure 17.4b). Given that the abbey church had been consecrated in 1065 and the dorter would have been amongst the first buildings to be constructed, a date in the early 1070s seems plausible. Although Warwick Rodwell (2009, pp. 155–9) has argued that the north end of the dorter undercroft (notably the Pyx Chamber) dates from the early 1060s, he suggests a date of

*Figure 17.3. The four types of capital on the free-standing piers of St John's Chapel: (a) chamfered block capital (Pier 4 from SW); (b) volute capital (Pier 8 from WNW); (c) double scallop capital (Pier 12 from NE); (d) mitred cushion capital (Pier 5 from SW).*

*c.* 1070–80 for the second phase comprising the south end of the undercroft and the upper level of the whole range, which is where the tau-cross capitals occur.

Although the St John's Chapel tau-cross capitals are more sophisticated in their design, they possess the same elements as the Westminster ones. The chamfers at the White Tower are decorated with concave leaf-like motifs which show much more finesse than the crude shapes found at Westminster Abbey. These foliate motifs are presumably a simplified, stylised form of the corner foliate volutes of classical Corinthian capitals.

It is argued below that the chamfered block capitals were carved in the first phase of building, before the major building break, and were probably set in position on top of their columns. One other capital may also have been carved in Phase 1 (Figure 17.3b). This capital derives from a different sculptural tradition. It is a volute capital, a type which ultimately derives from antique Corinthian capitals. Despite its distinct parentage, this capital shares many features with the chamfered block capitals, and there can be little doubt that it was produced by the same sculptural workshop. Its dimensions are similar, the springing of the corner volutes is likewise similar to the chamfers of the block capitals, and it is adorned with tau-crosses on each face. Arguably the most striking difference is in the inclusion of a tier of over-turned leaves forming a collarette just above the astragal.

Volute capitals enjoyed widespread use in the architecture of 11th-century Normandy, and the most obvious predecessors are found in the Caen churches, especially the nave of La Trinité, the north-west tower of Saint-Etienne, an area untouched by Ruprich-Robert's drastic restoration (Figure 17.5a), and the church of Saint-Nicolas (Figure 17.5b). Several English examples may however be adduced, notably the capitals of the chancel arch at Bramber (Figure 17.5c), possibly dating from 1073. More securely dated are

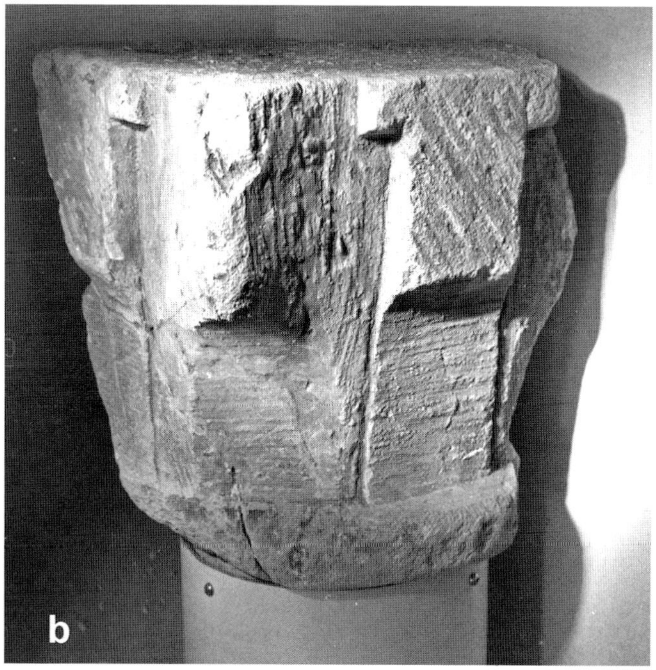

*Figure 17.4. (a) Jumièges, abbey church. Capital of north nave arcade; (b) tau-cross capital from the dorter range, Westminster Abbey.*

the crypt capitals of Lastingham church datable to *c.* 1080 (Figure 17.5d). However, these far-flung examples add nothing to the question of the date of the building break, given the relatively unchanging nature of chamfered block capitals and volute capitals.

Like the majority of the chamfered block capitals, the volute capital of Pier 8 was perhaps also set in position in Phase 1. Its position is significant, being one of the four capitals of the apse hemicycle, and the other three are also anomalous. Its counterpart on the north side of the apse (Pier 5) is a cushion capital made up of smaller pieces of stone, and is assigned to Phase 2. As for the intervening two piers (6 and 7), they are slimmer than all the others and are entirely built of Caen stone, but their bases and capitals were designed for piers of normal thickness, suggesting reconstruction in a design change in Phase 2.

The western respond capitals (Figure 17.6a–b) are also of the volute variety, though the actual volutes are small; in many respects these capitals could be regarded as variant forms of the chamfered block capitals. They are, however, more highly embellished than the free-standing block capitals, and their decoration includes pellet mouldings on the mid-vein of the leaves of the north-west capital, and pellet mouldings and chip-carving on their abaci. Importantly, these capitals occur above the building break, and are set in the white mortar characteristic of Phase 2. They were therefore not fixed in position until work on the chapel had resumed, and it is possible that they were not actually carved until that phase.

That this could be the case is certainly supported by the date of the best parallels for these capitals, namely the pier capitals from Anselm's 'Glorious Choir' at Canterbury, built in the 1090s (Figure 17.6c). Anselm's capitals owe their survival to being recycled in the crypt ambulatory by William of Sens nearly a century later. Like the St John's Chapel capitals they have tau-crosses on each face. In some respects the Canterbury capitals look more assured than those of the Tower, and could conceivably be of later date.

The most surprising architectural sculpture in St John's Chapel comprises the three cushion capitals, which immediately strike the viewer as being stylistically so out of keeping with the tau-cross capitals already described. It seems likely that their use, together with the constructional changes already noted, is indicative of a change in the team of masons involved in the project – a consequence of the major building break. Two types are represented: a pair of 'proto-scallop' capitals and a single mitred cushion capital. Although the latter is typologically earlier than the proto-scallops it was probably the last to be carved. It is made up of a number of pieces of stone – mostly Taynton but supplemented with Quarr and Caen stone – suggesting that there was not quite enough Taynton stone left to carve the last capital, so what emerged was a makeshift.

Cushion capitals are probably the commonest type used in early Anglo-Norman architecture after the Conquest. Somewhat surprisingly, the design, which developed in the Rhineland (Kubach 1989, pp. 198–202), appears to have come to England not from mainland Normandy but

*Figure 17.5. (a) Caen, Saint-Etienne. Volute capital in NW tower; (b) Caen, Saint-Nicolas, volute capital in nave; (c) Bramber, Sussex, volute capital on north side of chancel arch, (d) Lastingham (N Yorks), crypt, volute capital.*

north-east France. The earliest examples were possibly imported ready-carved from Marquise in the Pas-de-Calais (Gem 1987, pp. 95–7). The lost capitals from the crypt of St Augustine's, Canterbury, now represented only by a photograph, were mitred cushions, but the oldest extant examples are those at the west end of Lanfranc's crypt at Canterbury Cathedral (Figure 17.6d). Both these sets of capitals date from the earliest years of the 1070s. Thus, the last of the St John's capitals to be created was typologically the oldest. Clearly the capital is of no evidential value for dating the building break. The type was perhaps chosen because of the simplicity of the design, given that a single piece of stone of the required dimensions was apparently not available at this stage in the building project.

The two other cushion capitals are so-called 'proto-scallop' capitals, i.e. double cushions. The type is completely unknown in Normandy before the Conquest. Double, even triple block capitals are admittedly found in the Rheinland and but it seems highly unlikely that Anglo-Norman proto-scallops derive from these examples which probably result from parallel invention. The latter type continued in the 12th century at, for example, Rosheim in Alsace (Will 1965,

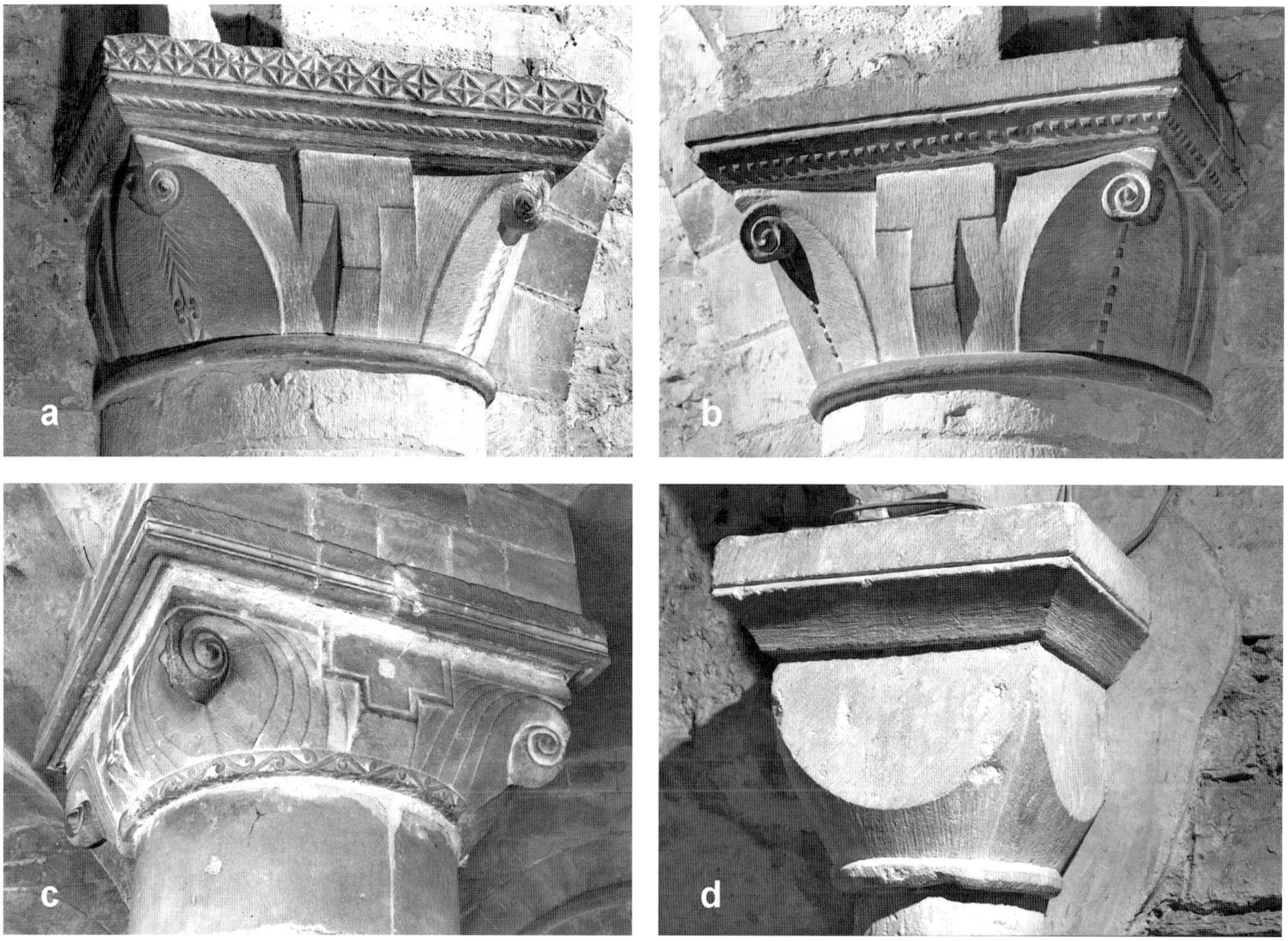


*Figure 17.6. (a) St John's Chapel, SW respond capital; (b) St John's Chapel, NW respond capital; (c) Canterbury Cathedral, crypt, recycled capital from the main level of the Glorious Choir; (d) Canterbury Cathedral, respond capital at west end of Lanfranc's crypt, c. 1070.*

pls 57–61; de Lasteyrie 1929, p. 613), or the west façade at Marmoutier (Busch 1963, pl. 185). Proto-scallops form part of a different lineage which goes back to the uniquely Anglo-Norman mitred cushion capital. The type would eventually cross the English Channel, and scallop capitals are notably found in the reconstructed clerestory of La Trinité, Caen, probably *c.* 1125.

Possibly the earliest proto-scallops in England are those found in the transepts of St Albans Abbey at gallery level (Figure 17.7a). The dating is not without ambiguity. According to Matthew Paris in the *Gesta Abbatum monasterii S Albani*, Abbot Paul started work on the church there in 1077 and completed everything within 11 years (Riley 1867–9, pp. i. 33–4). This is perhaps improbable, not least because the church was not consecrated until 1115, in the time of Abbot Richard. Matthew probably meant that the monks were able to move into the new church by 1088, which raises the question of whether the upper levels of the transepts had been completed by that date.

A date of 1088 is, however, slightly earlier than the first more securely dated examples. Amongst the earliest are those of the wall-shafts of Abbot Serlo's crypt at Gloucester Cathedral, formerly St Peter's Abbey, begun in 1089 (Figure 17.7b); of the chapter house arcade of Winchester Cathedral, probably shortly before the first consecration of the cathedral in 1093 (Figure 17.7c); and a single capital in the crypt of the Glorious Choir at Canterbury, after 1093 (Figure 17.7d), together with marking-out on a single cushion capital there in apparent preparation for sub-division into the double type. Also at Winchester, proto-scallops are found in a small area of the Romanesque nave that survived Wykeham's remodelling, but these form part of the second phase of the nave, built after the demolition of Old Minster in 1093–4.

There is no particular reason to suppose that the proto-scallop capitals found in St John's Chapel were state of the art innovations; rather, the new team responsible for the completion of the White Tower may have employed the

*Fig. 17.7. Late 11th-century double cushion (proto-scallop) capitals (a) St Alban's Abbey, east side of north transept gallery; (b) Gloucester Cathedral, crypt, respond capital; (c) Winchester Cathedral, chapter house arcade capitals; (d) Canterbury Cathedral, capital from crypt of the Glorious Choir.*

type because it was a tried and tested method of producing a capital of approximately the same overall dimensions as the earlier block and volute capitals used there. On balance therefore, a date of no earlier than *c.* 1090 seems possible for the resumption of works.

The location of these anomalous capitals is significant. They are found on the westernmost two free-standing piers on the south side, (Piers 11 and 12). Like the apse piers, already mentioned, Piers 11 and 12 are also anomalous in being constructed entirely of Caen stone, rather than the chequer Caen and Quarr stone that was the norm. It seems possible that construction of the latter piers was deferred for as long as possible so as to permit building materials to be craned over the south wall of the Tower rather than being brought up the stair vices at the Tower's corners. In the event, Piers 11 and 12 were not built until after the major building break; at the same time the piers in the apse chord were either built for the first time or rebuilt for reasons unknown.

Finally we should address the problem of the original intended disposition of the capitals. It is safe, I think, to assume that it was originally intended that there should be just two types of capital: chamfered block capitals and volute capitals, all with tau-crosses. Only one volute capital was carved, suggesting perhaps that it was the last to be produced before the major building break. That could suggest in turn that there were to be four volute types, and the most likely position for these would be around the altar. Only one is in its intended position. When work resumed after the break the two piers at the head of the apse (Piers 6 and 7) were rebuilt to a narrower profile, presumably for aesthetic reasons. One might have expected new capitals of appropriate size to be carved, but in fact two chamfered block capitals of the normal size were set on the thinner piers. These had presumably already been carved before the building break and were probably originally intended for Piers 11 and 12 – but the latter piers were not constructed until after the building break. This left three piers without capitals. New proto-scallops were carved for Piers 11 and 12, and the few bits of Taynton stone that had survived, eked out with Quarr and Caen stone, were used to create a standard mitred cushion capital for Pier 5.

## Bibliography


Busch, H. (1963) *Germania Romanica: Die hohe Kunst der romanischen Epoche* (Vienna, Schroll).

Crook, J. (2008) 'St John's Chapel', in E. Impey, ed., pp. 95–124.

Gem, R. (1987) 'Canterbury and the cushion capital: a commentary on passages from Goscelin's *De miraculis sancti Augustini*', in N. Stratford ed., *Romanesque and Gothic: Essays for George Zarnecki*, pp. 81–101 (Woodbridge, Boydell Press).

Impey, E., ed. (2008) *The White Tower* (New Haven and London, Yale University Press).

Kubach, H. E. (1989) *Romanische Baukunst am Rhein und Maas*. Architekturgeschichte und Kunstlandschaft, vol. 4 (Berlin, Deutsche Verlag für Kunstwissenschaft).

Lasteyrie, R. de (1929) (2nd ed.) *L'Architecture religieuse en France à l'époque romane* (Paris, Picard).

Riley, H. T., ed. (1867–9) *Gesta Abbatum Monasterii Sancti Albani*, 3 vols, Rolls Series (Public Record Office).

Rodwell, W. (2009) 'New glimpses of Edward the Confessor's abbey at Westminster', in R. Mortimer, ed., *Edward the Confessor: the Man and the Legend*, pp. 1516–7 (Woodbridge, Boydell Press).

Will, R. (1965) *Alsace Romane,* Collection La Nuit des Temps (La Pierre-qui-Vire, Editions Zodiaque).

# 18

## ANGLO-NORMAN ELITE OBJECTS FROM CASTLE AND COUNTRYSIDE

*Steven Ashley*

**Résumé**

*Pour la période allant de la Conquête jusque vers 1200, il n'existe que très peu d'accessoires vestimentaires et de biens personnels en comparaison des siècles précédents et suivants. Les trouvailles en notre possession sont une série d'objets du château, de la campagne, du manoir et du hall, reflétant le statut, les préoccupations et les plaisirs de la nouvelle élite dirigeante. Certains de ces objets portent des motifs décoratifs en forme de proto-armoiries ou de blasons et montrent également des influences d'Asie Centrale et d'Orient.*

*Un certain nombre d'objets étudiés ont été découverts dans ces contextes datés lors de l'excavation de châteaux et autres sites importants, et ces ensembles montrent une très grande cohérence, en effet prévisible, dans leur composition. Toutefois, les découvertes les plus récentes viennent de prospections par détection de métaux. C'est, du moins dans le Norfolk, le résultat de l'établissement de bonnes relations de travail avec les utilisateurs de détecteurs de métaux qui se poursuit depuis quatre décennies. Ceci a augmenté le nombre de trouvailles de cette période, dans les formes et les décors, sans pour autant modifier l'impression d'ensemble de la rareté relative du mobilier anglo-normand, dont peu d'éléments en outre proviennent des classes inférieures.*

*Les découvertes provenant des fouilles de châteaux et le matériel découvert plus récemment dans la campagne, en particulier l'exemple du Norfolk, sont considérés ici et groupés par thèmes. La mode des figures et styles exotiques, au sein de l'élite anglo-normand, indique les influences culturelles provenant d'un monde normand élargi et au-delà. L'insécurité et les incertitudes de la vie quotidienne peuvent également être décelées dans le rôle dual des animaux représentés sur une série d'objets, depuis les accessoires vestimentaires jusqu'aux pierres sculptées, autant marqueurs du statut social que protecteurs des biens et des personnes dans une fonction apotropaïque.*

In the period from the Conquest until *c.* 1200 there is a relative lack of finds of dress accessories and personal possessions in comparison with preceding and succeeding centuries (Hinton 1990d, p. 141; 2005, pp. 171–2; Ashley 2006; Egan 2009). Extant finds, a range of objects from castle, countryside, manor and hall, reflect the status, preoccupations and pleasures of the new ruling elite. Some of these objects bear decorative motifs employing proto-armorial or armorial devices and also demonstrate influences from Central Asia and the East (Ashley 2009; 2011 and in prep.).

A number of the finds under consideration were discovered in dated contexts during the excavation of castles and other high-status sites, and these assemblages exhibit a considerable degree of consistency and indeed predictability in their composition. However, most recently recorded finds come from metal-detecting. This is the result, in Norfolk at least, of the establishment of a good working relationship with metal detectorists which has continued over the last four decades. This has enhanced the range of finds for the period in terms of form and decoration without changing the overall picture of relative paucity of Anglo-Norman material, in which little is ascribable to the lower orders.

A selection of finds from castle excavations and more recently discovered material from the countryside, in particular examples from Norfolk, is considered here and grouped thematically. The illustrations are taken from the latter. Objects were found in Norfolk and are of copper alloy unless otherwise stated. The Norfolk Historic Environment Record (HER) number is appended to the parish name. Norfolk finds of contemporary objects produced in Limoges, such as figures of saints from chasses and fragments of crucifixes (e.g. those illustrated in Rogerson and Ashley 2011a, fig. 9, nos 54–7), have not been included.

## Furnishings

### *Bindings from boxes and caskets*

A large number of gilt copper-alloy binding strips were found in excavations on the bailey of the Norman motte-and-bailey castle at Goltho, Lincolnshire in a context dated to *c.* 1080–1150 (Goodall 1987, nos 18–60). These were associated with fragments of wood and bone plates representing the remains of a probable box or casket. At Ascot Doilly in Oxfordshire, during the excavation of the stone tower set within a small mound or motte, a number of similar binding strips were discovered lying on a floor sealed by the demolition of the structure, probably in *c.* 1180 (Jope and Threlfall 1959).

Bindings of this type have been recovered on many of the excavated Anglo-Norman castles that have produced good assemblages of material. These include Castle Acre (before *c.* 1180), where, as at Goltho, they comprised a large percentage of the copper alloy-finds (Goodall, A. R. 1982, fig. 43, nos 1–17). Articulated hinged strips of related type have been found in central Norfolk, such as an example from West Acre (Figure 18.1, 1, HER 3953). More elaborate still, are the mounts of extraordinary form with multiple strips or arms radiating from a central boss (so called 'Octopus' mounts), discovered at Baile Hill, York (constructed before 1070, out of use by the 14th century; Addyman and Priestly 1977, fig. 11, no. 82) and Lydford Castle, Devon (Goodall 1980, fig. 16, no. 1).

The surface decoration on many of these bindings is limited to oblique or transverse segmentation. However, a gilt copper-alloy binding from Winchester has an oval plate bearing a lion passant reguardant (Hinton 1990b) and a strip from Carleton Rode (Figure 18.1, 2, HER 50145) ends in an animal-head terminal. Other decorative terminals include an elaborate fleur-de-lis with palmettes from Marham (Figure 18.1, 3, HER 37216) and a human head or mask from Haveringland (Figure 18.1, 4, HER 44066).

These finds are clearly representative of elite or high-status objects: that is, boxes of wood or bone bound with gilt copper alloy and intended to contain precious personal possessions. What the contents comprised we can now only guess. The boxes themselves would have been covered in materials and decorated in ways that do not survive in the archaeological record. Wooden examples may have been carved, painted or covered in bone or ivory, leather or exotic coloured silks.

### *Gable mounts, hasps and padlocks*

Other finds of copper alloy relating to furniture comprise gable mounts such as an object from Salle (Figure 18.1, 5, HER 34990; cf. Hinton 1990b, fig. 221, no. 2363) surmounted by a large trefoil or fleur-de-lis and gilded and engraved; and possible cresting from a chasse (Runcton Holme, Figure 18.1, 6, HER 50139).

A series of mounts cast in the form of wyverns or dragons may have been employed as hasps. The largest and most elaborate example of this form of dragon mount, found at Monewden in Suffolk, is discussed by Daubney *et al.* (2005). The Monewden dragon, decorated with grooves and multiple drilled dots, represents an amphisbaena, a dragon with a second head at the end of its tail. However, in other respects its general form and method of attachment, with its distinctive integral right-angled peg projecting from the base, is reproduced in smaller Norfolk examples, from Grimston (Figure 18.1, 7, HER 13800; Gurney, 2006, fig. 7D), Wereham (Figure 18.1, 8, HER 33628) and Whissonsett (Figure 18.1, 9, HER 55990). A more complete example from Saxton with Scarthingwell in North Yorkshire has a separately cast bird riveted to the wyvern's back to act as a decorative handle (Portable Antiquities Scheme database SWYOR-761334).

Other hasps include a robust example from Great Dunham (Figure 18.2, 10, HER 45401), and another with a stylised animal-head terminal from Upwell (Figure 18.2, 11, HER 41358), and a bone hasp was recovered from the excavations at Castle Acre (Margeson 1982, p. 243, fig. 46, no. 9). A gilt copper-alloy keyhole escutcheon plate from Woodbastwick (Figure 18.2, 12, HER 51396) is decorated with four fleurs-de-lis radiating from the central perforation and must be re-used as both faces have traces of annular stamps forming the decoration.

Two padlocks from Hen Domen (occupied from the 1070s to the end of the 13th century) represent the more commonly found form (Higham and Rouillard 2000, fig. 5.6, nos 111–12) of which there are many examples from Norfolk. These include an eccentric variant from Postwick (HER 31762) whose case has been modified to look like a human head or mask (Figure 18.2, 13; Rogerson and Ashley 2009, pp. 567–8, fig. 10, no. 52). More elaborate padlocks, cast as horses, have been discovered by metal-detecting, with the example from Caston (Figure 18.2, 14, HER 51256) displaying possible lozengiform pendants suspended from the breast-band. These padlocks can be paralleled by a find from a 12th–early 13th-century context in Winchester (Biddle 1990, no. 3665) and others from Arwarton (Martin, Pendleton and Plouviez 1996, pp. 457 and 459, fig. 98A) and Butley, in Suffolk (photograph in the Norfolk Historic Environment Service Polaroid archive), and elsewhere.

### *Keys*

Many of the slide keys used in conjunction with padlocks would have been made of iron, and although present in abundance on excavated sites, such as at Castle Acre (Goodall, I. H. 1982, pp. 228, 230 and 232, fig. 40, nos

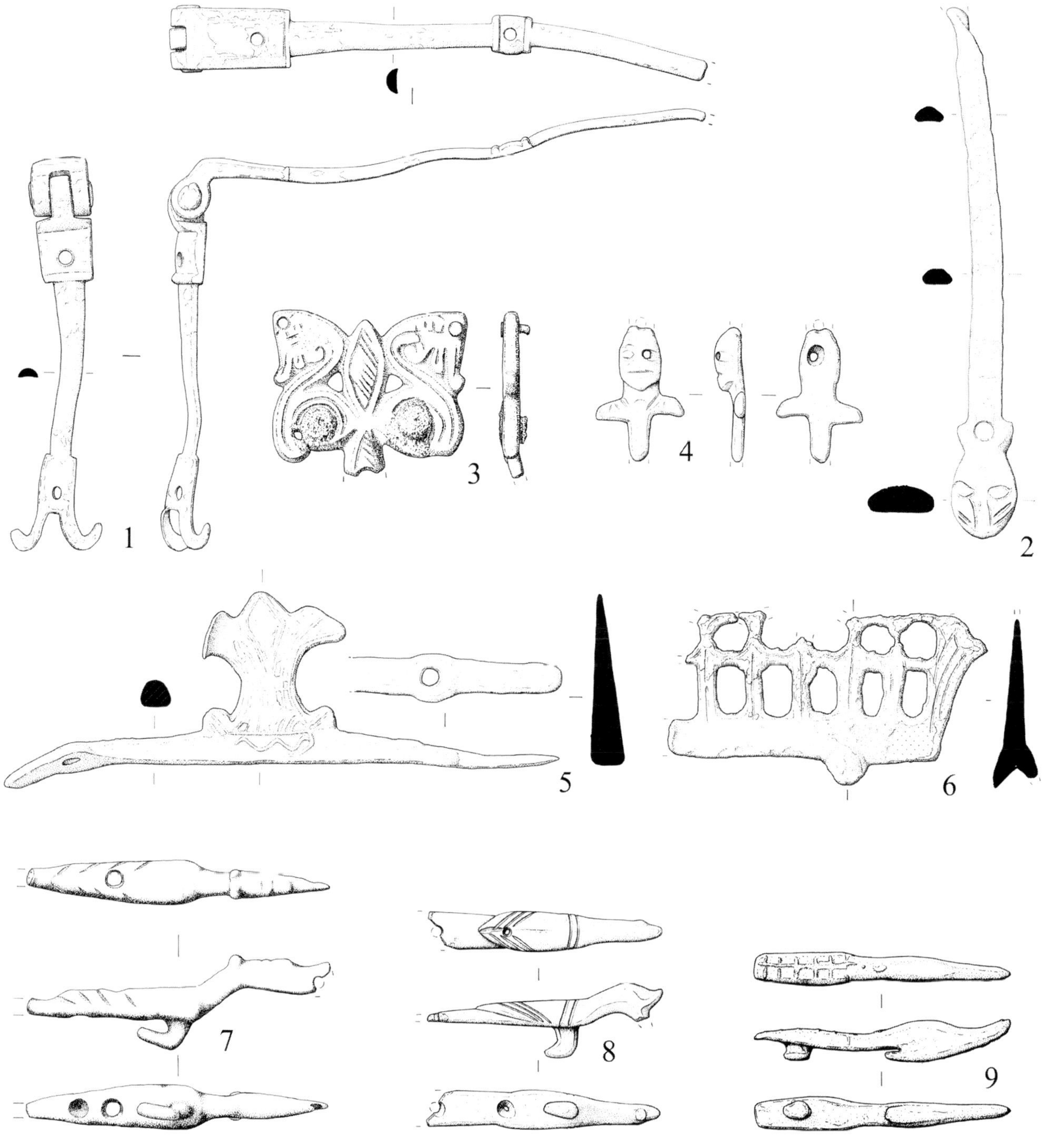


*Figure 18.1. Bindings, mounts and possible hasps from furniture, scale 1:1.*

81–101), they are less likely to be recovered from the plough soil. Others may have been of wood or bone (Egan 1998, pp. 88–9, fig. 63). Two copper-alloy examples from London have been published in Egan 1998, (fig. 74, nos 258–9). Copper-alloy rotary keys of simple form continued into the 13th century and beyond (Egan 1998, p. 111). Of at least two distinctive cast copper-alloy keys, that from Hevingham (HER 28514) is of Goodall's Type B, with the bit set centrally to the stem which springs from a highly stylised animal head at the junction with the bow (Figure 18.2, 15; Goodall 1990, no. 3724). The other is a fragment of a rotary key, from Keswick (Figure 18.2, 16, HER 25706), where the elaborate bow has sides cast in the form of stylised animal heads.

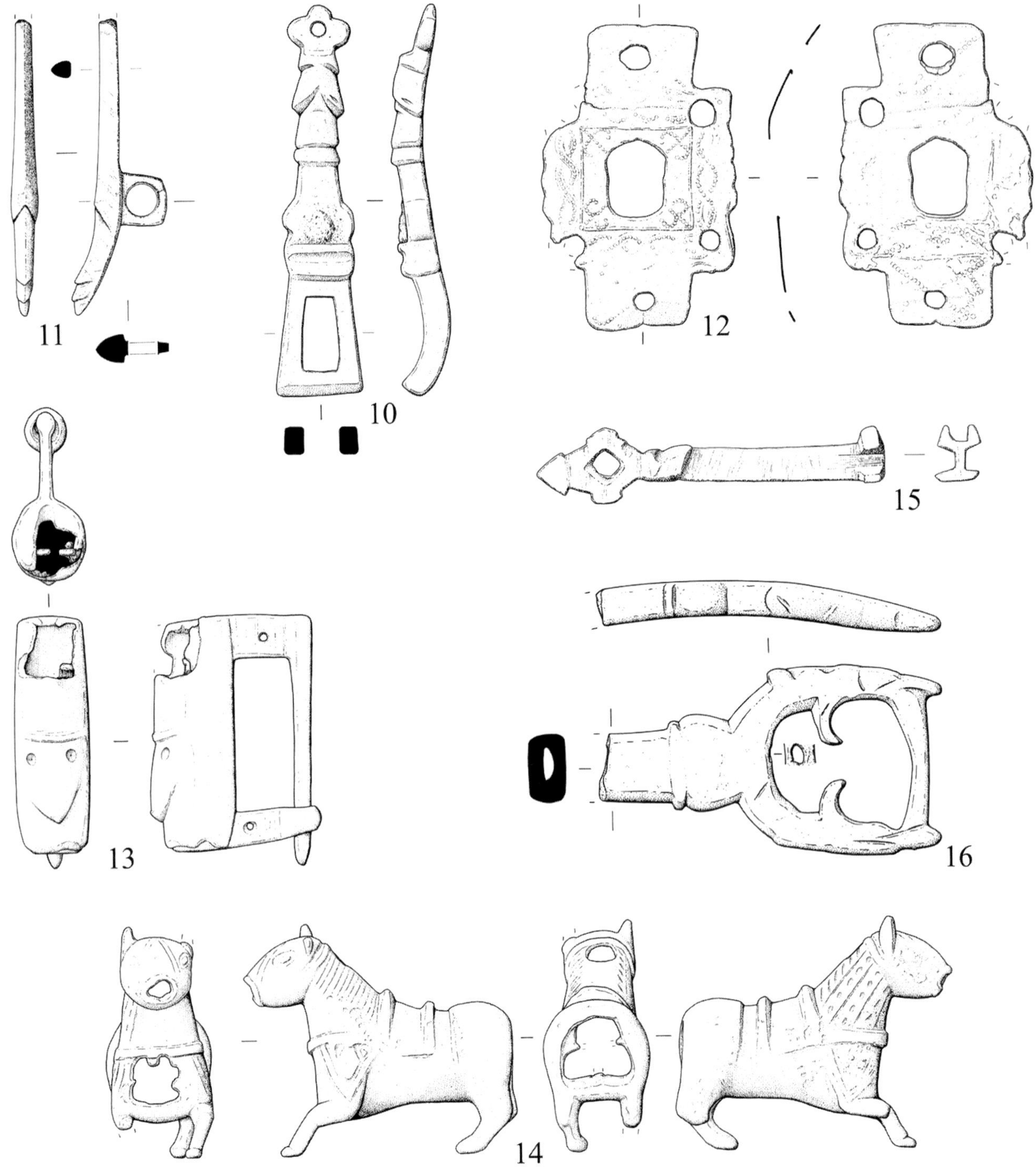


*Figure 18.2. Hasps, padlocks and keys, scale 1:1.*

## Household equipment

### *Cresset lamps and candlesticks*

The commonest form of artificial lighting was the cresset lamp (Ward Perkins 1940, pp. 174–6, fig. 54), made of pottery (Cherry 1984) or carved in stone like a lamp found in the early 12th-century layers of the heightening of the bailey rampart at Launceston Castle, Cornwall (Saunders 1978). Metal finds reveal other more sophisticated forms of lighting, such as a fragment of an ornate copper-alloy base of a Romanesque candlestick, found in Weasenham St Peter (Figure 18.3, 17, HER 43976). The hollow-cast openwork

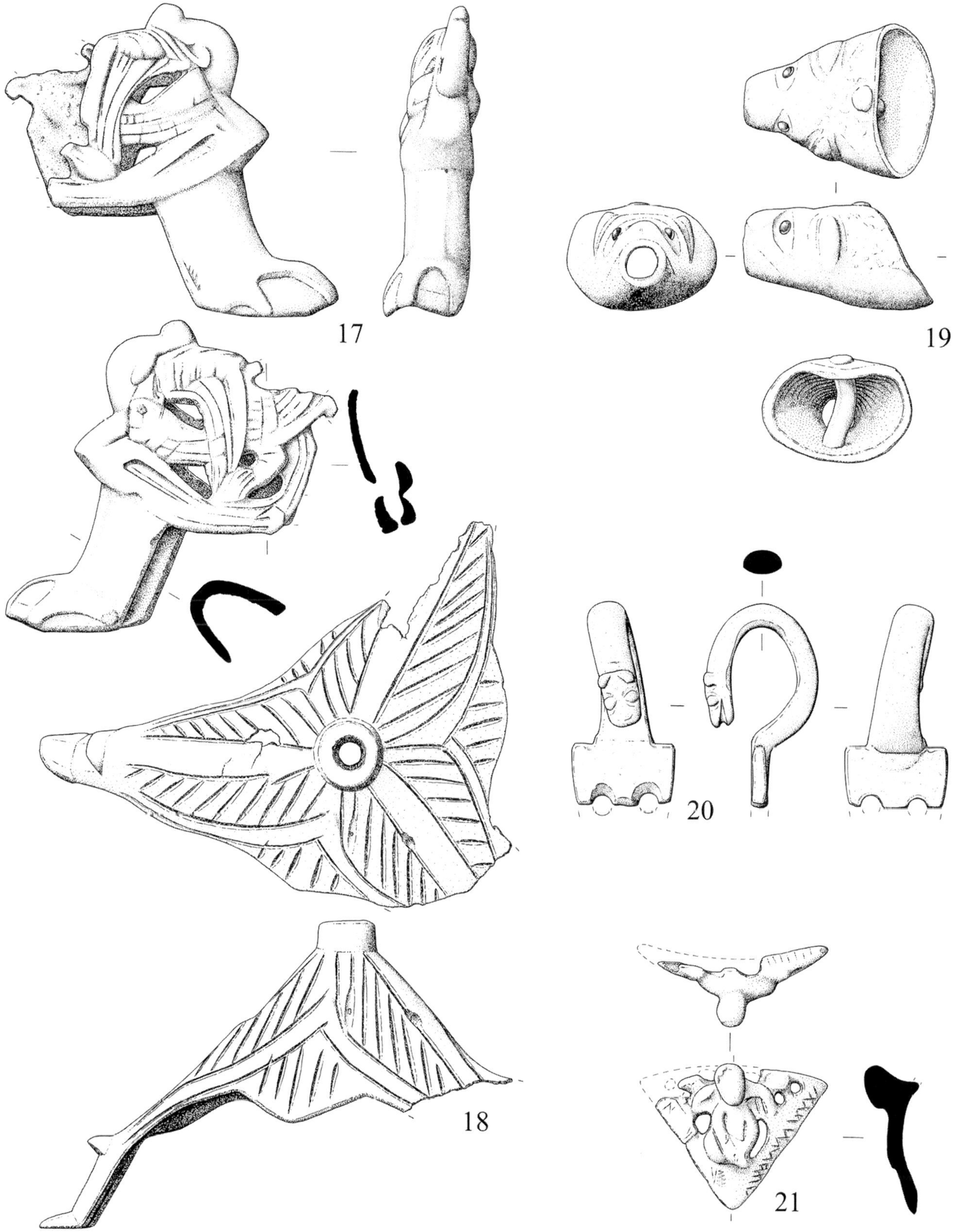


*Figure 18.3. Candlesticks and vessel mounts, scale 1:1.*

decoration comprises the remains of two wyverns entwined with strands of vegetation and with a plant-like tendril or possible animal head on the upper angle. Elements of the decoration (the strands and tendril) exhibit some late influence from the Scandinavian Ringerike style. It is similar in form to four matching Lotharingian candlesticks of the mid-12th century (Oddy, La Niece and Stratford 1986, pl. 7, nos 36 and 38). An English example of related type in the British Museum dates to *c.* 1130 (Stratford 1984b; Oddy, La Niece and Stratford 1986, pl. 8, no. 32).

A less ornate but perhaps rather more elegant candlestick base, found in Flixton, Suffolk (Portable Antiquities Scheme database NMS-DC4BF7), with engraved decoration and a socket at the apex to accommodate a separate shaft (Figure 18.3, 18), can be paralleled by a base from Haughmond Abbey near Shrewsbury belonging to the 2nd or 3rd quarter of the 12th century (Blair and Campbell 1979), and an enamelled example from Limoges of the late 12th or early 13th century (Boehm 1996).

### *Vessels and vessel mounts*

The overwhelming majority of vessels in everyday use would have been ceramic. Fragmentary contemporary metal vessels are not easily identified unless they bear distinctively Romanesque decoration. Norfolk examples include a hollow-cast copper-alloy animal head from Filby (Figure 18.3, 19, HER 49035), almost certainly a spout once attached by its substantial rivet to the sloping side of a vessel, possibly of leather. The eyes of the beast are both set with a pellet of dark blue glass.

An incomplete gilt hooked mount from Kenninghall (Figure 18.3, 20, HER 56281) was also once part of vessel, cf. an example from Coddenham in Suffolk (West 1998, pp. 20 and 135, fig. 19, no. 4). Animal-head terminals of similar form can be seen on a swivel, now in the British Museum (Stratford 1984a), belonging to the first half of the 12th century.

The openwork mount from Postwick (Figure 18.3, 21, HER 38152) is decorated with an angel which suggests its likely use on a censer, as seen for example on an extremely elaborate cast censer-cover in the British Museum of *c.* 1150–75 (Stratford 1984d).

## Weights and balances

Various forms of fiscal regulation may have taken place in and around castles. Nobles, sheriffs, commissioners and officers of the crown are likely to have undertaken the regulation of weights in the king's name, on a local, hundredal or county basis (Rosenthal 1964).

A bone tumbrel found at Castle Acre, dating to before 1175, is one of a number of such coin balances known from England, and there are others from Syria and Turkey, some of which can be seen in the collections of the Ashmolean Museum (Rogers 1993, p. 1). It may have been used by a reeve to check coins paid in tax (Margeson 1982, pp. 244–5, fig. 46, no. 11). The number of coins found on castle or other high status sites appears to be slightly higher than elsewhere (Hinton 1990d, p. 137). Castle Acre also produced a copper-alloy balance pan (Goodall, A. R. 1982, fig. 45, no. 49) and a copper-alloy stirrup from a balance, with ring-and-dot decoration (Goodall, A. R. 1982, fig. 45, no. 50). The latter finds a close parallel in an example discovered on excavations at Gloucester Castle (Darvill 1988, fig. 15, no. 360). A copper-alloy tumbrel with a typically Romanesque animal-head terminal from Hellesdon (Figure 18.4, 22,

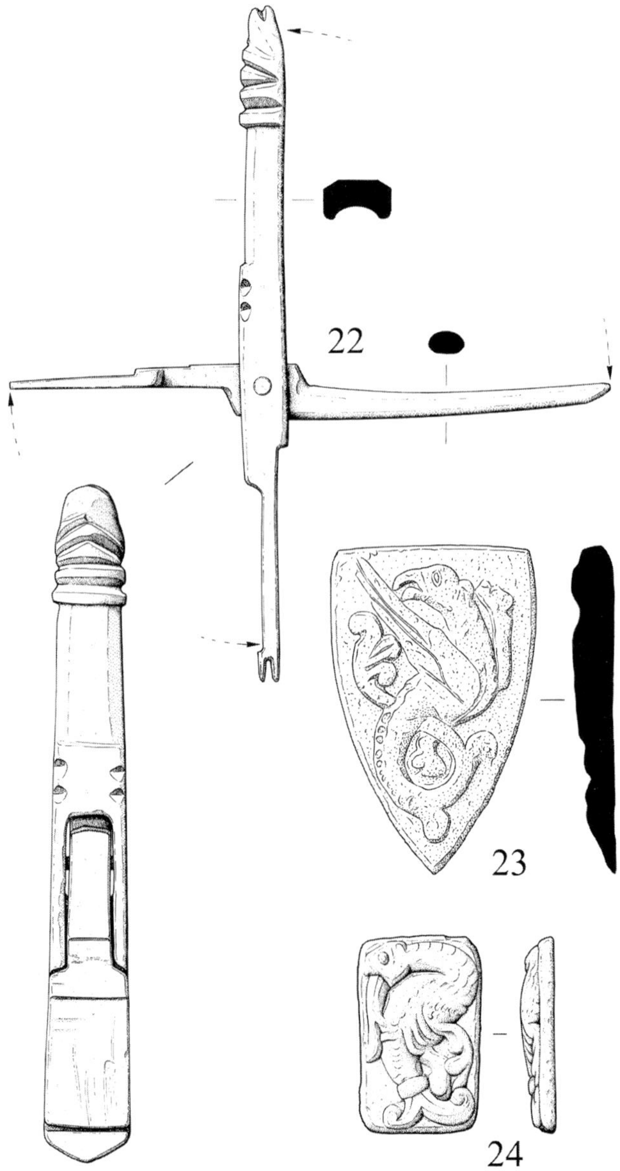


*Figure 18.4. Tumbrel and weights, scale 1:1.*

HER 8106) bears some resemblance to an example with an acorn finial from Anglesey (Redknap and Macdonald 2002).

A remarkable proto-armorial or armorial shield-shaped copper-alloy weight, bearing a wyvern cast in relief on the upper face, was found in Merton in 2002 (Figure 18.4, 23, HER 37113; Ashley 2008). At 26.21g, it is close to the significant unit of weight – 26.6g – identified from around 200 Hiberno-Norse finds from Dublin; many Late-Saxon/Anglo-Scandinavian weights from East Anglia conform to this Dublin unit (Mainman and Rogers, 2000, p. 2563). It is cast in the shape of a flat-topped or 'Norman convex' shield which first appeared towards the end of the 12th century (Grazebrooke 1890, pp. 17–8 and pl. 1, no. 4), of the type carried by some of the knights and warders in the hoard of walrus-ivory chessmen found on the Isle of Lewis (Stratford 1997, rep. 2001; pl. 24, Iv. Cat. 114 and pl. 30, Iv. Cat. 121). Similar shields can also be seen on the late 12th- or early 13th-century seals of David, Earl of Huntingdon (of 1185–1219) and William de Braose (of *c.* 1200) (Ellis 1978; 1981, pp. 234 and 1090).

The wyvern's foliate or acanthus leaf tail with its distinctive line of longitudinal beading can be paralleled in illuminated manuscripts (cf. Wormald 1945, p. 124; and Kauffmann 1984) and sculpture from the 11th and 12th centuries (Hicks 1993, pp. 263–5 and fig. 5.9, Zarnecki 1953, cat. nos 4 and pp. 71–2, and Stratford 1997 (revised 2001), Iv. Cat. 78).

Another contemporary copper alloy weight bearing a wyvern has recently come to light. An old find from Essex, previously unreported, it weighs 8.41g, close to one-third of the Dublin unit, and carries a wyvern in high relief with bifurcated tongue and tail (Figure 18.4, 24).

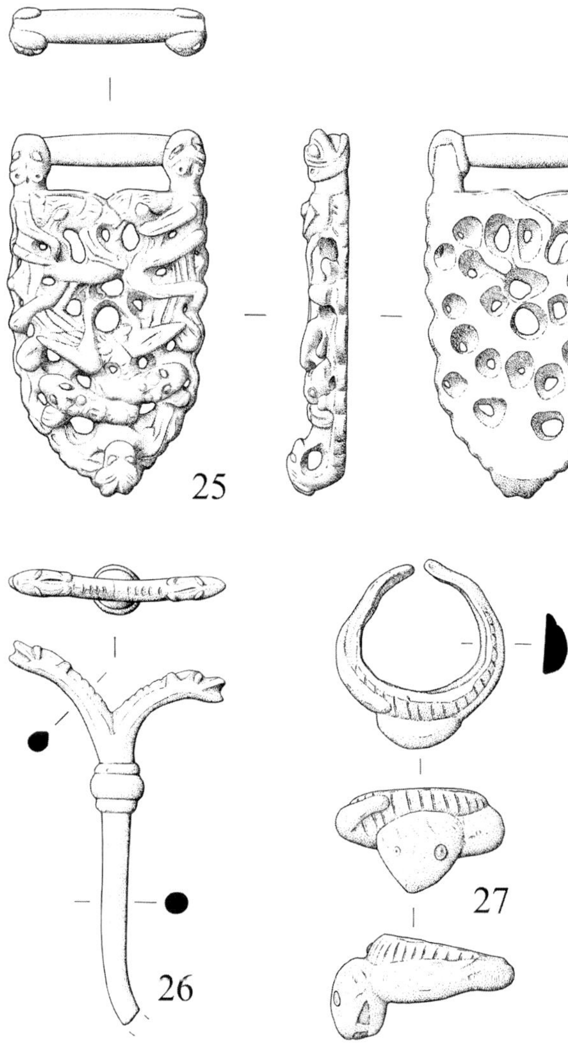


*Figure 18.5. Book-clasp, pin and finger ring, scale 1:1.*

## Books and book mounts

Magnificent leather book bindings survive from the 2nd half of the 12th century, with stamped decoration including men in combat, stags, wyverns, birds feasting on fish, lions, and confronted griffins with the Tree of Life amongst others (Foot 1984). These rare survivals hint at what may have been lost from other classes of leather artefact which do not survive.

A wonderfully exuberant cast copper-alloy openwork plate from a book-clasp was found in Quidenham (Figure 18.5, 25, HER 35413). Both ends of the narrowed bar for the strap are gripped in the mouths of winged lions with intertwined tails which themselves are interlaced with two long-necked winged creatures. A 5th creature's curved neck and head forms the terminal loop. The larger central hole in the plate may have fitted over a pin set into the wooden book cover, and a cord would have been threaded through the transverse hole formed by the curved animal head and neck. The handling of the openwork animal ornament on this plate is reminiscent of that found on objects of larger scale belonging to the early or mid-12th century such as candlesticks and censers (Stratford 1984b; Oddy, La Niece and Stratford 1986, pl. 7, nos 25, 36 and 38 and pl. 8, nos 31–4).

## Dress

### *Pins*

Twenty-four pins of bone and two of copper-alloy dating to *c.* 1085–1140, were recovered from excavations at Castle Acre (Margeson 1982). The short, hipped, bone pins have a variety of decorative heads, including unusual depictions of a small house and of a mouse, and were probably used as hair pins, those with a small loop at the apex being tied to secure them in place. Bone and ivory does not survive well in the plough-soil and contemporary examples of pins in other materials are rarely discovered. An incomplete bifurcated copper-alloy pin with two addorsed animal heads, found recently in Postwick (Figure 18.5, 26, HER 41365), is perhaps more likely to have been employed to secure an item of male dress than it is to have been used in a female hairstyle.

### *Finger rings*

The standard form of finger rings during the 12th century is 'stirrup-shaped', with others having an oval or rectangular bezel (Stratford 1984, e–g). Therefore, an example cast in the form of a grotesque serpent with its large head, one green glass eye (the other smaller socket is empty) and bared fangs, which was found in Upwell (Figure 18.5, 27, HER 29193) on the edge of the West Norfolk Fens, provides an interesting deviation from the norm.

### *Buckles*

A remarkable series of distinctively Romanesque buckles, with a concentration in Norfolk (ten have been found in the county, with 11 from elsewhere in England), has been published recently (Rogerson and Ashley 2011b). They show considerable wit and invention, with the hollow-cast copper-alloy gaping-mouthed beasts, perhaps lions, divided into two types, either swallowing the end of the strap or belt or with it emerging from the mouth as a tongue. Some of these heads have settings with inserted glass pellets for eyes, as on an example from Geldeston (Figure 18.6, 28, HER 52777).

Animal heads grip the ends of a narrowed pin-bar on four heavily cast copper alloy buckle frames – perhaps from sword belts – two of which were found in Fincham (Figure 18.6, 29, HER 25501 and Figure 18.6, 30, HER 38089), another, smaller example, in Methwold (Figure 18.6, 31, HER 5245) and the fourth was from a metal-detector survey at Bromholme Priory, Bacton (Figure 18.6, 32, HER 1073; Ashley 2006, fig. 1, no. 5). Two of these retain copper-alloy pins, with the point emerging from a cast animal head and a possible stylised animal head, and have an additional head on the outside edge of the frame notched to form a pin-rest. Four buckles of related type were found in Ashill (HER 30270), Hindringham (Figure 18.6, 33, HER 25672), Postwick (Figure 18.6, 34, HER 34967) and Norwich (Figure 18.6, 35, HER 156N, from an excavated early medieval context, Margeson 1993, pp. 25–6, fig. 13, no. 127). Although smaller than the sword belt buckles, they have animal-heads gripping the pin bar in a similar manner. The animal-heads on the frames from Hindringham and Postwick show some influence from the late Viking Ringerike style, and the buckles may be somewhat earlier than the larger examples, perhaps belonging to the 11th century and being their Late Saxon or earlier Anglo-Norman precursors. They are paralleled by a frame, with surviving plate and part of pin, from Winchester (Hinton 1990a, pp. 513–4, fig. 129, no. 1110).

An elaborate openwork buckle plate from Shipdham, displays a lion passant reguardant biting its tail and with its hindquarters charged with a cross potent (Figure 18.6, 36, HER 35321). The decoration of the lion's rear in this manner is derived from Eastern exemplars where the shoulder and/or the rump of a beast carries one of a range of devices, the significance of which is discussed towards the end of this paper.

Exotic proto-heraldic motifs with confronted lions and wyverns can be seen on a series of related later 12th- or 13th-century buckles, some flanking a floriated staff or Tree of Life, shown here on examples from Ringstead (Figure 18.7, 37, HER 44097), Heacham (Figure 18.7, 38, HER 51073) and Outwell (Figure 18.7, 39, HER 41077). The motif is also present on a buckle plate from Salle (Figure 18.7, 40, HER 34991), buckles from Emneth (Figure 18.7, 41, HER 39308) and Kenninghall (Figure 18.7, 42, HER 31412) and a recently published openwork plate with confronted wyverns and a Tree of Life from Houghton in Wiltshire (Burnett 2009).

However, none of the openwork buckle frames noted thus far can match the extraordinary artistry embodied in a fragmentary example found in Soham, Cambridgeshire (Figure 18.7, 43; Heslop and Ashley 2013, pp. 217–23). It comprises part of the cast outside edge, with curling lobed tendrils between two robed seated male figures. This remarkable frame is paralleled by a complete silver gilt example found in the Dune Hoard, Gotland (Swarzenski 1967, pl. 535; Fingerlin 1971, pp. 447–8 and 520, Kat. Nr. 467), and belongs to *c.* 1200.

Three buckle plates, from Heacham (Figure 18.7, 44, HER 37217), Litcham (Figure 18.7, 45, HER 15535) and Stoke Ferry (Figure 18.7, 46, HER 53725); have decoration derived from architectural motifs employing arcading with columns, arches and imposts. This decorative conceit is reinforced on two of these plates by arched perforations between the columns, similar to the decorative cresting for a casket or chasse on Figure 18.1, 6. A fourth plate, from Deopham (Figure 18.7, 47, HER 42552) has the openwork form with arched perforations but carries decoration which appears to be less obviously related to the architectural motif. Arcading, similar to that found on these plates, is present on a domestic hanging lamp in the Museum of London (Stratford 1984c), and on the base of an 11th- or 12th-century processional cross from Constantinople or Asia Minor, now in the Metropolitan Museum in New York (Wixom 1999). The form of the arches shown on the Stoke Ferry buckle plate is reminiscent of Mozarabic arches of the Spanish Romanesque (pers. comm. Stephen Heywood).

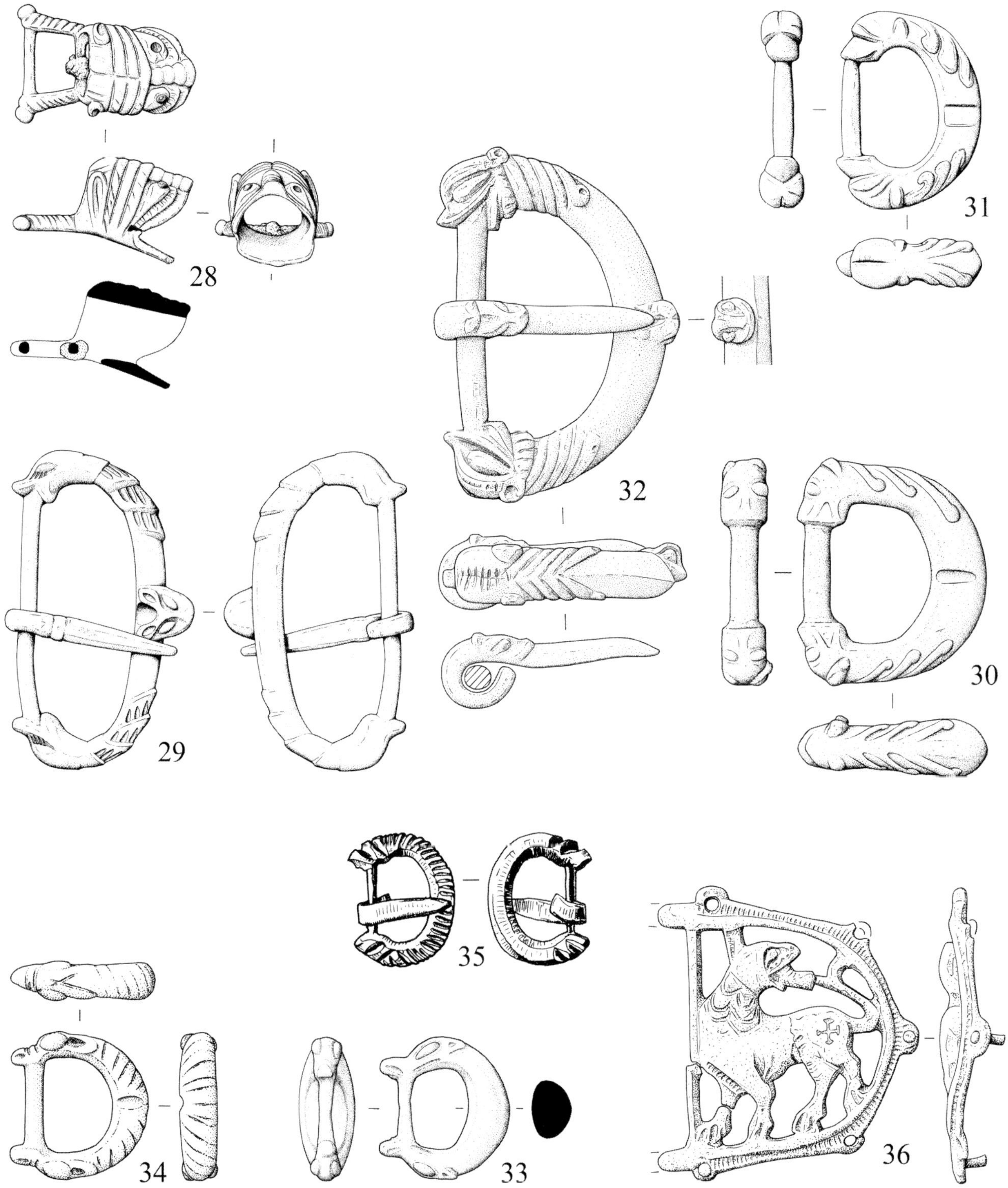


*Figure 18.6. Buckles, scale 1:1.*

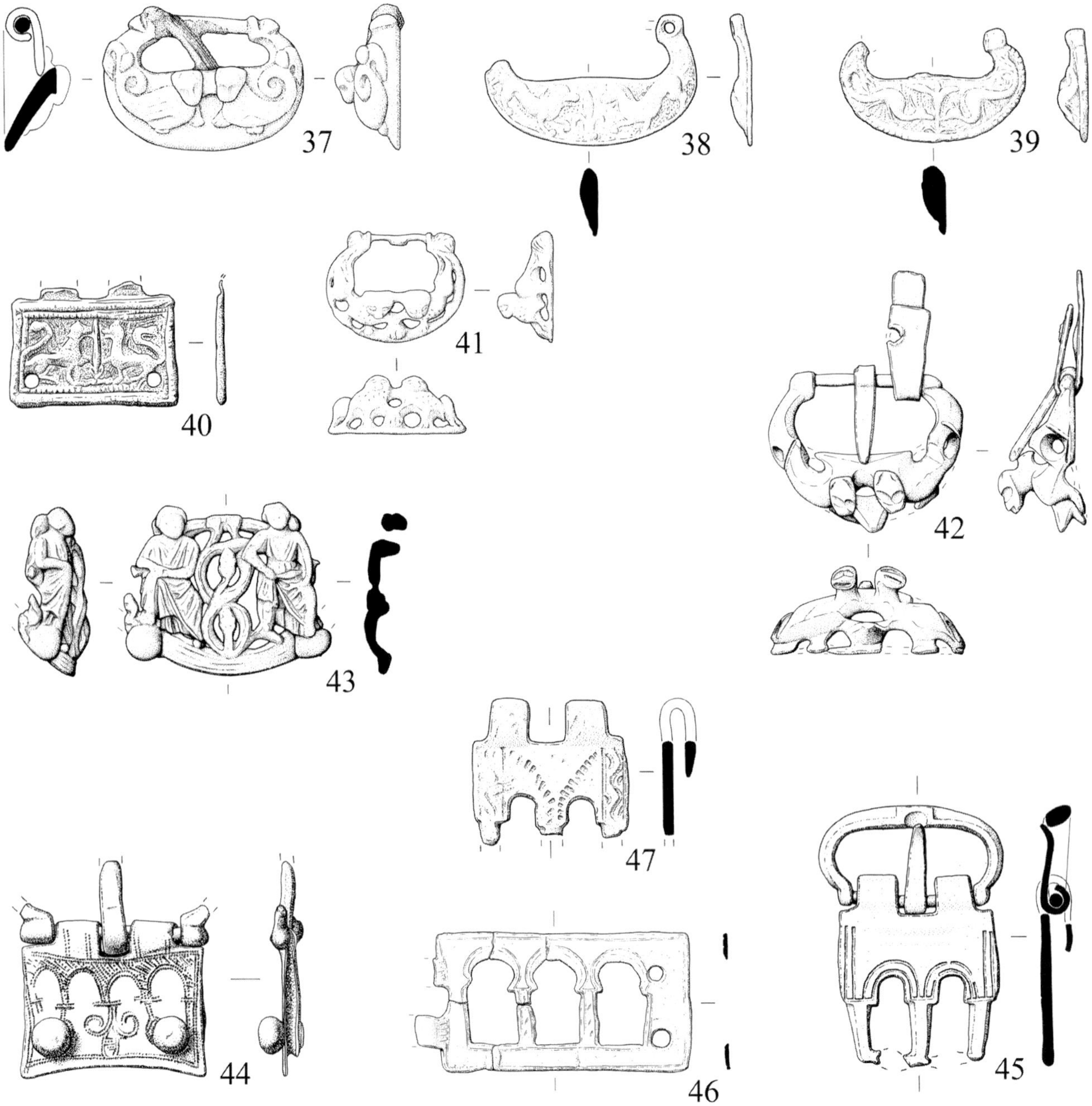


*Figure 18.7. Buckles, scale 1:1.*

### *Strap-ends*

A remarkable tongue-shaped strap-end from Norwich (Figure 18.8, 48, HER 55360) has faint indications of moulded ornament resembling lettering at the split attachment end and a symmetrical openwork design comprising two interlaced hounds engaged in the hunt. The manner of their depiction may represent part of the mid-11th-century transition from late Saxon and Anglo-Scandinavian art styles to post-conquest Romanesque. It belongs to Thomas's Class E unclassified type of which there is only one example in his recent survey (2004, no. 32), also openwork, from Hindolveston (Figure 18.8, 49, HER 22214). The latter shows a standing bull guardant on an openwork field in the upper part, and an enigmatic figure in the damaged lower part, both possibly representing figures from the zodiac. This unique gold strap-end is likely to date to the later 11th or early 12th century.

A small group of unusual heavily cast rectangular strap-ends with a thickened integral transverse bar at the terminal have been found in Norfolk. They are represented

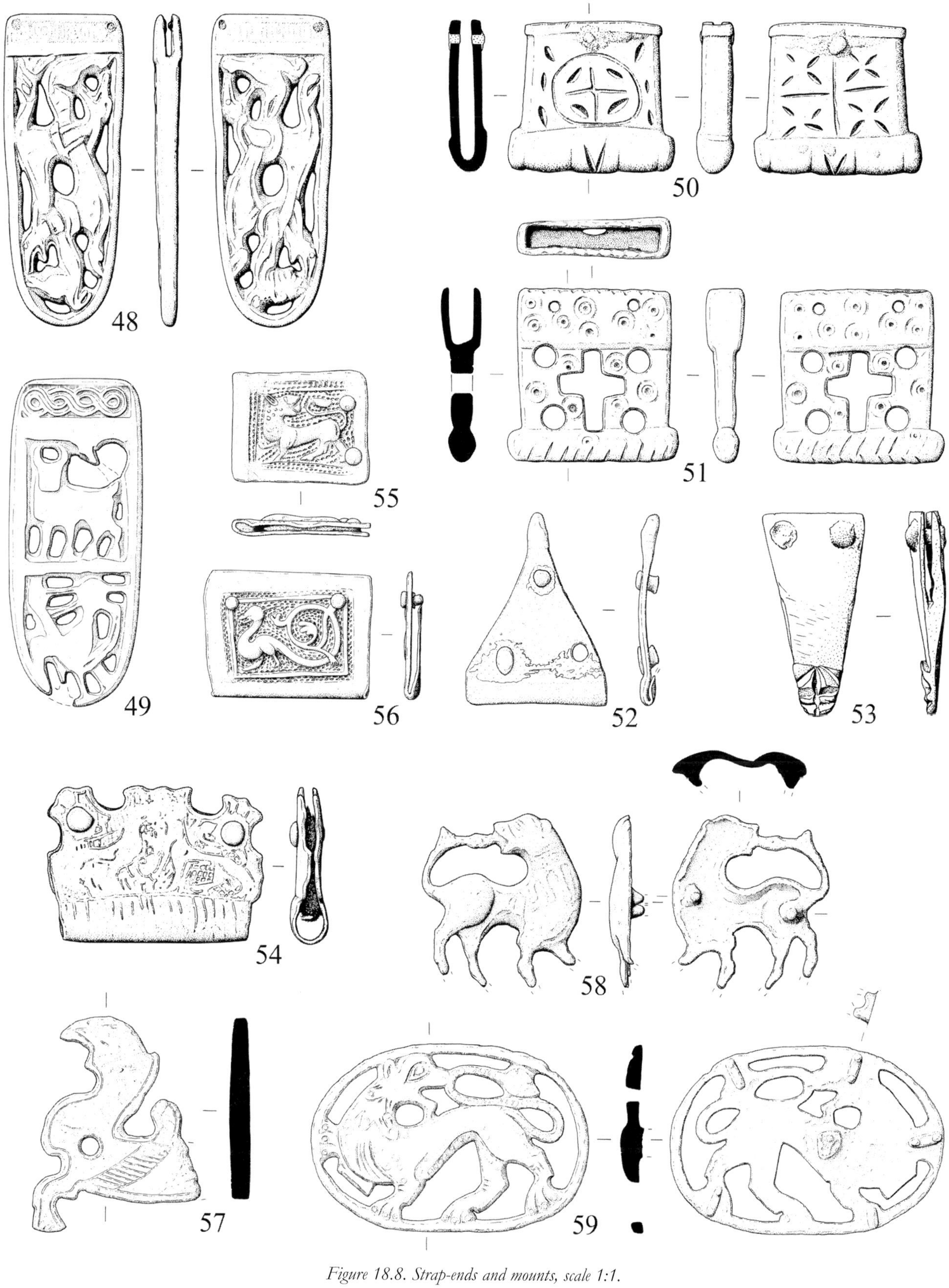


*Figure 18.8. Strap-ends and mounts, scale 1:1.*

here by examples from Attleborough (Figure 18.8, 50, HER 36381) and Ormsby St Margaret (Figure 18.8, 51, HER 24047). The dating of this group is uncertain, with elements of the decoration on the find from Ormesby being somewhat Roman in appearance, reminiscent of openwork key handles and with ring-and-dot decoration. A number of broadly similar although less heavily cast Roman strap-ends with socket, openwork terminal and ring-and-dot decoration have been found in Norfolk, at Burnham Market (HER 18496), and West Winch (HER 52685) for example. However, a date within the 12th century is most likely.

Other 12th-century strap-ends have animal-head terminals such as Fincham (Figure 18.8, 52, HER 25857), Shouldham (Figure 18.8, 53, HER 39658), and a gilt copper-alloy example from Great Moulton (Figure 18.8, 54, HER 56318) with notched attachment end is engraved with two confronted lions passant.

Two gilt relief-decorated strap-ends, one with a lion passant reguardant (Strumpshaw, Figure 18.8, 55, HER 54987), the other with a wyvern (Heacham, Figure 18.8, 56, HER 51335), are related to more commonly found buckle plates belonging to the late 12th or early 13th centuries (Egan and Pritchard 2002, fig. 72, no. 500 and an example from a private collection).

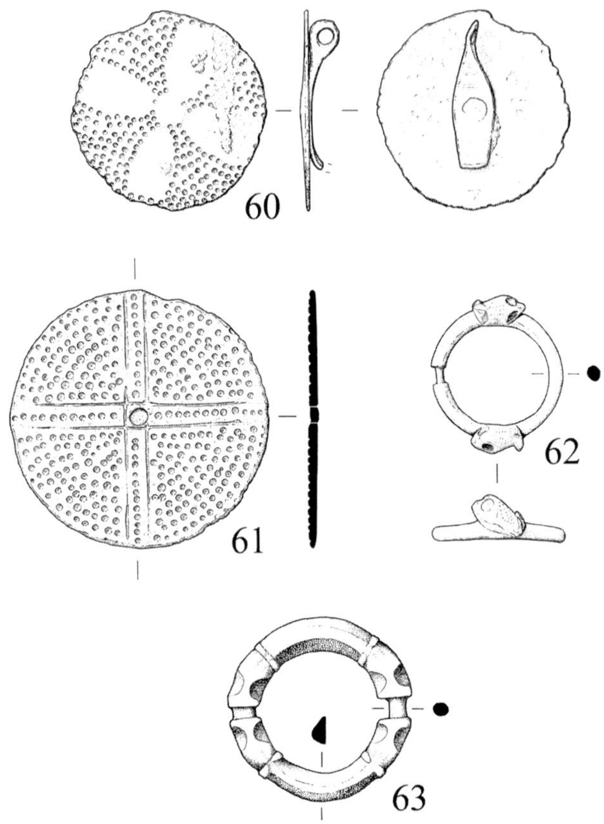


*Figure 18.9. Brooches, scale 1:1.*

### *Mounts*

A selection of belt, strap or harness mounts includes part of a highly unusual mount from Narford (Figure 18.8, 57, HER 54758), cast in the form of an exotic eagle-headed griffin with closed beak and 'rolled feather' ornament possibly derived from the Animal Style art of Central Asia (see Goldman 1960, pp. 321–2; Rudenko 1958).

The openwork mount with a lion biting his tail, from North Tuddenham (Figure 18.8, 58, HER 56284), is paralleled by a pair from Manuden, Essex (Portable Antiquities Scheme database ESS-B0C665). The lion is similar (although reversed) to one depicted on an unusual type of early 12th-century openwork buckle plate of which there are least three examples from Norfolk (see Figure 18.6, 36 and Ashley 2009, fig. 1). The oval mount from Spixworth (Figure 18.8, 59, HER 20913) has the remains of an unusually elaborate method of attachment on the reverse, comprising five radiating perforated lugs and the remains of a central shank.

### *Brooches*

Brooches are uncommon in the late 11th and first half of the 12th centuries. The falling-off in the number and variety of available types from the 9th and 10th centuries is dramatic. This trend also took place on the Continent as demonstrated by a graph shown in a recent German exhibition catalogue (Eggenstein *et al.* 2008, p. 142, Abb. 13). Amongst surviving brooches the splendid early shield-shaped gold piece with engraved lion rampant from Folkingham Castle stands out as exceptional (Cherry and Goodall 1985).

Two disc brooches from the cheaper end of the market found at Marham (Figure 18.9, 60, HER 34100), and Northrepps (Figure 18.9, 61, HER 55455), are decorated with multiple punched dots, forming a cross paty on the first (see Portable Antiquities database SF-3DA3D3 for another example, from Coddenham, Suffolk), and filling the field for an engraved cross on the second. Both probably belong to the later 11th or 12th century.

An annular brooch from a manorial site in Fransham (HER 24783, Ashley 2006, fig. 1, no. 7), with two large animal-heads projecting forward from the frame and another on the pin, has recently been paralleled by a remarkably similar although slightly smaller example from Morley (Figure 18.9, 62, HER 51542). Another annular brooch, from Postwick (Figure 18.9, 63, HER 38152), has opposed constrictions between two pairs of stylised confronted animal-heads.

### *Scabbard chapes*

Although few complete swords or daggers survive, fragments of distinctive late 11th- or 12th-century forms of scabbard chape are being recovered by detectorists. Some of these late 11th- and 12th-century forms were illustrated in an unpublished list of chapes by Anthony de Reuck in 1991. These include trapezoidal chapes with pairs of splayed projecting arms with perforated terminals similar to those excavated in Winchester (Hinton 1990c, nos 4030–1) and London (Egan and Pritchard 2002, fig. 83, no. 575, catalogued under 'strap-ends'). An incomplete example from Fransham (HER 20542) is illustrated here (Figure 18.10, 64).

Two similar incomplete chapes, from Hillington (Figure 18.10, 65, HER 29913) and Catfield (Figure 18.10, 66, HER 40986), show a human figure who may represent Samson, David or even Hercules, holding the head of a lion and attempting either to mount the beast or to wrestle it to the ground. However, the beast could also be interpreted as a fox or even a stag. Another incomplete openwork chape, from Shipdham (Figure 18.10, 67, HER 41710) depicts a knight on horseback facing left. The knight carries a kite-shaped shield and is wearing a hauberk and possibly a helmet. These elaborate openwork fragments represent the two different faces of a single form of chape. A complete example from Angel Court, in the City of London and now in the Museum of London (Spencer 1961, fig. 2) is asymmetrical. On this intact chape the knight has, in addition to his shield, a massive battle-axe held over his right shoulder, and a pair of decorated segmented bars with riveted terminals project at a slightly oblique angle to border one edge of the missing leather scabbard.

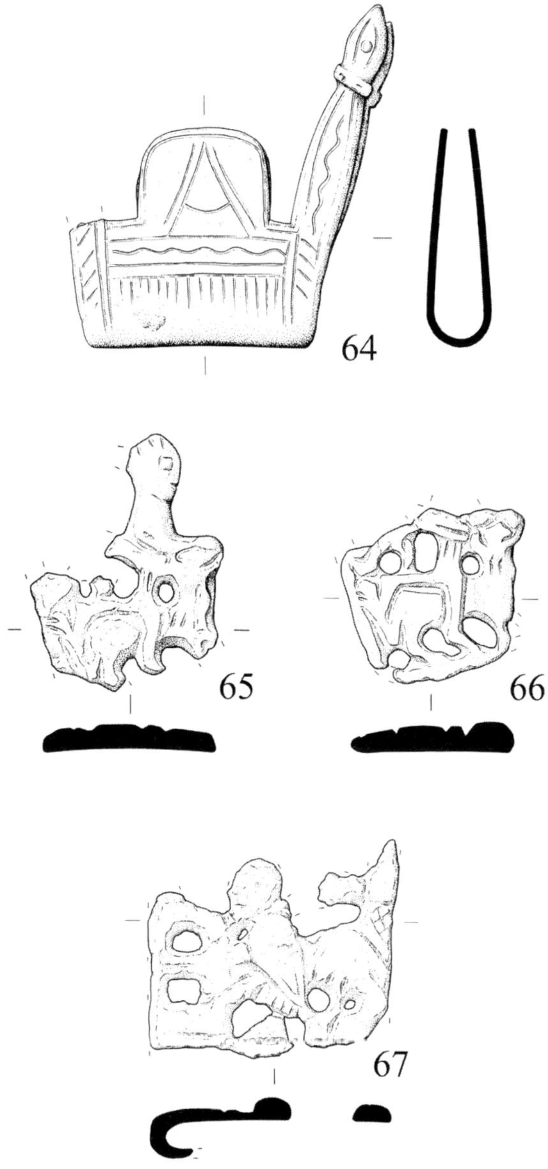


*Figure 18.10. Scabbard chapes, scale 1:1.*

## Horses, harness and hunting

### *Horse furniture*

Some types of what are now almost commonplace finds of Late Saxon stirrup-strap mounts, the subject of a national survey by D. Williams (1997), may continue into the late 11th and 12th centuries, or be Norman forms of this class of object (Ashley 2006, p. 105; Lewis 2007). Most examples display a lion, but a mount from Beeston with Bittering bears a rather more enigmatic beast, possibly a stag (Figure 18.11, 68, HER 44099).

Excavations at Rubercy Castle in Calvados, Normandy, which dates to *c.* 1150–1204, produced a range of finds which closely parallels those from castle excavations in England (Lorren 1981). Amongst this assemblage is a pair of openwork gilt copper-alloy horse harness pendants decorated with stamped annulets (Marin 1994), similar to an example found in Narborough (Figure 18.11, 69, HER 3932), which, in addition to traces of engraved decoration, has a separate claw bezel for a missing glass or stone setting. Another openwork pendant, found in Sedgeford (Figure 18.11, 70, HER 1079), originally with a smaller, separate, internal pendant, has elaborate architectural decoration comprising interlaced arcading, related to that seen on buckle plates (Figures 18.7, 44–7). It is paralleled by a fragment found in the adjacent parish of Heacham (Figure 18.11, 71, HER 51072), and by a recently discovered pendant with interlaced openwork arcading, central sexfoil, and a suspension stud in the form of an anthropomorphic mask, from Wimpole, Cambridgeshire (personal communication Angus Wainwright). All three have engraved detail accentuating the columns, arches and imposts. Intersecting arcading, as shown on the pendants from Sedgeford and Wimpole, was most commonly used

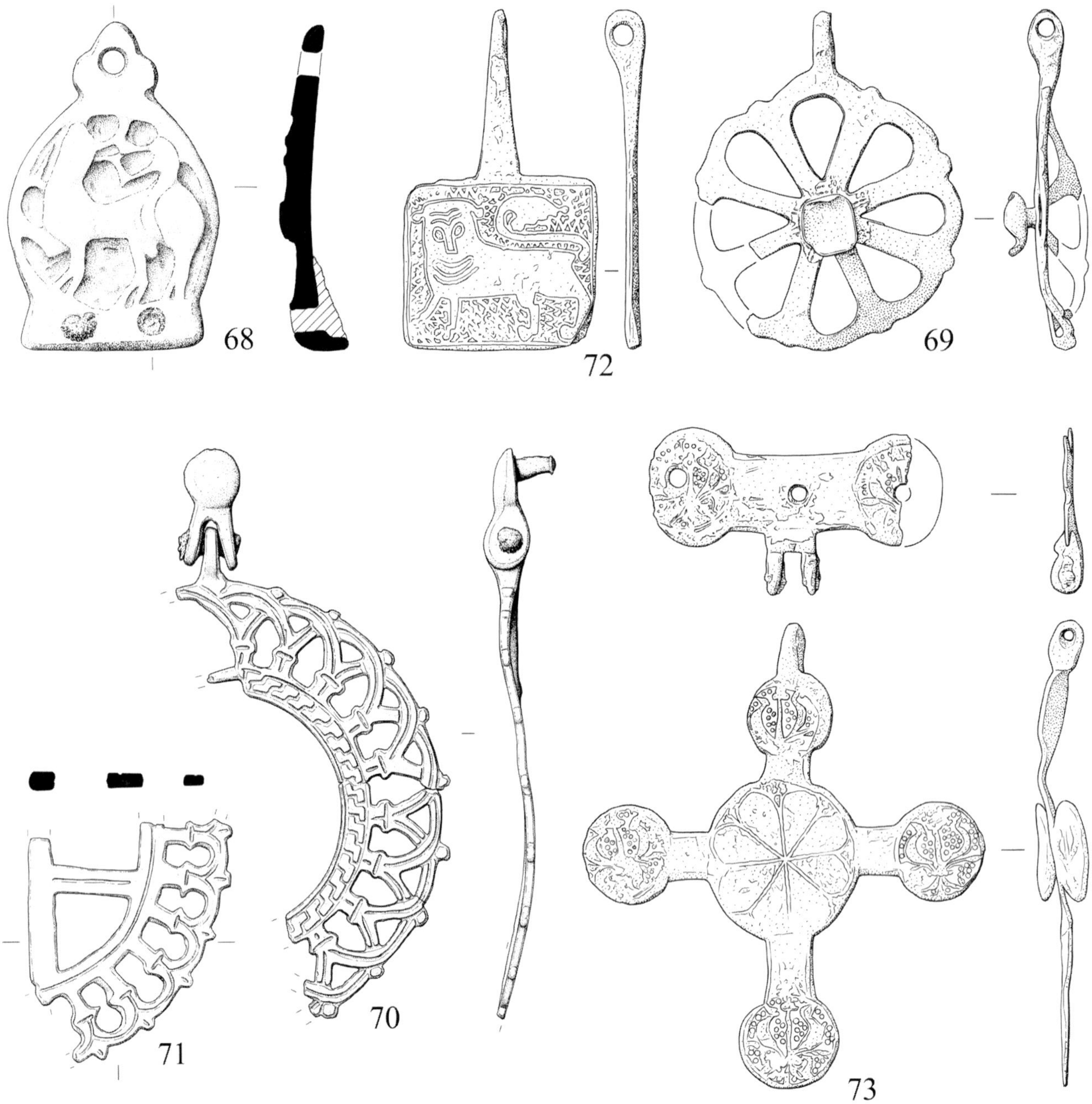


*Figure 18.11. Horse furniture, scale 1:1.*

between *c.* 1100–1140 and can be found on high status Romanesque buildings, e.g. Norwich Cathedral, on the transept (*c.* 1100) and West Range (*c.* 1120–1130).

A small number of pendants and mounts come from excavated castles in Britain, such as Hen Domen (a plain oval pendant with its suspension mount, misidentified as a strap-end; Higham and Rouillard, p. 104, fig. 5.6, no. 109), Castle Acre (Goodall, A. R. 1982, fig. 44, nos 35–7) and Castle Rising (Williams, V. 1997, pp. 88 and 93, fig. 60, no. 18), but the overwhelming majority have been found in rural situations lacking any secure archaeological context (Ashley 2002). This is unsurprising due to the essentially portable nature and relative fragility of this form of decorative horse gear. Almost invariably made of gilt copper-alloy with engraved and stamped decoration, 12th- and early 13th-century forms show considerable variety, a few examples of which are illustrated here, and others are figured and discussed in a survey of armorial horse furniture from Norfolk (Ashley 2002, figs 5–9). Decoration on some mounts and pendants comprises geometric arrangements that echo those of the earliest heraldry, with bends, checks, lozenges, foils and fleurs-de-lis. Others show lions, as on a square pendant from Hoxne or Mendham in Suffolk (Figure 18.11, 72), and another elaborately decorated cruciform pendant, from Colkirk (HER 37302) with its suspension mount, displays the Eurasian motif of addorsed birds flanking the Tree of Life (Figure 18.11, 73).

### *Swivels for leashes*

Swivels are likely to have had a number of related uses: for example, on the leashes of hunting dogs or lapdogs, with the smaller examples perhaps being used on straps for raptors when hawking.

A remarkable complete swivel was discovered on excavations at Dragon Hall, Norwich in 1997/8 (Cherry 2005). This elaborate openwork example has a central sphere with running acanthus leaf decoration and animal-head terminals on the loops. In a recent survey of Norfolk finds of swivels, at least 24 from a total of 34 examples have these distinctive animal-heads (Ashley 2006, p. 105). Since then many more swivels have been recorded, including one with elaborately modelled animal heads and decorative hemisphere from Scole (Figure 18.12, 74, HER 51835), and another, from Pulham Market (Figure 18.12, 75, HER 52999), with a pair of wyverns gripping a perforated disc, less accomplished versions of those employed on an extremely elaborate swivel 'from Cirencester', belonging to the first half of the 12th century, and now in the British Museum (Stratford 1984a).

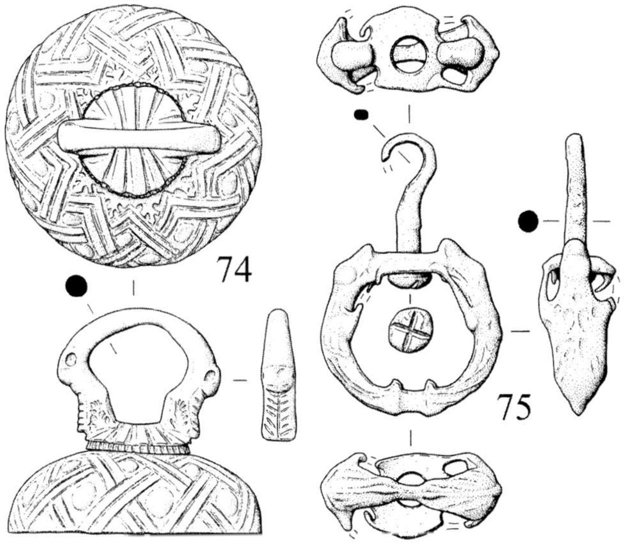


*Figure 18.12. Swivels, scale 1:1.*

## Exotic motifs and influences

### *Lions and wyverns*

The expanded range of objects for the 12th century discussed above displays a variety of decorative motifs which demonstrate exotic connections and exemplars. Amongst zoomorphic decoration lions and wyverns (dragons with two legs) predominate. Depictions of lions are derived from 11th-century manuscript illustrations and silks and textiles from Central Asia, China and the Byzantine Empire. They appear for example in the borders of the Bayeux Tapestry (Hicks 1993, pp. 252–4; Wilson 1985), on Norman dynastic tombs in Palermo, Sicily (Deér 1959, pp. 66–9) and on the fore-building of Norwich Castle (Bigod's tower), where two stone lions were displayed in a 'quasi-heraldic fashion' to guard the entrance in *c.* 1100 (Heslop 1994, p. 31 and figs 7 and 10).

Lions and wyverns have royal associations. The lion was readily associated with English kings from at least the reign of Henry II (Ailes 1982, pp. 54–63) and lions derived from or alluding to the royal arms become commonplace on later objects of personal dress, furniture and harness. This trend is certainly reinforced from 1198, when three lions passant guardant were adopted as the arms of England.

Wyverns appear in the Bayeux Tapestry, as King Harold's standard, (Wilson 1985, pl. 71; Renn 1993, p. 187), on Norman kite-shaped shields, on the prows of ships, and in the borders (Wilson 1985, on shields: pls 7, 12–13, 15, 70, on ships: pls 5, 6, 26, 33–34, 37, 40–43, and in the borders: pls 14, 17–18, 21, 25, 43–44, 57), and were later carried by the armies of King Stephen at Northallerton in 1138 (Lehmann-Brockhaus 1956, p. 6633), King Richard I, during the Third Crusade (1189–92), and King John (1199–1216), alongside the other English royal standards (Lofmark 1995, p. 54).

### *Shoulder ornament*

A notable openwork buckle-plate of the 1st half of the 12th century, from Shipdham (Figure 18.6, 36, HER 35321; Ashley 2006, fig. 1, no. 4; 2009), shows a lion passant reguardant with tail in mouth, its hindquarters charged with an engraved cross potent. This 'shoulder ornament' also appears on a piece of sculpture of *c.* 1120 from Thetford (Figure 18.13, HER 5752), which depicts a lion passant reguardant with a forked tail (Ashley 2011). Lions similarly charged with crosses potent can be found in the mosaic floor of the Abbey Church of Notre Dame, Ganagobie, in Provence (Barruol 1977, pls 28 and 30). The pavement was laid in *c.* 1135–73 and the style and subject matter of much of it is derived from Byzantine or other Eastern textiles or from painted copies of textiles in manuscripts. A remarkable example of a manuscript copy of an exotic textile can be found on a page from the Gospels of Otto III (*c.* 983–991). This shows a series of 14 differently coloured horizontal bands each with a repeat pattern, including pairs of confronted lions, griffins or wyverns with the Tree of Life, or Sassanian birds with ribbons (Goldschmidt 1928, vol. 2, pl. 48). Each of the lions displays a roundel on its rear. An earlier example of a cross used in a similar manner both to that on the Shipdham buckle plate and the Ganagobie mosaic can be seen on a Carthaginian mosaic of the late 5th–early 6th century AD which shows a mounted Vandal whose horse carries the device on its hindquarters (Buckton 1994, pp. 66–7, cat. no. 55(a)).

### *Confronted beasts and the Tree of Life*

The motif of pairs of confronted or addorsed birds or beasts flanking the Tree of Life, appears on a number of buckles and pieces of horse furniture described above. The Tree of Life is familiar from depictions on Assyrian stone carvings and cylinder seals from the 13th–7th centuries BC (Maxwell-Hyslop 1976). In central Asian shamanism the Tree of Life connects the earth to the heavens, crowned and winged sirens or griffins guard the Tree (Roxburgh 2005, p. 109). This motif can be seen on a fragment of a 12th-century ivory casket found at Old Sarum, Wiltshire, where two such griffins flank a rosette representing the Tree of Life (Armour 1995, p. 82). Imported silks from Central Asia, a conspicuously high status commodity, were the main mode of transmission for this motif. They depict pairs of confronted and addorsed beasts adopting heraldic poses and are often shown flanking a central tree. These Chinese influenced patterns in silk were copied in the Byzantine Empire, and became 'the accepted (and possibly the only acceptable) type' for traders and consumers of this élite material (Impey 1977, pp. 63–4). A recent note has highlighted the use of the heraldic fur, vair (formed from the pelts of squirrels) as a signifier of status in similar manner, in the Bayeux Tapestry and in 12th-century manuscripts (Phoenix 2010).

*Figure 18.13. Romanesque sculpture of a lion with 'shoulder ornament' from Thetford, Norfolk.*

An early imported silk decorated with pairs of panthers, birds and griffins, was found in the tomb of Edward the Confessor (Granger-Taylor 1994). Others survive converted for re-use as seal bags, such as those preserved in the treasury of the cathedral church of Canterbury (Robinson and Urquhart 1934).

The array of paired birds, beasts and monsters and other repeat pattern motifs such as fleurs-de-lis and double-headed eagles, carried on fine silks, provided nascent charges for the burgeoning noble fashion of armorial display in the 12th century. Likewise cloths with patterns formed by the woven structure of the material, comprising differently coloured vertical, horizontal, zigzag, chevronny or checky bands, were sometimes applied to the face of a knight's shield as signifiers of status, and must have had some influence on the development of early arms (see Davies 1979, pp. 120–4; 1984, pp. 2–9; Nickel 2002, p. 117 and figs X–45; Heslop forthcoming).

The fashion for exotic patterns and figures among the Anglo-Norman elite displays cultural influences from the wider Norman world and beyond. The insecurities and uncertainties of everyday life may also be reflected in the dual roles of beasts depicted on a range of objects, from dress accessories to sculpted stone, as both markers of status and in an apotropaic role as guardians of person and place.

## Acknowledgements

I am most grateful to Helen Geake, Andrew Rogerson and Melanie Rolfe for commenting on the text. The drawings are by Jason Gibbons with the exception of Figure 18.6, 35 which is taken from Margeson (1993, fig. 13, no. 127), and Figures 18.4, 23; 18.6, 32; 18.6, 36; 18.7, 40; 18.11, 69; 18.11, 72 and 18.11, 73 which are my own, as is the photograph (Figure 18.13). The figures were scanned by Mary Chester-Kadwell.

Corrigendum: The anthropomorphic fragment illustrated as Figure 18.1, 4 is probably part of an openwork buckle frame, cf. PAS database SF-E09EEO.

## Bibliography

Aberg, F. A. and Brown, A. E., ed. (1981) *Medieval Moated Sites in North-West Europe*, British Archaeological Report International Series 121 (Oxford).

Addyman, P. V. and Priestley, J. (1977) 'Baile Hill, York: a report on the Institute's excavations', *Archaeological Journal* 134, pp. 115–56.

Ailes, A. (1982) *The Origins of the Royal Arms of England: Their Development to 1199* (Reading, University of Reading Centre for Graduate Studies).

Armour, P. (1995) 'Griffins', in J. Cherry, ed., pp. 72–103.

Ashley, S. (2002) *Medieval Armorial Horse Furniture in Norfolk*, East Anglian Archaeology 101 (Dereham).

Ashley, S. (2006) 'Recent Finds of Anglo-Norman 'High-status' Objects from Norfolk', *Norfolk Archaeology* 45, pp. 105–8.

Ashley, S. (2008) 'A Wyvern on a twelfth-century armorial weight from Norfolk', *The Coat of Arms* 3rd Series 4(216), pp. 93–9.

Ashley, S. (2009) 'Lions charged with a cross potent: Central Asian 'shoulder ornament' on a twelfth-century buckle plate from Norfolk', *Coat of Arms* 3rd Series 5(217), pp. 1–6.

Ashley, S. (2011) 'A further example of Central Asian 'shoulder ornament', on a proto-heraldic sculpture of a lion from Thetford', *The Coat of Arms* 3rd Series 7(222), pp. 45–8.

Ashley, S. (in preparation) 'Birds and beasts and the Tree of Life: Eastern motifs on Anglo-Norman harness, dress accessories and other possessions'.

Barruol, G. (1977) 'Ganogobie' *Provence Romane*, pp. 97–164, Vol. 2, Collection La Nuit des Temps (La Pierre-qui-Vire, Editions Zodiaque).

Beaumont James, T. (2002) 'Medieval Britain and Ireland in 2001', *Medieval Archaeology* 46, pp. 125–264.

Beaumont James, T. (2005) 'Medieval Britain and Ireland in 2004', *Medieval Archaeology* 49, p. 323–473.

Beresford, G. (1987) *Goltho: the Development of an Early Medieval Manor c. 850–1150*, English Heritage Archaeological Report 4 (London, English Heritage).

Biddle, M.(1990) *Object and Economy in Medieval Winchester*, Winchester Studies 7ii (Oxford).

Blair, C. and Campbell, M. L. (1979) 'An eleventh-century latten candlestick, base and a thirteenth-century Limoges plaque from Hughmond Abbey, Shropshire', *Antiquaries Journal* 59(2), pp. 414–8, pl. lxxiii, a.

Boehm, B. D. (1996) '37. Candlestick', in T. Egan, pp. 156–7.

Bucton, D., ed. (1994) *Byzantium; Treasures of Byzantine Art and Culture from British Collections* (London, British Museum).

Burnett, L, (2009) 'Houghton' in J. Naylor, K. Leahy, and G. Egan, p. 340, fig. 6b.

Cherry, J. (1984) 'Lamp of pedestal form', in G. Zarnecki, J. Holt, and T. Holland, p. 351, no. 478.

Cherry, J., ed. (1995) *Mythical Beasts* (London, British Museum Press).

Cherry, J. (2005) 'Harness', in Shelley, pp. 115–7, fig. 76, no. 569.

Cherry, J. and Goodall J. (1985) 'A twelfth-century gold brooch from Folkingham Castle, Lincs', *Antiquaries Journal* 65(ii), pp. 471–2, pl. cvi, d–c.

Coad, J. and Streeten, A. D. F. (1982) 'Excavations at Castle Acre Castle, Norfolk, 1972–77: country house and castle of the Norman earls of Surrey', *Archaeological Journal* 139, pp. 138–301.

Darvill, T. (1988) 'Excavations on the site of the Early Norman Castle at Gloucester, 1983–84', *Medieval Archaeology* 32, pp. 1–49.

Daubney, A., Minter, F. and Robinson, J. (2005) 'Monewden', in Geake, pp. 342 and 345–6, fig. 7, c and d.

Davies, T. R. (1979) 'As it was in the beginning', *The Coat of Arms* New Series 3(109), pp. 114–24.

Davies, T. R. (1984) 'Diaper, paillé and papelonné', *The Coat of Arms* New Series 6(129), pp. 2–9.

De Reuck, A. (1991) *Dating Sword Chapes* (unpublished catalogue).

Deér, J. (1959) *The Dynastic Porphyry Tombs of the Norman Period in Sicily*, Dumbarton Oaks Studies 5 (Cambridge, Mass.).

D'Onofrio, M., ed. (1994) *I Normanni: Popolo d'Europa 1030–1200* (Venice, Marsilio).

Egan, G. (1998) *The Medieval Household: Daily Living c. 1150–c. 1450*, Medieval Finds from Excavations in London 6 (London).

Egan, G. and Pritchard, F. (2002) *Dress Accessories c. 1150–c. 1450*, Medieval Finds from Excavations in London 3 (London).

Egan, G. (2009) 'Material concerns: non-ceramic finds *c* 1050–1500', in Gilchrist and Reynolds, pp. 289–303.

Egan, T., ed. (1996) *Enamels of Limoges 1100-1350* (New York, Metropolitan Museum of Art).

Eggenstein, G., Börste, N., Zöller, H. and Zahn-Biemüller, E. (2008) *Eine Welt in Bewegung: Unterwegs zu Zentren des frühen Mittelalters* (Paderborn and Würzburg).

Ellis, R. H. (1978 and 1981) *Catalogue of Seals in the Public Record Office: Personal Seals*, Vols 1 and 2 (London, HMSO).

Fingerlin, I. (1971) *Gürtel des hohen und späten Mittelalters*, Kunstwissenschaftliche Studien Band XLVI (Munich and Berlin).

Foot, M. (1984) 'Bindings' in Zarnecki, Holt and Holland, pp. 342–9, nos 469–75.

Geake, H. (2002) 'Portable Antiquities Scheme', in Beaumont James, pp. 128–45.

Geake, H. (2005) 'Portable Antiquities Scheme', in Beaumont James, pp. 326–49.

Gilchrist, R. and Reynolds, A., ed. (2009) *Reflections: 50 Years of Medieval Archaeology 1957–2007* (Leeds, Maney).

Goldman, B. (1960) 'The development of the lion-griffin', *American Journal of Archaeology* 64(4), pp. 319–28.

Goldschmidt, A. (1928) *German Illumination*, 2 vols (Florence).

Goodall, A. R. (1980) 'Copper alloy objects', in A.D. Saunders, pp. 164–5.

Goodall, A. R. (1982) 'Objects of copper alloy', in J. Coad and A. D. F. Streeten, pp. 235–40.

Goodall, A. R. (1987) 'Medieval copper alloy', in G. Beresford, pp. 173–6.

Goodall, I. H. (1982) 'Iron objects', in J. Coad and A. D. F. Streeten, pp. 227–35.

Goodall, I. H. (1990) 'Locks and keys', in M. Biddle, pp.1001–36.

Granger-Taylor, H. (1994) '166 Silk from the tomb of Edward the Confessor', in D. Bucton, pp. 151–3.

Grazebrooke, G. (1890) *The dates of variously-shaped shields: with coincident dates and examples* (Liverpool).

Gurney, D. (2006) 'Archaeological finds in Norfolk in 2005', *Norfolk Archaeology* 45(i), pp. 112–23.

Heslop, T. A. (1994) *Norwich Castle Keep: Romanesque Architecture and Social Context* (Norwich, Centre of East Anglian Studies).

Heslop, T. A. (forthcoming) 'Courtliness and the Culture of Consumption' (1997 Slade Lectures, Cambridge).

Heslop, T. A. and Ashley, S. (2013) 'A fragment of a gilt bronze buckle frame from Soham, Cambridgeshire, and the Dune Hoard belt buckle in Stockholm', *Antiquaries Journal* 93, pp. 217–23.

Hicks, C. (1993) *Animals in Early Medieval Art* (Edinburgh, University Press).

Higham, R. and Rouillard, M. (2000) 'Metalwork and other material from the bailey excavations at Hen Domen 1960–1990', in R. Higham and P. Barker, pp. 98–110.

Higham, R. and Barker, P. (2000) *Hen Domen, Montgomery: A Timber Castle on the English-Welsh Border, A Final Report* (Exeter, University Press).

Hinton, D. A. (1990a) 'Buckles and buckle-plates', in M. Biddle, pp. 506–26.

Hinton, D. A. (1990b) 'Fittings from reliquaries and other fine caskets, i. gold, silver, lead or pewter, and copper-alloy fittings', in M. Biddle, pp. 762–80.

Hinton, D. A. (1990c) 'Chapes', in M. Biddle, pp. 1082–3.

Hinton, D. A. (1990d) *Archaeology, Economy and Society: England from the Fifth to the Fifteenth Century* (London, Seaby).

Hinton, D. A. (2005) *Gold and Gilt, Pots and Pins: Possessions and People in Medieval Britain* (Oxford, University Press).

Impey, O. (1977) *Chinoiserie: the impact of Oriental styles on Western art and decoration* (New York, Charles Scribner's Sons).

Jope, E. M. and Threlfall, R. I. (1959) 'The twelfth-century castle at Ascot Doilly, Oxfordshire: its history and excavation', *Antiquaries Journal* 39, pp. 219–73.

Kauffmann, C. M. (1984) 'Corpus of canon law' and 'St Jerome, Commentaries on the Old Testament', in G. Zarnecki, J. Holt and T. Holland, p. 107, nos 41–2.

Lehmann-Brockhaus, O. (1956) *Lateinische Schiftquellen zur Kunst in England, Wales und Schottland vom Jahre 901 bis zum Jahre 1307*, Vol. 3 (Munich)

Lewis, M. (2007) 'A new date for 'Class A, Type 11A' stirrup-strap mounts, and some observations on their distribution', *Medieval Archaeology* 51, pp. 178–84.

Lofmark, C. (1995) *A History of the Red Dragon* (Llanrwst, Gwasg Carreg Gwalch).

Lorren, C. (1981) 'The castle of Rubercy (Calvados) (*c.* 1150–1204)', in F. A. Aberg and A. E. Brown, ed., pp. 103–25.

Mainman, A. J. and Rogers, N. S. H. (2000) *Finds from Anglo-Scandinavian York*. Archaeology of York 17/4 (York).

Margeson, S. (1982) 'Worked bone', in J. Coad and A. D. F. Streeten, pp. 241–55.

Margeson, S. (1993) *Norwich Households: The Medieval and Post-Medieval Finds from Norwich Survey Excavations 1971–1978*, East Anglian Archaeology 58 (Norwich).

Marin, J-Y. (1994) 'Pendaglio di bardatura', in M. D'Onofrio, pp. 380–1, nos 13–14.

Martin, E., Pendleton, C. and Plouviez, J., ed. (1996) 'Archaeology in Suffolk 1995: archaeological finds', *Proceedings of the Suffolk Institute of Archaeology* 38, pp. 457–66.

Maxwell-Hyslop, K. R. (1976) 'The Assyrian 'Tree of Life': a western branch?', in J. V. S. Megaw, pp. 263–76.

Megaw, J. V. S. (1976) *To Illustrate the Monuments: Essays on Archaeology presented to Stuart Piggott* (London, Thames & Hudson).

Morley, B. and Gurney, D. (1997) *Castle Rising Castle, Norfolk*, East Anglian Archaeology 81 (Dereham).

Naylor, J., Leahy, K. and Egan, G. (2009) 'Medieval Britain and Ireland, 2008' *Medieval Archaeology* 53, pp. 327–46.

Nickel, H. (2002) 'The mutual influence of Europe and Asia in the field of arms and armour', in D. Nicolle, pp.107–25, figs x1–x73.

Nicolle, D. (2002) *Companion to Medieval Arms and Armour* (Woodbridge, Boydell).

Oddy, W. A., La Niece, S. and Stratford, N. (1986) *Romanesque Metalwork: Copper Alloys and their Decoration* (London, British Museum).

Phoenix, D. (2010) 'Garments so chequered' The Bible of Cîteaux, the Bayeux Tapestry and the Vair Pattern', *Antiquaries Journal* 90, pp. 195–210.

Redknap, M. and Macdonald, P. (2002) 'Foel Farm Park', in H. Geake, pp. 142 and 144, fig. 6d.

Renn, D. (1993) 'Burgeat and Gonfanon: two sidelights from the Bayeux Tapestry' *Anglo-Norman Studies* 16, 00–00.

Robinson, G. and Urquhart, H. (1934) 'Seal bags in the Treasury of the Cathedral Church of Canterbury', *Archaeologia* 84, pp. 163–211.

Rogers, D. J. (1993) *Tumbrels* Datasheet 16, Finds Research Group AD 700–1700 (London).

Rogerson, A. and Ashley, S. (2009) 'A Selection of finds from Norfolk recorded in 2009 and earlier', *Norfolk Archaeology* 45(iv), pp. 556–70.

Rogerson, A. and Ashley, S. (2011a) 'A Selection of finds from Norfolk recorded in 2011 and earlier', *Norfolk Archaeology* 46, pt. ii, pp. 248–62.

Rogerson, A. and Ashley, S. (2011b) 'Some medieval gaping-mouth beast buckles from Norfolk and elsewhere', *Medieval Archaeology* 55, pp. 299–302.

Rosenthal, J. T. (1964) 'The assizes of weights and measures in medieval England', *Western Political Quarterly* 17(3), pp. 409–22.

Roxburgh, D. J., ed. (2005) *Turks: a Journey of a Thousand Years* (London, Royal Academy of Arts).

Rudenko, S. J. (1958) 'The mythological eagle, the gryphon, the winged lion, and the wolf in the art of northern nomads', *Artibus Asiae*, 21(2), pp. 101–22.

Saunders, A. D. (1978) 'A stone lamp from Launceston Castle, Cornwall', *Antiquaries Journal* 58(ii), pp. 366–72, fig. 4.

Saunders, A. D. (1980) 'Lydford Castle, Devon', *Medieval Archaeology* 24, pp. 123–86.

Shelley, A. (2005) *Dragon Hall, King Street, Norwich: Excavations and Survey of a Late Medieval Merchant's Trading Complex*, East Anglian Archaeology 112 (Norwich).

Spencer, B. W. (1961) 'Two additions to the London Museum', *Transactions of London & Middlesex Archaeological Society* 20(4), pp. 214–7.

Stratford, N. (1984a) 'Double swivel for straps', in G. Zarnecki, J. Holt and T. Holland, p. 250, no. 248.

Stratford, N. (1984b) 'Foot of a candlestick', in G. Zarnecki, J. Holt and T. Holland, p. 250, no. 249.

Stratford, N. (1984c) 'Domestic lamp', in G. Zarnecki, J. Holt and T. Holland, p. 253, no. 258.

Stratford, N. (1984d) 'Censer-cover', in G. Zarnecki, J. Holt and T. Holland, p. 255, no. 261.

Stratford, N. (1984e) 'Seven gold finger-rings', in G. Zarnecki, J. Holt and T. Holland, pp. 290–1, nos 311–17.

Stratford, N. (1984f) 'Drawings of jewellery at St Albans', in G. Zarnecki, J. Holt and T. Holland, pp. 291–2, no. 318.

Stratford, N. (1984g) 'Six silver finger-rings from the Lark Hill hoard', in Zarnecki, Holt and Holland, p. 293, nos 320 a–f.

Stratford, N. (1986) 'Some recent acquisitions of medieval 'Limoges', in the British Museum', *Antiquaries Journal* 66(ii), pp. 380–2, pl. lxv, b–c.

Stratford, N. (1997, reprinted with revisions 2001) *The Lewis Chessmen and the Enigma of the Hoard* (London, British Museum).

Swarzenski, H. (1967) *Monuments of Romanesque Art; The Art of Church Treasures in North-western Europe* (London, Faber & Faber).

Thomas, G. (2004) *Late Anglo-Saxon and Viking-Age strap-ends 750–1100: Part 2* Datasheet 33, Finds Research Group AD 700–1700 (London).

Ward Perkins, J. B. (1940) *London Museum Medieval Catalogue* (London, Museum of London).

West, S. (1998) *A Corpus of Anglo-Saxon Material from Suffolk*, East Anglian Archaeology 84 (Ipswich).

Williams, D. (1997) *Late Saxon Stirrup-Strap Mounts*, Council for British Archaeology Research Report 111 (York).

Williams, V. (1997) 'The small finds', in B. Morley and D. Gurney, pp. 87–93.

Wilson, D. M. (1985) *The Bayeux Tapestry* (London, Thames & Hudson).

Wixom, W. D. (1999) 'Architectural base for a processional cross', in W. D. Wixom, pp. 85–6, no. 100.

Wixom, W. D., ed. (1999) *Mirror of the Medieval World* (New York).

Wormold, F. (1945) 'Decorated initials in English MSS. From A.D. 900 to 1100', *Archaeologia* 91, pp. 107–35.

Zarnecki, G. (1953) *Later English Romanesque sculpture 1140–1210* (London, Arts Council), cat. nos 4 and 71–2.

Zarnecki, G., Holt, J. and Holland, T., ed. (1984) *English Romanesque Art 1066–1200* (London, Arts Council).

# Index